Combinatorial Auctions

Combinatorial Auctions

edited by Peter Cramton, Yoav Shoham, and Richard Steinberg

The MIT Press
Cambridge, Massachusetts
London, England

MIT Press books may be purchased at special quantity discounts for business or sales promotional use. For information, please email special_sales@mitpress.mit.edu or write to Special Sales Department, The MIT Press, 55 Hayward Street, Cambridge, MA 02142.

This book was set in Stone Serif and Stone Sans on 3B2 by Asco Typesetters, Hong Kong. Printed and bound in the United States of America.

Library of Congress Cataloging-in-Publication Data

Combinatorial auctions / edited by Peter Cramton, Yoav Shoham, and Richard Steinberg.
    p. cm.
Includes bibliographical references and index.
ISBN 0-262-03342-9 (alk. paper)
1. Auctions. I. Cramton, Peter. II. Shoham, Yoav. III. Steinberg, Richard.
HF5476.C65   2005   381'.17—dc22   2005050499

10 9 8 7 6 5 4 3 2 1

To Benny Lehmann, whom we miss

Contents

Foreword

Vernon L. Smith

More than a quarter of a century ago, the federal government moved to deregulate airline routes, over the vigorous objections of all but two airlines. The political impetus was fueled by public realization that airline regulation had not benefited the airline passengers.

At the time, Stephen Rassenti was working on his Ph.D. in systems engineering, but he had minored in economics—theory, econometrics, and experimental economics. He was looking for a thesis topic, and I suggested that with airline route deregulation and the decision to sunset the Civil Aeronautics Board we were moving far and fast with no one thinking about the airports. Planes have to use runways to serve routes, and the airports were still regulated with a cumbersome political process for allocating runway rights. I proposed that Stephen, with his expertise in algorithms, work on the question of how you might design a smart computer-assisted market to solve this complex 0-1 combinatorial rights allocation problem. Bidders can naturally value packages of runway slots and can bid on them, but they need algorithm support so that the complex combinatorial problem of allocating elemental rights to the most efficient packages is simple for them. Their management problem is impossibly complex if they have to bid on package elements, obtain some, but not others, and then enter a secondary market to buy (or sell) the fragments that are not properly packaged. The basic idea was to engineer the market design to fit the management problem that businesses faced, and economize on transactions and strategizing costs. Stephen's solutions to this class of problems resulted in his dissertation (Rassenti 1981), and I think it is accurate to say this event launched the field of combinatorial auctions. More generically, Stephen had created the concept of the smart computer assisted exchange. Thus, as we noted at the time:

To our knowledge, this study constitutes the first attempt to design a "smart" computer-assisted exchange institution. In all the computer-assisted markets known to us in the field, as well as those studied in laboratory experiments, the computer passively records bids and contracts and routinely enforces the trading rules of the institution. The RSB mechanism has potential application to any market in which commodities are composed of combinations of elemental items (or characteristics). The distinguishing feature of our combinatorial auction is that it allows consumers to define the commodity by means of the bids tendered for alternative packages of elemental items. It eliminates the necessity for producers to anticipate, perhaps at substantial risk and cost, the commodity packages valued most highly in the market.... The experimental results suggest that: (a) the procedures of the mechanism are operational, i.e., motivated individuals can execute the required task with a minimum of instruction and training; (b) the extent of demand under revelation by participants is not large, i.e., allocative efficiencies of 98–99% of the possible surplus seem to be achievable over time with experienced bidders. This occurred despite repeated early attempts by inexperienced subjects to manipulate the mechanism and to engage in speculative purchases. (Rassenti, Smith, and Bulfin 1982, p. 672)

In 1976, we had "gone electronic" in the conduct of laboratory experiments at Arizona. What we learned over the next three years was the unanticipated ecological consequence of laboratory experience: human interactive experiments governed by a computer network enabled the accommodation of far larger message spaces, opened the way to the application of coordination and optimization algorithms to the messages of subjects, and facilitated their capacity to reach sophisticated equilibrium outcomes that they did not need to understand. Their expert system help was part of the overall design of the market mechanism.

From this very limited, modest, and hopeful beginning an exciting intellectual history followed, and this book is a truly important landmark in that development.

Stephen's 1981 results pale in comparison with what we have all learned since, and that learning continues unabated. What have we learned in and beyond the laboratory?

• The ideal incentive mechanism design should lead managers to a two-step procedure: (1) an estimation of the value of the auctioned item(s), followed by (2) a readiness to reveal this value in the form of a bid, if necessary, such action being a fair approximation to that which serves the interest of the bidder.

• Market design should focus on how to facilitate this procedure. Very complex market allocation problems for runway rights, gas in pipeline networks, energy on a high voltage grid, and so on, can be made simple for the participants. Humans make the value judgments, and smart markets handle the complexity.

• Participants are not required to be experts in anything except their own business uses of the auctioned items, and must apply what they know to determine the private values of those items. That must be their specialty and their focus, and strategizing should not be plainly required of them.

• Privacy is essential: public information on who is bidding for what, how much, and when, fosters manipulation, gaming, collusion, and inefficiency. It is a fantasy to think that such activities can be controlled by piecemeal auction rules adjusted after each auction based on complete information examples, good for teaching, but not for designing. The Federal Communication Commission's Simultaneous Multiple Round auction evolved over a sequence of field applications in which weaknesses and defects revealed in each application led to "fine tuning," followed by the observation of further problems leading to new "fixes," and so on. Each "fix," designed to limit a particular strategic exploitation, tended also to generate complexity and its attendant higher transactions' cost.

• This was precisely what had been learned in the laboratory in a series of elementary experiments that led to a sequence of increasingly complicated modifications of English procedures (McCabe, Rassenti, and Smith 1988; hereafter MRS). These experiments illustrated the potential for initiating the following dangerous design cycle. You begin with a precise theoretically "optimal" auction procedure—both of Vickrey's proposals for multiple unit English auctions seemed transparent. In implementation, you encounter behavioral incentives or "strategic" problems not considered as part of the original theory and likely intractable from a theoretical point of view. You come up with an intuitively plausible rule "fix" to provide a countervailing incentive. This creates a new problem requiring a new rule adjustment, and so on.

• In this study we found that all problems arose from a common feature: bidder control over price bids from the floor. These are issues not readily anticipated by formal analysis that can surface naturally in experiments, but make sense, ex post. The bottom line, transparently evident in the MRS results, is that if you want to do English multiple unit (incentive compatible) auctions, the way to do them is to use the English Clock. In forty-four English Clock auctions, only one failed to award the item to a highest value buyer. This method dominates all others in terms of efficiency. There can be no jump bidding because no one can bid a price.

• Thus, the MRS (p. 70) conclusion: "The English Clock is our best implementation and is likely to find acceptance in the field. This auction gives participants feedback during the auction … produces consistent pricing and very high efficiency, (and) can accommodate programmed (or electronic) … bidding." Essentially, the procedure works well because it removes from bidders the right to announce bids from the floor—they can only indicate willingness to be in, or out, at the standing price, and once out they cannot reenter (in the MRS implementation). Bidding from the floor invites jump bidding, collusion, and longer auctions. Avoid it by denying all opportunity and information that supports it. All the theoretical examples of incentive failure, manipulation, gaming, and bad outcomes that I know are based on complete information.

• Others have discovered through the hard knocks of experience the efficacy of English Clock Auctions, as in the nice chapter in this volume by Ausubel, Cramton, and Milgrom (chapter 5). They offer many elaborations eminently worthy of study.

• Elsewhere we report a Combo Clock (CC) auction that is easy for the participants, and places minimal computational requirements on the auctioneer (Porter et al. 2003). The optimization, if needed, is run only after all clocks have stopped and all information is submitted for processing. It trivially accommodates the sale of multiple units of multiple items. Bidders have complete freedom to move in and out of the auction bidding on any packages at will. It allows the bidder to impose logical constraints without increasing the computational burden during the auction. For example, a bidder may implement mutually exclusive bids and "if and only if" bids: the auction simply computes his demand for an item as the maximum number of units he could possibly win. The bidder is also free to blend current and previous clock prices in a current compound bid as long as part of the bid is at current clock prices. The CC auction may be the most flexible known combinatorial auction, but more testing is obviously in order. Moreover, *strategic behavior is controlled by feeding back only that information bidders need to know (item prices) in order to avoid bidding more than their maximum willingness to pay. For this purpose bidders do not need to know who is bidding, how many are bidding, and on which items or packages.* Hence, in auction environments where certain items have only one bidder—for example, timber and offshore petroleum tracts—this fact may still elicit full value bidding if every tract is potentially contestable, and bidders face much uncertainty about how active the bidding will be on any one item.

• The needs of the future are twofold: first, more laboratory tests by independent scholars, including explorations of alternative economic environments, with the objective of uncovering the Combo Clock's boundaries of validity—I believe that all mechanisms have limits to their robustness that can only be determined empirically, whether guided by theory or not; second, tests in the field where users must be persuaded to see the merits of strict security that enables bidding to be driven primarily by private information. This latter need will be particularly difficult because the problem was not addressed up front—early designers were all inexperienced—and users have become accustomed to the hope that ever more complex rules can control strategizing, without significantly increasing implementation costs for everyone.

• It is our understanding that the Freedom of Information Act and other legislation does not prevent complete bidder privacy in an auction until some time after the auction is completed.

• As economists our task is to emphasize that efficiency, not revenue, is the key criteria in economic systems design. For government sales of rights and assets, efficiency is the route to maximizing the creation of income and wealth in the economy, and that gives you more tax revenue tomorrow. To the extent that the FCC auctions have maximized revenue and contributed to the winner's curse, they have contributed to bankruptcies, spoiled the market for subsequent auctions, and reduced the generation of new wealth. For private auctions, public policy should lend support to programs for achieving efficient allocations.

It is a pleasure to commend the editors, who should be proud of having produced a volume likely to generate long lasting benefits to the growing market design community.

References

McCabe, Kevin A., Stephen J. Rassenti, and Vernon L. Smith (1988), "Testing Vickrey's and Other Simultaneous Multiple Unit Versions of the English Auction," revised 1989, in R. Mark Isaac, ed., *Research in Experimental Economics*, Vol. 4, 1991, Greenwich, CT: JAI Press, 45–79.

Porter, David, Stephen Rassenti, Anil Roopnarine, and Vernon Smith (2003), "Combinatorial Auction Design," *Proceedings of the National Academy of Sciences*, 100, 11153–11157.

Rassenti, Stephen J. (1981), "0-1 Decision Problems with Multiple Resource Constraints: Algorithms and Applications," Ph.D. thesis, University of Arizona.

Rassenti, Stephen J., Vernon L. Smith, and Robert L. Bulfin (1982), "A Combinatorial Auction Mechanism for Airport Time Slot Allocation," *Bell Journal of Economics*, 13, 402–417.

Acknowledgments

We gratefully acknowledge the conscientious work of the contributors, as well as the comments of many colleagues on previous drafts. Susan Powell, Ben Galin, Gaurav Raina, and Branimira Slavova provided invaluable editorial assistance. We would also like to thank Katherine Almeida at MIT Press.

Peter Cramton would like to acknowledge the support of the National Science Foundation. Yoav Shoham would like to acknowledge the support of the National Science Foundation and DARPA. Richard Steinberg would like to thank David Kreps, Stefanos Zenios, and the members of the Operations, Information, and Technology group at Stanford University Graduate School of Business for inviting him to spend his Michaelmas 2003 sabbatical leave with them. It was during this period that early work on this book was completed.

Combinatorial Auctions

Introduction to Combinatorial Auctions

Peter Cramton, Yoav Shoham, and Richard Steinberg

Combinatorial auctions are those auctions in which bidders can place bids on combinations of items, called "packages," rather than just individual items. The study of combinatorial auctions is inherently interdisciplinary. Combinatorial auctions are in the first place auctions, a topic economists have extensively studied.[1] Package bidding brings in operations research, especially techniques from combinatorial optimization and mathematical programming. Finally, computer science is concerned with the expressiveness of various bidding languages, and the algorithmic aspects of the combinatorial problem. The study of combinatorial auctions thus lies at the intersection of economics, operations research, and computer science. In this book, we look at combinatorial auctions from all three perspectives. Indeed, our contribution is to do so in an integrated and comprehensive way. The initial challenge in interdisciplinary research is defining a common language. We have made an effort to use consistent terminology throughout the book, with the most common terms defined in the glossary.

There are numerous examples of combinatorial auctions in practice. As is typical of many fields, practice precedes theory. Simple combinatorial auctions have been used for many decades in, for example, estate auctions. A common procedure is to auction the individual items, and then, at the end, to accept bids for packages of items. If a package bid exceeds the sum of the individual bids for the items in the package, then the items are sold as a package. In this book we consider a variety of much more general combinatorial auctions, but the key ingredient is the same as in this simple case: each bidder can submit bids on packages of items.

Recently, a variety of industries have employed combinatorial auctions. For example, they have been used for truckload transportation, bus routes, and industrial procurement, and have been proposed for airport arrival and departure slots, as well as for allocating radio spectrum for wireless communications services. Both the United States and Nigeria have conducted combinatorial auctions for radio spectrum. In each case, the compelling motivation for the use of a combinatorial auction is the presence of complementarities among the items that differ across bidders. For example, a trucker's cost of handling shipments in one lane depends on its loads in other lanes. Similarly, a mobile phone operator may value licenses in two adjacent cities more than the sum of the individual license values, because the operator's customers value roaming between cities.

I.1   Basic Auction Theory

Auction theory is among the most influential and widely studied topics in economics over the last forty years. Auctions ask and answer the most fundamental questions in economics: who should get the goods and at what prices? In answering these questions, auctions provide the micro-foundation of markets. Indeed, many modern markets are organized as auctions.

To understand the role of combinatorial auctions, it is useful to step back and think about auctions in general. Some auction types are familiar, such as the ascending-bid English auction used in many online consumer auctions, or the first-price sealed-bid auction used in many public procurements. More fundamentally, auctions are distinguished not only by the rules of the auction, such as ascending versus sealed bid, but by the auction environment. These combinatorial auctions can be studied in a wide range of auction environments. Important features, including the numbers of sellers and buyers, the number of items being traded, the preferences of the parties, and the form of the private information participants have about preferences all determine the auction environment.

The benchmark environment is the private value model, introduced by Vickrey (1961), which Ausubel and Milgrom (chapter 1 of this volume) discuss in detail. In the private value model, each bidder has a value for each package of items, and these values do not depend on the private information of the other bidders. Each bidder knows his values, but not the values of the other bidders. Vickrey's seminal paper, mentioned in his 1996 Nobel Prize in economics, introduced the independent private value model, demonstrated equilibrium bidding behavior in a first-price auction, and then showed that truthful bidding could be induced as a dominant strategy by modifying the pricing rule: let each bidder pay the social opportunity cost of his winnings, rather than his bid. Finally, he showed in an example what would later be proven generally as the revenue equivalence theorem: different auction mechanisms that result in the same allocation of goods yield the same revenue to the seller.

Thus, when auctioning a single item to n bidders, whose payoffs are linear in the bidder's valuation of the item and money ($u_i = v_i - p$, where u_i is bidder i's utility, v_i is i's value of the item, and p is the price paid for the item), and where each value is drawn independently from the same probability distribution, both the first-price and second-price auction award the item to the bidder with the highest value and yield the seller the same expected revenue.

Most of the chapters in this book use Vickrey's private value model, and many make use of the Vickrey pricing rule, at least as a benchmark for comparison with alternative mechanisms.

Wilson (1969) took auction theory in a new direction. He introduced the common value auction model, in which items have the same value to all bidders, but this value is uncertain and depends on the private information of all bidders. He derived the first analysis of equilibrium bidding with common values, demonstrating the importance of conditioning one's bid on the negative information winning implies, and thus avoiding what would later be called the winner's curse—the tendency for bidders, who do not understand that winning is bad news about one's estimate of value, to pay more than the item is worth.

Milgrom extended Wilson's early papers in several ways. Most importantly, he introduced an auction model with both private value and common value elements. The private value model of Vickrey and common value model of Wilson represent two extreme cases. These extreme models are useful in deriving strong theoretical results, but most practical auction environments have both private and common value elements. Milgrom (1981) showed the importance of the monotone likelihood ratio property in obtaining results in a realistic hybrid model.[2] In particular, the monotone likelihood ratio property, together with Wilson's assumption of conditional independence, means that 1) bidders use monotonic bidding strategies, and 2) that a monotonic strategy satisfying the first-order condition constitutes an equilibrium.

Milgrom's model led to the affiliated values model (Milgrom and Weber 1982), in which a bidder's value depends directly on the private information of all the bidders. The critical condition here, closely related to the monotone likelihood ratio property in Milgrom 1981, is that the bidders' signals, typically estimates of value, are affiliated random variables. This amounts to the plausible condition that if one bidder has a high signal of value, it is more likely that the signals of the other bidders are high. The paper shows that Vickrey's revenue equivalence result no longer holds when we introduce a common value element. In particular, the revenues from the standard auction formats differ and can be ranked. Formats such as ascending auctions, in which the price is linked to more affiliated private information, yield higher revenues.

The early work of Vickrey, Wilson, and Milgrom was largely focused on an equilibrium analysis and comparison of standard auction formats. Myerson led the development of mechanism design theory, which enables the researcher to characterize equilibrium outcomes of all auction mechanisms, and identify optimal mechanisms— those mechanisms that maximize some objective, such as seller revenues. His first application was to auctions. Myerson (1981) determined the revenue-maximizing auction with risk-neutral bidders and independent private information. He also proved a general revenue equivalence theorem that says that revenues depend fundamentally on how the items are assigned—any two auction formats that lead to the same assignment of the items yield the same revenues to the seller.

The trick in Myerson's analysis was recognizing that any auction can be represented as a direct mechanism in which bidders simultaneously report their private information and then the mechanism determines assignments and payments based on the vector of reports. For any equilibrium of any auction game, there is an equivalent direct mechanism in which bidders truthfully report types and agree to participate. Hence, without loss of generality we can look at incentive compatible and individually rational mechanisms to understand properties of all auction games. Incentive compatibility respects the fact that the bidders have private information about their values; individual rationality respects the bidders voluntary participation decision. This key idea is known as the revelation principle (Myerson 1979).

Myerson and Satterthwaite (1983) use this technique to prove the general impossibility of efficient bargaining when it is not common knowledge that gains from trade exist; that is, when it is not certain that a mutually beneficial agreement is possible. This same impossibility extends to auctions in which both sellers and buyers possess private information, although efficiency becomes possible when the traders jointly own the items (Cramton, Gibbons, and Klemperer 1987). Likewise, if the roles of buyer and seller are not fixed ex ante, but the traders may take on either role depending on price, then efficient mechanisms exist (Wilson 1993).

These early papers led to the rapid development of auction theory in the 1980s and 1990s. In addition, large empirical and experimental literatures have sprung from the theory. A number of articles and books summarize this work (e.g., McAfee and McMillan 1987; Kagel and Roth 1995; Klemperer 2000, 2004; Krishna 2002; and Milgrom 2004).

I.2   Combinatorial Auctions

A shortcoming of most of the work mentioned above (Milgrom 2004 is an exception) is the failure to recognize that in many auction environments bidders care in complex ways about the packages of items they win. The advantage of combinatorial auctions (CAs) is that the bidder can more fully express his preferences. This is particularly important when items are *complements*. Items are complements when a set of items has greater utility than the sum of the utilities for the individual items (for example, a pair of shoes is worth more than the value of a left shoe alone plus the value of a right shoe alone). The auction designer also derives value from CAs. Allowing bidders more fully to express preferences often leads to improved economic efficiency (allocating the items to those who value them most) and greater auction revenues.

However, alongside their advantages, CAs raise a host of questions and challenges. This book is devoted to discussing these questions, as well as the considerable progress made in answering them.

I.3   Types of Combinatorial Auctions

The book begins in part I with a description and analysis of various combinatorial auction mechanisms.

The most famous combinatorial auction is the combinatorial generalization of the Vickrey auction already mentioned, the Vickrey-Clarke-Groves (VCG) mechanism. Ausubel and Milgrom (chapter 1) explore the question of why the Vickrey auction, with its appealing theoretical properties, is seen so little in practice. In a VCG auction (also called a Vickrey auction), bidders report their valuations for all packages; items are allocated efficiently to maximize total value. Each winner pays the opportunity cost of his winnings: the incremental value that would be derived by assigning the bidder's items according to their next best use among the other bidders. In this way, a winning bidder achieves a profit equal to his incremental contribution to total value, and it is a dominant strategy for the bidder to truthfully report his values. Achieving efficiency in truth-dominant strategies is remarkable. Nonetheless, there are serious shortcomings. Most importantly, bidders are asked to express values for all packages without the aid of any information about prices. Also, when goods are not substitutes, seller revenues can be too low;[3] adding bidders or increasing bidder values can reduce seller revenue: chapter 1 also discusses other limitations of the Vickrey auction.

In chapter 2, Parkes examines iterative combinatorial auctions. A major motivation for an iterative process is to help the bidders express their preferences by providing provisional pricing and allocation information. This information helps the bidders focus their valuation efforts on options that are most relevant.

In chapter 3, Ausubel and Milgrom consider the ascending proxy auction (Ausubel and Milgrom 2002) as an alternative to the Vickrey auction. Each bidder submits valuation information to a proxy agent. The proxy agents bid iteratively, bidding on the most profitable package, whenever the proxy agent is not a provisional winner. The auction ends when no proxy agent who is not a provisional winner has a profitable bid. The ascending proxy auction allows for bidders to have budget constraints. In the absence of budget constraints, and when goods are substitutes for all bidders, the ascending proxy auction yields the same outcome as the Vickrey auction. More generally, the ascending proxy auction finds a bidder-optimal point in the core with respect to the reported preferences. Moreover, all bidder-optimal core points are Nash equilibria in the auction game, if we assume full information about values (each bidder knows the values of the other bidders). The ascending proxy auction addresses many of the drawbacks of the Vickrey auction in environments with some complements.

In chapter 4, Cramton studies the simultaneous ascending auction (SAA). The SAA is not a combinatorial auction, because bids in a SAA are placed for individual items, rather than packages of items. Yet the SAA has proven to be a highly effective method of auctioning many related items (see Cramton 1998, 2002; Milgrom 2004).

Simultaneous sale and ascending bids enable price discovery, which helps bidders build desirable packages of items. The SAA remains a useful benchmark for comparison with true combinatorial auctions.

In chapter 5, Ausubel, Cramton, and Milgrom propose the clock-proxy auction as a practical combinatorial design. A clock auction phase is followed by a best-and-final proxy round. The approach combines the simple and transparent price discovery of the clock auction with the efficiency of the proxy auction. Linear pricing is maintained as long as possible, but then is abandoned in the proxy round to improve efficiency and enhance seller revenues. The approach has many advantages over the simultaneous ascending auction. In particular, the clock-proxy auction has no exposure problem, eliminates incentives for demand reduction, and prevents most collusive bidding strategies. Without the best-and-final proxy round, the authors present an iterative combinatorial auction that can be implemented as a simple clock auction, avoiding all computational complexity issues in a process with highly useful price discovery (Ausubel and Cramton 2004). Over two dozen high-stake auctions in several countries and several industries have used this auction format recently.

Chapter 6 discusses a combinatorial auction procedure called PAUSE, proposed by Frank Kelly and Richard Steinberg, which relieves the auctioneer of having to face the "winner determination problem," discussed below, a computationally intractable problem. Under PAUSE, the burden of evaluating a combinatorial bid is transferred to the bidder making the bid; the auctioneer need only confirm the bid's validity, a computationally tractable problem. As a consequence, although PAUSE permits all combinatorial bids, the procedure is both computationally tractable for the auctioneer and transparent to the bidders. In their chapter, Land, Powell, and Steinberg focus specifically on bidder behavior under PAUSE.

I.4 Bidding and Efficiency

As mentioned above, combinatorial auctions give rise to a host of interesting questions and challenges. To begin with, there is the question of what should be the bidding language. Different choices vary in expressiveness and in simplicity. A bid in an auction is an expression of the bidder's preference for various outcomes. The most direct way of capturing such a preference is to have a bidder attach a monetary value to each possible allocation. This allows one to express all possible preferences, but it is not simple. Given n bidders and m items, it requires a bidder to submit a bid of size n^m. If we assume no externalities, so that each bidder cares only about the items he himself receives, the complexity drops to 2^m, which is still impractical for all but small m.

Part II of the book addresses both bidding languages and questions of efficiency. Auction theory generally assumes a fixed number of bidders with each bidder acting independently according to the rules of the auction. One simple deviation from this model is for a single bidder to act as multiple bidders. Such pseudonymous bidding is the subject of chapter 7. Yokoo shows that the Vickrey auction is not immune to this problem, unless a bidder submodularity condition is satisfied. And indeed, all efficient auctions suffer from this problem. It is sometimes profitable for a bidder to bid as multiple bidders, rather than one, and this undermines efficiency.

In chapter 8, Bikhchandani and Ostroy examine the connection between efficient auctions for many items and duality theory. The Vickrey auction can be thought of as an efficient pricing equilibrium, which corresponds to the optimal solution of a particular linear programming (LP) problem and its dual. A "buyers are substitutes" condition is necessary and sufficient for the pricing equilibrium to yield the Vickrey outcome. Thus, when buyers are substitutes, an efficient pricing equilibrium can be obtained with any LP algorithm. The simplex algorithm can be thought of as a static approach to determining the Vickrey outcome. Alternatively, the primal-dual algorithm can be thought of as a decentralized and dynamic method of determining the pricing equilibrium, as in the ascending proxy auction of chapter 3.

In chapter 9, Nisan examines a variety of bidding languages and their properties. For example, we see there that OR ("additive-or") bids, which allow the bidder to make *non-exclusive* offers on bundles, can capture all, and only, the super-additive valuations. In contrast, XOR ("exclusive-or") bids, which allow the bidder to make *exclusive* offers on bundles, can capture all valuations, though they may require an exponentially longer expression than the OR bids. However, asking an agent to disclose a full valuation function is often not necessary, because many parts of it might be irrelevant for computing the allocation.

In chapter 10, Sandholm and Boutilier look at ways in which the valuation function of agents can be elicited piecemeal, as needed by the auctioneer. One of the questions there is what form the queries may take. Sandholm and Boutilier consider several primary forms, including queries about absolute bundle values, queries about differences between two bundle values, a simple ordering on bundle values, and several others. Among the experimental results they show is the fact that in practice only a small fraction of the preferences need to be revealed. Among the theoretical results presented are some natural valuation classes where preferences can be elicited with a polynomial number of queries even in the worst case; the fact that even if the real preferences only fall approximately into these classes, an approximation can be found with a polynomial number of queries; and the fact that there can be super-exponential power in interleaving queries across agents (i.e., deciding what to ask an agent based on what others have revealed).

In chapter 11, Segal asks how many bits of information are required to compute an efficient allocation, regardless of the protocol used and disregarding issues of incentives. One result states that any mechanism that is guaranteed to compute an efficient allocation must necessarily also discover supporting prices (though these will in general be neither anonymous nor linear). The main question Segal addresses is how one can trade off the extent of communication required with the economic surplus gained. For example, the trivial protocol in which bidders communicate their value for the entire set of goods, which is allocated to the highest bidder (again, ignoring the issue of incentives), guarantees $1/n$ of the available surplus (where n is the number of bidders) while requiring a single bid from each bidder. A more elaborate mechanism yields $1/\sqrt{m}$ of the available surplus, where m is the number of goods. Interestingly, this is also a lower bound for any protocol whose running time is polynomial in m.

I.5 Complexity and Algorithmic Considerations

Once the bidding language is fixed, the question remains as to how to compute the allocation, given a set of bids. This problem, called the *winner determination problem* (WDP) has received considerable attention in the literature, and is the primary focus of part III.

In chapter 12, Lehmann, Müller, and Sandholm provide a precise formulation of the problem and explore its basic complexity properties. The problem is this: Given a set of bids in a combinatorial auction, find an allocation of items to bidders, including the possibility that the auctioneer retains some items, that maximizes the auctioneer's revenue. The problem, which is most naturally represented as an integer program (IP), is inherently complex. Specifically, it is NP-complete, meaning that a polynomial-time algorithm that is guaranteed to compute the optimal allocation is unlikely to exist. Even worse, the problem is not uniformly approximable, in the following sense: almost certainly there does not exist a polynomial-time algorithm and a constant d that, for all inputs, the algorithm produces an answer that is at least $1/d$ of the correct optimal answer.

We then follow this sobering introduction to the WDP with some good news. First, in chapter 13, Müller explores some constraints on the set of bids that ensure that a polynomial-time solution does exist. One such condition is for the constraint matrix to be *totally unimodular*. A special case of this is of *linear goods*; for example, if each bid is for some contiguous stretch of time on a shared machine, the problem can be solved in quadratic time. Then, in chapter 14, Sandholm looks at algorithms for solving the general problem. Although we know that in the worst case any algorithm will run in exponential time, there exist rules of thumb for searching the space of allocations that in practice allow us to solve large problems (for example, with hundreds of thousands of bids and tens of thousands of items). Sandholm concentrates on *complete* heuristics, ones that guarantee that an optimal solution is found but do not guarantee the running time.

The discussion of the WDP in chapters 12, 13, and 14 ignores issues of incentives. The optimization is assumed to be inherited from some mechanism, such as the VCG mechanism, but solved without regard to the originating mechanism. As discussed, these problems are computationally hard, and sometimes admit only suboptimal solutions. In chapter 15, Ronen looks at the impact of such suboptimal optimization on the incentive properties of mechanisms. For example, he shows that with suboptimal procedures, the VCG mechanism is no longer individually rational, nor is it incentive compatible. However, he presents a modification of VCG that restores individual rationality and, to a certain extent, incentive compatibility. The chapter covers several other topics, including a non-VCG mechanism that is computationally easy and incentive compatible, whose economic efficiency, in a restricted domain, is bounded from below by $1/\sqrt{m}$ where m is the number of goods.

In the final chapter of part III, chapter 16, Pekeč and Rothkopf consider appropriate ways to reduce or avoid computational difficulties in combinatorial auctions. The authors briefly review the computational issues in combinatorial auction design, the context of auction design including the information available to the designer, and properties that the auction designer must trade off in selecting the auction format and procedures. The major part of their chapter discuss opportunities for mitigating computational problems at four points in the auction: before bid submission, at the time of bid submission, after bid submission but before the announcement of a tentative set of winning bids, and after the announcement of a tentative set of winning bids.

I.6   Testing and Implementation

In part IV, we pick up the question of how to test experimentally the various proposed solutions to the WDP as well as how best to test and implement mechanisms from part I.

In chapter 17, Hoffman, Menon, van den Heever, and Wilson consider how best to implement the ascending proxy auction of chapter 3. They consider three approaches for accelerating the algorithm. The first involves working backward from the efficient allocation and starting with the Vickrey prices, which provide a lower bound on prices. The second approach, increment scaling, solves the problem with large bid increments and then backs up and solves the problem again with reduced increments until the desired accuracy is obtained. The third approach combines the previous two. These three approaches each dramatically reduce the number of iterations needed to determine the ascending proxy outcome.

In chapter 18, Leyton-Brown and Shoham present the *Combinatorial Auction Test Suite* (CATS). CATS is a publicly available software package that generates a variety of winner determination problems. Specifically, it implements several parameterized families of bid distributions, some based on real-world applications (such as transportation networks), and some on historical distributions used by researchers in the field. The goal of CATS is to serve as a uniform test suite for WDP algorithms, and it has been used widely in this capacity.

In chapter 19, Leyton-Brown, Nudelman, and Shoham use CATS to predict the running times of algorithms for the winner determination problem. The difficulty is that, because the problem is NP-complete, even the best heuristic procedures will take exponential time for some instances. In many applications, it is important to know in advance how long a given algorithm will run on a given instance (for example, an auction for energy production tomorrow needs to determine a schedule of operation well in advance of tomorrow). The authors describe how machine learning techniques can be used to predict this running time reliably, and which features of a given instance are most predictive of this running time. As a bonus, they also describe a portfolio approach to the WDP, whereby several competing algorithms are pressed into service, and for each instance the algorithm that is predicted to perform best is chosen.

I.7   Combinatorial Auctions in Practice

In their seminal paper on combinatorial auctions, Rassenti, Smith, and Bulfin (1982) present a sealed-bid combinatorial auction for the allocation of airport time slots (i.e., takeoff and landing slots) to competing airlines.[4] Even if landing slots are bundled with takeoff slots (much like left and right shoes are bundled), the need for a combinatorial auction follows from the differing ways that airlines value packages of slots: some are substitutes, some are complements, and the valuations vary across airlines. Although auctions, combinatorial or otherwise, have yet to be used to allocate scarce runway capacity, congestion at many major airports is becoming an increasingly difficult problem. The Federal Aviation Administration is now evaluating a combinatorial auction approach for New York's LaGuardia airport.

The final section of the book, part V, considers four important applications of combinatorial auctions. Chapter 20 takes up the topic of auctions for airport time slots. Ball, Donohue, and Hoffman provide suggestions for mechanisms for air transportation systems both to expand capacity and to assure that the current, limited capacity is used safely and efficiently. The authors begin by providing a description of the history of the U.S. aviation system, detail current procedures for allocating landing time slots, and explain how market-clearing mechanisms might be able to rectify many of the shortcomings of the current system. They include a presentation of some of the components that they believe are necessary to assure the success of combinatorial auctions in this setting.

In chapter 21, Caplice and Sheffi explore how combinatorial auctions are being used for the procurement of freight transportation services, focusing on those attributes of transportation that make combinatorial auctions especially attractive, as well as describing some of the unique elements of transportation auctions. They present such auctions first from the perspective of the auctioneer, that is, the shipper, then from the perspective of the bidder, or the carrier. This is followed by a discussion of the relationships between shippers and carriers, as the contracts that govern them have certain characteristics that distinguish them to some extent from auctions for other applications discussed elsewhere in the book. In fact, the types of bids used in transportation are distinctive to that industry, so there is an entire section discussing them. In this industry, the winner determination problem is known as the "Carrier Assignment Problem," the next topic in the chapter. Finally, the authors present lessons from practice.

In chapter 22, we move from the private sector to the public sector. As Cantillon and Pesendorfer explain, the London bus routes market provides an early example of the use of a combinatorial auction format in public procurement. The authority responsible for the provision and procurement of public transport services in the Greater London area—valued at $900 million—was London Regional Transport (LRT). The authors present the four major issues LRT faced. First, what set of contracts should be auctioned? Second, how should LRT auction these contracts? Third, who should be allowed to participate? Finally, which criteria should they use to award the contracts? The authors also discuss the motivations for submitting a package bid, a description of their data together with summary statistics, and finally their empirical analysis.

The final chapter of the book, chapter 23, discusses combinatorial auctions for industrial procurement, which is potentially one of the largest application domains for combinatorial auctions. As pointed out by the authors, Bichler, Davenport, Hohner, and Kalagnanam, CAs have already turned into a topic of interest for software vendors and procurement managers in the business-to-business domain. However, despite reports of the existence of a number of applications of combinatorial auctions in industrial procurement, documentation and public information on design details are rare—possibly because of efforts to protect proprietary information. This chapter describes current practice in this domain, including a case study at Mars, Inc.

I.8   Conclusion

The field of combinatorial auctions has grown rapidly in the past ten years. This volume aims to make this knowledge accessible to a broad group of researchers and practitioners. Our hope is that integrating the work from the three underlying disciplines of economics, operations research, and computer science will significantly enhance the development of the theory and application of this emerging field.

Notes

1. Operations researchers were also active contributors to the early work on auctions; see, for example, Friedman 1956 and Rothkopf 1969. Indeed, most of the early work on auctions first appeared in operations research journals.

2. A probability density function f satisfies the monotone likelihood ratio property if the ratio $f(v|t)/f(v|s)$ is weakly increasing in v for all $t > s$. Typically, $f(v|s)$ is the probability density of a bidder's value v conditional on the signal s (an estimate of value). Intuitively, the likelihood of high values increases with the estimate of value.

3. Goods are substitutes when increasing the price of one does not reduce demand for the other.

4. This was the first major paper on combinatorial auctions. It introduced many important ideas, such as the mathematical programming formulation of the auctioneer's problem, the connection between the winner determination problem and the set packing problem as well as the concomitant issue of computational complexity, the use of techniques from experimental economics for testing combinatorial auctions, and consideration of issues of incentive compatibility and demand revelation in combinatorial auctions.

References

Ausubel, Lawrence M. and Peter Cramton (2004), "Auctioning Many Divisible Goods," *Journal of the European Economic Association*, 2, 480–493, April–May.

Ausubel, Lawrence M. and Paul Milgrom (2002), "Ascending Auctions with Package Bidding," *Frontiers of Theoretical Economics*, 1, 1–42, ⟨www.bepress.com/bejte/frontiers/vol1/iss1/art1⟩.

Cramton, Peter (1998), "Ascending Auctions," *European Economic Review*, 42, 745–756.

Cramton, Peter (2002), "Spectrum Auctions," in Martin Cave, Sumit Majumdar, and Ingo Vogelsang, eds., *Handbook of Telecommunications Economics*, Amsterdam: Elsevier Science B.V., Chapter 14, 605–639.

Cramton, Peter, Robert Gibbons, and Paul Klemperer (1987), "Dissolving a Partnership Efficiently," *Econometrica*, 55, 615–632.

Friedman, Lawrence (1956), "A Competitive Bidding Strategy," *Operations Research*, 4, 104–112.

Kagel, John H. and Alvin E. Roth (1995), *The Handbook of Experimental Economics*, Princeton, NJ: Princeton University Press.

Klemperer, Paul (2000), *The Economic Theory of Auctions*, Cheltenham, UK: Edward Elgar.

Klemperer, Paul (2004), *Auctions: Theory and Practice*, Princeton, NJ: Princeton University Press.

Krishna, Vijay (2002), *Auction Theory*, San Diego, CA: Academic Press.

McAfee, R. Preston and John McMillan (1987), "Auctions and Bidding," *Journal of Economic Literature*, 25, 699–738.

Milgrom, Paul R. (1981), "Rational Expectations, Information Acquisition, and Competitive Bidding," *Econometrica*, 49, 921–943.

Milgrom, Paul (2004), *Putting Auction Theory to Work*, Cambridge: Cambridge University Press.

Milgrom, Paul R. and Robert J. Weber (1982), "A Theory of Auctions and Competitive Bidding," *Econometrica*, 50, 1089–1122.

Myerson, Roger B. (1979), "Incentive Compatibility and the Bargaining Problem," *Econometrica*, 47, 61–73.

Myerson, Roger B. (1981), "Optimal Auction Design," *Mathematics of Operations Research*, 6, 58–73.

Myerson, Roger B. and Mark A. Satterwaite (1983), "Efficient Mechanisms for Bilatteral Trading," *Journal of Economic Theory*, 29, 265–281.

Rassenti, Stephen J., Vernon L. Smith, and Robert L. Bulfin (1982), "A Combinatorial Auction Mechanism for Airport Time Slot Allocation," *Bell Journal of Economics*, 13, 402–417.

Rothkopf, Michael H. (1969), "A Model of Rational Competitive Bidding," *Management Science*, 15, 362–372.

Vickrey, William (1961), "Counterspeculation, Auctions, and Competitive Sealed Tenders," *Journal of Finance*, 16, 8–37.

Wilson, Robert (1969), "Competitive Bidding with Disparate Information," *Management Science*, 15, 446–448.

Wilson, Robert (1993), "Design of Efficient Trading Procedures," in Daniel Friedman and John Rust, eds., *The Double Auction Market: Institutions, Theories, and Evidence*, Reading, MA: Addison-Wesley Publishing Company, chapter 5, 125–152.

I Mechanisms

1 The Lovely but Lonely Vickrey Auction

Lawrence M. Ausubel and Paul Milgrom

1.1 Introduction

William Vickrey's (1961) inquiry into auctions and "counterspeculation" marked the first serious attempt by an economist to analyze the details of market rules and to design new rules to achieve superior performance. He demonstrated that a particular pricing rule makes it a dominant strategy for bidders to report their values truthfully, even when they know that their reported values will be used to allocate goods efficiently. Vickrey's discovery was largely ignored for a decade, but the floodgates have since opened. Dozens of studies have extended his design to new environments, developed his associated theory of bidding in auctions, and tested its implications using laboratory experiments and field data.

Despite the enthusiasm that the Vickrey mechanism and its extensions generate among economists, practical applications of Vickrey's design are rare at best. The classic English auction of Sotheby's and Christie's, in which bidders iteratively submit successively higher bids and the final bidder wins the item in return for a payment equaling the final bid, is closely related to Vickrey's second-price sealed-bid auction, but long predates it. Online auctions such as eBay, in which bidders commonly utilize proxy bids authorizing the auctioneer to bid up to specified prices on their behalf, more nearly resemble the Vickrey design for a single item; however, these remain true dynamic auctions, as online bidders who submit proxy bids generally retain the ability to raise their proxy bids later. The most general and novel version of Vickrey's design, which applies to sales in which different bidders may want multiple units of homogeneous goods—or packages of heterogeneous goods—remains largely unused.

Why is the Vickrey auction design, which is so lovely in theory, so lonely in practice? The answer, we believe, is a cautionary tale that emphasizes the importance of analyzing practical designs from many perspectives. Vickrey's design has some impressive theoretical virtues, but it also suffers from weaknesses that are frequently decisive. This chapter reviews the theoretical pluses and minuses of the Vickrey design, highlighting issues that cannot be ignored in developing practical auction designs.

1.2 Description of the General Vickrey (VCG) Design

Vickrey's original inquiry treated both auctions of a single item and auctions of multiple identical items, providing a mechanism in which it is a dominant strategy for bidders to report their values truthfully and in which outcomes are efficient. For a single item, the mechanism is often referred to as the *second-price sealed-bid auction*, or simply the *Vickrey auction*. Bidders simultaneously submit sealed bids for the item. The highest bidder wins the item, but (unlike standard sealed-bid tenders) the winner pays the amount of the second-highest bid. For example, if the winning bidder bids 10 and the highest losing bid is 8, the winner pays 8. With these rules, a winning bidder can never affect the price he pays, so there is no incentive for any bidder to misrepresent his value. From bidder n's perspective, the amount he bids determines only whether he wins, and only by bidding his true value can he be sure to win exactly when he is willing to pay the price.

In Vickrey's original treatment of multiple units of a homogeneous good, which may be available in either continuous or discrete quantities, each bidder is assumed to have monotonically nonincreasing marginal values for the good. The bidders simultaneously submit sealed bids comprising demand curves. The seller combines the individual demand curves in the usual way to determine an aggregate demand curve and a clearing price for S units. Each bidder wins the quantity he demanded at the clearing price. However, rather than paying the prices he bid or the clearing price for his units, a winning bidder pays the *opportunity cost* for the units won.

In the case of discrete units, an equivalent way to describe the multi-unit Vickrey auction is that each bidder submits a number of separate bids, each representing an offer to buy one unit. These individual bids describe the bidder's demand curve. The auctioneer accepts the S highest bids. If bidder n wins K units, then he pays the sum of the K highest rejected bids by other bidders. For example, if a bidder wins two units and the highest rejected bids by his competitors are 12 and 11, then the bidder pays 23 for his two units.

Another way to describe the rule is that the price a bidder pays for his rth unit is the clearing price that would have resulted if bidder n had restricted his demand to r units (all other bidders' behaviors held fixed). This equivalent description makes clear the opportunity-cost interpretation of the winners' payments. The total payment for bidder n is computed by summing this payment over all items won, in the case of discrete units, or by integrating this payment from 0 to the quantity won, in the case of continuous units.

The mechanism can be used as either a mechanism to sell (a standard auction) or as a mechanism to buy (a "reverse" auction). Described as a standard auction, the buyers generally pay a discount as compared to the clearing price. Described as a reverse auction, the sellers generally receive a premium as compared to the clearing price. Indeed, the main point of Vickrey's seminal article was that the government cannot establish a marketing agency to implement a dominant-strategy mechanism in two-sided markets without providing a subsidy: "The basic drawback to this scheme is, of course, that the marketing agency will be required to make payments to suppliers in an amount that exceeds, in the aggregate, the receipts from purchasers" (Vickrey 1961, p. 13).

Since Vickrey's original contribution, his auction design has been melded with the Clarke-Groves design for public goods problems.[1] The resulting auction design works for heterogeneous goods as well as homogeneous goods and does not require that bidders have nonincreasing marginal values. As with Vickrey's original design, this mechanism still assigns goods efficiently and still charges bidders the opportunity cost of the items they win. The main difference is that the amounts paid cannot generally be expressed as the sums of bids for individual items. The extended Vickrey mechanism goes by various names. Here, we call it the *Vickrey-Clarke-Groves* or *VCG mechanism*.

Formally, we can describe the VCG mechanism as follows. Let $\bar{x}$ be a vector of goods that a seller has on offer and let $v_n(x_n)$ denote bidder n's value for any nonnegative vector x_n. Each bidder $n = 1, \ldots, N$ reports a value function $\hat{v}_n$ to the auctioneer. The auctioneer then computes a value-maximizing allocation: $x^* \in \arg\max_{x_1,\ldots,x_N} \sum_n \hat{v}_n(x_n)$ subject to $\sum_n x_n \leq \bar{x}$. The price paid by a bidder n is then $p_n = \alpha_n - \sum_{m \neq n} \hat{v}_m(x_m^*)$, where $\alpha_n = \max\{\sum_{m \neq n} \hat{v}_m(x_m) | \sum_{m \neq n} x_m \leq \bar{x}\}$. Notice that α_n depends only on the value reports of the other bidders and not on what bidder n reports.

To illustrate the VCG mechanism, suppose that there are two items for sale (A and B) and two bidders. Each bidder $n = 1, 2$ submits bids: $\hat{v}_n(A)$ for item A; $\hat{v}_n(B)$ for item B; and $\hat{v}_n(AB)$ for the two items together. Assume without loss of generality that $\hat{v}_1(AB) \geq \hat{v}_2(AB)$ and $\hat{v}_1(A) + \hat{v}_2(B) \geq \hat{v}_1(B) + \hat{v}_2(A)$. If $\hat{v}_1(AB) > \hat{v}_1(A) + \hat{v}_2(B)$, then the outcome is that bidder 1 wins both items. Applying the formula, his payment is $\hat{v}_2(AB)$. However, if $\hat{v}_1(AB) > \hat{v}_1(A) + \hat{v}_2(B)$, then the outcome is that bidder 1 wins item A (with an associated payment of $\hat{v}_2(AB) - \hat{v}_2(B)$) and bidder 2 wins item B (with an associated payment of $\hat{v}_1(AB) - \hat{v}_1(A)$). In each case, the winner pays the opportunity cost of the items won, and his payment depends only on his opponent's reports.

The first theorem confirms that the general VCG mechanism still has the properties that it is a dominant strategy for each bidder to report its values truthfully and that the outcome in that event is an efficient one.

Theorem 1.1 Truthful reporting is a dominant strategy for each bidder in the VCG mechanism. Moreover, when each bidder reports truthfully, the outcome of the mechanism is one that maximizes total value.

Proof   Consider any fixed profile of reports, $\{\hat{v}_m\}_{m \neq n}$, for the bidders besides n. Suppose that when bidder n reports truthfully, the resulting allocation and payment vectors are denoted by x^* and p^*, but when bidder n reports $\hat{v}_n$, the resulting vectors are $\hat{x}$ and $\hat{p}$. When bidder n reports $\hat{v}_n$, its payoff is:

$$v_n(\hat{x}_n) - \hat{p}_n = v_n(\hat{x}_n) + \sum_{m \neq n} \hat{v}_m(\hat{x}_m) - \alpha_n$$

$$\leq \max \left\{ v_n(x_n) + \sum_{m \neq n} \hat{v}_m(x_m) \middle| \sum_m x_m \leq \bar{x} \right\} - \alpha_n$$

$$= v_n(x_n^*) + \sum_{m \neq n} \hat{v}_m(x_m^*) - \alpha_n$$

$$= v_n(x_n^*) - p_n^*. \tag{1.1}$$

The last line is bidder n's payoff from truthful reporting, so truthful reporting is always optimal. We omit the tedious but routine check that no other report is always optimal.

The last statement follows by construction of the mechanism.   ∎

1.3   Virtues of the VCG Mechanism

The VCG mechanism has several important virtues. The first is the dominant strategy property, which reduces the costs of the auction by making it easier for bidders to determine their optimal bidding strategies and by eliminating bidders' incentives to spend resources learning about competitors' values or strategies. Such spending is pure waste from a social perspective, because it is not needed to identify the efficient allocation, yet auction formats in which each bidder's best strategy depends on its opponents' likely actions can encourage it.

The dominant strategy property also has the apparent advantage of adding reliability to the efficiency prediction, because it means that the conclusion is not sensitive to assumptions about what bidders may know about each others' values and strategies. This is a distinctive virtue of the VCG mechanism. Theorems by Green and Laffont (1979) and by Holmstrom (1979) show that under weak assumptions, the VCG mechanism is the unique direct reporting mechanism with dominant strategies, efficient outcomes, and zero payments by losing bidders. Here, we report a version of Holmstrom's theorem. To prove it, we need one extra assumption that we have not needed so far, namely, that the set $\mathscr{V}$ of possible value functions is *smoothly path connected*. This means that given any two functions in $\mathscr{V}$, there is a smoothly parameterized family of functions $\{v(x, t)\}$ that lies wholly in $\mathscr{V}$, and connects the two functions. More precisely, for any two elements $v(\cdot, 0)$ and $v(\cdot, 1)$ in $\mathscr{V}$, there exists a path $\{v(\cdot, t)|t \in [0, 1]\}$ such that v is differentiable in its second argument and such that the derivative satisfies $\int_0^1 \sup_x |v_2(x, t)| \, dt < \infty$, where $v_2 \equiv \partial v/\partial t$ here denotes the partial derivative of v with respect to the second argument.

Theorem 1.2 If the set of possible value functions $\mathcal{V}$ is smoothly path connected and contains the zero function, then the unique direct revelation mechanism for which truthful reporting is a dominant strategy, the outcomes are always efficient, and there are no payments by or to losing bidders is the VCG mechanism.

Proof Fix any values for the bidders besides bidder n and consider any mechanism satisfying the assumptions of the theorem. If n reports the zero function, then his VCG allocation is zero and his payoff is also zero. Suppose that n reports some value function $v(\cdot, 1)$ and let $v(\cdot, 0)$ be the zero function. By construction, a bidder with values of zero for every package is a losing bidder at any efficient allocation. Let $\{v(\cdot, t) | t \in [0, 1]\}$ be a smooth path of value functions, as defined above.

Denote the total-value-maximizing allocation when n reports $v(\cdot, t)$ by $x^*(t)$ and let $V(t)$ denote n's corresponding payoff in the VCG mechanism: $V(t) = \max_s\{v(x_n^*(s), t) - p_n(s)\}$. By the envelope theorem in integral form (Milgrom and Segal 2002), $V(1) - V(0) = \int_0^1 v_2(x^*(t), t)\, dt$.

Let $\hat{p}(t)$ be the payments made under any other direct revelation mechanism for which truthful reporting is a dominant strategy, the outcomes are always efficient, and there are no payments by or to losing bidders. Let $\pi(t)$ denote n's payoff in the alternate mechanism when his value function is $v(\cdot, t)$: $\pi(t) = \max_s\{v(x_n^*(s), t) - \hat{p}_n(s)\}$. By the envelope theorem in integral form, $\pi(1) - \pi(0) = \int_0^1 v_2(x^*(t), t)\, dt = V(1) - V(0)$.

Because there are no payments by or to losing bidders, $\pi(0) = V(0) = 0$, so $v(x^*(1), 1) - \hat{p}_n(1) = \pi(1) = V(1) = v(x^*(1), 1) - p_n(1)$. Hence, $p_n(1) = \hat{p}_n(1)$; the payment rule must be the same as for the VCG mechanism. ∎

Another virtue of the VCG mechanism is its scope of application. Theorems 1.1 and 1.2 above do not impose any restrictions on the bidders' possible rankings of different outcomes. The basic rules of the Vickrey auction can be further adapted if the auctioneer wishes to impose some extra constraints. For example, the government seller in a spectrum auction may wish to limit the concentration of spectrum ownership according to some measure. Or the buyer in a procurement auction might want to limit its total purchases from first-time bidders or might want to ensure security by requiring that the total relevant capacity of its suppliers is at least 200 percent of the amount ordered. One can replace the constraint that $\sum_m x_m \leq \bar{x}$ by any constraint of the form $x \in X$ without affecting the preceding theory or arguments in any essential way.

A final virtue of the Vickrey auction is that its average revenues are not less than that from any other efficient mechanism, even when the notion of implementation is expanded to include Bayesian equilibrium. Below is a formal statement of this famous revenue equivalence theorem.

Theorem 1.3 Consider a Bayesian model in which the support of the set of possible value functions, $\mathcal{V}$, is smoothly path connected and contains the zero function. Suppose the bidder value functions are independently drawn from $\mathcal{V}$. If, for some mechanism, the Bayesian-Nash equilibrium outcomes are always efficient and there are no payments by or to losing bidders, then the expected payment of each bidder n, conditional on his value function $v_n \in \mathcal{V}$, is the same as for the VCG mechanism. In particular, the seller's revenue is the same as for the VCG mechanism.[2]

1.4   Weaknesses of the VCG Mechanism

Despite the attractiveness of the dominant-strategy property, the VCG mechanism also has several possible weaknesses:

- low (or zero) seller revenues;
- non-monotonicity of the seller's revenues in the set of bidders and the amounts bid;
- vulnerability to collusion by a coalition of losing bidders; and
- vulnerability to the use of multiple bidding identities by a single bidder.

Later this chapter will show that a simple and intuitive condition on individual bidders characterizes whether these deficiencies are present. In economic environments where every bidder has *substitutes preferences*, the above-listed weaknesses will never occur. However, if there is but a single bidder whose preferences violate the substitutes condition, then with an appropriate choice of values for the remaining bidders (even if the latter values are restricted to be additive), all of the above weaknesses will be present.

In what follows, we will limit attention to auctions of multiple items, in which different bidders may want different numbers or different packages of items. One obvious reason for the disuse of the VCG mechanism for large-scale applications with diverse items is the same as for other "combinatorial" or "package" auctions: complexity in all aspects of its implementation. The chapters of this book on the winner determination problem give some insights into the problem facing the auctioneer. There are also important difficulties facing the bidder in such auctions.

Complexity, however, cannot be the whole explanation of the rarity of the VCG mechanism. Combinatorial auctions of other kinds have been adopted for a variety of procurement applications, from school milk programs in Chile to bus route services in London, England. Small-scale combinatorial auctions are technically feasible, so we are forced to conclude that VCG rules have not been employed even when they are feasible.

Analyses of the VCG mechanism often exclude any discussion of the auction revenues. This is an important omission. For private sellers, revenues are the primary concern. Even in the government-run spectrum auctions, in which priorities such as allocational efficiency, promoting ownership by small businesses or women- or minority-owned businesses, rewarding innovation, and avoiding concentration of ownership are weighty considerations, one of the performance measures most emphasized by the public and politicians alike is the final auction revenue.[3]

Against this background, it is particularly troubling that the Vickrey auction revenues can be very low or zero, even when the items being sold are quite valuable and competition is ample. For example,[4] consider a hypothetical auction of two spectrum licenses to three bidders. Suppose that bidder 1 wants only the package of two licenses and is willing to pay $2 billion, whereas bidders 2 and 3 are both willing to pay $2 billion for a single license. The VCG mechanism assigns the licenses efficiently to bidders 2 and 3. The price paid by bidder 2 is the difference in the value of one license or two licenses to the remaining bidders. Because that difference is zero, the price is zero! The same conclusion applies symmetrically to bidder 3, so the total auction revenues are zero.

Notice that, in this example, if the government had sold the two licenses as an indivisible whole, then it would have had three bidders each willing to pay $2 billion for the combined license. That is ample competition: an ascending auction would have been expected to lead to a price of $2 billion. This revenue deficiency of the VCG mechanism is decisive to reject it for most practical applications.

Closely related to the revenue deficiency of the Vickrey auction is the non-monotonicity of seller revenues both in the set of bidders and in the amounts bid. In the preceding example, if the third bidder were absent or if its value for a license were reduced from $2 billion to zero, then the seller's revenues in the VCG auction would increase from $0 to $2 billion. This non-monotonicity is not only a potential public relations problem but also creates loopholes and vulnerabilities that bidders can sometimes exploit.

One is the Vickrey design's vulnerability to collusion, even by losing bidders. Let's illustrate this with a variant of the preceding example, in which bidder 1's values are unchanged but bidders 2 and 3 have their values reduced so that each is willing to pay only $0.5 billion to acquire a single license. The change in values alters the efficient allocation, making bidders 2 and 3 losers in the auction. However, notice that if the bidders each bid $2 billion for their individual licenses, then the outcome will be the same as above: each will win one license at a price of zero! This shows that the VCG mechanism has the unusual vulnerability that even losing bidders may possess profitable joint deviations, facilitating collusion in the auction.

A closely related stratagem is a version of shill bidding—a bidder's use of multiple identities in the auction—as chapter 7 of this book discusses.[5] To construct this example, let us replace bidders 2 and 3 of the preceding example by a single combined bidder whose values are $0.5 billion for a single license and $1 billion for the pair of licenses. Again, the efficient allocation assigns the licenses to bidder 1, so the combined bidder is destined to lose. However, if the auctioneer cannot keep track of the bidders' real identities, then the combined bidder could participate in the auction under two names—"bidder 2" and "bidder 3"—each of whom bids $2 billion for a single license. As we have already seen, the result is that bidders 2 and 3 win at a price of zero, so the combined bidder wins both licenses at a total price of zero.

A related difficulty with the VCG mechanism arises even if all the bidders play their dominant strategies, with no collusion or multiple identities. Suppose again that bidders 2 and 3 each value a single license at $2 billion, but that by combining operations they could increase the value of the package from $4 billion to $4 + X billion. If all bidders bid their values as in the original Vickrey analysis, then the unmerged bidders 2 and 3 would pay zero and earn a total profit of $4 billion. A merger by bidders 2 and 3 before the auction would raise the price from zero to $2 billion, so the firms would find it profitable to merge only if X > $2 billion. Thus, although the dominant strategy solution of the VCG mechanism provides the proper incentives for bidding with a fixed set of bidders, it distorts pre-auction decisions related to merging bidders.

Notice that, in each of these examples, bidder 1 has a value only for the entire package. If we modified the examples to make the licenses *substitutes* for bidder 1, for example, by specifying that bidder 1 was willing to pay $1 billion for each license rather than just $2 billion for the pair, then all of our conclusions would change. The seller's total revenue in the first example would be $2 billion, which is a *competitive* payment in the sense that the payoff outcome lies in the core.[6] This modification reverses all of the related examples, eliminating non-monotonicities in seller revenues, profitable joint deviations by losing bidders, the profitable use of multiple identities in bidding, and the bias against value-creating mergers.

The substitutes condition turns out to play a decisive role in characterizing the performance of the Vickrey auction. The formal analysis below develops that conclusion. We show that the kinds of problems described above cannot arise if all bidders are limited to having substitutes preferences. Moreover, if the possible bidder values include the additive values and if they are not restricted only to substitutes preferences, then there exist values profiles that exhibit all of the kinds of problems described above.

Before turning to that formal analysis, we illustrate some other, simpler drawbacks of the VCG auction design.

The Vickrey theory incorporates the very restrictive assumption that bidders' payoffs are quasi-linear. This requires that payoffs can be expressed as the value of the items received minus the payment made. In particular, it requires that there is no effective budget limit to constrain the bidders and that the buyer, in a procurement auction, does not have any overall limit on its cost of procurement. Although we have no data on how frequently these assumptions are satisfied, it appears that failures may be common in practice.

It is easy to see that the dominant strategy property breaks down when bidders have limited budgets.[7] For example, consider an auction in which each bidder has a budget of $1.2 billion to spend. Values are determined separately from budgets: they reflect the increment to the net present value of the bidder's profits if it acquires the specified spectrum licenses. Bidder A has values of $1 billion for a single license or $2 billion for the pair. Bidders B and C each want only one license. For bidder B, the value of a license is $800 million. Bidder C's value is unknown to the other bidders, because it depends on whether C is able to acquire a particular substitute outside of the auction. Depending on the circumstances, bidder C may be willing to pay either $1.1 billion or zero for a license. In a Vickrey auction, bidder A should win either two licenses or one, depending on the last bidder's decision. In either case, its total payment will be $800 million, so its budget is always adequate to make its Vickrey payment. Yet, if A's budget limit constrains it to bid no more than $1.2 billion for any package, then it has no dominant strategy. Suppose that bidders B and C adopt their dominant strategies, submitting bids equal to their values. Then, if bidder C bids zero, then A must bid less than $400 million for a single license (and, say, $1.2 billion for the package) to win both licenses and maximize its payoff. If instead bidder C bids $1.1 billion, then A must bid more than $800 million for a single license to win a single license and maximize its payoff. Because A's best bid depends on C's bid, A has no dominant strategy.

Vickrey auctions are sometimes viewed as unfair because two bidders may pay different prices for identical allocations. To illustrate, suppose there are two bidders and two identical items. Bidder 1 bids 12 for a single item and 13 for the package, whereas bidder 2 bids 12 for a single item and 20 for the package. The result is that each bidder wins one item, but the prices they pay are 8 and 1, respectively, even though the items are identical and each has made the same bid for the item it wins.

Rothkopf, Teisberg, and Kahn (1990) have argued that the VCG auction design presents a privacy preservation problem. Bidders may rationally be reluctant to report their true values, fearing that the information they reveal will later be used against them. For example, the public has sometimes been outraged when bidders for government assets are permitted to pay significantly less than their announced maximum prices in a Vickrey auction (McMillan 1994), and such reactions can lead to cancellations, renegotiations, or at least negative publicity. Modern systems of encryption make it technically feasible to verify the auction outcome without revealing the actual bids, so the privacy concern may seem less fundamental than the other weaknesses reported above. Moreover, the widespread use of proxy bidders, in which bidders are asked to report their values or maximum bids, in electronic auctions conducted by Google (for ad placements), eBay, Amazon, and others, establishes that privacy concerns are not always decisive.

Our entire discussion above has assumed the so-called "private values" model, in which each bidder's payoff depends solely on his own estimate of value and *not* on his opponents' estimates of value. This is appropriate, inasmuch as the classic theory of the Vickrey auction and the VCG mechanism is developed for a private values model. Without private values, they immediately lose their dominant-strategy property.[8] Moreover, serious problems may arise when applying Vickrey auctions in other frequently studied models. In the common value model of Milgrom (1981) and the "almost common value" model of Klemperer (1998), revenues can be nearly zero for a different reason than above, related to the extreme sensitivity of equilibria in the second price auction to the winner's curse. In the model of Bulow, Huang, and Klemperer (1999), the allocational efficiency of the second price auction design discourages entry by bidders who are unlikely to be part of the efficient allocation. The paucity of entry can be another reason for very low prices.

1.5   VCG Outcomes and the Core

Our discussion of the weaknesses of the VCG mechanism began with a three-bidder example in which the auction revenues were zero. Several of the subsequent weaknesses were built by varying this basic example. Because the zero revenues example was very special, a basic question will be: How low must revenue be before it is unacceptably low? We will adopt a competitive standard: the payoff outcome must lie in the core.

To justify the core as a competitive standard, suppose that two or more risk-neutral brokers compete to purchase the services of the auction participants. The broker's profits are defined to be the value of the hired coalition minus the wages paid to those hired. It then follows that the competitive equilibrium price vectors of such an economy are the same as the payoff vectors in the core of the game. The reason is simple. First, the requirement of equilibrium that the brokers do not lose money is identical with the core requirement that the payoff allocation (or "imputation") is feasible. Second, the requirement of equilibrium that no broker can earn positive profits by any feasible strategy coincides exactly with the core requirement that no coalition can block the payoff allocation. The conditions imposed by equilibrium on the price vector are thus the same as those imposed by the core on payoff profiles.

To investigate the relationship between VCG outcomes and the core, we introduce some notation. We first define the coalitional game (L, w) that is associated with the trading model. The set of players is $L = \{0, \ldots, |L| - 1\}$, with player 0 being the seller. The set of feasible allocations is X, for example, $X = \{(x_l)_{l \in L-0} : x_l \geq 0$ and $\sum_{l \in L-0} x_l \leq \bar{x}\}$. The coalitional value function is defined for coalitions $S \subset L$ as follows:

$$w(S) = \begin{cases} \max_{x \in X} \sum_{l \in S} v_l(x_l), & \text{if } 0 \in S, \\ 0, & \text{if } 0 \notin S. \end{cases} \tag{1.2}$$

The value of a coalition is the maximum total value the players can create by trading among themselves. If the seller is not included in the coalition, that value is zero.

The core of a game with player set L and coalitional value function $w(\cdot)$ is defined as follows:

$$Core(L,w) = \left\{ \pi : w(L) = \sum_{l \in L} \pi_l, w(S) \le \sum_{l \in S} \pi_l \text{ for all } S \subset L \right\}.$$

Thus, the core is the set of profit allocations that are feasible for the coalition of the whole and unblocked by any coalition.

Let $\bar{\pi}$ denote the *Vickrey payoff vector*: $\bar{\pi}_l = w(L) - w(L - l)$ for bidders $l \in L - 0$ and $\bar{\pi}_0 = w(L) - \sum_{l \in L - 0} \bar{\pi}_l$ for the seller. The next several theorems and their proofs are taken from Ausubel and Milgrom 2002.

Theorem 1.4 A bidder's Vickrey payoff $\bar{\pi}_l$ is l's highest payoff over all points in the core. That is, for all $l \in L - 0 : \bar{\pi}_l = \max\{\pi_l | \pi \in Core(L,w)\}$.

Proof The payoff vector defined by $\pi_0 = w(L - l)$, $\pi_l = w(L) - w(L - l)$, and $\pi_j = 0$, for $j \ne 0, l$, satisfies $\pi \in Core(L,w)$. Hence, $\bar{\pi}_l \le \max\{\pi_l | \pi \in Core(L,w)\}$.

Now suppose that π is a feasible payoff allocation with $\pi_l > \bar{\pi}_l$ for some $l \ne 0$. Then $\sum_{k \ne l} \pi_k = w(L) - \pi_l < w(L - l)$, so coalition $L - l$ blocks the allocation. Hence, $\pi \notin Core(L,w)$. ∎

A payoff vector in the core is *bidder optimal* if there is no other core allocation that all bidders prefer. It is *bidder dominant* if it is the bidders' unanimously most preferred point in the core. More precisely, let $\pi \in Core(L,w)$. We say that π is bidder optimal if there is no $\pi' \in Core(L,w)$ with $\pi' \ne \pi$ and $\pi'_l \ge \pi_l$ for every bidder l. We say that π is bidder dominant if every $\pi' \in Core(L,w)$ satisfies $\pi_l \ge \pi'_l$ for every bidder l.

Theorem 1.5 If the Vickrey payoff vector $\bar{\pi}$ is in the core, then it is the bidder-dominant point in the core. If the Vickrey payoff vector $\bar{\pi}$ is not in the core, then there is no bidder-dominant point in the core and the seller's Vickrey payoff is strictly less than the smallest of the seller's core payoffs.

Proof By theorem 1.4, $\bar{\pi}_l \ge \pi_l$ for all $\pi \in Core(L,w)$ and $l \in L - 0$. Hence, if the Vickrey payoff $\bar{\pi}$ is in the core, then it is bidder dominant.

Conversely, suppose that $\bar{\pi} \notin Core(L,w)$ and consider any $\hat{\pi} \in Core(L,w)$ and any j for whom $\hat{\pi}_j \ne \bar{\pi}_j$. By theorem 1.4, $\hat{\pi}_j < \bar{\pi}_j$, so $\hat{\pi}$ is not bidder dominant, and $\hat{\pi}_l \le \bar{\pi}_l$ for all $l \in L - 0$. So, $\bar{\pi}_0 = w(L) - \sum_{l \in L - 0} \bar{\pi}_l < w(L) - \sum_{l \in L - 0} \hat{\pi}_l = \hat{\pi}_0$. ∎

An equivalent way of expressing theorem 1.5 is that if the Vickrey payoff is in the core, then it is the unique bidder-optimal point in the core. Otherwise, there is a multiplicity of bidder-optimal points in the core—none of which is bidder dominant.

We thus find that the seller's revenues from the VCG mechanism are lower than the competitive benchmark unless the core contains a bidder-dominant point. Only then is the Vickrey payoff in the core, and only then does the seller get competitive payoff for its goods. The next tasks are to investigate when the Vickrey payoff is in the core and to show that, as in the examples, the VCG mechanism's other weaknesses hinge on these same conditions.

The style of our analysis is to treat conditions that are robust to certain variations in the underlying model. One might motivate this by imagining that the auction designer does not know who will bid in the auction or precisely what values the bidders will have. The next two sections deal with the uncertainties in sequence.

1.6   Conditions on the Coalitional Value Function

For this section, it is helpful to imagine that the seller knows the set of potential bidders L but does not know which of them will actually participate in the auction. The question we ask concerns conditions on the coalitional value function sufficient to ensure that the Vickrey outcome meets the competitive benchmark, that is, lies in the core, regardless of which bidders decide to participate. This sort of robustness property is both practically valuable and analytically useful, as we will see below.

To explore the question described above, we introduce the concept of a "restricted Vickrey payoff vector" $\bar{\pi}(S)$, which applies to the cooperative game in which participation is restricted to the members of coalition S. Thus, $\bar{\pi}_l(S) \equiv w(S) - w(S - l)$ for $l \in S - 0$ and $\bar{\pi}_0(S) \equiv w(S) - \sum_{l \in S - 0} \bar{\pi}_l(S)$. We also introduce our main condition for this section:

Definition 1.1   The coalitional value function w is *bidder-submodular* if for all $l \in L - 0$ and all coalitions S and S' satisfying $0 \in S \subset S'$, $w(S \cup \{l\}) - w(S) \geq w(S' \cup \{l\}) - w(S')$.

Theorem 1.6   The following three statements are equivalent:

1. The coalitional value function w is bidder-submodular.
2. For every coalition S that includes the seller, the (restricted) Vickrey payoff vector is in the core: $\bar{\pi}(S) \in Core(S, w)$.
3. For every coalition S that includes the seller, there is a unique bidder-optimal core point in the restricted game and, moreover:

$$Core(S, w) = \left\{ \pi_S | \sum_{l \in S} \pi_l = w(S), 0 \leq \pi_l \leq \bar{\pi}_l(S) \text{ for all } l \in S - 0 \right\} \qquad (1.3)$$

Proof   Define $\Pi_S = \{\pi_S | \sum_{l \in S} \pi_l = w(S), 0 \leq \pi_l \leq \bar{\pi}_l(S) \text{ for all } l \in S - 0\}$. Suppose that (1) holds. It follows from theorem 1.4 that $Core(S, w) \subset \Pi_S$. For the reverse inclusion, suppose $\pi_S \in \Pi_S$ and that $S = \{0, \ldots, s\}$, where $s = |S| - 1$. Let S' be a subcoalition of S including the seller, say, $S' = \{0, \ldots, k\}$. We show that the blocking inequality associated with coalition S' is satisfied. This follows because:

$$\sum_{l \in S'} \pi_l = w(S) - \sum_{l=k+1}^{s} \pi_l$$

$$\geq w(S) - \sum_{l=k+1}^{s} \bar{\pi}_l(S)$$

$$= w(S) - \sum_{l=k+1}^{s} [w(S) - w(S - l)]$$

$$\geq w(S) - \sum_{l=k+1}^{s} [w(\{0, \ldots, l\}) - w(\{0, \ldots, l-1\})]$$

$$= w(S) - [w(S) - w(S')]$$

$$= w(S') \tag{1.4}$$

The first step in equation 1.4 follows from the feasibility of π, the second from $\pi \in \Pi$, the third from the definition of $\bar{\pi}$, and the fourth from bidder submodularity. Hence, $(1) \Rightarrow (3)$.

It is immediate that $(3) \Rightarrow (2)$.

For $(2) \Rightarrow (1)$, we show the contrapositive. Suppose (1) fails, that is, w is not bidder submodular. Then, there exists a player i such that $w(S) - w(S - i)$ is not weakly decreasing in S. Hence, there is a coalition S' including the seller and players $i, j \in S' - 0$ such that $w(S') - w(S' - i) > w(S' - j) - w(S' - ij)$. So, $\sum_{l \in S' - ij} \bar{\pi}_l(S') = w(S') - \bar{\pi}_i(S') - \bar{\pi}_j(S') = w(S' - i) + w(S' - j) - w(S') < w(S' - ij)$. Thus, the payoff allocation $\bar{\pi}_{S'}$ is blocked by coalition $S' - ij$, that is, (2) also fails.   ∎

Theorem 1.6 gives a sharp and complete answer to our question: the seller can be sure that the VCG mechanism will satisfy the competitive benchmark regardless of which bidders participate exactly when the coalitional value function is bidder submodular.

1.7 Conditions on the Goods Valuation Functions

Coalitional values in an auction are not primitive objects. Rather, they are derived from individual bidders' package values using the formula of equation 1.2. Moreover, it is not usually reasonable to suppose that the auctioneer knows the coalitional value function or the bidders' values from which they are derived. Also, a model of bidder values can include the case where some potential bidders might not participate by including the possibility that bidder values are zero. It thus seems worthwhile to investigate the conditions on individual preferences that determine whether VCG pay-offs lie robustly in the core. As we have already hinted, the key to the analysis is the condition that goods are substitutes.

In discrete models, demands for goods are necessarily multivalued for some prices, so we need to modify the standard definition of substitutes to accommodate that. Thus, we shall say that *goods are substitutes* if they are substitutes on the restricted price do-main for which demand is single valued. In particular, goods are substitutes if the de-mand for each is nondecreasing in the prices of others on the relevant domain. Let v_l denote a buyer's value function for various packages and let $u_l(p) \equiv \max_z\{v_l(z) - p \cdot z\}$ define the corresponding indirect utility function. Then, the substitutes condition has a convenient dual representation, as follows.

Theorem 1.7   Goods are substitutes for bidder l if and only if the indirect utility func-tion $u_l(\cdot)$ is submodular.

Proof   The following three conclusions follow directly from a version of the envelope theorem.[9] First, the indirect utility function u_l is absolutely continuous and differentia-ble almost everywhere in each good's price p_m. Second, the partial derivative $\partial u_l/\partial p_m$ exists for precisely those price vectors p at which l's demand for good m is single valued. Third, at those prices p, $\partial u_l/\partial p_m = -x_{lm}(p)$, where $x_{lm}(p)$ is the quantity demanded of good m at price vector p (that is, $x_{lm}(p)$ is the mth coordinate of $x_l(p) = \arg\max_{\hat{x}_l}\{v_l(\hat{x}_l) - p \cdot \hat{x}_l\}$).

By definition, the substitutes condition is satisfied if and only if $x_{lm}(p)$ is non-decreasing in each p_j for $j \neq m$. Thus, goods are substitutes if and only if $\partial u_l/\partial p_m$ is nonincreasing in each p_j for $j \neq m$. This is equivalent to the conclusion that u_l is submodular.   ■

It is a familiar fact that when the valuation v_l is concave, it can be recovered from its dual, the indirect utility function. Recovery is not possible for general non-concave valuations, because there do not generally exist prices that correspond to each quantity vector being demanded. In this problem, however, where each good is unique and priced separately, there are prices that support any demand vector. Consequently, as the next lemma verifies, the usual formula applies to recover the goods valuation func-tion from the indirect utility function.

Lemma 1.1   Suppose $z \in \{0,1\}^N$, that is, all items are individually identified and priced. If the indirect utility function is $u(p) = \max_z\{v(z) - p \cdot z\}$, then the correspond-ing goods valuation function is:

$$v(z) = \min_{p \in \mathbb{R}_+^N}\{u(p) + p \cdot z\}. \tag{1.5}$$

Proof For all p and z, $u(p) \geq v(z) - p \cdot z$, so $v(z) \leq u(p) + p \cdot z$. Let B be a large number that exceeds the incremental value of any good to any package. Then, $v(z) \leq \min_{p \in [0,B]^N} \{u(p) + p \cdot z\}$. For any fixed $z \in \{0,1\}^N$, set $p_m = 0$ if $z_m = 1$ and $p_m = B$ if $z_m = 0$. By inspection, $u(p) = v(z) - p \cdot z$. So, $v(z) \geq \min_{p \in [0,B]^N} \{u(p) + p \cdot z\}$. Hence, $v(z) = \min_{p \in [0,B]^N} \{u(p) + p \cdot z\}$. ∎

Formula 1.5 is helpful for proving the following theorem.

Theorem 1.8 If goods are substitutes for all bidders, then the coalition value function is bidder submodular.

The proof formalizes the following intuitive argument: first, if goods are substitutes for each member of the coalition, then they are substitutes also for the coalition itself. Second, when a member is added to a coalition, if that member is assigned some goods, that leaves fewer goods available for the remaining members, which affects them like raising the prices of the reassigned goods. Because the goods are substitutes, this "price increase" raises the demand for all other goods, that is, the marginal values of additional good rises. Thus, the marginal value of goods to a coalition is increasing in coalition size. The incremental value of an extra member to the coalition is the new member's value of its package minus the coalition's opportunity cost of that package. Because that opportunity cost is increasing in coalition size, the value of a member is decreasing in the coalition size, which is equivalent to the statement that the coalition value function is bidder submodular.

Proof For any coalition S that includes the seller, the value for package z is $v_S(z) = \max\{\sum_{l \in S} v_l(x_l) | x \geq 0, \sum_{l \in S} x_l \leq z\}$ and the corresponding indirect utility function is:

$$u_S(p) = \max_z \{v_S(z) - p \cdot z\}$$

$$= \max_z \left\{ \max_{\{x \geq 0 | \sum x_l \leq z\}} \sum_{l \in S} v_l(x_l) - p \cdot z \right\}$$

$$= \max_{x \geq 0} \max_{z \geq \sum x_l} \left\{ \sum_{l \in S} v_l(x_l) - p \cdot x_l - p \cdot \left(z - \sum x_l\right) \right\},$$

$$= \max_{x \geq 0} \left\{ \sum_{l \in S} \{v_l(x_l) - p \cdot x_l\} \right\}$$

$$= \sum_{l \in S} \max_{x_l \geq 0} \{v_l(x_l) - p \cdot x_l\}$$

$$= \sum_{l \in S} u_l(p). \tag{1.6}$$

As a sum of submodular functions, $u_S(\cdot)$ is also submodular. (This corresponds to the step in the intuitive argument of establishing that if goods are substitutes for the individual bidders, then they are also substitutes for the coalition S.)

Consider a version of equation 1.5 that applies to the coalition S:

$$v_S(z) = \min_{p \in [0,B]^N} \{u_S(p) + p \cdot z\} \tag{1.7}$$

where B is a large number, exceeding every marginal valuation, so that constraining prices to lie below B leaves the minimum value unchanged for all z. The objective function in equation 1.7 is continuous, antitone ("weakly decreasing"), and submodular in p and has weakly decreasing differences in (p, S). Applying the Topkis monotonicity theorem, the set of minimizers has a maximum element $p(S|z)$, which is an isotone ("weakly increasing") function of S. (This corresponds roughly to the step in the intuitive argument that the marginal value of any good is increasing in coalition size. However, the next step is to show that the price $p(S|z)$ corresponds to the marginal value for goods m such that $z_m = 1$.)

Fix any good m. If $z_m = 0$, then, by inspection, $p_m(S|z) = B$. Next, suppose that $z_m = 1$. Let $\varepsilon > 0$ and $p'_\varepsilon = p(S|z) + \varepsilon 1_m$. By definition of $p(S|z)$, demand for good m at price vector p'_ε is zero. Because $p_m(S|z) = B$ for goods j for which $z_j = 0$, demand for these goods is still zero at price vector p'_ε. By the condition of substitutes, demand for the remaining goods is undiminished. Hence, $z - 1_m \in \arg\max_{z'} v_S(z') - p'_\varepsilon \cdot z'$ for all $\varepsilon > 0$. By the theorem of the maximum, the same must hold for $\varepsilon = 0$, that is, $z - 1_m \in \arg\max_{z'} v_S(z') - p(S|z) \cdot z'$. So $v_S(z - 1_m) - p(S|z) \cdot (z - 1_m) = v_S(z) - p(S|z) \cdot z$, and hence $p_m(S|z) = v_S(z) - v_S(z - 1_m)$.

Let $z^n = (1, \ldots, 1, 0, \ldots, 0)$ denote a vector with n initial 1s. Without loss of generality, we may reorder the items so that $z = z^m$ for some m. Then,

$$v_S(z^N) - v_S(z^m) = \sum_{j=m+1}^{n} (v_S(z^j) - v_S(z^{j-1})) = \sum_{j=m+1}^{n} p_j(S|z^j). \tag{1.8}$$

We have already established that $p_j(S|z)$ is isotone in S for all z, so by equation 1.8, $v_S(z^N) - v_S(z^m)$ is isotone in S as well.

Notice that $w(S \cup \{l\}) - w(S) = \max_z v_S(z) + v_l(M - z) - v_S(M)$. By the preceding paragraph, the right-hand expression is a maximum of isotone functions of S, so $w(S \cup \{l\}) - w(S)$ is itself isotone in S. Hence, w is bidder submodular. ∎

Thus, we have established that the substitutes condition for goods values is sufficient to conclude that the coalitional value function is bidder submodular. If the possible bidder values for goods include all the additive functions, then the same condition is also necessary. To state this result clearly, we introduce three sets of value functions for goods. Let $\mathscr{V}$ denote the set of value functions that are possible for bidders in the auction, $\mathscr{V}_{add}$ the set of additive value functions, and $\mathscr{V}_{sub}$ the set of value functions for which the goods are substitutes.

Theorem 1.9 Suppose that there are at least four possible bidders. Further suppose that there is a single unit of each kind and that $\mathscr{V}_{add} \subset \mathscr{V}$. Then the following three conditions are equivalent:

1. $\mathscr{V} \subset \mathscr{V}_{sub}$.
2. For every profile of bidder value functions drawn for each bidder from $\mathscr{V}$, the coalitional value function is bidder submodular.
3. For every profile of bidder value functions drawn for each bidder from $\mathscr{V}$, $\bar{\pi} \in Core(L, w)$.

Proof By theorems 1.8 and 1.6, (1) $\Rightarrow$ (2) $\Rightarrow$ (3). It remains to show that (3) $\Rightarrow$ (1).

Suppose that the substitutes condition fails for some $v_1 \in \mathscr{V}$, which we may take to be the value function of bidder 1. Then, there exist two goods, m and n, and a price vector, p, with $p_n, p_m > 0$, such that for all $\hat{p}_m$ such that $0 \leq \hat{p}_m < p_m$, there is a unique maximizer x' of $v_1(x) - (\hat{p}_m, p_{-m}) \cdot x$ satisfying $x'_n = x'_m = 1$, and for all $\hat{p}_m > p_m$, there is a unique maximizer x'' satisfying $x''_n = x''_m = 0$.[10] By Berge's theorem, it follows that at the price vector p, both x' and x'' are optimal. Moreover, any alternative bundle, x''', with the property that $x'''_m = 0$ and $x'''_n = 1$ is strictly suboptimal at price vector p.[11]

Because $\mathscr{V}_{add} \subset \mathscr{V}$, we may take buyers 2, 3, and 4 to have additive value functions as follows: $v_2(x) = \sum_{k \neq n, m} p_k x_k$; $v_3(x) = p_m x_m + p_n x_n$; and $v_4(x) = \hat{p}_m x_m$ where $\hat{p}_m > p_m$. Because x' is optimal for buyer 1 at price vector p above, $w(0123) = w(012)$. Because x'' is the unique optimum for buyer 1 at price vector $(p_{-m}, \hat{p}_m)$ and because $p_n > 0$, $w(01234) > w(0124)$. At the Vickrey payoffs, $\bar{\pi}_0 + \bar{\pi}_1 + \bar{\pi}_2 = w(01234) - (\bar{\pi}_3 + \bar{\pi}_4) = w(01234) - ([w(01234) - w(0124)] + [w(01234) - w(0123)]) = w(0123) + w(0124) - w(01234) < w(0123) = w(012)$. So, coalition 012 blocks the Vickrey payoff allocation and $\bar{\pi} \notin Core(L, w)$. ∎

One joint implication of theorems 1.8 and 1.9 is that if each bidder n is permitted to select its report *independently* from a set $\mathscr{V}_n$ of possible reports of value functions—and if all reports of additive values are allowed—then the substitutes condition is both necessary and sufficient to assure that the coalitional value function is bidder submodular (and that the Vickrey payoff allocation is contained in the core). Although some other authors have observed that there exist profiles of reports that jointly satisfy bidder submodularity but fail the substitutes condition for individual bidders, this observation can be misleading. The force of our theorems is that if the information available to the auction designer comes in the form of restrictions on the individual bidders' possible values and if the sets of possible values are "plausibly large," then the auctioneer cannot be sure that the Vickrey outcome lies in the core. The difficulty of ruling out very bad outcomes when goods may not be substitutes is enough to explain the reluctance of many to use the VCG auction design.

Theorem 1.9 is closely related to theorems about the existence of competitive equilibrium goods prices in models like this one. Indeed, Milgrom (2000) shows that if $\mathscr{V}_{add} \subset \mathscr{V}$, then a competitive equilibrium exists for every profile of bidder value functions drawn from $\mathscr{V}$ if and only if $\mathscr{V} \subset \mathscr{V}_{sub}$. Thus, possible failures of the substitutes condition are problematic for traditional market mechanisms as well as for the Vickrey mechanism.

In presenting our examples, we claimed that failures of the substitutes condition are also closely connected to possibilities for manipulation in the Vickrey auction, including collusion by losers and the profitable use of bidding with multiple identities. We now show how these possibilities are connected to a failure of monotonicity of revenues in the set of bidders.

We define an auction to exhibit *bidder monotonicity* if adding another bidder always (weakly) reduces existing bidders' equilibrium profits and (weakly) increases the seller's equilibrium revenues. Bidder monotonicity formalizes the familiar property of ordinary single-item private-values auctions that increasing bidder participation can only benefit the seller. The next theorem shows that the substitutes condition is sufficient for bidder monotonicity in the Vickrey auction, and for loser collusion and bidding with multiple identities to be unprofitable.[12] Moreover, the substitutes condition is also necessary for these conclusions if the set of bidder values is otherwise sufficiently inclusive.

Theorem 1.10 Suppose that there is a single unit of each kind and that $\mathscr{V}_{add} \subset \mathscr{V}$. Then the following four conditions are equivalent:[13]

1. $\mathscr{V} \subset \mathscr{V}_{sub}$.
2. For every profile of bidder value functions drawn from $\mathscr{V}$, the VCG mechanism exhibits bidder monotonicity.
3. For every profile of bidder value functions drawn from $\mathscr{V}$, any bidding with multiple identities is unprofitable in the Vickrey auction.
4. For every profile of bidder value functions drawn from $\mathscr{V}$, any joint deviation by losing bidders is unprofitable in the Vickrey auction.

Proof $(1) \Rightarrow (2)$ Let S, S' $(0 \in S \subset S' \subset L)$ be any nested sets of players that include the seller. As before, $\bar{\pi}(S)$ and $\bar{\pi}(S')$ denote the associated vectors of Vickrey payoffs. By theorem 1.8, if every bidder has substitutes preferences, then the coalitional value function is bidder submodular. Hence, for every bidder $l \in S - 0$, we have: $\bar{\pi}_l(S') = w(S') - w(S' - l) \leq w(S) - w(S - l) = \bar{\pi}_l(S)$. The bidder submodularity of the coalitional value function also implies that: $\sum_{l \in S' - S} \bar{\pi}_l(S') \leq w(S') - w(S)$ (see Ausubel and Milgrom 2002, footnote 35). Summing these inequalities, we conclude: $\bar{\pi}_0(S') = w(S') - \sum_{l \in S'-0} \bar{\pi}_l(S') \geq w(S) - \sum_{l \in S-0} \bar{\pi}_l(S) = \bar{\pi}_0(S)$, as required.

(1) $\Rightarrow$ (3)   Let v be any profile of reports, let x be the associated VCG allocation, and let $S \subset L - 0$ be any coalition of bidders. Suppose that the reports of every bidder $l \in L - S$ satisfy the substitutes condition. As the proof of theorem 1.8 shows, $v_{L-S}(\cdot)$ is also submodular, because if goods are substitutes for the individual bidders, then they are also substitutes for the coalition $L - S$. Now consider any bidder $k \in S$. Recall that $\bar{x}$ denotes the vector of goods being offered. Then $v_L(\bar{x}) = v_{L-S}(x_{L-S}) + v_{S-k}(x_{S-k}) + v_k(x_k)$ and $v_{L-k}(\bar{x}) \geq v_{L-S}(x_{L-S} + x_k) + v_{S-k}(x_{S-k})$, because it is feasible to reassign x_k to coalition $L - S$ in bidder k's absence. Therefore:

$$\bar{\pi}_k(L) = v_L(\bar{x}) - v_{L-k}(\bar{x}) \leq v_k(x_k) - [v_{L-S}(x_{L-S} + x_k) - v_{L-S}(x_{L-S})].$$

Because $\bar{\pi}_k(L) = v_k(x_k) - p_k$, where p_k denotes bidder k's payment in the VCG mechanism, this implies:

$$p_k \geq v_{L-S}(x_{L-S} + x_k) - v_{L-S}(x_{L-S}) \geq v_{L-S}(\bar{x}) - v_{L-S}(\bar{x} - x_k), \tag{1.9}$$

where the second inequality follows from the submodularity of $v_{L-S}(\cdot)$. (The intuition for inequality in equation 1.9 is that the price paid by bidder k for x_k must be at least the opportunity cost of denying these goods to coalition $L - S$.)

Now suppose that a given bidder utilizes "shills" (i.e., multiple identities). Let $S = \{1, \ldots, |S|\}$ denote the coalition of these shills. Then,

$$\sum_{k=1}^{|S|} p_k \geq \sum_{k=1}^{|S|} \left[v_{L-S}\left(\bar{x} - \sum_{j \in S-k} x_j \right) - v_{L-S}\left(\bar{x} - \sum_{j \in S} x_j \right) \right]$$

$$\geq \sum_{k=1}^{|S|} \left[v_{L-S}\left(\bar{x} - \sum_{j=1}^{k-1} x_j \right) - v_{L-S}\left(\bar{x} - \sum_{j=1}^{k} x_j \right) \right]$$

$$= v_{L-S}(\bar{x}) - v_{L-S}\left(\bar{x} - \sum_{j=1}^{|S|} x_j \right).$$

The first inequality follows from equation 1.9 and the second from the submodularity of v_{L-S}. The sum telescopes to the last term, which is the price that the bidder utilizing shills would pay to acquire the same allocation in the VCG mechanism without shills. Hence, the use of shills is unprofitable.

(1) $\Rightarrow$ (4)   Let v be the maximum value function for the coalition of winning bidders. Because goods are substitutes for the winning bidders, v is submodular. Suppose a coalition S of losing bidders deviates and acquires the bundles $(\hat{x}_l)_{l \in S}$. Using inequality 1.9, the Vickrey price paid by any losing bidder l to acquire its bundle is at least $v(\bar{x} - \sum_{k \in S-l} \hat{x}_k) - v(\bar{x} - \sum_{k \in S} \hat{x}_k) \geq v(\bar{x}) - v(\bar{x} - \hat{x}_l) \geq v_l(\hat{x}_l)$. The first inequality follows from inequality 1.9; the second follows because the middle expression is the Vickrey

price for a lone deviator l for bundle $\hat{x}_l$, which is less than its value (because l is a losing bidder). We conclude that no coalition of losing bidders has a profitable joint deviation.

(3) $\Rightarrow$ (1)   Suppose that the substitutes condition fails for some value function $v_1 \in V$, which we may take to be the value function of buyer 1. Then exactly as in the proof of theorem 1.9, there exist two goods, m and n, a price vector, p, and two bundles x' and x'', such that at price vector p, $\{x', x''\} = \arg\max\{v_1(x) - p \cdot x\}$, where $x'_n = x'_m = 1$ and $x''_n = x''_m = 0$. Let $\Delta = v(x''_{-n}, 1) - v(x'')$ be the incremental value of good n to buyer 1 at x''. Following the proof of theorem 1.9, we may take buyers 2 and 3 to have the additive value functions of $v_2(x) = \sum_{k \neq n,m} p_k x_k$ and $v_3(x) = p_m x_m + p_n x_n$. Observe that, in the sincere bidding equilibrium of the Vickrey auction, buyer 3 receives a payoff of zero. However, suppose that buyer 3 can enter an additional bid, $v_4(x) = (p_m + p_n - \Delta)x_m$, under the false name of buyer 4. With this bid, the shill buyer 4 wins good m for payment of p_m. Also, buyer 3 then wins good n for payment of $\Delta < p_n$, so the shill bidding is profitable for buyer 3.

(2) $\Rightarrow$ (1)   The construction in the preceding paragraph also provides a violation of bidder monotonicity. Adding buyer 4, now a real bidder, reduces the seller's revenues.

(4) $\Rightarrow$ (1)   The preceding construction also applies if buyer 4 is a real bidder but has value function $v_4(x) = p_m x_m$. In that case, it illustrates profitable collusion among losing bidders.   ∎

1.8 Conclusion

Although the VCG mechanism has virtues that are important for applications, it also suffers from serious weaknesses that limit its usefulness.

The most obvious disadvantages of the design are the complexity of the problem it poses to bidders, the reluctance of bidders to reveal their values, and the strategic issues posed by budget constraints. Complexity problems are universal in auctions where bidders are required to enumerate values associated with all subsets or the auctioneer must solve a large integer programming problem. Bidder reluctance to reveal values is most significant when that information might leak out and adversely affect other decisions or negotiations. Budget constraints are serious. If budget limits applied to bids, then, as we showed, they can destroy the dominant strategy property even when there is no chance that the price charged will exceed the bidder's budget.

In the case of homogeneous goods and nonincreasing marginal values, one can avoid these three disadvantages of a Vickrey auction by using the efficient ascending auction of Ausubel (2006, 2004), in which the auctioneer iteratively announces a price and bidders respond with quantities. Items are awarded at the current price whenever they are "clinched," in the sense that the aggregate demand of a bidder's opponents becomes less than the available supply. The price continues to be incremented until the market clears.

With private values, the Ausubel auction yields the same outcome as the multi-unit Vickrey auction: truthful reporting is a subgame perfect equilibrium of the game; and in a discrete formulation with incomplete information, it is the unique outcome of iterated elimination of weakly dominated strategies. In the Ausubel auction, privacy is preserved, because bidders never report their demands at any prices exceeding the clearing price. And the Ausubel auction performs better in the face of budget constraints, because bidders have the opportunity to reduce their demands to keep within their budgets as the bidding evolves.

When the items being sold may not be substitutes,[14] the VCG mechanism suffers from additional problems that are decisive for most practical applications. It can generate very low revenues—so low that the outcome is not in the core. Revenues can fall when additional bidders are introduced and/or when bidders' values are increased. Collusion is facilitated: even losing bidders can have profitable joint deviations. Also, bidders can sometimes profitably pose as multiple bidders, using pseudonyms to bid and increase their profits. If bidders can have any additive valuation functions, then these several additional problems can be excluded only when the goods are substitutes for the bidders. Thus, the problems are serious in the very case of complementary goods for which package bidding is believed to have its greatest potential payoff. Moreover, even when goods are substitutes, the VCG mechanism still has other imperfections. As we showed by example, it can discourage value-creating mergers among bidders.

For all of these reasons, it is useful to think of the VCG theory as a lovely and elegant reference point—but not as a likely real-world auction design. Better, more practical procedures are needed. We offer our own candidate designs in Ausubel and Milgrom 2002, and in chapters 3 and 5 of this book.

Notes

1. The Clarke-Groves design was introduced in Clarke 1971 and Groves 1973.

2. The proof of theorem 1.3 is similar to that for theorem 1.2, relying on the envelope theorem to determine the expected payoff of each type of each bidder. Williams (1999) proves more generally that optimization over the class of dominant-strategy mechanisms yields the same objective as optimization over the (larger) class of Bayesian mechanisms. Krishna and Perry (1997) show that the VCG mechanism maximizes the seller's revenues over the class of efficient mechanisms satisfying incentive compatibility and individual rationality.

3. However, Ausubel and Cramton (1999) argue that in the extreme case of an auction followed by a resale market in which all available gains from trade are realized, a focus solely on efficiency is appropriate.

4. This and all subsequent examples are drawn from Ausubel and Milgrom 2002.

5. See Sakurai, Yokoo, and Matsubara 1999, and Yokoo, Sakurai, and Matsubara 2000, 2004 for the original treatments of what they have called "false name bidding."

6. In the unmodified example, the Vickrey outcome was not in the core. The coalition consisting of the seller and bidder 1 could "block" the Vickrey outcome because, by themselves, they earn a coalition payoff of $2 billion, but the Vickrey outcome gave them only a payoff of zero.

7. Che and Gale (1998) analyze revenue differences among first-price and second-price auctions in the presence of budget constraints.

8. Ausubel (1999) describes a generalization of the multi-unit Vickrey auction to environments where bidders receive one-dimensional signals, and each bidder's values may depend on its opponents' signals. With bidders' values depending on opponents' signals, the efficient mechanism cannot possess the dominant-strategy property, but it retains the somewhat weaker property that truthful reporting is an *ex post* Nash equilibrium.

9. See Milgrom and Segal 2002, corollary 4.

10. The detailed construction begins by noting that, if the substitutes condition fails, then for any $\varepsilon > 0$, there exist two goods, m and n, and a price vector, $(\bar{p}_m, p_{-m})$, such that: i) buyer 1 has unique demands at price vector $(\bar{p}_m, p_{-m})$ and $x_{1n}(\bar{p}_m, p_{-m}) = 1$; and ii) buyer 1 has unique demands at price vector $(\bar{p}_m + \varepsilon, p_{-m})$ and $x_{1n}(\bar{p}_m + \varepsilon, p_{-m}) = 0$. Hence, there exists $p_m \in (\bar{p}_m, \bar{p}_m + \varepsilon)$ at which the demand for good n changes from 1 to 0. Furthermore, $x_{1m}(\bar{p}_m, p_{-m}) \neq x_{1m}(\bar{p}_m + \varepsilon, p_{-m})$, for otherwise (given the quasilinear preferences), the change in the price of good m would have no effect on buyer 1's demand for good n.

11. Otherwise, by inspection, x''' would also be optimal at any price vector $(\hat{p}_m, p_{-m})$ where $\hat{p}_m > p_m$, contradicting the uniqueness of the optimum at such prices.

12. Makoto Yokoo, Yuko Sakurai, and Shigeo Matsubara show in a series of papers (Sakurai, Yokoo, and Matsubara 1999; Yokoo, Sakurai, and Matsubara 2000, 2004; and chapter 7 of this volume) that false-name bidding is unprofitable under increasingly general conditions. The most general condition requires that the set of possible bidder valuations be restricted to ones for which the coalitional value function is bidder submodular. Theorem 1.9 of this chapter provides a condition on the primitive preferences that implies this property of the coalitional value function.

13. For models starting with a fixed number of bidders N, the proof establishes that $(1) \Rightarrow (2)$, $(1) \Rightarrow (3)$, $(1) \Rightarrow (4)$, $(2) \Rightarrow (1)$ and $(3) \Rightarrow (1)$, provided $N \geq 3$, and $(4) \Rightarrow (1)$, provided $N \geq 4$.

14. Note that, in the case of homogeneous goods, the substitutes condition reduces to the condition of nonincreasing marginal values that was considered in the previous two paragraphs.

References

Ausubel, Lawrence M. (1999), "A Mechanism Generalizing the Vickrey Auction," Working Paper, University of Maryland.

Ausubel, Lawrence M. (2006), "An Efficient Dynamic Auction for Heterogeneous Commodities," *American Economic Review*, forthcoming.

Ausubel, Lawrence M. (2004), "An Efficient Ascending-Bid Auction for Multiple Objects," *American Economic Review*, 94, 1452–1475.

Ausubel, Lawrence M. and Peter Cramton (1999), "The Optimality of Being Efficient," Working Paper, University of Maryland.

Ausubel, Lawrence M. and Paul Milgrom (2002), "Ascending Auctions with Package Bidding," *Frontiers of Theoretical Economics*, 1, 1–42 ⟨http://www.bepress.com/bejte/frontiers/vol1/iss1/art1⟩.

Bulow, Jeremy, Ming Huang, and Paul Klemperer (1999), "Toeholds and Takeovers," *Journal of Political Economy*, 107, 427–454.

Che, Yeon-Koo and Ian Gale (1998), "Standard Auctions with Financially Constrained Bidders," *Review of Economic Studies*, 65, 1–21.

Clarke, Edward H. (1971), "Multipart Pricing of Public Goods," *Public Choice*, 11, 17–33.

Green, Jerry and Jean-Jacques Laffont (1979), *Incentives in Public Decision Making*, North Holland: Amsterdam.

Groves, Theodore (1973), "Incentives in Teams," *Econometrica*, 41, 617–631.

Holmstrom, Bengt (1979), "Groves Schemes on Restricted Domains," *Econometrica*, 47, 1137–1144.

Klemperer, Paul (1998), "Auctions with Almost Common Values: The Wallet Game and Its Applications," *European Economic Review*, 42, 757–769.

Krishna, Vijay and Motty Perry (1997), "Efficient Mechanism Design," Working Paper, Penn State University.

McMillan, John (1994), "Selling Spectrum Rights," *Journal of Economics Perspectives*, 8, 145–162.

Milgrom, Paul R. (1981), "Rational Expectations, Information Acquisition, and Competitive Bidding," *Econometrica*, 49, 921–943.

Milgrom, Paul (2000), "Putting Auction Theory to Work: The Simultaneous Ascending Auction," *Journal of Political Economy*, 108, 245–272.

Milgrom, Paul (2004), *Putting Auction Theory to Work*, Cambridge: Cambridge University Press.

Milgrom, Paul and Ilya Segal (2002), "Envelope Theorems for Arbitrary Choice Sets," *Econometrica*, 70, 583–601.

Rothkopf, Michael H., Thomas J. Teisberg, and Edward P. Kahn (1990), "Why Are Vickrey Auctions Rare?" *Journal of Political Economy*, 98, 94–109.

Sakurai, Yuko, Makoto Yokoo, and Shigeo Matsubara (1999), "A Limitation of the Generalized Vickrey Auction in Electronic Commerce: Robustness against False-Name Bids," in *Proceedings of the Sixteenth National Conference on Artificial Intelligence (AAAI-99)*, 86–92.

Vickrey, William (1961), "Counterspeculation, Auctions, and Competitive Sealed Tenders," *Journal of Finance*, 16, 8–37.

Williams, Steven R. (1999), "A Characterization of Efficient, Bayesian Incentive Compatible Mechanisms," *Economic Theory*, 14, 155–180.

Yokoo, Makoto, Yuko Sakurai, and Shigeo Matsubara (2000), "The Effect of False-Name Declarations in Mechanism Design: Towards Collective Decision Making on the Internet," in *Proceedings of the Twentieth International Conference on Distributed Computing Systems* (*ICDCS-2000*), 146–153.

Yokoo, Makoto, Yuko Sakurai, and Shigeo Matsubara (2004), "The Effect of False-Name Bids in Combinatorial Auctions: New Fraud in Internet Auctions," *Games and Economic Behavior*, 46, 174–188.

2 Iterative Combinatorial Auctions

David C. Parkes

2.1 Introduction

Combinatorial auctions allow bidders to express complex valuations on bundles of items, and have been proposed in settings as diverse as the allocation of floor space in a new condominium building to individual units (Bayers 2000) and the allocation of take-off and landing slots at airports (Smith, in the foreword to this volume). Part V of this book describes many applications.

The promise of combinatorial auctions (CAs) is that they can allow bidders better to express their private information about preferences for different outcomes and thus enhance competition and market efficiency. Much effort has been spent on developing algorithms for the hard problem of winner determination once bids have been received (Sandholm, chapter 14 of this volume). Yet, preference elicitation has emerged as perhaps the key bottleneck in the real-world deployment of combinatorial auctions. Advanced clearing algorithms are worthless if one cannot simplify the bidding problem facing bidders.

Preference elicitation is a problem both because of the communication cost of sending bids to the auction and also because of the cost on bidders to determine their valuations for different bundles. The problem of communication complexity can be addressed through the design of careful bidding languages that provide expressive but concise bids (Nisan, chapter 9 of this volume). Non-computational approaches can also be useful, such as defining the good and bundle space in the right way in the first place (Pekeč and Rothkopf, chapter 16 of this volume).

However, even well-designed sealed-bid auctions cannot address the problem of hard valuation problems because they preclude the use of feedback and price discovery to focus bidder attention. There are an exponential number of bundles to value in CAs. Moreover, the problem of valuing even a single bundle can be difficult in many applications of CA technology. For instance, in the airport landing slot scenario (see Ball, Donohue, and Hoffman, chapter 20 of this volume) we should imagine that airlines are solving local scheduling, marketing, and revenue-management problems to determine their values for different combinations of slots.

Iterative combinatorial auctions are designed to address the problem of costly preference elicitation that arises due to hard valuation problems. An iterative CA allows
bidders to submit multiple bids during an auction and provides information feedback
to support adaptive and focused elicitation. For example, an ascending price auction
maintains ask prices and allows bidders to revise bids as prices are discovered. Significantly, it is often possible to determine an efficient allocation without bidders
reporting, or even determining, exact values for all bundles. In contrast, any efficient
sealed-bid auction requires bidders to report and determine their value for all feasible
bundles of goods.

This ability to mitigate the preference elicitation problem is a central concern in iterative CA design. But there are also a number of less tangible yet still important benefits:

• Iterative CAs can help to *distribute* the computation in an auction across bidders
through the interactive involvement of bidders in guiding the dynamics of the auction. Some formal models show the equivalence between iterative CAs and decentralized optimization algorithms (Parkes and Ungar 2000a; de Vries, Schummer, and
Vohra 2003). Iterative CAs can address concerns about *privacy* because bidders only
need to reveal partial and indirect information about their valuations.[1]
• *Transparency* is another practical concern in CAs. In the high-stakes world of wireless
spectrum auctions, the Federal Communications Commission (FCC) has been especially keen to ensure that bidders can verify and validate the outcome of an auction.
Although mathematically elegant, the VCG outcome can be difficult to explain to
bidders, and validation requires the disclosure and verification of many bids, both losing and winning. Thus, even as readily describable *implementations* of sealed-bid auctions, iterative CAs can offer some appeal (Ausubel and Milgrom 2002).
• The dynamic exchange of value information between bidders that is enabled within
iterative CAs is known to enhance revenue and efficiency in single item auctions with
correlated values (Milgrom and Weber 1982). Although little is known about the design of iterative CAs for correlated value problems, one should expect iterative CAs to
retain this benefit over their sealed-bid counterparts. Certainly, correlated value settings exist: consider the wireless spectrum auctions in which valuations are in part
driven by underlying population demographics and shared technological realities.

Yet, even with all these potential advantages, iterative CAs offer new opportunities
to bidders for manipulation. The biggest challenge in iterative CA design is to support
incremental and focused bidding without allowing new strategic behavior to compromise the economic goals of efficiency or optimality. For instance, one useful design
paradigm seeks to implement auctions in which straightforward bidding (truthful demand revelation in response to prices) is an ex post equilibrium. This equilibrium is
invariant to the private information of bidders, so that straightforward bidding is a
best response whatever the valuations of other bidders.

Steps can also be taken to minimize opportunities for signaling through careful control of the information that bidders can share during an auction. Finally, the benefits of iterative auctions disappear when bidders choose strategically to delay bidding activity until the last rounds of an auction. *Activity rules* (Milgrom 2000) can address this stalling and promote meaningful bidding during the early rounds of an auction.

The existing literature on iterative CAs largely focuses on the design of efficient auctions. Indeed, there are no known *optimal* (i.e., revenue-maximizing) general-purpose CAs, iterative or otherwise. As such, the canonical VCG mechanism (see chapter 1 of this volume) has guided the design of many iterative auctions.[2]

We focus mainly on *price-based* approaches, in which the auctioneer provides ask prices to coordinate the bidding process. We also consider alternative paradigms, including *decentralized protocols*, *proxied* auctions in which a bidding agent elicits preference information and automatically bids using a predetermined procedure, and *direct-elicitation* approaches.

In outline, section 2.2 defines competitive equilibrium (CE) prices for CAs, which may be nonlinear and non-anonymous in general. The section explains connections between CE prices, the core of the coalitional game, and the VCG outcome. Section 2.3 describes the design space of iterative CAs. Section 2.4 discusses price-based auctions, providing a survey of existing price-based CAs in the literature and a detailed case study of an efficient ascending price auction. Section 2.5 considers some alternatives to price-based design. Section 2.6 closes with a brief discussion of some of the open problems in the design of iterative combinatorial auctions, and draws some connections with the rest of this book.

2.2 Preliminaries

Let $\mathcal{G} = \{1, \ldots, m\}$ denote the set of items, and assume a private values model with $v_i(S) \geq 0$ to denote the value of bidder $i \in \mathcal{I} = \{1, \ldots, n\}$ for bundle $S \subseteq \mathcal{G}$. Note that set $\mathcal{I}$ does not include the seller. We assume free-disposal, with $v_i(T) \geq v_i(S)$ for all $T \supseteq S$, and normalization, with $v_i(\emptyset) = 0$. Let $\mathcal{V}$ denote the set of bidder valuations. Bidders are assumed to have quasi-linear utility (we also use *payoff* interchangeably with utility), with utility $u_i(S, p) = v_i(S) - p$ for bundle S at price $p \geq 0$. This assumes the absence of any budget constraints. Further assume that the seller has no intrinsic value for the items.

The efficient combinatorial allocation problem (CAP) solves:

$$\max_{S=(S_1,\ldots,S_n)} \sum_{i \in \mathcal{I}} v_i(S_i) \qquad\qquad [\text{CAP}(\mathcal{I})]$$

s.t. $S_i \cap S_j = \emptyset, \quad \forall i, j.$

Let S^* denote the efficient allocation. Also, we write $\text{CAP}(\mathcal{I}\backslash i)$ to denote the combinatorial allocation problem without bidder i.

2.2.1 Competitive Equilibrium Prices

We can consider a hierarchical structure for ask prices in CAs:

Linear   Prices $p_j \geq 0$, for $j \in \mathcal{G}$, define additive prices on bundles, with $p(S) = \sum_{j \in S} p_j$.

Nonlinear   Prices, $p(S) \geq 0$, for $S \subseteq \mathcal{G}$, allow $p(S) \neq p(S_1) + p(S_2)$, for some $S = S_1 \cup S_2$ and $S_1 \cap S_2 = \emptyset$.

Nonlinear and non-anonymous   Prices $p_i(S) \geq 0$, allow discriminatory pricing, with $p_i(S) \neq p_{i'}(S)$ for bidder $i \neq i'$, in addition to nonlinear prices.

In the following definitions we adopt $p_i(S)$ for notational convenience. We intend to allow (but not require) with this notation nonlinear and non-anonymous prices. For instance, linear prices p_j can be considered to induce prices $p_i(S) = \sum_{j \in S} p_j$ for bundle S and bidder i.

Competitive equilibrium prices extend the concept of Walrasian equilibrium prices to a CA. Let $\pi_i(S, p) = v_i(S) - p_i(S)$ denote bidder i's payoff from bundle S at prices p and $\Pi_s(S, p) = \sum_{i \in \mathcal{I}} p_i(S_i)$ denote the seller's revenue from allocation S at prices p.

Definition 2.1 Competitive Equilibrium   Prices, p, and allocation $S^* = (S_1^*, \ldots, S_n^*)$ are in competitive equilibrium (CE) if:

$$\pi_i(S_i^*, p) = \max_{S \subseteq \mathcal{G}}[v_i(S) - p_i(S), 0] \quad \forall i \tag{2.1}$$

$$\Pi_s(S^*, p) = \max_{S \in \Gamma} \sum_{i \in \mathcal{I}} p_i(S_i) \tag{2.2}$$

where Γ denotes the set of all feasible allocations.

A competitive equilibrium (p, S^*) is such that allocation S^* maximizes the payoff of every bidder and the seller given prices. Allocation S^* is said to be *supported* by prices p in CE.

Theorem 2.1   Allocation S^* is supported in competitive equilibrium if and only if S^* is an efficient allocation.

This welfare theorem follows from a simple linear-programming (LP) duality argument for suitably extended LP formulations of the CAP (Bikhchandani and Ostroy 2002; see also chapter 8 of this volume). Moreover, CE prices always exist for the CAP. For instance, prices $p_i = v_i$ trivially satisfy the CE conditions. The main new element in CAs is that these CE prices must sometimes be nonlinear and non-anonymous. Bikhchandani and Ostroy also show an equivalence between the core of the coalitional game and the set of CE prices. All core outcomes can be priced, and all CE prices correspond to core payoffs.

Many iterative CAs are designed to converge to CE prices, and as such it is important to characterize classes of valuations for which linear, and nonlinear but anonymous, CE prices exist. We will also see that it is *necessary* that an efficient CA must determine enough information about bidder valuations to define a set of CE prices, and *necessary* that a Vickrey auction determines enough information to define a set of *universal* CE prices.

For the existence of linear CE prices, it is sufficient (and almost necessary)[3] that valuations satisfy a *goods are substitutes* property (Kelso and Crawford 1982; Gul and Stacchetti 1999). This substitutes condition is defined indirectly, with respect to a *demand set*:

$$D_i(p) = \left\{ S : \pi_i(S, p) \geq \max_{T \subseteq \mathcal{G}} \pi_i(T, p), \pi_i(S, p) \geq 0, S \subseteq \mathcal{G} \right\}, \tag{2.3}$$

which includes all bundles that maximize a bidder's payoff at the prices.

Definition 2.2 Goods Are Substitutes Valuation v_i satisfies *goods are substitutes* if for all linear prices p, p' such that $p' \geq p$ (component-wise), and all $S \in D_i(p)$, there exists $T \in D_i(p')$ such that $\{ j \in S : p_j = p'_j \} \subseteq T$.

The goods are substitutes (or simply *substitutes*) condition requires that a bidder will continue to demand items that do not change in price as the price on other items increases. Substitutes valuations include *unit-demand* valuations with $v_i(S) = \max_{j \in S} \{v_{ij}\}$ for all S and value v_{ij} on item j in isolation, but preclude the possibility of items with complementary values (Lehmann, Lehmann, and Nisan 2003).

Conditions for the existence of nonlinear but anonymous CE prices are less well-understood, but sufficient conditions presented by Parkes (2001, theorem 4.7) include *supermodular* valuations, *single-minded* bidders that value a particular bundle, and bidders with *safe* valuations such that each pair of bundles with positive value to a bidder share at least one item. Consider, for example, a bidder in the FCC spectrum auction that definitely needs lower Manhattan, along with as many of the geographically neighboring licenses as possible.

2.2.2 Minimal Competitive Equilibrium Prices
In fact, many iterative CAs are designed to converge to *minimal* CE prices. This can be useful for two reasons. First, minimal CE prices on bundles in the efficient allocation correspond to VCG payments for a restricted class of valuations. In this case, we say that the CE prices *support* the VCG payments. Termination with CE prices that support

VCG payments brings straightforward bidding into an ex post equilibrium. Second, Ausubel and Milgrom (2002; see also chapter 3 of this volume) show that implementing minimal CE prices (corresponding to buyer-optimal core outcomes) avoids the problems that can occur with the VCG auction when VCG payments are not supported with minimal CE prices.

Definition 2.3 Minimal CE Prices Minimal CE prices minimize the seller's total revenue $\Pi_s(S^*, p)$ on the efficient allocation S^* across all CE prices.

A bidder's payment in the VCG mechanism is always less than or equal to the payment by that bidder at *any* CE price (Bikhchandani and Ostroy 2002). Thus, minimal CE prices always provide an upper-bound on VCG payments. Moreover, a bidder's VCG payment is equal to the CE price on his efficient bundle in some CE (Parkes and Ungar 2000b).

A characterization in terms of the coalitional value function explains when the VCG can be supported simultaneously to all bidders in the minimal CE.

Let $w(L)$ for $L \subseteq \mathscr{I}$ denote the *coalitional value* for a subset L of bidders, equal to the value of the efficient allocation for CAP(L). The *buyers are substitutes* (BAS) condition requires

$$w(\mathscr{I}) - w(\mathscr{I} \backslash K) \geq \sum_{i \in K}[w(\mathscr{I}) - w(\mathscr{I} \backslash i)], \quad \forall K \subset \mathscr{I}. \tag{BAS}$$

Theorem 2.2 (Bikhchandani and Ostroy 2002) A buyers are substitutes (BAS) coalitional value function is necessary and sufficient to support the VCG payments in competitive equilibrium.

In particular, the VCG payments are implemented in the minimal CE (or buyer-optimal core) when BAS holds, and buyer-optimal core payoffs are unique exactly when BAS holds.

A number of ascending price CAs can terminate with minimal CE prices given a slightly stronger condition, that of a *buyer-submodular* (BSM) coalitional value function:

$$w(L) - w(L \backslash K) \geq \sum_{i \in K}[w(L) - w(L \backslash i)], \quad \forall K \subset L, \forall L \subseteq \mathscr{I}. \tag{BSM}$$

Bikhchandani and Ostroy (see chapter 8 of this volume) refer to BSM as *buyers are strong substitutes*. Clearly, a BSM coalitional value function also satisfies BAS. But there are cases for which values satisfy BAS but not BSM (see Ausubel and Milgrom 2002, section 7, for example). Interestingly, substitutes valuations implies BSM and is almost necessary. Roughly, if at least one bidder does not satisfy substitutes then one can construct substitutes valuations for other bidders such that the coalitional value function fails BSM (see Ausubel and Milgrom, chapter 1 of this volume, for further discussion). Thus, the same conditions for the existence of a *linear* price equilibrium are sufficient and almost necessary for the existence of *some* price equilibrium (although perhaps nonlinear and non-anonymous) that supports the Vickrey outcome.[4]

2.2.3   Universal Competitive Equilibrium Prices

Experiments have suggested that BAS can often fail in realistic settings for CAs.[5] In these cases the VCG payments are not supported in any price equilibrium. We can still design price-based CAs by characterizing a stronger condition on CE prices that implies enough information to determine VCG payments from these prices. For this, we restrict attention to the *universal* CE prices (Parkes and Ungar 2002; Mishra and Parkes 2004).

Definition 2.4 Universal CE Prices   Prices p are Universal Competitive Equilibrium (UCE) prices if:

(a) Prices p are CE prices.
(b) Prices p_{-i} are CE prices for $\mathrm{CAP}(\mathscr{I}\backslash i)$, meaning they support some efficient allocation in $\mathrm{CAP}(\mathscr{I}\backslash i)$, for all bidders i.

where $p_{-i} = (p_1, \ldots, p_{i-1}, p_{i+1}, \ldots, p_n)$.

In words, prices are UCE when an efficient allocation for the restricted allocation problem without bidder i is supported with prices p_{-i}, for each bidder i removed in turn. Thus, UCE prices are CE prices in the main economy and in every marginal economy. Note that UCE prices need not require that the same allocation is supported in every marginal economy. The prices must support *some* efficient allocation in each marginal economy.[6]

UCE prices always exist, for example $p_i = v_i$, for all bidders i, are UCE prices. Moreover, a universal price equilibrium provides sufficient information about bidder valuations to compute the VCG outcome.

Theorem 2.3 (Parkes and Ungar 2002)   Given a UCE with prices p_{uce} and an efficient allocation S^*, the VCG payment to bidder i is computed as:

$$p_{\mathrm{vcg},i} = p_{\mathrm{uce},i}(S_i^*) - [\Pi_{\mathscr{I}}^*(p_{\mathrm{uce}}) - \Pi_{\mathscr{I}\backslash i}^*(p_{\mathrm{uce}})], \tag{2.4}$$

where $\Pi_L^*(p) = \max_{S \in \Gamma}(p_i(S_i))$ for bidders $L \subseteq \mathscr{I}$.

In the special case when prices are equal to valuations, this adjustment is equivalent to the standard definition of VCG payments.

2.2.4   Informational Requirements

Both CE and UCE prices have a central role in the preference elicitation problem. First, any auction that implements an efficient allocation must determine a set of CE prices. Second, any auction that implements the Vickrey outcome must determine a set of UCE prices. Segal (chapter 11 of this volume) provides an extended discussion.

Because the VCG auction is basically unique amongst the class of efficient auctions that take a zero payment from losing bidders (Ausubel and Milgrom, chapter 1 of this volume), these equivalences confirm the central role of prices in developing iterative CAs.

Theorem 2.4 (Parkes 2002; Nisan and Segal 2003)   A combinatorial auction realizes the efficient allocation if and only if the auction also realizes a set of CE prices and an allocation supported in the price equilibrium.

This result requires a technical condition of *privacy preservation*, which precludes bidders from making their valuations contingent on the valuations of other bidders (e.g., "My value for A is at least bidder 2's value for A").[7]

Theorem 2.5 (Parkes and Ungar 2002; Lahaie and Parkes 2004b)   A combinatorial auction realizes the VCG outcome if and only if the auction also realizes a set of UCE prices and an allocation supported in the price equilibrium of the main economy.

Parkes and Ungar (2002) first proved that UCE prices provide sufficient information. The necessary direction is due to Lahaie and Parkes (2004b). It is important to realize that the CE and UCE prices referenced in these results may only be realized implicitly and are not necessarily explicitly constructed in the auctions.

Considering minimal CE prices in particular, Mishra and Parkes (2004) note that minimal CE prices are universal if and only if BAS holds. In general, UCE prices are greater than the minimal CE prices because they must consider competition in the marginal economies in addition to the main economy.

The informational equivalence between the efficient outcome and the problem of discovering CE prices leads to a (largely negative) characterization of the worst-case communication complexity and preference-elicitation requirements of *any* efficient CA, iterative or otherwise (Segal, chapter 11 of this volume). On the other hand, iterative CAs are designed to have good elicitation properties on typical instances, whereas sealed-bid auctions must suffer the worst case every time. Moreover, this price equivalence suggests the central role of prices in the design of iterative CAs. Any protocol to determine the VCG outcome must (implicitly) determine UCE prices, so why not construct protocols to converge directly to UCE prices? We return to this theme in section 2.4.

2.2.5 Examples

The following examples illustrate the concept of CE and UCE prices and also serve to illustrate the principle that it is often unnecessary to receive complete information about bidder valuations to determine the Vickrey outcome. For each example, we define a space of valuations (that contain the true valuations) that provides sufficient information to determine the Vickrey outcome. The information is minimal—we call this a *minimal information set*—in the sense that no relaxed constraints on valuations are sufficient to pin down the Vickrey outcome.

Example 2.1 Consider a single-item auction with three bidders and values $(10, 8, 6)$. The efficient allocation assigns the item to bidder 1, and the Vickrey payment is $8. Prices $10 \geq p \geq 8$ are all in CE, and $p = \$8$ is the unique anonymous UCE price. Notice that the UCE price must be at least $8 to satisfy CE condition (1) for bidder 2 in $CAP(\{1, 2, 3\})$ but no greater than $8 to satisfy the same condition for bidder 2 in $CAP(\{2, 3\})$. The CE prices define a minimal information set, $\hat{\mathcal{V}}_1$, defined as the subset of valuations that satisfy constraints $\{v_1 \geq p, v_2 \leq p, v_3 \leq p, 10 \geq p \geq 8\}$. UCE prices imply additional information $\{v_2 = 8, v_3 \leq 8\}$, which together with $\hat{\mathcal{V}}_1$ is a minimal information set for the VCG outcome. Notice that an ascending price (i.e., English) auction can elicit this information if bidders 1 and 2 bid up the price to just above 8, at which point the auction terminates. Bidder 3 can remain silent.

Example 2.2 Consider a combinatorial allocation problem with items $\{A, B\}$ and five bidders (see table 2.1). The efficient allocation allocates A to bidder 1 and B to bidder 2 for a total value of 70. The VCG payments are $p_{\text{vcg}, 1} = 30 - (70 - 65) = 25$ and $p_{\text{vcg}, 2} = 40 - (70 - 55) = 25$. Table 2.1(b) illustrates an information set on bidder valuations, which is sufficient to compute the VCG outcome and minimal in the sense that no constraints can be relaxed. The following prices are UCE for any valuation in this

Table 2.1
Example 2.2: (a) Bidder valuations, with the efficient allocation indicated by *. (b) Minimal information on bidder valuations to compute the VCG outcome.

	A	B	AB	minimal information set
Bidder 1	30*	0	30	$v_1(A) \geq v_1(B)$, $v_1(A) \geq v_1(AB)$, $v_1(A) \geq 25$
Bidder 2	0	40*	40	$v_2(B) \geq v_2(A)$, $v_2(B) \geq v_2(AB)$, $v_2(B) \geq 25$
Bidder 3	0	20	40	$v_3(A) \leq 0$, $v_3(B) \leq 20$, $v_3(AB) \leq 40$
Bidder 4	25	0	25	$v_4(AB) \leq 25$
Bidder 5	0	25	25	$v_5(AB) \leq 25$

(a)   (b)

set: $p(A) = 25$, $p(B) = 25$, $p(AB) = 25$ to bidders $\{1, 2, 4, 5\}$ and prices $p_3(A) = 20$, $p_3(B) = 20$, $p_3(AB) = 40$ to bidder 3. In fact, these prices are also minimal CE prices and the discount computed in equation 2.4 is zero for bidders 1 and 2, and BAS is satisfied (because of the presence of bidders 4 and 5). Without these bidders, the BAS condition fails and the VCG payments become $p_{\text{vcg},1} = 0$ and $p_{\text{vcg},2} = 20$, which can be computed from UCE prices $p_1 = (20, 0, 20)$, $p_2 = (0, 40, 40)$ and $p_3 = (0, 20, 40)$. Additional information is needed from bidder 2 in this variation.

2.3 The Design Space for Iterative Combinatorial Auctions

The design space for iterative CAs is larger than for one-shot auctions. Important considerations include the design of information feedback to bidders and rules to guide the submission of bids. Cramton (chapter 4 of this volume) provides an in-depth discussion of many of these issues in the design of simultaneous ascending price auctions.

Let the *state* of an auction include all the information that is sufficient to define the future dynamics of the auction. For example, the state of an auction can define the ask prices, the provisional allocation, and also the bid improvement rules as they apply to particular bidders. Briefly, we can consider the role of the following design features:

Timing issues   Iterative auctions may be *continuous*, allowing bids to be submitted at any time with continual updates to the current provisional allocation and prices. Alternatively, iterative auctions may be *discrete*, or round-based, with the state updated periodically and with bidders provided with an opportunity to revise bids between rounds.

Continuous auctions can promote faster propagation of feedback information to bidders and help quickly to focus elicitation. However, continuous *combinatorial* auctions can be infeasible because the winner-determination problem must be resolved whenever a new bid is submitted. Continuous auctions also lead to high monitoring and participation costs for bidders. In comparison, discrete auctions allow an auctioneer to publish a *schedule* for rounds in the auction and bidders can plan when to allocate time to refine their values and bids.

Information feedback   Information feedback about the state of an auction can include information about the bids submitted and also aggregate information, such as price feedback and the current provisional allocation, to guide bidding. Information hiding is also possible, for example, with *rounding* to limit the potential for signaling between bidders and with limited and discriminatory reporting of bid information.

Information feedback policies make a tradeoff between serving the goal of providing effective bid guidance and minimizing the opportunity for collusion and other forms of manipulation through signaling and coordination.

Bidding rules   Ask prices are a common form of *bid improvement* rule, placing a lower-bound on the allowable bid price on a bundle. Bid improvement rules can also require a minimal *percentage improvement* over the current highest bid on a bundle, or over the total revenue in the next round given current bids. *Activity rules* (Milgrom 2000) introduce further restrictions, such as requiring that a bidder bids for a decreasing market share as prices increase during an auction. Ausubel, Cramton, and Milgrom (chapter 5 of this volume) provide an extended discussion of bid-improvement and activity rules.

Activity rules were introduced in the early FCC wireless spectrum auctions and proved important.[8] Decisions about appropriate rules are often guided by a tradeoff between providing *expressiveness* so that bidders can follow straightforward bidding strategies, while promoting early information exchange between bidders and limiting the opportunity for bidders to wait and snipe at the end of an auction. Computational considerations also matter; for example, linear prices can simplify the problem facing bidders in an auction (Kwasnica et al. 2005) but can be expensive to compute (Hoffman 2001).

Termination conditions   Auctions may close at a *fixed deadline*, perhaps with an opportunity for a final sealed-bid round of bidding (sometimes called a proxy round). Alternatively, auctions can have a *rolling closure* with the auction kept open while one or more losing bidders continue to submit competitive bids.

Fixed deadlines are useful in settings in which bidders are impatient and unwilling to wait a long time for an auction to terminate. However, fixed deadlines tend to require stronger activity rules to prevent the auction reducing to a sealed-bid auction with bids delayed until the final round. In comparison, researchers have shown that rolling closure rules promote early and sincere bidding.[9]

Bidding languages   A bid can be a complex object and expressed in terms of logical connectives (Nisan, chapter 9 of this volume). One popular bidding language is *exclusive-or* (XOR), in which bid (p_1, S_1) xor (p_2, S_2) xor ... xor (p_l, S_l) has semantics "I will buy *at most one* of these bundles" at the stated bid price. Another popular language is *additive-or* (OR) bidding languages, in which bid (p_1, S_1) or (p_2, S_2) or ... or (p_l, S_l) has semantics "I will buy *one or more* of these bundles" at the stated bid price. Bidding languages can also place constraints on the bid prices, for example by requiring *click-box bidding* in which bidders must submit bids from a menu.[10]

The expressiveness of a bidding language in an iterative CA must be considered together with the opportunity to refine bids during an auction. For instance, a language that is additive-or on *items* is not expressive in a one-shot CA but becomes expressive in an ascending auction when bidders can decommit from bids.[11] Bidding languages are often designed to support straightforward bidding with bidders able to state the bundle that maximizes their surplus in response to prices in each round.

Proxy agents   Proxy agents provide a still richer interface for iterative CAs (Parkes and Ungar 2000b; Ausubel and Milgrom 2002). Bidders can provide direct value information to an *automated bidding agent* that bids on their behalf within an auction. The bidder-to-proxy language should allow a bidder to express *partial* and *incomplete* information, to be refined during the auction, in order to realize the elicitation and price discovery benefits of an iterative auction.

Proxy agents can query a bidder actively when they have insufficient information to submit bids. Proxy agents can also facilitate faster convergence with rapid automated proxy rounds interleaved with bidder rounds. Mandatory proxy agents can be useful in restricting the strategy space available to bidders.

One concern in the design of proxy auctions is to determine when to allow proxy information to be revised and to determine the degree of consistency to enforce across revisions. An additional concern is that of *trust* and *transparency* because the bidding activity is transferred to automated agents.

2.4   Price-Based Iterative Combinatorial Auctions

Many iterative CAs are price based and provide ask prices to guide bidding. In this section we survey some of these auction designs. We limit our attention to auctions designed for valuations that are rich enough to include the substitutes valuations. As such, we exclude the assignment model in which bidders have unit-demand for items (see Bikhchandani and Ostroy, chapter 8 of this volume for a taxonomy that includes this case).

All the auctions that we discuss share the same high level structure:

In each round the auctioneer announces ask prices and a provisional allocation and requests new bids from bidders. The bids are used to formulate a new winner-determination problem and update the provisional allocation, and also to adjust ask prices and test for termination.

Table 2.2 provides a summary of the characteristics of some well-known auctions, stating properties for *straightforward* (nonstrategic) bidding. For the cases in which an auction terminates with the VCG outcome this assumption is justified in an ex post equilibrium, but otherwise one should expect incentives for demand reduction. The auctions are described in terms of the structure of the price space, the bidding language, and the method used to update prices.

We see a wide variety of prices, from simple prices on items (linear prices) to non-anonymous prices on bundles (non-anonymous and nonlinear). In addition, the auctions vary in the bids that a bidder can submit in each round: *OR-items*, an additive-or bid for multiple items; *XOR*, an exclusive-or bid for multiple bundles; *single*, a bid on a single bundle in each round; *OR*, an additive-or bid for multiple bundles. The *XOR* language has emerged as the definitive choice in recent designs.

The *price-update* methods, which characterize the rules by which prices are computed in each round, are broken down as follows:

Greedy update   The price is increased on some arbitrary set (perhaps all) of the over-demanded items or bundles.

Table 2.2
Price-based combinatorial auctions

Name	Valuations	Price Structure	Bidding Language	Price Update Method	Outcome
KC	substitutes	nonanon items	OR-items	greedy	CE
SAA	substitutes	items	OR-items	greedy	CE
GS	substitutes	items	XOR	minimal	min CE[12]
Aus	substitutes	items	single	greedy[a]	VCG
iBundle; Ascending-proxy[b]	BSM	nonanon bundles	XOR	greedy	VCG
...	general	...	...	...	min CE
dVSV	BSM	nonanon bundles	XOR	minimal	VCG
Clock-proxy	BSM	items (+ proxy)[c]	XOR	greedy	VCG
...	general	...	...	...	min CE
RAD	general	items	OR	LP-based	–
AkBA	general	anon bundles	XOR	LP-based	–
iBEA	general	nonanon bundles	XOR	greedy[d]	VCG
MP	general	nonanon bundles	XOR	minimal[d]	VCG

Note: Formal properties are stated for straightforward bidding, and with the most general class of valuations for which the property holds. Notation – in the *Outcome* column indicates that no formal properties have been established.

[a] Aus traces $n + 1$ trajectories.

[b] Ascending-proxy dynamics are identical to iBundle(3), although ascending-proxy emphasizes a sealed-bid proxy auction form.

[c] Clock-proxy is a hybrid design, with a linear-price clock auction followed by a sealed-bid ascending-proxy auction.

[d] Ascending price while the auction is open, followed by a downwards adjustment after termination.

KC (Kelso and Crawford 1982), GS (Gul and Stacchetti 2000), iBundle (Parkes and Ungar 2000a), dVSV (de Vries, Schummer, and Vohra 2003), RAD (Kwasnica et al. 2003), iBEA (Parkes and Ungar 2002), SAA (Milgrom 2000), Aus (Ausubel 2002), Ascending-proxy (Ausubel and Milgrom 2002), Clock-proxy (Ausubel, Cramton, and Milgrom, chapter 5), AkBA (Wurman and Wellman 2000), MP (Mishra and Parkes 2004).

Minimal update   The price is increased on a minimal set of *overdemanded items*, or based on the bids from a set of *minimally undersupplied bidders*.

LP-based   A linear program, formulated to find prices that are good approximations to CE prices given current bids, is used to adjust prices.

For linear prices, Demange, Gale, and Sotomayor (1986) in the assignment model and later Gul and Stacchetti (2000) for substitutes define a minimal update in terms of increasing the prices on a minimal overdemanded set of items.[13] Minimal price updates are adopted to drive prices toward minimal CE prices. De Vries, Schummer, and Vohra (2003) generalize this to define updates in terms of minimally under-supplied bidders[14] and define a minimal update for general CAs. All bidders in a mini-mally undersupplied set face higher prices on the bundles for which they submitted a bid.

RAD and A*k*BA adopt LP-based price updates and adjust prices to find good approxi-mations to CE prices given current bids and the current provisional allocation. RAD seeks linear and anonymous prices, whereas A*k*BA seeks nonlinear but anonymous price approximations. Formal convergence properties have not been proved for RAD or A*k*BA, although RAD reduces to a simultaneous ascending price auction for substi-tutes valuations.

The auctions that are able to implement the VCG outcome (for instance, Aus for substitutes and dVSV for BSM coalitional values) are interesting because they bring straightforward bidding into an equilibrium. Straightforward bidding is a best re-sponse, whatever the valuations of other bidders, as long as the other bidders also fol-low a straightforward (perhaps untruthful) bidding strategy. This ex post equilibrium concept is useful because it places no requirements on the knowledge that bidders have of the valuations of other bidders.

Winning bidders pay their final bid price in all auctions except Aus, *i*BEA, and MP. Aus allows for $(n+1)$ restarts and uses information elicited along each trajectory to de-termine the final payments. *i*BEA and MP terminate with UCE prices, at which point final payments are determined through downwards adjustments.

Auction *clock-proxy* (Ausubel, Cramton, and Milgrom, chapter 5 of this volume) is a hybrid auction. The first stage maintains item prices and runs an ascending-clock CA (see also Porter, Rassenti, and Smith 2003). This stage is used for price discovery and can be considered to construct approximate linear CE prices. The second stage is sealed-bid, with bids from the first stage combined with additional bids that must be consistent with bids from the clock phase.

2.4.1   Insufficiency of Simple Prices

It is interesting to consider what form of prices are necessary to implement efficient ascending CAs. Gul and Stacchetti (2000) first addressed this question in the setting of substitutes valuations. The authors provide a formal definition of an ascending CA, but limit attention to linear and anonymous prices. They show that there exists no ascending VCG auction with linear and anonymous prices for substitutes valuations. The auction due to Ausubel (2002) lies outside of this negative characterization because it uses $n + 1$ price trajectories.

Recently, Mishra and Parkes (2004) used the UCE-based price characterization to demonstrate that efficient ascending CAs require both non-anonymous and nonlinear prices, even for this case of substitutes valuations. The authors exhibit instances for which only non-anonymous and nonlinear UCE prices exist. As for sufficiency, auctions dVSV and *i*Bundle are examples of ascending VCG auctions for substitutes valuations that maintain these rich prices.

However, de Vries, Schummer, and Vohra (2003) extend the definition of ascending CAs in Gul and Stacchetti (2000) to allow for non-anonymous and nonlinear prices and obtain a negative result. When at least one bidder has a non-substitutes valuation an ascending CA cannot implement the VCG outcome even when the other bidders are restricted to substitutes and even with non-anonymous and nonlinear prices. Auctions *i*BEA and MP lie outside of this negative characterization because they allow a final downward adjustment to determine final prices.

Thus, with substitutes values but simple prices we must accept auctions with multiple trajectories or non-monotonic adjustments. Moreover, although rich prices extend the reach of ascending CAs to substitutes values we still need to accept multiple trajectories or non-monotonic adjustments to handle richer preferences than substitutes.

2.4.2 Primal-Dual Auction Design

Many traditional combinatorial optimization problems can be solved with primal-dual algorithms. A primal-dual approach uses linear-programming (LP) duality to formulate an optimization problem as a satisfaction problem. Strong LP duality states that a pair of feasible primal and dual solutions are optimal if and only if they satisfy *complementary slackness* (CS) conditions. We provide a brief review of LP theory at the end of this chapter, and refer the reader to Papadimitriou and Steiglitz 1998 for a textbook treatment.

In fact, primal-dual theory also provides a useful conceptual framework for the design of iterative price-based CAs. Prices are interpreted as a feasible dual solution and the provisional allocation is interpreted as a feasible primal solution. Bids provide sufficient information to formulate and solve *restricted* primal and dual problems, the *winner-determination* and *price-update* problems respectively (see figure 2.1). (For further discussion of this idea, see Parkes 2001, de Vries, Schummer and Vohra 2003, and Bikhchandani and Ostroy chapter 8 of this volume.)

Straightforward bidding is first assumed, and later justified by termination with VCG payments. The winner-determination problem uses information implicit in bids to compute a feasible solution that minimizes the violation of the CS conditions, and

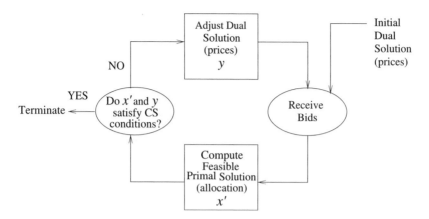

Figure 2.1
A primal-dual interpretation of an ascending CA.

price updates adjust the dual solution toward an optimal dual solution.[15] CS conditions have an exact equivalence with conditions 1 and 2 required for CE prices, and are satisfied on termination of an auction.

Constructively, primal-dual auction design requires the following steps:

1. Formulate an LP for the CAP that is integral, such that its optimal solution is a feasible allocation. The dual problem should allow convergence to UCE prices, or to minimal CE prices that support VCG payments in the case of BAS valuations.
2. Provide bidders with a bidding language that is expressive for straightforward bidding, and formulate a winner-determination problem to compute a feasible primal solution that minimizes the violation of CS conditions as represented in bids.
3. Terminate when the provisional allocation and ask prices satisfy CS conditions (and thus represent a CE), and also satisfy any additional conditions that are necessary to compute the VCG payments at termination (e.g., UCE conditions or minimal CE prices). Otherwise, adjust prices to make progress toward an optimal dual solution that satisfies these conditions.

The characterization of VCG payments in terms of minimal CE and UCE prices suggests two methods to adjust towards the VCG outcome. Figure 2.2 illustrates the methods, considering the price on bundles, S_1 and S_2, allocated to bidders 1 and 2 in the efficient outcome.

In case (a), the coalitional value function satisfies BSM and the VCG payments are supported at the minimal CE prices. Ascending CAs (such as dVSV) can converge monotonically to these prices and the VCG outcome. In case (b), the coalitional value function satisfies neither BSM nor BAS. Although each bidder's VCG payment is supported in some minimal CE, there is no single CE that supports the VCG payment to

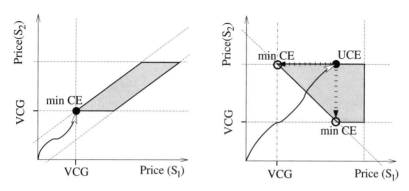

Figure 2.2
Adjusting toward the VCG outcome in price-based iterative CAs. CE prices lie within the shaded regions.

both bidders simultaneously. As illustrated, ascending CAs such as *i*BEA and MP can still converge monotonically to UCE prices from which the VCG outcome can be determined in a final adjustment.

The next section presents a case study of primal-dual methods to the design and analysis of the *i*Bundle auction.[16] In section 2.4.4 we return to the auctions in table 2.2, and discuss each in a little more detail.

2.4.3   Case Study: *i*Bundle

We will focus on variation *i*Bundle(2), in which prices are nonlinear but anonymous. This variation is efficient with straightforward bidding and an additional requirement that bidder strategies satisfy a "safety" property. Later, we also briefly describe *i*Bundle(3), which employs nonlinear and non-anonymous prices and is efficient without the safety condition.

The interested reader is referred to Parkes and Ungar 2000a and Parkes 2001 for additional details, including a description of *i*Bundle(d), which blends *i*Bundle(2) and *i*Bundle(3) and allows for price discrimination decisions to be made during the auction. In what follows, we will use *i*Bundle to refer to variation *i*Bundle(2) unless otherwise stated.

_i_Bundle(2): Anonymous Prices   *i*Bundle maintains ask prices on bundles and a provisional allocation and proceeds in rounds, indexed $t \geq 1$. In each round a bidder can submit XOR bids on bundles. In general, the bid price on a bundle must be at least the ask price. Bidders must resubmit bids on any bundle that they are winning in the current provisional allocation but can bid at the same price on such a bundle even if the ask price has since increased. A bidder can also bid at ε less than the ask price when making a "last-and-final" bid, at which point he can no longer improve the bid price. Equivalently, one can simply retain all bids from previous rounds. A bid at, or above, the current ask price is said to be *competitive*, and a bidder is competitive if he submits at least one competitive bid.

The winner-determination problem in each round is to compute a provisional allocation to maximize the seller's revenue given bids, with at most one bundle selected from the XOR bid of each bidder. Let $\mathcal{B}_i$ denote the bids from bidder i, and $p_{\text{bid},i}(S)$ denote the bid price on bundle $S \in \mathcal{B}_i$. Winner determination can be formulated as the following mathematical program:

$$\max_{x_i(S)} \sum_{i \in \mathcal{I}} \sum_{S \in \mathcal{B}_i} x_i(S) p_{\text{bid},i}(S)$$

$$\text{s.t.} \quad \sum_{S \in \mathcal{B}_i} x_i(S) \leq 1, \quad \forall i \tag{2.5}$$

$$\sum_{i \in \mathcal{I}} \sum_{S \in \mathcal{B}_i : j \in S} x_i(S) \leq 1, \quad \forall j \tag{2.6}$$

$$x_i(S) \in \{0, 1\}, \quad \forall i, \forall S \in \mathcal{B}_i.$$

Constraint 2.5 restricts the seller to selecting at most one bid from each bidder. Constraint 2.6 ensures the allocation is feasible. Ties are broken first to favor the allocation from the previous round and then to maximize the number of winning bidders.

*i*Bundle terminates when each competitive bidder receives a bundle in the provisional allocation. Otherwise, prices are increased by ε above the bid price on *all* bundles that receive a bid from some losing bidder in the current round, and the new allocation and prices are provided as feedback to bidders. Prices on other bundles are implicitly adjusted to satisfy free disposal, although only bundles that receive losing bids need to be explicitly quoted. On termination, the provisional allocation becomes the final allocation, and bidders pay their final bid prices.

*i*Bundle maintains feasible primal and dual solutions to an extended LP formulation of CAP and terminates with a CE outcome that satisfies CS conditions. The proof technique is inspired by Bertsekas' (1987) analysis of the AUCTION algorithm for the special case of unit-demand valuations.

Given ask prices, $p_i(S)$, to bidder i we define ε straightforward bidding in terms of an ε-demand set, ε-DS, which is:

$$\varepsilon D_i(p_i) = \left\{ S : v_i(S) - p_i(S) + \varepsilon \geq \max_{S'}(v_i(S') - p_i(S'), 0), \forall S \subseteq \mathcal{G} \right\}. \tag{ε-DS}$$

In words, bidders state in their bid all bundles that come within ε of maximizing their surplus given prices in each round. This reduces to straightforward bidding for a small enough ε.

Definition 2.5 Safety   The competitive bundles in the ε-demand set of each losing bidder in each round are non-disjoint, i.e., each pair of bundles shares at least one item.

For example, losing bids $\{(ABC, \$100), (CDE, \$50)\}$ from a single bidder satisfy safety, whereas losing bids $\{(ABC, \$100), (DE, \$50)\}$ from a single bidder fail the safety condition.

Theorem 2.6 (Parkes and Ungar 2000a) iBundle(2) terminates with an allocation that is within $3\min(n, m)\varepsilon$ of the efficient solution for ε-straightforward bidding strategies and with bid safety.

The first step of the proof is to introduce an extended LP formulation (LP$_2$) for CAP due to Bikhchandani and Ostroy (2002; see also chapter 8 of this volume). LP$_2$ is integral when the safety condition holds for straightforward bidding. The dual formulation (DLP$_2$) has variables that correspond to anonymous and nonlinear prices.

Let K denote the set of feasible partitions. For example, (A, B, C) and (AB, C) are feasible partitions for items ABC. Variable $y(k) = 1$ will indicate that the allocation must be restricted to bundles in partition $k \in K$. For example, if partition (AB, C) is selected, then the only valid allocations are those in which AB goes to some bidder and C to another bidder. We have:

$$\max_{x_i(S), y(k)} \sum_{S \subseteq \mathscr{G}} \sum_{i \in \mathscr{I}} x_i(S) v_i(S) \qquad [\text{LP}_2]$$

$$\text{s.t.} \quad \sum_{S \subseteq \mathscr{G}} x_i(S) \leq 1, \quad \forall i$$

$$\sum_{i \in \mathscr{I}} x_i(S) \leq \sum_{k \in K: S \in k} y(k), \quad \forall S$$

$$\sum_{k \in K} y(k) \leq 1$$

$$x_i(S), y(k) \geq 0, \quad \forall i, S, k$$

$$\min_{\pi_i, p(S), \Pi_s} \sum_{i \in \mathscr{I}} \pi_i + \Pi_s \qquad [\text{DLP}_2]$$

$$\text{s.t.} \quad \pi_i + p(S) \geq v_i(S), \quad \forall i, S$$

$$\Pi_s - \sum_{S \in k} p(S) \geq 0, \quad \forall k$$

$$\pi_i, p(S), \Pi_s \geq 0, \quad \forall i, S.$$

Dual variable $p(S)$ can be interpreted as the *ask price* on bundle S. Then, optimal $\pi_i^* = \max_S\{v_i(S) - p(S), 0\}$ defines the maximal payoff to bidder i across all bundles given prices, and optimal $\Pi_s^* = \max_{k \in K} \sum_{S \in k} p(S)$ defines the maximal revenue to the seller across all partitions given prices. This is also the maximal revenue across all allocations because prices are anonymous.

The dual problem sets prices to minimize the sum of the maximal payoff to each bidder and the maximal revenue to the seller. Optimal dual prices will correspond to CE prices whenever the primal LP is integral.

Interpret the provisional allocation and ask prices in a round of iBundle(2) as defining a feasible primal and a feasible dual solution (denoted $\hat{x}_i$, $\hat{y}$, $\hat{\pi}_i$, $\hat{p}$, and $\hat{\Pi}_s$). We can now establish termination with CS conditions for straightforward bidding strategies.

The first primal CS condition is:

$$\hat{x}_i(S) > 0 \Rightarrow \hat{\pi}_i + \hat{p}(S) = v_i(S), \quad \forall i, S. \tag{CS-1}$$

This states that any bundle allocated to bidder i must maximize his payoff across all bundles at the prices. Condition CS-1 is approximately satisfied in every round because the provisional allocation is selected with respect to bids, which are in turn drawn from ε demand sets. Formally, a relaxed form of condition CS-1 holds, with $\hat{x}_i(S) > 0 \Rightarrow \hat{\pi}_i + \hat{p}(S) \leq v_i(S) + 2\varepsilon$, for all i and S.

The second primal CS condition is:

$$\hat{y}(k) > 0 \Rightarrow \hat{\Pi}_s - \sum_{S \in k} \hat{p}(S) = 0, \quad \forall k. \tag{CS-2}$$

This states that the provisional allocation must maximize the seller's payoff (i.e., revenue) given the prices, across *all* feasible allocations and irrespective of bids received from bidders.

Bundle S has a *strictly* positive price if it is greater than the price on every bundle contained in S. Then, CS-2 follows from properties P1 and P2, which are maintained in each round of the auction:

(P1) All bundles with strict positive prices receive a bid from some bidder in every round.

(P2) One or more of the revenue-maximizing allocations in every round can be constructed from bids from different bidders.

Formally, P1 follows because one can show that a losing bidder will continue to bid for S in the next round, even at the higher price. Property P2 follows from the safety property, which prevents a single bidder from causing the price to increase on a pair of disjoint bundles. This is why we need the safety condition.

Combining P1 and P2, and together with ε-DS, we get a relaxed formulation of CS-2, with $\hat{y}(k) > 0 \Rightarrow \hat{\Pi}_s - \sum_{S \in k} \hat{p}(S) \leq \min(m, n)\varepsilon$, for all partitions $k \in K$.

Dual CS condition CS-3, states:

$$\hat{\pi}_i > 0 \Rightarrow \sum_{S \subseteq G} \hat{x}_i(S) = 1, \quad \forall i. \tag{CS-3}$$

In words, every bidder with positive payoff for some bundle at the current prices must receive a bundle in the provisional allocation. CS-3 is satisfied for all bidders that receive bundles in a particular round, but not for the losing bidders that are still competitive. However, CS-3 holds for every bidder on termination because at this point $\varepsilon\text{-DS} = \emptyset$ for all losing bidders.

CS-3 and CS-1 are equivalent to CE condition 2.1 and CS-2 together with an additional requirement that a provisional allocation is always selected is equivalent to CE condition 2.2.

Finally, we obtain an upper-bound on the worst-case efficiency error of *i*Bundle, in terms of the minimal bid increment ε. First, sum the approximate CS-1 condition over all bidders in the final allocation, and substitute $\hat{\pi}_i = 0$ for bidders not in the allocation by CS-3. This gives:

$$\sum_{i \in \mathscr{I}} \hat{\pi}_i \leq \sum_{i \in \mathscr{I}} v_i(\hat{S}_i) - \sum_{i \in \mathscr{I}} \hat{p}(\hat{S}_i) + 2\min(m, n)\varepsilon \tag{2.7}$$

$$\Rightarrow \hat{\Pi}_s + \sum_{i \in \mathscr{I}} \hat{\pi}_i \leq \sum_{i \in \mathscr{I}} v_i(\hat{S}_i) + 3\min(m, n)\varepsilon \tag{2.8}$$

where equation 2.7 follows because an allocation can include no more bundles than there are items or bidders, and equation 2.8 is by substitution of the ε-approximate CS-2 condition.

The LHS of equation 2.8 is the value of the final dual solution, and the first-term on the RHS is the value of the final primal solution. Now, $\hat{\Pi}_s + \sum_i \hat{\pi}_i \geq w(\mathscr{I})$, (the value of the optimal primal) by LP weak duality, and therefore $w(\mathscr{I}) \leq \hat{\Pi}_s + \sum_i \hat{\pi}_i \leq \sum_i v_i(\hat{S}_i) + 3\min(m, n)\varepsilon$. ∎

A complete proof must also show termination. The basic idea is to assume the auction never terminates and prove that a bidder must eventually submit a bid at a price above his valuation, assuming finite values and a finite number of items, from which we get a contradiction with straightforward bidding.

iBundle(3): Non-Anonymous Prices   *i*Bundle(3) is the variation of *i*Bundle in which each bidder faces non-anonymous prices in every round. The dynamics of *i*Bundle(3) with straightforward bidding are identical to that of Ausubel and Milgrom's (2002) ascending-proxy auction, although ascending-proxy is not described in price terms. *i*Bundle(3) is efficient for straightforward bidding with general values. Moreover, the auction will terminate with VCG outcomes for BSM coalitional value functions.

Let $p_{\text{ask},i}^t(S)$ denote the ask prices to bidder i in round t. Initially, $p_{\text{ask},i}^1(S) = 0$ for all bundles S and all bidders. Bids are received, and the winner determination problem solved, as in iBundle(2). Then, for each bidder not in the provisional allocation, the price *to that bidder* is increased by the minimal bid increment, $\varepsilon > 0$, above his bid price on all bundles submitted in that round, and adjusted for free-disposal.

It is now quite immediate to establish that iBundle(3) terminates in CE with straightforward bidding. The prices faced by a bidder in round t are parameterized by $\pi_i^t \geq 0$, which can be interpreted as the maximal payoff to the bidder in that round. The ask price on bundle S in round t is defined as:

$$p_{\text{ask},i}^t(S) = \max(0, v_i(S) - \pi_i^t). \tag{2.9}$$

Initially, $\pi_i^1 = \max_S\{v_i(S)\}$, for all i, and the price is zero on all bundles. The payoff π_i^t decreases monotonically during the auction and prices monotonically increase. The ε-DS for bidder i in round t includes every bundle for which $v_i(S) \geq \pi_i^t$, and increases monotonically across rounds. Eventually, when π_i^t is less than ε, the prices on each bundle are within ε of the bidder's value and he will bid for every bundle with positive value in his ε-DS.[17]

Condition CS-1 holds trivially in each round and CS-3 holds at termination, just as in iBundle(2). In addition, CS-2 holds in each round because of the special structure of prices: every bundle with a strict positive price receives a bid in a bidder's ε-DS. This does not require the safety condition.

Theorem 2.7 (Parkes and Ungar 2000a) iBundle(3) terminates with an allocation that is within $3\min(n,m)\varepsilon$ of the efficient allocation for ε-straightforward bidding strategies and with bid safety.

Theorem 2.8 (Ausubel and Milgrom 2002) iBundle(3) terminates with *minimal* CE prices and the VCG outcome for BSM valuations and straightforward bidding.

Proof Consider an arbitrary bidder j, and let $\bar{\pi}_j$ denote the bidder's payoff in the minimal CE prices. Refer to the bidders in the provisional allocation in round t as the *winning coalition*. We prove that the payoff, π_j^t to bidder j in any round t, satisfies $\pi_j^t \geq \bar{\pi}_j$. First, bidder j must be in the winning coalition in any round in which $\pi_j^t < \bar{\pi}_j$. To see this, consider a coalition $L \subset \mathscr{I}$, with $j \notin L$, and observe that the revenue to the seller from coalition L in round t is exactly $w(L) - \sum_{i \in L} \pi_i^t$ from equation 2.9. Then,

$$w(L) - \sum_{i \in L} \pi_i^t < w(L) - \sum_{i \in L} \pi_i^t + (\bar{\pi}_j - \pi_j^t)$$

$$= w(L) - \sum_{i \in L \cup \{j\}} \pi_i^t + w(\mathscr{I}) - w(\mathscr{I} \setminus j) \tag{2.10}$$

$$\leq w(L) - \sum_{i \in L \cup \{j\}} \pi_i^t + w(L \cup \{j\}) - w(L) \tag{2.11}$$

$$= w(L \cup \{j\}) - \sum_{i \in L \cup \{j\}} \pi_i^t$$

where equation 2.10 follows from the equivalence between maximal payoff and VCG payoff for BSM valuations and equation 2.11 follows from the BSM condition. Thus, the payoff to bidder j cannot fall more than ε below $\bar{\pi}_j$ (because the bidder always wins, and its prices are unchanged), and prices converge to the minimal CE prices as $\varepsilon \to 0$. ■

An ex post equilibrium is invariant to the values of bidders; that is, straightforward bidding is a game-theoretic equilibrium even once every bidder knows the values of other bidders.

Theorem 2.9 Straightforward bidding is an ex post equilibrium of iBundle(3), and the auction is efficient, for BSM valuations.

This result requires that the revealed preferences by a bidder are *consistent* with some valuation during the auction.[18] Given this, we can fix the reports v_{-i} of other bidders. If bidder i follows a straightforward strategy, the auction implements the VCG outcome because valuations satisfy BSM. Moreover, if bidder i reports some other valuation $\hat{v}_i \neq v_i$ the auction implements the efficient allocation for $(\hat{v}_i, v_{-i})$ and CE prices that are at least the bidder's Vickrey payment in that outcome. Thus, bidder i's best-response is straightforward bidding because the bidder's payoff in the truthful Vickrey outcome dominates his payoff in any other Vickrey outcome, and therefore also in this alternate CE outcome.

2.4.4 Ascending Price Combinatorial Auctions

Perhaps the defining feature of the iBundle family of auctions is that they allow non-linear, and sometimes non-anonymous, ask prices. Only the dVSV, iBEA, and MP auctions have a similarly rich class of prices. The other auctions in table 2.2 maintain simpler prices, typically anonymous and often linear.

In describing the auctions we group together auctions KC, SAA, GS, and Aus because they are all designed to handle the special case of substitutes valuations. Then we briefly discuss dVSV, which is designed for a BSM coalitional value function, and is presented in detail in Bikhchandani and Ostroy (chapter 8 of this volume). The ascending-proxy auction is a sealed-bid implementation of iBundle(3) with interesting theoretical properties, which we will discuss along with other proxied auctions in section 2.5.2 and which is presented in more detail by Ausubel and Milgrom (chapter 3 of this volume). Finally, we describe the clock-proxy, *i*BEA and MP auctions, which are designed for general valuations.

Special Case: Goods Are Substitutes   Recall that linear CE prices exist for substitutes valuations, but that nonlinear and non-anonymous prices are still required to support VCG payments, even for substitutes.

Auction KC was first described in the setting of a *matching problem*, with multiple firms and multiple workers. The matching problem can be reinterpreted as an allocation problem with each firm corresponding to a bidder and each worker to an item. Bidders can submit bids for multiple items in each round. Winner determination allocates all items that receive bids and prices are increased on overdemanded items. The auction converges to a competitive equilibrium outcome and an efficient allocation for straightforward bidding. Kelso and Crawford (1982) do not investigate strategic behavior or the relationship between the outcome and the VCG payoffs.

Auction SAA is closely related to KC in that bidders can submit bids for multiple items and the bid on an item must be repeated if it is winning. However, SAA maintains anonymous prices and is distinguished in its careful use of activity and bid-improvement rules. The auction design forms the basis of the series of FCC wireless spectrum auctions.

Auction GS adopts the same basic methodology as KC, except that prices are anonymous and increased on a set of *minimal* overdemanded items. This provides termination with minimal CE prices when bidders are straightforward. Just as in KC and SAA, these prices do not support the VCG outcome for substitutes valuations and straightforward bidding is not an equilibrium.

Auction Aus is unique amongst the auctions for substitutes valuations in its ability to terminate with the Vickrey outcome. Ausubel (2002) achieves this despite using only anonymous item prices by running $n + 1$ separate auctions, each with its own price trajectory. Information across each auction is used to adjust final payments to VCG payments. Let $(\mathscr{A}_{-1}, \ldots, \mathscr{A}_{-n}, \mathscr{A})$, denote the sequence of auctions in Aus, with bidder i excluded from participation in auction $\mathscr{A}_{-i}$. All bidders are invited to participate in the final auction. The allocation is determined in auction $\mathscr{A}$, but the payment by bidder i is determined from the price and bidding dynamics in auctions $\mathscr{A}_{-i}$ and $\mathscr{A}$. The dynamics in $\mathscr{A}_{-i}$ are used to adjust downwards the final payment for bidder i.

Bidder Submodular   Auction dVSV is similar to *i*Bundle, with bids for XOR sets of bundles and prices that are nonlinear and non-anonymous and increased based on bids from losing bidders. However, the price update rule is different. Auction dVSV increases prices on the set of minimally undersupplied bidders. This set can include bidders that are in the current provisional allocation, as well as losing bidders, and is different from the set of losing bidders on which prices are adjusted in *i*Bundle.

Although there has been no computational study, de Vries, Schummer, and Vohra (2003) argue by analogy to algorithms in the optimization literature that dVSV will converge in fewer rounds than *i*Bundle.[19] In *i*Bundle's favor is that the price-update step is simple to explain to bidders and easy to compute.

General-Purpose CAs RAD and A*k*BA are general-purpose ascending CAs, designed without restrictions on agent valuations. Although an equilibrium analysis is not available for either auction, their performance has been evaluated experimentally, through human-based laboratory studies and through computational simulation. Both auctions formulate an LP to adjust prices. A*k*BA provides nonlinear prices and supports an XOR bidding language, whereas RAD provides linear prices and supports an OR bidding language.

A competitive equilibrium perspective provides a unifying view of the auctions. Recall that CE prices in CAP must be both nonlinear and non-anonymous in general. One can interpret A*k*BA as an iterative procedure to determine anonymous and nonlinear prices that approximate CE prices, and RAD as an iterative procedure to determine anonymous and linear prices that approximate CE prices.

The bidding rules and winner-determination step in A*k*BA are much as in *i*Bundle. Each bidder submits an XOR bid, from which the winner-determination problem is formulated. A*k*BA differs from *i*Bundle in the price-update step, which is parameterized with $0 \le k \le 1$.

Let $S^t = (S_1^t, \ldots, S_n^t)$ denote the provisional allocation in round t, $p_{\text{ask}}^t(S)$ denote the ask price on S, $\Delta^t(S'', S') = p^t(S'') - p^t(S')$ denote the price difference between bundle S'' and bundle S', W^t denote the current winners, and $DS_i(p_{\text{ask}}^t)$ denote the bids submitted by bidder i in response to ask prices. A*k*BA computes prices for period $t + 1$ that will maintain CS condition (CS-1) for all bidders, given the demand-set information in their most recent bid.

In particular, prices $p_{\text{ask}}^{t+1}(S)$ are computed to satisfy:

a. $p_{\text{ask}}^{t+1}(S) \ge p^t(S)$, for all bundles $S \in S^t$ that receive bids from some losing bidder, $i \notin W^t$.

b. $\Delta^{t+1}(S'', S') \ge \Delta^t(S'', S')$ for any pair of bundles S'', S', such that S' is allocated to a winning bidder $i \in W^t$, and that bidder also bids on S''.

These prices are not unique in general, and A*k*BA breaks the tie by selecting a convex combination of prices, with $p_{\text{ask}}^{t+1}(S) = (1 - k)\underline{p}^{t+1}(S) + k\bar{p}^{t+1}(S)$, where $\underline{p}^{t+1}(S)$ and $\bar{p}^{t+1}(S)$ are the *minimal* and *maximal* prices that satisfy conditions a and b, for some parameter $0 \le k \le 1$.

Finally, new bids must improve the price by a minimal bid increment $\varepsilon > 0$ on at least one bundle. The $k = 1$ variation, with price adjustments $\bar{p}^{t+1}$ is thought to have better incentive properties (Wurman and Wellman 1999), and empirical analysis has demonstrated high efficiency with straightforward bidders (Wurman and Wellman 2000).

RAD provides an additive-or (OR) bidding language, and winner determination is formulated to allow multiple bids to be accepted from any one bidder (Kwasnica et al. 2005). Straightforward bidding is well defined for the OR language when valuations have additive-or semantics (e.g., when the bidder's value for a disjoint combination of packages is the sum of the individual package values).[20] However, this OR language is not always expressive for straightforward bidding. For example, a bidder with valuation $(AB, \$20)$, $(CD, \$20)$, $(ABCD, \$20)$ facing prices $(AB, \$10)$ and $(CD, \$10)$ cannot represent the bidder's best-response demand set (either AB or CD but not both).

RAD maintains linear and anonymous prices and formulates the price update as a series of LPs. The methodology is close in spirit to methods due to Rassenti, Smith, and Bulfin (1982), where approximate prices are computed in a one-shot CA.[21] Let $S^t = (S_1^t, \ldots, S_n^t)$ denote the provisional allocation computed in round t. RAD computes new linear prices that exactly match the bid price for all winning bids, with $\sum_{j \in S_i^t} p_{\text{ask}, j}^{t+1} = p_{\text{bid}, i}^t(S_i^t)$, and *minimize the maximal regret across losing bids*, with *regret* defined as the difference $\max\{0, p_{\text{bid}, i}^t(S) - \sum_{j \in S} p_{\text{ask}, j}^{t+1}\}$. Ties are broken first to lexicographically lower the regret on as many losing bids as possible, and then on prices for items in winning bids to maximize the minimal price on each such bundle. This procedure ensures a unique solution and is designed to provide bidders with informative signals.

Experimental results in a laboratory with human bidders demonstrate that RAD achieves higher efficiency than non-combinatorial auctions (Banks, Ledyard, and Porter 1989). In addition, RAD is demonstrated to terminate with fewer rounds than the SAA design, which typically has fewer rounds than simple ascending-bid CAs (Cybernomics 2000).

Auctions *i*BEA (Parkes and Ungar 2002) and MP (Mishra and Parkes 2004) are general purpose ascending Vickrey auctions. *i*BEA extends *i*Bundle(3) to adjust past the first set of CE prices and achieve UCE prices with straightforward bidding. This provides enough information to adjust downwards to VCG payments upon termination, bringing straightforward bidding into an ex post equilibrium for general values. Similarly, MP extends the minimal price update rule in dVSV, to ensure that the auction terminates with UCE prices. The same tradeoff occurs between *i*BEA and MP as occurs between *i*Bundle and dVSV. Although one should expect MP to converge more quickly than *i*BEA, each price update in *i*BEA is simple to compute and easier to explain to bidders.

2.5 Non-Price-Based Approaches

We survey three examples of non-price-based approaches to iterative CA design. These auctions do not require that bidders submit bids in response to ask prices. Instead, they include richer query models and are structured fundamentally different than ascending-price auctions. The auctions fall into one of the following categories:

Decentralized approaches   The winner determination problem is moved to the bidders, who are responsible for submitting bids and also computing allocations of items with high revenue given existing bids. The *Adaptive User Selection Mechanism* (AUSM) (Banks, Ledyard, and Porter 1989), a continuous auction which distributes winner determination to bidders, provides a canonical example.

Proxy auctions   Proxy agents, which automatically submit bids through a predetermined bidding procedure, provide an interface between bidders and an auction. Bidders provide incremental value information to proxy agents, which may query bidders actively.

Direct-elicitation approaches   (Conen and Sandholm 2001) Explicit queries are formulated by the auctioneer (perhaps in a decentralized way), and a bidder's strategy determines how to respond to these queries. Multiparty elicitation approaches ensure that information reported by one bidder can be used to refine the queries asked of another bidder.

There is perhaps some ambiguity between the proxy auctions approach and the direct-elicitation approach. We choose to reserve the term *proxy auction* to settings in which the proxy agents are restricted to following a straightforward bidding strategy in an auction protocol. Direct-elicitation methods may also distribute elicitation to individual proxy agents. However, the proxies in direct-elicitation interact with a richer centralized protocol (more akin to a computational procedure), that can itself be designed with knowledge that it will be interacting with automated proxy agents.

2.5.1   Decentralized Approaches: The AUSM Design

AUSM is a continuous auction that maintains a list of provisional winning bids and a *standby queue*. This standby queue contains bids that have been submitted but are not provisionally winning, and is designed to allow bidders to coordinate their bids. A bidder can always submit a bid to the queue and can also suggest a new combination of bids from the queue that provide more revenue than the current allocation. This proposed allocation becomes the new provisional allocation. The bidding language within the queue is implicitly *additive-or* and bidders are unable to place logical constraints between multiple bids in the queue. AUSM terminates after a period of quiescence.

AUSM distributes the winner-determination computation across the bidders. The auctioneer is only required to verify that a new provisional allocation is better than the current allocation and that it is formed from bids in the standby queue. Related ideas appear in the work of Brewer (1999) and the PAUSE auction (Land, Powell, and Steinberg, chapter 6 of this volume).

On one hand, this decentralization can remove a computational bottleneck from iterative CAs. On the other hand, this decentralization can bias the outcome in favor of technologically sophisticated bidders better able to solve larger optimization problems (see Pekeč and Rothkopf, chapter 16 of this volume, and Parkes and Shneidman 2004 for an additional discussion of the incentive aspects of decentralized approaches to solving the winner-determination problem).

Another potential concern with AUSM is that bidders must be able to process the disaggregated feedback provided in the auction, in the form of submitted bids. Nevertheless, AUSM has been demonstrated to provide better allocative efficiency than a noncombinatorial auction in experiments with human bidders (Banks, Ledyard, and Porter 1989).

2.5.2 Proxied Auctions

Proxied auctions include automated proxy agents that interface between bidders and the auctioneer and submit bids following a predetermined procedure. In an ascending CA, the proxies typically follow straightforward bidding strategies. If a proxy agent is following a *first-best* strategy (i.e., the bidding strategy that an agent would follow with full information about a bidder's value), then it must elicit enough information to compute a best-response to prices in each round.

At one extreme, each proxy agent can require direct and complete revelation at the start of the auction (Ausubel and Milgrom 2002; also chapter 3 of this volume). Of course, this reduces the auction to a sealed-bid auction. However, when combined with a bidder-to-proxy interface that allows bidders to provide incremental value information, proxied auctions suggest a paradigm shift in iterative CAs from *indirect* revelation (e.g., via best-response bids to prices) to incremental but *direct* revelation (Parkes 2001, section 7.5).

Proxy agents can maintain partial information about valuations. For instance, this information could be in the form of *exact values for a subset of bundles*, or *approximate values for each bundle*. Proxy agents can decide when to query and when to bid, based on a model of costly elicitation.

The bidder-to-proxy interface need not be constrained to logical languages such as XOR or OR, and can be adapted to suit the local problem of a bidder. For example, a bidder in a logistics problem can define the constraints and costs for his local business problem. The ability to support this kind of expressiveness can prove decisive in practice.[22]

In addition to enriching the bidding language, proxy auctions can also offer the following advantages:

a. Proxy auctions can restrict the dynamic strategies available to bidders, for example, by enforcing straightforward bidding based on reported valuations and by requiring consistent information-revelation to proxies (see section 7.5; Parkes 2001; and Ausubel and Milgrom 2002).

b. Proxy auctions offer opportunities for *accelerated* implementations of auctions, because there can be multiple fast "proxy rounds" of bidding interleaved with a few "human rounds" to refine proxy's value information. See Hoffman, Menon, van der Heever, and Wilson (chapter 17 of this volume); and Wurman, Zhong, and Cai 2004.[23]

In imposing strong activity rules, for instance to require that a bidder provides a consistent response to queries during an auction, one must allow for bidder mistakes and also for bidders that might be adjusting their beliefs about value as they receive feedback (e.g., in a *correlated value* setting). Ausubel, Cramton, and Milgrom (chapter 5 of this volume) advocate using a relaxed consistency rule to provide incentives for early demand revelation while allowing for these other effects.

2.5.3 Direct-Elicitation Approaches

A direct-elicitation approach formulates queries about bidder valuations, to which bidders are expected to respond (although not necessarily truthfully). Queries are typically interleaved across bidders so that the queries asked of one bidder can be selected given responses by other bidders. In this way, complete elicitation can be avoided through focused elicitation on interesting parts of the allocation space. Sandholm and Boutilier (chapter 10 of this volume) provide an extended discussion of direct-elicitation methods for the design of iterative CAs.

The query process in direct elicitation can be fully integrated within a winner-determination algorithm to determine whether enough information is available to implement an efficient allocation (e.g., Conen and Sandholm 2001). The query process may also be defined through an algorithmic technique that does not have a very natural analogue with traditional auction designs, such as *computational learning theory* (Zinkevich, Blum, and Sandholm 2003; Lahaie and Parkes 2004a).

Example queries can include: *"Is bundle S_1 preferred to bundle S_2?"; "Is your value on bundle S_1 at least $100?";* and *"What is your value on bundle S_1?"* The goal is to ask the minimal number of queries required to determine the efficient allocation and perhaps also to determine the VCG payments. Computing the VCG payments brings truthful response by bidders into an ex post equilibrium.

We know that any elicitation process must also determine CE prices if the goal is to determine an efficient allocation, and UCE prices if the VCG outcome is important (see section 2.2). Thus, one reasonable approach is explicitly *price based*, with elicitation structured as a search for CE prices. One can also consider an *allocation-based* approach, with elicitation structured as a search for the efficient allocation.

Price based   Query bidders until the value information is sufficient to verify a set of UCE prices and a supporting allocation for the main economy. For instance, one can simulate learning algorithms to elicit bidder valuations until they are known with enough accuracy to determine UCE prices (Lahaie and Parkes 2004a, 2004b).

Allocation based   Query bidders until the value information provides a certificate for the efficient allocation and the Vickrey payments. Use partial information to augment a search in allocation space, executing new queries to refine information that will resolve current uncertainty about the efficient allocation (Conen and Sandholm 2001; Hudson and Sandholm 2004).

As yet there are no published studies to compare the elicitation effectiveness and computational scalability of price-based approaches and allocation-based approaches. Price-based approaches may be fundamentally more scalable, with queries determined by solving optimization problems that are restricted by current bidder responses, for instance via winner-determination problems defined on bundles returned by best-response queries. In comparison, allocation-based approaches must strive to avoid maintaining an allocation graph that scales exponentially with the number of items.[24]

Price-based approaches are also naturally decentralized: in a proxied architecture, each proxy agent can elicit preference information independently until it has enough information to determine its best response to current prices. This best-response information can verify that an allocation is efficient even though each proxy knows nothing about the values of other bidders.

Recently, methods from computational learning theory (CLT) have been adapted to direct elicitation. CLT provides *membership* queries ("What is your value on bundle S?") and *equivalence* queries ("Is your valuation function $\hat{v}$? If not, identify a bundle S for which $\hat{v}(S)$ is incorrect."). In one approach, each proxy is responsible for learning the *exact* value function of a single bidder in isolation (Zinkevich, Blum, and Sandholm 2003; Blum et al. 2004). In another approach, Lahaie and Parkes (2004a) integrate CLT into price-based approaches and use *demand queries* to simulate equivalence queries. A demand query presents prices p and a bundle S, and asks whether S is in the demand set of the bidder at the prices. This coordinates elicitation across proxy agents and provides an elicitation method that can terminate as soon as CE prices are discovered and without learning values exactly.

2.6   Conclusion

Iterative CAs are of critical importance in addressing the problem of preference elicitation, which many view as the biggest issue to surmount in the real-world deployment of CAs. The sophisticated combinatorial optimization and pricing algorithms of CAs are impotent without rich bid information from bidders.

Iterative CAs focus elicitation, often through price discovery, and can find efficient allocations without bidders reporting, or even knowing, their exact value information. We emphasized price-based approaches, and in particular a primal-dual design paradigm. We also discussed canonical non price based approaches, including proxied- and direct-elicitation approaches.

For a related discussion of the primal-dual approach to auction design see chapter 8, and see also chapters 3, 5, and 6 of this volume for discussions of specific iterative CAs. Chapters 9, 10, and 11 relate to the discussion of bidding languages, elicitation, and communication complexity. Chapter 17 discusses methods to accelerate the computation of the outcome of a proxied ascending price CA.

Looking ahead, we see a number of outstanding problems in the design of iterative CAs:

• Introduce the *cost* of preference elicitation more explicitly into the auction design problem. Current methods are mainly *first best*, and seek to find an efficient allocation with as little information as possible. But what happens when this minimal information remains too costly for bidders to provide? This is the problem of designing *second best* auctions, which make the right tradeoff between the cost of information and the value of additional information in terms of improving the market allocation. Some initial progress has been made in the analysis of auction design with costly information (Compte and Jehiel 2000; Larson and Sandholm 2001; Fong 2003; Parkes 2004), and with bounded communication (Blumrosen and Nisan 2002; Blumrosen, Nisan, and Segal 2003), but much more work needs to be done.

• Design iterative CAs for which straightforward bidding is an ex post equilibrium, but which do not suffer from the well-known vulnerabilities of the VCG auction that Ausubel and Milgrom outline (chapter 1 of this volume). These auctions will necessarily not be allocatively efficient, but may be more desirable due to new robustness against manipulation by coalitions and improved revenue properties.

• Current iterative auctions for general valuations for which theoretical results are available use XOR bidding languages that are not concise enough to be usable for many real-world applications. We need iterative CAs that support richer bidding languages, for instance allowing side constraints, volume discounts, and other high-level bidding logic to be stated and then refined during the auction.

2.7 Appendix: LP Theory

Consider the linear program:

$$\max c^T x \tag{P}$$

$$\text{s.t.} \quad Ax \leq b$$

$$x \geq 0$$

where A is a $m \times n$ integer matrix, $x \in R^n$ is a n-vector, and c and b are n- and m-vectors of integers. Vectors are column-vectors, and notation c^T indicates the *transpose* of vector c, similarly for matrices. The primal problem [P] is to compute a feasible solution for x that maximizes the value of the objective function.

The dual program is constructed as:

$$\min b^T y \qquad \qquad \text{[D]}$$

$$\text{s.t.} \quad A^T y \geq c$$

$$y \geq 0$$

where $y \in R^m$ is a m-vector. The dual problem is to compute a feasible solution for y that minimizes the value of the objective function.

Let $V_{\text{LP}}(x) = c^T x$, the value of feasible primal solution x, and $V_{\text{DLP}}(y) = b^T y$, the value of feasible dual solution y.

Complementary-slackness conditions express logical relationships between the values of primal and dual solutions that are necessary and sufficient for optimality.

Definition 2.6 Complementary-Slackness   Complementary-slackness conditions constrain pairs of primal and dual solutions. *Primal* CS conditions state $x^T(A^T y - c) = 0$, or in logical form:

$$x_j > 0 \Rightarrow A^j y = c_j \qquad \qquad \text{(P-CS)}$$

where A^j denotes the jth column of A (written as a row vector to avoid the use of transpose). *Dual* CS conditions state $y^T(Ax - b) = 0$, or in logical form:

$$y_j > 0 \Rightarrow A_i x = b_i \qquad \qquad \text{(D-CS)}$$

where A_i denotes the ith row of A.

Theorem 2.10 Strong Duality   A pair of feasible primal, x, and dual solutions, y, are primal and dual optimal if and only if they satisfy the complementary-slackness conditions.

Proof   Primal CS holds iff $x^T(A^T y - c) = 0$, and Dual CS holds iff $y^T(Ax - b) = 0$. Equating, and observing that $x^T A^T y = y^T Ax$, we have P-CS and D-CS iff $x^T c = y^T b$, or $c^T x = b^T y$. The LHS is the value of the primal, $V_{\text{LP}}(x)$, and the RHS is the value of the dual, $V_{\text{DLP}}(y)$. By the strong duality theorem, $V_{\text{LP}}(x) = V_{\text{DLP}}(y)$ is a necessary and sufficient condition for the solutions to be optimal.   ■

Notes

1. One argument commonly made for why very few VCG mechanisms are seen in practice is that bidders are reluctant to reveal their complete and true valuations in a situation of long-term strategic interaction (Rothkopf, Teisberg, and Kahn 1990).

2. The observed vulnerabilities of the VCG auction can be viewed as problems intrinsic to the task of implementing *efficient* allocations in an ex post equilibrium in iterative CAs, given the uniqueness of the VCG auction among efficient auctions (see chapter 1 of this volume).

3. Goods are substitutes is the largest set containing unit-demand valuations (with $v_i(S) = \max_{j \in S}\{v_{ij}\}$ for all S, where v_{ij} is the value for item j in isolation) for which the existence of linear CE prices can be established (Gul and Stacchetti 1999).

4. Gul and Stacchetti (1999) show that there is often no linear price equilibrium that supports the VCG payments with substitutes valuations. On the other hand, linear prices can support the VCG outcome for unit-demand valuations (Leonard 1983).

5. Computational analysis on a broad test suite of problem instances demonstrated failure of buyers are substitutes in around 43 percent of instances (Parkes 2001, chapter 7, p. 216).

6. In fact, the UCE prices will support *all* efficient allocations in each marginal economy because prices that support any one efficient allocation support all.

7. Parkes (2002) uses *agent-independence* to refer to privacy preservation. Parkes also requires an additional technical requirement (*outcome-independence*), that is without loss of generality for "best-response bidding languages," which are expressive enough to simulate at least the following bids: *bundle S_1 is worth at least $100*; and *bundle S_1 is worth at least $50 more than bundle S_2*; and *bundle S_1 has value $200*.

8. The form of activity rule used in the FCC spectrum auctions is due to Paul Milgrom and Robert Wilson. The rule requires quantities bid in the auction are (weak) monotonically decreasing. Similar rules have since become standard in ascending CAs.

9. Roth and Ockenfels (2001) have studied the use of deadlines versus rolled closures, on eBay and Amazon Internet auctions, respectively. Bidders on Amazon bid earlier than on eBay, and many bidders on eBay wait until the last seconds of an auction to bid.

10. The FCC adopted click-box bidding in the light of evidence that bidders used the trailing digits for signaling in early wireless spectrum auctions.

11. Of course, arbitrary decommiting may be undesirable because it allows insincere bidding and cheap talk.

12. BAS holds and there is a set of minimal CE prices that will support the VCG outcome. However, Gul and Stacchetti's (2000) auction maintains item prices and a stronger condition, such as unit-demand valuations, is required for VCG payments to be supported with linear CE prices.

13. A set of items, $S' \subseteq \mathcal{G}$, are *overdemanded* when it is not possible to satisfy the demand sets of bidders that demand only items in S'.

14. A set $L \subseteq \mathcal{I}$ of bidders are *undersupplied* if not all bidders can be satisfied in the provisional allocation.

15. One can also imagine that each round of the auction closes the *duality gap* between the feasible primal and dual solutions. At termination the duality gap is zero, complementary slackness holds, and we have an efficient allocation and CE prices.

16. Recently, de Vries, Schummer, and Vohra (2003) observe a formal distinction between the *subgradient* approach adopted in *i*Bundle and the *primal-dual* approach adopted in dVSV and MP.

One can view subgradient methods as a specialization of primal-dual, and thus we prefer to continue to adopt the *primal-dual* terminology throughout this section.

17. Specifically, the bidder need only bid for bundles S for which there are no bundles $S' \subset S$ with $v_i(S') = v_i(S)$, i.e., taking advantage of sparse valuations.

18. A simple way to achieve consistency is to use a proxy agent interface. The proxy can follow a straightforward bidding strategy based on value information reported by a bidder. A bidder can provide additional information as needed but must be consistent during the course of the auction.

19. In particular, de Vries, Schummer, and Vohra (2003) note that *i*Bundle is more correctly a subgradient algorithm, whereas dVSV is a primal-dual algorithm. Primal-dual algorithms are inherently faster than subgradient algorithms in the optimization literature (Fisher 1981).

20. This property is satisfied by the "spatial fitting" environment used by Kwasnica et al. (2005) in experiments and introduced in Banks, Ledyard, and Porter (1989).

21. Graves, Schrage, and Sankaran (1993) have also described LP-based methods to provide price feedback in a multi-stage combinatorial auction procedure adopted at the University of Chicago Graduate Business School in the 1990s.

22. For instance, Kalagnanam, Bichler, Davenport, and Hohner (chapter 23) and Caplice and Sheffi (chapter 21) discuss the role of item prices coupled with volume discounts and complex bid-taker constraints in industrial procurement and logistics.

23. Indeed, FCC discussions have often cited the speed of iterative combinatorial auctions as one potential drawback in comparison with linear price auctions.

24. Current allocation-based algorithms cannot scale beyond a handful of bidders and tens of items (Hudson and Sandholm 2004). In comparison, ascending-price auctions readily scale to problems that push the limit of current winner-determination technology (Parkes and Ungar 2000a).

References

Ausubel, Lawrence M. (2002), "An Efficient Dynamic Auction for Heterogeneous Commodities," Working Paper, DE University of Maryland.

Ausubel, Lawrence M. and Paul Milgrom (2002), "Ascending Auctions with Package Bidding," *Frontiers of Theoretical Economics*, 1, 1–42 ⟨www.bepress.com/bejte/frontiers/vol1/iss1/art1⟩.

Bayers, Chip, "Capitalist Econstruction," *Wired Magazine*, 8.03, March.

Banks, Jeffrey S., John O. Ledyard, and David P. Porter (1989), "Allocating Uncertain and Unresponsive Resources: An Experimental Approach," *The RAND Journal of Economics*, 20, 1–25.

Benny Lehmann, Daniel Lehmann, and Noam Nisan (2003), "Combinatorial Auctions with Decreasing Marginal Utilities," *Games and Economic Behavior*, To appear.

Bertsekas, Dimitri P. (1987), *Dynamic Programming: Deterministic and Stochastic Models*, Upper Saddle River, NJ: Prentice-Hall.

Bikhchandani, Sushil and Joseph M. Ostroy (2002), "The Package Assignment Model," *Journal of Economic Theory*, 107, 377–406.

Blum, Avrim, Jeffrey Jackson, Tuomas Sandholm, and Martin Zinkevich (2004), "Preference Elicitation and Query Learning," *Journal of Machine Learning Research*, 5, 649–667.

Blumrosen, Liad and Noam Nisan (2002), "Auctions with Severely Bounded Communication," in *Proceedings of the 43rd Annual Symposium on Foundations of Computer Science (FOCS 2002)*, 406–415.

Blumrosen, Liad, Noam Nisan, and Ilya Segal (2003), "Multi-Player and Multi-Round Auctions with Severely Bounded Communication," in *Proc. 11th Annual European Symposium on Algorithms (ESA 2003)*, 102–113.

Brewer, Paul J. (1999), "Decentralized Computation Procurement and Computational Robustness in a Smart Market," *Economic Theory*, 13, 41–92.

Compte, Olivier and Philippe Jehiel (2000), "On the Virtues of the Ascending Price Auction: New Insights in the Private Value Setting," Discussion paper, CERAS and UCL.

Conen, Wolfram, and Tuomas Sandholm (2001), "Preference Elicitation in Combinatorial Auctions," in *Proc. 3rd ACM Conf. on Electronic Commerce (EC-01)*, pp. 256–259, New York: ACM Press.

Cybernomics (2000), "An Experimental Comparison of the Simultaneous Multiple Round Auction and the CRA Combinatorial Auction," Discussion paper, Report to the Federal Communications Commission. Available at ⟨http:/wireless.fcc.gov/⟩.

de Vries, Sven, James Schummer, and Rakesh V. Vohra (2003), "On Ascending Vickrey Auctions for Heterogeneous Objects," Working Paper, KS Northwestern University.

Demange, Gabrielle, David Gale, and Marilda Sotomayor (1986), "Multi-Item Auctions," *Journal of Political Economy*, 94, 863–872.

Fisher, Marshall L. (1981), "The Lagrangian Relaxation Method for Solving Integer Programming Problems," *Management Science*, 27, 1–18.

Fong, Kyna (2003), "Multi-Stage Information Acquisition in Auction Design," Undergraduate thesis, Harvard University. Available at ⟨http://www.eecs.harvard.edu/econcs⟩.

Graves, Robert L., Linus Schrage, and Jayaram Sankaran (1993), "An Auction Method for Course Registration," *Interfaces*, 23, 81–92.

Gul, Faruk and Ennio Stacchetti (1999), "Walrasian Equilibrium with Gross Substitutes," *Journal of Economic Theory*, 87, 95–124.

Gul, Faruk and Ennio Stacchetti (2000), "The English Auction with Differentiated Commodities," *Journal of Economic Theory*, 92, 66–95.

Hoffman, Karla (2001), "Issues in Scaling Up the 700 MHz Auction Design," Available at ⟨http://wireless.fcc.gov⟩.

Hudson, Benoît and Tuomas Sandholm (2004), "Effectiveness of Query Types and Policies for Preference Elicitation in Combinatorial Auctions," in *Third International Joint Conference on Autonomous Agents and Multiagent Systems (AAMS '04)*, 386–393.

Kelso, Alexander S. and Vincent P. Crawford (1982), "Job Matching, Coalition Formation, and Gross Substitutes," *Econometrica*, 50, 1483–1504.

Kwasnica, Anthony M., John O. Ledyard, David Porter, and Christine DeMartini (2005), "A New and Improved Design for Multiobject Iterative Auctions," *Management Science*, 51, 419–434.

Lahaie, Sébastien M. and David C. Parkes (2004a), "Applying Learning Algorithms to Preference Elicitation," in *Proceedings of the 5th ACM Conference on Electronic Commerce*, 180–188.

Lahaie, Sébastien M. and David C. Parkes (2004b), "Applying Learning Algorithms to Preference Elicitation in the Generalized Vickrey Auction," Discussion paper, Harvard University.

Larson, Kate and Tuomas Sandholm (2001), "Costly Valuation Computation in Auctions," in *Proceedings of Theoretical Aspects of Rationality and Knowledge VIII*, 169–182.

Leonard, Herman B. (1983), "Elicitation of Honest Preferences for the Assignment of Individuals to Positions," *Journal of Political Economy*, 91, 461–479.

Milgrom, Paul (2000), "Putting Auction Theory to Work: The Simultaneous Ascending Auction," *Journal of Political Economy*, 108, 245–272.

Milgrom, Paul R. and Robert J. Weber (1982), "A Theory of Auctions and Competitive Bidding," *Econometrica*, 50, 1089–1122.

Mishra, Debasis and David Parkes (2004), "Ascending Price Vickrey Auctions Using Primal-Dual Algorithms," Discussion paper, Harvard Univeristy.

Nisan, Noam and Ilya Segal (2003), "The Communication Requirements of Efficient Allocations and Supporting Prices," *Journal of Economic Theory*, To appear.

Papadimitriou, Christos H. and Kenneth Steiglitz (1998), *Combinatorial Optimization: Algorithms and Complexity*, Mineola, NY: Dover.

Parkes, David C. (2001), *Iterative Combinatorial Auctions: Achieving Economic and Computational Efficiency*, Ph.D. thesis, Department of Computer and Information Science, University of Pennsylvania ⟨http://www.eecs.harvard.edu/~parkes/diss.html⟩.

Parkes, David C. (2002), "Price-Based Information Certificates for Minimal-Revelation Combinatorial Auctions," in *Agent Mediated Electronic Commerce Workshop IV*, Julian Padget, Onn Shehory, David Parkes, Norman Sadeh, and William E1 Walsh, eds., LNAI 2531, Heidelberg: Springer-Verlag, 103–122.

Parkes, David C. (2005), "Auction Design with Costly Preference Elicitation," *Annals of Mathematics and AI*, 44, 269–302.

Parkes, David C. and Jeffrey Shneidman (2004), "Distributed Implementations of Vickrey-Clarke-Groves Mechanisms," in *Proc. 3rd Int. Joint Conf. on Autonomous Agents and Multi Agent Systems*, 261–268.

Parkes, David C. and Lyle H. Ungar (2000a), "Iterative Combinatorial Auctions: Theory and Practice," in *Proceedings of the 17th National Conference on Artificial Intelligence (AAAI-00)*, 74–81.

Parkes, David C. and Lyle H. Ungar (2000b), "Preventing Strategic Manipulation in Iterative Auctions: Proxy Agents and Price-Adjustment," in *Proc. 17th National Conference on Artificial Intelligence (AAAI-00)*, 82–89.

Parkes, David C. and Lyle H. Ungar (2002), "An Ascending-Price Generalized Vickrey Auction," Technical Report, Harvard University.

Porter, David, Stephen Rassenti, Anil Roopnarine, and Vernon Smith (2003), "Combinatorial Auction Design," *Proceedings of the National Academy of Sciences*, 100, 11153–11157.

Rassenti, Steve J., Vernon L. Smith, and Robert L. Bulfin (1982), "A Combinatorial Mechanism for Airport Time Slot Allocation," *Bell Journal of Economics*, 13, 402–417.

Roth, Alvin E. and Axel Ockenfels (2002), "Last-Minute Bidding and the Rules for Ending Second-Price Auctions: Evidence from eBay and Amazon Auctions on the Internet," *American Economic Review*, 92, 1093–1103.

Rothkopf, Michael H., Thomas J. Teisberg, and Edward P. Kahn (1990), "Why Are Vickrey Auctions Rare?" *Journal of Political Economy*, 98, 94–109.

Wurman, Peter R. and Michael P. Wellman (1999), "Equilibrium Prices in Bundle Auctions," in *Proc. AAAI-99 Workshop on Artificial Intelligence for Electronic Commerce*, 56–61.

Wurman, Peter R. and Michael P. Wellman (2000), "AkBA: A Progressive, Anonymous-Price Combinatorial Auction," in *Proc. Second ACM Conference on Electronic Commerce*, 21–29.

Wurman, Peter R., Jie Zhong, and Gangshu Cai (2004), "Computing Price Trajectories in Combinatorial Auctions with Proxy Bidding," *Electronic Commerce Research and Applications*, 3, 329–340.

Zinkevich, Martin, Avrim Blum, and Tuomas Sandholm (2003), "On Polynomial-Time Preference Elicitation with Value Queries," in *Proceedings of the 4th ACM Conference on Electronic Commerce*, 176–185.

3 Ascending Proxy Auctions

Lawrence M. Ausubel and Paul Milgrom

3.1 Introduction

Theoretical treatments of auctions usually analyze situations in which there is some particular item to be bought or sold and the question is what auction format to use. In real auctions, however, the important planning starts much earlier and is much more encompassing. For example, in a bankruptcy auction, the auctioneer may need to decide whether to sell an entire company as a single unit or its various assets individually, what guarantees to offer concerning the conditions of its physical assets, what kinds of financing terms to require, how much time to allow buyers to obtain needed regulatory or other approvals for the acquisition, and so on.

A similarly richer set of questions arises when a buyer runs a procurement auction. For example, when the Chilean government sought to buy milk for its school milk programs, it had to decide about the sizes of the regions to be served, whether to require bonding or other performance guarantees and at what levels, how to measure and reward quality, whether and how to account for differences in past performances of suppliers, and so on.

Often, these *packaging* decisions, which establish what will be bought or sold in the auction and how bids will be compared, are among the most critical decisions the auctioneer makes. Arguably, in the Chilean milk auction example, if the government were to specify that bids for service are to cover large areas of the nation, then smaller milk suppliers would effectively be precluded from bidding. At the same time, larger bidders, enjoying economies of scale in serving a large market, could pass on part of their cost savings by reducing their bids. Given these offsetting effects, how should the service areas be specified?

In the U.S. telecommunications spectrum auctions, sophisticated bidders anticipated the effects of packaging on the auction and lobbied the spectrum regulator for packages that served their individual interests. For example, the long-distance company MCI lobbied for a nationwide license that, it claimed, would enable cell phone companies to offer seamless coverage across the entire country. MCI knew that if such a nationwide license plan were adopted, it would exclude existing mobile telephone service providers from bidding, because those providers were ineligible to acquire new licenses covering areas that they already served. In the same proceeding, regional telephone companies such as Pacific Bell lobbied for licenses covering regional areas that fit well with their own business plans but poorly with the plans of MCI.[1]

Typically, the auctioneer does not know which packaging decision is optimal. Ideally, one would like to avoid predetermining the packaging decision, instead designing an auction mechanism that allows bidders with different plans to bid accordingly. In that way, competition among the bidders would determine not just the prices but the relevant packaging decisions as well.

The extra complexity involved in package auctions has been a serious barrier to implementation and other chapters of this book discuss it extensively. In this chapter, we set aside the issue of complexity to focus on other aspects of performance.

Many discussions of package auctions begin with what is variously called the Vickrey auction or the Vickrey-Clarke-Groves (VCG) mechanism.[2] As we described in chapter 1 of this volume, that mechanism and its extensions have their best performance when two conditions are satisfied: (1) the goods for sale are substitutes for all of the bidders; and (2) bidders face no effective budget constraints. When either of these conditions fail, however, the VCG mechanism can exhibit serious performance deficiencies. We have shown that when goods are not substitutes, VCG revenues can be low or zero; revenues can decrease as more bidders are added or as some bidders raise their bids; and shill bidding and collusion can become profitable strategies for the bidders. Also, when a bidder's budget constraint is binding, the VCG auction loses its dominant-strategy property, eliminating its greatest advantage over other designs.

A second alternative is simply to solicit sealed bids and to accept the combination of bids that maximizes the seller's revenue or minimizes its cost, subject to any relevant constraints. The payment rule is "first price" (i.e., each winning bidder pays the amount of the associated bid). The Chilean milk auction cited above was run in that way, and chapters 20–23 describe several related applications. Bernheim and Whinston (1986) develop a theory of sealed-bid, first-price package auctions. With complete information, this design has equilibria that are core allocations. However, this design has the same disadvantages as other static pay-as-bid auction formats, always forcing bidders to make guesses about the bids of others, and generally yielding inefficient outcomes in asymmetric environments with private information (including environments satisfying the substitutes condition).

In this chapter, we describe a third alternative, our ascending proxy auction, which retains some of the advantages while avoiding some of the disadvantages of the other two designs. We show that the new design duplicates the performance of the VCG mechanism when the two conditions described above hold, but leads to different results in general, avoiding the most serious shortcomings of the VCG mechanism when either condition fails. We will also show that, as with the first-price package auction design, it has full-information equilibria that are core allocations.

In its simplest form, the ascending proxy auction is a direct revelation mechanism.[3] Each bidder in the auction reports preferences for the contracts/packages that interest it to a proxy bidder (who may be an electronic proxy agent, or even the auctioneer), who then bids in a series of rounds on the bidder's behalf. At each round, if a given bidder is not among the provisional winners, the proxy makes whatever new bid that the bidder most prefers, according to his reported preferences. The auctioneer then considers all bids from the current and past rounds and selects his most preferred feasible collection of bids, where feasibility incorporates the constraint that the accepted bids can include at most one from each bidder. In the simplest case, the auctioneer's objective is to optimize the total price, but any other objective that leads to a unique choice is also allowed. The auctioneer's selected bids become the new provisional allocation—while the associated bidders are designated provisional winners—and the process is allowed to repeat until no new bids are submitted.

In the ascending proxy auction, both the nature of the packages or contracts between bidders and the seller and the bidders' preferences among these packages or contracts can be very general. In principle, a contract could specify a set of items, price, quality, closing date, and so on, and any bidder preferences over such contracts could be accommodated. Although sellers will, in practice, want to limit the complexity of bids, the generality of the theory highlights the breadth of potential applications. In particular, by varying the preferences, one can accommodate bidder budget limits or even financing limits that differentially constrain what the bidder can bid for different packages.

If there is just one item for sale and only price matters, the ascending proxy auction is similar to familiar Internet auctions, where a bidder may secretly confide its values to a proxy agent (or to the auctioneer), who bids on its behalf. The one important difference is that, in the ascending proxy auction, the use of the proxy bidder is mandatory.[4] As described in chapter 1, a single-item ascending auction with mandatory proxy bidding is strategically equivalent to the VCG mechanism for a single item (i.e., the second-price, sealed-bid auction). We show that the equivalence between the VCG mechanism and our ascending proxy auction extends to the entire range of environments in which the goods for sale are substitutes and bidders are not subject to any budget limits. This is the same as the range of environments on which the VCG mechanism avoids the problems described in chapter 1. The most interesting question then becomes how the ascending proxy auction performs generally, when the preceding assumptions do not apply.

Our analysis has two parts. The first part characterizes the main property of the mapping from bids to outcomes: we find that the auction generally yields a core allocation with respect to the preferences reported by the bidders and the seller. The second part of our analysis studies equilibrium. We show, using an equilibrium refinement, that when preferences are quasi-linear and budget limits do not apply, the set of equilibrium allocations coincides with the set of bidder-optimal core allocations.

For additional detail about the ascending proxy auction, see Ausubel and Milgrom 2002, on which this chapter is based, or Milgrom 2004, which discusses additional applications and other related auction designs. Ausubel and Milgrom 2001 further describes some aspects of the ascending proxy auction technology.

3.2   Modeling the Ascending Proxy Auction

Denote the set of participants in the auction by $\{0, 1, \ldots, L\}$, where 0 denotes the seller and $l \neq 0$ denotes a bidder. Let X_l denote the finite set of *contracts* available to bidder l. For example, in a spectrum allocation problem, X_l would contain pairs, each consisting of a set of spectrum licenses and an associated price. In that case, the relevant set X_l is finite if prices are described by positive integers and l faces some overall budget limit. For the Brewer-Plott (1996) train scheduling problem, a shipper's contract specifies a train's departure and arrival times, its direction of travel, and a price. For a procurement problem in which the eventual quantity to be purchased is uncertain, a seller's contract specifies a range of permitted quantities and an associated price schedule and may also specify contract terms concerning quality, delivery, guarantees, and so on. As described in the next section, the model even applies to public decisions with transfers, in which case each X_l is a set of pairs describing the joint decision and l's transfer.

In the environments we have described, an *allocation* is described by a profile of contracts $x = (x_1, \ldots, x_L)$. A *feasible* allocation is an element of the non-empty set $F \subset X_1 \times \cdots \times X_L$. For a spectrum allocation problem, F would constrain the seller to sell each license to at most one bidder. For the Brewer-Plott train scheduling problem, F would constrain the set of train schedules so that no trains will crash and safe spacing requirements are satisfied.

In the ascending proxy auction, *bids* are the contracts that the bidders propose. We limit attention here to modeling auctions with voluntary trade. This means that for each bidder l, the "null offer" $\varnothing_l$ is always included in X_l. For simplicity, we assume that $(\varnothing_1, \ldots, \varnothing_L) \in F$. This means that the seller is not compelled to sell anything to anyone, which ensures that there is always at least one feasible allocation for the seller.

Suppose that each bidder l ranks any allocations x based only on its own contract x_l and let $\succ_l$ denote a strict preference ordering over the finite set X_l.[5,6] In the proxy auction, the bidder reports such a preference ordering to its proxy bidder. The auctioneer specifies a preference ordering $\succ_0$ over the set of feasible bid profiles F. Given any set of bidders S, denote the set of feasible bid profiles for the coalition consisting of those bidders and the seller by $F_S = \{x \in F | x_l = \varnothing_l$ for all $l \notin S\}$.

Once the bidders report their preferences, the *ascending proxy auction* operates in a series of rounds, where the state variable for the auction is the profile $(B_l^t)_{l=1,\ldots,L}$ of bid sets and the provisional allocation x_0^t. The seller initializes the bid sets by entering the null bid on each bidder's behalf: $B_l^0 = \{\varnothing_l\}$ and initializes the provisional allocation x_0^0 by assigning each bidder its null contract: $x_{0l}^0 = \varnothing_l$. Each round t of the ascending proxy auction proceeds as described below, in which the notation "max" applied to any choice set is defined with respect to the chooser's reported preference ordering.

1. For each bidder, determine the set of *available new bids*, A_l^t, which comprises the individually rational bids not yet made: $A_l^t = X_l - \{x_l | x_l \prec_l \varnothing_l\} - B_l^{t-1}$.
2. Any bidder l who is not a provisional winner and who has not exhausted its profitable bids offers its $\succ_l$-most preferred contract in A_l^t. Formally, $[x_{0l}^t = \varnothing_l, A_l^t \neq \varnothing] \Rightarrow B_l^t = B_l^{t-1} \cup \{\max A_l^t\}$.
3. All other bidders make no new bids: $[x_{0l}^t \neq \varnothing_l \text{ or } A_l^t = \varnothing] \Rightarrow B_l^t = B_l^{t-1}$.
4. If there are no new bids at round t $(B^t = B^{t-1})$, then the auction terminates and the provisional allocation x_0^t becomes the final allocation. Otherwise $(B^t \neq B^{t-1})$, the auctioneer determines its current feasible set, $F^t = F \cap \bigcap_{l=1}^{L} \{x | x_l \in B_l^t\}$, selects its $\succ_0$-most-preferred element $x_0^{t+1} = \max F^t$, and iterates with round $t+1$.

The ascending proxy algorithm determines a mapping from reported preferences to allocations. The first step in the analysis is to establish a key property of that mapping, namely, that it picks points in the core.

Theorem 3.1   The allocation determined by the ascending proxy auction is a stable allocation (and hence an NTU-core allocation) with respect to the reported preferences.[7]

Proof   Let T be the final round and let x_0^T be the allocation determined by the ascending proxy auction. By construction, x_0^T is individually rational for bidders ($x_l^T = \varnothing$ or $x_l^T \succ_l \varnothing$) and because only the null allocation is feasible for coalitions excluding the seller, no coalition of bidders alone can block x_0^T. It therefore suffices to show that no coalition of the seller and one or more bidders can block.

Let S be any non-empty set of bidders. Suppose $x \in F_S$, so that for all $l \notin S$, $x_l = \varnothing_l$. Contrary to our conclusion, suppose that the coalition consisting of the seller and the bidders in S blocks x_0^T with x, that is, $x \succ_0 x_0^T$ and for all $l \in S$, $x_l = x_{0l}^T$ or $x_l \succ_l x_{0l}^T$. Consider the components of the auction outcome x_0^T. By construction, whether l is a losing bidder ($x_{0l}^T = \varnothing_l$) or a winning bidder ($x_{0l}^T \neq \varnothing_l$), by the end of the auction, the proxy for l in the auction has made every bid that l weakly prefers to x_{0l}^T. In particular, the proxy has bid x_l, so $x_l \in B_l^T$. Hence, $x \in F^T = \bigcap_{l=1,\ldots,L} \{x | x_l \in B_l^T\} \cap F$. Then, by step 4 of the algorithm, it cannot be that $x \succ_0 x_0^T$, contradicting the hypothesis that x_0^T is blocked.   ∎

Theorem 3.1 provides an important hint about how the ascending proxy auction is related to the Vickrey auction. In chapter 1 of this volume, we showed that the Vickrey auction leads generally to core allocations only if the goods for sale are substitutes and bidder budgets are unlimited. Failure of the outcome to lie in the core, we showed, is associated with low seller revenues, non-monotonic prices (adding bidders or increasing bidder values may reduce prices), existence of profitable shill-bidding opportunities by individual bidders,[8] and existence of profitable joint deviations by groups of losing bidders.

Theorem 3.1 and its proof are closely related to similar results and proofs about deferred acceptance algorithms in matching theory (for example, see Gale and Shapley 1962; Kelso and Crawford 1982; and Roth and Sotomayor 1990). In all of these algorithms, one side of the market makes a sequence of bids and continues to add bids when its old bids are rejected. Further connecting the results is Hatfield and Milgrom's (2005) finding that, if the final allocation from such a *cumulative offer process* is feasible, then it is a stable allocation.

3.3   The Transferable Utility Case

Theorem 3.1's conclusion that the outcome is a stable allocation (and hence an NTU core allocation) with respect to reported preferences has three important limitations. First, it does not identify which NTU core outcome among the possibly many such outcomes is selected. Second, it is silent about whether or when the reported preferences are likely to coincide with or even resemble the bidders' actual preferences, which importantly affects the interpretation of the result. Third, it is silent about how the outcome relates to the NTU core when bidders play an equilibrium strategy that misreports their actual preferences. To answer the associated questions, we specialize the model and introduce additional assumptions.

Our first change is to focus attention on the case in which the auction is conducted by a seller who ranks feasible collections of bids according to their total price. In this setting, an allocation is a pair (z, p) where $z = z_0 = (z_1, \dots, z_L)$ is a *decision* and p is a vector of *cash transfers*. In a typical package auction, the decision describes which bidder gets which goods, but there are other possibilities as well. For example, in a club or social organization, z may describe the levels of investment in club facilities and amenities and the ascending proxy auction may be used to decide both z and which bidders will be members. In this setting, it is convenient to apply the feasibility criterion to the decision z, rather than to the allocation (z, p). The condition in the club version of the problem that all "members" enjoy the same services $\hat{z}$ is $F \subset \bigcup_{\hat{z} \in \hat{Z}} \{(z_1, \dots, z_L) | (\forall l) z_l \in \{\hat{z}, \varnothing_l\}\}$.

We assume that the bidders' valuations are quasi-linear, so we can write a bidder's payoff as $v_l(z) - p_l$ or $v_l(z_l) - p_l$. In this *transferable utility* case, the total payoff is

$\sum_{l=1}^{L} v_l(z_l)$ and variations in the payment profile p transfer utility among the participants.

Finally, to reinforce the idea that there is just one seller, we assume that if $z = (z_1, \ldots, z_L) \in F$ is a feasible decision, then so is $(\varnothing_l, z_{-l})$. This ensures that one can exclude bidder l and its contract without affecting the feasibility of the sale, as is the case in many package auctions.

The ascending proxy auction modeled in the preceding section uses finite feasible sets for the bidders. In the transferable utility case, it simplifies the analysis to imagine that the monetary unit is very small, so that the NTU core is closely approximated by the traditional transferable utility (TU) core. We will make our arguments below as if this approximation were exact. Also, because the theory was based on the assumption that seller preferences are strict, we need a method to resolve ties. Many different procedures are satisfactory. For example, it suffices to imagine that the seller breaks ties by adding a negligibly small, random, negative amount to each bid.

To describe the TU core, one must first define the coalitional game (L, w) that is associated with the trading model. The set of players is just as above: $L = \{0, \ldots, L\}$. The coalitional value function is defined as follows:

$$
w(S) = \begin{cases} \max_{x \in X} \sum_{l \in S} v_l(x_l), & \text{if } 0 \in S, \\ 0, & \text{if } 0 \notin S. \end{cases} \tag{3.1}
$$

The value of a coalition is the maximum total value the players can create by trading among themselves. If the seller is not included in the coalition, that value is zero.

In TU games, it is traditional to define the core by suppressing the allocation and focusing on the imputed payoffs, or *imputations*, associated with any feasible allocation. The TU core in this case is a set of payoffs, as follows:

$$
Core(L, w) = \left\{ \pi : w(L) = \sum_{l \in L} \pi_l, w(S) \le \sum_{l \in S} \pi_l \text{ for all } S \subset L \right\}. \tag{3.2}
$$

As new bids are introduced in the ascending proxy auction, the bidders move down their preference lists, so the payoff associated with each new bid is less than that associated with all earlier bids by the same bidder. It is convenient to track the progress of the auction in terms of the payoff associated with each bidder's most recent bid. Let π_l^t be that payoff for bidder l at round t. The highest bid that l has made for decision z_l by round t is within one bid increment of $\max(0, v_l(z_l) - \pi_l^t)$. In our calculations below, we treat this estimate of the bid as exact.

Imagine that the seller regards the auction as serving two purposes. First, the auction identifies a coalition to utilize the seller's goods and the bidders' additional resources and expertise. Second, it determines how to distribute the value created by the winning coalition. From that perspective, at every round of the auction, there is an implicit bid by every coalition of bidders for the seller's goods. Given our previous formula describing the bids, the maximum total price offered at round t by coalition S is $\max_{z \in F} \sum_{l \in S-0} \max(0, v_l(z_l) - \pi_l^t) = \sum_{l \in S-0} \max(0, v_l(z_{Sl}^*) - \pi_l^t)$. Notice that if coalition S includes any bidder n for whom $v_n(z_{Sn}^*) - \pi_n^t < 0$, then the coalition $S - n$ bids as much as coalition S by using the same allocation among its continuing members (and setting $z_{S-n,n}^* = \varnothing_n$). If π_0^t is the highest total bid at round t, then

$$\max_S \left(w(S) - \sum_{l \in S-0} \pi_l^t \right) = \pi_0^t, \tag{3.3}$$

so for all S, $w(S) \leq \sum_{l \in S} \pi_l^t$. This means that in the transferable utility game with coalitional value function w, no coalition can block the payoff vector π^t. At the last round T, the auction payoff vector π^T is the one associated with the actual final allocation, so it is also feasible and hence a core payoff imputation.

This analysis suggests an interesting interpretation of the proxy auction for the transferable utility case. For concreteness, think of the bidders in the auction as workers seeking employment and the seller in the auction as a supplier of capital assets. Imagine that there is a large set of competing brokers who may hire workers and buy assets from the seller to run a business. Each broker considers only one combination of workers whom it might employ. At round t, a typical bidder l demands a payoff or "wage" of π_l^t and a broker representing coalition S is driven by competition with identical brokers to offer $w(S) - \sum_{l \in S-0} \pi_l^t$ to acquire the seller's capital. At each round, there is a provisional winning coalition S, and workers not in that coalition are unemployed. Any unemployed workers who have demanded positive wages reduce their wage demands by one unit, and the brokers then bid again. The process continues iteratively; it ends when a competitive equilibrium wage vector is found.

In this interpretation, the auction is simply a *tatonnement* device to identify a competitive equilibrium. A TU core imputation is a vector of competitive equilibrium prices specifying a wage for each worker and a price for the seller's bundle of assets. The TU core conditions state that the winning broker just breaks even and that there exist no profit opportunities for any broker at the given prices.

With transferable utility, we have the following special case of theorem 3.1:

Theorem 3.2 In the transferable utility model, the payoff imputation determined by the ascending proxy auction is a core imputation with respect to the reported preferences.

3.4 Profit-Target Strategies and Equilibrium

We turn next to our analysis of bidder incentives and equilibrium. Our first result shows that one can sometimes limit attention to the class of π_l-*profit-target* or *semi-*

sincere strategies, in which a bidder reports its value for each decision z to be $\max(0, v_l(z) - \pi_l)$.[9] That is, l reduces all of its reported values by essentially the same fixed amount π_l, which may be regarded as its minimum profit target. We say "essentially" because negative values are reported to be zero.

Theorem 3.3 In the transferable utility model, given any pure strategy profile for the other bidders, bidder n has a best reply that is a profit-target strategy.

Proof Fix bidder n and any pure strategy report profile $\hat{v}_{-n}$ for the competing bidders. Define $\Pi_n(\hat{v})$ to be n's profit for any report profile $\hat{v}$. Let $\pi_n = \max_{\hat{v}_n} \Pi_n(\hat{v})$ be n's maximum profit, $v_n^* \in \arg\max_{\hat{v}_n} \Pi_n(\hat{v})$ be any best reply, and z^* be the corresponding decision selected by the ascending proxy auction. Because the outcome is in the core, for all decisions z, $\sum_{l=1}^{L} \hat{v}_l(z^*) \geq \sum_{l=1}^{L} \hat{v}_l(z)$. Also, because n pays $v_n(z^*) - \pi_n$, we have $\hat{v}_n(z^*) \geq v_n(z^*) - \pi_n$.

Consider n's π_n-profit-target reporting strategy: $\tilde{v}_n(z) = \max(0, v_n(z) - \pi_n)$. Because bids are nonnegative, we have that for all z, $\tilde{v}_n(z^*) + \sum_{l \neq n} \hat{v}_l(z^*) \geq \sum_{l \neq n} \hat{v}_l(z)$. So, the decision z selected when n reports is one for which $0 \leq v_n(z) - \pi_n$, that is, n is a winning bidder and pays a price of at most $\tilde{v}_n(z)$. It follows that its profit is at least $v_n(z) - \tilde{v}_n(z) = \pi_n$, so the π_n-profit-target reporting strategy is also a best reply. ∎

Profit-target strategies are of interest for several reasons. First, if all bidders adopt such strategies and if the selected decision is not one for which any losing bidder l has set $\pi_l = 0$, then the decision maximizes total values, that is, it is efficient. Second, a bidder who uses such a strategy bids its full incremental value for changing from any decision z to any alternative decision z', which means it cannot be part of any collusive, price reducing agreement. For example, suppose the decision concerns the allocation of two licenses. Suppose, given the bids, bidder 1 wins the first license and bidder 2 the second. If bidder 1 adopts any profit target strategy, then bidder 2 must pay at least 1's incremental value, $v_1(12) - v_1(1)$, to win license 2. The conclusion in theorem 3.3 that each bidder always has a best reply that is a profit-target strategy means that there does not exist any profile of reports for the other bidders that can deter the bidder from bidding aggressively, offering to pay up to their full incremental values for different or extra licenses. More generally, within the rules of the proxy auction, there is no strategy profile that can deter a bidder from bidding to change the predicted decision to one that he prefers.

The next theorem identifies full information Nash equilibria of the ascending proxy auction in profit-target strategies. The equilibrium outcome will be a *bidder-optimal point in the core*, meaning that the payoff profile $\pi \in Core(L, w)$ and that there is no $\pi' \in Core(L, w)$ with $\pi' \neq \pi$ and $\pi'_l \geq \pi_l$ for every bidder l. Notice that the outcome is a bidder-optimal core allocation with respect to the bidders' *actual* preferences. In particular, the outcome is efficient and has the desirable revenue properties associated with core allocations. This duplicates a property by Bernheim and Whinston (1986) previously identified for sealed-bid, first-price package auctions.

Theorem 3.4   In the transferable utility model, for every bidder-optimal point π in the core, the strategy profile in which each bidder l plays its π_l-profit target strategy is a Nash equilibrium with associated profit vector π. Moreover, if $\tilde{v}$ is a Nash equilibrium in semi-sincere strategies at which losing bidders bid sincerely, then $\pi(\tilde{v})$ is a bidder-optimal point in $Core(L, w)$.

Proof   Suppose that the proposed strategy profile is not an equilibrium. Then there is some player l and some unilateral deviation for that player that leads to a winning coalition T ($T \ni l$) and profit outcome vector $\hat{\pi}$. For bidder l, $\hat{\pi}_l > \pi_l$, and for all bidders $k \in T$, the proxy strategies imply that $\hat{\pi}_k \geq \pi_k$.

Because π is bidder-optimal, there is a coalition S such that $l \notin S$ and $w(S) = \sum_{k \in S} \pi_k$ (otherwise, for some $\varepsilon > 0$, there would be a point in the core at which l gets $\pi_l + \varepsilon$, the seller gets $\pi_0 - \varepsilon$, and others payoffs are as specified by π, contradicting bidder optimality). Let $\beta(S)$ and $\beta(T)$ denote the highest total revenue associated with bids by the bidders in coalitions S and T during the proxy auction, given the specified deviation by bidder l. We show that $\beta(S) > \beta(T)$, contradicting the hypothesis that T is the winning coalition. Indeed, using equation 3.3:

$$\beta(S) \geq w(S) - \sum_{k \in S-0} \max(\pi_k, \hat{\pi}_k)$$

$$> w(S) - \sum_{k \in S-0} \pi_k - \sum_{k \in T-0} \max(0, \hat{\pi}_k - \pi_k)$$

$$= \pi_0 - \sum_{k \in T-0} \max(0, \hat{\pi}_k - \pi_k)$$

$$\geq w(T) - \sum_{k \in T-0} \pi_k - \sum_{k \in T-0} \max(0, \hat{\pi}_k - \pi_k)$$

$$= w(T) - \sum_{k \in T-0} \hat{\pi}_k$$

$$= \beta(T). \tag{3.4}$$

The first step in equation 3.4 follows from the proxy rules: any losing bidders in S stop bidding only when their potential profits reach the specified levels. The strict inequality in the second step follows because $l \in T \backslash S$ and $\hat{\pi}_l > \pi_l$. The third step follows by selection of S, the fourth because $\pi \in Core(L, w)$, and the fifth and sixth by the definitions of T, $\hat{\pi}$, and $\beta(T)$.

If π is not bidder optimal in the core, then there exists l and $\pi'_l > \pi_l$ such that $(\pi'_l, \pi_{-l}) \in Core(L, w)$. Bidder l can deviate by reporting $\max\{\tilde{v}_l - \pi_l + \pi'_l, 0\}$ instead of reporting $\tilde{v}_l$, thereby increasing its profits to π'_l. ∎

The examples in chapter 1 showed that Vickrey auction outcomes can fail to be in the core because seller revenues are too low. That conclusion, and the connection to matching theory, may seem to suggest that bidder-optimal outcomes are seller-pessimal ones, that is, outcomes that minimize the seller's revenues among all core allocations.

Here is a counter-example to refute that suggestion. There are three items for sale, denoted by A, B, and C. The following table describes values for various packages:

Bidder	A	B	C	AC	BC
1	2				
2		2			
3			10		
4				8	8

We identify payoffs by a five-vector with the payoff of the seller (player 0) listed first. Using the tabulated values, let us verify that $X = (8, 2, 2, 2, 0)$ and $Y = (10, 0, 0, 4, 0)$ are bidder-optimal core allocations. Observe first that X and Y are individually rational and feasible, with a total payoff of 14.

Any blocking coalition must involve the seller and pay him more than 8, so we may limit attention to coalitions with value strictly exceeding 8. We may further limit attention to minimal coalitions with any particular value.

There are six coalitions that meet these criteria. Coalition 0123 is the unique minimal coalition with value 14 and it receives 14 at both of the identified imputations, so it does not block. Coalitions 013 and 023 have value 12 and receive 12 or 14 at the two imputations, so they do not block. Coalitions 014 and 024 have value 10 and receive 12 or 14 at the two imputations, whereas coalition 03 has value 10 and receives 10 or 14 at the two imputations, so none of those coalitions block. We conclude that the imputations X and Y are unblocked and hence are core imputations.

Imputation X, in which the seller gets 8, is seller pessimal, because: (1) bidder 4 must get zero at every core imputation; and (2) the coalition 04 must get at least 8. Hence, X is a bidder-optimal core imputation. At imputation Y, bidder 3 gets his Vickrey payoff of 4, which, as we found in chapter 1, is his best core payoff. So, any bidder-preferred core imputation must have the form $(10 - x - y, x, y, 4, 0)$. If $x > 0$, this imputation is blocked by coalition 024 and if $y > 0$, it is blocked by coalition 014. Because any bidder-preferred imputation is blocked, Y is a bidder-optimal core imputation.

This example identifies two-bidder optimal core allocations with different values for the seller, so bidder optimality is not the same as seller pessimality.

3.5 When Sincere Bidding Is an Equilibrium

We found in chapter 1 that if the Vickrey payoff vector is an element of the core, then there is a unique bidder-optimal point in the core, which eliminates a fundamental bargaining problem among the bidders. It might then seem that under this condition each bidder could simply use the straightforward bidding strategy and this would yield an equilibrium corresponding to the unique bidder-optimal point. However, this conclusion is not quite right, as the following example demonstrates.

Suppose that there are four spectrum licenses. In order to understand that the following bidder valuations are sensible, it is helpful to depict the licenses as follows:

←Geographic Space→

| West-20 | East-20 |
| West-10 | East-10 |

↑ Bandwidth ↓

There are five bidders. Bidder 1 desires a 10-MHz band of spectrum covering both East and West. Bidders 2 and 3 desire a 20-MHz band of spectrum covering both East and West. Bidder 4 wants the full 30-MHz of spectrum in the East. Bidder 5 wants the full 30-MHz of spectrum in the West. Thus:

$v_1(\text{West-10}, \text{East-10}) = 10$,

$v_2(\text{West-20}, \text{East-20}) = 20$,

$v_3(\text{West-20}, \text{East-20}) = 25$,

$v_4(\text{East-20}, \text{East-10}) = 10$,   and

$v_5(\text{West-20}, \text{West-10}) = 10$,

with all singletons and all other doubletons valued at zero.

Observe that the Vickrey payoff vector, (20, 10, 0, 5, 0, 0), is an element of the core, corresponding to Bidder 3 paying 20 for his desired licenses and Bidder 1 paying 0 for his desired licenses. Nevertheless, straightforward bidding is likely to lead Bidder 1 to pay a positive price.[10] In the ascending proxy auction, Bidder 1 could do better by setting profit target at or slightly below his Vickrey profit, ensuring that he never pays a substantial positive price for his licenses.

3.5.1 Bidder-Submodular Values

In this subsection and the next, we explore conditions under which there is a truthful reporting equilibrium of the ascending proxy auction. In this subsection, we investigate a restriction on the coalitional value function that implies that truthful reporting is an equilibrium. In the next subsection, we explore a corresponding condition on valuation of goods.

In chapter 1, we defined the coalitional value function w to be *bidder submodular* if bidders are more valuable when added to smaller coalitions than when added to larger coalitions. Formally, the condition is that for all $l \in L - 0$ and all coalitions S and S' satisfying $0 \in S \subset S'$, $w(S \cup \{l\}) - w(S) \geq w(S' \cup \{l\}) - w(S')$.[11]

Since Shapley (1962), bidder submodularity has been called the condition that "bidders are substitutes," but that description does not coincide with the usual economic meaning of substitutes. For suppose there were a labor market in which the bidders could be hired and a seller who hired bidders to form coalition S earned a profit of $w(S)$ minus the total wages paid. The bidder-submodularity condition is necessary, but not sufficient, for bidders to be substitutes in that labor market. For example, with three bidders, suppose that $w(02) = w(03) = 1$, $w(01) = w(023) = w(012) = w(013) = w(0123) = 2$, and all other values are zero. By inspection, w is bidder submodular. Bidders, however, are not substitutes, because changing the wage profile from $(1.7, 0.8, 0.8)$ to $(1.7, 1, 0.8)$ changes the hiring decision from $(0, 1, 1)$ to $(1, 0, 0)$. That is, *increasing* the wage of bidder 2 *reduces* the demand for bidder 3, contrary to the standard economic definition of substitutes.

In theorem 1.6 of chapter 1, we established that the following three statements are equivalent:

1. The coalitional value function w is bidder submodular.
2. For every coalition S that includes the seller, the restricted Vickrey payoff vectors all lie in the cores of the corresponding restricted games:

$$\bar{\pi}(S) \in Core(S, w).$$

3. For every coalition S that includes the seller, there is a unique core point that is unanimously preferred by the buyers and, indeed:

$$Core(S, w) = \left\{ \pi_S \Big| \sum_{l \in S} \pi_l = w(S), 0 \leq \pi_l \leq \bar{\pi}_l(S) \text{ for all } l \in S - 0 \right\}. \tag{3.5}$$

Here we establish an additional result about bidder-submodular values.

Theorem 3.5 Suppose that the coalitional value function is bidder submodular. Then, truthful reporting is a Nash equilibrium strategy profile of the ascending proxy auction and leads to the Vickrey outcome: $\pi^T = \bar{\pi}$.

Proof We first establish that truthful reporting leads to the Vickrey payoff vector. Suppose there is some round t at which $\pi_l^t < \bar{\pi}_l$. We show that l is necessarily part of the winning coalition at that round. Let S be any coalition including the seller but not bidder l. Then,

$$w(S) - \sum_{k \in S} \pi_k^t < w(S) - \sum_{k \in S} \pi_k^t + (\bar{\pi}_l - \pi_l^t)$$

$$= w(S) - \sum_{k \in S \cup \{l\}} \pi_k^t + w(L) - w(L - l)$$

$$\leq w(S) - \sum_{k \in S \cup \{l\}} \pi_k^t + w(S \cup l) - w(S)$$

$$= w(S \cup \{l\}) - \sum_{k \in S \cup \{l\}} \pi_k^t. \tag{3.6}$$

So, l's profit π_l^t is at least $\bar{\pi}_l$ minus one bid increment ε. Taking the bid increment to zero for the ascending proxy auction proves that for $l \neq 0$, $\pi_l^T \geq \bar{\pi}_l$, and the reverse inequality follows from theorem 1.4 of chapter 1.

Second, we show that truthful reporting is a best response to all other bidders reporting truthfully. For any bidder l and any report by that bidder, theorem 1.4 of chapter 1 implies that the payoff to coalition $L - l$ is at least $w(L - l)$. Because the total payoff to all players is at most $w(L)$, l's payoff to any strategy is bounded above by $\bar{\pi}_l = w(L) - w(L - l)$, which is the payoff that results from truthful reporting. ∎

3.5.2 When Goods Are Substitutes

In the preceding subsection, we studied bidder submodularity, which is a restriction on the coalition value function. In auction models, however, coalition values are not primitive—they are derived from individual package values. It is therefore natural to ask: What conditions on bidder valuations *imply* bidder submodularity of the coalitional value function?

A key to the answer lies in a characterization of bidder submodularity that we developed earlier. In theorem 1.9 of chapter 1, we established that if there are at least four bidders and if the set of possible bidder values $\mathcal{V}$ includes all additive values, then the following three conditions are equivalent:

1. $\mathcal{V}$ includes only valuations for which goods are substitutes.
2. For every profile of bidder value functions drawn for each bidder from $\mathcal{V}$, the coalitional value function is bidder submodular.
3. For every profile of bidder value functions drawn for each bidder from $\mathcal{V}$, $\bar{\pi} \in Core(L, w)$.

According to this theorem, if goods are substitutes for each bidder, then the coalitional value function is bidder submodular. Consequently, theorem 3.5 can be recast in terms of substitutes preferences, as follows.

Theorem 3.6 If goods are substitutes for all bidders, then truthful reporting is a Nash equilibrium strategy profile of the ascending proxy auction and leads to the generalized Vickrey outcome: $\pi^T = \bar{\pi}$. Moreover, if bidders are restricted to report preferences such that goods are substitutes, and if bidder l's actual preferences have the property that goods are substitutes, then it is a *dominant strategy* for bidder l to report truthfully.

The theorem also has a converse. If we include any goods values for which goods are not substitutes, then we cannot ensure that the coalition value function is bidder submodular, so the theory of the preceding subsection does not apply. What is more, we also cannot ensure that the Vickrey outcome is a core outcome, so there cannot be an incentive for bidders to report truthfully in the ascending proxy auction. The reason is that, as observed in chapter 1, the Vickrey auction is the unique auction that, on a wide class, has the dominant-strategy property, leads to efficient outcomes, and takes only a zero payment from losing bidders.

When goods are not substitutes, the theorem implies that the ascending proxy auction necessarily departs from the VCG results, because it selects core allocations with respect to reported preferences, whereas the VCG mechanism does not. Unlike the VCG mechanism, the proxy auction does not have a dominant-strategy solution in every private-values environment. However, the proxy auction has some offsetting advantages, at least at its full-information equilibrium.

3.6   Comparisons of the Vickrey and Ascending Proxy Auctions

In chapter 1, we found that the failure of the substitutes condition and of bidder submodularity was closely connected to some extreme possibilities for manipulation in the Vickrey auction, including shill bidding and loser collusion. We also established that these possibilities for manipulation were intimately related to a failure of monotonicity of revenues in the set of bidders.

These shortcomings of the Vickrey auction contrast sharply with the properties of the ascending proxy auction. For the latter, to check bidder monotonicity, we need to identify the "equilibrium revenues." We focus attention on the equilibrium of the proxy auction that is consistent with the selection in theorem 3.4 and that minimizes revenues among those. Using the characterization of the theorem, the minimum equilibrium revenue is min π_0, subject to $\sum_{l \in S} \pi_l \geq v(S)$ for every coalition $S \subset L$. It is straightforward to see that introducing additional bidders or increasing the reports of existing bidders must (weakly) increase π_0 in this formulation. Suppose that

$\hat{v}_l(\cdot) \geq v_l(\cdot)$ for all $l \in L - 0$. Consider any profit allocation $(\hat{\pi}_l)_{l \in L}$ that satisfies $\sum_{l \in S} \hat{\pi}_l \geq \hat{v}(S)$ for all $S \subset L$. Observe that $\sum_{l \in S} \hat{\pi}_l \geq v(S)$ is also satisfied for all $S \subset L$, implying that the minimum π_0 (subject to $\sum_{l \in S} \pi_l \geq v(S)$) is weakly lower than the minimum $\hat{\pi}_0$ (subject to $\sum_{l \in S} \hat{\pi}_l \geq \hat{v}(S)$). In this sense, the ascending proxy auction satisfies bidder monotonicity.

One weakness of the Vickrey auction is its susceptibility to collusion, even by coalitions of losing bidders. The ascending proxy auction is clearly immune to loser collusion. Let S be any coalition of losing bidders. Then the prices paid by the complementary set, $L \backslash 0 \backslash S$, of bidders in the ascending proxy auction sum to at least $w(S)$; otherwise, coalition S would outbid the winners. So, to become winning bidders, members of the coalition S would have to raise their total winning bid above $w(S)$, suffering a loss in the process. Hence, a coalition consisting only of losing bidders has no profitable deviation.

A more severe failing of the Vickrey auction is its susceptibility to shill bidders; that is, a bidder can sometimes increase its payoff by employing two or more agents to bid on its behalf. The ascending proxy auction is immune to the use of shills in the following sense: given any pure strategy profile for the bidders besides l, there is a best reply for bidder l that does not use shill bids. In particular, this implies that at any pure strategy Nash equilibrium, there is no gain to any deviation using shill bids, in contrast with the result for Vickrey auctions.

Because this result can be proved using the same reasoning as for theorem 3.3, we simply sketch the argument here. Bidder l, or its several agents acting together, can acquire a set of goods A in the ascending proxy auction only if its final bid for that set exceeds the incremental value of A to the coalition $L - l$. This minimum price for A can only be increased by adding losing bidders to the coalition $L - l$, so bidder l cannot reduce its minimum price for any bundle it might acquire by using shills. Moreover, bidder l can win the bundle A at the minimum price by bidding just for A and offering the incremental value. Therefore, bidder l can achieve its maximum payoff using a strategy that does not employ shills.

We have made each of the above comparisons using one of two assumptions: either goods are substitutes or bidders have complete information about values. Although there are no theorems to identify how far our conclusions extend to environments where both conditions fail, there are robust examples showing that there is a class of environments with incomplete information and without the substitutes property that still have properties similar to those that we have described.

To illustrate, consider the following incomplete information, private-values extension of an example from chapter 1. There are two items and two bidders. Bidder 1 wants only the package of two licenses and values it at v_1, which is a random variable with support $[0, 3]$. Bidder 2 values each license singly at v_2 and values the package of two licenses at $2v_2$, where v_2 is a random variable with support $[0.3, 0.7]$. Each bidder i

knows the realization of v_i but only the distribution of v_j ($j \neq i$). In the Vickrey auction, if bidder 1 is expected to report its value truthfully, then bidder 2 would benefit by participating in the auction under two names—say, "bidder 2" and "bidder 3"—each of whom bids \$3 for a single license. The result would be that bidder 2 receives both licenses for a price of zero, which is the same conclusion as in the complete information case.

By contrast, in the proxy auction, it is optimal for bidder 2 to bid straightforwardly, that is, to bid v_2 for each single license and to bid $2v_2$ for the package of two licenses. If bidder 2 instead bids using two identities, his optimal strategy is still to place bids that sum to $2v_2$ for the package of two licenses. In either event, the result is that bidder 2 receives both licenses if and only if $2v_2 \geq v_1$, and then for a price of v_1. In this example with private information and without substitutes preferences for bidder 1, the Vickrey auction remains vulnerable to shill bidding, whereas the ascending proxy auction implements the Vickrey outcome without that vulnerability.

3.7 Conclusion

Our analysis of the ascending package auction may explain the efficient outcomes that sometimes emerge in experiments with package bidding and entail new predictions as well. If bidders bid "straightforwardly," the auction outcome is not only efficient, but also a core allocation of the exchange game.

The ascending proxy auction is a new kind of deferred acceptance algorithm, related to the algorithms studied in matching theory. Unlike the sealed-bid, first-price package auction, this new design duplicates the advantages of the Vickrey auction in environments where goods are substitutes, but the new auction design also has significant advantages compared to the Vickrey auction.

First, the ascending proxy auction avoids the very low revenues possible in the Vickrey auction, because the former always selects core allocations both when bidders bid straightforwardly and at their full information equilibria. By contrast, the Vickrey auction is assured to select core allocations only when goods are substitutes.

Second, the ascending proxy auction also avoids much of the vulnerability of the Vickrey auction to shill bids and to collusion by coalitions of losing bidders. Whereas a bidder in a Vickrey auction may sometimes find it profitable to bid under multiple names, there exists no pure strategy profile in the ascending proxy auction that ever makes such a behavior advantageous. And, whereas losing bidders in a Vickrey auction can sometimes collude profitably, that is never possible at the identified equilibria of the ascending proxy auction.

Third, the ascending proxy auction can be implemented as a multi-stage process, in which bidders first specify initial proxy values and later have one or more opportunities to revise their proxy bids. That implementation, like other sequential communication protocols, economizes on the amount of information that bidders need to communicate. It may also economize on bidders' costs of evaluating packages by allowing them to focus their efforts on the packages that they have a reasonable chance to win based on the bids made by competitors earlier in the auction.

In addition to the basic ascending proxy auction, we have also introduced a generalized version that applies for much more general preferences and constraints than the standard Vickrey model permits. For example, it applies to models in which bidders are budget constrained and to procurement problems with their characteristic complex constraints and multifaceted selection criteria. With complex auctioneer preferences, the Vickrey auction may not even apply, and with bidder budget constraints it may lead to inefficient outcomes, but the generalized ascending proxy auction selects allocations in the NTU core. We believe that this family of auction designs holds considerable promise for a variety of practical applications.

Notes

1. For a more complete account of the pre-auction positioning, see Milgrom 2004, chapter 1.

2. Vickrey (1961) originally treated auctions with multiple units of a homogeneous product, whereas Clarke (1971) and Groves (1973) treated public choice problems. In particular, the Clarke-Groves treatment explicitly includes both the auctions Vickrey studied and auctions of multiple heterogeneous objects. For auction applications, we use "VCG mechanism" and "Vickrey auction" interchangeably.

3. The main ideas underlying the ascending proxy auction and its analysis were introduced by Ausubel (1997, 1999, 2000), Milgrom (2000a,b), Parkes and Ungar (2000), Parkes (2001) and Ausubel and Milgrom (2002).

4. Some of our results continue to hold when the bidder retains some discretion to modify its proxy instructions, but we limit attention here to the pure proxy case.

5. This formulation rules out "value interdependencies" in which one bidder's information might affect another bidder's choices. This assumption would not apply if, for example, the rankings of outcomes depend on the resolution of common uncertainties about technology or demand. See Milgrom and Weber 1982.

6. In the case of public decisions with transfers, as described below, each x_l describes the joint decision and l's transfer. This allows the bidder to express preferences over a joint decision.

7. An allocation x is *stable* if 1) it is feasible ($x \in F$), 2) it is individually rational for each bidder and for the seller, and 3) there exists no S and allocation $y \in F_S$ such that $y \succ_0 x$ and for all $l \in S$, $y_l \succ_l x_l$ or $y_l = x_l$. The notion of blocking used to define the NTU core replaces 3) with the weaker requirement that there exists no S and allocation $y \in F_S$ such that $y_l \succ_l x_l$ for all $l \in S \cup \{0\}$, ruling out the possibility that $y_l = x_l$ for some $l \in S$.

8. See Yokoo, Sakurai, and Matsubara 2004, and chapter 7 of this volume for an alternative treatment of shills and "false name bidding."

9. The "semi-sincere" rubric arises because the bidder's reports of *relative* valuations are truthful, but his reports of *absolute* valuations may be untruthful (i.e., shaded). In the NTU generalization, semi-sincere strategies rank every pair of outcomes accurately except pairs that include the null (nonparticipation) outcome; semi-sincere strategies may report the null outcome to be higher in the bidder's ranking than it actually is.

10. For example, if each bidder raises his bid by the same bid increment whenever he is not a provisional winner, we see that (so long as bidder 2 remains in the auction), coalition $\{1, 2\}$ is a provisional winner one-quarter of the time, coalition $\{1, 3\}$ is a provisional winner one-quarter of the time, and coalition $\{4, 5\}$ is a provisional winner half of the time. With starting prices of zero, straightforward bidding would lead bidder 1 to bid 10, bidders 2 and 3 to bid 15 each, and bidders 4 and 5 to bid 10 apiece. At this point, bidders 4 and 5 drop out of the auction, and so there is nothing further to induce bidder 1 to raise his bid. But he has already, irrevocably, reached a bid of 10; when his bidder-Pareto-optimal core payment equals 0. If bidder 1 had instead limited his bidding to 0, he still would have won the West 10 and East 10 licenses.

11. This condition was introduced in Shapley's 1962 treatment of the assignment problem. It was shown to imply that there is a unique bidder-optimal core point (coinciding with the Vickrey payoff) in theorem 3 of Ausubel 1997, which was superceded and improved upon by theorem 7 of Ausubel and Milgrom 2002. The predecessor theorem also included the following necessary condition for the uniqueness of a bidder-optimal core point: $w(L) - w(L - S) \geq \sum_{l \in S-0}(w(L) - w(L - l))$ for all coalitions S $(0 \in S \subset L)$. Bikhchandani and Ostroy (2002) subsequently developed the implications of these conditions for dual problems to the package assignment problem.

References

Ausubel, Lawrence M. (1997), "On Generalizing the English Auction," unpublished working paper ⟨http://www.ausubel.com/⟩.

Ausubel, Lawrence M. (1999), "Computer Implemented Methods and Apparatus for Auction," U.S. Patent No. 5,905,975, issued 18 May 1999.

Ausubel, Lawrence M. (2000), "Computer Implemented Methods and Apparatus for Auction," U.S. Patent No. 6,021,398, issued 1 Feb. 2000.

Ausubel, Lawrence M. and Paul Milgrom (2001), "System and Method for a Dynamic Auction with Package Bidding," International Patent Application No. PCT/US02/16937.

Ausubel, Lawrence M. and Paul Milgrom (2002), "Ascending Auctions with Package Bidding," *Frontiers of Theoretical Economics* 1, 1–42 ⟨http://www.bepress.com/bejte/frontiers/vol1/iss1/art1⟩.

Bernheim, B. Douglas and Michael Whinston (1986), "Menu Auctions, Resource Allocation and Economic Influence," *Quarterly Journal of Economics*, 101, 1–31.

Bikhchandani, Sushil and Joseph M. Ostroy (2002), "The Package Assignment Model," *Journal of Economic Theory*, 107, 377–406.

Brewer, Paul J. and Charles R. Plott (1996), "A Binary Conflict Ascending Price (BICAP) Mechanism for the Decentralized Allocation of the Right to Use Railroad Tracks," *International Journal of Industrial Organization*, 14, 857–886.

Clarke, Edward H. (1971), "Multipart Pricing of Public Goods," *Public Choice*, 11, 17–33.

Gale, David and Lloyd S. Shapley (1962), "College Admissions and the Stability of Marriage," *American Mathematical Monthly*, 69, 9–15.

Groves, Theodore (1973), "Incentives in Teams," *Econometrica*, 41, 617–631.

Hatfield, John W. and Paul Milgrom (2005), "Auctions, Matching and the Law of Aggregate Demand," *American Economic Review*, to appear.

Kelso, Alexander S. and Vincent P. Crawford (1982), "Job Matching, Coalition Formation, and Gross Substitutes," *Econometrica*, 50, 1483–1504.

Milgrom, Paul (2000a), "Putting Auction Theory to Work: The Simultaneous Ascending Auction," *Journal of Political Economy*, 108, 245–272.

Milgrom, Paul (2000b), "Putting Auction Theory to Work: Ascending Auctions with Package Bidding," unpublished working paper.

Milgrom, Paul (2004), *Putting Auction Theory to Work*, Cambridge: Cambridge University Press.

Milgrom, Paul R. and Robert J. Weber (1982), "A Theory of Auctions and Competitive Bidding," *Econometrica*, 50, 1089–1122.

Parkes, David C. (2001), *Iterative Combinatorial Auctions: Achieving Economic and Computational Efficiency*, Ph.D. thesis, Department of Computer and Information Science, University of Pennsylvania ⟨http://www.eecs.harvard.edu/~parkes/diss.html⟩.

Parkes, David C. and Lyle H. Ungar (2000), "Iterative Combinatorial Auctions: Theory and Practice," in *Proceedings of the 17th National Conference on Artificial Intelligence (AAAI-00)*, 74–81.

Roth, Alvin E. and Marilda A. Oliveira Sotomayor (1990), *Two-Sided Matching: A Study in Game-Theoretic Modeling and Analysis*, Cambridge: Cambridge University Press.

Shapley, Lloyd (1962), "Complements and Substitutes in the Optimal Assignment Problem," *Naval Research Logistics Quarterly*, 9, 45–48.

Vickrey, William (1961), "Counterspeculation, Auctions and Competitive Sealed Tenders," *Journal of Finance*, 16, 8–37.

Yokoo, Makoto, Yuko Sakurai, and Shigeo Matsubara (2004), "The Effect of False-Name Bids in Combinatorial Auctions: New Fraud in Internet Auctions," *Games and Economic Behavior*, 46, 174–188.

4 Simultaneous Ascending Auctions

Peter Cramton

4.1 Introduction

This chapter examines one of the most successful methods for auctioning many related items—the simultaneous ascending auction. This auction form was first developed for the U.S. Federal Communications Commission's spectrum auctions, beginning in July 1994, and has subsequently been adopted with slight variation for dozens of spectrum auctions worldwide, resulting in revenues in excess of $200 billion. The method, first proposed by Paul Milgrom, Robert Wilson, and Preston McAfee, has been refined with experience, and extended to the sale of divisible goods in electricity, gas, and environmental markets. Here I describe the method and its extensions, provide evidence of its success, and suggest what we can learn from the years of experience conducting simultaneous ascending auctions.

It might seem odd for the simultaneous ascending auction to appear as a method for combinatorial auctions, because a key feature of the simultaneous ascending auction, at least in its basic form, is the requirement that bids be for individual items, rather than packages of items. As a result, the simultaneous ascending auction exposes bidders to the possibility that they will win some, but not all, of what they desire. In contrast, all the other combinatorial auction methods discussed in this book eliminate this exposure problem by allowing bidders to bid on packages of items. Nonetheless, I view the simultaneous ascending auction not as a historical curiosity to be supplanted by more powerful combinatorial methods, but as an essential method any auction designer should have in his toolkit. The simultaneous ascending auction (and its variants) will remain the best method for auctioning many related items in a wide range of circumstances, even settings where some of the goods are complements for some bidders, so the exposure problem is a real concern.

This is not to say that true combinatorial auctions—those that allow package bids—are not also important. They are. Rather, my point is that there are many situations where the simultaneous ascending auction will do a sufficiently good job in limiting the exposure problem that its other advantages (especially simplicity and price discovery) make it a preferred auction method. In other settings, where complementarities are both strong and varied across bidders, package bids are needed to improve the efficiency of the auction mechanism.

The simultaneous ascending auction is a natural generalization of the English auction when selling many goods. The key features are that all the goods are on the block at the same time, each with a price associated with it, and the bidders can bid on any of the items. The bidding continues until no bidder is willing to raise the bid on any of the items. Then the auction ends with each bidder winning the items on which it has the high bid, and paying its bid for any items won.

The reason for the success of this simple procedure is the excellent price discovery it affords. As the auction progresses bidders see the tentative price information and condition subsequent bids on this new information. Over the course of the auction, bidders are able to develop a sense of what the final prices are likely to be, and can adjust their purchases in response to this price information. To the extent price information is sufficiently good and the bidders retain sufficient flexibility to shift toward their best package, the exposure problem is mitigated—bidders are able to piece together a desirable package of items, despite the constraint of bidding on individual items rather than packages.

Perhaps even more importantly, the price information helps the bidders focus their valuation efforts in the relevant range of the price space. Standard auction models, which assume that each bidder costlessly knows his valuation for every possible package (or at least knows how his valuation depends on the information of others in the case of non-private value models), ignore this benefit of price discovery. However, in practice, determining values is a costly process. When there are many items, determining precise values for all possible packages is not feasible. Price discovery focuses the bidders' valuation efforts to the relevant parts of the price space, improving efficiency and reducing transaction costs.

To further mitigate the exposure problem, most simultaneous ascending auctions allow bidders to withdraw bids. This enables bidders to back out of failed aggregations, shifting bids to more fruitful packages. However, I find that bid withdrawals often facilitate undesirable gaming behavior, and thus the ability to withdraw bids needs to be constrained carefully. It is my view that price discovery—not bid withdrawal—is the more effective way to limit the exposure problem in simultaneous ascending auctions.

Since July 1994, the Federal Communications Commission (FCC) has conducted dozens of spectrum auctions with the simultaneous ascending format, raising tens of billions for the U.S. Treasury. The auctions assigned thousands of licenses to hundreds of firms. These firms provide a diversity of wireless communication services now enjoyed by a majority of the population. The FCC is not alone. Countries throughout the world are now using auctions to assign spectrum. Indeed, the early auctions in Europe for third-generation (3G) mobile wireless licenses raised nearly $100 billion. Auctions have become the preferred method of assigning spectrum, and most have been simultaneous ascending auctions (see Cramton 1997 and Milgrom 2004 for a history of the auctions).

There is now substantial evidence that this auction design has been successful. Resale of licenses has been uncommon, suggesting the auction assignment is nearly efficient. Revenues often have exceeded industry and government estimates. The simultaneous ascending auction may be partially responsible for the large revenues. Revealing information in the auction process reduces bidder uncertainty, and the bidders can safely bid more aggressively. Also, revenues may increase to the extent the design enables bidders to piece together more efficient packages of items.

Despite the general success, the simultaneous ascending auctions have experienced a few problems from which one can draw important lessons. One basic problem is the simultaneous ascending auction's vulnerability to revenue-reducing strategies in situations where competition is weak. Bidders have an incentive to reduce their demands in order to keep prices low, and to use bid signaling strategies to coordinate on a split of the items. I identify problems with the simultaneous ascending auctions, and discuss how to minimize these problems.

I begin by motivating the design choices in a simultaneous ascending auction and discuss an important extension, the simultaneous clock auction, for the sale of many divisible goods. Then I describe typical rules, including many important details. Next I examine the performance of the simultaneous ascending auction, identifying both strengths and weaknesses of the approach. I discuss many refinements to the auction method, which have been introduced from early experience.

4.2 Auction Design

The critical elements of the simultaneous ascending auction are 1) open bidding, 2) simultaneous sale, and 3) no package bids. These features create a Walrasian pricing process that yields a competitive equilibrium provided 1) items are substitutes, 2) bidders are price takers, and 3) bid increments are negligible (Milgrom 2000, 2004). Of course, these conditions do not hold in practice. Some degree of market power is common, at least some items are complements, and getting the auction to conclude in a manageable number of rounds requires bid increments in the 5 to 10 percent range.

Still, the simultaneous ascending auction does perform well in practice largely because of the benefits of price discovery that come from open bidding and simultaneous sale. These benefits take two forms. First, in situations where bidder values are interdependent, price discovery may reduce the winner's curse and raise revenue (Milgrom and Weber 1982). Bidders are able to bid more aggressively, because they have better information about the item's value. More importantly, when many items are for sale, the price discovery lets bidders adapt their bidding and analysis to the price information, which focuses valuation efforts and facilitates the aggregation of a complementary package of items.

The alternative of sequential sale limits information available to bidders and limits how the bidders can respond to information. With sequential auctions, bidders must guess what prices will be in future auctions when determining bids in the current auction. Incorrect guesses may result in an inefficient assignment when item values are interdependent. A sequential auction also eliminates many strategies. A bidder cannot switch back to an earlier item if prices go too high in a later auction. Bidders are likely to regret having purchased early at high prices, or not having purchased early at low prices. The guesswork about future auction outcomes makes strategies in sequential auctions complex, and the outcomes less efficient.

The Swiss wireless-local-loop auction conducted in March 2000 illustrates the difficulties of sequential sale. Three nationwide licenses were sold in a sequence of ascending auctions. The first two licenses were for a 28-MHz block; the third was twice as big (56 MHz). Interestingly, the first license sold for 121 million francs, the second for 134 million francs, and the third (the large license) sold for 55 million francs. The largest license sold for just a fraction of the prices of the earlier licenses.

Almost all the simultaneous ascending auctions conducted to date do not allow package bids. Bids are only for individual items. The main advantages of this approach is simplicity and anonymous linear prices. The auction is easily implemented and understood. The disadvantage is the exposure problem. With individual bids, bidding for a synergistic combination is risky. The bidder may fail to acquire key pieces of the desired combination, but pay prices based on the synergistic gain. Alternatively, the bidder may be forced to bid beyond his valuation in order to secure the synergies and reduce loss from being stuck with the dogs. Bidding on individual items exposes bidders seeking synergistic combinations to aggregation risk.

Not allowing package bids can create inefficiencies. For example, suppose there are two bidders for two adjacent parking spaces. One bidder with a car and a trailer requires both spaces. He values the two spots together at $100 and a single spot as worth nothing; the spots are perfect complements. The second bidder has a car, but no trailer. Either spot is worth $75, as is the combination; the spots are perfect substitutes. Note that the efficient outcome is for the first bidder to get both spots for a social gain of $100, rather than $75 if the second bidder gets a spot. Yet any attempt by the first bidder to win the spaces is foolhardy. The first bidder would have to pay at least $150 for the spaces, because the second bidder will bid up to $75 for either one. Alternatively, if the first bidder drops out early, he will "win" one spot, losing an amount equal to his highest bid. The only equilibrium is for the second bidder to win a single spot by placing the minimum bid. The outcome is inefficient, and fails to generate revenue. In contrast, if package bids are allowed, then the outcome is efficient. The first bidder wins both with a bid of $75 for the package.

This example is extreme to illustrate the exposure problem. The inefficiency involves large bidder-specific complementarities and a lack of competition. In most spectrum auctions conducted to date, the complementarities were less extreme and the competition was greater.

Unfortunately, allowing package bids creates other problems. Package bids may favor bidders seeking large aggregations due to a variant of the threshold problem. Continuing with the last example, suppose that there is a third bidder who values either spot at $40. Then the efficient outcome is for the individual bidders to win both spots for a social gain of $75 + 40 = \$115$. But this outcome may not occur when values are privately known. Suppose that the second and third bidders have placed individual bids of $35 on the two spots, but these bids are topped by a package bid of $90 from the first bidder. Each bidder hopes that the other will bid higher to top the package bid. The second bidder has an incentive to understate his willingness to push the bidding higher. He may refrain from bidding, counting on the third bidder to break the threshold of $90. Because the third bidder cannot come through, the auction ends with the first bidder winning both spaces for $90.

Package bidding also adds complexity. Unless the complementarities are large and heterogeneous across bidders, a simultaneous ascending auction without package bids may be preferred.

4.2.1 Clock Auctions
An important variation of the simultaneous ascending auction is the simultaneous clock auction, discussed in greater detail in chapter 5. The critical difference is that bidders simply respond with quantities desired at prices specified by the auctioneer. Clock auctions are especially effective in auctioning many divisible goods. There is a clock for each divisible good indicating its tentative price per unit quantity. Bidders express the quantity desired at the current prices. For those goods with excess demand the price is raised and bidders again express their desired quantities at the new prices. This process continues until supply just equals demand. The tentative prices and assignments then become final.

If we assume no market power and bidding is continuous, then the clock auction is efficient with prices equal to the competitive equilibrium (Ausubel and Cramton 2004).

Discrete, rather than continuous, rounds means that issues of bid increments, ties, and rationing are important. This complication is best handled by allowing bidders in each round to express their demand curves for all points along the line segment between the start of round prices and the end of round prices. Allowing a rich expression of preferences within a round makes bid increments, ties, and rationing less important. Because preferences for intermediate prices can be expressed, the efficiency loss associated with the discrete increment is less, so the auctioneer can choose a larger bid increment, resulting in a faster and less costly auction process.

A second practical consideration is market power. Although some auction settings approximate the ideal of perfect competition, most do not. The auction design needs to address market power issues. Two useful instruments are information policy and reserve pricing. By controlling the information that the bidders receive after each round of the auction, the auctioneer can enhance the desirable properties of price and assignment discovery, while limiting the scope for collusive bidding. Reserve pricing serves two roles, providing price discipline in the absence of competition and discouraging collusion by limiting the maximum gain from successful collusion.

4.3   Typical Rules

The simultaneous ascending auction works as follows. A group of items with strong value interdependencies are up for auction at one time. A bidder can bid on any collection of items in any round, subject to an activity rule that determines the bidder's current eligibility. The auction ends when a round passes with no new bids on any item. This auction form was thought to give the bidders flexibility in expressing values and building packages of items. I describe common rules below.

Quantity cap   To promote competition in the aftermarket, a bidder often is limited in the quantity he can win.

Payment rules   Payments are typically received at least at two times: a refundable deposit before the bidding begins and a final payment for items won. The refundable deposit often defines the bidder's initial eligibility—the maximum quantity of items that the bidder can bid for. A bidder interested in winning a large quantity of items would have to submit a large deposit. The deposit provides some assurance that the bids are serious. Some auctions require bidders to increase the deposit as bids increase.

Minimum bid increments   To assure that the auction concludes in a reasonable amount of time, minimum bid increments are specified. Bid increments are adjusted in response to bidder behavior. Typically, the bid increments are between 5 and 20 percent.

Activity rule   The activity rule is a device for improving price discovery by requiring a bidder to bid in a consistent way throughout the auction. It forces a bidder to maintain a minimum level of activity to preserve current eligibility. A bidder desiring a large quantity at the end of the auction (when prices are high) must bid for a large quantity early in the auction (when prices are low). As the auction progresses, the activity requirement increases, reducing a bidder's flexibility. The lower activity requirement early in the auction gives the bidder greater flexibility in shifting among packages early on when there is the most uncertainty about what will be obtainable.

Number of rounds per day   A final means of controlling the pace of the auction is the number of rounds per day. Typically, fewer rounds per day are conducted early in the auction when the most learning occurs. In the later rounds, there is much less bidding activity, and the rounds can occur more quickly.

Stopping rule   A simultaneous stopping rule gives the bidders maximum flexibility in pursuing backup strategies. The auction ends if a single round passes in which no new bids are submitted on any item. In auctions with multiple stages (later stages have higher activity requirements), the auction ends when no new bids are submitted in the final stage. Few or no bids in an earlier stage shifts the auction to the next stage.

Bid information   The most common implementation is full transparency. Each bidder is fully informed about the identities of the bidders and the size of the deposits. High bids and bidder identities are posted after each round. In addition, all bids and bidder identities are displayed at the conclusion of each round, together with each bidder's eligibility.

Bid withdrawal   To limit the exposure problem, the high bidders can withdraw their bids subject to a bid withdrawal penalty. If a bidder withdraws its high bid, the auctioneer is listed as the high bidder and the minimum bid is the second highest bid for that item. The second highest bidder is in no way responsible for the bid, as this bidder may have moved on to other items. If there are no further bids on the item, the auctioneer can reduce the minimum bid. To discourage insincere bidding, there are penalties for withdrawing a high bid. The penalty is the larger of 0 and the difference between the withdrawn bid and the final sale price. This penalty is consistent with the standard remedy for breach of contract. The penalty equals the damage suffered by the seller as a result of the withdrawal.

4.4   Performance of the Simultaneous Ascending Auction

Because we do not observe the values firms place on items, it is impossible to assess directly the efficiency of the simultaneous ascending auction from field data. Nonetheless, we can indirectly evaluate the auction design from the observed behavior in spectrum auctions (Cramton 1997; McAfee and McMillan 1996). I focus especially on the three U.S. PCS broadband auctions, which I refer to as the AB auction, the C auction, and the DEF auction, indicating the blocks of spectrum that were assigned in each. This spectrum is used to provide mobile wireless voice and data communications.

Revenue is a first sign of success, and auction revenues have been substantial—typically exceeding industry and government estimates. The simultaneous ascending auction may be partially responsible for the large revenues. By revealing information in the auction process, the winner's curse is reduced, and the bidders can bid more aggressively. Also, revenues may increase to the extent the design enables bidders to piece together more efficient packages of items.

A second indicator of success is that the auctions tended to generate market prices. Similar items sold for similar prices. In the narrowband auctions, the price differences among similar licenses were at most a few percent and often zero. In the first broadband auction, where two licenses were sold in each market, the prices differed by less than one minimum bid increment in forty-two of the forty-eight markets.

A third indicator of success is the formation of efficient license aggregations. Bidders did appear to piece together sensible license aggregations. This is clearest in the narrowband auctions. In the nationwide narrowband auction, bidders buying multiple bands preferred adjacent bands. The adjacency means that the buffer between bands can be used for transmission, thus increasing capacity. The two bidders that won multiple licenses were successful in buying adjacent bands. In the regional narrowband auction, the aggregation problem was more complicated. Several bidders had nationwide interests, and these bidders would have to piece together a license in each of the five regions, preferably all on the same band, in order to achieve a nationwide market. The bidders were remarkably successful in achieving these aggregations. Four of the six bands sold as nationwide aggregations. Bidders were able to win all five regions within the same band. Even in the two bands that were not sold as nationwide aggregations, bidders winning multiple licenses won geographically adjacent licenses within the same band.

Large aggregations were also formed in the PCS broadband auctions. Bidders tended to win the same band when acquiring adjacent licenses. In the AB auction, the three bidders with nationwide interests appeared to have efficient geographic coverage when one includes their cellular holdings. The footprints of smaller bidders also seem consistent with the bidders' existing infrastructures. In the C-block auction, bidders were able to piece together contiguous footprints, although many bidders were interested in stand-alone markets.

Ausubel et al. (1997) analyze the AB and C auction data to see if there is evidence of local synergies. Consistent with local synergies, these studies find that bidders did pay more when competing with a bidder holding neighboring licenses. Hence, bidders did bid for synergistic gains and, judging by the final footprints, often obtained them.

The two essential features of the simultaneous ascending auction design are (1) the use of multiple rounds, rather than a single sealed bid, and (2) simultaneous, rather than sequential sales. The goal of both of these features is to reveal information and then give the bidders the flexibility to respond to the information. There is substantial evidence that the auction was successful in revealing extensive information. Bidders had good information about both prices and assignments at a point in the auction where they had the flexibility to act on the information (Cramton 1997). The probability that a high bidder would eventually win the market was high at the midpoint of each auction. Also the correlation between mid-auction and final prices was high in each auction. Information about prices and assignments improved throughout each auction and was of high quality before bidders lost the flexibility to move to alternative packages.

The absence of resale also suggests that the auctions were highly efficient. In the first two years of the PCS auctions, there was little resale. GTE was the one exception. Shortly after the AB auction ended, GTE sold its AB winnings for about what it paid for the licenses. Apparently there was a shift in corporate strategy away from PCS.

4.5   Demand Reduction and Collusive Bidding

Despite the apparent success of these auctions, an important issue limiting both efficiency and revenues is demand reduction and collusive bidding. These issues become important in multiple-item auctions. The efficiency results from single-item auctions do not carry forward to the multiple-item setting. In an ascending auction for a single item, each bidder has a dominant strategy of bidding up to his private valuation. Hence, the item always goes to the bidder with the highest value. If, instead, two identical items are being sold in a simultaneous ascending auction, then a bidder has an incentive to stop bidding for the second item before its marginal valuation is reached. Continuing to bid for two items raises the price paid for the first. As a result, the bidder with the highest value for the second item may be outbid by a bidder demanding just a single unit.

For example, suppose there are two identical items and two bidders (Large and Small). Large has a value of $100 per item ($200 for both); whereas Small has a value of $90 for one item and values the second at $0. In a simultaneous ascending auction with a reserve price less than $80, the unique equilibrium outcome is for each to bid for a single item, so that the auction ends at the reserve price. Large prefers ending the auction at the reserve price, winning a single item for a profit of more than $20, because to win both items Large would have to raise the price on both items above $90 (it is a dominant strategy for Small to bid up to $90 on each), which results in a profit of less than $20. The demand reduction by Large harms both efficiency and seller revenues.

This logic is quite general. In multi-unit uniform-price auctions, typically every equilibrium is inefficient (Ausubel and Cramton 2002). Bidders have an incentive to shade their bids for multiple units, and the incentive to shade increases with the quantity being demanded. Hence, large bidders will shade more than small bidders. This differential shading creates an inefficiency. The small bidders will tend inefficiently to win items that the large bidders should win. The intuition for this result is analogous to why a monopolist's marginal revenue curve lies below its demand curve: bringing more items to market reduces the price received on all items. In the auction, demanding more items raises the price paid on all items. Hence, the incentive to reduce demand.

One can view the simultaneous ascending auction as an ascending-bid version of a uniform-price auction. Certainly, for items that are close substitutes, the simultaneous ascending auction has generated near uniform prices. However, the incentives for demand reduction and collusive bidding likely are more pronounced in an ascending version of the uniform-price auction (Cramton and Schwartz 2002; Ausubel and Schwartz 1999). To illustrate this, consider a simple example with two identical goods and two risk-neutral bidders. Suppose that for each bidder the marginal value of winning one item is the same as the marginal value of winning a second item. These values are assumed independent and private, with each bidder drawing its marginal value from a uniform distribution on [0, 100]. First consider the sealed-bid uniform price auction where each bidder privately submits two bids and the highest two bids secure units at a per-unit charge equal to the third highest bid. There are two equilibria to this sealed-bid auction: a demand-reducing equilibrium where each bidder submits one bid for $0 and one bid equal to its marginal value; and a sincere equilibrium where each bidder submits two bids equal to its marginal value. The sincere equilibrium is fully efficient in that both units will be awarded to the bidder who values them more. The demand-reducing equilibrium, however, raises zero revenue (the third highest bid is zero) and is inefficient because the bidder with the higher value wins only one unit.

Next consider the same setting, but using an ascending version of the auction. Specifically, view the ascending auction as a two-button auction where there is a price clock that starting from price 0 increases continuously to 100. The bidders depress the buttons to indicate the quantity they are bidding for at every instant. The buttons are "non-repushable," meaning a bidder can decrease but not increase its demand. Each bidder observes the price and can observe how many buttons the opponent is depressing. The auction ends at the first price such that the total number of buttons depressed is less than or equal to two. This price is the clearing price. Each bidder will win the number of units he demands when the auction ends, and is charged the clearing price for each unit won. In this game, if dominated strategies are eliminated, there is a unique equilibrium in which the bidding ends at a price of zero, with both bidders demanding just a single unit. The reason is that each bidder knows that if it unilaterally decreases its bidding to one unit, the other bidder will instantaneously end the auction, as argued above. But because the bidder prefers the payoff from winning one unit at the low price over the expected payoff of winning two units at the price high enough to eliminate the other bidder from the auction, the bidder will immediately bid for just one unit, inducing an *immediate* end to the auction. Thus, the only equilibrium here is analogous to the demand-reducing equilibrium in the sealed-bid uniform-price auction. The efficient equilibrium does not obtain. This example shows that the incentives to reduce demand can be more pronounced in an open auction, where bidders have the opportunity to respond to the elapsed bidding. The 1999 German GSM spectrum auction, which lasted just two rounds, illustrates this behavior (Jehiel and Moldovanu 2000; Grimm, Riedel, and Wolfstetter 2002).

This example is meant to illustrate that in simple settings with few goods and few bidders, bidders have the incentive to reduce demand. Direct evidence of demand reduction was seen in the nationwide narrowband auction. The largest bidder, PageNet, reduced its demand from three of the large licenses to two, at a point when prices were still well below its marginal value for the third unit (Cramton 1995). PageNet felt that if it continued to demand a third license, it would drive up the prices on all the others to disadvantageously high levels.

An examination of the bidding in the AB auction is suggestive that the largest bidders did drop out of certain markets at prices well below plausible values, as a result of either demand reduction or tacit collusion.

Further evidence of demand reduction comes from the C auction. One large bidder defaulted on the down payment, so the FCC reauctioned the licenses. Interestingly, the licenses sold for 3 percent more than in the original auction. Consistent with demand reduction, NextWave, the largest winner in the C auction, bought 60 percent of the reauctioned spectrum. This occurred despite the fact that NextWave was not the second highest bidder on any of these licenses in the original auction. NextWave was able to bid aggressively in the reaction, knowing that its bidding would have no affect on prices in the original auction.

Engelbrecht-Wiggans and Kahn (1998) and Brusco and Lopomo (2002) show that for an auction format such as the FCC's, where the bidding occurs in rounds and bidding can be done on distinct units, that there exist equilibria where bidders coordinate a division of the available units at low prices relative to own values. Bidders achieve these low-revenue equilibria by threatening to punish those bidders who deviate from the cooperative division of the units. The idea in these papers is that bidders have the incentives to split up the available units ending the auction at low prices.

With heterogeneous goods and asymmetric bidders in terms of budgets, capacities, and current holdings of complementary goods, it is unlikely that bidders would be aware of a simple equilibrium strategy that indicates which items to bid on and which to avoid. However, bidders in the FCC auctions, especially the DEF auction, took advantage of signaling opportunities to coordinate how to assign the licenses. With signaling, bidders could indicate which licenses they most wanted and which licenses they would be willing to forgo. Often this communication took the form of punishments.

Cramton and Schwartz (2002) examine collusive bidding strategies in the DEF auction. During the DEF auction, the FCC and the Department of Justice observed that some bidders used bid signaling to coordinate the assignment of licenses. Specifically, some bidders engaged in *code bidding*. A code bid uses the trailing digits of the bid to tell other bidders on which licenses to bid or not bid. Because bids were often in millions of dollars, yet were specified in dollars, bidders at negligible cost could use the last three digits—the trailing digits—to specify a market number. Often, a bidder (the sender) would use these code bids as retaliation against another bidder (the receiver) who was bidding on a license desired by the sender. The sender would raise the price on some market the receiver wanted, and use the trailing digits to tell the receiver on which license to cease bidding. Although the trailing digits are useful in making clear which market the receiver is to avoid, *retaliating bids* without the trailing digits can also send a clear message. The concern of the FCC is that this type of coordination may be collusive and may dampen revenues and efficiency.

The DEF auction was especially vulnerable to collusive bidding, because it featured both small markets and light competition. Small markets enhanced the scope for splitting up the licenses. Light competition increased the possibility that collusive bidding strategies would be successful. Indeed, prices in the DEF auction were much lower than prices in the two earlier broadband PCS auctions, as well as subsequent auctions.

From a strategic viewpoint, the simultaneous ascending auction can be thought of as a negotiation among the bidders. The bidders are negotiating how to split up the licenses among themselves, but only can use their bids for communication. The auction ends when the bidders agree on the division of the licenses. Retaliating bids and code bids are strategies to coordinate on a split of the licenses at low prices. In addition, bidders with a reputation for retaliation may scare off potential competitors.

Cramton and Schwartz (2002) found that bidders who commonly use these strategies paid less for the spectrum they ultimately won. Further evidence that retaliation was effective in reducing prices is seen by the absence of arbitrage between the identical D and E blocks in each market. In particular, there was a tendency for bidders to avoid AT&T, a large bidder with a reputation for retaliation. If bidders did not care about the identity of the high bidder, they would arbitrage the prices of the D and E blocks, and bid against AT&T if the other block was more expensive. This did not happen. Even when the price of the other block was 50 percent higher, bidders bid on the higher priced block 27 percent of the time, rather than bid against AT&T.

Following the experience in the DEF auction, the FCC restricted bids to a whole number of bid increments above the standing high bid. This eliminates code bidding, but it does nothing to prevent retaliating bids. Retaliating bids may be just as effective as code bids in signaling a split of the licenses, when competition is weak.

The auctioneer has many instruments to reduce the effectiveness of bid signaling. These include:

• Concealing bidder identities   This prevents the use of targeted punishments against rivals. Unless there are strong efficiency reasons for revealing identities, anonymous auctions may be preferable.

• Setting high reserve prices   High reserve prices reduce the incentive for demand reduction in a multiple-item auction, because as the reserve price increases the benefit from reducing demands falls. Moreover, higher reserve prices reduce the number of rounds that the bidders have to coordinate a split of the licenses and still face low prices.

• Offering preferences for small businesses and non-incumbents   Competition is encouraged by favoring bidders that may otherwise be disadvantaged ex ante. In the DEF auction, competition for the D and E license could have been increased by extending small business preferences to the D and E blocks, rather than restricting the preferences to the F block.

• Offering larger licenses   Many small licenses are more easily split up. At the other extreme, a single nationwide license is impossible to split up. Such extreme bundling may have negative efficiency consequences, but improve revenues.

The inefficiencies of demand reduction can be eliminated with a Vickrey auction or more practically with an ascending proxy auction or a clock-proxy auction (see Ausubel and Milgrom 2002; and chapters 1, 3, and 5 of this volume).

4.6   Lessons Learned and Auction Enhancements

The FCC auction rules have evolved in response to the experience of several dozen auctions. An examination of this evolution is instructive. Despite many enhancements, the FCC spectrum auctions have retained the same basic structure, a strong indication of an excellent initial design. The intent of the changes were to reduce speculative bidding, to avoid collusion, and to speed the auction along.

Elimination of installment payments   A serious inefficiency in the C auction was speculative bidding caused by overly attractive installment payment terms. Bidders only had to put down 5 percent of their bids at the end of the auction, a second 5 percent at the time of license award, and then quarterly installment payments at the ten-year Treasury rate with interest-only payments for the first six years. These attractive terms favor bidders that are speculating in spectrum. If prices go up, the speculators do well; if prices fall, the speculators can walk away from their down payments. Indeed, spectrum prices did fall after the C auction, and most of the large bidders in the C auction defaulted on the payments. As a result of this experience, the FCC no longer offers installment payments. Bids must be paid in full when the licenses are awarded.

Click-box bidding   Bidders in FCC auctions no longer enter bids in dollars. Rather, the bidder indicates in a click-box the number of bid increments from 1–9 that it wishes to bid above the standing high bid. If the standing high bid is 100 and the minimum bid increment is 10 percent, then the allowable bids would be 110, 120 ... 190, corresponding to the allowable increment bids of 1, 2 ... 9. This approach solves two problems. First, it eliminates code bidding. Bidders can no longer use the trailing digits of bids to signal to other bidders who should win what. Second, it reduces the possibility of mistaken bids. There were several instances of bidders adding too many zeros to the end of their dollar bids. Click-box bidding permits substantial jump bids but not gross mistakes.

The downside of click-box bidding is the greater possibility of tie bids. This turns out not to be a serious problem. Although ties do occur early in the auction, it is unlikely that the final bid on a license involves a tie. Still, ties do occur, and so the FCC tie-breaking rule takes on greater importance. The FCC initially broke ties with the time stamp. Bids entered earlier have preference. Because bidders often have a mild preference for being the standing high bidder, it is common for bidders to race to enter their bids early in the round to win ties. Such behavior is undesirable, and so the FCC now uses a random tie-breaking rule.

License-specific bid increments   In early auctions, the FCC used the same percentage increment for all licenses. This was fine for auctioning a handful of similar licenses. However, when auctioning hundreds of heterogeneous licenses, it was found that some licenses would have a lot of bidding activity and others would have little activity. To speed the auction along, it makes sense to use larger bid increments for more active licenses. In recent auctions, the FCC adjusts the bid increments for each license based on the license's history of bid activity, using an exponential smoothing formula. Percentage increments tend to range between 5 and 20 percent, depending on prior activity. More active licenses have a larger increment.

Limit the use of withdrawals   Bid withdrawals were introduced to permit bidders to back out of a failed aggregation. The DEF auction had 789 withdrawals. Few if any of these withdrawals were related to failed aggregations. Rather, most of the withdrawals appear to have been used as a strategic device, in one of three ways: 1) as a signal of the bidder's willingness to give up one license in exchange for another, 2) as part of a parking strategy to maintain eligibility without bidding on desired licenses, and 3) to acquire near the end of the auction more preferred licenses that seem to free up after the decline of another bidder. The undesirable use of withdrawals was also observed in other auctions. As a result, the FCC now only allows withdrawals in at most two rounds of the auction for any bidder. This enables the bidder to back out of up to two failed aggregations, and yet prevents the frequent strategic use of withdrawals.

Faster rounds   The FCC's auction system now permits much faster rounds than the initial implementation. In many auctions, bidding activity is slow in the later part of the auction. Hence, being able to conduct twenty or more rounds per day is important in speeding the auction along.

Minimum opening bids   Early FCC auctions did not use minimum opening bids; any opening bid greater than zero was acceptable. The FCC now sets substantial minimum opening bids. These bid limits both increase the pace and reduce the potential for collusion. By starting at a reasonably high level, the bidders have fewer rounds to resolve their conflicts at low prices, thus reducing the benefit of collusive strategies.

4.7   Conclusion

A simultaneous ascending auction is a sensible way to auction many items. This approach has been used with great success in many high-stake auctions in the last ten years to auction spectrum, energy, and pollution permits. The process yields a competitive equilibrium in simple settings. Evidence from practice suggests that the desirable properties of the design are largely robust to practical complications, such as mild complementarities. However, when competition is weak, then there is a tendency for collusive bidding strategies to appear, especially in the fully transparent implementation in which all bids and bidder identities are revealed after each round.

When some items are complements, the simultaneous ascending auction suffers from the exposure problem, because package bids are not allowed. To limit this problem, the auction rules typically allow the withdrawal of standing high bids. This allows a bidder to back out of a failed aggregation. Interestingly, an examination of withdrawals in the FCC spectrum auctions reveals that the withdrawals typically were not used for this desired purpose, but rather were mostly for undesirable bid signaling. As a result, current auctions limit a bidder's withdrawals to occur in just a few rounds of the auction.

Recent experience with simultaneous ascending auctions suggests that there are many advantages to the clock variation (Ausubel and Cramton 2004). Most importantly, this greatly reduces the ability of bidders to engage in tacit collusion through bid signaling. Demand reduction remains a problem in the standard clock auction; however, demand reduction can be eliminated by adding a final proxy round at the end of the clock auction. This innovation is the subject of the next chapter.

Acknowledgments

I gratefully acknowledge the support of National Science Foundation Grants SES-01-12906 and IIS-02-05489.

References

Ausubel, Lawrence M. and Peter Cramton (2002), "Demand Reduction and Inefficiency in Multi-Unit Auctions," University of Maryland Working Paper 96-07, revised July 2002.

Ausubel, Lawrence M. and Peter Cramton (2004), "Auctioning Many Divisible Goods," *Journal of the European Economic Association*, 2, 480–493, April–May.

Ausubel, Lawrence M., Peter Cramton, R. Preston McAfee, and John McMillan (1997), "Synergies in Wireless Telephony: Evidence from the Broadband PCS Auctions," *Journal of Economics and Management Strategy*, 6, 497–527.

Ausubel, Lawrence M. and Paul Milgrom (2002), "Ascending Auctions with Package Bidding," *Frontiers of Theoretical Economics*, 1, 1–42 ⟨www.bepress.com/bejte/frontiers/vol1/iss1/art1⟩.

Ausubel, Lawrence M. and Jesse A. Schwartz (1999), "The Ascending Auction Paradox," Working Paper, University of Maryland.

Brusco, Sandro and Giuseppe Lopomo (2002), "Collusion via Signalling in Simultaneous Ascending Bid Auctions with Heterogeneous Objects, with and without Complementarities," *Review of Economic Studies*, 69, 407–436.

Cramton, Peter (1995), "Money out of Thin Air: The Nationwide Narrowband PCS Auction," *Journal of Economics and Management Strategy*, 4, 267–343.

Cramton, Peter (1997), "The FCC Spectrum Auctions: An Early Assessment," *Journal of Economics and Management Strategy*, 6, 431–495.

Cramton, Peter and Jesse Schwartz (2002), "Collusive Bidding in the FCC Spectrum Auctions," *Contributions to Economic Analysis & Policy*, 1 ⟨www.bepress.com/bejeap/contributions/vol1/iss1/art11⟩.

Engelbrecht-Wiggans, Richard and Charles M. Kahn (1998), "Multi-Unit Auctions with Uniform Prices," *Economic Theory*, 12, 227–258.

Grimm, Veronika, Frank Riedel, and Elmar Wolfstetter (2002), "Low Price Equilibrium in Multi-Unit Auctions: The GSM Spectrum Auction in Germany," *International Journal of Industrial Organization*, 21, 1557–1569.

Jehiel, Philippe and Benny Moldovanu (2000), "A Critique of the Planned Rules for the German UMTS/IMT-2000 License Auction," Unpublished Working Paper, University of Bonn.

McAfee, R. Preston and John McMillan (1996), "Analyzing the Airwaves Auction," *Journal of Economic Perspectives*, 10, 159–176.

Milgrom, Paul (2000), "Putting Auction Theory to Work: The Simultaneous Ascending Auction," *Journal of Political Economy*, 108, 245–272.

Milgrom, Paul (2004), *Putting Auction Theory to Work*, Cambridge: Cambridge University Press.

Milgrom, Paul R. and Robert J. Weber (1982), "A Theory of Auctions and Competitive Bidding," *Econometrica*, 50, 1089–1122.

5 The Clock-Proxy Auction: A Practical Combinatorial Auction Design

Lawrence M. Ausubel, Peter Cramton, and Paul Milgrom

5.1 Introduction

In this chapter we propose a method for auctioning many related items. A typical application is a spectrum sale in which different bidders combine licenses in different ways. Some pairs of licenses may be substitutes and others may be complements. Indeed, a given pair of licenses may be substitutes for one bidder but complements for another, and may change between substitutes and complements for a single bidder as the prices of the other licenses vary. Our proposed method combines two auction formats—the clock auction and the proxy auction—to produce a hybrid with the benefits of both.

The *clock auction* is an iterative auction procedure in which the auctioneer announces prices, one for each of the items being sold. The bidders then indicate the quantities of each item desired at the current prices. Prices for items with excess demand then increase, and the bidders again express quantities at the new prices. This process is repeated until there are no items with excess demand.

The *ascending proxy auction* is a particular package bidding procedure with desirable properties (see Ausubel and Milgrom 2002, and chapter 3 of this volume). The bidders report values to their respective proxy agents. The proxy agents iteratively submit package bids on behalf of the bidders, selecting the best profit opportunity for a bidder given the bidder's inputted values. The auctioneer then selects the provisionally winning bids that maximize revenues. This process continues until the proxy agents have no new bids to submit.

The clock-proxy auction is a hybrid auction format that begins with a clock phase and ends with a final proxy round. First, bidders directly submit bids in a clock auction, until there is no excess demand for any item. Then bidders have a single opportunity to input proxy values. The proxy round concludes the auction. All bids are kept live throughout the auction. There are no bid withdrawals. The bids of a particular bidder are mutually exclusive. There is an activity rule throughout the clock phase and between the clock phase and the proxy round.

There are three principal motivations behind our clock-proxy auction proposal. First, Porter et al. (2003) precede us in proposing a particular version of a "combinatorial" clock auction for spectrum auctions, and they provide experimental evidence in its support. Second, the recent innovation of the proxy auction provides a combinatorial auction format suitable for related items such as spectrum. Unlike pure clock auctions, whose anonymous linear prices are not generally rich enough to yield efficient outcomes even with straightforward bidding, the proxy auction leads to efficient outcomes and it yields competitive revenues when bidding is straightforward. It also has some desirable individual and group incentive properties. However, the theoretical development of the proxy auction treats only a sealed-bid procedure, omitting opportunities for bidder feedback and price discovery. Third, our own version of a clock auction has been implemented in the field for products such as electricity in recent years with considerable success (see Ausubel and Cramton 2004). This empirical success in the field suggests that the clock phase would be a simple and effective device for providing essential price discovery in advance of a final proxy round. During the clock phase, bidders learn approximate prices for individual items as well as packages (summing the individual prices). This price information helps bidders focus their valuation analysis on packages that are most relevant.

An important benchmark for comparison is the simultaneous ascending auction (see Cramton, chapter 4 of this volume; Milgrom 2000, 2004). This auction form performs well when items are substitutes and competition is strong. The clock phase by itself also does well in this simple setting and, in particular, the outcome is similar to that of a simultaneous ascending auction. However, the addition of the proxy auction round should be expected to handle complications, such as complements, collusion, and market power, much better than the simultaneous ascending auction. In environments—including many spectrum auctions—where such complications are present, the clock-proxy auction is likely to outperform the simultaneous ascending auction both on efficiency and revenues.

We begin by motivating and describing the clock phase. Then we examine the proxy phase. Finally we combine the two together in the clock-proxy auction, describing the important role played by both phases, comparing the auction with the simultaneous ascending auction, and discussing implementation issues. Some aspects of the auction technology are further described by Ausubel and Milgrom (2001), Ausubel, Cramton, and Jones (2002), and Milgrom (2004).

5.2 Clock Phase

The simultaneous clock auction is a practical implementation of the fictitious "Walrasian auctioneer." The auctioneer announces anonymous linear prices. The bidders respond with quantities desired at the specified prices. Then the prices are increased for items in excess demand, while other prices remain unchanged. This process is repeated until there is no excess demand for any item.

The clock phase has several important benefits. First, it is simple for the bidders. At each round, the bidder simply expresses the quantities desired at the current prices. Linear pricing means that it is trivial to evaluate the cost of any package—it is just the inner product of the prices and quantities. Limiting the bidders' information to a reporting of the excess demand for each item removes much strategizing. Complex bid signaling and collusive strategies are eliminated, as the bidders cannot see individual bids, but only aggregate information. Second, unlike the original Walrasian auction, it is monotonic. This monotonicity contributes to the simplicity of the auction and ensures that it will eventually terminate. Finally, the clock phase produces highly useable price discovery, because of the item prices (linear pricing). With each bidding round, the bidders get a better understanding of the likely prices for relevant packages. This is essential information in guiding the bidders' decision making. Bidders are able to focus their valuation efforts on the most relevant portion of the price space. As a result, the valuation efforts are more productive. Bidder participation costs fall and efficiency improves.

The weakness of the clock auction is its use of linear pricing at the end of the auction. This means that, to the extent that there is market power, bidders will have an incentive to engage in demand reduction to favorably impact prices. This demand reduction implies that the auction outcome will not be fully efficient (Ausubel and Cramton 2006). When goods are substitutes, the clock auction can restore efficiency by utilizing a "clinching" rule instead of linear pricing (Ausubel 2002, 2004). However, in environments with complementary goods, a clock auction with a separate price quoted for each individual item cannot by itself generally avoid inefficiency. The proxy phase will eliminate this inefficiency.

There are several design choices that will improve the performance of the clock phase. Good choices can avoid the exposure problem, improve price discovery, and handle discrete rounds.

5.2.1   Avoiding the Exposure Problem

One important issue in clock auctions is how to treat quantity changes that, if accepted, would make aggregate demand less than supply. For example, for a particular item, demand may equal supply, so the price of the item does not increase, but the increased price of a complementary item may lead the bidder to reduce the quantity it demands. In both clock auctions and the related simultaneous ascending auctions, the usual rule has been to prohibit quantity reductions on items for which the price does not increase, but this creates an exposure problem when some items are complements. Our design allows a bidder to reduce quantity for any item so long as the price has increased on some item the bidder had demanded. This rule eliminates the exposure problem. The bidder is given the flexibility to drop quantity on items for which there is no price increase.

Another case arises when demand is greater than supply for a particular item, so the price increases, and one or more bidders attempt to reduce their demands, making demand less than supply. The common approach in this case is to ration the bidders' reductions so that supply equals demand. However, this again creates an exposure problem when some items are complements. Our approach is not to ration the bidders. All reductions are accepted in full.

The reason for the common restrictions on quantity reductions is to avoid undersell (ending the auction at a point where demand is less than supply). However, these restrictions create an exposure problem. Bidders may be forced to purchase quantities that do not make sense given the final price vector. We eliminate these restrictions and avoid the exposure problem. The consequence is the possibility of undersell in the clock phase, but this is of little importance, as the proxy round can resolve any undersell.

We have conducted over twenty high-stake clock auctions using this rule for electricity products, some of which are substitutes and some of which are complements. These are clock-only auctions without a proxy round. However, because the auctions are conducted quarterly, any undersell in the current auction is added to the quantities in the next auction. Our experience has been that undersell typically is slight (only a few percent of the total). The one exception was an auction in which there was a large negative market price shock near the end of the auction, which resulted in undersell of about fifty percent.

With our rule, the clock auction becomes a package auction. For each price vector, the bidder expresses the package of items desired without committing itself to demanding any smaller package.

All bids in the clock phase are kept live in the proxy round. Including these bids has two effects. It potentially increases revenues after the proxy phase by expanding choices in the winner determination problem, and it encourages sincere bidding in the clock phase, because bidders are on the hook for all earlier bids.

5.2.2 Improving Price Discovery

In auctions with more than a few items, the sheer number of packages that a bidder might buy makes it impossible for bidders to determine all their values in advance. Bidders adapt to this problem by focusing most of their attention on the packages that are likely to be valuable relative to their forecast prices. A common heuristic to forecast package prices is to estimate the prices of individual items and to take an inner product with quantities to estimate the likely package price. Clock auctions with individual prices assist bidders in this *price discovery* process.

Several recent proposed combinatorial auction procedures, such as the RAD procedure studied by Kwasnica et al. (2005), produce approximate shadow prices on individual items to help guide bidders. The clock auction just does this directly.

Price discovery is undermined to the extent that bidders misrepresent their demands early in the auction. One possibility is that bidders will choose to underbid in the clock phase, hiding as a "snake in the grass" to conceal their true interests from their opponents. To limit this form of insincere bidding, the U.S. Federal Communications Commission (FCC) introduced the Milgrom-Wilson activity rule, and similar activity rules have since become standard in both clock auctions and simultaneous ascending auctions. In its most typical form, a bidder desiring large quantities at the end of the auction must bid for quantities at least as large early in the auction, when prices are lower.

Some clock auctions have performed well in the laboratory without any activity rule (Porter et al. 2003). We suspect that this is because of the limited information that the bidders have about the preferences and plans of the other bidders. This lack of information makes it difficult for participants to know how best to deviate from the straightforward strategy of bidding to maximize profits, ignoring one's impact on prices. In practice, activity rules appear to be important, because of the more detailed knowledge bidders have about the preferences of others and hence a better sense of the benefits of deviating from straightforward bidding. The first U.S. broadband auction is a good example of an auction where the activity rule played an important role (McAfee and McMillan 1996; Cramton 1997).

The most common activity rule in clock auctions is monotonicity in quantity. As prices rise, quantities cannot increase. Bidders must bid in a way that is consistent with a weakly downward sloping demand curve. This works well when auctioning identical items, but is overly restrictive when there are many different products. If the products are substitutes, it is natural for a bidder to want to shift quantity from one product to another as prices change, effectively arbitraging the price differences between substitute products.

A weaker activity requirement is a monotonicity of aggregate quantity across a group of products. This allows full flexibility in shifting quantity among products in the group. This is the basis for the FCC's activity rule. Each license has a number of bidding units associated with it, based on the size of the license. A bidder's activity in a round is the sum of the bidding units of the licenses on which the bidder is active—either the high bidder in the prior round or placing a valid bid in the current round. This aggregate activity level must exceed or equal a specified percentage (the activity requirement) of the bidder's current eligibility (typically, 60 percent in the first stage, 80 percent in the second, and 100 percent in the third stage). Otherwise, the bidder's eligibility in all future rounds is reduced to its activity divided by the activity requirement. Additionally, a bidder has five waivers. A bidder can use a waiver in a round to prevent its eligibility from being reduced in the round.

A weakness of the rule based on monotonicity of aggregate quantities is that it assumes that quantities are readily comparable. For example, in the FCC auctions, the quantity associated with a license is the bandwidth of the license times the population covered (MHz-pop). If prices on a per MHz-pop basis vary widely across licenses, as often is the case, bidders may have an incentive to bid on cheap licenses to satisfy the activity rule. This distortion in bidding compromises price discovery.

We propose an alternative activity rule based on revealed preference that does not require any aggregate quantity measure. The rule is derived from standard consumer theory. Consider any two times, denoted s and t ($s < t$). Let p^s and p^t be the price vectors at these times, let x^s and x^t be the associated demands of some bidder, and let $v(x)$ be that bidder's value of the package x. A sincere bidder prefers x^s to x^t when prices are p^s:

$$v(x^s) - p^s \cdot x^s \geq v(x^t) - p^s \cdot x^t$$

and prefers x^t to x^s when prices are p^t:

$$v(x^t) - p^t \cdot x^t \geq v(x^s) - p^t \cdot x^s.$$

Adding these two inequalities yields the *revealed preference activity rule*:

(RP) $(p^t - p^s) \cdot (x^t - x^s) \leq 0.$

At every time t, the bidder's demand x^t must satisfy RP for all times $s < t$.

For the case of a single good, RP is equivalent to the condition that as price goes up, quantity cannot increase; that is, bids must be consistent with a weakly downward-sloping demand curve.

Now suppose there are many goods, but all the goods are perfect substitutes in some fixed proportion. For example, the FCC is auctioning 2-MHz licenses and 20-MHz licenses. Ten 2-MHz blocks substitute perfectly for one 20-MHz block. In this simple case, we would want RP to do the same thing it does when the perfect substitutes are auctioned as a single good, and it does so.

First, suppose that all prices are consistent with the rate of substitution (e.g., the 20-MHz block is ten times as expensive as the 2-MHz block) and all are increasing by the same percentage. The bidder then only cares about the total quantity in MHz and does not care about which goods are purchased. In this case, RP allows the bidder to substitute arbitrarily across goods. RP is satisfied with equality so long as the bidder maintains the same total MHz in response to the higher prices, and inequality if the bidder reduces total MHz.

Second, suppose that the prices are not consistent with the rate of substitution. Say the price on the 2-MHz block increases too fast relative to the 20-MHz block. The bidder then wants to shift all its quantity to the 20-MHz block, and RP allows this: because the 20 MHz is relatively cheaper, RP gives the bidder more credit for dropping quantity on the 2-MHz blocks than the bidder is debited for the increase in the 20-MHz block. It might seem that the mispricing allows the bidder to expand quantity somewhat, but this is not the case. Because RP is required with respect to all previous bids, the bidder would be constrained by its maximum quantity the last time the 20-MHz block was the best value.

We conclude that RP does just the right thing in the case of perfect substitutes. The activity rule is neither strengthened nor weakened by alternative product definitions.

Now suppose some goods are perfect complements in fixed proportion. For example, in an electricity auction, the bidder wants to maintain a 2-to-1 ratio between baseload product and peakload product. If there are just these two products, then the bidder just cares about the weighted sum of the product prices. As prices increase, the bidder certainly satisfies RP by maintaining the same quantities or by reducing the quantities in the desired ratio; however, the bidder is unable to increase quantities. RP does just the right thing in the case of perfect complements.

If we combine the two cases above so that some goods are perfect substitutes and some are perfect complements, then RP still does the right thing. Bidders will want to shift quantity to the cheapest substitute in building the package of complements. Shifting away from substitute products for which price is increasing too quickly yields a credit that exceeds the debit from shifting toward the relatively cheap product. Hence, this is allowed under RP. Moreover, RP prevents a bidder who always bids on the cheapest among substitutes goods from expanding its quantity of complementary goods as prices rise.

It is useful to compare RP with the current FCC activity rule, which ignores prices and simply looks at aggregate quantity in MHz-pop. "Parking" is the main problem created by the current rule: to maintain flexibility, a bidder has an incentive to bid on underpriced products or low-value products with high quantity, rather than to bid on products that it actually wants to buy. The bidder does this for two reasons: (1) to keep the prices on desired products from increasing too quickly, while maintaining the flexibility to expand demand on products for which competitor demands fall off faster than expected; and (2) to maintain the flexibility to punish a rival by shifting bidding for the rival's desired markets if the rival bids for the bidder's desired markets. Thus, parking is motivated by demand reduction and tacit collusion. But the clock implementation mitigates collusion, because bidders see only excess demand; they do not have the information to know when retaliation is needed, where the retaliation should occur, or how to avoid retaliation. And the final proxy round mitigates demand reduction. Hence, we should expect parking to be much less of a problem in the clock implementation.

The greatest damage from parking comes from price distortions that exclude the high-value bidder from winning an item. Under the FCC rule, bidders are most tempted to park on low-price, high-quantity licenses. These prices may get bid up to the point where the efficient winner drops out, because they enable the parking bidder to bid later on other licenses. In contrast, the RP rule does not allow a bidder to increase its quantity for another license unless there is excess demand for the parking license. Thus, parking is only effective when bidding on underpriced goods. But parking on underpriced goods does no harm; it simply serves to increase the price of the underpriced good. Hence, the revealed-preference activity rule has important advantages over the current FCC activity rule.

The revealed-preference activity rule may appear more complex than the FCC rule based on aggregate quantity. However, it still can be displayed in the same simple way on the bidder's bid entry screen. As the bid is entered, an activity cell indicates the amount of slack in the tightest RP constraint, and changes to red when the constraint is violated. Moreover, to the extent that the revealed preference activity rule eliminates complex parking strategies, the rule may be simpler for bidders.

5.2.3   Handling Discrete Rounds

Although in theory one can imagine implementing an ascending auction in continuous time, this is hardly ever done in practice. Real clock auctions use discrete rounds for two important reasons. First, communication is rarely so reliable that bidders would be willing to be exposed to a continuous clock. A bidder would find it unsatisfactory if the price clock swept past the bidder's willingness to pay because of a brief communication lapse. Discrete rounds are robust to communication problems. Discrete rounds have a bidding window of significant duration, rarely less than ten minutes and sometimes more than one hour. This window gives bidders time to correct any communication problems, to resort to back-up systems, or to contact the auctioneer and have the round extended. Second, a discrete round auction may improve price discovery by giving the bidders an opportunity to reflect between rounds. Bidders need time to incorporate information from prior rounds into a revised bidding strategy. This updating is precisely the source of price discovery and its associated benefits.

An important issue in discrete-round auctions is the size of the bid increments. Larger bid increments enable the auction to conclude in fewer rounds, but the coarse price grid potentially introduces inefficiencies. Large increments also introduce incentives for gaming as a result of the expanded importance of ties. But using small increments, especially in an auction with many clocks, can greatly increase the number of rounds and, hence, the time required to complete the auction. Bidders generally prefer a shorter auction, which reduces participation costs. It also reduces exposure to market price movements during the auction. This is especially relevant in securities and energy auctions for which there are active secondary markets of close substitutes, and for which underlying price movements could easily exceed the bid increments.

Fortunately, it is possible to capture nearly all of the benefits of a continuous auction and still conduct the auction in a limited number of rounds, using the technique of intra-round bids. With intra-round bids, the auctioneer proposes tentative end-of-round prices. Bidders then express their quantity demands in each auction round at all price vectors along the line segment from the start-of-round prices to the proposed end-of-round prices. If, at any time during the round, the prices reach a point at which there is excess supply for some good, then the round ends with those prices. Otherwise, the round ends with the initially proposed end-of-round prices.

Consider an example with two products. The start-of-round prices are 90, 180, and end-of-round prices are 100, 200. The bidder decides to reduce quantity at two price points (40 percent and 60 percent) between the start-of-round and end-of-round prices, as shown below:

Price Point	Product 1		Product 2	
	Price	Quantity	Price	Quantity
0%	90	8	180	4
40%	94	5	188	4
60%	96	5	192	2
100%	100	5	200	2

The auctioneer aggregates all the bids and determines whether any products clear at price points of up to 100 percent. If not, then the process repeats with new end-of-round prices based on excess demand. If one or more products clear, then we find the first product to clear. Suppose the bidder's drop from 8 to 5 at the 40 percent price point causes product 1 to clear, but product 2 has not yet cleared at the 40 percent price point. Then the current round would post at the 40 percent price point. The next round would have start-of-round prices of 94, 188 (the prices at the 40 percent price point) and, perhaps, end-of-round prices of 94, 208. The price of product 1 stops increasing, as there is no longer excess demand.

Following this exact approach means that the clock phase will typically have more rounds than products. This works fine in an environment where there are multiple units of a relatively limited number of products (all of which are assigned the same price). However, this could be an issue in FCC auctions with hundreds of unique licenses requiring independent prices. In that event, the auctioneer may wish to adopt an approach of settling for approximate clearing in the clock phase in order to economize on the number of rounds.

This use of intra-round bids avoids the inefficiency associated with a coarser price grid. It also avoids the gaming behavior that arises from the increased importance of ties with coarser prices. The only thing that is lost is the within-round price discovery. However, within-round price discovery is much less important than the price discovery that occurs between rounds.

The experience from a number of high-stakes clock auctions indicates that intra-round bidding lets the auctioneer conduct auctions with several products in about ten rounds, with little or no loss from the discreteness of rounds (Ausubel and Cramton 2004). These auctions can be completed in a single day. By way of contrast, early spectrum auctions and some electricity auctions without intra-round bids took weeks or even months to conclude. In a few instances, the longer duration was warranted due to the enormous uncertainty and extremely high stakes, but generally speaking, intra-round bids would have reduced the bidding costs without any meaningful loss in price discovery.

5.2.4 End of the Clock Phase

The clock phase concludes when there is no excess demand on any item. The result of the clock phase is much more than this final assignment and prices. The result includes all packages and associated prices that were bid throughout the clock phase. Due to complementarities, the clock phase may end with substantial excess supply for many items. If this is the case, the final assignment and prices may not provide a good starting point for the proxy phase. Rather, bids from an earlier round may yield an assignment with higher revenue. (When calculating revenues excess supply should be priced at the reserve price, which presumably represents the seller's opportunity cost of selling the item.)

A sensible approach is to find the revenue maximizing assignment and prices from all the bids in the clock phase. This point is found by backing up the clock to the price point where revenue is at its maximum. The revenue maximizing prices from the clock phase can serve as reasonable lower bounds on prices in the proxy phase. That is, the minimum bid on each package is calculated as the inner product of the revenue maximizing prices and the quantities of items in the package.

In some cases the auctioneer may decide to end the clock phase early—with some excess demand on one or more items. This would be done when the total revenue ceases to increase or when revenue improvements from successive clock rounds are sufficiently small. With the proxy phase to follow, there is little loss in either revenues or efficiency from stopping, say when revenue improvements are less than one-half percent for two consecutive rounds. At this point price discovery is largely over on all but the smallest items. Giving the auctioneer the discretion to end the clock phase early also enables the auction to follow a more predictable schedule.

5.3 Proxy Phase

Like the clock auction, the proxy auction is based on package bids. However, the incentives are quite different. The main difference is the absence of anonymous linear prices on individual items. Only packages are priced—and the prices may be bidder specific.

This weakens price discovery, but the proxy phase is not about price discovery. It is about providing the incentives for efficient assignment. All the price discovery occurs in the clock phase. The second main difference is that the bidders do not bid directly in the proxy phase. Rather, they submit values to the proxy agents, who then bid on their behalf using a specific bidding rule. The proxy agents bid straightforwardly to maximize profits. The proxy phase is a last-and-final opportunity to bid.

The proxy auction works as follows (see Ausubel and Milgrom 2002, and chapter 3 of this volume). Each bidder reports his values to a proxy agent for all packages that the bidder is interested in. Budget constraints can also be reported. The proxy agent then bids in an ascending package auction on behalf of the real bidder, iteratively submitting the allowable bid that, if accepted, would maximize the real bidder's profit (value minus price), based on the reported values. The auction in theory is conducted with negligibly small bid increments. After each round, provisionally winning bids are determined that maximize seller revenue from compatible bids. All of a bidder's bids are kept live throughout the auction and are treated as mutually exclusive. The auction ends after a round with no new bids (see chapter 17 of this volume, and Day and Raghavan 2004 for practical methods to implement the proxy phase).

The advantage of this format is that it ends at a core allocation for the reported preferences. Denote the coalition form game (L, w) where L is the set of players ($l = 0$ is the seller and the rest are the bidders) and $w(S)$ is the value of coalition S. Let X denote the set of feasible allocations $(x_l)_{l \in L}$. If S excludes the seller, then $w(S) = 0$; if S includes the seller, then

$$w(S) = \max_{x \in X} \sum_{l \in S} v_l(x_l).$$

The Core(L, w) is the set of all imputations π (payoffs imputed to the players based on the allocation) that are feasible for the coalition of the whole and cannot be blocked by any coalition S; that is, for each coalition S, $\sum_{l \in S} \pi_l(x_l) \geq w(S)$.

Theorem 5.1 (Ausubel and Milgrom 2002, Parkes and Ungar 2000) The payoff vector π resulting from the proxy auction is a core imputation relative to the reported preferences: $\pi \in \text{Core}(L, w)$.

Core outcomes exhibit a number of desirable properties, including (1) efficiency, and (2) competitive revenues for the seller. Thus, the theorem shows that the proxy auction is not subject to the inefficiency of demand reduction: no bidder can ever reduce the price it pays for the package it wins by withholding some of its losing bids for other packages. The theorem also includes the idea that the seller earns competitive revenues: no bidder or coalition of bidders is willing to bid more for the seller's goods. Ausubel and Milgrom (2002, theorems 2 and 14) establish the core outcome result, whereas Parkes and Ungar (2000, theorem 1) independently demonstrate the efficiency of outcomes of an ascending proxy auction without addressing the issue of the core.

A payoff vector in the core is said to be *bidder optimal* if there is no other core allocation that all bidders prefer. If the items are substitutes, then the outcome of the proxy auction coincides with the outcome of the Vickrey auction and with the unique bidder-optimal point in the core. If the goods are not substitutes, then the Vickrey payoff is not generally in the core and the proxy auction yields an outcome with higher seller revenues.

Theorem 5.2 (Ausubel and Milgrom 2002) If π is a bidder-optimal point in the Core(L, w), then there exists a full-information Nash equilibrium of the proxy auction with associated payoff vector π.

These equilibria may be obtained using strategies of the form: bid your true value minus a nonnegative constant on every package. We emphasize that this conclusion concerns full-information Nash equilibrium: bidders may need to know π to compute their strategies.

Two important advantages of the proxy auction over the Vickrey auction are that the prices and revenues are monotonic (increasing the set of bidders leads to higher prices) and the payoffs are competitive. To illustrate the comparative weaknesses of the Vickrey auction, suppose there are two identical items and two bidders. Bidder 1 values the pair only at $2.05. Bidder 2 wants a single item only and has a value of $2. The Vickrey auction awards the pair to bidder 1 for a price of $2, which is the opportunity cost incurred by not assigning an item to bidder 2. So far, the outcome is unproblematic.

Let us now add a bidder 3 with the same values as bidder 2. In this case, the Vickrey auction awards the items to bidders 2 and 3. Bidder 2's Vickrey price is the opportunity cost of its good to the other participants, which is $2.05 − 2.00 = $0.05. Bidder 3's price is the same. Total revenues fall from $2.00 to $0.10. Moreover, the new outcome is not in the core, because the coalition of the seller and bidder 1 could both do better by making a private deal, for example by trading the package at a price of $1. By way of contrast, adding a bidder in the proxy auction can never reduce seller revenues.

5.4   The Clock-Proxy Auction

The clock-proxy auction begins with a clock auction for price discovery and concludes with the proxy auction to promote efficiency.

The clock auction is conducted with the revealed-preference activity rule until there is no excess demand on any item. The market-clearing item prices determine the initial minimum bids for all packages for all bidders. Bidders then submit values to proxy agents, who bid to maximize profits, subject to a relaxed revealed-preference activity rule. The bids from the clock phase are kept live as package bids in the proxy phase. All of a bidder's bids, both clock and proxy, are treated as mutually exclusive. Thus, the auctioneer obtains the provisional winning bids after each round of the proxy phase by including all bids—those submitted in the clock phase as well as those submitted in the proxy phase—in the winner determination problem and by selecting at most one provisional winning bid from every bidder. As usual, the proxy phase ends after a round with no new bids.

5.4.1 Relaxed Revealed-Preference Activity Rule

To promote price discovery in the clock phase, the proxy agent's allowable bids must be constrained by the bidder's bids in the clock phase. The constraint we propose is a relaxed version of the revealed preference activity rule.

First, we restate revealed preference in terms of packages and the associated minimum bids for the packages. Consider two times s and t ($s < t$). Suppose the bidder bids for the package S at time s and T at time t. Let $P^s(S)$ and $P^s(T)$ be the package price of S and T at time s; let $P^t(S)$ and $P^t(T)$ be the package price of S and T at time t; and let $v(S)$ and $v(T)$ be the value of package S and T. Revealed preference says that the bidder prefers S to T at time s:

$$v(S) - P^s(S) \geq v(T) - P^s(T)$$

and prefers T to S at time t:

$$v(T) - P^t(T) \geq v(S) - P^t(S).$$

Adding these two inequalities yields the revealed preference activity rule for packages:

$$(\text{RP}') \quad P^t(S) - P^s(S) \geq P^t(T) - P^s(T).$$

Intuitively, the package price of S must have increased more than the package price of T from time s to time t, for otherwise, at time t, S would be more profitable than T.

Notice that the constraint RP′ is automatically satisfied at any two times in the proxy phase, because the proxy agent is required to bid to maximize profits. However, an activity rule based on RP′ is too strict when comparing a time s in the clock phase with a time t in the proxy phase. Due to the linear pricing in the clock phase, the bidders have an incentive to reduce demands below their true demands. One purpose of the proxy phase is to let the bidders undo any inefficient demand reduction that would otherwise occur in the clock phase and to defect from any collusive split of the items that would otherwise take place. Hence, it is important to let the bidders expand their demands in the proxy phase. The amount of expansion required depends on the competitiveness of the auction.

We propose a *relaxed revealed-preference activity rule*:

$$(\text{RRP}) \quad \alpha[P^t(S) - P^s(S)] \geq P^t(T) - P^s(T).$$

At every time t in the proxy phase, the proxy agent is permitted to bid on the package T only if RRP is satisfied for every package S bid at time s in the clock phase. The proxy agent bids to maximize profits, subject to satisfying RRP relative to all prior bids.

The auctioneer chooses the parameter $\alpha > 1$ based on the competitiveness of the auction. For highly competitive auctions, little demand reduction is likely to occur in the clock phase and α can be set close to 1. On the other hand, if there is little competition (and high concentration), then a higher α is appropriate.

It is possible to state RRP in terms of a restriction on the value function v reported to the proxy, rather than on the bids. Intuitively, a bidder's reported value for a package is constrained by all of its bids in the clock phase. In particular, if the bidder bid on some package S but not T at some time s, then it may not claim at the proxy phase that a bid on T would have been much more profitable, as formalized by the inequality: $v(T) - P^s(T) \leq \alpha(v(S) - P^s(S))$. Under this version of RRP, a bidder is required to state in the proxy phase a value for each package on which the bidder has already bid in the clock phase. The advantage of this approach is that it allows the proxies to bid accurately according to the bidders' reported values while still imposing consistency across stages.

5.4.2 Why Include the Clock Phase?

The clock phase provides price discovery that bidders can use to guide their calculations in the complex package auction. At each round, bidders are faced with the simple and familiar problem of expressing demands at specified prices. Moreover, because there is no exposure problem, bidders can bid for synergistic gains without fear. Prices then adjust in response to excess demand. As the bidding continues, bidders get a better understanding of what they may win and where their best opportunities lie.

The case for the clock phase relies on the idea that it is costly for bidders to determine their preferences. The clock phase, by providing tentative price information, helps focus a bidder's decision problem. Rather than consider all possibilities from the outset, the bidder can instead focus on cases that are important given the tentative price and assignment information. Although the idea that bidders can make information processing decisions in auctions is valid even in auctions for a single good (Compte and Jehiel 2000), its importance is magnified when there are many goods for sale, because the bidder's decision problem is then much more complicated. Rather than simply decide whether to buy at a given price, the bidder must decide which goods to buy and how many of each. The number of possibilities grows exponentially with the number of goods. Price discovery can play an extremely valuable role in guiding the bidder through the valuation process.

Price discovery in the clock phase makes bidding in the proxy phase vastly simpler. Without the clock phase, bidders would be forced either to determine values for all possible packages or to make uninformed guesses about which packages were likely to be most attractive. Our experience with dozens of bidders suggests that the second outcome is much more likely; determining the values of exponentially many packages becomes quickly impractical with even a modest number of items for sale. Using the clock phase to make informed guesses about prices, bidders can focus their decision making on the most relevant packages. The bidders see that they do not need to consider the vast majority of options—they are excluded by the prices established in the clock phase. The bidders also get a sense of what packages are most promising, and how their demands fit in the aggregate with those of the other bidders.

In competitive auctions where the items are substitutes and competition is strong, we expect the clock phase to do most of the work in establishing prices and assignments—the proxy phase would play a limited role. When competition is weak, demand reduction may lead the clock phase to end prematurely, but this problem is corrected at the proxy stage, which eliminates incentives for demand reduction. If the clock auction gives the bidders a good idea of likely package prices, then expressing a simple approximate valuation to the proxy is made easier. For example, with global economies of scope, a bidder might report to his proxy bidder a value for each item, a fixed cost of operation, and a limit on the number of items acquired. This is just an example, but it serves to highlight that simple valuation functions might serve well once the range of likely package prices is limited.

5.4.3 Why Include the Proxy Phase?

The main advantage of the proxy phase is that it pushes the outcome toward the core, that is, toward an efficient allocation with competitive payoffs for the bidders and competitive revenues for the seller.

In the proxy phase, there are no incentives for demand reduction. A large bidder can bid for large quantities without the fear that doing so will adversely impact the price the bidder pays.

The proxy phase also mitigates collusion. Any collusive split of the items established in the clock phase can be undone in the proxy phase. The relaxed activity rule means that the bidders can expand demands in the proxy phase. The allocation is still up for grabs in the proxy phase.

The clock-proxy auction has some similarities with the Anglo-Dutch design initially proposed for (but not ultimately used in) the United Kingdom's third-generation mobile wireless auction (Klemperer 2002). Both formats have an ascending auction followed by a sealed-bid last-and-final round. However, the motivation for the last-and-final round is quite different. In the Anglo-Dutch design, the last round has pay-as-bid pricing intended to introduce inefficiency, so as to motivate inefficient bidders to participate in the auction (and perhaps increase auction revenues). In the clock-proxy auction, the last round is more similar to Vickrey pricing and is intended to promote efficiency, rather than prevent it. The relaxed activity rule in the proxy round, however, does encourage the undoing of any tacit collusion in the clock phase, and in this sense is similar to the last-and-final round of the Anglo-Dutch design.

The proxy phase will play a more important role to the extent that competition is limited and complementarities are strong and varied across bidders. Then it is more likely that the clock phase will end prematurely. However, in competitive auctions, the proxy phase may not be needed.

A potential problem with a clock-only auction under our proposed rules arises from a bidder's ability to reduce quantity on products even when the price of a product does not go up. This may appear to create a "free withdrawal" and a potential source of gaming. For example, a bidder might bid up the price on a competitor's preferred license to the point where the competitor drops out. Then the strategic bidder reduces quantity on this product. Alternatively, the bidder might bid up the price and then drop quantity before the competitor drops out.

Two features mitigate this potential problem. First, the revealed-preference activity rule makes it risky for a bidder to overbid on items that the bidder does not want. Unlike the activity rule based on aggregate quantity, the bidder dropping quantity on a product for which the price has not increased is not given any credit in the RP inequality and hence has no ability to expand demand on another product. Second, the preferred approach would be to run the winner-determination-problem at the end among *all* prior bids. Hence, the strategic bidder may find that it is obligated to purchase items that it does not want. (Of course, if goods are mostly substitutes, then one simply could prevent quantity reductions for goods that have cleared.)

5.4.4 Two Examples

We illustrate our answers to "Why include the clock phase?" and "Why include the proxy phase?" with two examples.

In our first example, there are two items and two bidders. Bidder 1 wants just a single item and values it at v_1. Bidder 2 wants up to two items and values each at v_2 (valuing the package of two items at $2v_2$). The private values v_1 and v_2 are drawn independently from the uniform distribution on $[0, 1]$. Each bidder i knows the realization of v_i but only the distribution of v_j ($j \neq i$). In the clock auction, this is a classic example of demand reduction. For simplicity, assume that the clock price ascends continuously. Bidder 1's weakly dominant strategy is to bid a quantity of 1 at all prices up to v_1 and then to drop to a quantity of 0. Bidder 2 has a choice whether to bid initially for a quantity of two, or to bid for only one unit and cause the price clock to stop at zero. A straightforward calculation shows that bidding for only one unit and obtaining a zero price maximizes bidder 2's expected payoff, establishing that this is the unique equilibrium (Ausubel and Cramton 2002, p. 4).

Thus, conducting only a clock phase is disastrous for the seller; revenues equal zero and the outcome of each bidder winning one unit is inefficient whenever $v_2 > v_1$.

However, suppose that the clock phase is followed by a proxy round, using a parameter $\alpha \geq 2$ in the relaxed revealed-preference activity rule. Because the substitutes condition is satisfied in this example, the bidders' dominant strategies in the proxy round are each to bid their true values. Thus, the clock-proxy auction yields the bidder-optimal core outcome, and the seller earns revenues of $\min\{v_1, v_2\}$. Nothing of consequence occurs in the clock phase, and the proxy phase yields the desirable outcome by itself.

In our second example, there are m items and n bidders ($n > m$). Each bidder i values item k at v_{ik}. But bidder i has value for only a single item, and so for example if bidder i received both items k and l, his value would be only $\max\{v_{ik}, v_{il}\}$. The values v_{ik} are random variables with support $[0, 1]$. Each bidder i knows the realization of v_{ik} ($k = 1, \ldots, m$), but only the distribution of v_{jk} ($j \neq i$) ($k = 1, \ldots, m$). In the clock auction, because bidders have demand for only a single item, each bidder's dominant strategy is to bid a quantity of one on an item k such that $v_{ik} - p_k = \max_{l=1,\ldots,m}\{v_{il} - p_l\}$ and to bid a quantity of zero on all other items. Therefore, the clock phase concludes at the Vickrey outcome, which is also the predicted outcome of the proxy phase (because the substitutes condition is satisfied). Thus, the clock-proxy auction again yields the bidder-optimal core outcome. This time the clock phase yields the desirable outcome by itself, and nothing further occurs in the proxy phase.

If the bidders find it costly to determine their values, the clock phase may find the outcome without the need for bidders to calculate all their values. For example, suppose $m = 2$ and $n = 3$ and the bidders' estimated value pairs are $(2, 4)$, $(3, 8)$ and $(7, 2)$, but each bidder knows each of its values only to within ± 1, without further costly investment. In the clock phase, bidder 1 will be the first to face the need to invest in learning its exact values. If he does so, the auction will end at prices of 2 and 4 without the second and third bidder ever needing to make that investment. Price discovery at the clock phase saves bidders 2 and 3 from the need to determine their full values for the proxy stage.

5.4.5 Comparison with the Simultaneous Ascending Auction

The simultaneous ascending auction as implemented by the FCC is an important benchmark of comparison, given its common use in auctioning many related items (see Cramton, chapter 4 of this volume). The clock auction is a variant of the simultaneous ascending auction in which the auctioneer specifies prices and the bidders name quantities. There are several advantages to the clock implementation.

The clock auction is a simpler process than the simultaneous ascending auction. Bidders are provided the minimal information needed for price discovery—the prices and the excess demand. Bidders are not distracted by other information that is either extraneous or useful as a means to facilitate collusion.

The clock auction also can take better advantage of substitutes, for example, using a single clock for items that are near perfect substitutes. In spectrum auctions, there is a tendency for the spectrum authority to make specific band plans to facilitate the simultaneous ascending auction. For example, anticipating demands for a large, medium, and small license, the authority may specify a band plan with three blocks—30 MHz, 20 MHz, and 10 MHz. Ideally, these decisions would be left to the bidders themselves. In a clock auction, the bidders could bid the number of 2-MHz blocks desired at the clock price. Then the auction would determine the band plan, rather than the spectrum authority. This approach is more efficient and would likely be more competitive, because all bidders are competing for all the bandwidth in the clock auction. With the preset band plan, some bidders may be uninterested in particular blocks, such as those that are too large for their needs.

Clock auctions are faster than a simultaneous ascending auction. Simultaneous ascending auctions are especially slow near the end, when there is little excess demand. For example, when there are six bidders bidding on five similar licenses, then it typically takes five rounds to obtain a one bid-increment increase on all items. In contrast, in a clock auction, an increment increase takes just a single round. Moreover, intra-round bids allow larger increments, without introducing inefficiencies, because bidders still can express demands along the line segment from the start-of-round prices to the end-of-round prices.

The clock auction limits collusion relative to the simultaneous ascending auction. Signaling how to split up the items is greatly limited. Collusive strategies based on retaliation are not possible, because bidder-specific quantity information is not given. Further, the simultaneous ascending auction can have a tendency to end early when an obvious split is reached, but this cannot happen in the clock auction, because the bidders lack information about the split. Also there are fewer rounds to coordinate a split.

The clock auction, as described here, eliminates the exposure problem. As long as at least one price increases, a bidder can reduce quantity on his other items. The bid is binding only as a full package. Hence, the bidder can safely bid for synergistic gains.

The clock-proxy auction shares all these advantages of the clock auction, and in addition promotes core outcomes. The proxy phase further mitigates collusion and eliminates demand reduction. The cost of the proxy phase is added implementation complexity. Also the absence of linear pricing reduces the transparency of the auction. It is less obvious to a bidder why he lost. Nonetheless, the auctioneer at the conclusion of the auction can disclose sufficient information for the bidders to determine the outcome without revealing any supramarginal values.

5.4.6 Combinatorial Exchange

Like other package auctions, the clock-proxy auction is designed for settings with a single seller. With multiple sellers and no item prices, there is an additional problem to solve: how to divide the auction revenues. For example, if separate sellers own items A and B, and if all the bidders want to buy items A and B together, with no interest in these separate and separately owned items, the auction itself can provide no information about how to allocate the revenue from the winning bid among the sellers. The revenue-sharing rule has to be determined separately, and there is no simple and completely satisfactory solution to this problem.

The clock-proxy auction can be extended to handle exchanges with one passive seller and many active buyers and sellers. A natural application is the auctioning of encumbered spectrum (Cramton, Kwerel, and Williams 1998; Kwerel and Williams 2002). The spectrum authority would be the passive seller, selling overlay licenses. Incumbents are (potentially) the active sellers, selling their existing rights. In this setting, one can adapt the clock-proxy auction very simply. An incumbent seller's bid would reflect an offer to sell a package. Formally, its bid would specify the goods it offers as negative quantities in the clock phase and would specify negative quantities and prices in the proxy stage. In principle, one could even allow bids in which an incumbent offers to exchange its good for another good plus or minus some compensating payment, where the package is expressed by a vector of positive and negative numbers.

Alternative designs differ in how they divide auction revenues and in what bids sellers are allowed to make. For example, one possibility is to fix the items to be sold at the proxy stage as those that were not acquired by their original owners at the clock stage. Final revenues would then be distributed to sellers in proportion to the prices from the clock stage. Another possibility is to allow the sellers to bid in every stage of the auction, essentially negotiating what is sold and how revenues are to be split through their bidding behavior. A third possibility is to allow sellers to set reserve prices and to use those to divide revenues among the sellers.

These alternative designs split revenues differently, so they create different incentives for incumbents to report exaggerated values. The result will be differences in the likelihood of a successful sale. So far, theory provides little guidance on which choice is best, beyond indicating that the problem can sometimes be a hard one. If there are many sellers whose goods are sufficiently good substitutes, then the problem may not be too severe. This strongly suggests that the most important issue for the FCC in making the package exchange a success is careful attention to the incumbents' rights, to make their goods as substitutable as possible.

5.4.7 Implementation Issues

We briefly discuss four of the most important implementation issues.

Confidentiality of Values One practical issue with the proxy phase is confidentiality of values. Bidders may be hesitant to bid true values in the proxy phase, fearing that the auctioneer would somehow manipulate the prices with a "seller shill" to push prices all the way to the bidders' reported values. Steps need to be taken to assure that this cannot happen. A highly transparent auction process helps to assure that the auction rules are followed. Auction software can be tested and certified that it is consistent with the auction rules. At the end of the auction, the auctioneer can report all the bids. The bidders can then confirm that the outcome was consistent with the rules. In addition, there is no reason that the auctioneer needs to be given access to the high values. Only the computer need know.

A further step to protect the privacy of high values is to allow a multiround implementation of the proxy phase. The critical feature of the proxy phase is that the relative values are locked. If bidders do not want to reveal their final values, that can be handled. In a multiround version of the proxy phase, bidders must freeze the relative values of the packages they name but can periodically authorize a fixed dollar increase in all of their bids. With this approach, the auction becomes an ascending, pay-as-bid package auction.

Price Increments in the Clock Phase   When auctioning many items, one must take care in defining the price adjustment process. This is especially true when some goods are complements. Intuitively, undersell in the clock phase is minimized by having each product clear at roughly the same time. Otherwise price increases on complementary products can cause quantity drops on products that have already cleared. Thus, the goal should be to come up with a price adjustment process that reflects relative values as well as excess demand. Moreover, the price adjustment process effectively is resolving the threshold problem by specifying who should contribute what as the clock ticks higher. To the extent that prices adjust with relative values the resolution of the threshold problem will be more successful.

One simple approach is to build the relative value information into the initial starting prices. Then use a percentage increase, based on the extent of excess demand. For example, the percentage increment could vary linearly with the excess demand, subject to a lower and upper limit.

Expression of Proxy Values   Even with the benefit of the price discovery in the clock phase, expressing a valuation function in the proxy phase may be difficult. When many items are being sold, the bidder will need a tool to facilitate translating preferences into proxy values. The best tool will depend on the circumstances.

At a minimum, the tool will allow an additive valuation function. The bidder submits a demand curve for each item. The value of a package is then found by integrating the demand curve (adding the marginal values) up to the quantity of the item in the package, and then adding over all items. This additive model ignores all value interdependencies across items; it assumes that the demand for one item is independent of the demand for other items. Although globally (across a wide range of quantities) this might be a bad assumption, locally (across a narrow range of quantities) this might be a reasonable approximation. Hence, provided the clock phase has taken us close to the equilibrium, so the proxy phase is only doing some fine-tuning of the clock outcome, then such a simplistic tool may perform reasonably well. And of course it performs very well when bidders actually have additive values.

A simple extension of the additive model allows the bidder to express perfect substitutes and complements within the additive structure. For example, items A and B may be designated perfect complements in the ratio 1 to 3 (one unit of A is needed for three units of B). Then the bidder expresses a demand curve for A and B (with the 1-to-3 ratio always maintained). Items C and D may be designated perfect substitutes in the ratio 2 to 1 (two Cs equal one D). Then the bidder expresses a demand curve for C or D (with all quantity converted to C-equivalent). This extension effectively allows the bidder to redefine the items in such a way to make the additive model fit. For example, in a spectrum auction, a bidder for paired spectrum will want to express a demand for paired spectrum. This can be done by designating the upper and lower channels as perfect complements, but then the blocks of paired spectrum as perfect substitutes. A bidder for unpaired spectrum would designate all channels as perfect substitutes, and then express a single demand curve for unpaired spectrum.

Demand curves typically are expressed as step functions, although in some contexts piece-wise linear demand curves are allowed. Bidders should be able to specify whether quantity can be rationed. For example if a bidder drops quantity from 20 to 10 at a price of $5, does this mean the bidder is just as happy getting 14 units as 10 units or 20 units when the price is $5 per unit, or does the bidder only want exactly 10 units at a price of $5, and exactly 20 units at a price of $4.99? Is there a minimum quantity that the bidder must win for the item to have value?

Beyond this, the tool should allow for the inclusion of bidder constraints. Budget constraints are the most common: do not bid more than X. Other constraints may be on quantities: only value A if you win B. This constraint arises in spectrum auctions when a bidder has secondary regions that have value only if the primary regions are won.

The bidders' business plans are a useful guide to determine how best to structure the valuation tool in a particular application. Business plans are an expression of value to investors. Although the details of the business plans are not available to the auctioneer, one can construct a useful valuation tool from understanding the basic structure of these business plans.

Calculating Prices in the Proxy Phase   The proxy phase is a sealed-bid auction. At issue is how best to calculate the final assignment and prices. The final assignment is easy. This is just the value maximizing assignment given the reported values. The harder part is determining the prices for each winning package. The clock phase helps by setting a lower bound on the price of each package. Given these starting prices, one approach would be to run directly the proxy auction with negligible bid increments. With many items and bidders this would require voluminous calculations.

Fortunately, one can accelerate the process of calculating prices using various methods (see Hoffman et al., chapter 17 of this volume; Day and Raghavan 2004; Wurman et al. 2004). First, as David Parkes suggested, package prices for all bidders can start at "safe prices," defined as the maximum bid on the package by any losing bidder. Second, prices can increase in discrete jumps to the point where a bidder starts or stops bidding on a particular package. Although these methods have not yet been fully developed, calculating the prices in the proxy phase likely can be done with many items and bidders in an expedient manner.

The precise process for calculating the prices is especially important when some items are complements, because then there will be a set of bidder-optimal points in the core, and the price process will determine which of these points is selected.

5.5   Conclusion

We propose the clock-proxy auction for auctioning many related items—a simultaneous clock auction followed by a last-and-final proxy round. The basic idea is to use anonymous linear prices as long as possible to maximize price discovery, simplicity, and transparency. The clock phase also greatly facilitates the bidders' valuation analysis for the proxy round, because the analysis can be confined to the relevant part of the price space identified in the clock phase. Finally, unlike the simultaneous ascending auction, the clock auction does not suffer from the exposure problem.

For highly competitive auctions of items that are mostly substitutes, the clock auction without the proxy round will perform well. Indeed a clock auction without a proxy round may be the best approach in this setting, as it offers the greatest simplicity and transparency, while being highly efficient.

With limited competition or items with a complex and varied structure of complements, adding the proxy phase can improve the auction outcome. In particular, a core outcome is achieved. Seller revenues are competitive and the allocation is efficient. The demand reduction incentive present in the clock phase is eliminated. Most importantly, adding the proxy round does no harm: in the simplest settings where the clock auction alone performs well, adding the proxy round should not distort the outcome. The proxy round simply expands the settings in which the auction performs well.

Acknowledgments

This research was inspired by the Federal Communications Commission's efforts to develop a practical combinatorial auction for its spectrum auctions. We are especially grateful to Evan Kwerel for his insights and encouragement.

References

Ausubel, Lawrence M. (2006), "An Efficient Dynamic Auction for Heterogeneous Commodities," *American Economic Review*, forthcoming.

Ausubel, Lawrence M. (2004), "An Efficient Ascending-Bid Auction for Multiple Objects," *American Economic Review*, 94, 1452–1475.

Ausubel, Lawrence M. and Peter Cramton (2002), "Demand Reduction and Inefficiency in Multi-Unit Auctions," University of Maryland Working Paper 96-07, revised July 2002.

Ausubel, Lawrence M. and Peter Cramton (2004), "Auctioning Many Divisible Goods," *Journal of the European Economic Association*, 2, 480–493, April–May.

Ausubel, Lawrence M., Peter Cramton, and Wynne P. Jones (2002), "System and Method for an Auction of Multiple Types of Items," International Patent Application No. PCT/US02/16937.

Ausubel, Lawrence M. and Paul Milgrom (2001), "System and Method for a Dynamic Auction with Package Bidding," International Patent Application No. PCT/US01/43838.

Ausubel, Lawrence M. and Paul Milgrom (2002), "Ascending Auctions with Package Bidding," *Frontiers of Theoretical Economics*, 1, 1–42 ⟨http://www.bepress.com/bejte/frontiers/vol1/iss1/art1⟩.

Compte, Olivier and Philippe Jehiel (2000), "On the Virtues of the Ascending Price Auction: New Insights in the Private Value Setting," Discussion Paper, CERAS and VCL.

Cramton, Peter (1997), "The FCC Spectrum Auctions: An Early Assessment," *Journal of Economics and Management Strategy*, 6, 431–495.

Cramton, Peter, Evan Kwerel, and John Williams (1998), "Efficient Relocation of Spectrum Incumbents," *Journal of Law and Economics*, 41, 647–675.

Day, Robert W. and S. Raghavan (2004), "Generation and Selection of Core Outcomes in Sealed-Bid Combinatorial Auctions," Working Paper, University of Maryland.

Klemperer, Paul (2002), "What Really Matters in Auction Design," *Journal of Economic Perspectives*, 16, 169–189.

Kwasnica, Anthony M., John O. Ledyard, David Porter, and Christine DeMartini (2005), "A New and Improved Design for Multi object Iterative Auctions," *Management Science*, 51, 419–434.

Kwerel, Evan R. and John R. Williams (2002), "A Proposal for the Rapid Transition to Market Allocation of Spectrum," Working Paper, Office of Plans and Policy, FCC.

McAfee, R. Preston and John McMillan (1996), "Analyzing the Airwaves Auction," *Journal of Economic Perspectives*, 10, 159–176.

Milgrom, Paul (2000), "Putting Auction Theory to Work: The Simultaneous Ascending Auction," *Journal of Political Economy*, 108, 245–272.

Milgrom, Paul (2004), *Putting Auction Theory to Work*, Cambridge: Cambridge University Press.

Parkes, David C. and Lyle H. Ungar (2000), "Iterative Combinatorial Auctions: Theory and Practice," in *Proceedings of the 17th National Conference on Artificial Intelligence (AAAI-00)*, 74–81.

Porter, David, Stephen Rassenti, Anil Roopnarine, and Vernon Smith (2003), "Combinatorial Auction Design," *Proceedings of the National Academy of Sciences*, 100, 11153–11157.

Wurman, Peter R., Jie Zhong, and Gangshu Cai (2004), "Computing price Trajectories in Combinatorial Auctions with Proxy Bidding," *Electronic Commerce Research and Applications*, To appear.

6 PAUSE: A Computationally Tractable Combinatorial Auction

Ailsa Land, Susan Powell, and Richard Steinberg

6.1 Introduction

Kelly and Steinberg (1997, 2000) describe an iterative combinatorial auction procedure called PAUSE (Progressive Adaptive User Selection Environment) that on the one hand permits all package bids, but on the other is both computationally tractable for the auctioneer and transparent to the bidders. The underlying principle is that because the inherent computational complexity of package bidding cannot be eliminated (see Lehmann, Müller, and Sandholm, chapter 12 of this volume), the computational burden of evaluating a package bid is transferred from the auctioneer to the bidder making the package bid. The auctioneer no longer faces the winner determination problem.

PAUSE progresses in stages. In stage 1, a simultaneous ascending auction is held for all the items; thus bidders can submit bids on one or more individual items, but no package bidding is allowed. After stage 1, package bids are allowed; however, now bids cannot be submitted in isolation. Each bidder is required to submit his bids as part of a *composite bid*, which is a set of non-overlapping package bids (including individual bids) that cover all the items in the auction. Of course, in general a bidder will be interested in bidding on only a subset of items in the auction—and in any given round, perhaps only a subset of these. However, for the items on which he has no interest in bidding, the bidder fills out his composite bid by making use of prior bids by any of the bidders.

The following example illustrates how composite bids are formed. There are six items in the auction, α, β, γ, α', β', γ', where stage 1 ended with a bid of 5 on each item by bidders A, B, C, D, E, F, respectively; thus with a revenue to the auctioneer from these six bids totalling 30. In the current round there are standing bids of 10 by bidder A on the package $\alpha\alpha'$, 20 by B on the package $\beta\beta'$, and 15 by C on $\gamma\gamma'$, with a revenue to the auctioneer from these three bids totalling 45. Bidder A has a high valuation for the package $\alpha\beta\gamma$, and places a composite bid consisting of a bid from himself of 35 on the package $\alpha\beta\gamma$, together with the earlier bids of 5 each on α', β', and γ' from bidders D, E, and F, respectively, with revenue to the auctioneer of 50 from bidder A's composite bid.

6.1.1 Properties of PAUSE

The PAUSE procedure is progressive in the usual sense that the auction is concluded
only when no bidder wishes to submit a higher bid (Vickrey 1961, 1962). However, it
is progressive in another sense as well: there is a maximum allowable *size* for a package,
that is, the number of component items, which increases over the course of the auction. This feature helps mitigate the "threshold problem" (see the appendix to this
chapter).

PAUSE is conducted in an environment similar to the AUSM (Adaptive User Selection Mechanism) of Banks, Ledyard, and Porter (1989) in that, in order to form their
package bids, bidders make use of each others' bids. However, there are several important differences between PAUSE and AUSM.[1] We have already mentioned the most significant of these, that in PAUSE a bidder is not permitted to place a package bid on its
own, but must submit it as part of a composite bid comprised of a collection of disjoint
package bids that cover all the items in the auction.

Three important consequences of composite bid submission are: (1) the auctioneer is
relieved of the combinatorial burden of having to piece together individual bids and
needs simply to choose the best valid composite bid; (2) each losing bidder can compare his bid with the winning composite bid to see why he lost; and (3) at the conclusion of the auction, no bidder would prefer to exchange his allocation with that of
another bidder. These features are called, respectively, *computational tractability*, *transparency*, and *envy-freeness*.[2]

In the PAUSE procedure, when a bidder places a bid on a package, he is offering to
serve all the items on that package or none of them. Thus, the bid is in a sense a contingent bid. As Kelly and Steinberg (2000) pointed out, however, PAUSE can allow for
more general forms of contingency though the use of *Boolean bids* (see glossary). However, the format of the Boolean bid would need to be specified such that, given a set of
items, it would be computationally tractable to evaluate the value of the bid for that set
of items (with the value being zero if the set of items is not consistent with the Boolean
bid). Bidder behavior in PAUSE with the allowance of Boolean bids would be an area
for future research.

Kelly and Steinberg (2000) had presented PAUSE as a *two-stage* auction, consisting of
stage 1, with bidding only on individual items; and stage 2, with composite bids on
blocks of maximum size 2 in substage 1, of maximum size 3 in substage 2, and so forth.
Here we make a terminological simplification and present PAUSE as a *multistage* auction consisting of stage 1, with bidding only on individual items; stage 2, with composite bids on blocks of maximum size 2; stage 3, with composite bids on blocks of
maximum size 3; and so forth. Note that stage 1 facilitates price discovery, whereas
stages $k \geq 2$ facilitate realization of bidder synergies.

Kelly and Steinberg (2000) focus for the most part on issues of concern to the auctioneer, including bounds on the number of rounds in PAUSE, as well as how the pro-

cedure prevents "jump bidding" and mitigates both the threshold problem and the problem of signaling. They also discussed issues of implementation, testing, and validation. Although the PAUSE procedure applies to combinatorial auctions in general, Kelly and Steinberg presented it in the context of assigning Universal Service obligation to competing telephone companies.[3] For that application, the U.S. Federal Communications Commission required that the procedure include some additional features, most significantly the allowance for multiple winners.

6.1.2 Overview of This Chapter

In this chapter, we present the PAUSE auction procedure generally, without reference to any specific application. In section 6.2, for ease of exposition, we describe the main features of the PAUSE procedure. The appendix gives a detailed description of the procedure. Section 6.2 also includes the assumptions of the analysis that we conduct in section 6.3, where we present new material in which we begin to examine bidder behavior under the procedure by considering in detail a fairly general case of a two-item combinatorial auction. Section 6.4 describes two methods by which the PAUSE procedure can allow for multiple winners. Section 6.5 concludes.

6.2 Description of PAUSE

6.2.1 Structure of the Auction

PAUSE is a multistage combinatorial bidding auction procedure on m items. Stage 1 is run as a simultaneous ascending auction, with bidders submitting bids on individual items.[4] Each stage k, for $k = 2, 3, \ldots, m$, is run as a multiround combinatorial auction, with each bidder submitting a single *composite bid* in a round. A composite bid covers *all* the items in the auction, but can include prior bids by any of the bidders. There is a *minimum bid increment*, $\varepsilon > 0$.

Formally, a *composite bid* **T** consists of: (1) a *partition* of the set of items into (nonempty) subsets called *blocks*; (2) an *assignment* mapping each block to both a bidder and the bidder's bid price on that block; and (3) an *evaluation*, which is the sum of the bid prices on all the blocks in the partition. There is a key restriction on composite bids: none of the blocks comprising a composite bid made in stage k can have cardinality exceeding k. Note that this means that the final stage $k = m$ allows bids on the block consisting of all the items in the auction. Note the distinction between a package and a block. A block refers to an individual item or package that has been submitted as a component of a composite bid.

At the end of the final round of stage 1, the leading bid on each item is registered in a database to its respective owner. This database is accessible to all the bidders. At the end of each round in stages $k \geq 2$, each new leading bid on each block is registered in the database to its respective owner, and the highest valid composite bid is accepted as the standing composite bid. Thus, in each round of stage $k \geq 2$, the auctioneer accepts *one* composite bid from among all the composite bids submitted, but updates the database with *all* valid bids on blocks from among *all* the composite bids submitted.

6.2.2   Terminology and Notation

Let $\Omega = \{\alpha, \beta, \ldots\}$ denote the set of *items*, where $|\Omega| = m$. Let A, B, C, ... denote the bidders, where X and Y denote generic bidders.

A composite bid T that the auctioneer accepts at the conclusion of a round becomes the *standing composite bid* at the beginning of the next round. The *incumbent* bidder on a block b is the bidder with the leading (i.e., high) bid on that block, whether or not that bid is active.

At the end of a round, if bidder X has submitted a bid for block b, we denote the bid price as $p_X(b)$.

Let z denote the revenue accruing to the auctioneer at a specified point in the auction; let z^k denote the revenue accruing to the auctioneer at the end of stage k. At the end of stage 1, z^1 is the sum of the standing bids on each of the items in Ω; at the end of stages $k \geq 2$, z^k is the sum of the bids on each block contained in the standing composite bid T.

6.2.3   Bidder Payoff

In general, bidders will have different valuations for blocks. Let $v_X(b)$ denote the valuation by bidder X of block b. Denote by $\pi_X(b)$ the *payoff to bidder* X *on block* b:

$$\pi_X(b) = v_X(b) - p_X(b).$$

Let $\Pi_X(T)$ denote the *payoff to bidder* X *with respect to composite bid* T, that is, the sum over the blocks of T on which X is the incumbent bidder of X's valuation for the block minus X's bid on the block. Thus, we have:

$$\Pi_X(T) = \sum_{b \in T} \delta_X(b) \cdot \pi_X(b),$$

where $\delta_X(b) = 1$ if X is the incumbent bidder on block b and is 0 otherwise.

6.2.4   Assumptions of Analysis

We assume that there are no budget constraints. We make four additional simplifying assumptions. The first two concern the structure of the auction, the third pertains to bidder behavior, and the fourth is a relatively mild assumption that insures that tie composite bids do not occur:

1. The auction of m items will operate for m stages;
2. There is no limit to the number of rounds in a stage;

3. All bidders engage in straightforward bidding, i.e., a bidder will place the minimum bid that maximizes his payoff given the current auction prices; in particular, no bidder will place a bid which, if accepted, would leave him with a negative payoff;

4. At the end of a stage there is a unique composite bid on offer to the auctioneer.

6.3 Illustration of a Two-Item Auction

6.3.1 Motivation and Assumptions

In this section, we illustrate bidder behavior under the PAUSE procedure by considering in detail a fairly general case of a two-item combinatorial auction. If the items of the auction are partitioned into blocks such that each block is assigned to a bidder, then the sum of the valuations for the bidders on their respective blocks is called the *combinatorial evaluation* or, more simply, the *evaluation*, of the items relative to that partition and assignment.

We consider the case of two items, α and β, where the bidders have nonnegative valuations for the individual items and for the package $\alpha\beta$. We are assuming that there is nonnegative synergy for the package $\alpha\beta$ for all bidders. In the sequel, we will use the term "package" more generally to refer to either the combination of two items or to a single item. At the end of the auction, either the two items will assigned individually to bidders, or they will be assigned as a package to a single bidder. We will use the terms *highest valuation* and *second highest valuation* to refer to the valuations for a specific package among all the bidders.

Let there be five bidders: A, B, C, D, and E. Table 6.1 gives the specific pattern of valuations that we consider, where the highest valuation over all bidders of the item α is denoted by a and the second highest valuation by p_α; the highest valuation for the item β is denoted by b and the second highest valuation by p_β. Thus, A has the highest valuation for α, B has the highest valuation for β, and E has the second highest valuation for each of α and β. Bidders C and D have similar valuation structures to each other, where we will distinguish them by assuming $c > d$.

Table 6.1

Valuations

		A	B	C	D	E	
Package	α	a	0	0	0	p_α	$p_\alpha < a$
	β	0	b	0	0	p_β	$p_\beta < b$
	$\alpha\beta$	a	b	c	d	$p_\alpha + p_\beta$	$c > d$

At the end of the auction, either the two items will be assigned individually to bidders, or the package of two items will be assigned to a single bidder. A combinatorial evaluation for the items of this auction is a total bid price for both items, either as the price on the two items taken as a package, or as the sum of the prices of the two items taken individually. The possible valuations for the items by the bidders are:

- for the two items taken individually: $a + b$, $p_\alpha + b$, $p_\beta + a$, $p_\alpha + p_\beta$;
- for the two items taken as a package: a, b, c, d, $p_\alpha + p_\beta$.

It follows from the assumption of straightforward bidding, that is, assumption 3 of section 6.2.4, that each bidder will employ the following bidding policy:

1. Bidding in stage 1 for the individual items for which his valuation is positive; and
2. Not bidding in stage 2 for the package if his synergy on the package is zero.

6.3.2 Stages 1 and 2

In stage 1, each item is won by the bidder with the highest valuation at a price equal to the second highest valuation. Thus, we can immediately write the stage 1 results:

A wins α at a price of p_α, B wins β at a price of p_β.

We denote these prices and their owners by $p_A(\alpha)$ and $p_B(\beta)$, therefore the auctioneer's revenue z^1 at the end of stage 1 is given by:

$$z^1 = p_A(\alpha) + p_B(\beta).$$

The payoff to bidder A is $v_A(\alpha) - p_A(\alpha) = a - p_A(\alpha)$, to bidder B is $v_B(\beta) - p_B(\beta) = b - p_B(\beta)$, and to each of bidders C, D, and E is zero. That is:

Bidder	A	B	C	D	E
Bidder Payoff	$a - p_A(\alpha)$	$b - p_B(\beta)$	0	0	0

All the bidders know that, as A won α in stage 1, then the only bidder who could increase the individual bid for item α is bidder A; similarly for bidder B and item β. As a consequence, should A or B submit a composite bid (as is shown below could happen), its valuation will be $a + b$; such a composite bid dominates composite bids whose valuations are $p_\alpha + b$ and $p_\beta + a$.

We now continue with stage 2 with possible valuations for the items, α and β, either individually or as a package, of:

c, d, $a + b$, $p_\alpha + p_\beta$.

Denote the minimum bid increment set by the auctioneer by ε. Bidder E, aware that he cannot submit a bid that will improve the auctioneer's revenue, drops from the bidding. Bidder A knows that if necessary he could submit a composite bid of

[A: $(A, \alpha, p_A(\alpha) + \varepsilon), (B, \beta, p_B(\beta))$].

That is, A submits item α from himself at a price of $p_A(\alpha) + \varepsilon$ and item β from B at a price of $p_B(\beta)$. This yields a revenue to the auctioneer of $p_A(\alpha) + p_B(\beta) + \varepsilon = z^1 + \varepsilon$. Similarly, bidder B knows that if necessary he could submit a composite bid of

[B: $(A, \alpha, p_A(\alpha)), (B, \beta, p_B(\beta) + \varepsilon)$]

with a revenue to the auctioneer of $z^1 + \varepsilon$. Bidders C and D with zero payoff at the end of stage 1 have an incentive to bid. However, if $z^1 > c + \varepsilon$, neither will make a bid, so there is no bidding in stage 2. In this situation, $a + b > p_\alpha + p_\beta > c > d$; the auctioneer will receive a revenue of $p_\alpha + p_\beta$.

We will assume that $z^1 < c + \varepsilon$. We will discuss first the case when $d < p_\alpha + p_\beta$ where there will be three active bidders in stage 2, and second the case when $d > p_\alpha + p_\beta$ where there will be four active bidders in stage 2 (as follows from assumption 4 of section 6.2.4, $d \neq p_\alpha + p_\beta$).

6.3.3 Three Active Bidders

In this case, where $d < p_\alpha + p_\beta$, the possible bidders are A, B, and C; the possible valuations are $a + b$ and c, where $a + b > z^1$ and $c > z^1$.

Bidder C with a zero payoff at the end of stage 1 will submit a composite bid of

[C: $(C, \alpha\beta, p_A(\alpha) + p_B(\beta) + \varepsilon)$]

with a revenue to the auctioneer of $z^1 + \varepsilon$. Let $\hat{\Pi}_{YX}$ denote the *potential payoff* to bidder X if bidder Y's composite bid were to be accepted. The potential payoff $\hat{\Pi}_{CX}$ of each of bidders X = A, B, and C as a consequence of C's submitted bid is

Bidder	A	B	C
C's bid	0	0	$c - p_A(\alpha) - p_B(\beta) - \varepsilon$

Potential Bidder Payoff

Bidder A, realizing that his potential payoff accruing from C's bid is zero, that is $\hat{\Pi}_{CA} = 0$, submits a composite bid of

[A: $(A, \alpha, p_A(\alpha) + 2\varepsilon), (B, \beta, p_B(\beta))$]

with a revenue to the auctioneer of $z^1 + 2\varepsilon$. That is, A submits item α from himself at a price of $p_A(\alpha) + 2\varepsilon$ and item β from B at a price of $p_B(\beta)$. Similarly bidder B submits a composite bid of

[B: $(A, \alpha, p_A(\alpha)), (B, \beta, p_B(\beta) + 2\varepsilon)$]

with a revenue to the auctioneer of $z^1 + 2\varepsilon$. The potential payoffs of each bidder as a consequence of A's and B's bids are

Bidder	A	B	C
A's bid	$a - p_A(\alpha) - 2\varepsilon$	$b - p_B(\beta)$	0
B's bid	$a - p_A(\alpha)$	$b - p_B(\beta) - 2\varepsilon$	0

Potential Bidder Payoff

Bidder C, realizing that his potential payoff accruing from both A's and B's bids is zero, that is $\hat{\Pi}_{AC} = 0$ and $\hat{\Pi}_{BC} = 0$, submits a composite bid of

$$[C: (C, \alpha\beta, p_A(\alpha) + p_B(\beta) + 3\varepsilon)]$$

with a revenue to the auctioneer of $z^1 + 3\varepsilon$. The potential payoffs $\hat{\Pi}_{CX}$ of each bidder as a consequence of C's submitted bid are

Bidder	A	B	C
C's bid	0	0	$c - p_A(\alpha) - p_B(\beta) - 3\varepsilon$

Potential Bidder Payoff

Both bidders A and B, realizing independently that their potential payoff accruing from C's bid is zero, independently submit the identical composite bid of

$$[A, B: (A, \alpha, p_A(\alpha) + 2\varepsilon), (B, \beta, p_B(\beta) + 2\varepsilon)]$$

with a revenue to the auctioneer of $z^1 + 4\varepsilon$. The potential payoffs of each bidder as a consequence of A's and B's bids are

Bidder	A	B	C
A's bid	$a - p_A(\alpha) - 2\varepsilon$	$b - p_B(\beta) - 2\varepsilon$	0
B's bid	$a - p_A(\alpha) - 2\varepsilon$	$b - p_B(\beta) - 2\varepsilon$	0

Potential Bidder Payoff

Bidder C responds to these bids with a composite bid of

$$[C: (C, \alpha\beta, p_A(\alpha) + p_B(\beta) + 5\varepsilon)]$$

to which A and B respond, and so on. Table 6.2 summarizes the sequence of bids in stage 2, where r denotes the number of the round.

We set $\theta = r\varepsilon$. Here θ represents the minimum incremental increase in the auctioneer's revenue after r rounds. We assume that ε is sufficiently small that $(r + 2/2)\varepsilon$ and $(r - 2/2)\varepsilon$ can be approximated by $(r/2)\varepsilon$, that is, by $(1/2)\theta$. Thus, the stage 2 bid for C will be:

$$[C: (C, \alpha\beta, p_A(\alpha) + p_B(\beta) + \theta)]$$

and the stage 2 bids for A and B can be taken to be:

Table 6.2

Stage 2 Bidding

Round, r	Auctioneer's Revenue	Bids
1	$z^1 + \varepsilon$	$[C: (C, \alpha\beta, p_A(\alpha) + p_B(\beta) + \varepsilon)]$
2	$z^1 + 2\varepsilon$	$[A: (A, \alpha, p_A(\alpha) + 2\varepsilon), (B, \beta, p_B(\beta))]$ $[B: (A, \alpha, p_A(\alpha)), (B, \beta, p_B(\beta) + 2\varepsilon)]$
3	$z^1 + 3\varepsilon$	$[C: (C, \alpha\beta, p_A(\alpha) + p_B(\beta) + 3\varepsilon)]$
4	$z^1 + 4\varepsilon$	$[A: (A, \alpha, p_A(\alpha) + 2\varepsilon), (B, \beta, p_B(\beta) + 2\varepsilon)]$ $[B: (A, \alpha, p_A(\alpha) + 2\varepsilon), (B, \beta, p_B(\beta) + 2\varepsilon)]$
5	$z^1 + 5\varepsilon$	$[C: (C, \alpha\beta, p_A(\alpha) + p_B(\beta) + 5\varepsilon)]$
6	$z^1 + 6\varepsilon$	$[A: (A, \alpha, p_A(\alpha) + 4\varepsilon), (B, \beta, p_B(\beta) + 2\varepsilon)]$ $[B: (A, \alpha, p_A(\alpha) + 2\varepsilon), (B, \beta, p_B(\beta) + 4\varepsilon)]$
7	$z^1 + 7\varepsilon$	$[C: (C, \alpha\beta, p_A(\alpha) + p_B(\beta) + 7\varepsilon)]$
8	$z^1 + 8\varepsilon$	$[A: (A, \alpha, p_A(\alpha) + 4\varepsilon), (B, \beta, p_B(\beta) + 4\varepsilon)]$ $[B: (A, \alpha, p_A(\alpha) + 4\varepsilon), (B, \beta, p_B(\beta) + 4\varepsilon)]$
$\vdots$	$\vdots$	$\vdots$
r odd	$z^1 + r\varepsilon$	$[C: (C, \alpha\beta, p_A(\alpha) + p_B(\beta) + r\varepsilon)]$
$r \equiv 2 \pmod 4$	$z^1 + r\varepsilon$	$[A: \left(A, \alpha, p_A(\alpha) + \frac{r+2}{2}\varepsilon\right), \left(B, \beta, p_B(\beta) + \frac{r-2}{2}\varepsilon\right)]$ $[B: \left(A, \alpha, p_A(\alpha) + \frac{r-2}{2}\varepsilon\right), \left(B, \beta, p_B(\beta) + \frac{r+2}{2}\varepsilon\right)]$
$r \equiv 0 \pmod 4$	$z^1 + r\varepsilon$	$[A: \left(A, \alpha, p_A(\alpha) + \frac{r}{2}\varepsilon\right), \left(B, \beta, p_B(\beta) + \frac{r}{2}\varepsilon\right)]$ $[B: \left(A, \alpha, p_A(\alpha) + \frac{r}{2}\varepsilon\right), \left(B, \beta, p_B(\beta) + \frac{r}{2}\varepsilon\right)]$

$$[A, B: (A, \alpha, p_A(\alpha) + (1/2)\theta), (B, \beta, p_B(\beta) + (1/2)\theta)]$$

with a revenue to the auctioneer, in each case, of $z^1 + \theta$. The potential payoffs from these bids are

Bidder	A	B	C
A's bid	$a - p_A(\alpha) - \frac{1}{2}\theta$	$b - p_B(\beta) - \frac{1}{2}\theta$	0
B's bid	$a - p_A(\alpha) - \frac{1}{2}\theta$	$b - p_B(\beta) - \frac{1}{2}\theta$	0
C's bid	0	0	$c - p_A(\alpha) - p_B(\beta) - \theta$

Potential Bidder Payoff

Because no bidder will allow his payoff to fall below zero, the maximum value of θ that will arise from C's bids is $\theta_C = c - p_A(\alpha) - p_B(\beta)$; the maximum from A's bids is $\theta_A = 2(a - p_A(\alpha))$; and from B's is $\theta_B = 2(b - p_B(\beta))$. Thus, the maximum value of θ is $\min\{\theta_A, \theta_B, \theta_C\}$, at which value a bidder will *drop* from the bidding as his payoff will become zero.

We will consider the order in which the bidders will drop from the bidding. We assume, without loss of generality, that $\theta_A < \theta_B$. That is, $a - p_A(\alpha) < b - p_B(\beta)$, so bidder A drops before bidder B. There are three cases of the order of dropping, depending on whether C drops last, second, or first:

Case 1: A, B, C;   Case 2: A, C, B;   and   Case 3: C, A, B.

Cases 1 and 2 In cases 1 and 2, bidder A is the first bidder to drop. This happens when θ reaches $2(a - p_A(\alpha))$. We denote the number of rounds by r', that is $r'\varepsilon = 2(a - p_A(\alpha))$. Bidder A will not submit a bid at this round, r', as this will give him zero payoff; however, bidder C submits the bid

[C: $(C, \alpha\beta, p_A(\alpha) + p_B(\beta) + 2(a - p_A(\alpha)))$]

giving a revenue to the auctioneer of $z^1 + 2(a - p_A(\alpha))$. At round $r' + 1$ bidder A drops out, because a successful bid would leave him with a negative payoff. However, B bids

[B: $(A, \alpha, a), (B, \beta, p_B(\beta) - p_A(\alpha) + a + \varepsilon)$],

giving a revenue to the auctioneer of $z^1 + 2(a - p_A(\alpha)) + \varepsilon$.

We now reset the round counter, r, renumbering the round at which bidder A drops out (i.e., round $r' + 1$) to be 1. Bidder C responds in round 2, with

[C: $(C, \alpha\beta, p_A(\alpha) + p_B(\beta) + 2(a - p_A(\alpha)) + 2\varepsilon)$].

The auction continues with bids from B and C. At round r bidder B bids

[B: $(A, \alpha, a), (B, \beta, p_B(\beta) - p_A(\alpha) + a + r\varepsilon)$]

and at round $r + 1$ bidder C bids

[C: $(C, \alpha\beta, p_B(\beta) + 2a - p_A(\alpha) + (r + 1)\varepsilon)$].

From our previous assumption about the size of ε it follows that $(r + 1)\varepsilon$ may be approximated by $r\varepsilon$, which we denote, as before, by θ. The bids can be considered to be

[B: $(A, \alpha, a), (B, \beta, p_B(\beta) - p_A(\alpha) + a + \theta)$]   and

[C: $(C, \alpha\beta, p_B(\beta) + 2a - p_A(\alpha) + \theta)$].

with a revenue to the auctioneer of $z^1 + 2(a - p_A(\alpha)) + \theta$. The potential payoffs from these bids are

Bidder	A	B	C
B's bid	0	$b - p_B(\beta) + p_A(\alpha) - a - \theta$	0
C's bid	0	0	$c - p_B(\beta) - 2a + p_A(\alpha) - \theta$

Potential Bidder Payoff

The maximum value of θ that will arise from B's bids is $\theta_B = b - p_B(\beta) - a + p_A(\alpha)$ and the maximum from C's bids $\theta_C = c - p_B(\beta) - 2a + p_A(\alpha)$.

Case 1   Here, after the drop of bidder A, bidder B is the next bidder to drop so $\theta_B < \theta_C$, that is,

$$b - p_B(\beta) - a + p_A(\alpha) < c - p_B(\beta) - 2a + p_A(\alpha),$$

giving $b + a < c$. Bidder B drops from the bidding when θ reaches $b - p_B(\beta) - a + p_A(\alpha)$ giving the auctioneer a revenue of $a + b$. Bidder C wins stage 2 with a composite bid of

$[C: (C, \alpha\beta, a + b)]$.

Thus the auctioneer achieves a revenue of $a + b$. The payoffs at the end of stage 2 are

Bidder	A	B	C
Payoff	0	0	$c - (a + b)$

Case 2   Here, after the drop of bidder A, bidder C is the next bidder to drop so $\theta_C < \theta_B$, that is,

$$c - p_B(\beta) - 2a + p_A(\alpha) < b - p_B(\beta) - a + p_A(\alpha),$$

giving $c < a + b$. Bidder C drops from the bidding when θ reaches $c - p_B(\beta) - 2a + p_A(\alpha)$, giving the auctioneer a revenue of c. Bidder B wins stage 2 with a composite bid of

$[B: (A, \alpha, a), (B, \beta, c - a)]$.

Thus the auctioneer achieves a revenue of c. The payoffs at the end of stage 2 are

Bidder	A	B	C
Payoff	0	$b - (c - a)$	0

Case 3   Here, bidder C is the first bidder to drop, followed by bidder A. This happens when $\theta_C < \theta_A$, that is $c - p_A(\alpha) - p_B(\beta) < 2(a - p_A(\alpha))$; combining this with the assumption $a - p_A(\alpha) < b - p_B(\beta)$ gives $c < a + b$.

In the interests of concision, the analysis presented here is not in terms of ε; it is given instead in terms of θ. When θ reaches $c - p_A(\alpha) - p_B(\beta)$, then C's potential payoff becomes zero and C drops from the bidding. The revenue to the auctioneer is $z^1 + c - p_A(\alpha) - p_B(\beta) = c$. Stage 2 is won by the identical independent composite bids of A and B:

$$[A, B: (A, \alpha, (1/2)[c + p_A(\alpha) - p_B(\beta)]), (B, \beta, (1/2)[c - p_A(\alpha) + p_B(\beta)])],$$

giving the auctioneer a revenue of c. The payoffs at the end of stage 2 are

Bidder	A	B	C
Payoff	$a - \frac{1}{2}[c + p_A(\alpha) - p_B(\beta)]$	$b - \frac{1}{2}[c - p_A(\alpha) + p_B(\beta)]$	0

6.3.4   Four Active Bidders

In the case where $d > p_\alpha + p_\beta$, the possible bidders are A, B, C, and D; the possible valuations are $a + b$, c and d, where $a + b > z^1$, $c > d > z^1$.

If $d < z^1$ then D does not bid in stage 2 and the bidding proceeds as in the three-bidder analysis presented in the previous section. Otherwise, when $d > z^1$, D submits a composite bid of

$$[D: (D, \alpha\beta, p_A(\alpha) + p_B(\beta) + \theta)],$$

with revenue to the auctioneer of $z^1 + \theta$. Bidders A, B, and C submit the composite bids described in the three-bidder case above. The potential payoffs from all these bids are

Bidder	A	B	C	D
A's bid	$a - p_A(\alpha) - \frac{1}{2}\theta$	$b - p_B(\beta) - \frac{1}{2}\theta$	0	0
B's bid	$a - p_A(\alpha) - \frac{1}{2}\theta$	$b - p_B(\beta) - \frac{1}{2}\theta$	0	0
C's bid	0	0	$c - p_A(\alpha) - p_B(\beta) - \theta$	0
D's bid	0	0	0	$d - p_A(\alpha) - p_B(\beta) - \theta$

Potential Bidder Payoff

The maximum values of θ that arise from the bids are

Bidder X	A	B	C	D
θ_X	$2(a - p_A(\alpha))$	$2(b - p_B(\beta))$	$c - p_A(\alpha) - p_B(\beta)$	$d - p_A(\alpha) - p_B(\beta)$

The maximum value of θ is $\min\{\theta_A, \theta_B, \theta_C, \theta_D\}$ at which value a bidder will drop from the bidding as his payoff will become zero.

We will consider the order in which the bidders will drop from the bidding. We assume, as before, that $\theta_A < \theta_B$, that is $a - p_A(\alpha) < b - p_B(\beta)$; thus bidder A drops out before bidder B. Because d is the second highest valuation for $\alpha\beta$, it follows that $\theta_D < \theta_C$, so bidder D drops out before bidder C. There are six cases of the order of dropping:

Case 1: D, A, B, C;   Case 2: D, A, C, B;   Case 3: D, C, A, B;
Case 4: A, D, C, B;   Case 5: A, D, B, C;   Case 6: A, B, D, C.

Cases 1, 5 and 6 are equivalent to case 1 of the three-bidder analysis; cases 2 and 4 are equivalent to case 2 of the three-bidder analysis; and case 3 is case 3 of the three-bidder analysis. In cases 1, 2, and 3, bidder D is the first to drop, whereas in cases 4, 5, and 6 bidder A is first.

Cases 1, 2, and 3   In these cases, bidder D is the first bidder to drop out. Though the second bidder to drop out is not always bidder A, the condition $\theta_D < \theta_A$ holds, that is, $d - p_A(\alpha) - p_B(\beta) < 2(a - p_A(\alpha))$. Combining this with the assumption $a - p_A(\alpha) < b - p_B(\beta)$ gives $d < a + b$.

Case 1   Here, after bidder D drops from the bidding, the auction continues as in case 1 of the three-bidder analysis. The valuations are $d < a + b < c$; the auction terminates with the bid [C: $(C, \alpha\beta, a + b)$]. The auctioneer achieves revenue of $a + b$.

Case 2   Here, after bidder D drops from the bidding, the auction continues as in case 2 of the three-bidder analysis. The valuations are $d < c < a + b$; the auction terminates with the bid [B: $(A, \alpha, a), (B, \beta, c - a)$]. The auctioneer achieves a revenue of c.

Case 3   Here, after bidder D drops from the bidding, the auction continues as in case 3 of the three-bidder analysis. The valuations are $d < c < a + b$; the auction terminates with the bid

$$[A, B: (A, \alpha, (1/2)[c + p_A(\alpha) - p_B(\beta)]), (B, \beta, (1/2)[c - p_A(\alpha) + p_B(\beta)])].$$

The auctioneer achieves a revenue of c.

Cases 4, 5, and 6   In these cases, bidder A is the first to drop when θ reaches $2(a - p_A(\alpha))$. Resetting θ, the bids are

$$[B: (A, \alpha, a), (B, \beta, p_B(\beta) - p_A(\alpha) + a + \theta)],$$

$$[C: (C, \alpha\beta, p_B(\beta) + 2a - p_A(\alpha) + \theta)]$$

$$[D: (D, \alpha\beta, p_B(\beta) + 2a - p_A(\alpha) + \theta)]$$

with a revenue to the auctioneer of $z^1 + 2(a - p_A(\alpha)) + \theta$. The maximum values of θ that arise from the bids are

Bidder X	B	C	D
θ_X	$b - p_B(\beta) + p_A(\alpha) - a$	$c - p_B(\beta) - 2a + p_A(\alpha)$	$d - p_B(\beta) - 2a + p_A(\alpha)$

Case 4   Here, after A drops from the bidding, the auction continues with C and B bidding, as in case 2 of the three-bidder analysis, and bidder D also bidding for $\alpha\beta$. The order $\theta_D < \theta_C < \theta_B$ gives the valuations $d < c < a + b$. The auction terminates with the bid $[B: (A, \alpha, a), (B, \beta, c - a)]$, giving the auctioneer a revenue of c.

Cases 5 and 6   Here, after A drops from the bidding, the auction continues with C and B bidding, as in case 1 of the three-bidder analysis, and bidder D also bidding for $\alpha\beta$. In case 5 the order $\theta_D < \theta_B < \theta_C$ gives the valuations $d < a + b < c$. The auction terminates with the bid $[C: (C, \alpha\beta, a + b)]$, giving the auctioneer a revenue of $a + b$.

In case 6, the order $\theta_B < \theta_D < \theta_C$ gives the valuations $a + b < d < c$. The auction terminates with the bid $[C: (C, \alpha\beta, d)]$, giving the auctioneer a revenue of d.

6.3.5   Remark on the Two-Item Auction
We have considered in detail bidder behavior for two items and a particular pattern of valuations. Observe that the bidders A and B, when participating in stage 2, will find themselves repeatedly submitting identical composite bids. This is interesting for two reasons. First, bidders A and B are interested in two different items on which they have, in general, different valuations. Second, this behavior arises purely from bidder self-interest and is not the result of either explicit or tacit collusion.

6.4   Multiple Winners

The analysis thus far has assumed an item to be indivisible. However, there are circumstances, such as telecommunications customers in a service area, where this assumption could be relaxed at the instigation of the auctioneer.

Let us suppose that a number of bidders can share an item. At the end of stage 1, the auctioneer can announce the number of multiple winners on each item as determined by an *outcome rule*. For example, the auctioneer might choose to employ the outcome rule proposed by Milgrom (1996):[5] 1) If at least one competing bid is within G_1 percent of the highest bid, then all who bid within G_1 percent of the highest bid are designated as winners; 2) if no competing bid is within G_1 percent, but one bid is within G_2 percent, then the two highest bidders are winners; and 3) if no bid is within G_2 percent, then there is a single winner, viz., the highest bidder. The number of multiple winners on each item ϕ at the end of stage 1 is denoted by $g(\phi)$. Before the start of stage 2, item ϕ is replaced by $g(\phi)$ items, $\phi_1, \phi_2, \ldots, \phi_{g(\phi)}$, each corresponding to $1/g(\phi)$ portion of the original item ϕ.

At the conclusion of the last stage of the auction, the $g(\phi)$ winners on item ϕ are each awarded a $1/g(\phi)$ share of the item ϕ. It is essential that, before the start of stage 2, that is, before the package bidding begins, the auctioneer specifies the rules that need to be satisfied by a valid composite bid in a manner that the bidders, as well as the auctioneer, can check.

6.4.1 Alternative Structure for Stage 1

The method by which the number of multiple winners are determined as described above is consistent with Milgrom (1996) who showed that, in a setting with a single item or where all the items are independent (i.e., have no synergies), an optimal auction design entails endogenous market structure. In contrast, we describe here a modification to PAUSE, where the first stage is conducted as a sealed-bid auction.

The bidders   Each bidder submits a *panel* of bids, made known only to the auctioneer, for each individual item in which he has an interest. The panel of bids on a given item from bidder X is $(c(1, X), c(2, X), \ldots, c(g, X), \ldots, c(G, X))$. Here $c(g, X)$ is the price bidder X requires to be one of g multiple winners on the item, and G is the maximum number of winners the auction authority will allow on the item. (We would expect the sequence $\{g \cdot c(g, X)\}$ to be nonincreasing in g.)

The auctioneer   If the auctioneer generally prefers winners of greater multiplicity g, then he will discount the bids accordingly; specifically, let $f(g)$ be the auctioneer's g-*competitor discount factor*, where $f(1) = 0$ and where the function $f(g)$ is nonincreasing in g.

Multiple winners   After all the sealed bids have been submitted, for each item the auctioneer goes through the following simple procedure. First, he computes $C(g) = g \cdot c'(g)$, where $c'(g)$ is the largest term in the set $\Pi(g) = \{c(g, 1), c(g, 2), \ldots\}$. Second, he computes $g^* = \arg\max\{(1 + f(g)) \cdot C(g)\}$. Third, he announces that the number of multiple winners for that item is g^*, that the stage 1 winning bids on the item are those bids from the set $\Pi(g)$ achieving at least $C(g^*)/g^*$, and that the price level for each bid on the item is $C(g^*)/g^*$. Denote the number of multiple winners on each item, ϕ, at the end of stage 1 by $g(\phi)$. The fourth and final step occurs shortly before the start of stage 2: the auctioneer replaces item ϕ by $g(\phi)$ items $\phi_1, \phi_2, \ldots, \phi_{g(\phi)}$, each allocated a nominal fraction of the item equal to $1/g(\phi)$.

6.5 Conclusion

We have described the PAUSE combinatorial auction procedure Kelly and Steinberg (2000) devised. The presentation here makes no assumptions about the application of the procedure. In order to understand the workings of the auction, we have considered in detail bidder behavior for an illustrative case consisting of two items and a particular pattern of valuations, where there are either three or four active bidders.

Recently, interest has developed in *two-way combinatorial auctions* or *combinatorial exchanges*; these generalize combinatorial auctions by allowing players to simultaneous buy and sell items. See papers from the Third Combinatorial Bidding Conference (2003). This appears to be a natural extension for the PAUSE auction procedure, and would be worthy of future investigation.

Acknowledgments

The authors would like to thank Richard Gibbens for his helpful comments.

6.6   Appendix: Detailed Description of PAUSE

6.6.1   Composite Bids

Let $\Omega = \{\alpha, \beta, \ldots\}$ denote the set of *items*, where $|\Omega| = m$. Let $A, B, C, \ldots, X, \ldots$ denote the bidders. Label *packages* $k \in K(\Omega)$, where $K(\Omega)$ is the set of (non-empty) subsets of Ω. Let

$$K_q = \{k \in K(\Omega) : 1 \le |k| \le q\},$$

where $|k|$ denotes the number of items in package k, that is, the *size* of k. Thus K_q denotes the set of packages up to size q.[6] A *partition* $\mathbf{P} = \{b_1, b_2, \ldots, b_r\}$ is a collection of packages called *blocks* $b_1, b_2, \ldots, b_r \in K(\Omega)$ such that $\bigcup_{i=1}^{r} b_i = \Omega$, and $b_i \cap b_j = \emptyset$ for $i \ne j$. If a bidder, X, places a bid at price $p(b)$ on a block b of size k, then the triple $(X, b, p(b))$ is called a *block bid*.

A *composite bid* by bidder X is a collection of disjoint block bids that cover all the items of the auction. Note that such a composite bid will, in general, contain block bids of other bidders in addition to one or more bids from bidder X. More formally, a composite bid comprises a partition

$$\mathbf{P} = (b_1, b_2, \ldots, b_r)$$

together with an *evaluation*

$$(E(\mathbf{P}); p(b_1), p(b_2), \ldots, p(b_r))$$

where

$$E(\mathbf{P}) = \sum_{i=1}^{r} p(b_i).$$

Thus, a composite bid consists of $3r + 1$ pieces of information (in addition to the identity of the bidder placing the composite bid), capable of registration in a database.

The first piece of information is the total value of the composite bid, $E(\mathbf{P})$. The remaining $3r$ pieces of information are, for each i $(i = 1, 2, \ldots, r)$:

1. the specification of the block b_i;
2. the bid $p(b_i)$ on the block b_i;
3. the identity of the bidder for block b_i.

All $3r + 1$ pieces of information are available from the database to all bidders.

6.6.2 Specification of the Auction Mechanism

Stage 1: Bidding on Individual Assets

The Bidders Each bidder submits bids on one or more items. In each round there is an *improvement margin requirement*:

The new bid must improve on the previous best bid on that item by at least ε and strictly less than 2ε.

The Auctioneer In each round, for each item the auctioneer confirms that a bid on that item is *valid* by verifying *increment validity*:

The bid satisfies the bounds of the improvement margin requirement.

In each round, the highest valid bid on each item is accepted. The stage ends when bidding ends on all items.[7] At the conclusion of the stage, the leading (i.e., high) bids on the items are registered in a database to their respective owners.

Activity Rules PAUSE may or may not incorporate activity rules in each stage of the auction. A bidder's current *activity* is a measure based on the new bids and his standing bids. These rules restrict the eligibility of a bidder with insufficiently high activity to place bids later on in the auction. (See Kelly and Steinberg 2000 for details about suggested activity rules for the PAUSE procedure, as well as discussion of the related issues of bid waivers and bid withdrawals.)

Stage $k \geq 2$: Package Bidding

The Bidders Each bidder submits a single composite bid, $\mathbf{T}$ (which, by definition, covers all the items in the auction). In each round there is an *improvement margin requirement*:

Let $w(\mathbf{T})$ denote the number of *new* bids in the composite bid. The new evaluation must improve on the previous best evaluation by *at least* $w(\mathbf{T})\varepsilon$ and *strictly less than* $2w(\mathbf{T})\varepsilon$ (i.e., an average improvement per block of at least ε but less than 2ε).

In stage k, each component b_i of a bidder's partition $\mathbf{P} = \{b_1, b_2, \ldots, b_r\}$ is restricted to $b_i \in \mathbf{K}_k$, where $p(b_i)$ is either a new bid for block b_i, or a registered bid.

The Auctioneer In each round, the auctioneer checks that a composite bid is *valid* by checking:

1. Bid validity Each bid which is asserted to be registered in the database is indeed so registered, and that new bids identify correctly the bidder for block b_i, and satisfy $b_i \in \mathbf{K}_k$;

2. Evaluation validity The value, $E(\mathbf{P})$, of the composite bid is indeed equal to $\sum_{i=1}^{r} p(b_i)$, the sum of the bids on each of its blocks and

3. Increment validity The value of the composite bid, $E(\mathbf{P})$, satisfies the bounds of the improvement margin requirement.

At the end of each round in stages $k \geq 2$, the new collection of valid bids on all the blocks from all the bidders is registered in the database to their respective owners, and the highest valid composite bid is accepted as the standing composite bid. Thus, in each round, the auctioneer accepts *one* composite bid from among all the composite bids submitted by the bidders, but updates the database with *all* valid bids on blocks from among *all* the bidders. A stage ends when bidding ceases.

6.6.3 Prevention against Jump Bidding and Mitigation of the Threshold Problem

McAfee and McMillan (1996) report a potential problem with simultaneous, multiple-round auctions, called *jump bidding*. This is the tactic of a bidder entering bids far above that required by the minimum bid increment, the intention of which is to warn weaker rivals against competing on specific items. Kelly and Steinberg (2000) call this, more specifically, *price-jump bidding*. This is to distinguish it from another tactic, which they call *block-jump bidding*, in which a bid by a powerful bidder for a block of several items could be effective at preventing small bidders from piecing together a comparable composite bid, which is known as the *threshold problem*.

In PAUSE, the improvement margin requirement reduces the possibility of price-jump bidding. The progression of allowable block size prevents block-jump bidding and mitigates the threshold problem.[8]

Notes

1. See Parkes (chapter 2, section 2.5 of this volume) for more on the AUSM design.

2. The concept of envy-freeness is due to Foley (1967), although the term itself was introduced later. We are grateful to Andrzej Skrzypacz for pointing out the envy-freeness property of PAUSE.

3. Also, for purposes of their telecommunications application, PAUSE was presented in the form of a one-sided procurement auction, i.e., a *reverse auction*.

4. For more on the simultaneous ascending auction, see Cramton (chapter 4 of this volume).

5. This is in fact a generalization of Milgrom's outcome rule; he specified particular values corresponding in our notation to $G_1 = 15$ and $G_2 = 25$.

6. More generally, we can allow restrictions on the types of bids allowed. Label *packages* $k \in K(\Omega, A)$, where $K(\Omega, A)$ is a set of subsets of Ω defined by a set of *attributes* A that are computationally tractable for the auctioneer to verify for each member of $K(\Omega, A)$. Label $K_q = \{k \in K(\Omega, A) : 1 \leq |k| \leq q\}$, where $|k|$ denotes the number of items in package k, i.e., the *size* of k. Thus K_q denotes the set of packages up to size q possessing attributes A. (Example attribute: "Items of a package must be geographically contiguous.")

7. Stage 1 can be divided into substages along the line of Simultaneous Ascending Auction structure used by the U.S. Federal Communications Commission (McAfee and McMillan 1996), where progressively more severe activity rules are imposed over stages.

8. For an example of how the absence of the upper bound on the improvement margin requirement can favor bidders seeking large aggregations, see Cramton (chapter 4, section 4.2 of this volume).

References

"Third Combinatorial Bidding Conference," FCC and SIEPR, Aspen Institute's Wye River Conference Center, Queenstown, Maryland November 21–23, 2003. Available at ⟨http://wireless.fcc.gov/⟩.

Banks, Jeffrey S., John O. Ledyard, and David P. Porter (1989), "Allocating Uncertain and Unresponsive Resources: An Experimental Approach," *RAND Journal of Economics*, 20, 1–25.

Foley, Duncan C. (1967), "Resource Allocation and the Public Sector," *Yale Economic Essays*, 7, 45–98.

Kelly, Frank and Richard Steinberg (1997), "A Combinatorial Auction with Multiple Winners for COLR," University of Cambridge, Cambridge, England. (Submitted *ex parte* 18 March 1997 by Citizens for a Sound Economy Foundation to U.S. Federal Communications Commission re CC Docket No. 96–45, Federal-State Board on Universal Service.)

Kelly, Frank and Richard Steinberg (2000), "A Combinatorial Auction with Multiple Winners for Universal Service," *Management Science*, 46, 586–596.

McAfee, R. Preston and John McMillan (1996), "Analyzing the Airwaves Auction," *Journal of Economic Perspectives*, 10, 159–175.

Milgrom, Paul (1996), Statement attached to GTE's Comments in response to questions, Federal Communications Commission. Notice of Proposed Rulemaking, Federal-State Joint Board on Universal Service, CC Docket No. 96–45, Washington, D.C.

Vickrey, William (1961), "Counterspeculation, Auctions, and Competitive Sealed Tenders," *Journal of Finance*, 16, 8–37.

Vickrey, William (1962), "Auction and Bidding Games," in *Recent Advances in Game Theory*, The Princeton University Conference, 15–27.

II   Bidding and Efficiency

7 Pseudonymous Bidding in Combinatorial Auctions

Makoto Yokoo

7.1 Introduction

In this chapter, we discuss the effect of pseudonymous bidding in combinatorial auctions. Although the Internet provides an excellent infrastructure for executing combinatorial auctions, we must consider the possibility of new types of manipulation. For example, a bidder may try to profit from submitting multiple bids using pseudonyms, perhaps by submitting bids from multiple email addresses. Such an action is very difficult to detect, because identifying each participant on the Internet is virtually impossible. We call a bid made under a pseudonym a *pseudonymous bid*. Also, we call a protocol *pseudonymous-bid-proof* if truth telling without the use of pseudonymous bids is a dominant strategy for each bidder.

Many researchers have discussed the problems resulting from collusion (McAfee and McMillan 1987, 1992; Milgrom and Weber 1982; Milgrom 2000). Compared with collusion, a pseudonymous bid is easier to execute on the Internet because getting another identifier such as an email address is cheap. We can consider pseudonymous bidding as a very restricted subclass of collusion.

Some researchers have proposed a concept called *group-strategy-proof* to study another restricted subclass of general collusion (Müller and Satterthwaite 1985; Moulin and Shenker 1996). An auction protocol is group-strategy-proof if there exists no group of bidders that satisfies the following condition:

- By deviating from truth telling, each member in the group obtains at least the same utility compared with the case of truth telling, whereas at least one member of the group obtains a better utility compared with the case of truth-telling.

Group-strategy-proof and pseudonymous-bid-proof are independent concepts; that is, a group-strategy-proof protocol is not necessarily pseudonymous-bid-proof, and vice versa. We discuss this in more detail in section 7.5.

In this chapter, we examine the effect of pseudonymous bids on combinatorial auctions. We can summarize the results presented in this chapter as follows:

- The Vickrey-Clarke-Groves (VCG) mechanism (see chapter 1 of this volume), which is strategy proof and Pareto efficient if there exists no pseudonymous bid, is not pseudonymous-bid-proof.
- There exists no pseudonymous-bid-proof combinatorial auction protocol that satisfies Pareto efficiency.
- We identify one sufficient condition where the VCG mechanism is pseudonymous-bid-proof, i.e., a surplus function is *bidder submodular* (see chapter 1).
- We show a pseudonymous-bid-proof protocol called the Leveled Division Set (LDS) protocol.

Sakurai, Yokoo, and Matsubara (1999) and Yokoo, Sakurai, and Matsubara (2000a, 2004) introduced the concept of pseudonymous bids (also called false-name-bids). Yokoo, Sakurai, and Matsubara 2000b, 2001a, 2001b presented the LDS protocol. Yokoo, Sakurai, and Matsubara (2001d), Terada and Yokoo (2003), and Iwasaki, Yokoo, and Terada (2003) discuss pseudonymous-bid-proof multi-unit auction protocols. Also, Yokoo, Sakurai, and Matsubara (2001c) and Sakurai and Yokoo (2003) discuss the effects of pseudonymous bids in double auctions.

In the rest of this chapter, we first develop the model of a combinatorial auction in which pseudonymous bids are possible (section 7.2). Next, we examine the effect of pseudonymous bids in combinatorial auctions (section 7.3), and we provide a sufficient condition for the VCG mechanism to be pseudonymous-bid-proof (section 7.3.3). Finally, we present a pseudonymous-bid-proof protocol called the Leveled Division Set (LDS) protocol (section 7.4).

7.2 Formalization

In this section, we formalize a combinatorial auction protocol in which pseudonymous bids are possible. Our model is based on that presented by Monderer and Tennenholtz (2000), but we have modified 17 to handle pseudonymous bids.

7.2.1 Specification of Model

Assume there is a set of bidders $N = \{1, 2, \ldots, n\}$. We assume agent 0 is an auctioneer, who is willing to sell a set of goods $A = \{a_1, a_2, \ldots, a_l\}$. Each bidder i has his preferences over the subsets of A. Formally, we model this by supposing that bidder i privately observes a type θ_i, which is drawn from a set Θ. We assume a *quasi-linear, private value* model with *no allocative externality*, defined as follows:

Definition 7.1   The utility of bidder i, when i obtains a subset of goods $B \subseteq A$ and a monetary transfer t_i, is represented as $v(B, \theta_i) + t_i$.

We assume that the evaluation value v is normalized by $v(\emptyset, \theta_i) = 0$. Also, we assume *free disposal*, that is, $v(B', \theta_i) \geq v(B, \theta_i)$ for all $B \subseteq B'$. Furthermore, for the auctioneer 0 we assume $v(B, \theta_0) = 0$ for any subset of goods B.

To formalize the concept of pseudonymous bids, we introduce a set of identifiers M and an indexed partition ϕ such that $\phi(i)$ is the set of identifiers available to bidder i.

Definition 7.2 There exists a set of identifiers $M = \{id_1, id_2, \ldots, id_m\}$. Furthermore, there exists an indexed partition $\phi : N \to 2^M \backslash \emptyset$, which assigns to each bidder i a set $\phi(i)$ of identifiers, where $|\phi(i)| \geq 1$, $\bigcup_i \phi(i) = M$, and $\phi(i) \cap \phi(j) = \emptyset$ for $i \neq j$.

We assume $\phi(i)$ is also the private information of bidder i. Therefore, the set of signals is represented as $T = \Theta \times (2^M \backslash \emptyset)$, where the signal of bidder i is $(\theta_i, \phi(i)) \in T$.

In other words, a bidder can submit multiple bids pretending to be multiple bidders, but a bidder cannot impersonate another real, existing bidder. Also, the auctioneer 0 has no knowledge of ϕ and each bidder i only knows $\phi(i)$ and does not know $\phi(j)$ for $j \neq i$.

Next, we define a combinatorial auction protocol. For simplicity, we restrict our attention to *almost anonymous mechanisms*, in which obtained results are invariant under permutation of identifiers except for the cases of ties. We describe the condition that an almost anonymous mechanism must satisfy for the cases of ties later. Also, we restrict our attention to auction protocols in which the set of messages for each identifier is $\Theta \cup \{0\}$, where 0 is a special symbol used for "nonparticipation." The fact that this restriction does not harm the generality of our results does not follow directly form the revelation principle, because the signal of a bidder is a pair $(\theta_i, \phi(i))$, and not just θ_i. We comment on this usage of the revelation principle in section 7.2.2.

Definition 7.3 A *combinatorial auction protocol* is defined by $\Gamma = (k(\cdot), t(\cdot))$. We call $k(\cdot)$ the *allocation function* and $t(\cdot)$ the *transfer function*. Let us represent a profile of types, each of which is declared under each identifier as $\theta = (\theta_{id_1}, \theta_{id_2}, \ldots, \theta_{id_m})$, where $\theta_{id_i} \in \Theta \cup \{0\}$. Here 0 is a special type declaration used when a bidder is not willing to participate in the auction. Hence:

$k(\theta) = (k_0(\theta), k_{id_1}(\theta), \ldots, k_{id_m}(\theta))$, where $k_{id_i}(\theta) \subseteq A$.

$t(\theta) = (t_0(\theta), t_{id_1}(\theta), \ldots, t_{id_m}(\theta))$, where $t_0(\theta), t_{id_i}(\theta) \in \mathbf{R}$,

where $\mathbf{R}$ is the set of real numbers. Here, $t_0(\theta)$ represents the revenue of the auctioneer and $-t_{id_i}(\theta)$ represents the payment of id_i. Here, $k_0(\theta)$ represents the unallocated items.

We assume the following constraints are satisfied.

Allocation feasibility constraints: *For all $i \neq j$, $k_{id_i}(\theta) \cap k_{id_j}(\theta) = \emptyset$, $k_{id_i}(\theta) \cap k_0(\theta) = \emptyset$,*

and $k_{id_j}(\theta) \cap k_0(\theta) = \emptyset$. Also, $\bigcup_{i=1}^{m} k_{id_i}(\theta) \cup k_0(\theta) = A$.

Budget constraint: $t_0(\theta) = - \sum\limits_{1 \leq i \leq m} t_{id_i}(\theta)$.

Nonparticipation constraint: *For all i, if $\theta_{id_i} = 0$, then $k_{id_i}(\theta) = \emptyset$ and $t_{id_i}(\theta) = 0$.*

Also, in an almost anonymous mechanism, we assume for the cases of ties, the following condition is satisfied:

For a declared type profile $\theta = (\theta_{id_1}, \theta_{id_2}, \ldots, \theta_{id_m})$, if $\theta_{id_i} = \theta_{id_j}$, then $v(k_{id_i}(\theta), \theta_{id_i}) + t_{id_i}(\theta) = v(k_{id_j}(\theta), \theta_{id_j}) + t_{id_j}(\theta)$ holds.

We define the fact that an allocation function is Pareto (or ex post) efficient as follows.

Definition 7.4 An allocation function $k(\cdot)$ is *Pareto efficient* if for all $k = (k_0, k_{id_1}, \ldots, k_{id_m})$, which satisfies the allocation feasibility constraints,

$$\sum\limits_{1 \leq i \leq m} v(k_{id_i}(\theta), \theta_{id_i}) \geq \sum\limits_{1 \leq i \leq m} v(k_{id_i}, \theta_{id_i})$$

holds. Let us denote a Pareto efficient allocation function as $k^*(\cdot)$.

A strategy of a bidder is defined as follows.

Definition 7.5 A strategy s of bidder i is a function $s : T \to (\Theta \cup \{0\})^M$ such that $s(\theta_i, \phi(i)) \in (\Theta \cup \{0\})^{|\phi(i)|}$ for every $(\theta_i, \phi(i)) \in T$. That is, $s(\theta_i, \phi(i)) = (\theta_{i,1}, \ldots, \theta_{i,m_i})$, where $\theta_{i,j} \in \Theta \cup \{0\}$ and $|\phi(i)| = m_i$.

We denote a profile of types for identifiers $M \backslash \phi(i)$ as $\theta_{\sim i}$. Also, we denote a profile of types for $\phi(i)$ declared by bidder i as $(\theta_{i,1}, \ldots, \theta_{i,m_i})$. Also, we denote a combination of these two type profiles as $((\theta_{i,1}, \ldots, \theta_{i,m_i}), \theta_{\sim i})$.

When a declared type profile is $\theta = ((\theta_{i,1}, \ldots, \theta_{i,m_i}), \theta_{\sim i})$, the utility of bidder i is represented as $v(sk_i(\theta), \theta_i) + st_i(\theta)$, where $sk_i(\theta) = \bigcup_{id_j \in \phi(i)} k_{id_j}(\theta)$ and $st_i(\theta) = \sum_{id_j \in \phi(i)} t_{id_j}(\theta)$.
We define a (weakly) dominant strategy of bidder i as follows.

Definition 7.6 For bidder i, a strategy $s^*(\theta_i, \phi(i)) = (s^*_{i,1}, \ldots, s^*_{i,m_i})$ is a *dominant strategy* if for all type profiles $\theta_{\sim i}$, $(\theta_{i,1}, \ldots, \theta_{i,m_i})$, where $\theta = ((s^*_{i,1}, \ldots, s^*_{i,m_i}), \theta_{\sim i})$, $\theta' = ((\theta'_{i,1}, \ldots, \theta'_{i,m_i}), \theta_{\sim i})$, $v(sk_i(\theta), \theta_i) + st_i(\theta) \geq v(sk_i(\theta'), \theta_i) + st_i(\theta')$ holds.

7.2.2 Definition of Pseudonymous-Bid-Proof Protocols and the Revelation Principle

In a traditional setting where there exists no pseudonymous bid, we say a direct revelation mechanism is truthfully implementable (in dominant strategies) or strategy-proof, when truthfully declaring his type is a dominant strategy for each bidder (Mas-Colell,

Whinston, and Green 1995). By contrast, in the problem setting in this chapter, each bidder can submit multiple types in a mechanism. We define a pseudonymous-bid-proof mechanism/protocol (or a truthfully implementable mechanism/protocol in dominant strategies with the possibility of pseudonymous bids) as follows.

Definition 7.7 We say a mechanism is *pseudonymous-bid-proof* when for all bidders i, $s^*(\theta_i, \phi(i)) = (\theta_i, 0, \ldots, 0)$ is a dominant strategy.

Because we assume a protocol/mechanism is almost anonymous, we can assume without loss of generality that each bidder uses only the first identifier.

Bidder i can declare $(0, \ldots, 0)$, that is, nonparticipation in the auction. In this case, the utility of i becomes 0. Therefore, our definition that a mechanism is pseudonymous-bid-proof includes *individual rationality* (or *participation constraint*), which requires that the utility of each bidder must be nonnegative.

In a traditional setting without pseudonymous bids, the revelation principle holds that if there exists a mechanism that implements a social choice function f in dominant strategies, then f is truthfully implementable. In other words, without loss of generality we can restrict our attention to strategy-proof mechanisms. In the rest of this section, we discuss the meaning of the revelation principle when pseudonymous declarations are possible.

When pseudonymous bids are possible, the private information of each bidder is not only his type that determines the evaluation values of goods, but also a set of his identifiers $\phi(i)$. Therefore, in general, a direct revelation mechanism needs to ask not only a type, but also a set of identifiers a participant can use.

Formally, in a general mechanism, a social choice x is chosen from a set of alternatives X. We can assume a social choice function takes a set of pairs, where each pair consists of a type of each participant and a set of identifiers he can use and return a selected social choice, that is, $f(\{(\theta_1, \phi(1)), \ldots, (\theta_n, \phi(n))\}) = x$.

It is rather straightforward to show that the revelation principle holds for such a social choice function. The revelation principle holds in a general mechanism, which is not necessarily almost anonymous.

Also, if we assume a mechanism is almost anonymous, there is no difference among identifiers, thus only the number of identifiers $m_i = |\phi(i)|$ affects the social choice. Furthermore, if we assume the social choice function f is invariant to the number of identifiers a participant can use, we can omit the declarations of identifiers. In this case, because the outcome of the direct mechanism does not rely on the identities, the mechanism in which bidders report types but not identifiers is strategically equivalent to the direct revelation mechanism, so truthful reporting of types is again a dominant strategy. Thus, the revelation principle holds for a mechanism introduced in this section, which asks only a type of each participant and does not ask a set of identifiers.

7.3   Vickrey-Clarke-Groves (VCG) Mechanism and Pseudonymous Bidding

7.3.1   Vulnerability of VCG Mechanism

In this section, we first examine the effect of pseudonymous bids in the Vickrey-Clarke-Groves (VCG) mechanism.

The Vickrey-Clarke-Groves (VCG) mechanism (see chapter 1 of this volume), also called the Generalized Vickrey Auction Protocol (Varian 1995), is defined as follows. For notational simplicity, we sometimes omit the subscript of an allocation when the meaning is obvious—for example, we use $v(k^*(\theta), \theta_{id_j})$ to represent $v(k^*_{id_j}(\theta), \theta_{id_j})$.

Definition 7.8   In the VCG mechanism, $k^*(\cdot)$ is used for determining the allocation, and the transfer function is determined as follows.

$$t_{id_i}(\theta) = \left[\sum_{j \neq i} v(k^*(\theta), \theta_{id_j})\right] - \left[\sum_{j \neq i} v(k^*_{-id_i}(\theta), \theta_{id_j})\right]$$

where $k^*_{-id_i}(\theta)$ is an allocation k that maximizes $\sum_{j \neq i} v(k_{id_j}, \theta_{id_j})$.

In short, in the VCG mechanism, each bidder is required to pay the decreased amount of the surplus, that is, the sum of the gross utilities, of other bidders caused by his participation.

We describe how the VCG mechanism works in the following example.

Example 7.1   Three bidders (bidder 1, bidder 2, and bidder 3) are bidding for two goods, a_1 and a_2. The evaluation values of a bidder are represented as a triplet (the evaluation value for good a_1 only, the evaluation value for good a_2 only, the evaluation value for both a_1 and a_2):

- bidder 1: $(7, 0, 7)$
- bidder 2: $(0, 0, 12)$
- bidder 3: $(0, 7, 7)$.

We assume there are four identifiers. Bidder 1 can use two identifiers, whereas bidders 2 and 3 can use only one identifier. If each bidder declares his true type using a single identifier, bidder 1 and bidder 3 will receive good a_1 and good a_2, respectively. The payment of bidder 1 is calculated as $12 - 7 = 5$, because the sum of the gross utilities of other bidders when bidder 1 participates is 7, whereas the sum of the gross utilities of other bidders when bidder 1 does not participate would be 12. Bidder 3's payment is also equal to 5.

If there are no pseudonymous bids, the VCG mechanism is strategy proof: for each bidder, truthfully revealing his type is a dominant strategy. Now, we show an example where the VCG mechanism is not pseudonymous-bid-proof.

Example 7.2 Assume the same setting as the previous example, but the evaluation values of bidder 1 are different and bidder 3 is not interested in the auction.

- bidder 1: $(7, 7, 14)$
- bidder 2: $(0, 0, 12)$
- bidder 3: $(0, 0, 0)$.

In this case, if bidder 1 uses a single identifier, he can obtain both goods, and the payment is equal to 12. However, bidder 1 can create the situation basically identical to example 7.1 by using another identifier and splitting his bid. In this case, the payment becomes $5 + 5 = 10$. Therefore, for bidder 1, using a pseudonymous bid is profitable.

7.3.2 Impossibility of Pareto Efficient Pseudonymous-Bid-Proof Protocols

We showed that the VCG is vulnerable against pseudonymous-bid manipulations. The next question is, is it possible to construct a mechanism that is pseudonymous-bid-proof and Pareto efficient, either by modifying the VCG or by using completely different ideas? The following proposition is a non-existence theorem that provides a negative answer to this question.

Proposition 7.1 In combinatorial auctions, there exists no pseudonymous-bid-proof auction protocol that satisfies Pareto efficiency.

Proof We will prove the proposition by presenting a generic counter-example assuming there exists a pseudonymous-bid-proof, Pareto efficient protocol.

Let us assume that there are two goods, a_1 and a_2, and three bidders, denoted by bidder 1, bidder 2, and bidder 3. The evaluation values of a bidder are represented as a triplet: the evaluation value for good a_1 only, the evaluation value for good a_2 only, the evaluation value for both a_1 and a_2. We assume there are four identifiers. Bidder 1 can use two identifiers, whereas bidders 2 and 3 can use only one identifier.

- bidder 1: $(b, 0, b)$
- bidder 2: $(0, 0, b + c)$
- bidder 3: $(0, b, b)$.

Let us assume $b > c$. According to Pareto efficiency, bidder 1 gets good a_1 and bidder 3 gets good a_2. Let p_b denote the payment of bidder 1.

If bidder 1 declares his evaluation value for good a_1 as $b' = c + \varepsilon$, the allocation does not change. Let $p_{b'}$ denote bidder 1's payment in this situation. The inequality $p_{b'} \leq b'$ should hold; otherwise, if bidder 1's true evaluation value for good a_1 were b', truth telling would not be a dominant strategy because bidder 1 is not willing to participate if $p_{b'} > b'$. Furthermore, because truth telling is a dominant strategy, $p_b \leq p_{b'}$ should hold. These assumptions lead to $p_b \leq c + \varepsilon$. The condition for bidder 3's payment is identical to that for bidder 1's payment.

Next, we assume another situation where bidder 3 is not interested in the auction:

- bidder 1: $(b, b, 2b)$
- bidder 2: $(0, 0, b + c)$
- bidder 3: $(0, 0, 0)$.

According to Pareto efficiency, both goods go to bidder 1. Let us denote the payment of bidder 1 by p_{2b}. If bidder 1 uses a pseudonymous bid and splits his bid, the same result as in the previous case can be obtained. Because the protocol is pseudonymous-bid-proof, the following inequality must hold, otherwise, bidder 1 can profit by using another identifier and splitting his bid: $p_{2b} \leq 2 \times p_b \leq 2c + 2\varepsilon$.

On the other hand, let us consider the following case:

- bidder 1: $(d, d, 2d)$
- bidder 2: $(0, 0, b + c)$
- bidder 3: $(0, 0, 0)$.

Let us assume $c + \varepsilon < d < b$, and $b + c > 2d$. According to Pareto efficiency, both goods go to bidder 2. Consequently, the utility of bidder 1 is 0. However, if bidder 1 declares his evaluation values as b, b, $2b$ instead of d, d, $2d$, both goods go to bidder 1 and the payment is $p_{2b} \leq 2c + 2\varepsilon$, which is smaller than $2d$, bidder 1's true evaluation value of these two goods. Therefore, bidder 1 can increase the utility by overstating his true evaluation values.

Thus, in combinatorial auctions, there exists no pseudonymous-bid-proof auction protocol that satisfies Pareto efficiency.   ∎

Note that proposition 7.1 holds in more general settings. The proof relies on the model defined in definition 7.2, but it does not require the assumption of free disposal. Also, the proof does not rely on the fact that the mechanism is almost anonymous.

Alternatively, proposition 7.1 can be derived using theorem 1.2 in chapter 1, which shows that, under weak assumptions, the VCG is the unique mechanism that is strategy proof, Pareto efficient, and has zero payments by losing bidders. Because a pseudonymous-bid-proof protocol must satisfy the nonparticipation constraint, losing bidders make no positive payments. Also, if a protocol is not strategy proof, it cannot be pseudonymous-bid-proof.

7.3.3   Condition Where VCG Becomes Pseudonymous-Bid-Proof

To derive a sufficient condition where the VCG mechanism is pseudonymous-bid-proof, we introduce the following function.

Definition 7.9 For a set of bidders and their types $Y = \{(y_1, \theta_{y_1}), (y_2, \theta_{y_2}), \ldots\}$ and a set of goods $B \subseteq A$, we define surplus function U as follows. Denote $K_{B,Y}$ as a set of feasible allocations of B to Y. Then:

$$U(B, Y) = \max_{k \in K_{B,Y}} \sum_{(y_i, \theta_{y_i}) \in Y} v(k_{y_i}, \theta_{y_i}).$$

In particular, for the set of all goods A, we abbreviate $U(A, Y)$ as $U_A(Y)$.

Definition 7.10 We say $U_A(\cdot)$ is bidder-submodular if for all sets of bidders X, X', Y, where $X \subseteq X'$, the following condition holds:

$$U_A(X \cup Y) - U_A(X) \geq U_A(X' \cup Y) - U_A(X').$$

This is equivalent to the fact that the coalition value function is *bidder submodular*, introduced in chapter 1. This condition is called *concavity* in Sakurai, Yokoo, and Matsubara 1999 and in Yokoo, Sakurai, and Matsubara 2000a, 2004.

The following proposition holds.[1]

Proposition 7.2 The VCG mechanism is pseudonymous-bid-proof if the following conditions are satisfied.

- Θ satisfies that $U_A(\cdot)$ is bidder submodular for all bidders with types in Θ.
- Each declared type is in $\Theta \cup \{0\}$.

The second condition, that is, the declared (not necessarily true) type also must be in $\Theta \cup \{0\}$, is required by the following reason. Even if bidders' true types satisfy the bidder-submodularity condition, if bidder i declares a false type so that the bidder-submodularity condition is violated (although doing so is not rational for bidder i), it is possible that using pseudonymous bids is profitable for another bidder j.

To prove proposition 2, we first prove the following proposition.

Proposition 7.3 Assume $U_A(\cdot)$ is bidder submodular and the declared types also satisfy the bidder-submodular condition. Then, if a bidder uses two identifiers, the bidder can obtain more (or the same) utility by using a single identifier.

Proof Assume bidder 1 can use two identities id_1 and id_2. Also, let us assume bidder 1 declares type θ_{id_1} for id_1 and type θ_{id_2} for id_2.

Let us represent a type profile $\theta = (\theta_{id_1}, \theta_{id_2}, \theta_{id_3}, \ldots, \theta_{id_m})$, where $\theta_{id_1}, \theta_{id_2}, \theta_{id_3}, \ldots, \theta_{id_m}$ are declared types.

The monetary transfer received by bidder 1 is the sum of:

$$t_{id_1}(\theta) = \left[\sum_{j \neq 1} v(k^*(\theta), \theta_{id_j})\right] - \left[\sum_{j \neq 1} v(k^*_{-id_1}(\theta), \theta_{id_j})\right]$$

and

$$t_{id_2}(\theta) = \left[\sum_{j \neq 2} v(k^*(\theta), \theta_{id_j})\right] - \left[\sum_{j \neq 2} v(k^*_{-id_2}(\theta), \theta_{id_j})\right].$$

Now, let us assume that bidder 1 uses only a single identifier id_1, and declares his type as θ'_{id_1}, so that the following condition is satisfied for all bundle B:

$$v(B, \theta'_{id_1}) = v(B, \theta_{id_1}) + v(B, \theta_{id_2}).$$

Now, the declared type profile is $\theta' = (\theta'_{id_1}, 0, \theta_{id_3}, \ldots, \theta_{id_m})$.

Obviously, $k^*_{id1}(\theta) \cup k^*_{id2}(\theta) = k^*_{id1}(\theta')$ holds; that is, the goods bidder 1 obtains do not change.

The monetary transfer received by bidder 1 is:

$$t_{id_1}(\theta') = \left[\sum_{j \neq 1} v(k^*(\theta'), \theta_{id_j})\right] - \left[\sum_{j \neq 1} v(k^*_{-id_1}(\theta'), \theta_{id_j})\right].$$

We are going to prove that $t_{id_1}(\theta') \geq t_{id_1}(\theta) + t_{id_2}(\theta)$, that is, the monetary transfer becomes larger when bidder 1 uses one identifier.

Let us denote $Y = \{(id_3, \theta_{id_3}), \ldots, (id_m, \theta_{id_m})\}$.

$$t_{id_1}(\theta') - t_{id_1}(\theta) - t_{id_2}(\theta)$$

$$= \left[\sum_{j \neq 1} v(k^*(\theta'), \theta_{id_j})\right] - \left[\sum_{j \neq 1} v(k^*_{-id_1}(\theta'), \theta_{id_j})\right]$$

$$- \left(\left[\sum_{j \neq 1} v(k^*(\theta), \theta_{id_j})\right] - \left[\sum_{j \neq 1} v(k^*_{-id_1}(\theta), \theta_{id_j})\right]\right)$$

$$- \left(\left[\sum_{j \neq 2} v(k^*(\theta), \theta_{id_j})\right] - \left[\sum_{j \neq 2} v(k^*_{-id_2}(\theta), \theta_{id_j})\right]\right)$$

$$= U_A(Y \cup \{(id_1, \theta_{id_1}), (id_2, \theta_{id_2})\}) - v(k^*(\theta), \theta_{id_1}) - v(k^*(\theta), \theta_{id_2})$$

$$- U_A(Y) - (U_A(Y \cup \{(id_1, \theta_{id_1}), (id_2, \theta_{id_2})\}) - v(k^*(\theta), \theta_{id_1}))$$

$$+ U_A(Y \cup \{(id_2, \theta_{id_2})\}) - (U_A(Y \cup \{(id_1, \theta_{id_1}), (id_2, \theta_{id_2})\}) - v(k^*(\theta), \theta_{id_2}))$$

$$+ U_A(Y \cup \{(id_1, \theta_{id_1})\})$$

$$= U_A(Y \cup \{(id_1, \theta_{id_1})\}) + U_A(Y \cup \{(id_2, \theta_{id_2})\})$$

$$- U_A(Y) - U_A(Y \cup \{(id_1, \theta_{id_1}), (id_2, \theta_{id_2})\}).$$

By the bidder-submodular condition, the following formula is satisfied:

$$U_A(Y \cup \{(id_1, \theta_{id_1}), (id_2, \theta_{id_2})\}) - U_A(Y \cup \{(id_1, \theta_{id_1})\}) \leq U_A(Y \cup \{(id_2, \theta_{id_2})\}) - U_A(Y).$$

By transposition, we obtain:

$$0 \leq U_A(Y \cup \{(id_1, \theta_{id_1})\}) + U_A(Y \cup \{(id_2, \theta_{id_2})\}) - U_A(Y) - U_A(Y \cup \{(id_1, \theta_{id_1}), (id_2, \theta_{id_2})\}).$$

Therefore, we obtain:

$$t_{id_1}(\theta') \geq t_{id_1}(\theta) + t_{id_2}(\theta). \qquad \blacksquare$$

By repeatedly applying proposition 7.3, we can show that if a bidder is using more than two identities, he can obtain more (or the same) utility by using a single identifier.

Now, let us examine the meanings of the bidder-submodularity condition. First, we show one sufficient condition for U_A being bidder-submodular, that is, the gross substitutes condition. The definition of this condition is as follows (Gul and Stacchetti 1999; Kelso and Crawford 1982).

Definition 7.11   Given a price vector $p = (p_{a_1}, \ldots, p_{a_l})$, we denote

$$D_i(p) = \left\{ B \subset A : v(B, \theta_i) - \sum_{a_j \in B} p_{a_j} \geq v(C, \theta_i) - \sum_{a_j \in C} p_{a_j}, \forall C \subset A \right\}.$$

$D_i(p)$ represents the collection of bundles that maximize the net utility of bidder i under price vector p. Then, we say that the gross substitutes condition is satisfied, if for any two price vectors p and p' such that $p' \geq p$, $p'_{a_j} = p_{a_j}$, and $a_j \in B \in D_i(p)$, then there exists $B' \in D_i(p')$ such that $a_j \in B'$.

In short, the gross substitutes condition states that if good a_j is demanded with price vector p, it is still demanded if the price of a_j remains the same, whereas the prices of some other goods increase. The key property that makes the gross substitutes condition so convenient is that in an auction that satisfies the gross substitutes condition, Walrasian equilibria exist (Kelso and Crawford 1982).

One special case where the gross substitutes condition holds is a multi-unit auction (i.e., in which multiple units of an identical good are auctioned) in which the marginal utility of each unit is constant or diminishes.

Instead of showing directly the fact that the gross substitutes condition implies bidder submodular, we introduce another sufficient condition called submodularity over goods.

We define U to be *submodular over goods* for a set of bidders as follows.

Definition 7.12 We say U is submodular over goods for a set of bidders X, if the following condition is satisfied for all sets $B \subseteq A$ and $C \subseteq A$:

$$U(B,X) + U(C,X) \geq U(B \cup C, X) + U(B \cap C, X).$$

The following proposition holds.

Proposition 7.4 If U is submodular over goods for all set of bidders $X \subseteq N$, then U_A is bidder submodular.

Proof Let us choose three mutually exclusive subsets of bidders Y, Z', W. Also, let us assume in an allocation that maximizes $U(A, Y \cup Z' \cup W)$, that B_Y, $B_{Z'}$, and B_W are allocated to Y, Z', and W, respectively. Because we assume free disposal, we can assume $A = B_Y \cup B_{Z'} \cup B_W$, that is, that each good is allocated to some bidder. The following formula holds:

$$U(A, Y \cup Z' \cup W) = U(B_Y, Y) + U(B_{Z'}, Z') + U(B_W, W).$$

Also, the following formula holds:

$$U(A, Y \cup W) \geq U(B_Y \cup B_{Z'}, Y) + U(B_W, W).$$

The right side represents the surplus when allocating $B_Y \cup B_{Z'}$ to bidders Y and B_W to bidders W. This inequality holds because the left side is the surplus of the best allocation including this particular allocation.

Similarly, the following formula holds:

$$U(A, Y \cup Z') \geq U(B_Y \cup B_W, Y) + U(B_{Z'}, Z').$$

By adding these two formulae, we obtain the following formula:

$$U(A, Y \cup W) + U(A, Y \cup Z')$$
$$\geq U(B_Y \cup B_{Z'}, Y) + U(B_Y \cup B_W, Y) + U(B_{Z'}, Z') + U(B_W, W).$$

From the fact U is submodular over goods, the following formula holds:

$$U(B_Y \cup B_{Z'}, Y) + U(B_Y \cup B_W, Y) \geq U(A, Y) + U(B_Y, Y).$$

From these formulae, we obtain the following formula:

$$U(A, Y \cup W) + U(A, Y \cup Z')$$
$$\geq U(A, Y) + U(B_Y, Y) + U(B_{Z'}, Z') + U(B_W, W)$$
$$\geq U(A, Y) + U(A, Y \cup Z' \cup W).$$

By setting $Z = Y \cup Z'$, we get $U_A(Z \cup W) - U_A(Z) \leq U_A(Y \cup W) - U_A(Y)$. ∎

The condition that U is submodular over goods can be considered as a kind of a "necessary" condition for U_A to be bidder-submodular, and so the following proposition holds.

Proposition 7.5 If U is not submodular over goods for a set of bidders X and a set of goods B and C, that is, $U(B,X) + U(C,X) < U(B \cup C, X) + U(B \cap C, X)$, then we can create a situation where for a set of bidders Y, although U is submodular over goods for Y, U_A is not bidder submodular for $X \cup Y$, where $A = B \cup C$.

Proof We assume for a set of bidders X and a set of goods B and C, where $B \cup C = A$, and $U(B,X) + U(C,X) < U(B \cup C, X) + U(B \cap C, X)$ holds.

Let us assume for each good $a_i \in A \backslash B$, there exists bidder $i \notin X$, who is interested in only a_i, and his evaluation value for a_i is larger than $U(A, X)$. Let us denote a set of these bidders as W. Similarly, let us assume for each good $a_j \in A \backslash C$, there exists bidder $j \notin X$, who is interested in only a_j, and his evaluation value for a_j is larger than $U(A, X)$. Let us denote a set of these bidders as Z. It is clear that U is submodular over goods for $W \cup Z$, because these bidders are *unit demand consumers*, and satisfies the gross substitutes condition (Gul and Stacchetti 1999).

It is clear that in the allocation that maximizes $U_A(X \cup W \cup Z)$, $A \backslash B$ are allocated to bidders in W, $A \backslash C$ are allocated to bidders in Z, and $B \cap C$ are allocated to bidders in X.

Also, for $X \cup W$, it is clear that in the allocation that maximizes $U_A(X \cup W)$, $A \backslash B$ are allocated to bidders in W, and B are allocated to bidders in X. Similarly, in the allocation that maximizes $U_A(X \cup Z)$, $A \backslash C$ are allocated to bidders in Z, and C are allocated to bidders in X.

Thus, the following formulae hold:

$$U_A(X \cup W) = U(A \backslash B, W) + U(B, X)$$

$$U_A(X \cup Z) = U(A \backslash C, Z) + U(C, X)$$

$$U_A(X \cup W \cup Z) = U(A \backslash B, W) + U(A \backslash C, Z) + U(B \cap C, X).$$

From these formulae and the assumption $U(B,X) + U(C,X) < U(B \cup C, X) + U(B \cap C, X)$, the following formula holds:

$$U_A(X \cup W) + U_A(X \cup Z)$$

$$= U(A \backslash B, W) + U(B, X) + U(A \backslash C, Z) + U(C, X)$$

$$= U_A(X \cup W \cup Z) - U(B \cap C, X) + U(B, X) + U(C, X)$$

$$< U_A(X \cup W \cup Z) + U(B \cup C, X)$$

$$= U_A(X \cup W \cup Z) + U_A(X).$$

Thus, the bidder-submodular condition is violated because $U_A(X \cup W) - U_A(X) < U_A(X \cup Z \cup W) - U_A(X \cup Z)$.
∎

This proposition is similar to theorem 1.9 in chapter 1, which shows that if the possible bidder valuations include additive valuations, then the gross-substitute condition is necessary to guarantee bidder submodularity.

Note that the fact that U is not submodular over goods for some set of bidders X does not necessarily mean that the bidder-submodular condition will be violated for all situations that involve a set of bidders X. For example, if all bidders have all-or-nothing evaluation values for goods a_1 and a_2, where for all i, $v(\{a_1\}, \theta_i) = v(\{a_2\}, \theta_i) = 0$, whereas $v(\{a_1, a_2\}, \theta_i) > 0$, clearly, U is not submodular over goods, but we can create a situation where U_A is bidder submodular.

Gul and Stacchetti (1999) show that if the evaluation value v for each bidder satisfies the gross substitutes condition and monotonicity, then the surplus function U is submodular. Therefore, if the evaluation value v for each bidder satisfies the gross substitutes condition and monotonicity, which is satisfied if we assume free disposal, then U_A is bidder submodular. Also, theorem 1.8 in chapter 1 shows that the gross substitutes condition implies bidder submodular. As a result, the VCG mechanism is pseudonymous-bid-proof if the gross substitutes condition is satisfied.

Note that as Gul and Stacchetti (1999) show, even if the evaluation value v for each bidder is submodular, this is not sufficient to guarantee that U is submodular over goods.

7.4   Design of Pseudonymous-Bid-Proof Protocol

In this section, we present a pseudonymous-bid-proof protocol called the Leveled Division Set (LDS) protocol (Yokoo, Sakurai, and Matsubara 2001b).

7.4.1   Basic Ideas

There exists a rather trivial protocol that is pseudonymous-bid-proof: selling all goods in one bundle and using the second price sealed-bid auction protocol to determine the winner and his payment. We call this simple protocol the *set protocol*. Clearly, this protocol is pseudonymous-bid-proof, as only one bidder can receive goods and submitting additional bids only increases the payment of the winner.

Selling goods in one bundle makes sense if all goods are complementary for all bidders; the utility of a set of goods is larger than the sum of the utilities of having each good separately. However, if goods are substitutable for some bidders, that is, if the utility of a set of goods is smaller than the sum of the utilities of having each good separately, the set protocol is wasteful; the social surplus and the revenue of the seller can be significantly worse than that for the VCG.

Let us consider a simple case where there are two goods a_1 and a_2. To increase the social surplus, we must design a protocol where goods can be sold separately in some cases. To guarantee that the protocol is pseudonymous-bid-proof, the following condition must be satisfied.

Necessary condition   If a_1 and a_2 are sold separately to different bidders, then the sum of the payments must be larger than the highest declared evaluation value for the set of a_1 and a_2.

This is a necessary (but not sufficient) condition to guarantee pseudonymous-bid-proofness; if this condition is not satisfied, there is a chance that a single bidder is using two pseudonyms to obtain these goods. However, designing a pseudonymous-bid-proof protocol satisfying this condition is not easy. For example, the following simple protocol is not pseudonymous-bid-proof.

Vulnerable protocol   Determine tentative winners and payments using the VCG. If a_1 and a_2 are sold separately to different bidders, and the sum of the payments does not satisfy the necessary condition, then sell the goods in one bundle, otherwise, use the results of the VCG.

Assume the situation in example 7.1. Because the result of the VCG does not satisfy the necessary condition, both goods are sold to bidder 2. However, bidder 1 can create the following situation using pseudonyms 4 and 5.

- bidder 1: $(7, 0, 7)$
- bidder 2: $(0, 0, 12)$
- bidder 3: $(0, 7, 7)$
- bidder 4: $(5.2, 0, 5.2)$
- bidder 5: $(0, 6.9, 6.9)$.

In this case, using the VCG, a_1 is allocated to bidder 1 and a_2 is allocated to bidder 3, and bidder 1 pays 5.2 and bidder 3 pays 6.9; thus the necessary condition is satisfied. Clearly, bidder 1 prefers this result because he can obtain a_1 by paying 5.2 and his utility becomes $7 - 5.2 = 1.8$, whereas bidder 1 cannot obtain any good when he does not submit pseudonymous bids.

As this example shows, if a bidder can submit pseudonymous bids, then it is rather easy to manipulate the payments of other bidders. In this case, bidder 1 manipulates the result by forcing bidder 3 to pay more by submitting a pseudonymous bid. In essence, we must solve the difficult dilemma of satisfying the above condition on payments without using the second highest evaluation values, which are essential to calculating the payments.

We can solve this dilemma by utilizing *reservation prices* of goods: the seller does not sell a good if the payment for the good is smaller than the reservation price. Let us assume the reservation prices of a_1 and a_2 are r_1 and r_2, respectively. In this protocol, we sell goods separately only when the highest declared evaluation value for the set is smaller than $r_1 + r_2$. Also, the payment for each good is always larger than or equal to the reservation price. Clearly, this protocol satisfies the necessary condition. In the following, we will show how this idea can be introduced into the VCG.

7.4.2 Specification of Leveled Division Set (LDS) Protocol

We first show the sketch of the Leveled Division Set (LDS) protocol. In the LDS protocol, the auctioneer determines a leveled division set (table 7.1). This leveled division set describes the possible way for dividing goods among different bidders. In level 1, all goods are sold in one bundle. Goods are divided into smaller bundles as the level increases. The auctioneer chooses the level according to the declared evaluation values of bidders, then uses the VCG within the level to determine the winners and payments.

In the following, we are going to define several terms and notations. To aid readability, we use two different types of parentheses, ( ) and { }, to represent sets.

- Define a division, which is a set of bundles, $D = \{B | B \subseteq A\}$, where $\forall B, B' \in D$ and $B \neq B'$, $B \cap B' = \emptyset$ holds.[2]
- For each good a_j, the reservation price r_j is defined.
- For a bundle B, we define $R(B)$ as $\sum_{a_j \in B} r_j$.

A *leveled division set* is defined as follows:[3]

- Levels are defined as $1, 2, \ldots, max\_level$.
- For each level i, a division D_i is defined.

A leveled division set must satisfy the following three conditions:

- $D_1 = \{A\}$—the division of level 1 consists of a bundle of all goods.
- For each level and its division, a union of multiple bundles in a division is always included in a division of a smaller level, i.e., $\forall i > 1$, $\forall D' \subseteq D_i$, where $|D'| \geq 2$, $B_u = \bigcup_{B \in D'} B$, then there exists a level $j < i$, with a division D_j, where $B_u \in D_j$.
- For each level and its division, each bundle in a division is not included in a division of a different level,[4] i.e., $\forall i, \forall B \in D_i, \forall j \neq i, B \notin D_j$.

Table 7.1

Examples of leveled division sets

	instance 1	instance 2	instance 3
level 1	$\{(a_1, a_2)\}$	$\{(a_1, a_2, a_3)\}$	$\{(a_1, a_2, a_3, a_4)\}$
level 2	$\{(a_1), (a_2)\}$	$\{(a_1, a_2)\}$	$\{(a_1, a_2, a_3)\}$
level 3		$\{(a_2, a_3)\}$	$\{(a_2, a_3, a_4)\}$
level 4		$\{(a_1, a_3)\}$	$\{(a_1, a_4)\}$
level 5		$\{(a_1), (a_2), (a_3)\}$	$\{(a_1), (a_4), (a_2, a_3)\}$

Figure 7.1 shows examples of leveled division sets. Instance 1 shows one instance where there are two goods (a_1 and a_2), and instance 2 and instance 3 show instances where there are three and four goods, respectively.

In the following, let us assume agent 0 is a *dummy bidder*, whose evaluation value of the good a_j is equal to the reservation price r_j. For a division $D = \{B_1, B_2, \ldots\}$ and one feasible allocation of goods $k = (k_{id_1}, k_{id_2}, \ldots, k_{id_m})$, we say k is allowed under D if the following conditions are satisfied:

1. Multiple goods that belong to the same bundle in a division must be allocated to the same bidder, i.e., $\forall B \in D$, $\forall a_i, a_{i'} \in B$, if $a_i \in k_{id_j}$, then $a_{i'} \in k_{id_j}$ holds.
2. If two goods belong to different bundles in a division, they must be allocated to different bidders, except for the case where they are allocated to the dummy bidder 0, i.e., $\forall B, B' \in D$, where $B \neq B'$, $\forall a_i \in B$, $\forall a_{i'} \in B'$, either $a_i \in k_{id_j}$, $a_{i'} \in k_{id_{j'}}$, where $id_j \neq id_{j'}$, or $a_i \in k_0$, $a_{i'} \in k_0$ holds.
3. If a good does not belong to any bundle in the division, it must be allocated to the dummy bidder 0, i.e., $\forall a_i$, if $\forall B \in D$, $a_i \notin B$ holds, then $a_i \in k_0$.

Note that we allow the case where some bundle is allocated to the dummy bidder 0.

Also, we define *allowed allocations* in level i (denoted as K_i) as a set of allocations that are allowed under D_i.

To execute the LDS protocol, the auctioneer must predefine the leveled division set and the reservation prices of goods. Let us assume for identifier x, the declared (not necessarily true) type is θ_x. We assume that for the dummy bidder 0, $v(B, \theta_0) = R(B)$ holds.

To search the level in which goods should be sold, the auctioneer calls the procedure LDS(1). LDS(i) is a recursive procedure defined as follows, which returns the pair of the allocation and transfer (k, t).

Procedure LDS(i)

Case 1 If there exists exactly one bidder $x \in N$ whose evaluation values satisfy the following condition: $\exists B_x \in D_i$, where $v(B_x, \theta_x) \geq R(B_x)$,

then let $(k^i, t^i) \leftarrow \text{VCG}(i)$ and $(k^{i+1}, t^{i+1}) \leftarrow \text{LDS}(i+1)$,
if $v(k_x^i, \theta_x) + t_x^i \geq v(k_x^{i+1}, \theta_x) + t_x^{i+1}$,
then return (k^i, t^i),
else return (k', t'), where $k_x' = k_x^{i+1}$, $t_x' = t_x^{i+1}$, $k_0' = A \backslash k_x^{i+1}$,
$t_0' = -t_x^{i+1}$, for $y \neq 0 \wedge y \neq x$, $k_y' = \emptyset$, $t_y' = 0$. **end if; end if;**

Case 2 If there exist at least two bidders $x_1, x_2 \in N$, $x_1 \neq x_2$ whose evaluation values satisfy the following condition:

$\exists B_{x_1} \in D_i$, $\exists B_{x_2} \in D_i$, where $v(B_{x_1}, \theta_{x_1}) \geq R(B_{x_1})$,
$v(B_{x_2}, \theta_{x_2}) \geq R(B_{x_2})$,
then return VCG(i). **end if;**

Case 3 otherwise:

if $i = max\_level$
then return (k, t), where $k_0 = A$, $t_0 = 0$, for $y \neq 0$, $k_y = \emptyset$, $t_y = 0$,
else return LDS($i + 1$). **end if;**

Procedure VCG(i) Choose an allocation $k^*(\theta) \in K_i$ such that it maximizes $\sum_{0 \leq y \leq m} v(k^*(\theta), \theta_y)$. The payment of bidder x (represented as p_x) is calculated as:

$$\left[\sum_{y \neq x} v(k^*(\theta), \theta_y) \right] - \left[\sum_{y \neq x} v(k^*_{-x}(\theta), \theta_y) \right]$$

where $k^*_{-x}(\theta) \in K_i$ is the allocation that maximizes the sum of all bidders' (including the dummy bidder 0) evaluation values except that of bidder x.

return (k^i, t^i), where for $1 \leq y \leq m$, $k^i_y = k^*_y(\theta)$, $t_y = -p_y$,
$k^i_0 = k^*_0(\theta)$, $t^i_0 = \sum_{1 \leq y \leq m} p_y$.

If case 1 is applied for bidder x, we say bidder x is a *pivotal* bidder. In this case, we compare the results obtained by the procedure VCG(i) and LDS($i + 1$), and choose the one that gives the larger utility for bidder x. When choosing the result of LDS($i + 1$), we do not assign any good, nor transfer money, to bidders other than x, although the assigned goods for bidder x and his payment are calculated as if goods were allocated to the other bidders.

Note that the procedures in VCG(i) are equivalent to those in the VCG, except that the possible allocations are restricted to K_i. We say that the *applied level* of the LDS protocol is i if the result of VCG(i) is used.

7.4.3 Examples of Protocol Application

Example 7.3 Let us assume there are two goods a_1 and a_2, the reservation price of each good is 50, the leveled division set is defined as instance 1 in Figure 7.1, and the evaluation values of bidders are defined as follows:

	a_1	a_2	a_1, a_2
bidder 1	80	0	110
bidder 2	0	80	105
bidder 3	60	0	60

Because there exist two bidders whose evaluation values for the set are larger than the sum of the reservation prices (i.e., 100), the condition in case 2 of LDS(1) is satisfied; bidder 1 obtains both goods by paying 105. Note that this allocation is not Pareto efficient. In the Pareto efficient allocation, bidder 1 obtains a_1 and bidder 2 obtains a_2.

Example 7.4 The problem setting is basically equivalent to example 7.3, but the evaluation values are defined as follows:

	a_1	a_2	a_1, a_2
bidder 1	80	0	80
bidder 2	0	80	80
bidder 3	60	0	60

There exists no bidder whose evaluation value of the set is larger than 100. In this case, the condition in case 3 of LDS(1) is satisfied, and then the condition in case 2 of LDS(2) is satisfied. As a result, bidder 1 obtains a_1 and bidder 2 obtains a_2. Bidder 1 pays 60, and bidder 2 pays the reservation price 50.

Example 7.5 The problem setting is basically equivalent to example 7.3, but the evaluation values are defined as follows:

	a_1	a_2	a_1, a_2
bidder 1	80	0	110
bidder 2	0	80	80
bidder 3	60	0	60

There exists only one bidder whose evaluation value of the set is larger than 100. The condition in case 1 of LDS(1) is satisfied; bidder 1 is the pivotal bidder. Bidder 1 prefers the result of LDS(2), obtaining only a_1 (with the payment 60), to the result of VCG(1), obtaining both a_1 and a_2 (with the payment 100). Therefore, bidder 1 obtains a_1 and pays 60.

Note that in example 7.5, a_2 is not allocated to any bidder. This might seem wasteful, but this is necessary to guarantee that the protocol is pseudonymous-bid-proof. In example 7.3, if bidder 2 declares his evaluation value for the set as 80, the situation becomes identical to example 7.5. If we allocate the remaining good a_2 to bidder 2, under-bidding becomes profitable for bidder 2.

Example 7.6 There are three goods a_1, a_2, and a_3. The reservation price for each is 50, and the leveled division set is defined as instance 2 in figure 7.1. The evaluation values of bidders are defined as follows:

	a_1	a_2	a_3	a_1, a_2	a_2, a_3	a_1, a_3	a_1, a_2, a_3
bidder 1	60	30	30	90	60	90	120
bidder 2	30	60	30	90	90	60	120
bidder 3	30	30	60	60	90	90	120

The condition in case 2 of LDS(5) is satisfied. Bidders 1, 2, 3 obtain a_1, a_2, a_3, respectively, and each pays the reservation price 50.

7.4.4 Proof of Pseudonymous-Bid-Proofness

We will prove the following proposition.

Proposition 7.6 The LDS protocol is pseudonymous-bid-proof.

To prove proposition 7.6, we use the following lemmas.

Lemma 7.1 In the LDS protocol, the payment of bidder x who obtains a bundle B is larger than (or equal to) the sum of the reservation prices $R(B)$.

The proof is as follows. Let us assume that the applied level is i. The payment of bidder x (represented as p_x) is defined as $p_x = [\sum_{y \neq x} v(k^*(\theta), \theta_y)] - [\sum_{y \neq x} v(k^*_{-x}(\theta), \theta_y)]$, where $k^*_{-x}(\theta) \in K_i$ is the allocation that maximizes the sum of all bidders' (including the dummy bidder 0) evaluation values except that of bidder x. The set of allocations K_i considered at level i contains an allocation k', which is basically the same as $k^*(\theta)$, but all goods in B (that are allocated to bidder x in k^*) are allocated to the dummy bidder 0 rather than x. The following formula holds:

$$\sum_{y \neq x} v(k', \theta_y) = \sum_{y \neq x} v(k^*(\theta), \theta_y) + R(B).$$

Because $k^*_{-x}(\theta)$ is the allocation that maximizes the sum of all bidders' evaluation values (including the dummy bidder) except x in K_i, $\sum_{y \neq x} v(k', \theta_y) \leq \sum_{y \neq x} v(k^*_{-x}(\theta), \theta_y)$ holds. Thus, the following formula holds:

$$p_x = \sum_{y \neq x} v(k^*_{-x}(\theta), \theta_y) - \sum_{y \neq x} v(k^*(\theta), \theta_y)$$

$$\geq \sum_{y \neq x} v(k', \theta_y) - \sum_{y \neq x} v(k^*(\theta), \theta_y) = R(B).$$

Lemma 7.2 In the LDS protocol, a bidder cannot increase his utility by submitting pseudonymous bids.

Proof Let us assume that bidder x uses two pseudonyms x' and x'' to obtain two bundles $B_{x'}$ and $B_{x''}$, respectively. Also, let us assume that the applied level is i. From lemma 7.1, the payments $p_{x'}$ and $p_{x''}$ satisfy $p_{x'} \geq R(B_{x'})$ and $p_{x''} \geq R(B_{x''})$. Now, let us assume that bidder x declares the evaluation value $R(B)$ for the bundle $B = B_{x'} \cup B_{x''}$ by using a single identifier. From the condition of a leveled division set, there exists a level $j < i$, where $B \in D_j$ holds. In this case, the condition in case 1 of LDS(j) is satisfied; that is, only bidder x declares evaluation values that are larger than or equal to the sum of reservation prices. Thus, $\sum_{y \neq x} v(k^*_{-x}(\theta), \theta_y) = R(A)$, and $\sum_{y \neq x} v(k^*(\theta), \theta_y) = R(A) - R(B)$ hold. As a result, the payment becomes $R(B) = R(B_{x'}) + R(B_{x''}) \leq p_{x'} + p_{x''}$, that is, the payment of bidder x becomes smaller than (or equal to) the case where bidder x uses two pseudonyms. Similarly, we can show that even when a bidder uses more than two identifiers, the payment of such a bidder would become smaller (or remain the same) if the bidder uses only one identifier.

Lemma 7.2 states that pseudonymous bids are not effective in the LDS protocol. Now, we are going to show that truth telling is the dominant strategy for each bidder assuming that each bidder uses a single identifier.

The following lemma holds.

Lemma 7.3 When there exists no pseudonymous bid, and the applied level of the LDS protocol remains the same, a bidder can maximize his utility by declaring his true type.

The proof is basically identical to the strategy-proofness of the VCG mechanism.

Next, we show that a bidder cannot increase his utility by changing the applied level.

Lemma 7.4 A bidder cannot increase his utility by over-bidding so that the applied level decreases.

The proof is as follows. Let us assume that when bidder x truthfully declares his type, the applied level is i, and by over-bidding, the applied level is changed to $j < i$. In that case, for each bundle B included in the division of level j, bidder x's evaluation value of B must be smaller than the sum of the reservation prices $R(B)$; otherwise, level j is applied when bidder x tells the truth. On the other hand, by lemma 7.1, the payment for a bundle B is always larger than the sum of the reservation prices $R(B)$, which means that bidder x cannot obtain a positive utility by over-bidding.

Lemma 7.5 A bidder cannot increase his utility by under-bidding so that the applied level increases.

The proof is as follows. Bidder x can increase the applied level only in the following two cases:

1. Bidder x is the pivotal bidder when bidder x truthfully declares his type.
2. By under-bidding, another bidder y becomes the pivotal bidder.

In the first case, let us assume if bidder x tells the truth, bidder x becomes the pivotal bidder at level i. Also, let us assume the applied level becomes $j > i$ when bidder x does under-bidding. If bidder x prefers the result of VCG(j) to VCG(i), then LDS($i + 1$) must return the result of VCG(j) in case 1 of LDS(i) when bidder x tells the truth. Therefore, under-bidding is meaningless. In the second case, bidders other than y cannot obtain any goods; the utility of bidder x becomes 0. In both cases, bidder x cannot increase his utility by under-bidding.

From these lemmas, we obtain proposition 7.6.   ■

When proving lemma 7.2, we use the second condition of the leveled division set, that is, a union of multiple bundles must appear in an earlier level. In other words, the leveled division set is constructed so that a bidder who is willing to buy larger bundles has a higher priority. Therefore, submitting pseudonymous bids and buying goods separately does not make sense at all.

7.4.5 Efficiency of LDS Protocol

In the LDS protocol, we can expect that the social surplus and the revenue of the seller can vary significantly according to the leveled division set and reservation prices. In this section, we show how the social surplus changes according to the reservation prices using a simulation in a simple setting where there are only two goods a_1 and a_2, and the leveled division set is defined as instance 1 in table 7.1.

We determine the evaluation values of bidder x by the following method.

• Determine whether the goods are substitutable or complementary for bidder x, i.e., with probability p, the goods are substitutable, and with probability $1 - p$, the goods are complementary.
• When the goods are substitutable: for each good, randomly choose his evaluation value from within the range of $[0, 1]$. The evaluation value of the set is the maximum of the evaluation value of a_1 and that of a_2 (having only one good is enough).
• When the goods are complementary: the evaluation value of a_1 or a_2 is 0. Randomly choose the evaluation value of the set from within the range of $[0, 2]$ (all-or-nothing).

Figure 7.1 shows the result where $p = 0.5$ and the number of bidders N is 10. We created 100 different problem instances and show the average of the social surplus by varying the reservation price. Both a_1 and a_2 have the same reservation price. For comparison, we show the social surplus of the VCG (assuming there exists no pseudo-

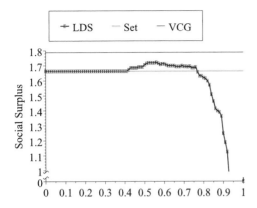

Figure 7.1
Comparison of social surplus ($p = 0.5$).

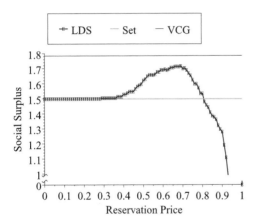

Figure 7.2
Comparison of social surplus ($p = 0.7$).

nymous bid), the Pareto efficient social surplus,[5] and the social surplus of the set proto-col. Figure 7.2 shows the result where $p = 0.7$.

When the reservation price is small, the results of the LDS protocol are identical to the set protocol. We can see that by setting an appropriate reservation price the obtained social surplus becomes larger than that for the set protocol. When the probability that the goods are substitutable becomes large, the difference between the set protocol and the VCG, and the difference between the set protocol and the LDS protocol also be-come large.

7.5 Discussion

As described in section 7.1, researchers have previously proposed a concept called *group-strategy-proof* to study another restricted subclass of general collusion. Group-strategy-proof and pseudonymous-bid-proof are independent concepts. We can show an example where a protocol is pseudonymous-bid-proof, but not group-strategy-proof.

Let there be two goods a_1 and a_2, and two bidders 1 and 2. We assume $\Theta = \{\theta_1, \theta_2, \theta_3, \theta_4\}$, where the evaluation values for these types are represented as follows:

- θ_1: $(10, 9, 18)$
- θ_2: $(9, 10, 18)$
- θ_3: $(10, 0, 10)$
- θ_4: $(0, 10, 10)$

Each of these types satisfies the gross substitutes condition, because when the number of goods is two, the fact that the evaluation value is subadditive, that is, $v(\{a_1\}, \theta_i) + v(\{a_2\}, \theta_i) \geq v(\{a_1, a_2\}, \theta_i)$, implies the gross substitutes condition (Kelso and Crawford 1982). Thus, as the previous section showed, the VCG mechanism is pseudonymous-bid-proof in this example.

However, the VCG mechanism is not group-strategy-proof. Let us assume the type of bidder 1 is θ_1 and the type of bidder 2 is θ_2. By truth telling, bidders 1 and 2 obtain a_1 and a_2, respectively, and each pays 8, thus the utility of each bidder is $10 - 8 = 2$. On the other hand, let us assume bidder 1 declares his type as θ_3 and bidder 2 declares his type as θ_4, in which both bidders understate their evaluation values of one good.

Then, the payment becomes 0, and the utility of each bidder becomes $10 - 0 = 10$. Thus, the utility of each bidder increases by deviating from truth telling, so the VCG mechanism is not group-strategy-proof in this case.

Next, let us show an example where a protocol is group-strategy-proof, but not pseudonymous-bid-proof. Let us assume an auction of a single item, single unit. Clearly, the following protocol is group-strategy-proof:[6]

- The auctioneer sets a reservation price p. The winner is chosen randomly from the bidders whose declared evaluation value is larger than p. The winner pays p.

However, this protocol is not pseudonymous-bid-proof. A bidder can increase his chance of winning by submitting multiple bids.

One shortcoming of the LDS protocol is that when the leveled division set and reservation prices are not determined appropriately, there is a chance that some goods cannot be sold. In that case, the social surplus and the revenue of the seller might be smaller than that for the set protocol. Yokoo, Sakurai, and Matsubara (2001a) discuss a method for heuristically finding a good leveled division set.

One advantage of the LDS protocol over the VCG is that it requires less communication/computation costs. To execute the VCG, the bidder must declare his evaluation values for all possible bundles. Also, the seller must solve a complicated optimization problem to determine the winners and their payments. In the LDS protocol, the allowed bundles are predetermined, and bidders need to submit bids only for these bundles. Furthermore, the search space of the possible allocations is much smaller than the search space that one must considere in the VCG.[7]

Rothkopf, Pekeč, and Harstad (1998) present the idea of restricting the possible bundles that bidders can submit so as to allow efficient winner determination in combinatorial auctions. The leveled division set introduced in this chapter is intended to guarantee robustness against pseudonymous bids, and there is no direct relationship between the leveled division set and the methods of dividing goods described by Rothkopf, Pekeč, and Harstad (1998).

7.6 Conclusion

In this chapter, we studied the effect of pseudonymous bidding on combinatorial auction protocols. First, we developed a formal model of combinatorial auction protocols in which pseudonymous bidding are possible. Then, we showed that the VCG mechanism is not pseudonymous-bid-proof. Next, we showed a generalized counter-example that illustrates there exists no pseudonymous-bid-proof combinatorial auction protocol that satisfies Pareto efficiency. Then, we identified one sufficient condition where the VCG mechanism is pseudonymous-bid-proof, that is, a surplus function is bidder-submodular. Further, we described a pseudonymous-bid-proof protocol called the Leveled Division Set (LDS) protocol.

Notes

1. Theorem 1.10 in chapter makes a similar claim.

2. Note that we do not require $\bigcup_{B \in D} B = A$ holds, i.e., satisfying $\bigcup_{B \in D} B \subseteq A$ is sufficient.

3. We describe a simplified version of the LDS protocol described in Yokoo, Sakurai, and Matsubara 2001b. In the original protocol, we can place multiple divisions, i.e., a division set, to each level.

4. This condition is not contradictory to the second condition, because the second condition involves the union of multiple bundles.

5. We cannot tell the result of the VCG when bidders can submit pseudonymous bids, because there exists no dominant strategy equilibrium.

6. Note that this protocol does not fit the definitions used in this chapter, because this is a randomized mechanism.

7. Of course, we cannot achieve a Pareto efficient allocation because we restrict the possible allocations.

References

Gul, Faruk and Ennio Stacchetti (1999), "Walrasian Equilibrium with Gross Substitutes," *Journal of Economic Theory*, 87, 95–124.

Iwasaki, Atsushi, Makoto Yokoo, and Kenji Terada (2003), "A Robust Open Ascending-Price Multi-Unit Auction Protocol against False-Name Bids," in *Proceedings of the Fourth ACM Conference on Electronic Commerce (EC-2003)*, 85–92.

Kelso, Alexander S. and Vincent P. Crawford (1982), "Job Matching, Coalition Formation, and Gross Substitutes," *Econometrica*, 50, 1483–1504.

Mas-Colell, Andreu, Michael D. whinston, and Jerry R. Green (1995), *Microeconomic Theory*, New York: Oxford University Press.

McAfee, R. Preston and John McMillan (1987), "Auction and Bidding," *Journal of Economic Literature*, 25, 699–738.

McAfee, R. Preston and John McMillan (1992), "Bidding Rings," *American Economic Review*, 82, 579–599.

Milgrom, Paul (2000), "Putting Auction Theory to Work: The Simultaneous Ascending Auction," *The Journal of Political Economy*, 108, 245–272.

Milgrom, Paul R. and Robert J. Weber (1982), "A Theory of Auctions and Competitive Bidding," *Econometrica*, 50, 1089–1122.

Monderer, Dov and Moshe Tennenholtz (2000), "Asymptotically Optimal Multi-Object Auctions," working paper.

Moulin, Hervé and Schott Shenker (1996), "Strategyproof Sharing of Submodular Costs: Budget Balance versus Efficiency," ⟨http://www.aciri.org/shenker/cost.ps⟩.

Müller, Eitan and Mark A. Satterthwaite (1985), "Strategy-Proofness: The Existence of Dominant-Strategy Mechanisms," in Leonid Hurwicz, David Schmeidler, and Ugo Sonnenschein, eds., *Social Goals and Social Organization*, Cambridge: Cambridge University Press, 131–171.

Rothkopf, Michael H., Aleksandar Pekeč, and Ronald M. Harstad (1998), "Computationally Manageable Combinational Auctions," *Management Science*, 44, 1131–1147.

Sakurai, Yuko, and Makoto Yokoo (2003), "A False-Name-Proof Double Auction Protocol for Arbitrary Evaluation Values," in *Second International Joint Conference on Autonomous Agents and Multiagent Systems (AAMAS-2003)*, 329–336.

Sakurai, Yuko, Makoto Yokoo, and Shigeo Matsubara (1999), "A Limitation of the Generalized Vickrey Auction in Electronic Commerce: Robustness against False-Name Bids," in *Proceedings of the Sixteenth National Conference on Artificial Intelligence (AAAI-99)*, 86–92.

Terada, Kenji and Makoto Yokoo (2003), "False-Name-Proof Multi-Unit Auction Protocol Utilizing Greedy Allocation Based on Approximate Evaluation Values," in *Proceedings of the Second International Conference on Autonomous Agents and Multiagent Systems (AAMAS-2003)*, 337–344.

Varian, Hal R. (1995), "Economic Mechanism Design for Computerized Agents," in *Proceedings of the First USENIX Workshop on Electronic Commerce*, July 11–12, New York.

Yokoo, Makoto, Yuko Sakurai, and Shigeo Matsubara (2000a), "The Effect of False-Name Declarations in Mechanism Design: Towards Collective Decision Making on the Internet," in *Proceedings of the Twentieth International Conference on Distributed Computing Systems (ICDCS-2000)*, 146–153.

Yokoo, Makoto, Yuko Sakurai, and Shigeo Matsubara (2000b), "Robust Combinatorial Auction Protocol against False-Name Bids," in *Proceedings of the Seventeenth National Conference on Artificial Intelligence (AAAI-2000)*, 110–115.

Yokoo, Makoto, and Yuko Sakurai, and Shigeo Matsubara (2001a), "Bundle Design in Robust Combinatorial Auction Protocol against False-Name Bids," in *Proceedings of 17th International Joint Conference on Artificial Intelligence (IJCAI-2001)*, 1095–1101.

Yokoo, Makoto, Yuko Sakurai, and Shigeo Matsubara (2001b), "Robust Combinatorial Auction Protocol against False-Name Bids," *Artificial Intelligence*, 130, 167–181.

Yokoo, Makoto, Yuko Sakurai, and Shigeo Matsubara (2001c), "Robust Double Auction Protocol against False-Name Bids," in *Proceedings of the 21st International Conference on Distributed Computing Systems (ICDCS-2001)*, 137–145.

Yokoo, Makoto, Yuko Sakurai, and Shigeo Matsubara (2001d), "Robust Multi-Unit Auction Protocol against False-Name Bids," in *Proceedings of 17th International Joint Conference on Artificial Intelligence (IJCAI-2001)*, 1089–1094.

Yokoo, Makoto, Yuko Sakurai, and Shigeo Matsubara (2004), "The Effect of False-Name Bids in Combinatorial Auctions: New Fraud in Internet Auctions," *Games and Economic Behavior*, 46, 174–188.

Yokoo, Makoto, Yuko Sakurai, and Shigeo Matsubara (2005), "Robust Double Auction Protocol against False-Name Bids," *Decision Support Systems*, 39, 241–252.

8 From the Assignment Model to Combinatorial Auctions

Sushil Bikhchandani and Joseph M. Ostroy

8.1 Introduction

The goal of this chapter is to describe efficient auctions for multiple, indivisible objects in terms of the duality theory of linear programming. Because of their well-known incentive properties, we shall focus on Vickrey auctions.[1] These are efficient auctions in which buyers pay the social opportunity cost of their purchases and consequently are rewarded with their (social) marginal product.[2] We use the assignment model to frame our analysis.

We will divide the exposition into static and dynamic parts. By "static," we shall mean the characterization of a combinatorial sealed-bid auction as a *pricing equilibrium*. Pricing equilibria correspond to optimal solutions to the primal and dual of a certain linear programming (LP) problem. We shall give necessary and sufficient conditions, called *buyers are substitutes* (formulated by Shapley 1962), for the existence of a pricing equilibrium that yields the outcome of a Vickrey auction.

Algorithms for solving LP problems imply that the static characterization has a "dynamic" counterpart. But the simplex algorithm, for example, has the drawback that buyers' preferences must be available to the implementor; information must be centralized. Among the methods for solving LP problems, the primal dual algorithm is noteworthy because its informational requirements can be decentralized. The implementor can act as an auctioneer who calls out prices—otherwise known as feasible solutions to the dual—who requires no information about buyers' preferences. Using only knowledge of their own preferences, each buyer makes utility maximizing bids based on those prices; and the auctioneer/implementor uses that information to adjust prices. By starting the algorithm at zero prices, the primal dual method can be interpreted as an ascending price auction.

The results reported here can be regarded as the grafting of two related ideas to form a useful hybrid. In linear programming, the primal dual algorithm was originally developed for the assignment model (see section 8.2). In economics, the algorithm is the law of supply and demand, the story of how market prices adjust to establish equilibrium.

In the auction problem, the metaphorical auctioneer of the market is replaced by a literal entity, as well as a detailed procedure adjusting prices to bids. A complicating factor in the auction problem ignored in the law of supply and demand is that bidders should have an incentive to bid truthfully. These incentive requirements conflict with the linearity and anonymity of pricing with which the law is normally identified.[3] Nevertheless, we can extend the logic of prices adjusting to excess demands beyond its traditional boundaries to meet the added challenge of incentive compatible pricing.

Ausubel (2004) formulated an ingenious ascending price auction for homogeneous goods with diminishing marginal utility to implement a Vickrey scheme, which can be described as nonlinear version of the law of supply and demand. Bikhchandani and Ostroy (2002b) show that the indivisible commodity version of Ausubel's auction is a primal dual algorithm.

Heterogeneous commodities present new challenges. The LP formulation of Bikhchandani and Ostroy (2002a) addresses these. The optimal solutions to the dual linear program correspond to pricing equilibria with possibly nonlinear and non-anonymous prices. A decentralized procedure, such as the primal dual algorithm for solving the LP, which approaches the pricing equilibrium corresponding to the social opportunity cost point (from below) would yield an incentive compatible decentralized auction.

Parkes and Ungar (2000a) and Ausubel and Milgrom (2002) independently developed an ascending price auction for heterogeneous goods (see also Parkes, chapter 2 of this volume and Ausubel and Milgrom, chapter 3 of this volume). Parkes and Ungar show that it converges to an efficient outcome, and Ausubel and Milgrom prove that under a condition called buyers are submodular, a slightly stronger version of the buyers are substitutes condition, the auction is incentive compatible and converges to the social opportunity cost point. De Vries, Schummer, and Vohra (2003) construct an incentive compatible primal dual auction that builds upon ideas in Demange, Gale, and Sotomayor (1986) and the LP formulation of Bikhchandani and Ostroy (2002a).

Section 8.2 describes the basic results for the assignment model, and sections 8.3–8.6 for the combinatorial auction model. Section 8.3 defines the combinatorial auction model and pricing equilibria. Section 8.4 provides a necessary and sufficient condition for the equivalence between pricing equilibrium and the sealed-bid Vickrey auction. Section 8.5 illustrates an LP formulation of the auction model. Section 8.6 describes an ascending price auction as a primal dual algorithm for solving the LP. Section 8.7 concludes with a perspective on the work of others, viewed through this LP framework.

8.2   The Assignment Model

The basic building block for our analysis is the assignment model. In common with combinatorial auctions, the assignment model concerns allocations with indivisibilities. Even though an optimal assignment is an integer programming problem, it is amenable to analysis as an LP problem because it has an *integral* optimal solution. A variant of the assignment model was the origin of one of the earliest application of LP (Kantorovich 1942). The assignment model was also the first (modern) application of the core of a game to economics (Shapley 1955), and the core itself is an integral solution to an LP problem. Use of the primal dual algorithm is hardly coincidental because that algorithm was first developed to solve the assignment model (Kuhn 1955). Demange, Gale, and Sotomayor (1986) formulated a particular application of the algorithm to implement a version of the ascending price auction in which buyers receive their Vickrey payoffs.

Normally, the assignment model is presented by taking the payoffs of pairwise matches as given. For economic applications, however, it is essential to provide a commodity representation of those payoffs.

Let $I = B \cup S$, where B, the set of buyers, has n elements and S, the set of sellers, has m elements. Buyers are indexed by $b \in B$, sellers are indexed $s \in S$, and agents (buyers or sellers) are indexed $i \in I$. Let $C = \{1, \ldots, m\}$ be the set of commodities having the same cardinality as S. Denote by $\mathbf{1}_c \in \mathbb{R}^m$, $c = 1, \ldots, m$, the vector with zeroes in all components except the cth, which has value 1.

The utility of buyer $b \in B$ for consuming commodity bundle $z_b \in \mathbb{R}^m$ is $v_b(z_b) \geq 0$. For each b, the set of possible z_b will be restricted to

$$Z^1 = \{\mathbf{1}_c : c = 1, \ldots, m\} \cup \{\mathbf{0}\}.$$

This commodity representation is distinguished by the restriction that each buyer wishes to purchase at most one object, called the *unit demand* assumption. There is also a unit supply restriction for sellers. Let $v_s(z_s) \leq 0$ be the utility to seller $s \in S$ of supplying the bundle $z_s \in \mathbb{R}^m$. For each s, the set of possible z_s is

$$Z^s = \{\mathbf{1}_s, \mathbf{0}\},$$

that is, seller s is the only supplier of commodity $c = s$. As a normalization, assume $v_b(\mathbf{0}) = v_s(\mathbf{0}) = 0$. Consequently, if b is matched with s, they could jointly obtain

$$v_{bs} = \max_{z \in Z^s}\{v_b(z) + v_s(z)\} \geq 0.$$

Throughout we assume that utility is *quasi-linear* in the commodity z_i and the amount of the money commodity, τ_i, that i pays or receives, which is to say that $u_i(z_i, \tau_i) = v_i(z_i) + \tau_i$. Thus, the utility of no trade is zero: $u_i(\mathbf{0}, 0) = 0$. Further, buyers can supply any (negative) money quantity required.

Let $p \in \mathbb{R}^m$ denote prices for each of the m commodities. The utility maximizing choice by b at prices p is $v_b^*(p) = \max_{z_b \in Z^1}\{v_b(z_b) - p \cdot z_b\}$.[4] The utility maximizing choice by s at p is $v_s^*(p) = \max_{z_s \in Z^s}\{v_s(z_s) + p \cdot z_s\}$.

Definition 8.1 A *Walrasian equilibrium* for the commodity representation of the assignment model is a $(p, (z_b), (z_s))$ such that

- $v_b(z_b) - p \cdot z_b = v_b^*(p)$ for all b
- $v_s(z_s) + p \cdot z_s = v_s^*(p)$ for all s
- $\sum_{b \in B} z_b = \sum_{s \in S} z_s$.

The first two conditions stipulate utility maximization subject to prices and a budget constraint $\tau_b = -p \cdot z_b$ representing the transfer from the buyer and $\tau_s = p \cdot z_s$ being the transfer to the seller. The third condition is "market-clearance," the objects demanded equal the objects supplied.

The LP version of the commodity representation of the assignment model is:

$$\vartheta(1_I, 0) = \max \sum_{b \in B} \sum_{z_b \in Z^1} v_b(z_b)x_b(z_b) + \sum_{s \in S} \sum_{z_s \in Z^s} v_s(z_s)x_s(z_s),$$

subject to:

$$\sum_{z_b \in Z^1} x_b(z_b) = 1, \quad \forall b$$

$$\sum_{z_s \in Z^s} x_s(z_s) = 1, \quad \forall s$$

$$\sum_b \left(\sum_{z_b \in Z^1} z_b x_b(z_b) \right) - \sum_s \left(\sum_{z_s \in Z^s} z_s x_s(z_s) \right) = 0$$

$$x_b(z_b), x_s(z_s) \geq 0, \quad \forall b, \forall z_b \in Z^1, \forall s, \forall z_s \in Z^s.$$

The quantity $x_b(z_b)$ is the amount of z_b consumed by b and the quantity $x_s(z_s)$ is the amount of z_s supplied by s. The expression $\vartheta(1_I, 0)$ is the optimal value as a function of the right-hand side constraints: 1_I is the restriction that there is one each of the individuals in I and $0 \in \mathbb{R}^m$ stands for the requirement that the demands of buyers for each of the m commodities must be exactly offset by the supplies of sellers.

An integral solution satisfies the above constraints *and* $x_b(z_b), x_s(z_s) \in \{0, 1\}$. Such a requirement implies that for each b, $x_b(z_b) = 1$ for exactly one z_b, and for each s, $x_s(z_s) = 1$ for exactly one z_s. If $z_b = 1_s$ then $z_b - z_s = 0$, that is, b and s are matched. Because 0 is a possible choice by a buyer or seller, integral solutions do not require that all buyers and sellers be matched. Indeed, if $n \neq m$, they cannot be.

Let v_I be the maximum to the above problem when integral constraints are imposed. Therefore, $\vartheta(\mathbf{1}_I, 0) \geq v_I$. A key feature of the assignment model is that

$$\vartheta(\mathbf{1}_I, 0) = v_I,$$

that is, there always exists integer optimal solutions to the LP problem.

The dual of this LP problem is:

$$\min\left(\sum_{b \in B} y_b + \sum_{s \in S} y_s\right),$$

subject to:

$$y_b + p \cdot z_b \geq v_b(z_b), \quad \forall b, z_b \in Z^1$$

$$y_s - p \cdot z_s \geq v_s(z_s), \quad \forall s, z_s \in Z^s.$$

The dual constraints of the LP problem mirror utility maximization in Walrasian equilibrium. For each b, $y_b \geq v_b(z_b) - p \cdot z_b$, for all z_b. Hence, $y_b \geq v_b^*(p)$; and because y_b is to be minimized, y_b can be equated with $v_b^*(p)$. Similarly, for y_s and $v_s^*(p)$.

The assignment model also defines a game in characteristic function form, and from that its core is obtained. Because the only groupings of productive individuals are matches between buyers and sellers, we can bypass those formalities and concentrate on the equivalent notion of a "stable matching."

If the number of buyers is not equal to the number of sellers, add dummies to the smaller set to make them equal. For concreteness, define a dummy as having 0 as the only feasible trade. Let π be a matching of buyers to sellers, that is, $\pi : B \to S$ is one-to-one and onto. There is an evident equivalence between a π and an integral solution to the LP problem.

The core of the assignment model is a stable matching defined by a $(\pi, (y_b), (y_s))$ such that $\pi(b) = s$ implies $y_b + y_s = v_{bs}$ and $\pi(b) \neq s'$ implies $y_b + y_{s'} \geq v_{bs'}$.

The various notions described above coincide:

Proposition 8.1 (Assignment Model Equivalence)   The following are equivalent:

a. $(p, (z_b), (z_s))$ is a Walrasian equilibrium where $y_b = v_b^*(p)$ and $y_s = v_s^*(p)$

b. $(z_b), (z_s)$ is an integral optimal solution to the primal and $(y_b), (y_s)$ and p is an optimal solution to the dual

c. $(\pi, (y_b), (y_s))$ belongs to the core of the assignment game.

Koopmans and Beckman (1957) established the equivalence of (a) and (b), using a result in von Neumann 1953, which showed that an LP version of the assignment model has integer solutions. The equivalence of (a) and (c) is due to Shapley and Shubik (1972).

The assignment model has another remarkable property that it shares with Vickrey auctions. Recall that $v_I(= \vartheta(\mathbf{1}_I, \mathbf{0}))$ is the maximum total gains for the individuals in I. Let v_{-b} be the maximum total gains without buyer b. This can be obtained as $v_{-b} = \vartheta(\mathbf{1}_I - \mathbf{1}_b, \mathbf{0}))$, or equivalently by forcing $x_b(\cdot) \equiv 0$. Define the *marginal product* of b as

$$MP_b = v_I - v_{-b}.$$

The aggregate resources in the assignment model are $\mathbf{1}_C$. If b were to obtain $z = \mathbf{1}_c$, the resources available to the others would be $\mathbf{1}_C - \mathbf{1}_c$. Let

$$V_{-b}(\mathbf{1}_C - \mathbf{1}_c) = \max\left\{\sum_{i \neq b} v_i(z_i) : \sum_{i \neq b} z_i = \mathbf{1}_C - \mathbf{1}_c\right\}$$

be the maximum total gains in the model without b when their aggregate resources are $\mathbf{1}_C - \mathbf{1}_c$. Note that $v_{-b} = V_{-b}(\mathbf{1}_C)$ and

$$v_I = \max_{z_b \in Z^1}\{v_b(z_b) + V_{-b}(\mathbf{1}_C - z_b)\}$$

$$= \max\left\{\max_c\{v_b(\mathbf{1}_c) + V_{-b}(\mathbf{1}_C - \mathbf{1}_c)\}, V_{-b}(\mathbf{1}_C)\right\}.$$

Define the *social opportunity cost* of giving one unit of c to b as the minimum amount of money the remaining individuals would be willing to accept to give one unit of c to b, that is,

$$\Delta V_{-b}(\mathbf{1}_c) = V_{-b}(\mathbf{1}_C) - V_{-b}(\mathbf{1}_C - \mathbf{1}_c).$$

If they were to receive $\Delta V_{-b}(\mathbf{1}_c)$, the remaining individuals would be exactly as well off as if they had kept those resources, namely $v_{-b} = V_{-b}(\mathbf{1}_C)$.

The lesson of the Vickrey-Clarke-Groves approach to incentive compatibility is that when a buyer is required to pay the social opportunity cost of his trade (equivalently, receive a payoff equal to his marginal product), the buyer has the incentive to report his characteristics truthfully. And, opportunities for profitable misrepresentations are created when a buyer pays more than the social opportunity cost.

One can readily establish that

Proposition 8.2 (Marginal Product Pricing Inequality) For every Walrasian equilibrium price p,

$$p \cdot \mathbf{1}_c = p_c \geq \Delta V_{-b}(\mathbf{1}_c), \quad \forall b, \forall c.$$

Consequently,

$$MP_b \geq v_b^*(p), \quad \forall b.$$

When the inequality is strict, prices are manipulable. However, for each buyer there is a most favorable Walrasian equilibrium in which that buyer reaches the upper bound on his payoff beyond which he cannot manipulate.

Proposition 8.3 (One at a Time Property; Makowski and Ostroy 1987)   For any $b \in B$ there exists a Walrasian equilibrium price p^b such that

$$\text{MP}_b = v_b^*(p^b).$$

Prices p^b are the best for b, i.e., $v_b^*(p^b) = \text{MP}_b$, but another buyer $\hat{b}$ might think otherwise, that is, $v_{\hat{b}}^*(p^b) < \text{MP}_{\hat{b}}$. Let $\hat{p}^{\hat{b}}$ be the best Walrasian equilibrium for $\hat{b}$. For any two price vectors p and $\hat{p}$, define $\min\{p, \hat{p}\}$ as the vector consisting of the element by element $\min\{p_c, \hat{p}_c\}$. The assignment model guarantees that as far as the buyers are concerned, there need not be any conflict because of the following:

Proposition 8.4 (Lattice Property; Shapley and Shubik 1972)   If p and $\hat{p}$ are Walrasian equilibrium prices so is $\min\{p, \hat{p}\}$.

Combining propositions 8.3 and 8.4,

Proposition 8.5 (Buyers Get Their MPs; Gretsky, Ostroy, and Zame 1999)   There is an equilibrium price $\underline{p}$ such that for all b, if buyer b receives commodity c,

$$\underline{p}_c = \Delta V_{-b}(\mathbf{1}_c);$$

and therefore

$$\text{MP}_b = v_b^*(\underline{p}).$$

Similar conclusions can be obtained for the sellers. Of course, it is typically not possible for both buyers and sellers to get their marginal products. This fact is implicitly recognized in the auction model, below, where the seller is treated asymmetrically as less than fully strategic in his actions and hence not requiring the same kind of incentive payments as the buyers.

Crawford and Knoer (1981) and Demange, Gale, and Sotomayor (1986) provide ascending price auctions that implement the smallest Walrasian price. As each buyer gets his marginal product, the auction is incentive compatible. One of the auctions in Demange, Gale, and Sotomayor 1986 is a primal dual algorithm on an LP formulation of the assignment model.

Fix a price vector $p = (p_1, p_2, \ldots, p_c, \ldots, p_C)$ and let $D_b(p)$ be the demand set of buyer b at these prices. Let $M \subseteq C$. Let $R(M)$ be the set of individuals such that $\emptyset \neq D_b(p) \subseteq M$ for all $b \in R(M)$. A subset of objects M is *overdemanded* if $|R(M)| > |M|$. A necessary and sufficient condition for the existence of a feasible assignment in which every buyer is assigned an element of his demand set is that there is no overdemanded set of objects. This follows from Hall's theorem (see Gale 1960, p. 144). The Demange, Gale, and Sotomayor ascending-price auction described below raises prices of a minimal (w.r.t. set inclusion) overdemanded set:

Step 0   Start with price zero for each object.
Step 1   Buyers report their demand sets at current prices. If there is no overdemanded set, go to step 3; otherwise go to step 2.
Step 2   Choose a minimal overdemanded set. Raise prices of all objects in this set until some buyer changes his demand set. Go to step 1.
Step 3   Assign each buyer an object in his demand set at current prices. Stop.

In the following sections, the above properties of the assignment model serve as important guideposts for extending efficient and incentive compatible auctions beyond the unit demand assumption. To do this, we must clear an obvious hurdle.

The Walrasian equilibria and associated LP problem underlying the assignment model yield linear and anonymous prices for commodities. That such prices suffice for sealed-bid and ascending price implementations of Vickrey auctions is a consequence of the unit demand assumption. In contrast, Vickrey payments are known to be typically discriminatory, that is, the average amount an individual pays may depend on the quantity purchased, and two buyers purchasing the same objects may pay different amounts. To deal with multiple units of homogeneous objects and, *a fortiori* with multiple units of heterogeneous objects, the notion of Walrasian equilibrium and its corresponding LP problem must be reformulated to allow a greater variety of pricing than is needed in the assignment model, or that is normally associated with price-taking behavior and Walrasian equilibrium.[5]

8.3   The Combinatorial Auction Model

In this and the remaining sections we shall construct the parallels between the assignment and auction models. The participants in the auction are $I = \{s\} \cup B$, where s is the seller and $B = \{1, \ldots, n\}$ are the buyers. As in the previous section, denote by $i \in I$ a buyer or seller, and by b a member of B.

Let $\mathbb{Z}_+$ be the nonnegative integers and $\mathbb{Z}_+^m$ its m-fold Cartesian product. A commodity bundle assigned to b is denoted $z_b \in \mathbb{Z}_+^m$. An allocation of indivisible commodities to buyers is $Z = (z_b)$. The aggregate endowment of indivisible quantities of the m objects initially held by the seller is $\omega \in \mathbb{Z}_+^m$. The set of feasible assignments from the seller to the buyers is therefore

$$\mathcal{Z} = \left\{ Z = (z_1, z_2, \ldots, z_b, \ldots, z_n) : \sum_{b \in B} z_b \leq \omega \right\}.$$

The utility to b of z_b is $v_b(z_b)$. Assume that $v_b(\cdot)$ is weakly monotonic on $\mathbb{Z}_+^m$ and, as a normalization, $v_b(0) = 0$.

The cost to the seller of supplying Z is $v_s(Z)$, where $v_s(Z) = v_s(Z')$ if $\sum_{b \in B} z_b = \sum_{b \in B} z_b'$, i.e., $v_s(Z) = v_s(\sum z_b)$.

It will be convenient to write the total utility from any $Z \in \mathscr{Z}$ as

$$\left(\sum_{i \in I} v_i\right)(Z) = \left(\sum_{b \in B} v_b\right)(Z) + v_s(Z),$$

rather than as $\sum_b v_b(z_b) + v_s(\sum_{b \in B} z_b)$.

The auction model is therefore described by $(\mathscr{Z}, \{v_i\})$.

8.3.1   Special Cases

Unit demands   As section 8.2 described, $z_b \in Z^1$. There are several sellers in the assignment model and each is assumed to have one unit of their own commodity so that the aggregate endowment of commodities $\omega = 1_C$. In the auction version of the assignment model, a single seller controls ω.

Homogeneous objects   Assume $m = 1$, whereas ω is an arbitrary element of $\mathbb{Z}_+$.

Multiple units of heterogeneous objects   The auction model above allows for the seller to have multiple units of several commodities and for buyers' utilities to be similarly unrestricted. Hence, v_b is defined for $z_b \in \mathbb{Z}_+^m$, where m can be greater than 1 and z_b need not be less than or equal to 1_C. Unless otherwise indicated, that is the setting described below.

8.3.2   Pricing Equilibria in the Auction Model

Let $P_b(z_b)$ be the money payment by b for the allocation z_b. Thus, b receives the total (or net) utility $v_b(z_b) - P_b(z_b)$ from the allocation z_b.

Define

$$v_b^*(P_b) = \max_{z_b}\{v_b(z_b) - P_b(z_b)\}$$

as the indirect utility of b facing pricing schedule $P_b(\cdot)$.

Let $(\sum_{b \in B} P_b)(Z) = \sum_{b \in B} P_b(z_b)$ where $Z = (z_b)$. Given the pricing schedules P_b for each b, the utility maximizing choice of assignments by the seller is

$$v_s^*\left(\sum_{b \in B} P_b\right) = \max_{Z \in \mathscr{Z}}\left\{v_s(Z) + \left(\sum_{b \in B} P_b\right)(Z)\right\}.$$

Whereas each b is concerned only with the benefits and costs of the bth component of Z, the seller is interested in the entire assignment. The term $(\sum_{b \in B} P_b)(Z)$ is reminiscent of the supplier of a public good who offers the bundle Z to buyers and collects $P_b(z_b)$ from each one. The similarity arises from the possibility of price discrimination.

Just as the supplier of a public good can charge different prices to different buyers, so can the seller in a combinatorial auction. For example, the seller can receive different payments for the same quantities delivered to different buyers and the seller's average revenue from any single buyer can vary with the quantities purchased. The difference, of course, is that unlike the supplier of a public good, the seller who gives the bundle z_b to buyer b cannot also supply those same objects to any other buyer.

Definition 8.2 $(Z = (z_b), \{P_b\})$ is a *pricing equilibrium* for the auction model $(\mathscr{Z}, \{v_i\})$ if

- $v_b(z_b) - P_b(z_b) = v_b^*(P_b)$
- $v_s(Z) + (\sum_{b \in B} P_b)(Z) = v_s^*(\sum_{b \in B} P_b)$
- $Z \in \mathscr{Z}$.

Pricing equilibrium is a variation on Walrasian equilibrium. In fact, we have

Definition 8.3 $(Z, \{P_b\})$ is a *Walrasian equilibrium* for the auction model $(\mathscr{Z}, \{v_i\})$ if it is a *pricing equilibrium* and there exists a $p \in \mathbb{R}^m$ such that for all b and z,

$$P_b(z) = p \cdot z.$$

Pricing equilibrium is therefore an extension of Walrasian equilibrium in which each buyer chooses a z_b to maximize utility subject to a budget constraint in which prices depend on both b and z, while the seller maximizes utility subject to a revenue function that permits discriminatory pricing.

The concept of pricing equilibrium *could be* used to describe "first degree price discrimination," in which the seller seeks to extract the maximum possible gains from the buyers, as if the seller knew the buyers' utility functions and the seller could prevent resale. In fact, we will use it to illustrate the very opposite, in the sense that the buyers will receive the maximum—not the minimum—surplus consistent with pricing equilibrium and consequently have an incentive to reveal their utilities in a sealed-bid auction or bid straightforwardly in an ascending price auction. In the remainder of this section, we describe some of its relevant features.

An allocation Z is *efficient* for the auction model $(\mathscr{Z}, \{v_i\})$ if it achieves the maximum total gains

$$v_I = \max_{Z \in \mathscr{Z}} \left(\sum_{i \in I} v_i \right) (Z).$$

It is readily seen that for any $\{P_b\}$, $v_b^*(P_b) \geq v_b(z_b) - P_b(z_b)$ and $v_s^*(\sum_{b \in B} P_b) \geq v_s(Z) + (\sum_{b \in B} P_b)(Z)$. These inequalities lead directly to the conclusion that, as with standard Walrasian equilibrium,

Proposition 8.6 (Bikhchandani and Ostroy 2002a) All pricing equilibria are efficient.

Let

$$v_{-b} = \max_{Z \in \mathscr{Z}} \left(\sum_{i \neq b} v_i \right)(Z),$$

be the maximum total gains in the auction model without b. Again, the marginal product of b is

$$MP_b = v_I - v_{-b}.$$

We shall want to compare the utility each b receives in a pricing equilibrium with that buyer's marginal product.

If b were to obtain z, the resources available to the others would be $\omega - z$. Let

$$V_{-b}(\omega - z) = \max \left\{ \left(\sum_{i \neq b} v_i \right)(Z) : \sum_{b' \neq b} z_{b'} = \omega - z \right\}$$

be the maximum total gains in the model without b when their aggregate resources are $\omega - z$. The difference between this and the assignment model is that here ω is not necessarily $\mathbf{1}_C$ and z is not necessarily $\mathbf{1}_c$. Nevertheless, again $v_{-b} = V_{-b}(\omega)$ and

$$v_I = \max_{z_b \in \mathbf{Z}_+^m} \{v_b(z_b) + V_{-b}(\omega - z_b)\}.$$

Again the *social opportunity cost* of giving z to b is

$$\Delta V_{-b}(z) = V_{-b}(\omega) - V_{-b}(\omega - z).$$

If the individuals other than b were to receive $\Delta V_{-b}(z)$, they would be exactly as well off as if they had kept those resources, namely v_{-b}.

The analog of proposition 8.2 for the auction model is:

Proposition 8.7 (MP Pricing Equilibrium Inequality; Bikhchandani and Ostroy 2002a) If $(Z, \{P_b\})$ is a pricing equilibrium, then

$$P_b(z_b) \geq \Delta V_{-b}(z_b).$$

Consequently,

$$MP_b \geq v_b^*(P_b).$$

Proposition 8.7 says that in any pricing equilibrium buyers pay at least as much as the social opportunity cost of their purchases, and possibly more. If the buyer's payment does equal the social opportunity cost of the purchase, it must be that among all pricing equilibria the buyer is paying the minimum, that is,

$$\min_{P_b} \ P_b(z_b) = \Delta V_{-b}(z_b),$$

among all equilibrium $P_b(\cdot)$.

Definition 8.4 An *MP pricing equilibrium* (for buyers) is a pricing equilibrium $(Z, \{\underline{P}_b\})$ with the added property that for all b,

$$\underline{P}_b(z_b) = \Delta V_{-b}(z_b).$$

Equivalently,

$$v_b(z_b) - \underline{P}_b(z_b) = MP_b.$$

8.4   Sealed-Bid Vickrey Auctions as Pricing Equilibria

The characterizing property of a Vickrey auction is that buyers pay the social opportunity cost of their purchases. As in the assignment model (proposition 8.3), for any one buyer there is always a pricing equilibrium in which that buyer makes his Vickrey payment.

Proposition 8.8 (One at a Time Property; Parkes and Ungar 2000b)   For any $b^0 \in B$, there exists a pricing equilibrium $(Z, \{P_b\})$ such that

$$P_{b^0}(Z) = \Delta V_{-b^0}(z_{b^0}),$$

and consequently,

$$v_{b^0}^*(P_{b^0}) = MP_{b^0}.$$

Unlike the assignment model, however, a pricing equilibrium for which all buyers pay their social opportunity cost need not exist (see example 5.1 in Bikhchandani and Ostroy 2002a). The following qualification gives necessary and sufficient conditions for a pricing equilibrium to satisfy that condition.

For $R \subseteq B$, let

$$v_{-R} = \max_{Z \in \mathcal{Z}} \left(\sum_{i \in B \backslash R} v_i \right)(Z)$$

be the maximum gains without the buyers in R. Define the marginal product of R as

$$MP_R = v_I - v_{-R}.$$

In other words, v_{-R} and MP_R are extensions of v_{-b} and MP_b to include subsets of buyers other than singletons.

Following Shapley (1962), who established this property for the assignment model,

Definition 8.5 *Buyers are substitutes* if for every $R \subseteq B$,

$$MP_R \geq \sum_{b \in R} MP_b.$$

Proposition 8.9 (Vickrey Auctions as Pricing Equilibrium; Bikhchandani and Ostroy 2002a) An MP pricing equilibrium exists if and only if buyers are substitutes.

Let $\hat{B} \subset B$ and for $b \in \hat{B}$, let $MP_b(\hat{B}) \equiv \max_{Z \in \mathscr{Z}}(\sum_{i \in \hat{B}} v_i)(Z) - \max_{Z \in \mathscr{Z}}(\sum_{i \in \hat{B} \setminus b} v_i)(Z)$ be the marginal product of b in $\hat{B} \cup s$. Similarly, for $R \subset \hat{B}$, $MP_R(\hat{B})$ is the marginal product of R in $\hat{B} \cup s$.

Definition 8.6 *Buyers are strong substitutes* if for every $R \subseteq \hat{B} \subseteq B$,

$$MP_R(\hat{B}) \geq \sum_{b \in R} MP_b(\hat{B}).$$

Ausubel and Milgrom (2002) (see also chapter 3 of this volume) use the term "buyer submodularity" instead of "buyers are strong substitutes."

8.4.1 MP Pricing Equilibria in Various Auction Models

Single object auction   This is the simplest and best known example. Assuming the seller's valuation is zero and buyers valuation are such that $v_1 \geq v_2 \geq \cdots v_n \geq 0$, a pricing equilibrium is described by single p and $z_1 \neq 0$ such that $v_1 \geq p \geq v_2$. When $p = v_2$, buyer 1 pays the social opportunity cost of the object.

Unit demands   Assume buyers' demands are in Z^1. The unit demand assumption implies that without loss of generality, pricing equilibrium can be limited to those $P_b(\cdot)$ for which there exists $p \in \mathbb{R}^m$ such that for all b and z_b, $P_b(z_b) = p \cdot z_b$, that is, to Walrasian equilibria. Proposition 8.5 implies that the pricing equilibrium $(Z, \underline{p})$ satisfies the requirement of proposition 8.9, confirming the fact that buyers are always substitutes in the assignment model.

Homogeneous units   With multiple units of a homogeneous object, let

$$\Delta v_b(z_b) = v_b(z_b + 1) - v_b(z_b)$$

be the increase in utility from adding one more unit to the purchases of buyer b. Buyer b exhibits *diminishing marginal utility* if $z' > z$ implies $\Delta v_b(z') \leq \Delta v_b(z)$. *The buyers are substitutes condition is satisfied if each v_b exhibits diminishing marginal utility* (Bikhchandani and Ostroy 2002a). Conversely, when there is a buyer who does not exhibit diminishing marginal utility, examples in which the buyers are substitutes condition is not satisfied are readily constructed.

Unlike the single object and unit demand models in which linear anonymous prices characterize Vickrey payments, when there are multiple units of a homogeneous commodity a single price will not do. The social opportunity cost function $\Delta V_{-b}(z)$ varies nonlinearly with z and also varies with b. It therefore requires the full level of generality of pricing equilibrium, along with the hypothesis of diminishing marginal utility, to capture Vickrey payments.

Multiple units of heterogeneous commodities   Pricing equilibria always exist for auction models, and for any one b there is always a smallest pricing equilibrium $\underline{P}_b$ such that the buyer's price coincides with the Vickrey payment. However, unless the buyers are substitutes condition is satisfied, there will be a conflict between choosing the smallest pricing equilibrium for one buyer and the smallest for another. A condition proposed by Kelso and Crawford (1982) suffices to eliminate that conflict.

Kelso and Crawford considered the following many-to-one variant of the assignment model. On one side of the market, each seller can offer one unit of his own good (his labor). On the other side, buyers can employ more than one worker. Interpret $v_b(z_b)$ as the output of employer b hiring workers z_b. Walrasian equilibrium in this many-to-one model combines the price-taking behavior of the sellers in the assignment model with the price-taking behavior of buyers in the heterogenous object auction model. To ensure the existence of such an equilibrium, they assumed that v_b satisfies *gross substitutes*: If the prices of some but not all commodities increase, there is always a utility maxmizing demand in which the goods that do not rise in price continue to be demanded. More formally, if $v_b(z) - p \cdot z = v_b^*(p)$ and $p' \geq p$, then there exists a z' such that $v_b(z') - p' \cdot z' = v_b^*(p')$ and $z_c' \geq z_c$ for those c such that $p_c = p_c'$.

The gross substitutes condition guarantees the existence of Walrasian equilibrium, a particular form of pricing equilibrium. By proposition 8.7, the payments that buyers (employers) make will be at least as large as their social opportunity costs. Because prices are restricted to be linear, however, there may be no Walrasian equilibrium for which *any* buyer makes his Vickrey payments. Nevertheless, gross substitutes is relevant to our analysis:

Proposition 8.10 (Bikhchandani et al. 2002; Ausubel and Milgrom 2002)   If each v_b satisfies the gross substitutes condition, then buyers are strong substitutes.

Therefore, even though Walrasian equilibrium is not generally compatible with buyers paying the social opportunity costs of their purchases, conditions guaranteeing the existence of Walrasian equilibrium imply the existence of a pricing equilibrium that does.

8.5   LP Formulation of the Auction Model

The set of pricing equilibria for the auction model corresponds to the set of *integral* optimal solutions to the primal and the set of optimal solutions to the dual of an LP problem. The LP connection implies that one can use LP algorithms to find pricing equilibria. This section is therefore the bridge between the sealed-bid or static approach and the ascending price or dynamic approach to pricing equilibria and Vickrey auctions.

To construct the LP problem defined by the auction model $(\mathcal{Z}, \{v_i\})$, regard (b, Z) as an "activity," the unit value of which is written as $v_b(Z) \equiv v_b(z_b)$. Similarly, (s, Z) is an activity, the unit value of which is $v_s(Z)(=0)$. The LP problem is:

$$\vartheta(\mathbf{1}_I, \mathbf{0}_L) = \max_{Z \in \mathcal{Z}} \left[v_s(Z)x(s, Z) + \sum_{b \in B} v_b(Z)x(b, Z) \right]$$

subject to

$$\sum_{Z \in \mathcal{Z}} x(b, Z) = 1, \quad \forall b$$

$$\sum_{Z \in \mathcal{Z}} x(s, Z) = 1$$

$$x(b, Z) - x(s, Z) = 0, \quad \forall (b, Z)$$

$$x(b, Z), x(s, Z) \geq 0.$$

The quantity $x(b, Z)$ represents the level of operation of the "activity" (b, Z), and similarly for $x(s, Z)$. For each buyer, there is a constraint stipulating that his total participation among all Z must be 1 and there is a similar constraint for the seller, for a total of $n + 1$ constraints for which the RHS is 1. The third line of constraints says that for each (b, Z), the level of participation by b in Z, $x(b, Z)$, must be the same as the level of participation by s in Z, $x(s, Z)$. Letting d be the number of elements Z in $\mathcal{Z}$, there are $L = nd$ third line constraints. The expression $\vartheta(\mathbf{1}_I, \mathbf{0}_L)$ is the optimal value function of the LP problem as a function of its RHS constants. This LP problem has $\mathbf{1}_I$ in common with the LP problem defining the assignment model, but its vector of zero constraints is of a different dimension. (Note: both models use I to describe the participants, even though the number of sellers in the two models differs.)

An integer feasible solution is an $\{x(b, Z), x(s, Z)\}$ satisfying the above constraints and $x(b, Z), x(s, Z) \in \mathbb{Z}_+$. For the constraints above, integrality implies there exists exactly one Z such that $x(b, Z) = 1$, $\forall b$ and $x(s, Z) = 1$. The value v_I is precisely the optimal value subject to the integer restriction. Because the LP problem includes the integer feasible solutions, $\vartheta(\mathbf{1}_I, \mathbf{0}_L) \geq v_I$. Inspection of the constraint set reveals that the integer solutions are in fact its extreme points, from which it follows that like the assignment model, there is always an *integral optimal solution*,

$$\vartheta(\mathbf{1}_I, \mathbf{0}_L) = v_I.$$

The dual is:

$$\min \sum_{b \in B} y_b + y_s,$$

subject to

$$y_b + P_b(Z) \geq v_b(Z), \quad \forall (b, Z)$$

$$y_s - \left(\sum_{b \in B} P_b \right)(Z) \geq v_s(Z), \quad \forall Z.$$

Rewriting the dual constraints, for each b, $y_b \geq v_b(Z) - P_b(Z)$, $\forall Z$, and $y_s \geq v_s(Z) + (\sum_{b \in B} P_b)(Z)$, $\forall Z$. Because y_b and y_s are to be minimized, we can set $y_b = v_b^*(P_b)$ and $y_s = v_s^*(\sum_{b \in B} P_b)$. Therefore, the dual can be rewritten as

$$\min_{\{P_b\}} \sum_{b \in B} v_b^*(P_b) + v_s^* \left(\sum_{b \in B} P_b \right).$$

This reduction leads to:

Proposition 8.11 (LP Equivalence; Bikhchandani and Ostroy 2002a) $(Z, \{P_b\})$ is a pricing equilibrium for the auction model $(\mathscr{L}, \{v_i\})$ if and only if Z is an integral optimal solution to the primal and $\{P_b\}$ is an optimal solution to the dual, i.e., $y_b = v_b^*(P_b)$ for all b and $y_s = v_s^*(\sum_{b \in B} P_b)$.

The integral optimality observed above, along with the evident existence of optimal solutions to this LP problem, implies the existence of pricing equilibria.

8.5.1 LP and the Core

In the assignment model, the core corresponds to the set of optimal solutions to the dual. The same conclusion holds for the auction model.

For the auction model, recall that $I = \{s\} \cup B$, where $B = \{1, \ldots, n\}$. The game theoretic characteristic function for an auction model is described by the collection $\{v_T : T \subseteq I\}$, where $v_\emptyset = 0$, and for non-empty T,

$$v_T = \vartheta(\mathbf{1}_T, \mathbf{0}_L) = \begin{cases} \max\limits_{Z \in \mathscr{Z}} \left(\sum\limits_{i \in T} v_i \right)(Z), & \text{if } s \in T, \\ 0, & \text{otherwise.} \end{cases}$$

The core of $\{v_T\}$ is the set of those (y_i) such that (i) $\sum_{i \in T} y_i \geq v_T$ for all T and (ii) $\sum_{i \in I} y_i = v_I$. If $(Z, \{P_b\})$ is a pricing equilibrium, proposition 8.11 implies that setting $y_b = v_b^*(P_b)$ for all b and $y_s^* = v_s^*(\sum_{b \in B} P_b)$, y will satisfy (i) and (ii). The converse also holds.

Proposition 8.12 (Core Equivalence; Bikhchandani and Ostroy 2002a) For any (y_i) in the core of the characteristic function $\{v_T\}$ defined by the auction model $(\mathcal{Z}, \{v_i\})$, there exists a pricing equilibrium $(Z, \{P_b\})$ such that $y_b = v_b^*(P_b)$ for all b and $y_s^* = v_s^*(\sum_{b \in B} P_b)$.

8.6 An Ascending Price Auction

The logic of dual algorithms is familiar to economists as the idea that prices adjust to excess demand. But the application of that price adjustment rule is identified with linear, anonymous prices. What is remarkable here is that the principle can be applied more generally.

There are two types of dual algorithms that lend themselves to an auction implementation—the subgradient algorithm and the primal dual algorithm. It is easier to find a direction of (dual) price change in a subgradient algorithm, whereas a restricted primal and restricted dual linear program must be solved to obtain a price change in a primal dual algorithm. The payoff to this additional computation in the primal dual algorithm is that at each iteration price changes can be large. In a subgradient algorithm, on the other hand, assurance of close proximity to an optimal solution requires that price changes be small. Thus, a subgradient algorithm has weaker convergence properties. The ascending price auction in Parkes and Ungar 2000a and Ausubel and Milgrom 2002 is a subgradient algorithm. See Parkes (chapter 2 of this volume) and Ausubel and Milgrom (chapter 3 of this volume) for a description and properties of this auction. We describe the primal dual auction of de Vries, Schummer, and Vohra (2003), which builds upon ideas in Demange, Gale, and Sotomayor (1986) and the LP formulation in Bikhchandani and Ostroy 2002a.

Note that any $\{P_b\}$ defines a feasible solution to the dual. If buyers and sellers faced those prices, they could announce utility maximizing demands and supplies. In particular, buyer b is only concerned with the z_b component of Z, whereas all the z_b would be relevant for the seller. If prices are such that the amounts buyers wish to purchase exceeds the amount the seller wishes to supply, the primal dual algorithm proposes an adjustment in $\{P_b\}$ to reduce excess demands. When prices are such that each of the buyers together with the seller choose the same Z, that would only be possible if the Z were a feasible solution to the primal. In that case, the primal dual algorithm would stop. And one can readily verify that in such a case the value of the primal would equal the value of the dual and hence an optimal solution would be achieved.

A primal dual algorithm applied to the auction model could begin with any dual feasible solution and converge to some optimal solution to the primal and dual. As far as overall efficiency is concerned, there would be no reason to choose one version of the algorithm over another because they would differ only with respect to the distribution of the gains from trade, not its total. For example, starting from prices that are too high, one could construct a primal dual algorithm mimicking a descending price auction leading to the highest prices at which the commodities could be sold. This would require the willing cooperation of the buyers bidding straightforwardly even though that information would be used against them. But, just as it is commonly presumed that without sufficient information about buyers, a seller cannot enforce "first degree" or perfect price discrimination, here we presume that buyers would bid strategically to lower the prices they pay. To preclude such behavior, it is desirable to have an auction in which each buyer can rely on the fact that the information gleaned from his bidding is used in his favor both with respect to the seller and with respect to the information supplied by the other bidders. This will be the case if buyers understand that they will pay no more than the social opportunity cost of their purchases; that is, buyers make their Vickrey payments.

If the buyers are substitutes condition is satisfied, there will exist a lowest pricing equilibrium $\{\underline{P}_b\}$ such that if Z is an efficient assignment, $\underline{P}_b(z_b)$ is the social opportunity cost of z_b for all b. Consequently, starting from prices that are too low and adjusting upwards, that is, creating an ascending price auction, one can construct a primal dual algorithm that converges to $\{\underline{P}_b\}$. If the buyers are strong substitutes condition is not satisfied, then in any pricing equilibrium there will be at least one buyer paying more than his social opportunity cost. This buyer would have incentive to shade his bids.

In the remainder of this section, we outline the ascending-price auction for the heterogeneous object auction model, due to de Vries, Schummer, and Vohra (2003) that leads to the Vickrey payments when buyers are strong substitutes. We follow this with a simple illustrative example describing the step by step details.

8.6.1 The Auction Algorithm

Define utility maximizing demands for b at prices P_b as

$$D_b(P_b) = \{z_b : v_b(z_b) - P_b(z_b) = v_b^*(P_b)\}.$$

The auctioneer uses this information as follows:

a. For any $\{P_b\}$, the set of price consistent feasible assignments $\Phi(\{P_b\}) \subset \mathscr{Z}$ is defined as

$$Z \in \Phi(\{P_b\}) \text{ such that } z_b \neq \mathbf{0} \text{ implies } z_b \in D_b(P_b).$$

b. Among the price consistent feasible assignments, the set of revenue maximizing feasible assignments for the seller at $\{P_b\}$ is

$$\bar{\Phi}(\{P_b\}) = \arg\max\left\{\left(\sum_{b\in B}P_b\right)(Z) : Z \in \Phi(\{P_b\})\right\}.$$

c. A set of buyers T is *unsatisfied* at prices $\{P_b\}$ if there does not exist a revenue maximizing feasible assignment that simultaneously satisfies the demands of all buyers in T. That is, if $\hat{Z}$ is an assignment such that $\hat{z}_b \in D_b(\{P_b\})$ for all $b \in T$, then $\hat{Z} \notin \bar{\Phi}(\{P_b\})$. There may be several unsatisfied sets of buyers at prices $\{P_b\}$. Accordingly, let $\underline{T}$ be a *minimally unsatisfied* set of buyers if no subset of $\underline{T}$ is unsatisfied, and let $\underline{B}(\{P_b\})$ be the set of minimally unsatisfied sets of buyers at prices $\{P_b\}$. $\underline{B}(\{P_b\}) = \emptyset$ if and only if $(Z, \{P_b\})$ is a pricing equilibrium for all efficient assignments Z.

Assume that buyers' valuations are discrete, that is, for all b, $v_b(z_b) \in k^{-1}\mathbb{Z}_+$ for some integer k. To simplify further, assume $k = 1$ so that valuations are integral.

The steps of the auction/algorithm are as follows:[6]

Step 0   Set $t = 1$. Start with prices $P_b^1(z_b) = 0$ for all b and z_b.

Step 1   Buyers report $D_b(P_b^t)$, from which the auctioneer constructs $\underline{B}(\{P_b^t\})$ following (a)–(c) above. If $\underline{B}(\{P_b^t\}) = \emptyset$, go to step 3. If not, select a $\underline{T}^t \in \underline{B}(\{P_b^t\})$ go to step 2.

Step 2   For each $b \in \underline{T}^t$ and $z_b \in D_b(P_b^t)$, set $P_b^{t+1}(z_b) = P_b^t(z_b) + 1$. Let $t \leftarrow t + 1$. Go to step 1.

Step 3   Each b receives a $z_b \in D_b(P_b^t)$ and the auction ends.

This auction is a primal dual algorithm on the LP formulation of the auction model. It converges to a pricing equilibrium (whether or not buyers are substitutes). If buyers are strong substitutes, then the auction is incentive compatible and it is an ascending price implementation of the Vickrey auction.

Proposition 8.13 (Primal Dual Auction; de Vries, Schummer, and Vohra 2003)   If buyers are strong substitutes, then the above algorithm implements the Vickrey auction, i.e., it converges to a MP pricing equilibrium.

8.6.2 An Example

There are three buyers, 1, 2, and 3, and two indivisible objects, a and b. Buyers' reservation utilities and Vickrey payments are in table 8.1. At the unique efficient assignment, buyer 1 gets b and 3 gets a.

The auction starts with all prices equal to zero. Buyers' demand $\underline{ab}$ at these prices; in addition, $\underline{a}$ is also in buyer 3's demand set (see table 8.2). The set $\bar{\Phi}(\{P_b^1\})$ consists of feasible assignments that give $\underline{ab}$ to one buyer and nothing to the other two and the feasible assignment that gives $\underline{a}$ to buyer 3 and nothing to the other two. Any pair of buyers is minimally unsatisfied; we select the first two buyers and raise by one unit prices of all elements in their demand sets, that is, raise prices of $\underline{ab}$ for buyers 1 and 2. Table 8.3 shows the start of round 2.

Table 8.1

Buyer utilities

z	$\underline{a}$	$\underline{b}$	$\underline{ab}$	Marginal Product	Vickrey payment
$v_1(z)$	2	3	4	1	2
$v_2(z)$	2	2	4	0	0
$v_3(z)$	3	1	3	1	2

Table 8.2

Round 1

Start of round 1	$\{P_b^1\}$			Demand sets
$p_1^1(z)$	0	0	0	$D_1(p_1^1) = \{\underline{ab}\}$
$p_2^1(z)$	0	0	0	$D_2(p_2^1) = \{\underline{ab}\}$
$p_3^1(z)$	0	0	0	$D_3(p_3^1) = \{\underline{a}, \underline{ab}\}$
$\bar{\Phi}(\{P_b^1\}) = (\underline{ab}, 0, 0), (0, \underline{ab}, 0), (0, 0, \underline{a}),$ & $(0, 0, \underline{ab})$				
$\underline{B}(\{P_b^1\}) =$ any pair of buyers. Select $\{1, 2\}$				

Now, $\underline{b}$ is added to buyer 1's demand set.[7] Observe that $\{3\}$ is a minimally un-satisfied set of buyers because for any $Z \in \bar{\Phi}(\{P_b^2\})$, we have $z_3 = 0$, whereas $D_3(p_3^2) = \underline{a}, \underline{ab}$. Select the minimally unsatisfied set $\{1, 2\}$ and increment prices of objects in these two buyers' demand sets.

From table 8.4 we see that at the start of round 3, the minimally unsatisfied sets are the same as at start of round 2; select $\{1, 2\}$ again.

The demand sets at start of round 4 (table 8.5) are the same as at the end of round 3; however, $\{3\}$ is the only minimally unsatisfied set of buyers. Thus, in round 4, prices at which $\underline{a}$ and $\underline{ab}$ are available to buyer 3 are incremented by one unit.

Table 8.6 indicates that $(\underline{b}, 0, \underline{a})$ is added to the set of revenue maximizing feasible assignments at the start of round 5. Now, the only minimally unsatisfied set in round 5 is $\{2, 3\}$. After incrementing prices for buyers 2 and 3, there are no unsatisfied buyers. The prices $\{P_b\}$ implement the Vickrey outcome (table 8.7).

8.7 Conclusion

Our goal has been to explore the properties of heterogeneous object auctions as exten-sions of the assignment model. The essential common thread between the assignment

Table 8.3

Round 2

Start of round 2	$\{P_b^2\}$			Demand sets
$p_1^2(z)$	0	0	1	$D_1(p_1^2) = \{\underline{b}, \underline{ab}\}$
$p_2^2(z)$	0	0	1	$D_2(p_2^2) = \{\underline{ab}\}$
$p_3^2(z)$	0	0	0	$D_3(p_3^2) = \{\underline{a}, \underline{ab}\}$
$\bar{\Phi}(\{P_b^2\}) = (\underline{ab}, 0, 0)$ & $(0, \underline{ab}, 0)$ $\underline{B}(\{P_b^2\}) = \{1, 2\}$ & $\{3\}$. Select $\{1, 2\}$				

Table 8.4

Round 3

Start of round 3	$\{P_b^3\}$			Demand sets
$p_1^3(z)$	0	1	2	$D_1(p_1^3) = \{\underline{a}, \underline{b}, \underline{ab}\}$
$p_2^3(z)$	0	0	2	$D_2(p_2^3) = \{\underline{a}, \underline{b}, \underline{ab}\}$
$p_3^3(z)$	0	0	0	$D_3(p_3^3) = \{\underline{a}, \underline{ab}\}$
$\bar{\Phi}(\{P_b^3\}) = (\underline{ab}, 0, 0)$ & $(0, \underline{ab}, 0)$ $\underline{B}(\{P_b^3\}) = \{1, 2\}$ & $\{3\}$. Select $\{1, 2\}$				

Table 8.5

Round 4

Start of round 4	$\{P_b^4\}$			Demand sets
$p_1^4(z)$	1	2	3	$D_1(p_1^4) = \{\underline{a}, \underline{b}, \underline{ab}\}$
$p_2^4(z)$	1	1	3	$D_2(p_2^4) = \{\underline{a}, \underline{b}, \underline{ab}\}$
$p_3^4(z)$	0	0	0	$D_3(p_3^4) = \{\underline{a}, \underline{ab}\}$
$\bar{\Phi}(\{P_b^4\}) = (\underline{b}, \underline{a}, 0), (\underline{ab}, 0, 0)$ & $(0, \underline{ab}, 0)$ $\underline{B}(\{P_b^4\}) = \{3\}$				

Table 8.6

Round 5

Start of round 5	$\{P_b^5\}$			Demand sets
$p_1^5(z)$	1	2	3	$D_1(p_1^5) = \{\underline{a}, \underline{b}, \underline{ab}\}$
$p_2^5(z)$	1	1	3	$D_2(p_2^5) = \{\underline{a}, \underline{b}, \underline{ab}\}$
$p_3^5(z)$	1	0	1	$D_3(p_3^5) = \{\underline{a}, \underline{ab}\}$
$\bar{\Phi}(\{P_b^5\}) = (\underline{b}, \underline{a}, 0), (\underline{b}, 0, \underline{a}), (\underline{ab}, 0, 0) \ \& \ (0, \underline{ab}, 0)$ $\underline{B}(\{P_b^5\}) = \{2, 3\}$				

Table 8.7

End of auction

End of auction	$\{\underline{P}_b\}$			Demand sets
$p_1(z)$	1	2	3	$D_1(p_1) = \{\underline{a}, \mathbf{b}, \underline{ab}\}$
$p_2(z)$	2	2	4	$D_2(p_2) = \{\mathbf{0}, \underline{a}, \underline{b}, \underline{ab}\}$
$p_3(z)$	2	0	2	$D_3(p_3) = \{\underline{a}, \underline{b}, \underline{ab}\}$
$\bar{\Phi}(\{\underline{P}_b\}) = (\underline{b}, 0, \underline{a})$ $\underline{B}(\{\underline{P}_b\}) = \emptyset$				

and auctions models is that both exhibit integer optimal solutions in their respective linear programming formulations. In both models,

- Optimal solutions to the primal and dual can be identified as pricing equilibria.
- The dual solutions can be identified with the core, and hence with pricing equilibria.
- The primal dual algorithm can be used to implement an ascending price auction.

One contrast between the two models is:

- Integral optimality is a built-in feature of the linear programming formulation of the assignment model, whereas in the combinatorial auction model the linear program must be specifically tailored to achieve it.

This first contrast leads to a second:

- Pricing equilibria in the assignment model are characterized by anonymous pricing, whereas in the combinatorial auction model pricing equilibria are nonlinear and non-anonymous.

Table 8.8

Efficient, ascending price auctions in private value models

Model/Paper	Buyers are substitutes?	Implement MP Pricing equilibrium?	Incentive compatible?	Ascending-price Vickrey Auction?
Assignment model (CK, DGS)	Yes	Yes (smallest Walrasian equilibrium)	Ex post incentive compatible (EPIC)	Yes
Homogenous objects, diminishing marginal utility (A1)	Yes	Yes	EPIC	Yes
Minimum spanning tree (BdVSV)	Yes	Yes	EPIC	Yes
Heterogeneous objects, gross substitute preferences (KC, GS, M)	Yes	No (Walrasian but not MP pricing eq.)	No	No
Heterogeneous objects, gross substitute preferences (A2, AM, dVSV, PU)	Yes	Yes	EPIC	Yes
Heterogeneous objects, no restriction on preferences (AM, PU)	No	No (MP pricing eq. need not exist)	Nash equilibrium under complete information	No

A1, Ausubel (2004); A2, Ausubel (2002); AM, Ausubel and Milgrom (2002); BdVSV, Bikhchandani, de Vries, Schummer, and Vohra (2002); CK, Crawford and Knoer (1981); DGS, Demange, Gale, and Sotomayor (1986); dVSV, de Vries, Schummer, and Vohra (2003); GS, Gul and Stacchetti (2000); KC, Kelso and Crawford (1982); M, Milgrom (2000); PU, Parkes and Ungar (2000a).

And this, in turn, leads to a difference with respect to our characterization of the outcome of a Vickrey auction where buyers pay the social opportunity cost of their purchases, called an MP pricing equilibrium.

• In the assignment model, MP pricing equilibria (for buyers) always exists because the buyers are substitutes condition is always satisfied, whereas in the auction model the buyers are substitutes condition must be assumed, either directly or derived from a prior condition such as gross substitutes on buyers' utilities.

One can use the linear programming framework to describe research on efficient, ascending price auctions in private value models. The rows in table 8.8 list several models and the papers analyzing them. In the first five rows, buyers are substitutes. Thus, an MP pricing equilibrium exists; the ascending-price auctions that are incentive compatible are exactly the ones that implement an MP pricing equilibrium. In the assignment model, the smallest Walrasian equilibrium is MP pricing. In a combinatorial auction model, Walrasian equilibrium is not typically compatible with MP pricing. Therefore, the ascending-price auctions by Kelso and Crawford (1982), Gul and Stacchetti (2000), and Milgrom (2000) that implement Walrasian equilibria are not incentive compatible—typically buyers pay more than their social opportunity costs. The auctions in Parkes and Ungar (2000a), Ausubel and Milgrom (2002), and de Vries, Schummer, and Vohra (2003) in the last row implement pricing equilibria. Because buyers need not be substitutes, MP pricing equilibrium need not exist and therefore the Vickrey outcome need not be implemented.

Thus, a number of combinatorial ascending price auctions have important features in common: they implement pricing equilibria; the auction itself is often a primal dual algorithm on an LP formulation of the underlying exchange economy; and they are incentive compatible if and only they implement an MP pricing equilibrium. These features should serve as useful guidelines in comparing common value auctions and in addressing future challenges in auction theory.

Acknowledgments

We are grateful to Sven de Vries, David Parkes, Jim Schummer, Rakesh Vohra, and two anonymous referees for helpful comments. Bikhchandani gratefully acknowledges support from the National Science Foundation.

Notes

1. See also Ausubel and Milgrom, chapter 1 of this volume.

2. Such a scheme mimics the reward principle in a perfectly competitive market. See Makowski and Ostroy 1987.

3. See Kelso and Crawford 1982, Bikhchandani and Mamer 1997, and Gul and Stacchetti 1999.

4. If $z_b = 1_c$, then $p \cdot z_b = p_c$, i.e., $p \cdot z_b$ is the dot product of p and z_b.

5. An exception is Makowski (1979), who gives a nonlinear, non-anonymous version of Walrasian equilibria.

6. In this auction, the packages in the demand sets of buyers in a minimal unsatisfied set play the role of a minimal overdemanded set of objects in the ascending price auction for the assignment model described in section 8.2.

7. Under the rules of the auction, the demand sets of buyers are non-decreasing; that is once in the demand set, a package never leaves it.

References

Ausubel, Lawrence M. (2004), "An Efficient Ascending-Bid Auction for Multiple Objects," *American Economic Review*, 94, 1452–1475.

Ausubel, Lawrence M. (2002), "An Efficient Dynamic Auction for Heterogeneous Commodities," Working Paper, University of Maryland.

Ausubel, Lawrence M. and Paul Milgrom (2002), "Ascending Auctions with Package Bidding," *Frontiers of Theoretical Economics*, 1, 1–42. Available at ⟨http://www.bepress.com/bejte/frontiers/vol1/iss1/art1⟩.

Bikhchandani, Sushil and John W. Mamer (1997), "Competitive Equilibrium in an Exchange Economy with Indivisibilities," *Journal of Economic Theory*, 74, 385–413.

Bikhchandani, Sushil and Joseph M. Ostroy (2002a), "The Package Assignment Model," *Journal of Economic Theory*, 107, 377–406.

Bikhchandani, Sushil and Joseph M. Ostroy (2002b), "Ascending Price Vickrey Auctions," *Games and Economic Behavior*, To appear.

Bikhchandani, Sushil, Sven de Vries, James Schummer, and Rakesh Vohra (2002), "Linear Programming and Vickrey Auctions," in *Mathematics of the Internet: E-Auction and Markets*, Brenda Dietrich, Rakesh V. Vohra, eds., New York: Springer Verlag, pp. 75–115.

Crawford, Vincent P. and Elsie M. Knoer (1981), "Job Matching with Heterogeneous Firms and Workers," *Econometrica*, 49, 437–450.

Demange, Gabrielle, David Gale, and Marilda Sotomayor (1986), "Multi-Item Auctions," *Journal of Political Economy*, 94, 863–872.

de Vries, Sven, James Schummer, and Rakesh Vohra (2003), "On Ascending Vickrey Auctions for Heterogeneous Objects," Working Paper, Northwestern University.

Gale, David (1960), *The Theory of Linear Economic Models*, Chicago: University of Chicago Press.

Gretsky, Neil, Joseph M. Ostroy, and William Zame (1999), "Perfect Competition in the Continuous Assignment Model," *Journal of Economic Theory*, 88, 60–118.

Gul, Faruk and Ennio Stacchetti (1999), "Walrasian Equilibrium with Gross Substitutes," *Journal of Economic Theory*, 87, 95–124.

Gul, Faruk and Ennio Stacchetti (2000), "The English Auction with Differentiated Commodities," *Journal of Economic Theory*, 92, 66–95.

Kantorovich, Leonid V. (1942), "On the Translocation of Masses," *Doklady Akad. Navk S.S.S.R.*, 37, 199–201. Translated in *Management Science*, 5, October 1958, 1–4.

Kelso, Alexander S. and Vincent P. Crawford (1982), "Job Matching, Coalition Formation, and Gross Substitutes," *Econometrica*, 50, 1483–1504.

Koopmans, Tjallings C. and Martin Beckman (1957), "Assignment Problems and the Location of Economic Activities," *Econometrica*, 25, 53–76.

Kuhn, Harold W. (1955), "The Hungarian Method for the Assignment Problem," *Naval Research Logistics Quarterly*, 2, 83–97.

Makowski, Louis (1979), "Value Theory with Personalized Trading," *Journal of Economic Theory*, 20, 194–212.

Makowski, Louis and Joseph M. Ostroy (1987), "Vickrey-Clarke-Groves Mechanisms and Perfect Competition," *Journal of Economic Theory*, 42, 244–261.

Milgrom, Paul (2000), "Putting Auction Theory to Work: The Simultaneous Ascending Auction," *Journal of Political Economy*, 108, 245–272.

Parkes, David C. and Lyle H. Ungar (2000a), "Iterative Combinatorial Auctions: Theory and Practice," in *Proceedings of the 17th National Conference on Artificial Intelligence (AAAI-00)*, 74–81.

Parkes, David C. and Lyle H. Ungar (2000b), "Preventing Strategic Manipulation in Iterative Auctions," in *Proceedings of the 17th National Conference on Artificial Intelligence (AAAI-00)*, 82–89.

Shapley, Lloyd (1955), "Markets as Cooperative Games," RAND Corporation working paper P-629, Santa Monica, CA.

Shapley, Lloyd (1962), "Complements and Substitutes in the Optimal Assignment Problem," *Naval Research Logistics Quarterly*, 9, 45–48.

Shapley, Lloyd and Martin Shubik (1972), "The Assignment Game I: The Core," *International Journal of Game Theory*, 1, 111–130.

von Neumann, John (1953), "A Certain Zero-Sun Two-Person Game Equivalent to the Optimal Assignment Problem," in *Contributions to the Theory of games*, Vol. 2, Harold Kuhn and Albert Tucker (eds.), Princeton: Princeton University Press, 5–12.

9   Bidding Languages for Combinatorial Auctions

Noam Nisan

9.1   Introduction

This chapter concerns the issue of the *representation* of bids in combinatorial auctions. Theoretically speaking, bids are simply abstract elements drawn from some space of strategies defined by the auction. Every implementation of a combinatorial auction (and, in fact, every other game) must define how each possible bid is actually represented using the underlying communication technology. As the representation details have no strategic implications, the issue of representation is often ignored. However, it may not be ignored in combinatorial auctions due to the underlying complexity of bids: the space of possible bids in combinatorial auctions is usually huge, as large as the space of possible valuations. Specifying a valuation in a combinatorial auction of m items, requires providing a value for each of the possible $2^m - 1$ non-empty subsets. A naive representation would thus require $2^m - 1$ real numbers to represent each possible bid. It is clear that this would be very inconvenient in practice even for ten-item auctions, and completely impractical for more than about two dozen items.

We will thus look for more convenient *bidding languages* that will allow us to encode "common" bids more succinctly. The exact details of the communication technology are not important, the only point being that communication is always achieved using finite strings of characters. A bidding language is thus simply a mapping from the abstract mathematical space of possible bids into the set of finite strings of characters. The exact choice of the set of characters does not matter much as long as it is finite, and may be taken practically to be the set of a hundred or so ASCII characters, or more theoretically, to be the boolean set $\{0, 1\}$.

This puts us in a "syntax vs. semantics" situation common in logic and in computer science. A *language* assigns a semantic meaning (in our case, a bid) to each well-formed syntactic element (in our case, word in the bidding language). The language specification matters and needs to be studied to the extent that it affects our ability to constructively handle the semantic items of interest. Bidding languages for combinatorial auctions have always been implicit in any implementation of combinatorial auctions. They were first studied explicitly and in a general and formal way by Nisan (2000).

9.1.1 Representation of Real Numbers

A standard technical detail that needs to be taken care of before we proceed is the fact that finite strings of characters cannot represent infinite-precision real numbers. We will ignore this issue by actually assuming the opposite: that a single real number *may* be represented in a finite number of characters. One may formalize this in various mathematical ways, for example, by assuming that all real numbers in bids are given in *finite* precision, for example, using sixty-four bits. (This is certainly enough for all practical applications, allowing a micro-penny precision on trillion-dollar auctions.)

9.1.2 Bids vs. Valuations

Each combinatorial auction mechanism may define an arbitrary space of possible bids. This space of bids is identical to the space of valuations when the mechanism is a direct revelation mechanism, as is commonly the case. However, this is not mandatory and, in principle, the space of bids may be quite different from the space of valuations. Of course, a player's bid will always be a function of his valuation, but still not necessarily equivalent to it. However, in almost all studied single-round auctions, the bid space is essentially equivalent to the valuation space. In such cases, bids *are* valuations. Indeed, in all studied bidding languages, the bidding language is really a *valuation language*—a syntactic representation of valuations. We use the name "bidding language" rather than the more precise "valuation language" due to the main intended use of such languages—bidding.

A bidding language can now provide a side benefit: classify valuations according to their complexity. "Simple valuations" have short representations, whereas "complex valuations" require long representations. A collection of bidding languages may yield a qualitative classification according to the set of bidding languages in which the valuation has sufficiently succinct representation. Such syntactic classifications may be useful alongside the various semantic classifications of valuations.

9.1.3 Information-Theoretic Limitations

From the outset we should notice that it is impossible to allow encoding *all* possible valuations succinctly. This is due to simple information theoretic reasons: there are fewer than 2^t strings of bits of length strictly less than t, and thus not all elements from a space of size 2^t can be represented using strings of length less than t. The size of the space of all valuations on m items (with each real number limited to finite precision) is exponential in 2^m. It follows that in any bidding language some valuation (actually, almost all valuations) requires encoding length that is exponential in m. Our interest would thus be not in attempting succinctly to represent all valuations but rather only succinctly to represent *interesting* ones.

9.1.4 Expressiveness vs. Simplicity

When attempting to choose or design a bidding language we are faced with the same types of tradeoffs common to all language design tasks: *expressiveness vs. simplicity*. On one hand, we would like our language to express important valuations well; on the other hand, we would like it to be as simple as possible. Let us look closer at these two requirements.

We would first want our valuation language to be *fully expressive*, that is, to be able to express *every* valuation. We would then want to ensure that "important" valuations have succinct representations. In any intended use there are some valuations that may be realistically those of some bidder—these are the important ones for this application. Other valuations are unlikely to appear in this application, hence their encoding length is not an issue. Unfortunately, it is quite hard to characterize this set of "realistic" valuations: not only is it application-specific and not general, but also there is very little empirical evidence from real combinatorial auctions.

We are thus left with two possible ways to choose the "important" valuations for which we aim to give short representations. The "soft" approach attempts guessing various types of valuations that would seem to be natural and realistic in many settings. A language that can more succinctly represent more of these valuations would be considered better. The "hard" approach attempts comparing the expressive power of various bidding languages, formally proving relations between representation lengths in different languages. One language would be better than another if it can succinctly express any valuation that the other may.

The notion of the simplicity of a language has two components: an intuitive one and a technical one. First, the language must "look" simple to humans. Humans should be able to intuitively understand what a bid in the language means, as well as how to represent a valuation. This requirement may be somewhat relaxed, allowing such simplicity to emerge only with the use of "software crutches" in the form of computerized agents. Technically, simplicity should mean that all computational tasks associated with the valuations should be as easy as possible—the most obvious such task being winner determination when bids are presented in this language.

One would expect the goals of expressiveness and simplicity to be relatively conflicting, as the more expressive a language is, the harder it becomes to handle it. A well-chosen bidding language should aim to strike a good balance between these two goals.

9.1.5 The Rest of the Chapter

We follow the standard notations used in most of this book: our combinatorial auction is on a set of m items. A valuation v provides a real value $v(S)$ for each subset S of the items. We assume that $v(\emptyset) = 0$ and that for $S \subseteq T$ we have that $v(S) \leq v(T)$.

We start, in section 9.2, by providing some examples of valuations that we consider natural. In no way is this meant to be a comprehensive list of types of valuations that we wish our bidding languages to express, but rather just a representative sample. Section 9.3 discusses the main paradigm for bidding languages: exclusive and non-exclusive combinations of package bids. Section 9.4 describes some extensions and special cases. Section 9.5 shortly describes the associated computational complexity issues. Section 9.6 contains the technical proofs for the theorems in section 9.3. Finally, section 9.7 concludes.

9.2 Some Examples of Valuations

We present here a few examples of valuations that seem to be natural and are used below as examples. Some of these valuations are symmetric, with all items are identical (at least from the point of view of the bidder), whereas other valuations are not. For symmetric valuations v, the value $v(S)$ depends only on the size of the set of items obtained S.

9.2.1 Symmetric Valuations

The simple additive valuation   The bidder values any subset of k items at value k. That is, $v(S) = |S|$.

The simple unit demand valuation   The bidder desires any single item, and only a single item, and values it at 1. Thus $v(S) = 1$ for all $S \neq \emptyset$.

The simple K-budget valuation   Each set of k items is valued at k, as long as no more than K items are obtained. That is, $v(S) = \min(K, |S|)$.

Intuitively, each single item is valued at 1, but the total budget available to the bidder is K.

The majority valuation   The bidder values at 1 any majority (i.e., set of size at least $m/2$) of the items and at 0 any smaller number of items.

The general symmetric valuation   Let $p_1, p_2, \ldots, p_m$ be arbitrary nonnegative numbers. The price p_j specifies how much the bidder is willing to pay for the j'th item won. Thus $v(S) = \sum_{j=1}^{|S|} p_j$.

In this notation, the simple additive valuation is specified by $p_j = 1$ for all j. The simple unit demand valuation is specified by $p_1 = 1$ and $p_j = 0$ for all $j > 1$. The simple K-budget valuation is specified by $p_j = 1$ for $j \leq K$ and $p_j = 0$ for $j > K$. The majority valuation is specified by $p_{m/2} = 1$ and $p_j = 0$ for $j \neq m/2$.

A downward sloping symmetric valuation   A symmetric valuation is called downward sloping if $p_1 \geq p_2 \cdots \geq p_m$.

9.2.2 Asymmetric Valuations

An additive valuation   The bidder has a value v^j for each item j, and he values each subset as the sum of the items in it. That is, $v(S) = \sum_{j \in S} v^j$.

The unit demand valuation   The bidder has a value v^j for each item j, but desires only a single item. Thus $v(S) = \max_{j \in S} v^j$.

The monochromatic valuation   There are $m/2$ red items and $m/2$ blue items for sale. The bidder requires items of the same color (be it red or blue), and values each item of that color at 1. Thus the valuation of any set of k blue items and l red items ($|S| = k + l$) is $\max(k, l)$.

The one-of-each-kind valuation   There are $m/2$ pairs of items. The bidder wants one item from each pair and values it at 1. Thus, the valuation of a set S that contains k complete pairs and l singletons ($|S| = 2k + l$) is $k + l$.

9.3   Exclusive and Non-Exclusive Bundle-Bids

In this section we present the leading paradigm for bidding in combinatorial auctions: making sets of bids for "bundles" of items, where the bid for the different bundles can be either exclusive or non-exclusive. This paradigm seems to be intuitive and is often used without even formally defining the underlying bidding language. Sandholm 2002a and Fujishima, Leyton-Brown, and Shoham 1999 explicitly used basic bidding languages of this form and Nisan (2000) gave the general classification.

9.3.1   Basic Bidding Languages

We first start by defining the most basic types of bids—those that desire a single bundle of items.

Atomic Bids   Each bidder can submit a pair (S, p) where S is a subset of the items and p is the price that he is willing to pay for S. Thus $v(T) = p$ for $S \subseteq T$ and $v(T) = 0$ otherwise. Such a bid is called an atomic bid.

Lehmann, O'Callaghan, and Shoham (2002) called atomic bids single-minded bids. It is clear that many simple bids cannot be represented at all in this language; for example, it is easy to verify that an atomic bid cannot represent even the simple additive valuation on two items.

OR Bids   Each bidder can submit an arbitrary number of atomic bids, that is, a collection of pairs (S_i, p_i), where each S_i is a subset of the items, and p_i is the maximum price that the bidder is willing to pay for that subset. Implicit here is that he is willing to obtain any number of disjoint atomic bids for the sum of their respective prices. Thus an OR bid is equivalent to a set of separate atomic bids from different bidders. More formally, for a valuation $v = (S_1, p_1)\ OR \ldots OR\ (S_k, p_k)$, the value of $v(S)$ is defined to be the maximum over all possible valid collections W, of the value of $\sum_{i \in W} p_i$, where W is valid if for all $i \neq j \in W$, $S_i \cap S_j = \emptyset$.

The OR bidding language cannot represent all valuations. It is easy to verify that the following proposition completely characterizes the descriptive power of OR bids.

Proposition 9.1 OR bids can represent all bids that don't have any substitutabilities, i.e., those where for all $S \cap T = \emptyset$, $v(S \cup T) \geq v(S) + v(T)$, and only them.

In particular, OR bids cannot represent the simple unit demand valuation on two items.

XOR Bids Each bidder can submit an arbitrary number of pairs (S_i, p_i), where S_i is a subset of the items, and p_i is the maximum price that he is willing to pay for that subset. Implicit here is that he is willing to obtain at most one of these bids. More formally, for a valuation $v = (S_1, p_1) \, XOR \ldots XOR \, (S_k, p_k)$, the value of $v(S)$ is defined to be $\max_{i|S_i \subseteq S} p_i$.

Proposition 9.2 XOR-bids can represent all valuations.

The term XOR bids is taken from Sandholm (2002a), and is commonly used despite the fact that purists may object to the confusion with the totally different boolean exclusive-or function. As we have seen, XOR bids can represent everything that OR bids can represent, as well as some valuations that OR bids cannot represented—those with substitutabilities. Yet, the representation need not be succinct: there are valuations that can be represented by very short OR bids and yet the representation by XOR bids requires exponential size.

Definition 9.1 The size of a bid is the number of atomic bids in it.

Proposition 9.3 Any additive valuation on m items can be represented by OR bids of size m. The simple additive valuation requires XOR bids of size 2^m.

9.3.2 Combinations of OR and XOR

Although both the OR and XOR bidding languages are appealing in their simplicity, it seems that each of them is not strong enough to succinctly represent many desirable simple valuations. A natural attempt is to combine the power of OR bids and XOR bids. In this subsection we investigate such combinations.

OR-of-XORs Bids Each bidder can submit an arbitrary number of XOR-bids, as defined above. Implicit here is that he is willing to obtain any number of these bids, each for its respectively offered price.

Sandholm (2002b) called OR-of-XORs bids OR-XOR bids. OR-of-XORs bids generalize both plain XOR bids and plain OR bids. The following example is a non-obvious example of their power and demonstrates that OR-of-XOR bids can succinctly express some valuations that cannot be succinctly represented by either OR-bids or XOR-bids alone.

Lemma 9.1 (Nisan 2000)   OR-of-XORs bids can express any downward sloping symmetric valuation on m items in size m^2.

Proof   For each $j = 1, 2, \ldots, m$ we will have a clause that offers p_j for any single item. Such a clause is a simple XOR-bid, and the m different clauses are all connected by an OR. Because the p_j's are decreasing, we are assured that the first allocated item will be taken from the first clause, the second item from the second clause, and so on.   ∎

The fact that the valuation is downward sloping, $p_1 \geq p_2 \geq \cdots \geq p_n$, is important: the majority valuation (which is not downward sloping) requires exponential size OR-of-XORs bids. Theorem 9.8 will show this exponential lower bound for an even more general language, OR^*-bids.

One may also consider the dual combination: XOR-of-OR bids. Intuitively, these types of bids seem somewhat less natural than OR-of-XOR bids, but, as we will see, they can also be useful.

XOR-of-ORs Bids   Each bidder can submit an arbitrary number of OR-bids, as defined above. Implicit here is that the bidder is willing to obtain just one of these bids.

An example where XOR-of-ORs bids are more powerful than OR-of-XORs bids is the monochromatic valuation. XOR-of-ORs bids require only size m: "(OR of all blues) XOR (OR of all reds)." By contrast, OR-of-XORs require exponential size for this, as the following theorem, whose proof appears in section 9.6, shows.

Theorem 9.1 (Nisan 2000)   The monochromatic valuation requires size of at least $2 \cdot 2^{m/2}$ in the OR-of-XORs bidding language.

On the other hand, for other valuations the OR-of-XORs language may be exponentially more succinct. We have already seen that OR-of-XORs bids can succinctly represent any downward sloping symmetric valuation, and, so in particular, the simple K-budget valuation. In contrast, we have the following theorem, whose proof we postpone to section 9.6.

Theorem 9.2 (Nisan 2000)   Fix $K = \sqrt{m}/2$. The K-budget valuation requires size of at least $2^{m^{1/4}}$ in the XOR-of-ORs bid language.

It is natural at this point to consider not just OR-of-XORs and XOR-of-ORs, but also arbitrarily complex combinations of ORs and XORs. We will define valuations obtained from general OR/XOR formulae over atomic bids. This general definition also formalizes the semantics of the OR-of-XORs and XOR-of-ORs languages discussed above. The general definition treats OR and XOR as operators on valuations. The XOR operator allows taking any one of the two operands, and the OR operator allows partitioning the items between the two operands. Formally,

Definition 9.2 Let v and u be valuations, then $(v \ XOR \ u)$ and $(v \ OR \ u)$ are valuations and are defined as follows:

- $(v \ XOR \ u)(S) = \max(v(S), u(S))$.
- $(v \ OR \ u)(S) = \max_{R, T \subseteq S, R \cap T = \emptyset} v(R) + u(T)$.

OR/XOR Formulae Bids Each bidder may submit a OR/XOR formula specifying his bid. OR/XOR formulae are defined recursively in the usual way using OR and XOR operators, where the operands are either atomic bids (specifying a price p for a subset S) or recursively, OR/XOR formulae.

Notice that all previously mentioned bidding languages are special types of OR/XOR formulae bids, where the formulae are restricted to a specific syntactic form. In particular, the previous two lemmas provide examples of valuations that can be represented succinctly by general OR/XOR formulae but require exponential size OR-of-XOR bids or alternatively XOR-of-OR bids. A single valuation that requires exponential size for both OR-of-XORs bids and XOR-of-OR bids can be obtained by defining a valuation that combines the monochromatic valuation on the first $m/2$ items and the K-budget valuation on the second $m/2$ items.

9.3.3 OR Bids with Dummy Items

We now introduce the bidding language of our choice. Fujishima, Leyton-Brown, and Shoham (1999) introduced this language in order to allow XOR bids to be expressed as a variant of OR bids; Nisan (2000) exposed its full power. The idea in this bidding language is to allow the bidders to introduce "dummy" items into the bidding. These items will have no intrinsic value to any of the participants, but they will be indirectly used to express constraints. The idea is that a XOR bid $(S_1, p_1) \ XOR \ (S_2, p_2)$ can be represented as $(S_1 \cup \{d\}, p_1) \ OR \ (S_2 \cup \{d\}, p_2)$, where d is a dummy item.

Let M be the set of items for sale; we let each bidder i have its own set of dummy items D_i, which only he can bid on.

OR* Bids Each bidder i can submit an arbitrary number of pairs (S_l, p_l), where each $S_l \subseteq M \cup D_i$, and p_l is the maximum price that he is willing to pay for that subset. Implicit here is that he is willing to obtain any number of disjoint bids for the sum of their respective prices.

An equivalent but more appealing "user interface" may be put on the OR* language as follows: users may enter atomic bids together with "constraints" that signify which bids are mutually exclusive. Each one of these constraints is then simply interpreted as a dummy item that is added to the pair of mutually exclusive bids. Despite its apparent simplicity, this language turns out to be the most efficient one so far and can simulate all bidding languages presented so far, including general OR/XOR formulae.

Theorem 9.3 (Nisan 2000) Any valuation that can be represented by OR/XOR formula of size s, can be represented by OR* bids of size s, using at most s^2 dummy items.

The proof is postponed to section 9.6 and may be directly converted into a "compiler" that takes OR/XOR formulae bids and converts them to OR* bids. The following theorem shows that even the OR* language has its limitations. We postpone the proof to section 9.6.

Theorem 9.4 The majority valuation requires size of at least $\binom{m}{m/2}$ in the OR* bid language.

One of the appealing features of OR* bids is that despite their power, they "look just like" regular OR-bids, on a larger set of items. Winner determination algorithms that expect to see OR-bids will directly thus be able to handle OR* bids as well.

9.4 Extensions and Special Cases

So far we have discussed the basic standard constructs used in bidding languages. In this section we first shortly describe various possible extensions, and then shortly discuss some important special cases.

9.4.1 Additional Constructs

We have so far started with simple atomic bids and used two "combining operators" on valuations: OR and XOR. One may think of many other ways of constructing valuations from combinations of simpler valuations. We now shortly mention some of those that seem to "make sense."

Logical Languages We start by considering the basic building blocks. We have so far used only the very simple atomic bids. In general, we should be able to take any monotone boolean predicate $f : \{0,1\}^m \to \{0,1\}$, and assign a value p to any bundle that satisfies this predicate (identifying a boolean vector $b \in \{0,1\}^m$ with the set of items

$\{j|b_j = 1\}$). Formally, the logical valuation $v = (f, p)$ is given by $v(S) = p$ if $f(S) = 1$ and $v(S) = 0$ otherwise. These valuations can then further be combined by OR and XOR operations as well as other constructs presented below.

Naturally, at this point one might ask how can f be represented. The most natural representation would be to use monotone boolean formulae (Hoos and Boutlier 2000). The most general representation would be to allow general boolean circuits. The comparison between the many various possibilities puts us well into the field of boolean complexity theory (see, e.g., Wegner 1987).

Budget Limits   Given a valuation, we can think of limiting it up to some given "budget" k—bundles that used to receive a higher valuation are now valued at the budget limit. Formally: the valuation $v' = \text{Budget}_k(v)$ is defined by $v'(S) = \min(v(S), k)$.

Limits on Number of Items   Given a valuation, we can think of limiting it up to some maximum number k of obtained items. Valuations of larger sets of items are truncated by ignoring the extra items. Formally: the k-satiated valuation $v' = \text{Sat}_k(v)$ is defined by $v'(S) = \max_{s' \subseteq S, |s'| \leq k} v(s')$.

Semantics for AND: ALL and MIN   Certainly, the name of the "OR" construct suggests that we should have an "AND" construct as well. There is probably no truly satisfying definition of an AND construct on valuations. The most natural definition, called ALL by Zinkevich, Blum, and Sandholm (2003), takes value 0 (zero) to mean failure, and uses addition to combine non-failed values. Formally, the valuation $v = v_1$ ALL v_2 is defined by $v(S) = 0$ if $v_1(S) = 0$ or if $v_2(S) = 0$, and otherwise $v(S) = v_1(S) + v_2(S)$. An alternative semantics is to simply take point-wise minimum. Formally: the valuation $v = v_1$ MIN v_2 is defined by $v(S) = \min(v_1(S), v_2(S))$.

k-OR   The OR and XOR operators can be viewed as extreme cases of a general construct that allows combinations of at most k valuations from a given set of t valuations. In this respect, XOR is the case $k = 1$, whereas OR is the case with $k = t$. Formally: the valuation $v = \text{OR}_k(v_1 \dots v_t)$ is defined by $v(S) = \max_{S_1 \dots S_k} \sum_{j=1}^{k} v_{i_j}(S_j)$, where $S_1 \dots S_k$ form a partition of the items, and $i_1 < i_2 \cdots < i_k$.

Operators with Associated Prices   It is sometimes natural to "factor out" parts of the values of bundles in a way that represents how the value is derived. For example, consider the valuation giving value 101 to item A and 102 to item B (let's ignore the value of the pair AB). This valuation could have been obtained by the following logic: "Any item will give me a benefit of 100, and I also get a side benefit of 1 from A and 2 from B." One can think of suggesting this using a syntax such as $([(A, 1)OR(B, 2)], 100)$. Boutlier and Hoos (2001) suggested a general language using such constructs.

9.4.2 Special Cases

Symmetric Valuations   Clearly the case where all items are identical (at least for the bidder) is of special interest. In this case the value of a subset is fully determined by the size of the subset, that is, by the number of items won. Auctions where this is guaranteed to be the case for all bidders are in fact just multi-unit (single-good) auctions. Symmetric valuations can be fully represented by a vector of m numbers $v_1 \leq \cdots \leq v_m$, with $v(S) = v_{|S|}$. Equivalently and more intuitively they can be represented by the vector of marginal values $p_i = v_i - v_{i-1} \geq 0$ as section 9.2 showed above.

When the symmetric valuation is downward sloping, that is, $p_i \geq p_{i+1}$ for all i, this same information may be provided in a natural economic format by a *demand curve d*, where $d(p)$ denotes the number of items desired at price p per item, the largest value of i such that $p_i < p$. This demand curve may be fully specified by giving the value of d only for the finite set of values p where $d(p)$ changes. This representation may be more concise than providing the full vector of marginal values in cases where the p_is are not strictly decreasing but rather remain constant for long intervals.

Combinations of Singleton Valuations   An interesting class of valuations is those obtained by restricting the atomic bids to be *singleton bids*, or, atomic bids (S, p) where $|S| = 1$. ORs of such singleton valuations are exactly the additive valuations, and XORs of singleton valuations are the unit demand valuations. Lehmann, Lehmann, and Nisan (2001) studied more complex combinations of singleton bids: OR of XORs of singletons, termed OXS bids, and XOR of ORs of singletons, termed XOS bids. None of these languages is fully expressive, as all XOR and OR combinations of singleton bids are complement-free (i.e., satisfy $v(S \cup T) \leq v(S) + v(T)$). The expressive power of these classes (without any limitations on succinctness) was shown to form a proper hierarchy within the class of complement-free valuations.

Theorem 9.5 (Lehmann, Lehmann, and Nisan 2001)   The following sequence of strict containments holds: $\mathrm{GS} \subset \mathrm{OXS} \subset \mathrm{SM} \subset \mathrm{XOS} \subset \mathrm{CF}$. Here, GS is the class of (gross-)substitute valuations, SM the class of submodular valuations, and CF the class complement-free valuations.

Network Valuations   In many cases, the items for sale are network resources. Specifically and formally, they may be viewed as edges in some underlying graph. In many such cases, bidders will pay a given price for any bundle of items that has some specific property in the underlying graph. In such cases, a bidding language can simply allow the description of the desired property together with the price offered. For example, consider a bidder who requires to send a message from vertex s to vertex t in the underlying graph. For this, he must acquire a set of edges that consists of a directed path from s to t. In this case, the bidding language should simply allow specifying s, t, and a price p. Similar examples include a bidder that desires a spanning tree of a particular subset of vertices, a set of edges with enough flow capacity, and so on.

9.5 Computational Complexities of Bidding Languages

Once a bidding language has been fixed, various desired operations on valuations become computations over strings, and one can study their computational complexity. There are various such operations of which we should mentioned at least three:

1. Expression   Given another representation of a valuation v, express v in the bidding language. This task of course depends on the "other representation of which the most interesting one is the intuitive non-formal way by which people *know* their preferences.
2. Winner determination   Given a set of valuations $\{v_i\}$, find the allocation (i.e., a partition of the items) $\{S_i\}$ that maximizes the total value: $\sum_i v_i(S_i)$.
3. Evaluation   Given a valuation v, and a "query" about it, answer the query. The most basic type of query to consider is the *value query*: Given a set S, determine $v(S)$. Another important query is the *demand query*: Given a set of item prices $\{p_i\}$, find the set that maximizes $v(S) - \sum_{i \in S} p_i$. One may consider other types of queries as well, of course.

We will not discuss further the question of expression complexity due to its non-formal nature. It is certainly an important topic for experimental evaluation.

9.5.1   Complexity of Winner Determination

Part III (chapters 12–16) of this book study the question of winner determination at length. Here we only wish to point out the basic computational characteristics: even the simplest bidding language, one allowing atomic bids only, gives an NP-complete optimization problem. Even the strongest language that we have studied still gives "just" an NP-complete problem, as can be easily seen by the fact that from the point of view of winner determination, bids in the OR* language look exactly like collections of simple atomic bids. Thus from a "high-level" point of view, winner determination complexity is basically independent of the bidding language choice. Of course, in real applications we do expect stronger bidding languages to require more effort, and more refined analysis will uncover such differences.

Important exceptions that we must mention are those bidding languages that give rise to polynomial-time solvable winner determination problem. Chapter 14 studies these cases, and we mention here just two: XOR-bids when there are a constant number of bidders (using simple exhaustive search) and OXS-bids (using bipartite maximum-weight matching).

9.5.2 Complexity of Evaluation

We would now like to address the question of the algorithmic difficulty of interpreting a bid. Let us start with the simplest queries, value queries: given a valuation v in one of the bidding languages defined above, how difficult is it to calculate, for a given set of items S, the value $v(S)$? One would certainly hope that this algorithmic problem (just of interpreting the bid—not of any type of allocation) is easy.

This is indeed the case for the atomic bidding language as well as the XOR bidding language. Unfortunately, this is not true of all other bidding languages presented above, starting from the OR bidding language. Given an OR bid:

$$v = (S_1, p_1) \ OR \ (S_2, p_2) \ OR \dots OR \ (S_k, p_k),$$

computing the value $v(S)$ for a subset S is exactly the same optimization problem as allocating S among many different bidders (S_i, p_i), a problem that is NP-complete. Thus, theoretically speaking, almost all languages considered are "too strong"—even a simple value query cannot be answered on them. However, it seems that practically, this is not a problem: either allocation between the different clauses is practically easy, or else the difficulty gets merged into the hardness of winner determination.

Now let us consider demand queries: given a valuation v and a set of "item prices" $p_1 \dots p_m$, find the set that maximizes $v(S) - \sum_{i \in S} p_i$. It is again easy to verify that for the atomic bidding language as well as for the XOR bidding language this is still solvable in polynomial time. This problem is NP-complete for stronger languages, starting with the OR language. In general, one may observe that demand queries are always at least as hard as value queries:

Lemma 9.2 In any bidding language, a value query may be reduced to demand queries (via a polynomial-time Turing reduction).

Proof   First, we can reduce a value query to a sequence of "marginal value" queries: given a subset S and an item $i \notin S$, evaluate $v(i|S) = v(S \cup \{i\}) - v(S)$. The reduction is simply using the recursive algorithm: $v(\emptyset) = 0$ and $v(S \cup \{i\}) = v(S) + v(i|S)$.

A marginal value query $v(i|S)$ can be reduced to demand queries using the item prices: $p_j = 0$ for $j \in S$ and $p_j = \infty$ for $j \notin S \cup \{i\}$. The demand query will answer S for every $p_i > v(i|S)$ and will answer $S \cup \{i\}$ for $p_i < v(i|S)$. The value of $v(i|S)$ can thus be found using binary search (assuming finite precision). ∎

9.5.3 Complete Bidding Languages

At this point it may become natural to consider "complete" bidding languages, that is, languages that can efficiently simulate "all" bidding languages from some class. The natural choice would be a bidding language that allows submitting arbitrary polynomial-time computable *programs* as valuations. What is not clear is what these programs should compute. The natural answer is that such "program bids" should answer value queries: accept as input a set S and return, in polynomial time, the value $v(S)$. This natural choice is not entirely satisfying for two reasons: 1) This does not give enough power to a winner determination algorithm that accepts several such bids: almost nothing nontrivial can be done with value queries alone. 2) As previously mentioned, in most bidding languages, value queries are NP-complete. It follows that such a polynomial-time computable program will *not* be able to simulate, for example, even the OR language.

We may then contemplate two alternatives, each attempting to address one of these issues. The first would be to require these program-bids to answer other queries as well, for example, demand queries. This may enable winner determination algorithms to function using better information, as Bartal, Gonen, and Nisan (2003) studied. On the other hand, this would only further make simulation of other bidding languages harder. The other approach, suggested by Nisan (2000), is to weaken the query semantics and make it "nondeterministic": such a query will accept a set S and a "witness" w, and must output some value $v(S, w)$. The only requirement is that $v(S) = \max_w v(S, w)$. One may verify that all bidding languages considered in this chapter have such nondeterministic value queries, and may thus be simulated by such program-bid language.

9.6   Proofs of Theorems from Section 9.3

Proof (of theorem 9.1)   Consider a fixed OR-of-XORs bid representing the monochromatic valuation. Let us call each of the XOR expressions in the bid a clause. Each clause is composed of atomic bids to be called in short, atoms. Thus an atom is of the form (S, p) where S is a subset of the items. We can assume without loss of generality that each atom in the bid is monochromatic, because otherwise removing such non-monochromatic atoms cannot distort the representation of the monochromatic valuation. Also, for no atom can we have $p > |S|$, because otherwise the valuation of S will be too high. Thus we can also assume without loss of generality that for all atoms $p = |S|$, because otherwise that atom can never be "used" in the valuation of any set T, because that would imply too low a valuation for T.

We can now show that all atoms must be in the same clause. Assume not, if two blue atoms are in different clauses, then any red atom cannot be in the same clause with both of them. If a red atom $(p = |T|, T)$ and a blue atom $(p = |S|, S)$ are in different clauses, then because the clauses are connected by an OR, then the valuation given by the bid to $S \cup T$ must be at least $|S| + |T|$, in contradiction to the definition of the monochromatic valuation.

Thus the whole bid is just a single XOR clause, and because every subset S of the red items and every subset S of the blue items must get the valuation $|S|$, it must have its own atom in the XOR clause. Because there are $2^{m/2}$ blue subsets and $2^{m/2}$ red subsets, the theorem follows.   ∎

Proof (of theorem 9.2) Consider a XOR-of-ORs bid representing the K-budget valuation. Let us call each of the OR expressions in the bid a clause. Each clause is composed of atomic bids, in short, atoms. Thus an atom is of the form (S, p) where S is a subset of the items. Let us call a set of size K, a K-set, and an atom of a K-set, a K-atom. Let t be the number of clauses in the bid and l the number of atoms in the largest bid.

First, for no atom (p, S) can we have $p > |S|$, because otherwise the valuation of S will be too high. Thus we can also assume without loss of generality that for all atoms $p = |S|$, because otherwise that atom can never be "used" in the valuation of any set T, because that would imply too low a valuation for T.

For every K-set S, the valuation for S must be obtained from one of the clauses. This valuation is obtained as an OR of disjoint atoms $S = \bigcup_i S_i$. We will show that if the clause size $l \leq 2^{m^{1/4}}$, then each clause can yield the valuation of at most a fraction $2^{-m^{1/4}}$ of all K-sets. Thus the number of clauses must satisfy $t \geq 2^{m^{1/4}}$, obtaining the bound of the lemma.

Fix a single clause. Now consider whether some K-set S is obtained in that clause via a disjoint union $S = \bigcup_i S_i$, of at least $m^{1/4}$ atoms.

If such a set S does not exist, then all K-sets S whose valuation is obtained by this clause are obtained by a union of at most $m^{1/4}$ atoms. Thus the total number of K-sets S obtained by this clause is bounded from above by $\binom{l}{m^{1/4}}$. As a fraction of all possible K-sets this is $\binom{l}{m^{1/4}} / \binom{m}{K}$, which, with the choice of parameters we have, is bounded from above by $2^{-m^{1/4}}$.

Otherwise, fix an arbitrary K-set S that obtains its valuation as a disjoint union of at least $m^{1/4}$ atoms $S = \bigcup_i S_i$. The main observation is that any other K-set T whose valuation is obtained by this clause must intersect each one of these sets S_i, as otherwise the valuation for $T \cup S_i$ would be too high! Let us bound from above the number of possible such sets T. A randomly chosen K-set T has probability of at most Kc/m to intersect any given set S_i of size c. For all $S_i \subseteq S$, this is at most $1/4$, because $c \leq K = \sqrt{m}/2$. The probability that it intersects all these $m^{1/4}$ sets S_i is thus at most $4^{-m^{1/4}}$ (the events of intersecting with each S_i are not independent, but they are negatively correlated, hence the upper bound holds). Thus the fraction of K-sets T that can be obtained by this clause is at most $4^{-m^{1/4}} \leq 2^{-m^{1/4}}$.   ∎

Proof (of theorem 9.3) We prove by induction on the formula structure that a formula of size s can be represented by an OR* bid with s atomic bids. We then show that each atomic bid, in the final resulting OR* bid, can be modified as to not to include more than s dummy items in it.

Induction: The basis of the induction is an atomic bid, which is clearly an OR* bid with a single atomic bid. The induction step requires handling the two separate cases: OR and XOR.

To represent the XOR of several OR* bids as a single OR* bid, we simply merge the clauses of the different OR* bids into a single OR* bid.

To represent the XOR of several OR* bids as a single OR* bid, we introduce a new dummy item x_{ST} for each pair of atomic bids (S, p) and (T, q) that are in two different original OR* bids. For each bid (S, p) in any of the original OR* bids, we add to the generated OR* bid an atomic bid $(S \cup \{x_{ST}|T\}, p)$, where T ranges over all atomic bids in all of the other original OR* bids.

It is clear that the inductive construction constructs a OR* bid with exactly s clauses in it, where s is the number of clauses in the original OR/XOR formula. The number of dummy items in it, however, may be exponentially large. However, we can remove most of these dummy items. One can see that the only significance of a dummy item in an OR* bid is to disallow some two (or more) atomic bids to be taken concurrently.

Thus we may replace all the existing dummy items with at most $\binom{s}{2}$ new dummy items, one for each pair of atomic bids that cannot be taken together (according to the current set of dummy items). This dummy item will be added to both of the atomic bids in this pair.   ∎

Proof (of theorem 9.4)   First note that no subset of the real items of size smaller than $m/2$ can appear with a non-zero valuation in the bid (whatever the associated phantom items are). Now, because every set of the real items of size $m/2$ should have valuation 1, and they cannot get that valuation indirectly from subsets, then this set must appear as one of the atoms in the OR* bid.   ∎

9.7   Conclusion

The core of this chapter was the presentation and formal definition of several bidding languages. We formally studied these languages in terms of their expressive power. The main formal results are of two types: either a simulation result showing that one language is at least as good as another, or a separation result exhibiting a valuation that can be described succinctly in one language, but not in another one. Most attention was given to bidding languages that use combinations of bids on bundles of items; we also mentioned several extensions and important special cases.

The most important computational task associated with a bidding language is solving the winner determination problem among such bidders. We hardly touched this issue in this chapter, as it is the subject of part III of this book. We shortly discussed other computational issues.

References

Bartal, Yair, Rica Gonen, and Noam Nisan (2003), "Incentive Compatible Multi Unit Combinatorial Auctions," in *Proceedings of the 9th Conference on Theoretical Aspects of Rationality and Knowledge*, 72–87.

Boutilier, Craig and Holger H. Hoos (2001), "Bidding Languages for Combinatorial Auctions," in *Seventeenth International Joint Conference on Artificial Intelligence (IJCAI-01)*, 1211–1217.

Fujishima, Yuzo, Kevin Leyton-Brown, and Yoav Shoham (1999), "Taming the Computational Complexity of Combinatorial Auctions: Optimal and Approximate Approaches," in *Proceedings of IJCAI'99*, 548–553.

Hoos, Holger H. and Craig Boutlier (2000), "Solving Combinatorial Auctions Using Stochastic Local Search," in *Proceedings of the 17th National Conference on Artificial Intelligence*, 22–29.

Lehmann, Daniel, Liadan I. O'Callaghan, and Yoav Shoham (2002), "Truth Revelation in Approximately Efficient Combinatorial Auctions," in *Journal of the JACM*, 49, 577–602.

Lehmann, Benny, Daniel Lehmann, and Noam Nisan (2001), "Combinatorial Auctions with Decreasing Marginal Utilities," in *Proc. 3rd ACM Conference on Electronic Commerce ACM Press*, 18–28. *Games and Economic Behavior*, To appear.

Nisan, Noam (2000), "Bidding and Allocation in Combinatorial Auctions," in *Proceedings of the 2nd ACM Conference on Electronic Commerce*, 1–12.

Sandholm, Tuomas (2002a), "Algorithm for Optimal Winner Determination in Combinatorial Auctions," *Artificial Intelligence*, 135, 1–54.

Sandholm, Tuomas (2002b), "eMediator: A Next Generation Electronic Commerce Server," *Computational Intelligence*, 18, 656–676.

Wegner, Ingo (1987), *The Complexity of Boolean Functions*, Stuttgart: John Wiley and Sons.

Zinkevich, Martin, Avrim Blum, and Tuomas W. Sandholm (2003) "On Polynomial-Time Preference Elicitation with Value Queries," in *Proceedings of the 4th ACM Conference on Electronic Commerce*, 176–185.

10 Preference Elicitation in Combinatorial Auctions

Tuomas Sandholm and Craig Boutilier

10.1 Motivation and Introduction

The key feature that makes combinatorial auctions (CAs) most appealing is the ability for bidders to express complex preferences over collections of items, involving complementarity and substitutability. It is this generality that makes providing the input to a CA extremely difficult for bidders. In effect, each bidder must provide his *valuation function* over the space of all bundles of items. More precisely, with m items for sale, there are $2^m - 1$ bundles over which a bidder may have to provide bids.

Requiring all of this information from all bidders is undesirable for several reasons. First, determining one's valuation for any specific bundle can be computationally demanding (Sandholm 1993, 2000; Parkes 2005; Larson and Sandholm 2001), thus requiring this computation for exponentially many bundles is impractical. Second, communicating exponentially many bids can be prohibitive (e.g., w.r.t. network traffic).[1] Finally, agents may prefer not to reveal their valuation information for reasons of privacy or long-term competitiveness (Rothkopf, Teisberg, and Kahn 1990).

Researchers have proposed several approaches for addressing the problem. Ascending CAs (see, for example, Parkes 1999; Wurman and Wellman 2000; Ausubel and Milgrom 2002; Parkes, chapter 2 of this volume; and Ausubel and Milgrom, chapter 3 of this volume), provide one means of minimizing the information requirements on bidders by posting prices (sometimes implicitly) on all bundles and asking bidders to reveal their demands at the current prices.[2] Conen and Sandholm (2001) have recently proposed a more general approach, where the auctioneer (or *elicitor*), instead of requesting bids on all bundles, asks bidders for very limited, and ideally *relevant*, information about their valuations. Through *incremental* querying, the auctioneer gradually builds up a partial model of bidder valuations, one that becomes more refined with each query, until it is possible to determine an optimal allocation. Adopting a query strategy in which previously revealed information guides the selection of subsequent queries focuses elicitation on pertinent information. Ideally, one can determine an optimal allocation despite the fact that each bidder's valuation function has only been partially revealed. One can view ascending CAs as a special case of this model.

The preference elicitation problem in CAs is in many ways the same as that faced in decision analysis and multiattribute utility theory (Keeney and Raiffa 1976). Indeed, the preferences expressed by bids can be seen as a multiattribute utility function in which each item is an attribute. One way to deal with the exponential bid space is to assume some structure in utilities. For instance, it is common to assume utility can be expressed as the additive combination of independent local value functions for each attribute; researchers have also proposed and used much more flexible yet compact representations (Keeney and Raiffa 1976), including graphical models (Bacchus and Grove 1995; Boutilier, Bacchus, and Brafman 2001). The use of structured models that exploit the same intuitions has been developed in CAs under the guise of *bidding languages* (Nisan, chapter 9 of this volume). In such models, one takes advantage of the fact that a utility function over an exponential outcome space (or bundle space) can sometimes be expressed with far fewer parameters. Toward the end of this chapter we present methods for elicitation in CAs that exploit such structure in individual valuation functions.

Compact models still do not address the issue of the cost of precisely computing the parameters of the model in question. Again, the analogous problem in decision analysis—the fact that humans have a hard time precisely assessing utilities—has drawn considerable attention (Keeney and Raiffa 1976; Kahneman and Tversky 1979; Saaty 1980; Dyer 1972; White, Sage, and Dozono 1984; Salo and Hämäläinen 2001; Chajewska, Koller, and Parr 2000; Boutilier 2002; Wang and Boutilier 2003). Typically, in practical decision analysis, one asks comparison queries of various sorts (which require only yes/no responses) rather than direct evaluation queries. These impose bounds on utility parameters, and a number of these queries are asked until a single decision is proven to be optimal, or the user can be presented a manageable Pareto optimal set for selection. In practice, optimal decisions can be found with very limited elicitation of the utility function.

A key feature that distinguishes the preference elicitation problem in CAs from traditional preference elicitation is the fact that certain information about the preferences of one bidder may be irrelevant given the preferences of others. For instance, suppose bidder b has expressed that he prefers bundle X to bundle Y, and that bundle X is worth no more than \$100. Should the auctioneer have information about other agents that ensures revenue greater than \$100 can be obtained for Y, asking for b's valuation for Y serves no useful purpose. Thus, careful interleaving of queries among different bidders can offer potential reductions in the amount of information that needs to be elicited (Conen and Sandholm 2001). This is not always the case—as we discuss below, worst-case results exist that show, in general, the amount of communication required to realize an optimal allocation is exponential, equivalent to at least one bidder revealing his entire valuation for all bundles (Nisan and Segal 2005). But we will see that careful elicitation, can, in practice, offer significant savings. Such multiagent considerations give most work on elicitation in CAs a rather different character than techniques in decision analysis.

The multiagent considerations naturally apply to the more standard single-item auctions as well. Recent work has focused on the question of how to limit the amount of valuation information provided by bidders, for example, by (adaptively) limiting the precision of the bids that are specified (Grigorieva et al. 2002; Blumrosen and Nisan 2002). The motivation for the work can be seen as largely the same as work on preference elicitation in CAs. Of course, the problem is much more acute in the case of CAs, due to the combinatorial nature of valuation space.

We begin in section 10.2 with a discussion of a general framework for elicitation, and describe relevant concepts such as certificates and incentives. Section 10.3 deals with a class of elicitation algorithms that use the concept of a *rank lattice*. We discuss instantiations of the more general framework in section 10.4, focusing on methods that make no assumptions about valuation structure, and then section 10.5 deals with methods that exploit structured valuations. We conclude with discussion of future directions.

10.2   A General Elicitation Framework

We begin by describing the basic CA setting, and propose a general model in which we can cast most forms of incremental elicitation. We also describe several concepts that have a bearing on most elicitation techniques.

10.2.1   The Setting

Consider a setting with one benevolent seller (auctioneer or arbitrator) and n buyers (bidders). The seller has a set $M = \{1, \ldots, m\}$ of indivisible, distinguishable items to sell (we assume no reservation value). Any subset of the items is called a *bundle*. The set of bidders is $N = \{1, \ldots, n\}$.

Each bidder has a valuation function $v_i : 2^M \to \mathbb{R}$ that states how valuable any given bundle is to that bidder. Let $v_i(\emptyset) = 0$ for all i. These valuations are private information. We make the standard quasilinearity assumption: the utility of any bidder i is $u_i(X_i, p_i) = v_i(X_i) - p_i$, where $X_i \subseteq M$ is the bundle he receives and p_i is the amount that he has to pay.

A *collection* $(X_1, \ldots, X_n)$ states which bundle X_i each bidder i receives. If some bidders' bundles overlap, the collection is infeasible. An *allocation* is a feasible collection (i.e., each item is allocated to at most one bidder).

We will study elicitors that find a welfare maximizing allocation (or in certain settings, a Pareto efficient allocation). An allocation X is *welfare maximizing* if it maximizes

$\sum_{i=1}^{n} v_i(X_i)$ among all allocations. An allocation X is *Pareto efficient* if there is no other allocation Y such that $v_i(X_i) \geq v_i(Y_i)$ for each bidder i and strictly greater for at least some bidder i.

10.2.2 Elicitors

By *preference elicitation* in CAs we refer to a process by which the auctioneer queries bidders for specific information about their valuations. If we think of elicitation as a distinct process, we can view the auctioneer as augmented with an *elicitor* (most practically embodied in software) that determines what queries to pose. Given any sequence of responses to previous queries, the elicitor may decide to ask further queries, or stop and (allow the auctioneer to) determine a feasible (possibly optimal) allocation and payments. Most models and algorithms of elicitation in CAs studied to date can be cast as instantiations of the following general algorithm:

1. Let C_t denote information the elicitor has regarding bidder valuation functions after iteration t of the elicitation process. C_0 reflects any prior information available to the auctioneer.
2. Given C_t, either a) terminate the process, and determine an allocation and payments; or b) choose a set of (one or more) queries Q_t to ask (one or more) bidders.
3. Update C_t given response(s) to query set Q_t to form C_{t+1}, and repeat.

This framework is, of course, too general to be useful without addressing some key questions. All specific algorithms for elicitation that we survey take a concrete stance on each of the following issues.

First, what queries is the elicitor allowed to pose? Examples considered in the literature include rank queries ("What is your second-most preferred bundle?"), order queries ("Is bundle a preferred to bundle b?"), bound queries ("Is bundle a worth at least p?"), value queries ("What is bundle a worth?"), and demand queries ("If the prices for—some or all—bundles were $\vec{p}$, which bundle would you buy?"). When evaluating the effectiveness of elicitation, we generally care about the number of queries required to determine an optimal allocation. This must be considered carefully, because powerful queries such as "What is your valuation?" trivialize the problem. Thus it is natural to compare the number of queries the elicitor asks on a specific problem instance to the number of the *same type* of queries needed to realize full revelation.

Second, how is information about bidder valuations represented? This is tied intimately to the permitted query types, because different queries impose different types of constraints on possible valuations. For instance, if one uses only bound queries, then upper and lower bounds on valuations (and allocations) must be maintained. This question also depends on structural assumptions that the elicitor makes about valuations. The query types above exploit no structural information (because they ask only about bundles); but if one can assume, say, that a bidder's valuation function is linear, then queries can be directed toward parameters of the valuation function. Furthermore, the representation of the consistent valuation functions can be much more compact. Finally, one might use probabilistic representations to reflect priors over valuations, for instance, to decide which queries are most likely to be useful.

Finally, the issue of termination is critical: when does the elicitor have enough information to terminate the process? Naturally, determination of an optimal or approximately optimal allocation (w.r.t. the responses offered) should be possible. However, incentive properties must also be accounted for (see below). Ideally, mechanisms should also account for the costs of elicitation (e.g., communication costs, or computational/cognitive costs imposed on the bidders).

10.2.3 Certificates
Because the aim of incremental elicitation is to determine optimal allocations without full valuation information, it is critical to know when *enough* information has been elicited. A *certificate* is a set of query-answer pairs that prove that an allocation is optimal.[3] The form of certificates naturally depends on the types of queries one is willing to entertain. For example, when the objective is to find a welfare-maximizing allocation, the elicitor clears the auction if, given the information received, he can infer that one allocation is worth at least as much as any other. A *minimal certificate* is a certificate that would cease to be a certificate if any query-answer pair were removed from it. A *shortest certificate* for a specific problem instance is a certificate that has the smallest number of query-answer pairs among all certificates.[4]

10.2.4 Handling Incentives
Motivating the bidders to answer elicitor queries truthfully is a key issue; if the bidders lie, the resulting allocation may be suboptimal. It is well known that the Vickrey-Clarke-Groves (VCG) mechanism (Vickrey 1961; Clarke 1971; Groves 1973) makes truth telling each bidder's dominant strategy.[5] (See Ausubel and Milgrom, chapter 1 and Ronen, chapter 15 of this volume for discussions of incentives.) However, the VCG mechanism, as generally defined, requires complete "up front" revelation of each bidder's valuation (in sealed-bid fashion).

When using incremental elicitation, motivating bidders to answer queries truthfully is more difficult, as elicitor queries may leak information to the bidder about the answers that other bidders have given (depending on the elicitor's query policy). For instance, a bidder may condition his response on the precise sequence of queries asked by inferring that the current query is deemed necessary by the elicitor given responses to queries by other bidders. This makes the bidders' strategy spaces richer, and can provide incentive to reveal untruthfully.

Conen and Sandholm (2001) describe a methodology by which one can structure incremental elicitation mechanisms so that answering queries truthfully is an *ex post equilibrium*: bidding truthfully is each bidder's best strategy, given that the other bidders bid truthfully. The elicitor asks enough queries to determine not only the welfare-maximizing allocation, but also VCG payments.[6] Using the welfare-maximizing allocation and VCG payments so constructed, the elicitor induces all bidders to answer their queries truthfully.[7]

A related approach to handling incentives in auctions involves proving that myopic best-responding is an ex post equilibrium in ascending auctions (Gul and Stacchetti 2000). This approach has also been used in multi-unit (Ausubel 2005) and combinatorial auctions (Ausubel 2002). Another related approach uses proxy bidders in CAs: the proxies carry out myopic best response strategies in an ascending auction. In that case, revealing valuation information to the proxies truthfully on an as-needed basis is an ex post equilibrium (Parkes 2001).

Incentive-Compatible *Push-Pull* Mechanisms   To improve revelation efficiency, the elicitor can, apart from querying (or *pulling* information), allow bidders to provide unsolicited information (i.e., *push* information), and treat it as if he had asked the corresponding query. Revelation through bidder push can be effective because the bidder has information (about his own valuation) that the elicitor does not. Revelation through elicitor pull can be effective because the elicitor has information that the bidder doesn't (about others' valuations). Because both modes have their strengths, the hybrid push-pull method can help reduce the amount of revelation compared to pure push or pull.

Bidders can also refuse to answer some of the elicitor's queries (e.g., if they are too hard to answer). As long as enough information is revealed to determine the optimal allocation and VCG payments, truth telling is an ex post equilibrium. Thus, incentive properties remain intact despite the fact that the bidders can pass on queries and "answer" queries that the elicitor did not ask.[8] In the rest of this chapter, we only consider *pull* mechanisms.

10.2.5   Constraint Network

Although different elicitation algorithms may require different means of representing the information obtained by bidders, Conen and Sandholm (2001) describe a fairly general method for representing an incompletely specified valuation function that supports update with respect to a wide variety of queries, and inference by the elicitor. A *constraint network* is a labeled directed graph consisting of one node for each bundle b representing the elicitor's knowledge of the preferences of a bidder. A *directed edge* (a, b) indicates that bundle a is (known to be) preferred to bundle b. Each node b is labeled with an interval $[LB_i(b), UB_i(b)]$, where $LB_i(b)$ is the greatest lower bound the elicitor can prove on the true $v_i(b)$ given the answers received to queries so far, and $UB_i(b)$ is

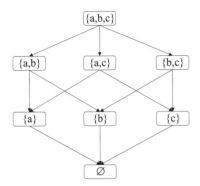

Figure 10.1
A constraint network for a single bidder with 3 items a, b, and c encoding free disposal.

the least upper bound. By transitivity, the elicitor knows that a is preferred to b, denoted $a \succeq b$, if there is a directed path from a to b or if $LB_i(a) \geq UB_i(b)$.

The free disposal assumption allows the elicitor to add the edges (a, b) to any constraint network for any $a \subseteq b$, as figure 10.1 shows. Responses to order queries can be encoded by adding edges between the pair of bundles compared, whereas value and bound queries can be encoded by updating the bounds. When bounds are updated, new lower bounds can readily be propagated "upstream" and new upper bounds "downstream."

The constraint network representation is useful conceptually, and can be represented explicitly for use in various elicitation algorithms. But its explicit representation is generally tractable only for small problems, because it contains 2^m nodes (one per bundle), and an average outdegree of $m/2$.

10.3 Rank Lattice-Based Elicitors

We begin with discussion of a class of elicitors that use the notion of a *rank lattice* (Conen and Sandholm 2001, 2002c). Rank-lattice elicitors adopt specific query policies that exploit the topological structure inherent in the problem to guide the elicitation of bidders' preferences.

Conceptually, bundles can be ranked for each bidder from most to least preferred. This gives a unique rank for each bundle for each bidder (assuming no indifference). Let $b_i(r_i)$ be the bundle that bidder i has at rank r_i. In other words, $b_i(1)$ is the bidder's most preferred bundle, $b_i(2)$ second-most, and so on. A *rank vector* $r = [r_1, r_2, \ldots, r_n]$ represents the allocation of $b_i(r_i)$ to bidder i. Naturally, some rank vectors correspond to feasible allocations and some to infeasible collections. The value of a rank vector r is $v(b(r)) = \sum_i v_i(b_i(r_i))$. A rank vector $[r_1, r_2, \ldots, r_n]$ *dominates* rank vector $[r'_1, r'_2, \ldots, r'_n]$ if

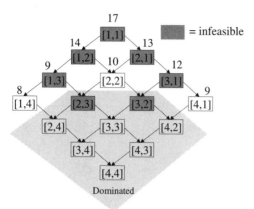

Figure 10.2
Rank lattice for two bidders, 1 and 2, and two items, A and B, with the following value functions: v1(AB) = 8, v1(A) = 4, v1(B) = 3, v1(;) = 0, v2(AB) = 9, v2(B) = 6, v2(A) = 1, v2(;) = 0. Gray nodes are infeasible. The shaded area is the set of nodes dominated by feasible nodes. Above each node is its value.

$r_i \le r_i'$ for all bidders $i \in N$. The set of rank vectors together with the domination relation define the *rank lattice*, as depicted in figure 10.2.

If a feasible collection (i.e., allocation) is not dominated by another allocation in the rank lattice, it is Pareto efficient (i.e., if the elicitor knew only the ranks of all bundles of all bidders, but had no valuation information, each such nondominated allocation is potentially optimal; see the three white nodes in figure 10.2). Welfare-maximizing allocations (in this example, rank vector [2, 2]) can be determined using the values only of allocations in this set.

Because no allocation that lies below another in the rank lattice can be a better solution to the allocation problem, Conen and Sandholm (2001, 2002b, c) propose a series of search algorithms to find optimal allocations that exploit this fact to guide the elicitation process. Intuitively, rank-based elicitors construct relevant parts of the rank lattice by traversing the lattice in a top-down fashion, asking queries in a "natural" order. Because the rank lattice has 2^{mn} nodes, careful enumeration is critical, because the entire rank lattice cannot be examined in any but the smallest problems. Within the general elicitation model, these methods rely on rank, value, and "relative" bound queries, and assume no structure in valuations.

10.3.1 Using Rank and Value Queries
The PAR (Pareto optimal) algorithm (Conen and Sandholm 2002c) is a top-down search algorithm that uses rank queries to find all Pareto efficient allocations. It initially

asks every bidder for his most preferred bundle, constructing the collection $(1, \ldots, 1)$ that sits atop the rank lattice. As the search progresses, the elicitor asks one new query for every successor that it "constructs" in the rank lattice by asking one of the bidders for the next most preferred bundle. Specifically, starting with $(1, \ldots, 1)$ in the *fringe*, PAR chooses a node from the fringe, adds it to the Pareto efficient set if it is feasible; if not, its children are added to the fringe. At each stage, all nodes in the fringe that are dominated by a Pareto optimal node are removed. The algorithm terminates when the fringe is empty. At termination, all Pareto optimal solutions have been identified.[9] PAR can be augmented to produce a welfare-maximizing outcome by asking value queries of all bundles that occur in the Pareto efficient set. This variant is called MPAR (maximizing PAR).

The EBF (efficient best first) algorithm (Conen and Sandholm 2002c) is designed to find a welfare-maximizing allocation under the standard assumption of transferable and quasi-linear utility. As with PAR, it asks for each bidder's bundles in most-to-least-preferred order. However, EBF also asks for bundle *values*. These values give the search algorithm additional guidance as to which nodes to expand. The algorithm starts from the root and always expands the fringe node of highest value, while pruning provably dominated nodes. The first feasible node reached is optimal.

Unlike typical best-first search, EBF cannot always determine which node on the fringe has highest value (and thus should be expanded) given its current information; thus further elicitation is generally required. Conen and Sandholm define a simple (nondeterministic) subroutine for node expansion that defines an elicitation policy where the elicitor picks an arbitrary node from the fringe and elicits just enough information to determine its value, until it can prove which node on the fringe has highest value. Interestingly, because the elicitor uses constraint network inference to propagate value bounds, one can determine the best node in the fringe without knowing its precise value or the identity of the bundles that make it up. Determining feasibility then requires that the elicitor ask rank queries to determine each unknown $b_i(r_i)$.

Conen and Sandholm show that MPAR and EBF are, in a sense, as effective as possible in their uses of information, within the restricted class of *admissibly equipped* elicitors. An elicitor is *admissible* if it always finds a welfare-maximizing allocation; both EBF and MPAR are admissible. An elicitor is *admissibly equipped* if it can perform *only* the following operations: a) determine the welfare of a given collection (by asking bidders for their valuations for relevant bundles); b) determine whether a given collection is feasible or not (by asking bidders for the bundles at that rank vector); and c) determine the next unvisited direct successors of a collection in the lattice.

Theorem 10.1 (Conen and Sandholm 2002c) No admissible, admissibly equipped, deterministic elicitor requires fewer feasibility checks on every problem instance than EBF.

This result does not depend on the specific instantiation of the nondeterministic node-expansion strategy used by EBF.

Theorem 10.2 (Conen and Sandholm 2002c) No admissible, admissibly equipped, deterministic algorithm that only calls the valuation function for feasible collections requires fewer calls than MPAR.

This result restricts elicitors to asking for the valuation of feasible collections. It also counts valuation calls to collections, as opposed to individual bundle-bidder pairs. In practice, we care about the latter and have no reason to restrict the elicitor to queries about feasible collections.

Although EBF and MPAR are as effective as any admissible, admissibly equipped elicitor, Conen and Sandholm (2002c) show that worst-case behavior for both algorithms (hence for any algorithm in this class) is quite severe. Specifically, MPAR needs to query the value of n^m allocations in the worst case, whereas EBF must call the valuation routine on $(2^{mn} - n^m)/2 + 1$ collections.

The practical effectiveness of these algorithms is strongly dependent on the number of items and agents. Maintaining an explicit constraint network for each bidder and rank lattice can be problematic, because the former (i.e., number of bundles) grows exponentially with the number of items, and the latter grows exponentially with the number of relevant bundles. The hope is that by clever elicitation, EBF will obviate the need to construct anything but a very small portion of the rank lattice. Unfortunately, EBF shows rather poor empirical performance in this regard (Hudson and Sandholm 2004): the *elicitation ratio*—the ratio of the number of queries asked by an elicitor to the total number of queries required by full revelation—is rather poor. On small problems (from two to four bidders, two to eleven items), the ratio drops with the number of items, but quickly approaches 1 as the number of bidders increases (and is close to one with as few as four bidders). This is not surprising, because bidders tend to win smaller, low-ranked bundles when the number of participants is large, forcing enumeration of large parts of the lattice.

One benefit of examining the lattice top-down occurs when considering VCG payments. Once EBF terminates, no additional queries are needed to determine VCG payments.

Theorem 10.3 (Conen and Sandholm 2002c) No information in addition to the information already obtained by EBF is necessary to determine the VCG payments.

10.3.2 Differential Elicitation
Conen and Sandholm (2002b) propose variants of the EBF algorithm in which the elicitor asks bidders for the *differences between valuations* rather than absolute valuations.

Such *differential elicitation* methods require bidders to reveal less about their valuations. The elicitor asks rank queries (i.e., what bundle has rank k), and either *differential value queries* of the form "What is the difference between the value of bundle b and your most preferred bundle?" or *differential bound queries* of the form "Is the difference between the value of bundle b and your most preferred bundle greater than δ?"

The general differential elicitation algorithm is a modification of EBF. The key observation is that the optimal allocation minimizes the aggregated loss in utility of each bidder relative to his most preferred bundle. The algorithm therefore iteratively elicits differences between valuations relative to the (unspecified, maximum) valuation for the highest ranking bundle. We focus on the use of differential bound queries, and suppose that there is some small "accounting unit" ε such that all valuations must differ by some integral multiple of ε.

The algorithm EBF-DE proceeds like EBF differing only in its use of differential bound queries rather than value queries, and its strategy for expanding nodes. For any specific bundle-bidder pair, EBF-DE asks queries for that bundle in increasing order of difference (e.g., is the difference between the value of b and your most preferred bundle greater than 0? ε? 2ε? etc.). If the bidder responds yes, this establishes a lower bound on the difference; if no, this establishes the precise difference. These lower bounds can be used to reason about domination in the rank lattice, because the lower bounds on loss (relative to the optimal bundle) for each bidder can be summed to obtain a lower bound on the aggregate loss.[10] EBF-DE ensures a welfare-maximizing allocation is found. Furthermore, like EBF, we have:

Proposition 10.1 (Conen and Sandholm 2002b) No information in addition to that obtained by EBF-DE is necessary to determine VCG payments.

10.4 Elicitation with Unstructured Valuations

Elicitors that exploit rank lattices have a very restricted, inflexible form of query policy, intimately intertwined with the elicitor's lattice representation of the information gleaned from bidders. In this section, we describe work that offers more flexible approaches to elicitation along the lines of the general elicitation framework described in section 10.2.2. We focus here on the case of unstructured valuations, deferring discussion of structured valuations to section 10.5.

Conen and Sandholm (2001) describe a general framework for unstructured preferences in which the elicitor's knowledge is organized as a set of *candidates*. A candidate $c = \langle c_1, c_2, \ldots, c_n \rangle$ is any allocation (i.e., feasible collection) that, given the responses to queries so far, is potentially optimal. Given the nature of the queries considered below, one can generally impose upper and lower bounds on the value associated with each allocation in the candidate set.

One can obviously view the problem of elicitation as a game against nature, in which an optimal elicitor constructs an optimal strategy (or contingency plan) where nature chooses valuations for the bidders, thus dictating responses to the queries prescribed by the optimal policy.[11] This can be solved using tree search, but this is clearly impractical except for tiny problems (Hudson and Sandholm 2004). This has led the development of heuristic methods for elicitation, as we now describe.

10.4.1 Value Queries

Hudson and Sandholm (2004) consider various instantiations of the general elicitation framework in which the elicitor is restricted to asking *value queries*, in which a bidder is asked to reveal his valuation $v_i(b)$ of a specific bundle b. This sets the value of b for bidder i and can be used to set upper and lower bounds on other bundles using constraint network inference (section 10.2.5). Note that without edges in the constraint network (e.g., due to free disposal), information about the value of one bundle provides no information on the value of others. All of the value-query policies considered ask each bidder for the value of the *grand bundle M* consisting of all items, because it imposes an upper bound on the value of all bundles—Hudson and Sandholm (2004) give formal justification for eliciting the grand bundle. They also investigate the potential savings of several elicitation policies relative to the $Q = n(2^m - 1)$ value queries required by full elicitation. We let q_{min} denote the shortest certificate for a specific problem instance (here, the fewest value queries an omniscient elicitor could ask).

The *random elicitation policy* simply asks random value queries (whose answers cannot yet be inferred given the answers so far) until a optimal allocation can be determined.

Theorem 10.4 (Hudson and Sandholm 2004)   For any given problem instance, the expected number of value queries q that the random elicitation policy asks is at most $(q_{min}/(q_{min} + 1))(Q + 1)$.

This upper bound guarantees relatively minor savings in elicitation because q_{min} increases with the number of agents and items. However, the pessimistic nature of the proof—that there is one minimal certificate—gives hope that in practice random elicitation may perform better than suggested. Experiments (see figure 10.3) show that, although the elicitation ratio q/Q is less than 1, and slowly decreases with the number of items, it generally offers little savings over full elicitation (Hudson and Sandholm 2004).

The *random allocatable policy* improves on the random policy by restricting the set from which a query will be randomly selected. Note that the elicitor might know that a bundle b will not be allocated to bidder i before he knows the bidder's precise valuation for the bundle. This occurs when the elicitor knows of a different allocation that it

elicitation ratio

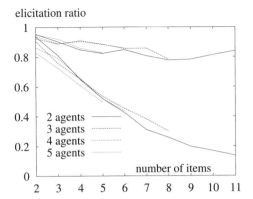

Figure 10.3
Top: Random elicitation policy. Bottom: Random allocatable policy.

can prove will generate at least as much value as any allocation that allocates b to agent i. If the elicitor cannot (yet) determine this (i.e., if there is a candidate in which $c_i = b$), then the bundle-bidder pair ·is deemed *allocatable*. The random allocatable policy is identical to the random policy with a restriction to allocatable bundle-bidder pairs. Hudson and Sandholm (2002, 2004) provide a characterization of situations in which restricting queries to allocatable pairs can and cannot lessen the effectiveness of the random policy. This restriction can never lessen the effectiveness by more than a factor of 2. Empirically, they show that the random allocatable policy performs dramatically better than the random policy, that the proportion of queries asked drops quickly with the number of items, and is unaffected by the number of bidders (see figure 10.3).

The *high-value candidate* policy (Hudson and Sandholm 2004) relies on the following intuition: to prove an allocation is optimal, we require a sufficiently high lower bound on it, and sufficiently low upper bounds on all other allocations. By only picking from high-value candidates, the high-value candidate elicitor is biased toward queries that (we expect) need to be asked anyway. In addition, by picking from those queries that will reduce as many values as possible, it is also biased toward reducing upper bounds.

More precisely, let C_{max} be the set of *high-value candidates*, those with the greatest upper bound. For each $(b, i) \in C_{max}$, let *sub-bundles*(b, i) be the number of other bundles in C_{max} whose value might be affected upon eliciting $v_i(b)$, that is, those $(b', i) \in C_{max}$ for which $b \supset b'$ and $LB_i(b) < UB_i(b')$. The elicitor asks value queries by choosing uniformly at random among the (b, i) with the most sub-bundles. Empirically, Hudson and Sandholm (2004) show that the high-value candidate elicitor performs better than the random allocatable elicitor (see figure 10.4 for illustrative results); it achieves an elicitation ratio of only 24 percent with eight items and three agents, as opposed to 30 percent for the random allocatable policy and 78 percent for the random policy.

elicitation ratio

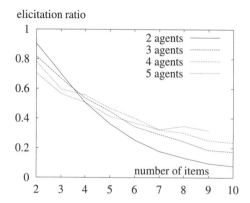

Figure 10.4
High-value candidate elicitation policy. The legend is in the order of the plot lines at two items.
The elicitation ratio falls with increasing number of items, but grows with increasing number of
agents, when there are more items than agents (see Hudson and Sandholm (2004) for details).

Hudson and Sandholm (2004) also evaluate the performance of an *omniscient* elicitor, one that knows each bidder's valuation function, but must ask a set of queries
whose responses constitute a minimal certificate for the instance in question.[12] The
performance of the omniscient elicitor provides an instance-specific lower bound on
that of any real elicitor.

The policies described above require intensive computation, especially if the candidate set is represented explicitly, as this scales poorly with the number of agents. Pruning of dominated candidates after any query response requires time quadratic in the
number of candidates, whereas determining the best query (e.g., in the high-value candidate policy) and termination requires linear time, a tremendous burden, because
there may be as many as n^m candidates.[13]

Candidates need not be represented explicitly. Query selection can be accomplished
by repeatedly solving an efficient integer program (IP) to compute the value of the
highest valued candidate (Hudson and Sandholm 2004). With reasonable caching, the
implicit approach can be several orders of magnitude faster than the explicit candidate
representation.

Finally, Hudson and Sandholm (2004) address the question of whether there exist
universal elicitors, that is, elicitors that save revelation on all instances (excluding those
where even the omniscient elicitor must reveal everything).

Definition 10.1 A *universal revelation reducer* is an elicitor with the following property:
given any problem instance, it guarantees (always in the deterministic case; in expectation over the random choices in the randomized case) saving some elicitation over full

revelation—provided the shortest certificate is shorter than full revelation. Formally: if $q_{min} < Q$, the elicitor makes $q < Q$ queries.

By theorem 10.4, the unrestricted random elicitor is a universal revelation reducer. In contrast:

Theorem 10.5 (Hudson and Sandholm 2004)   No deterministic value query policy is a universal revelation reducer.

10.4.2 Order Queries

In some applications, bidders might need to expend great (say, cognitive or computational) effort to determine their valuations precisely (Sandholm 1993; Parkes 2005; Sandholm 2000; Larson and Sandholm 2001), but might easily be able to see that one bundle is preferable to another. In such settings, it is natural to ask bidders *order queries*, that is, which of two bundles, b or b', they prefer. A response to this query induces a new (direct) domination relation in the constraint network for the bidder. Naturally, by asking only order queries, the elicitor cannot compare the valuations of one agent with those of another, so it generally cannot determine a welfare-maximizing allocation. However, order queries can be helpful when interleaved with value queries.

Hudson and Sandholm (2004) propose an elicitation policy that combines value and order queries by simply alternating between the two, starting with an order query. Whenever an order query is to be asked, the elicitor computes all tuples (b, b', i) where bundles b and b' are each allocated to bidder i in some candidate, and where the elicitor knows neither $b' \succeq b$ nor $b \succeq b'$, and asks the order query corresponding to a random such tuple. Value queries are chosen randomly from among allocatable bundle-bidder pairs (as in the random allocatable policy above).

To compare the effectiveness of this policy against value-query-based policies, one needs to assess the relative "costs" of order and value queries. If order queries are cheap, it is worth mixing the two; otherwise, using value queries alone is better. An experiment by Hudson and Sandholm suggests that (when the random allocatable policy is used to select value queries) the break-even point occurs when an order query costs about 10 percent of the cost of a value query.

An advantage of the mixed value-order policy is that it does not depend as critically on free disposal. Without free disposal, any policy that uses value queries only would have to elicit all values. Order queries, on the other hand, can create useful edges in the constraint network, which the elicitor can use to prune candidates.

Conen and Sandholm (2001) present several other algorithms within the general elicitation framework that use combinations of value, order, and rank queries. Researchers have also demonstrated the effectiveness of elicitation in combinatorial reverse auctions (Hudson and Sandholm 2003) and in combinatorial exchanges (Smith, Sandholm, and Simmons 2002).

10.4.3 Bound-Approximation Queries

In many settings, the bidders can more readily estimate their valuations than accurately compute them; and often the more accurate the estimate, the more costly it is to determine. This might be the case, for example, if bidders determine their valuations using anytime algorithms (Larson and Sandholm 2001). To account for this, Hudson and Sandholm (2004) introduce the use of *bound-approximation queries* for CAs, where the elicitor asks a bidder i to tighten its upper bound $UB_i(b)$ or lower bound $LB_i(b)$ on the value of a given bundle b.[14] This allows for elicitation of a more incremental form than that provided by value queries. The model Hudson and Sandholm study is one in which the elicitor can provide a hint as to how much time to spend refining this bound.

The *bound-approximation query policy* considered is one in which the elicitor determines the best query as follows: for each (b, i) pair, it (optimistically) assumes that the answer $z = UB_i(b)$ will be provided to a lower bound query (thus moving the lower bound maximally); conversely, it (optimistically) assumes that the answer $z = LB_i(b)$ will be provided to an upper bound query. The best query is that whose sum of (assumed) changes over all candidates is maximal. The policy was tested using a model of bound refinement that allowed for diminishing returns of computational effort: the marginal rate at which the bound is tightened reduces with the amount of computational effort expended. Experiments (Hudson and Sandholm 2002) show on small problems that this policy can reduce overall computation cost as the number of items grows (and is independent of the number of agents).

Hudson and Sandholm (2003) have empirically studied the question of VCG payments in the general elicitation framework for value, order, and bound-approximation queries. Unlike the EBF elicitor, in which VCG payments are obtained as a side effect due to the rigid query order, the general model will usually require additional queries. Experimentally, once a specific elicitor found the optimal allocation (and its value), each bidder i was removed from consideration in turn, and the elicitation algorithm was continued without candidates that allocated items to i, thus allowing the optimal allocation opt_{-i} (and value) without i, hence VCG payments, to be computed.

The two-agent case requires almost no additional elicitation: opt_{-i} simply allocates the grand bundle M to the agent that was not removed. Thus at most four additional values are needed over what is necessary to compute the optimal allocation: $v_1(opt_1)$, $v_1(M)$, $v_2(opt_2)$, and $v_2(M)$. Although this argument does not generalize to more than two agents, in practice, relatively little extra information is needed. For example, the elicitation ratio of the bound-approximation policy is 60 percent at three agents and five items, and determining VCG payments only increases the elicitation ratio to 71 percent. Similarly, that of the value and order policy only increases from 48 percent to 56 percent.

10.4.4   Demand Queries

Demand queries form another interesting, naturally occurring class of queries. In a demand query the elicitor asks bidder i: "If the prices on bundles $S \subseteq M$ were p_i (where $p_i : 2^M \rightarrow \mathbb{R}$), which bundle S would you buy?" In practice, prices are explicitly quoted only on a small subset of the bundles; the price of any other bundle is implicitly defined based on the prices of its subsets, for example, $p_i(S) = \max_{S' \subseteq S} p_i(S')$. The bidder would answer with the profit-maximizing bundle $\max_{S \subseteq M} v_i(S) - p_i(S)$.

One can distinguish demand query elicitors along several dimensions:

1. Does the elicitor adopt *anonymous pricing*, by offering the same prices $p_i(S) = p(S)$ to all bidders, or *discriminatory pricing*, offering different prices $p_i(S)$ to different bidders i?
2. Are *bundle prices* used, or *item prices*? Item prices associate a price $p_i(k)$ with each item k, with $p_i(S) = \sum_{k \in S} p_i(j)$.[15]
3. How does the elicitor chooses the next query to ask?

Ascending (combinatorial) auctions—in which prices increase during the auction—can be seen as a special case of the general elicitation framework which use demand queries in a very specific way. There has been considerable research on ascending CAs, much of it focused on structured valuations of various types. Indeed, most work on elicitation using demand queries arises in the context of ascending CAs. We briefly overview here results dealing with general, unstructured valuations, and return to the question of structured valuations in the next section. In this volume, Parkes (chapter 2) and Ausubel and Milgrom (chapter 3) discuss ascending CAs in further detail. Segal (chapter 11) addresses elicitation using demand queries.

An important strand of research is the design of ascending CAs for general valuations (e.g., Parkes 1999a; DeMartini et al. 1999; Wurman and Wellman 2000). There are ascending discriminatory bundle-price auctions that yield optimal allocations in this general setting. They can be understood as linear programming algorithms for the winner determination problem: primal-dual algorithms (de Vries, Schummer, and Vohra 2003) or subgradient algorithms (Parkes and Ungar 2000; Ausubel and Milgrom 2002). Additional conditions on the valuation functions need to be satisfied for the auctions to also yield VCG prices (de Vries, Schummer, and Vohra 2003; see also Parkes, chapter 2, and Ausubel and Milgrom, chapter 3 of this volume). It is unknown whether any *anonymous* bundle-price auction guarantees optimality (Nisan 2003), though for restrictive definitions of "auction," the insufficiency of anonymous prices has been shown (Parkes, chapter 2 of this volume). (See Bikhchandani and Ostroy 2002 for a discussion of competitive equilibria with anonymous bundle-prices.) Item-price demand queries can be used to efficiently simulate any value query (the converse is not true) (Nisan 2003). (However, to answer a demand query, a bidder may need to solve his planning problems for a large number of bundles, if not all of them; a value query can be answered based on one plan.) Therefore, the optimal allocation can always be found using item-price demand queries, but the number of queries needed (shortest certificate) is exponential in some instances. Furthermore, even in some instances where a polynomial number of item-price demand queries constitutes a certificate, no *ascending* item-price auction (even a discriminatory one) can find the optimal allocation (Nisan 2003).

Taken together, Blum et al. (2004) and Lahaie and Parkes (2004) show that bundle-price queries have drastically more power than item-price queries. As Nisan (2003) pointed out, any reasonable ascending bundle-price auction will terminate within a pseudopolynomial number of queries:

$s \cdot n \cdot$ (highest-bid/minimum-bid-increment).

Here s is the number of maximum number of terms required to express any bidder's valuation in the *XOR* language (introduced in Sandholm 2002; see also Nisan, chapter 9 of this volume). Furthermore, using bundle-price demand queries (where only poly-nomially many bundles are explicitly priced) and value queries together, the optimal allocation can be found in a number of queries that is polynomial in m, n, and s (Lahaie and Parkes 2004), using techniques from computational learning theory (see section 10.5.3). On the other hand, there is a nontrivial lower bound for *item-price* demand queries:

Theorem 10.6 (Blum et al. 2004)   If the elicitor can only use value queries and item-price demand queries, then $2^{\Omega(\sqrt{m})}$ queries are needed in the worst case to determine the optimal allocation. This holds even if each bidder's valuation, represented in the XOR-language, has at most $O(\sqrt{m})$ terms.

Nisan and Segal (2005) address the communication complexity of CAs, in particular, the possibility that clever elicitation can reduce the need for a bidder to specify a valu-ation function over all bundles. Their main results are negative: reduction in commu-nication complexity is not (generally) possible. Although they do not rely on specific query types, these results demonstrate the importance of supporting, "personalized" prices for all bundles.[16] In particular, Nisan and Segal demonstrate that any communi-cation protocol must reveal supporting prices; stated very roughly:

Proposition 10.2 (Nisan and Segal 2005)   A communication protocol with message space M realizes an efficient allocation rule if and only if there exists a (personalized) price vector (over bundles) for each $m \in M$ realizing a price equilibrium.

This generalizes an earlier result of Parkes (2002), who considers a more restricted query language (and explores the relationship to ascending auctions and demand queries). The notion of *dual utilities* (under mild normalization and quasi-linearity assumptions) is then used to provide a lower bound on communication. More precisely, assume a two-bidder problem and let V_1 be space of valuations of the first bidder and V_2 the second. For any $v_1 \in V_1$, we say $v_2 \in V_2$ is the *dual* of v_1 if and only if the social welfare of every allocation is identical given $\langle v_1, v_2 \rangle$.

Theorem 10.7 (Nisan and Segal 2005)   If for each $v_1 \in V_1$, there is a dual $v_2 \in V_2$, then any efficient communication protocol requires at least $\log |V_1|$ bits.

For a CA, one can apply the dual notion to show that:

Theorem 10.8 (Nisan and Segal 2005)   The dimension of the message space in any efficient protocol for a CA with m items (with general valuations) is at least $2^m - 1$.

This means that the communication required is at least that of one agent revealing his full valuation. This bound is tight for two agents, but an upper bound for more than $n > 2$ agents of $(n - 1)(2^m - 1)$ is known not to be tight. Nisan and Segal also describe a wide variety of approximation results (see Segal, chapter 11 of this volume, for further details).

We have seen that in practice, full revelation is sometimes prevented by careful incremental elicitation. These results show, however, that in general, this cannot be the case (relative to the entire valuation of one agent). We will see the impact of these results in the case of structured valuations below.

10.5   Elicitation with Structured Valuations

Despite the worst-case complexity of preference elicitation for general valuations, for certain restricted classes, the elicitor can learn the function v_i (even in the worst case) using a number of queries that is polynomial in the number of items. Many of these results build upon work in computational learning theory (COLT) (Angluin 1988; Angluin, Hellerstein, and Karpinski 1993; Bshouty et al. 1994; Bshouty, Hancock, and Hellerstein 1995).

Many of these classes are rich enough to exhibit both complementarity and substitutability. When valuations can be elicited with polynomially many (reasonable) queries, a natural approach to elicitation is to first determine each bidder's valuation completely, and then determine an allocation (and payments), rather than attempt to save elicitation effort (relative to full revelation). We will, however, see approaches that attempt to save elicitation effort even when valuations are themselves compactly specifiable.

10.5.1 General Results

Nisan and Segal (2005) provide some very powerful worst-case results for general valuations, as discussed above. They also provide results for a number of restricted valuation classes. Significantly, using the notion of a dual valuation, they are able to show that any restricted valuation class that includes its dual valuations requires a message space that allows the specification of a full valuation in the restricted space. Thus specific results are derived for homogeneous valuations, additive valuations, submodular valuations (using a modified notion of dual), and substitute valuations (a lower bound based on additive valuations).

10.5.2 Value Queries

Zinkevich, Blum, and Sandholm (2003) define the class of *read-once valuations* and show that elicitation of such a valuation is effective with value queries. A read-once valuation, analogous to a read-once formula, is a function that can be represented as a tree, where the items being auctioned label the leaves, together with the bidder's valuations for the individual items. The function's output value is obtained by feeding in a bundle S of items to the leaves and reading the valuation $v_i(S)$ from the root. A leaf sends the item's valuation up the tree if the item is included in S; otherwise the leaf sends 0. The nodes of the trees can use different types of gates. A SUM node sums the values of its inputs; a MAX node takes the maximum value of its inputs; an ALL node sums its inputs *unless* one of the inputs is zero, in which case the output is 0. Read-once valuations can capture many natural preferences, but are not fully expressive.

Theorem 10.9 (Zinkevich, Blum, and Sandholm 2003) If a bidder has a read-once valuation with SUM, MAX, and ALL gates only, it can be learned using $O(m^2)$ value queries.

Consider also the setting where a bidder's valuation function is a δ-approximation of a read-once function: given that the valuation function is v, there exists a read-once function v' such that for all sets S, we have $|v(S) - v'(S)| < \delta$.

Theorem 10.10 (Zinkevich, Blum, and Sandholm 2003) Let v be a δ-approximation of a read-once function consisting of MAX and SUM gates only. Then a function v' can be learned in $m(m-1)/2$ value queries such that for any set of items S', we have $|v'(S') - v(S')| < 6\delta|S'| + \delta$.

Zinkevich, Blum, and Sandholm (2003) consider more general gates from which to build valuation circuits: MAX_l gates, which output the sum of the l highest inputs; $ATLEAST_k$ gates, which output the sum of its inputs if there are at least k positive inputs, and 0 otherwise; and $GENERAL_{k,l}$ gates, which generalize all of these gates by returning the sum of its highest l inputs if at least k of its inputs are positive, and returns 0 otherwise (we assume $k \leq l$).

Theorem 10.11 (Zinkevich, Blum, and Sandholm 2003)   If a bidder has a read-once valuation with $GENERAL_{k,l}$ gates only, it can be learned using a polynomial number of value queries.

Although read-once valuations can be exactly learned in a polynomial number of queries, finding the optimal allocation of items to just two bidders with known read-once valuations is NP-hard (Zinkevich, Blum, and Sandholm 2003). It is polynomially solvable if one of the two bidders has an additive valuation function.

Another restricted, but polynomially elicitable valuation class is that of *toolbox valuations*. Here, each bidder has an explicit list of k bundles $S_1, \ldots, S_k$, with values $v_1, \ldots, v_k$ respectively. The value given to a generic set S' is assumed to be the *sum* of values of the S_i contained in S', that is, $v(S') = \sum_{S_i \subseteq S'} v_i$. These valuations are natural if, for example, the items are tools or capabilities and there are k tasks to perform that each require some subset of tools. The value of a set of items to the agent is the sum of the values of the tasks that the agent can accomplish with those items.

Theorem 10.12 (Zinkevich, Blum, and Sandholm 2003)   If a bidder has a toolbox valuation, it can be learned using $O(mk)$ value queries.

Conitzer, Sandholm, and Santi (2003) and Santi, Conitzer, and Sandholm (2004) introduced other valuation classes learnable in a polynomial number of value queries. These include valuations where items have at most k-wise dependencies, and certain other valuations. Furthermore, if two classes of valuations are each learnable in a polynomial number of queries, then so is their union—even though the elicitor does not know in advance in which of the two classes (or both) the bidder's valuation belongs. Santi, Conitzer, and Sandholm (2004) also present severely restricted valuation classes where learning nevertheless requires an exponential number of value queries. They also give first steps toward a characterization of polynomial learnability of valuation functions.

Power of Interleaving Queries among Agents   Because we can efficiently elicit read-once and tool-box valuations, we may be inclined to simply elicit the entire valuation of each bidder and then optimize. However, as with the elicitation algorithms discussed above, we might also consider how to exploit the existence of multiple agents to obviate the need for full elicitation. Blum et al. (2004) consider a two-bidder setting in which each bidder desires some subset of bundles, where each of the desired bundles contains at most $\log_2 m$ items. Each bidder's valuation is 1 if he gets at least one of the desired bundles, and 0 otherwise. Observe that there are $\binom{m}{\log m}$ bundles of size $\log m$, so some members of this class cannot be represented in $poly(m)$ bits. So, a valuation function in this class can require a super-polynomial number of value queries to learn. However, a polynomial number of value queries suffices for finding the optimal allocation:

Theorem 10.13 (Blum et al. 2004)   In the setting described above, the optimal allocation can be determined in a number of value queries polynomial in m.

The approach involves randomly proposing even splits of the items between the two bidders. Because they prefer small bundles, an allocation where both bidders are satisfied is found in a small number of proposals, with high probability. Blum et al. (2004) also present a way to derandomize this protocol.

Another example by Blum et al. (2004) shows that for some valuation classes, learning the bidders' valuations is hard, whereas eliciting enough to find the optimal allocation is easy—*even though the valuation functions have short descriptions.* Consider an "almost threshold" valuation function. It is defined by specifying a bundle S'. This bundle in turn defines a valuation function that is 1 for any bundle of size greater than or equal to $|S'|$, except for S' itself, and is 0 otherwise.

Proposition 10.3 (Blum et al. 2004)   If a bidder has an almost threshold valuation function, it can take at least $\binom{m}{\lceil m/2 \rceil - 1}$ value queries to learn it.

Theorem 10.14 (Blum et al. 2004)   In a setting with two bidders, if both of them have almost threshold valuation functions, then the optimal allocation can be determined in $4 + \log_2 m$ value queries.

This demonstrates that there is super-exponential power in deciding what to elicit from a bidder based on the answers received from other bidders so far.[17] On the other hand, Blum et al. (2004) also present a sufficient condition on valuation classes under which the ability to allocate the items optimally using a polynomial number of value queries implies the ability to learn the bidders' valuation functions exactly using a polynomial number of value queries.

10.5.3   Demand Queries

As mentioned, most research on demand queries takes place in the context of ascending CAs. In this setting, considerable research has focused on valuation classes under which ascending item-price auctions yield an optimal allocation. For example, suppose items are *substitutes*: increasing the price on one item does not decrease the demand on any other item. It is well known that in this setting, some vector of anonymous item prices (i.e., *Walrasian prices*) constitutes a certificate. Researchers have developed several ascending CAs for (subclasses of) substitutes (Kelso and Crawford 1982; Gul and Stacchetti 2000; Ausubel 2002). Furthermore, there is a novel mechanism for substitutes that requires polynomial number of item-price demand queries in the worst case (Nisan and Segal 2005), it asks queries in an unintuitive way that does not resemble ascending auctions.

Lahaie and Parkes (2004) provide a novel use of demand queries for elicitation of concisely representable valuations. Again drawing parallels with work in COLT, they show how one can use any query learning model to elicit preferences effectively. Specifically, they use the results of Nisan and Segal (2005) to argue that complexity of preference elicitation should exhibit dependence on the size of the representation of a bidder's valuation function in a suitable representation language. By drawing a strong analogy between value queries and *membership queries* in COLT (as do Blum et al. 2004) and demand queries and *equivalence queries*, Lahaie and Parkes show that any class of valuations can be elicited effectively if they can be learned efficiently:

Definition 10.2 (Lahaie and Parkes 2004)   Valuation classes $V_1, \ldots, V_n$ can be *efficiently elicited* using value and demand queries if there is an algorithm L and polynomial p such that, for any $\langle v_1, \ldots, v_n \rangle \in V_1 \times \cdots \times V_n$, L outputs an optimal allocation for $\langle v_1, \ldots, v_n \rangle$ after no more than $p(size(v_1, \ldots, v_n), n, m)$ value and demand queries.

Theorem 10.15 (Lahaie and Parkes 2004)   Valuation classes $V_1, \ldots, V_n$ can be efficiently elicited using value and demand queries if each V_i can be efficiently learned using membership and equivalence queries.

Lahaie and Parkes describe an algorithm that basically simulates an efficient concept learning algorithm on each of the classes V_i until a point is reached at which the algorithm requires an equivalence of each bidder. Then a demand query is posed using (individualized) bundle prices using current hypothesized valuations. This continues until all bidders accept the proposed bundles at the proposed prices. As a result, this algorithm does not necessarily determine each agent's valuation fully, and thus genuinely relies on the joint valuations of all bidders to guide the interaction process. Polynomial communication complexity is also shown for efficiently elicitable valuation classes. Lahaie and Parkes apply these results to show that various classes of valuation functions can be efficiently elicited.

Among the classes of functions Lahaie and Parkes (2004) consider are *t-sparse polynomials*, where each bidder i has a valuation that can be expressed as a polynomial (over variables corresponding to items) with at most t_i terms. This representation is fully expressive, but is especially suitable for valuations that are "nearly additive," and can thus be represented with few terms. Drawing on existing algorithms from learning theory, they show that only polynomially many queries are needed to learn each valuation.

They exhibit the power of bundle-price demand queries in their treatment of XOR valuations. In contrast to the results of Blum et al. (2004), which use only item-price demand queries (and value queries), we have:

Theorem 10.16 (Lahaie and Parkes 2004)   The class of XOR valuations can be elicited with polynomially many value and (bundle-price) demand queries.

Finally, they consider linear-threshold representations, involving the *r-of-S* expressions: a bundle has value 1 if it contains at least r of the items specified in S, and 0 otherwise (majority valuations are a special case). These can also be learned efficiently using demand queries only (no value queries).

10.6 Conclusion

Preference elicitation for CAs is a nascent research area, but one of critical importance to the practical application of CAs. Though strong worst-case results are known, preliminary evidence suggests that, in practice, incremental elicitation can sometimes reduce the amount of revelation significantly compared to direct mechanisms. In certain natural valuation classes, even the worst-case number of queries is polynomial. Furthermore, as we presented, in some settings there is super-exponential power in deciding what to ask a bidder based on what other bidders have expressed so far. This offers considerable promise for research in the area, and new developments that will push the use of incremental elicitation into practice.

Future research should study concise, yet powerful (and potentially application-specific) query types and new elicitation policies. Most importantly, elicitors must be designed that address the tradeoffs among a number of different problem dimensions. Among these are:

1. Bidder's evaluation complexity   In many CAs, the main bottleneck is to have the bidders determine (through information acquisition or computation of plans) their valuations. The mechanism should be frugal in requiring such effort. This requires a model

of how hard alternative queries are to answer (see, e.g., bound-approximation queries, section 10.4.3). Sandholm (2000) and Larson and Sandholm (2001) present more sophisticated and strategic models.

2. Privacy A: Amount of information revealed to the auctioneer (less seems better)   This gets addressed to some extent by optimizing (1). However, when there is a tradeoff between (1) and (2), one might be able to tune the elicitor for (1), and obtain privacy using complementary techniques. For example, the elicitor could be run as a trusted third party that only reveals the optimal allocation (and payments) to the auctioneer. Alternatively, it is sometimes possible to avoid the auctioneer's learning unnecessary information by using cryptographic techniques such as secure function evaluation (e.g., Naor, Pinkas, and Sumner 1999).

3. Privacy B: Amount of information revealed to other bidders   There is a tradeoff between revelation to the elicitor and revelation to other bidders. If the elicitor decides which query to ask based on what other bidders have stated so far, less information needs to be revealed to the elicitor. Yet it is exactly that conditioning that causes the elicitor to leak information across bidders (Conitzer and Sandholm 2002b). An elicitor could control that tradeoff by controlling the extent of the conditioning.

A different idea is to determine the outcome without an auctioneer, that is, via the agents communicating with each other directly. When relying on computational intractability assumptions, it is possible to devise protocols that accomplish this fully privately: no coalition of agents can learn anything about preferences of the remaining agents (except which outcome is chosen overall) (Brandt 2003). Without intractability assumptions, fully private protocols only exist for a restricted class of mechanisms. There are protocols for first-price sealed-bid auctions, but none can exist for second-price (Vickrey) auctions (Brandt and Sandholm 2004b). It is also possible for agents to *emulate* a preference elicitor fully privately (Brandt and Sandholm 2004b).

4. Communication complexity   Reducing the number of bits transmitted (Nisan and Segal 2005) is useful, and is usually roughly in line with (1). However, when there is a tradeoff between (1) and (4), it seems that in practice it should be struck in favor of (1): if a bidder can afford to evaluate a bundle, he will also be able to communicate the value.

5. Elicitor's computational complexity   There are two potentially complex activities an elicitor will necessarily face: deciding what query to ask next, and deciding when to terminate (and which allocation(s) to return). In the elicitor designs presented in the general elicitation framework of this chapter, these operations required determining the undominated candidate allocations (complexity can creep in at the stage of assimilating a new answer into the elicitor's data structures, or in using those data structures to determine domination, or both). In some elicitation policies, determining the next query to ask can be complex beyond that. For example, even for the omniscient elicitor, finding a shortest certificate (which, in turn, allows one to ask an optimal query)

seems prohibitively complex. For some elicitors, determining when to terminate may also be hard beyond the hardness of maintaining the candidates.

6. Elicitor's memory usage   For example, maintaining the list of candidates explicitly becomes prohibitive at around ten items for sale. The implicit candidate representation technique that we discussed exemplifies how memory usage can be traded off against time in order to move to larger auctions.

7. Mechanism designer's objective   The designer could settle for a second-best solution in order to address criteria (1)–(6). For example, one might terminate before the optimal allocation is found, when the cost of further elicitation is likely to outweigh the benefit. (Handling the incentives in that approach seems tricky because the VCG scheme requires optimal allocation.) Furthermore, the mechanism could even be designed for the specific prior at hand, and it could be designed automatically using a computer (e.g., Conitzer and Sandholm 2002a). Although research on automated mechanism design has focused on direct-revelation mechanisms so far, the approach could be extended to sequential mechanisms with an explicit elicitation cost. When communication and/or computational complexity becomes prohibitive, the revelation principle ceases to apply, and there can even be benefit in moving to mechanisms with insincere equilibrium play (Conitzer and Sandholm 2004).

Acknowledgments

Parts of this research were funded by CombineNet, Inc., parts by NSF CAREER Award IRI-9703122 and NSF grants IIS-9800994, ITR IIS-0081246, ITR IIS-0121678, ITR IIS-0427858, and parts by NSERC.

Notes

1. See Blumrosen and Nisan 2002 for a discussion of this point even in the case of single valuations.

2. Parkes, chapter 2, and Ausubel and Milgrom chapter 3 of this volume detail ascending CAs.

3. This differs slightly from the notion of certificate Parkes (2002) defines, where a certificate is a subspace of valuation functions that are consistent with the queries and their answers.

4. With multiple query types, we could account for the "cost" of different queries.

5. This ceases to hold if bidders can decide how much effort to invest in determining their own valuations (e.g., via information acquisition or computing) (Sandholm 2000).

6. The elicitor has to ask enough queries to be able to determine the welfare-maximizing allocations (among the remaining bidders) with each bidder removed. This imposes an additional elicitation burden (see the discussion of certificates, above).

7. Reichelstein (1984) already studied implications of incentive compatibility constraints on certificate complexity, and used the VCG mechanism. That work was very different because (1) it only studied single-shot communication, so the issue of the elicitor leaking information across bidders did not arise; (2) it assumed a nondeterministic communication complexity model where, in effect, the elicitor is omniscient, knowing all the bidders' preferences in advance; (3) there was only one good to be traded; and (4) that good was divisible.

8. However, if agents can endogenously decide whether to use costly deliberation to determine their own and others' valuations, then, in a sense, there exists no truth-promoting mechanism that avoids counterspeculation unless the mechanism computes valuations for the agents, or is trivial, i.e., ignores what agents reveal (Larson and Sandholm 2004).

9. This assumes no indifference; otherwise, a subset of Pareto optimal allocations is found.

10. Conen and Sandholm (2002b) consider other variants of EBF-DE, e.g., using differential value queries to request the precise difference or using bisection search on difference size. Some variants of EBF-DE are very similar to the iBundle(3) iterative auction (Parkes 1999a).

11. We contrast an optimal elicitor, which does not know the responses a priori, with an *omniscient* elicitor, which does and simply needs to produce a certificate.

12. In the worst case, exponential communication is required to find an (even approximately) optimal allocation in a CAs—no matter what query types and elicitation policy one uses (Nisan and Segal 2005).

13. Hudson and Sandholm (2003) present techniques for speeding up the determination of domination.

14. Parkes (2005) proposed such queries for one-object auctions.

15. One idea is to use *coherent prices*, where the price for a bundle may not exceed the sum of prices of the bundles in any partition of the bundle, and the prices for super-bundles of the bundles in the optimal allocation are additive (Conen and Sandholm 2002a).

16. Because of this connection, we discuss these general results in the context of demand queries, though the results do not rely on the use of demand queries for elicitation.

17. An exponential communication *and computation* gap has been demonstrated in settings other than CAs (Conitzer and Sandholm 2004).

References

Angluin, Dana (1988), "Queries and Concept Learning," *Machine Learning*, 2(4): 319–342.

Angluin, Dana, Lisa Hellerstein, and Marek Karpinski (1993), "Learning Read-Once Formulas with Queries," *Journal of the ACM*, 40, 185–210.

Ausubel, Lawrence M. (2004), "An Efficient Ascending-Bid Auction for Multiple Objects," *American Economic Review*, 94, 1452–1475.

Ausubel, Lawrence (2002), "An Efficient Dynamic Auction for Heterogenous Objects," Working Paper, University of Maryland.

Ausubel, Lawrence M. and Paul Milgrom (2002), "Ascending Auctions with Package Bidding," *Frontiers of Theoretical Economics*, 1, 1–42. 〈http://www.bepress.com/bejte/frontiers/vol1/iss1/art1〉.

Bacchus, Fahiem and Adam Grove (1995), "Graphical Models for Preference and Utility," in *Conference on Uncertainty in Artificial Intelligence*, 3–10.

Bikhchandani, Sushil and Joseph M. Ostroy (2002), "The Package Assignment Model," *Journal of Economic Theory*, 107, 377–406.

Blum, Avrim, Jeffrey Jackson, Tuomas Sandholm, and Martin Zinkevich (2004), "Preference Elicitation and Query Learning," *Journal of Machine Learning Research*, 5, 649–667.

Blumrosen, Liad and Noam Nisan (2002), "Auctions with Severely Bounded Communication," in *Proceedings of the 43rd Annual Symposium on Foundations of Computer Science (FOCS 2002)*, 406–415.

Boutilier, Craig (2002), "A POMDP Formulation of Preference Elicitation Problems," in *National Conference on Artificial Intelligence*, 239–246.

Boutilier, Craig, Fahiem Bacchus, and Ronen Brafman (2001), "UCP-Networks: A Directed Graphical Representation of Conditional Utilities," in *Conference on Uncertainty in Artificial Intelligence*, 56–64.

Brandt, Felix (2003), "Fully Private Auctions in a Constant Number of Rounds," in R. N. Wright (ed.), *Conference on Financial Cryptography*, volume 2742 of *Lecture Notes in Computer Science*, p. 223–238. Berlin: Springer.

Brandt, Felix and Tuomas Sandholm (2004a), "On Correctness and Privacy in Distributed Mechanisms," in *Agent-Mediated Electronic Commerce Workshop*, 1–14.

Brandt, Felix and Tuomas Sandholm (2004b), "(Im)Possibility of Unconditionally Privacy-Preserving Auctions," in *International Conference on Autonomous Agents and Multi-Agent Systems*, 810–817.

Bshouty, Nader, Thomas Hancock, and Lisa Hellerstein (1995), "Learning Arithmetic Read-Once Formulas," *SIAM Journal on Computing*, 24(4): 706–735.

Bshouty, Nader, Thomas Hancock, Lisa Hellerstein, and Marek Karpinski (1994), "An Algorithm to Learn Read-Once Threshold Formulas, and Transformations between Learning Models," *Computational Complexity*, 4, 37–61.

Chajewska, Urszula, Daphne Koller, and Ronald Parr (2002), "Making Rational Decisions Using Adaptive Utility Elicitation," in *National Conference on Artificial Intelligence*, 363–369.

Clarke, Edward H. (1971), "Multipart Pricing of Public Doods," *Public Choice*, 11, 17–33.

Conen, Wolfram and Tuomas Sandholm (2001), "Preference Elicitation in Combinatorial Auctions," in *Proceedings of the 3rd ACM Conference on Electronic Commerce (EC-01)*, New York: ACM Press, 256–259.

Conen, Wolfram and Tuomas Sandholm (2002a), "Coherent Pricing of Efficient Allocations in Combinatorial Economies," in *International Conference on Autonomous Agents and Multi-Agent Systems*, 254–260.

Conen, Wolfram and Tuomas Sandholm (2002b), "Differential-Revelation VCG Mechanisms for Combinatorial Auctions," in *Agent-Mediated Electronic Commerce Workshop*, volume 2531 of *Lecture Notes in Computer Science*, pp. 34–51. Berlin: Springer.

Conen, Wolfram and Tuomas Sandholm (2002c), "Partial-Revelation VCG Mechanism for Combinatorial Auctions," in *National Conference on Artificial Intelligence*, 367–372.

Conitzer, Vincent and Tuomas Sandholm (2002a), "Complexity of Mechanism Design," in *Conference on Uncertainty in Artificial Intelligence*, 103–110.

Conitzer, Vincent and Tuomas Sandholm (2002b), "Vote Elicitation: Complexity and Strategy-Proofness," in *National Conference on Artificial Intelligence*, 392–397.

Conitzer, Vincent and Tuomas Sandholm (2004), "Computational Criticisms of the Revelation Principle," in *Conference on Logic and the Foundations of Game and Decision Theory*.

Conitzer, Vincent, Tuomas Sandholm, and Paolo Santi (2003), "Combinatorial Auctions with Wise Dependent Valuations," mimeo, October.

de Vries, Sven, James Schummer, and Rakesh Vohra (2003), "On Ascending Vickrey Auctions for Heterogeneous Objects," Working Paper, Northwestern University.

Dyer, J. S. (1972), "Interactive Goal Programming," *Management Science*, 19, 62–70.

Grigorieva, Elena, Jean-Jacques Herings, Rudolf Müller, and Dries Vermeulen (2002), "The Private Value Single Item Bisection Auction," Research Memorandum 51, METEOR, Maastricht.

Groves, Theodore (1973), "Incentives in Teams," *Econometrica*, 41, 617–631.

Gul, Faruk and Ennio Stacchetti (2000), "The English Auction with Differentiated Commodities," *Journal of Economic Theory*, 92, 66–95.

Hudson, Benoit and Tuomas Sandholm (2002), "Effectiveness of Preference Elicitation in Combinatorial Auctions," in *Agent-Mediated Electronic Commerce Workshop*, 386–393.

Hudson, Benoit and Tuomas Sandholm (2003), "Generalizing Preference Elicitation in Combinatorial Auctions," in *Second International Joint Conference on Autonomous Agents and Multi Agent Systems*, 1014–1015.

Hudson, Benoît and Tuomas Sandholm (2004), "Effectiveness of Query Types and Policies for Preference Elicitation in Combinatorial Auctions," in *Third International Joint Conference on Autonomous Agents and Multi Agent Systems (AAMAS04)*, 386–393.

Kahneman, David and Amos Tversky (1979), "Prospect Theory: An Analysis of Decision under Risk," *Econometrica*, 21, 263–291.

Keeney, Ralph and Howard Raiffa (1976), *Decisions with Multiple Objectives: Preferences and Value Trade-offs*, New York, Wiley.

Kelso, Alexander S. and Vincent P. Crawford (1982), "Job Matching, Coalition Formation, and Gross Substitues," *Econometrica*, 50, 1483–1504.

Kwasnica, Anthony M., John O. Ledyard, Dave Porter, and Christine DeMartini (2005), "A New and Improved Design for Multiobject Iterative Auctions," *Management Science*, 51, 419–434.

Lahaie, Sebastién and David Parkes (2004), "Applying Learning Algorithms to Preference Elicitation," in *Proceedings of the 5th ACM Conference on Electronic Commerce*, 180–188.

Larson, Kate and Tuomas Sandholm (2001), "Costly Valuation Computation in Auctions," in *Proceedings of Theoretical Aspects of Rationality and Knowledge VIII*, 169–182.

Larson, Kate and Tuomas Sandholm (2004), "Designing Auctions for Deliberative Agents," in *Agent-Mediated Electronic Commerce Workshop*, 225–238. A short, newer version: *Strategic Deliberation and Truthful Revelation: An Impossibility Result* in ACM-EC-04.

Naor, Moni, Benny Pinkas, and Reuben Sumner (1999), "Privacy Preserving Auctions and Mechanism Design," in *ACM Conference on Electronic Commerce*.

Nisan, Noam (2003), "The Power and Limitations of Item Price Combinatorial Auctions," Slides from the FCC Combinatorial Bidding Conference, Queenstown, MD, Nov. 21–23.

Nisan, Noam and Ilya Segal (2003), "The Communication Requirements of Efficient Allocations and Supporting Prices," *Journal of Economic Theory*, To appear.

Parkes, David C. (2001), *Iterative Combinatorial Auctions: Achieving Economic and Computational Efficiency*, PhD thesis, University of Pennsylvania.

Parkes, David C. (2005a), "Price-Based Information Certificates for Minimal-Revelation Combinatorial Auctions," in *Agent Mediated Electronic Commerce Workshop IV*, Julian Padget, Onn Shehory, David Parkes, Norman Sadeh, and William El Walsh, eds., LNAI 2531, pp. 103–122. Heidelberg: Springer-Verlag.

Parkes, David C. (1999), "iBundle: An Efficient Ascending Price Bundle Auction," in *Proceedings of the 1st ACM Conference on Electronic Commerce*, 148–157.

Parkes, David C. (2005b), "Auction Design with Costly Preference Elicitation," *Annals of Mathematics and AI*, Special Issue on the Foundations of Electronic Commerce, To appear.

Parkes, David C. and Lyle H. Ungar (2000), "Iterative Combinatorial Auctions: Theory and Practice," in *Proceedings of the 17th National Conference on Artificial Intelligence*, 74–81.

Reichelstein, Stefan (1984), "Incentive Compatibility and Informational Requirements," *Journal of Economic Theory*, 34, 32–51.

Rothkopf, Michael H., Thomas J. Teisberg, and Edward P. Kahn (1990), "Why Are Vickrey Auctions Rare?" *Journal of Political Economy*, 98, 94–109.

Saaty, Thomas L. (1980), *The Analytic Hierarchy Process*. New York: McGraw-Hill.

Salo, Ahti and Raimo Hämäläinen (2001), "Preference Ratios in Multiattribute Evaluation (PRIME)—Elicitation and Decision Procedures under Incomplete Information," *IEEE Trans. on Systems, Man and Cybernetics*, 31(6): 533–545.

Sandholm, Tuomas (1993), "An Implementation of the Contract Net Protocol Based on Marginal Cost Calculations," in *Eleventh National Conference on Artificial Intelligence*, 256–262.

Sandholm, Tuomas (2000), "Issues in Computational Vickrey Auctions," *International Journal of Electronic Commerce*, 4, 107–129.

Sandholm, Tuomas (2002), "Algorithm for Optimal Winner Determination in Combinatorial Auctions," *Artificial Intelligence*, 135, 1–54.

Santi, Paolo, Vincent Conitzer, and Tuomas Sandholm (2004), "Towards a Characterization of Polynomial Preference Elicitation with Value Queries in Combinatorial Auctions," in *Conference on Learning Theory*, 1–16.

Smith, Trey, Tuomas Sandholm, and Reid Simmons (2002), "Constructing and Clearing Combinatorial Exchanges Using Preference Elicitation," in *AAAI-02 Workshop on Preferences in AI and CP: Symbolic Approaches*, 87–93.

Vickrey, William (1961), "Counterspeculation, Auctions, and Competitive Sealed Tenders," *Journal of Finance*, 16, 8–37.

Wang, Tianhan and Craig Boutilier (2003), "Incremental Utility Elicitation with the Minimax Regret Decision Criterion," in *International Joint Conference on Artificial Intelligence*, 309–316.

White III, Chelsea, Andrew Sage, and Shigeru Dozono (1984), "A Model of Multiattribute Decisionmaking and Trade-Off Weight Determination under Uncertainty," *IEEE Transactions on Systems, Man and Cybernetics*, 14(2): 223–229.

Wurman, Peter R. and Michael P. Wellman (2000), "AkBA: A Progressive, Anonymous-Price Combinatorial Auction," in *Second ACM Conference on Electronic Commerce*, 21–29.

Zinkevich, Martin, Avrim Blum, and Tuomas Sandholm (2003), "On Polynomial-Time Preference Elicitation with Value Queries," in *Proceedings of the 4th ACM Conference on Electronic Commerce*, 176–185.

11 The Communication Requirements of Combinatorial Allocation Problems

Ilya Segal

11.1 Introduction

A combinatorial auction must elicit enough information about bidders' preferences to find a desirable (e.g., efficient or approximately efficient) allocation. The mechanism design literature has used the revelation principle to restrict attention to mechanisms in which bidders reveal their true preferences (see Ausubel and Milgrom, chapter 1 of this volume). However, full revelation of a bidder's preferences requires naming a willingness to pay for each of the $2^m - 1$ possible nonempty combinations of the m items. Already with $m = 20$, this would involve the communication of more than one million numbers, which is beyond the capabilities of any auction participant.

Recognition of the communication problem has prompted researchers to propose simpler mechanisms, in which valuations are not fully revealed. For example, in the iterative auctions and preference elicitation mechanisms suggested in other chapters of this book (chapters 2–6, 8, and 10), at each stage a bidder is asked to reveal only a small amount of information—for example, his valuation for a given bundle or his optimal bundle at given prices. The hope is that such designs could achieve or at least approximate efficiency, while using only a small number of queries.[1] But is this hope justified? What information needs to be communicated to find an efficient or approximately efficient allocation, and how extensive must this communication be?

A central idea of this chapter is that in order to find an efficient allocation, it is necessary to communicate supporting prices. One can trace intellectual origins of this idea to Hayek (1945), who argued that prices succinctly summarize the knowledge of "particular circumstances of time and place," which is too enormous to be communicated to a central planner. Hurwicz (1977) and Mount and Reiter (1974) formalized Hayek's intuition by showing that in classical convex economies, the Walrasian price mechanism verifies the efficiency of a proposed allocation while communicating as few real variables as possible among all "regular" mechanisms. Furthermore, Jordan (1982) showed that the Walrasian mechanism is a unique voluntary mechanism with this property. However, these results do not apply to *nonconvex* economies with indivisible goods, in which (1) a linear-price equilibrium typically does not exist, and (2) the regularity restriction used in the literature precludes the communication of discrete allocations.[2] Also, this literature focused on achieving exact efficiency, and did not examine the potential communication savings from allowing approximate efficiency.

Nisan and Segal (2003, henceforth NS) recently examined these issues. They demonstrated that any communication mechanism that finds an efficient allocation must also discover supporting prices (which are in general personalized and nonlinear). (Parkes 2002 obtained a similar result for a restricted class of communication languages.) The result holds even if the agents are truthful (i.e., follow the prescribed reporting strategies).

The NS result implies that the simpler "nondeterministic" problem of *verifying* an efficient allocation is exactly that of announcing supporting prices, and its communication burden is the minimal size of a price space that ensures the existence of a price equilibrium. For example, in a convex exchange economy, there always exists an equilibrium with prices that are Walrasian (i.e., anonymous and linear), which are easy to communicate. In the CA problem, by contrast, it proves impossible to reduce the price space substantially while ensuring equilibrium existence. Specifically, NS show that at least one real-valued price must be named for each of the $2^m - 1$ possible combinations of items, and so the communication of supporting prices is at least as hard as full revelation of one agent's preferences. This is impractical with as few as twenty items.

Given the hardness of exact efficiency, one may ask how closely the one can approximate maximal surplus using less communication. Because any given approximation can be achieved by transmitting discretized valuations, one should measure its communication burden with the number of transmitted bits, as in the computer science field of communication complexity.[3] An exact characterization of the tradeoff between the number of transmitted bits and the realized surplus would be quite difficult. Instead, the literature provides upper and lower communication bounds for the communication burden of a given surplus approximation, and examines the asymptotic behavior of the communication burden as the numbers of items and agents go to infinity and as the required approximation error goes to zero.

One can obtain an upper bound on the communication burden by examining a specific mechanism. For example, the "bundled auction," which sells all items as a bundle to the highest bidder, guarantees $1/n$th of the available surplus while requiring each bidder to send only one number. NS show that guaranteeing a better approximation requires exponential communication in m.[4] This remains true even if improvement is required only *on expectation*, for *some* joint probability distribution over valuations (and even if communication is measured as the *expected* number of bits transmitted).

The lower bounds of NS imply that one can achieve exact or approximate efficiency in CAs with many items only in cases in which the agents' preferences (or probability distribution over them) are known a priori to lie in a certain class. One example is given by valuations satisfying the "substitute property" of Kelso and Crawford (1982). With such valuations, a Walrasian equilibrium exists; furthermore, NS show that it can be found with (truly) polynomial deterministic communication. However, the substitute property is quite restrictive. NS show for the somewhat larger class of "submodular" valuations (i.e., those exhibiting diminishing marginal utility of items), efficiency still requires very extensive communication, and a fast (so-called "fully polynomial") approximation is impossible.

NS also examine the problem of allocating m *identical* items, in which they find a drastic difference between the communication burden of exact efficiency (at least m real numbers) and that of approximation within any given ε (only $O(\log m)$ bits). Furthermore, they construct a so-called "fully polynomial" approximation scheme, even for the case of a *divisible* homogeneous good, in which, as Calsamiglia (1977) shows, exact efficiency would require infinitely-dimensional communication. Thus, in this particular case, one can achieve an enormous savings in communication with only a slight sacrifice in economic efficiency.

This chapter formulates the communication problem and describes the above results in more detail, as well as discusses the extensions of the analysis to procurement auctions, deterministic communication, incentive-compatible communication, and general social choice problems.

11.2 The Allocation Problem and Communication

11.2.1 The Allocation Problem
Let $N = \{1, \ldots, n\}$ denote the set of agents (with $n \geq 2$ to avoid the trivial case) and $K = \{1, \ldots, k\}$ denote the set of allocations. An agent's *valuation* assigns a real number to each allocation, and is therefore represented with a vector in $\mathbb{R}^k$. The class of possible valuations of agent $i \in N$ is denoted by $U_i \subset \mathbb{R}^k$. Agent i's valuation $u_i \in U_i$ is assumed to be his privately observed "type." A *state* is a valuation profile $(u_1, \ldots, u_n) \in U \equiv U_1 \times \cdots \times U_n \subset \mathbb{R}^{nk}$.

The goal is to implement an *allocation rule*, which is a nonempty-valued correspondence $F : U \twoheadrightarrow K$.[5] For each state $u \in U$, the allocation rule describes the nonempty subset $F(u) \subset K$ of "desirable" allocations. For example, the *efficient* allocation rule, which selects the allocations maximizing the sum of the agents' valuations (*total surplus*), is given by[6]

$$F^*(u) = \arg\max_{j \in K} \sum_{i \in N} u_{ij} \quad \forall u \in U.$$

11.2.2 Communication Protocols

We now describe communication procedures that solve the allocation problem. It is well known that communication can be shortened by letting agents send messages sequentially rather than simultaneously. For example, an agent need not report his valuation for allocation j if previous messages have made it clear that j stands no chance of being efficient.[7] Therefore, we must consider multistage communication.

In the language of game theory, a general communication protocol is described with an extensive form message game as well as each agent's strategy in this game (complete action plan contingent on his type and observed history). Instead of payoffs, the game assigns allocations to terminal nodes (and so is more properly called a "game form," or "mechanism"). The agents are assumed to follow the prescribed strategies (I discuss their incentives to do so in subsection 11.5.4). Such communication protocols are called "deterministic" because the message an agent sends at a given information set is fully determined by his type and the preceding messages. A protocol *realizes* allocation rule F if in every state $u \in U$ it achieves a terminal node to which an allocation from $F(u)$ is assigned.

Characterizing deterministic communication protocols would be very hard. One can simplify analysis by considering what is known as "nondeterministic communication" in computer science and as the "verification scenario" in economics. Imagine an omniscient oracle who knows the true state u, and consequently knows a "desirable" allocation $j \in F(u)$, but has to prove to an ignorant outsider that j is indeed desirable. He carries out the proof by publicly announcing a message $w \in W$. Each agent i either accepts or rejects the message, doing this on the basis of his own type u_i. Acceptance of message w by all agents must prove to the outsider that allocation j is desirable. This communication is called "nondeterministic" because it does not "determine" a desirable allocation, but simply verifies that a candidate allocation is desirable.

A famous economic example of nondeterministic communication is the Walrasian equilibrium. The "Walrasian auctioneer," who announces the equilibrium allocation and prices, plays the role of the oracle. Each agent accepts the announcement if and only if his allocated consumption bundle maximizes his utility under the announced prices. The classical welfare theorems say that one can use Walrasian equilibria to verify Pareto efficiency in convex exchange economies.

Observe that any deterministic communication can be represented as nondeterministic simply by letting all the messages be sent by the oracle instead of the agents, and having each agent accept the message sequence if and only if all the messages sent in his stead are consistent with his strategy given his type. The oracle's message space W is thus identified with the set of the protocol's possible message sequences (terminal nodes). Therefore, any lower bound on the communication requirements of nondeterministic protocols applies to deterministic protocols as a particular case. This is the main justification for our focus on nondeterministic communication. Another justification is that one can view a nondeterministic protocol as a steady state of a deterministic iterative adjustment protocol (e.g., Walrasian "tâtonnement"), whose fast convergence may sometimes be assured (see subsection 11.5.2 for more detail).

Formally, nondeterministic communication is defined as follows:

Definition 11.1 A *nondeterministic communication protocol* is a triple $\Gamma = \langle W, \mu, h \rangle$, where W is the message set, $\mu : U \twoheadrightarrow W$ is the message correspondence, and $h : W \to K$ is the outcome function, and the message correspondence μ has the following properties:

- Existence: $\mu(u) \neq \emptyset$ for all $u \in U$,
- Privacy Preservation: $\mu(u) = \bigcap_i \mu_i(u_i)$ for all $u \in U$, where $\mu_i : U_i \twoheadrightarrow W$ for all $i \in N$.

Protocol Γ *realizes* allocation rule $F : U \twoheadrightarrow K$ if $h(\mu(u)) \subset F(u)$ for all $u \in U$.

Existence means that an acceptable message exists in each state. *Privacy preservation* follows from the fact that each agent does not observe other agents' types when making his acceptance decision; thus the set of messages acceptable to him is a function $\mu_i(u_i)$ of his own type u_i only.[8] Finally, the definition of realization says that the acceptance of a message w by all agents proves to the outsider that $h(w) \in F(u)$.

Definition 11.1 has a nice interpretation in terms of geometric properties of the subsets $\mu^{-1}(w)$ of the state space U, each such subset being the event in which a given message w occurs. In this interpretation, described by Kushilevitz and Nisan (1997), existence requires that the collection $\{\mu^{-1}(w)\}_{w \in W}$ of such events cover the state space U. Privacy preservation requires that each element of the covering be a product set $\mu_1^{-1}(w) \times \cdots \times \mu_n^{-1}(w)$—a "rectangle" in computer science parlance. Realization requires that for each rectangle $\mu^{-1}(w)$ from the covering, there exists a single outcome $h(w)$ that is "desirable" on the whole rectangle (in computer science parlance, the rectangle is "monochromatic").

11.2.3 The Burden of Discrete and Continuous Communication

The deterministic (nondeterministic) communication burden of an allocation rule is defined as the minimal communication burden of a deterministic (respectively, nondeterministic) protocol realizing it. The communication burden of a protocol is naturally defined as the length of the realized message sequence, that is, the number of messages sent in the course of the protocol. Because this number may vary across states, for now we focus on the "worst-case" communication burden—the maximum length of the message sequence over all states (see subsection 11.5.3 for some average-case results). For this measure to be interesting, we must require that all communication to be encoded with "elementary" messages, which convey a fixed amount of information.

The computer science literature on communication complexity considers discrete communication, in which an elementary message conveys one bit (binary digit) (Kushilevitz and Nisan 1997).[9] In particular, in the nondeterministic case, the minimal binary encoding of the oracle's message from set W takes $\log_2 |W|$ bits.

The case of continuous communication should allow for real-valued elementary messages. We also want to allow finite-valued messages (say, to communicate discrete allocations), but not count them toward the communication burden. Thus, the worst-case burden of continuous communication is defined as the maximum number of real-valued elementary messages sent in the course of the protocol. In the nondeterministic case, we can identify the communication burden with the dimension of the oracle's message space W, which must thus be endowed with a topology.

A well-known quandary in continuous communication is the possibility of smuggling multidimensional information in a one-dimensional message (e.g., using the inverse Peano function). Note, however, that with such "smuggling," a small error in the message would yield a huge error in its meaning. To avoid this, NS define a metric on messages based on their meaning: they define the distance between messages w and w' as the Hausdorff distance between the events $\mu^{-1}(w)$ and $\mu^{-1}(w')$ in which they occur.[10] The metric dimension of space W, denoted by dim W, then serves as a measure of the communication burden.[11] With this definition, any coding of messages from W with d real numbers that prevents small errors in the code from drastically distorting the meaning (formally, the inverse of the code is Lipszhitz continuous) must have $d \geq W$ (Edgar 1990, exercise 6.1.9[1]). Thus, dim W is the relevant measure of communication burden if the communication must be robust to small transmission errors, due either to analog noise or to discretization ("quantization").[12]

11.3   Efficient Communication and Supporting Prices

One way to verify the efficiency of an allocation is by announcing supporting prices:

Definition 11.2   A pair $(p, j) \in \mathbb{R}^{nk} \times K$, where $j \in K$ is the proposed allocation and $p \in \mathbb{R}^{nk}$ is a list of personalized allocation prices, is a *price equilibrium* in state $u \in U$ if

$$u_{ij} - p_{ij} \geq u_{ij'} - p_{ij'} \quad \text{for all } i \in N, \, j' \in K, \tag{11.1}$$

$$\sum_{i \in N} p_{ij} \geq \sum_{i \in N} p_{ij'} \quad \text{for all } j' \in K. \tag{11.2}$$

Let $E(u) \subset \mathbb{R}^{nk} \times K$ denote the set of price equilibria in state u.

Inequalities 11.1 says that the proposed allocation maximizes each agent's utility net of the announced prices. Inequality 11.2 can be interpreted as requiring that the proposed allocation maximize the designer's revenue under the announced prices.

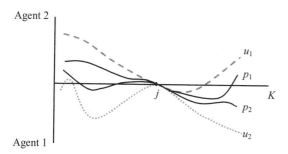

Figure 11.1
Price equilibrium.

Figure 11.1 illustrates a price equilibrium with $n = 2$ agents. Without loss of generality we normalize both agents' utilities and prices for the equilibrium allocation j to zero, and graph agent 1's valuations and prices for all allocations in the downward direction, and those of agent 2 in the upward direction. (The economic interpretation of figure 11.1 is as an "Edgeworth box" whose vertical dimension represents the split of money between the two agents and whose horizontal dimension represents the allocations. In this interpretation, u_1 and u_2 depict the agents' respective indifference curves passing through the equilibrium point, and p_1 and p_2 depict the boundaries of their respective budget sets.) Inequalities 11.2 say that the curve representing p_1 must lie above that representing p_2, and inequalities 11.1 that the curve representing u_1 is above that for p_1 and the line representing u_2 is below that for p_2.

Mas-Colell (1980) first suggested this general notion of price equilibrium, and it was later used for combinatorial allocation problems (Bikhchandani and Ostroy, chapter 8 of this volume). A well-known observation, referred to as the *First Welfare Theorem*, is that any price equilibrium allocation is efficient. In figure 11.1, efficiency simply means that curve u_1 must lie above curve u_2. In general, efficiency is seen by adding up, for any given alternative allocation j', inequalities 11.1 for all $i \in N$ and inequality 11.2.

The First Welfare Theorem allows one to verify efficiency with a *price protocol*, whose message space is $W \subset \mathbb{R}^{nk} \times K$, whose message correspondence is $\mu(u) = E(u) \cap W$, and whose outcome function is $h(p, j) = j$. Note that there are many different price protocols described by different message spaces, that is, different feasible price-allocation pairs. Any price protocol satisfies *privacy preservation* by construction, as each agent verifies his inequalities in 11.1 using his own type only, and any agent can verify in 11.2. Thus, if a message space W is large enough that a price equilibrium from W to exists in all states, the size of W provides an upper bound on the burden of efficient nondeterministic communication. (Namely, it is $\log_2|W|$ bits for discrete communication, and dim W for continuous communication.)

One might think that there exist some efficient communication protocols that are distinct from, and perhaps much simpler than, price protocols. However, NS establish that this is not the case—any efficient communication protocol must reveal supporting equilibrium prices:[13]

Proposition 11.1 Communication protocol $\Gamma = \langle W, \mu, h \rangle$ realizes the efficient allocation rule F^* if and only if there exists an assignment $p : W \to \mathbb{R}^{nk}$ of prices to messages such that protocol $\langle W, \mu, \langle p, h \rangle \rangle$ realizes the price equilibrium correspondence E.

The "if" statement of the proposition is the First Welfare Theorem. The "only if" statement can be thought of as a strengthening of the traditional *Second Welfare Theorem*, which says only that for any efficient allocation we can construct supporting prices *given full information about the economy*. (For general price equilibria, the construction is trivial: for example, we can take prices $p^i = u^i$ for all agents i.) The Second Welfare Theorem is not a very useful result, because with full information, an efficient allocation can be implemented directly, without using prices. In contrast, proposition 11.1 says not only that supporting prices exist, but also that they must be revealed by *any* efficient communication, not just by full revelation.

Figure 11.2 illustrates the "only if" part of proposition 11.1 for two agents, which depicts their valuations in the same way as figure 11.1. Suppose that a message w verifies that allocation j is efficient. Consider the two agents' valuations that are consistent with message w. By *privacy preservation*, j must be efficient in any state in which each agent's valuation is consistent with w. Graphically, this means that any valuation curve of agent 1 consistent with w (u_1' and u_1'' in the figure) must lie above any valuation curve of agent 2 consistent with w (u_2' and u_2'' in the figure). Therefore, letting agent 1's price curve p_1 be the lower envelope of his valuation curves consistent with w, and letting agent 2's price curve p_2 be the *upper* envelope of his valuation curves consistent with w, p_1 will lie above p_2, and thus the prices will satisfy condition 11.2.

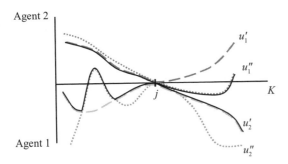

Figure 11.2
Revelation of prices.

Also, by construction, these prices satisfy condition 11.1 in all states consistent with w (states $[u_1', u_2']$, $[u_1', u_2'']$, $[u_1'', u_2']$, and $[u_1'', u_2'']$ in the figure). Thus, on the basis of a message w verifying j, we have constructed a price equilibrium supporting j in all states in which w occurs.

Proposition 11.1 implies that the nondeterministic communication burden of the efficient allocation rule F^* is *exactly* the minimum size of a price-allocation space W ensuring the existence of an equilibrium from $W \subset \mathbb{R}^{nk} \times K$. Although finding such a minimal space is in general a hard problem, below we derive some upper and lower bounds for it in specific cases (and in some of these cases the two bounds match).

11.4 The Combinatorial Allocation Problem

We now specialize to the *combinatorial allocation (CA) problem*, in which $M = \{1, \dots, m\}$ denotes the set of items to be allocated among the agents, and so the allocation space is $K = N^m$. Thus, $j(l)$ denotes the agent holding item $l \in M$ in allocation $j \in K$.

NS impose several standard restrictions on valuations (which can only reduce the communication burden):

• **No externalities (NE):** For each i and each $u_i \in U_i$, there exists $v_i : 2^m \to \mathbb{R}$ such that $u_i(j) = v_i(j^{-1}(i))$ for each $j \in K$.

In words, each agent i's utility is a function v_i of the bundle $j^{-1}(i)$ allocated to him. We will now call v_i the agent's valuation, and let $V_i \subset \mathbb{R}^{2^m}$ denote the class of his possible valuations. The state space can then be represented by $V = V_1 \times \cdots \times V_n$.

Each $v_i \in V_i$ is also assumed to satisfy the following restrictions:

• **Normalization (N):** $v_i(\emptyset) = 0$.
• **Free disposal (FD):** $v_i(S)$ is nondecreasing in $S \subset M$.
• **Boundedness (B):** Either $v_i(M) = 0$ or $v_i(M) \in [\gamma, 1]$, for some parameter $\gamma > 0$.

N is without loss of generality, and it serves to rule out distinct valuations that differ only by a constant, thus describing the same preferences. FD and B are not needed for the analysis of exact efficiency, but play a role in the analysis of approximation (see note 16 below). Given that the analysis is invariant to scale, the choice of the upper bound as 1 is arbitrary. The lower bound γ can be viewed as a parameter of the problem along with n and m, but its value will be irrelevant for most results. Let $V_{\text{gen}} \subset \mathbb{R}^{2^m}$ denote the class of all valuations satisfying NE, N, FD, and B. We will also consider more restricted valuation classes below.

11.4.1 A "Fooling Set" Lower Bound on Communication
Suppose we have a subset $V^{\text{f}} \subset V$ of states such that no two distinct states from V^{f} share a price equilibrium. Proposition 11.1 then implies that no two distinct states from V^{f} share a message in any efficient protocol. A set V^{f} with this property is known

as a "fooling set" in computer science and as a "set with the uniqueness property" in the economic literature. The size of a fooling set provides a lower bound on the size of the message space in any efficient protocol.

NS construct a fooling set that consists of the states in which the total surplus is constant across all allocations. Here we illustrate the construction for the CA problem with $n = 2$ agents. For any valuation $v \in V_{\text{gen}}$ of agent 1, let agent 2 have the *dual valuation* described by

$$\tilde{v}(S) = v(M) - v(M \backslash S) \quad \text{for all } S \subset M.$$

In state $(v, \tilde{v})$, all allocations of the items between the two agents are efficient. However, in any price equilibrium (p, j) in this state, the prices faced by the two agents must coincide with their valuations up to a constant (this can be seen formally from inequalities 11.1 and 11.2, or geometrically from Figure 11.1, by observing that the two agents' valuation curves coincide, and the price curves are squeezed in between). Therefore, two distinct states, $(v, \tilde{v})$ and $(v', \tilde{v}')$, cannot share a price equilibrium; hence, the set of such states forms a fooling set. This argument implies

Proposition 11.2 Suppose that $n = 2$, and that for any $v \in V_1$, $\tilde{v} \in V_2$. Then, if V_1 is a finite set, any efficient protocol transmits at least $\log_2 |V_1|$ bits, and otherwise its message space dimension is at least dim V_1.

In particular, because for every general valuation $v \in V_{\text{gen}}$ the dual valuation is in V_{gen}, proposition 11.2 implies

Proposition 11.3 In the combinatorial allocation problem with general valuations, the dimension of the message space in any efficient protocol is at least dim $V_{\text{gen}} = 2^m - 1$.

Intuitively, with general valuations, any efficient protocol must communicate all possible price vectors for all bundles for a given agent, which requires the communication of $2^m - 1$ real numbers—as long as a full description of the agent's valuations. This lower bound is tight for $n = 2$, because once agent 1's valuations are revealed, agent 2 can announce an efficient allocation. The exact communication burden for $n > 2$ remains an open question.[14]

11.4.2 Approximation and Discretization
Approximate efficiency may require less communication than exact efficiency. This section discusses how to analyze the communication burden of approximate efficiency. To be consistent with the computer science literature, we use an approximation measure that is invariant to the utility units. Specifically, letting

$$S(v) = \max_{j \in K} \sum_i v_i(j^{-1}(i))$$

denote the maximum surplus available in state v, we define the allocation rule F_r^* realizing approximation ratio $r \in [0, 1]$ as follows:[15,16]

$$F_r^*(v) = \left\{ j \in K : \sum_i v_i(j^{-1}(i)) \geq rS(u) \right\}.$$

By construction, $F_1^* = F^*$ (the efficient allocation rule), and $F_r^*(v)$ is nonincreasing in r in the set inclusion order.

One can evaluate the communication burden of F_r^* by examining the communication burden of the exactly efficient allocation rule F^* in a discretized problem. Indeed, suppose we ask the agents to round off all valuations to multiples of $\delta > 0$ and then follow a protocol Γ that realizes efficiency for the rounded-off valuations. Letting n' be the number of agents with non-null valuations, the sum of rounded-off utilities for every allocation is within $n'\delta/2$ from the true surplus at this allocation; hence, the maximization of this sum results in a surplus loss of at most $n'\delta$. Because the maximum available surplus is bounded below by $n'\gamma$, we realize approximation ratio $1 - \delta/\gamma$, using as much communication as in Γ. In particular, full revelation of valuations rounded off with a sufficiently fine precision achieves an approximation ratio arbitrarily close to 1.

Discretization also allows one to bound the communication burden of approximation *from below*. For this purpose, consider the state space V^δ consisting of those valuations from V that are multiples of δ. Because any misallocation in problem V^δ loses at least surplus δ, and the maximum available surplus is bounded above by n, realizing an approximation ratio higher than $1 - \delta/n$ in problem V^δ is equivalent to realizing exact efficiency. Realizing the same approximation ratio in the continuous problem V requires at least as much communication. This observation will allow us to bound below the communication burden of approximating efficiency in problem V by applying proposition 11.2 to problem V^δ.

To describe the dependence of the communication burden on the desired approximation as well as on the parameters of the problem, the computer science literature on approximation algorithms (see, e.g., Vazirani 2001) has used the following three concepts, listed from weaker to stronger:

• A *polynomial approximation scheme* (PAS) in some parameters is a protocol that for any given $\varepsilon > 0$ realizes approximation ratio $1 - \varepsilon$ using a number of bits that is polynomial in the parameters.

• A *fully polynomial approximation scheme* (FPAS) in some parameters is a protocol that for any $\varepsilon > 0$ realizes approximation ratio $1 - \varepsilon$ using a number of bits that is polynomial in ε^{-1} and the parameters.

- A *truly polynomial approximation scheme* (TPAS) in some parameters is a protocol that for any $\varepsilon > 0$ realizes approximation ratio $1 - \varepsilon$ using a number of bits that is polynomial in $\log \varepsilon^{-1}$ and the parameters.

PAS achieves an arbitrarily close approximation with polynomial communication, but does not stipulate how the communication burden depends on the approximation error. In contrast, in FPAS and TPAS, the error must shrink sufficiently fast with the number of bits transmitted. An example of FPAS is an ascending-bid auction for one item with a minimum bid increment $\varepsilon > 0$. At each price level starting from $p = \gamma$, the auction asks each agent to send one bit—"in" or "out." If at least one agent sends "in," the price is incremented by ε. The auction stops when all agents send "out," assigning the item to (one of) the agent(s) who sent "in" in the previous stage. If the agents send "in" if and only if their valuations exceed the current price, the auction is exactly efficient for the discretized problem V^ε, and it realizes approximation ratio $1 - \varepsilon/\gamma$ for the continuous problem. Because number of price increments is bounded above by ε^{-1}, the total (worst-case) number of transmitted bits is $n\varepsilon^{-1}$.

TPAS requires a much faster approximation than FPAS—the error must now shrink exponentially with the number of bits transmitted. An example of TPAS is a sealed-bid auction of one item, in which the agents submit their valuations rounded off to a multiple of $\varepsilon > 0$. The auction is exactly efficient for the discretized problem V^ε, and it realizes approximation ratio $1 - \varepsilon/\gamma$. Because it takes $\log_2 \varepsilon^{-1}$ bits to transmit a valuation rounded off to a multiple of ε, the total number of transmitted bits is $n \log_2 \varepsilon^{-1}$.

We obtained our TPAS example by taking a fully efficient continuous protocol and asking the agents to round off their messages. This technique can be generalized: given a d-dimensional continuous protocol realizing approximation ratio r, rounding off the messages yields a TPAS to approximation ratio r whose communication burden is proportional to d. Intuitively, rounding off a message results in an allocation that is desirable for some state that is not too far from the true state, and therefore the efficiency loss is not too large. Formally, NS establish the following result:[17]

Proposition 11.4 If there exists a protocol realizing approximation ratio r in the CA auction problem with a message space of upper box dimension[18] $d > 0$, then for any $\varepsilon > 0$ there exists a nondeterministic protocol realizing approximation ratio $r - \varepsilon$ using $C(\varepsilon)$ bits, with $C(\varepsilon) \sim d \log \varepsilon^{-1}$ as $\varepsilon \to 0$.

The Proposition offers a justification for using the metric dimension of the message space in a continuous protocol to measure the communication burden even if real-life communication is a discrete TPAS.[19] However, there may also exist non-TPAS approximation schemes that are much faster than what the best exactly efficient continuous protocol would suggest (see subsection 11.4.6 for an example).

The Proposition also implies that if we have continuous communication that is polynomial in some parameters and realizes approximation ratio r, then the discretized protocol is a TPAS for r in the same parameters. In such a case we will also say that the discretized protocol is a "truly polynomial protocol realizing approximation ratio r."

11.4.3 Application: General Valuations

We have already argued using the fooling set approach that the communication burden of exact efficiency with general valuations is at least $2^m - 1$ real variables (proposition 11.3). To bound below the communication burden of approximation, we apply the same logic to the discretized problem V^1_{gen}, in which the agents' valuations for all bundles are either 0 or 1. Only counting those valuations in V^1_{gen} that have $v(S) = 0$ for $|S| < m/2$ and $v(S) = 1$ for $|S| > m/2$, we see that $|V^1_{\text{gen}}| \geq 2^{\binom{m}{m/2}}$.[20] Because for $n = 2$ any protocol for V^1_{gen} realizing an approximation ratio higher than $1 - \delta/n = 1/2$ must be exactly efficient, by proposition 11.2 it must transmit at least $\log_2 |V^1_{\text{gen}}| \geq \binom{m}{m/2}$ bits, which grows exponentially with m.

Observe that approximation ratio $1/n$ can be realized by auctioning off all items as a bundle to the highest bidder. (Indeed, the bundled auction realizes surplus $\max_i v_i(M)$, which bounds above any single agent's utility at any allocation.) Thus, we have shown that for $n = 2$, any improvement upon the bundled auction still requires exponential communication with m. NS extend this result to $n > 2$, though using a different technique, based on a reduction to the approximate set packing problem:

Proposition 11.5 In the CA problem with general valuations, realizing an approximation ratio higher than $1/n$ requires communicating at least $\ln 2 \cdot \exp\{m/(2n^2) - 2\ln n\}$ bits.

Compare this result with the findings of Lehmann, O'Callaghan, and Shoham (2002) and Holzman et al. (2004), who suggest "simple" protocols improving upon the bundled auction. For example, Holzman et al. (2004) note that auctioning off the items in two equal-sized bundles achieves approximation ratio $2/m$ for any n, thus improving upon the bundled auction when $m < 2n$ (splitting M into more bundles allows further improvement). The "greedy" polynomial-time approximation algorithm suggested by Lehmann et al. (2002) can be adapted into a communication protocol realizing approximation ratio $1/\sqrt{m}$, which improves upon the bundled auction when $m < n^2$.[21] Observe that these improvements do not contradict proposition 11.5: intuitively, the proposition implies that when the number of agents is either fixed or grows slower than $\sqrt{m}$ as $m \to \infty$, "simple" protocols (i.e., polynomial in m) cannot improve over the bundled auction. The protocol of Lehmann et al. (2002) offers a matching upper bound: when the number of agents grows faster than $\sqrt{m}$, simple protocols *can* improve over the bundled auction, though all of them realize a vanishing share of the available surplus as $m \to \infty$.

11.4.4 Application: Submodular Valuations

Here each agent's valuation space $V_i = V_{\text{sm}}$ is the set of all valuations $v \in V_{\text{gen}}$ for which the marginal benefit of each item $l \in M$, $v(S \cup l) - v(S)$, is nonincreasing in $S \subset M$.[22] Proposition 11.2 cannot be applied to this case directly, because the dual of a submodular valuation is not submodular unless both are additive. NS circumvent this problem by constructing a subspace of valuations $\tilde{V} \subset V_{\text{sm}}$ with the property that in any state $(v^1, v^2) \in \tilde{V} \times \tilde{V}$, any efficient allocation involves an even split of items, that is, lies in $\tilde{K} = \{j \in K : |j^{-1}(1)| = m/2\}$. Furthermore, for each $v \in \tilde{V}$ NS construct its "quasi-dual" valuation $\hat{v} \in \tilde{V}$ in such a way that the set of efficient allocations in state $(v, \hat{v})$ is exactly $\tilde{K}$. Application of proposition 11.2 with the two agents' valuations restricted to $\tilde{V}$ and the allocations restricted to $\tilde{K}$ then yields

Proposition 11.6 In the CA problem with submodular valuations, the dimension of the message space in any efficient protocol is at least $|\tilde{K}| - 1 = \begin{pmatrix} m \\ m/2 \end{pmatrix}$.

Intuitively, with submodular valuations, any efficient protocol must at least communicate prices for all even splits of items, and the number of such splits is exponential in m. By considering a discretized problem $\tilde{V}^{1/m}$, NS also bound below the communication burden of approximation:

Proposition 11.7 In the CA problem with submodular valuations, realizing an approximation ratio higher than $1 - 1/(2m)$ requires communicating at least $\begin{pmatrix} m \\ m/2 \end{pmatrix} - 1$ bits.

Proposition 11.7 implies that a FPAS in m is impossible (otherwise it could be used to realize approximation ratio $1 - 1/(2m)$ with polynomial communication in m). In particular, an ascending-bid auction with m per-item prices and bid increment ε cannot approximate efficiency within ε, because the auction's worst-case complexity would be $nm\varepsilon^{-1}$, and so it would be a FPAS. Yet, it is not known whether there exists a PAS—that is, whether any approximation ratio less than one can be achieved with polynomial communication in n, m. The only known polynomial approximation protocol is the (deterministic) "greedy" protocol of Lehmann, O'Callaghan, and Shoham (2001), which realizes approximation ratio 1/2.

11.4.5 Application: Substitute Items

Here each agent's valuation space $V_i = V_{\text{sub}}$ is the set of valuations $v \in V_{\text{gen}}$ whose indirect utility function $\max_{S \subset M}(v(S) - \sum_{l \in S} p_l)$ is submodular in $p \in \mathbb{R}_+^m$.[23] Because $V_{\text{sub}} \subset V_{\text{sm}}$ (see Gul and Stacchetti 1999), the dual of a substitute valuation is not one, except when both are *additive*, i.e., take the form $v(S) = \sum_{l \in S} \phi_l$ for some $\phi \in \mathbb{R}^m$. Let V_{add} denote the class of additive valuations. Because $V_{\text{add}} \subset V_{\text{sub}}$, and the dual of an additive valuation is itself, proposition 11.2 implies that the dimension of the message space in an efficient protocol is at least dim $V_{\text{add}} = m$. This lower bound is attained by the *Walrasian* price protocol in which prices are restricted to be additive (i.e., per item) and anonymous (Kelso and Crawford 1982; Gul and Stacchetti 1999).

The Walrasian protocol is nondeterministic, leaving open the question of how to *find* an equilibrium. Several ascending-price auction protocols reaching Walrasian equilibria have been proposed (Bikhchandani and Ostroy, chapter 8 of this volume), but all of them are only FPAS. NS improve upon such protocols by offering a deterministic TPAS, which is based on solving the dual problem (find prices to *minimize* the total surplus subject to the constraints that no agent can increase his utility at the current prices) with a separation-based linear programming algorithm (such as the ellipsoid method). Because each constraint in the dual problem depends on the valuation of a single agent, at each stage of the algorithm each agent is asked to report a bundle giving him a higher net utility than his "target utility" at the current prices. The protocol continues as long as one of the agents makes such a report. Running the protocol on discretized valuations yields an approximate solution to the dual and primal problems.

11.4.6 Application: Homogeneous Items

Here each agent's valuation space $V_i = V_h$ is the set of valuations $v \in V_{\text{gen}}$ that satisfy $v(S) = \phi(|S|)$ for all $S \subset M$, where $\phi : \{0, \ldots, m\} \to \mathbb{R}$. That is, agents care only about the number of items they receive. Because the dual of a homogeneous valuation is homogeneous, proposition 11.2 implies

Proposition 11.8 In the combinatorial allocation problem with homogeneous valuations, the dimension of the message space in any efficient protocol is at least dim $V_h = m$.

By contrast, full revelation of valuations rounded off to multiples of δ requires each agent to communicate only the $\lfloor \delta^{-1} \rfloor$ points in $\{0 \ldots m\}$ at which his discretized valuation jumps, each of which is transmitted with $\log_2(m + 1)$ bits. This communication realizes approximation ratio $1 - \delta/\gamma$:

Proposition 11.9   In the combinatorial allocation problem with homogeneous valuations, for any $\delta > 0$, approximation ratio $1 - \delta/\gamma$ is realized by full revelation of valuations rounded off to multiples of δ, which takes at most $n\lfloor \delta^{-1} \rfloor \log_2(m+1)$ bits.

Because by the proposition full revelation of valuations rounded off to multiples of $\varepsilon\gamma$ realizes approximation ratio $1 - \varepsilon$ using at most $n\lfloor \varepsilon^{-1}\gamma^{-1} \rfloor \log_2(m+1)$ bits, this gives a FPAS in $\log m$. In particular, any given approximation error can be achieved using $O(\log m)$ bits, which is exponentially smaller than the number of real variables required for exact efficiency. A finite counterpart of this observation (formally stated in NS) is that when m is large and we have a discrete protocol that achieves a close approximation of efficiency, a small reduction in inefficiency requires an enormous increase in communication.

Compare these results with those of Calsamiglia (1977), in which instead of m indivisible items there is one unit of an infinitely divisible good. In this case, V is the space of nondecreasing functions $v : [0, 1] \rightarrow [0, 1]$, and so dim $V = \infty$. Proposition 11.2 then implies that efficiency requires an infinite-dimensional message space, re-deriving Calsamiglia's (1977) result.[24] Notwithstanding this pessimistic result, proposition 11.9 allows to construct a FPAS for Calsamiglia's model by allocating the goods in properly chosen discrete units, provided that the agents' valuation functions satisfy a mild strengthening of continuity (e.g., Hölder continuity of any degree would suffice).

11.5   Remarks and Extensions

11.5.1   The Procurement Problem

The procurement problem is the combinatorial allocation problem in which the items are procured *from* the agents, and the goal is to *minimize* the total cost. Denoting agent i's cost of procuring bundle $S \subset M$ by $c_i(S)$, the total cost of allocation $j \in N^M$ is $\sum_i c_i(j^{-1}(i))$. The analysis of exact efficiency in the procurement problem is exactly the same as in the "selling" problem considered before, but the analysis of approximation differs. Define realizing approximation factor $r \geq 1$ as guaranteeing a total cost at most r times the minimum possible, and suppose that the agents' costs satisfy restrictions N, FD, and B.

Consider the setting with two agents whose costs take only values 0 or 1. Here realizing *any* finite approximation factor requires realizing the total cost of zero whenever possible, which is equivalent to exact efficiency and requires exponential communication in m by the argument of proposition 11.2. One can achieve better approximation when costs are known to be *subadditive*, i.e., satisfying $c^i(S \cup T) \leq c^i(S) + c^i(T)$ for all $S, T \subset M$. Nevertheless, even for this case, Nisan (2002) shows that a $c \log m$-approximation for any constant $c < 1/2$ requires communication that is exponential in m. A matching upper bound obtains using the following iterative procedure based on Lovász's (1975) classical algorithm for approximate set covering: Ask each player i to announce a subset S^i of yet unprocured items that minimizes his average cost $c_i(S_i)/|S_i|$, along with the minimum average cost itself, and procure the set with the minimum average cost across agents. Repeat until all items are procured.

11.5.2 Deterministic Communication

So far we have focused on the burden of nondeterministic communication (NDC), but in practice we can only implement deterministic communication (DC). Although in some instances we were able to bound the DC burden above by suggesting a specific protocol, in general it remains unclear by how much it can exceed the NDC burden. For the case of discrete communication, the gap between DC and NDC has been studied in the communication complexity literature. The gap can be exponential for general allocation rules:

Example 11.1 Consider the CA problem with $n = 2$ firms (agents) and $m = 3q$ workers (items). Each worker speaks a single language, and there are $2q$ languages in total, of which q are spoken by a single worker, and q spoken by two workers. Firm 1 knows privately all workers' languages, and it receives value 1 from employing a pair of workers who speak the same language. Firm 2 does not know or care about workers' languages; it receives value 1 from employing a particular group of $q - 1$ workers, which it knows privately. There is free disposal of workers. Note that there always exists an allocation of workers to firms yielding the maximal total surplus 2. An NDC protocol can verify this allocation with $2 \log_2 m$ bits: announce a pair of workers going to firm 1 with the others going to firm 2, and let each firm verify that its profit is 1. However, the DC complexity of realizing efficiency is asymptotically proportional to m. This follows from the result on the DC complexity of the "pair-disjointness" correspondence derived in Kushilevitz and Nisan (1997, section 5.2).

However, in some well-known allocation problems the gap between deterministic and nondeterministic communication burdens proves to be small. This is trivially true when even nondeterministic communication proves almost as hard as full revelation (e.g., in the CA problem with general valuations). More interestingly, the gap is also small in some cases in which the communication burden is much lower than full revelation. A famous case is given by convex economies with the "gross substitute" property, in which the deterministic "tâtonnement" process originally proposed by Walras converges quickly to a Walrasian equilibrium (Mas-Colell et al. 1995, section 17.H). Similarly, subsection 11.4.5 of this chapter describes a TPAS for the CA problem with substitute items.

Most protocols described in this book (chapters 2–6, 8, and 10) operate by asking a sequence of *demand queries*, which ask an agent to report his preferred bundle given a bundle-price vector $p : 2^M \to \mathbb{R}$ that is a function of the agents' previous reports. However, Nisan and Segal (2004) find that restricting attention to such demand-query protocols can increase the deterministic communication burden exponentially:[25]

Example 11.2 Suppose we have $n = 2$ agents, and each agent i's valuation class consists of valuations $v_i : 2^M \to \mathbb{R}$ satisfying $v_i(S) \in \{0, 1\}$ for all $S \subset M$, with $v_i(S) = 0$ for $|S| \leq m/2$, $v_i(S) = 1$ for $|S| \geq m/2$, and

$$|\{S \subset M : |S| = m/2, v_i(S) = 1\}| > \frac{1}{2} \binom{m}{m/2}.$$

Then finding an efficient allocation is equivalent to finding an even split $(S, N \setminus S)$ of items such that $v_1(S) = v_2(N \setminus S) = 1$ (and such a split always exists). Nisan and Segal (2004) demonstrate a protocol that does this using no more than $4m^2$ bits. On the other hand, they prove that any efficient demand-query protocol asks at least $1/2 \binom{m}{m/2} - 1$ queries in the worst case. They also show that, for *some* joint probability distribution over such valuations, any expected-surplus improvement upon the bundled auction must still use an expected number of queries that is exponential in m.[26]

These findings are especially surprising in light of proposition 11.1, which allows one to restrict attention to demand queries without increasing the *nondeterministic* communication burden. It seems important to characterize the classes of valuations (or probability distributions over them) for which demand queries can be used without a large increase in the deterministic communication burden, as well as examine which more general kinds of queries could be useful for general valuations.

11.5.3 Average-Case Analysis

Given a probability distribution over the state space, we can relax the notion of approximation to the requirement that the *expected* surplus be close to maximal. At the same time, we can count the expected rather than worst-case number of bits transmitted, which allows a savings from coding more frequent messages with fewer bits (as in Shannon's [1948] information theory). This average-case approach is known as *distributional* communication complexity, because the results clearly depend on the assumed distribution of the states of the world. For example, if the distribution puts all weight on a single state, then an efficient outcome is known without any communication. Thus, it is only interesting to consider distributions that are sufficiently diffuse so that no outcome has a high a priori probability of being efficient. NS show that for *some* such distributions, the communication burden of any improvement over the bundled auction still grows exponentially with the number of items:

Proposition 11.10 In the combinatorial allocation problem, for each n and m there exists a joint probability distribution over valuation profiles $(v^1, \ldots, v^n)$ such that for any $\varepsilon > 0$, realizing fraction $1/n + \varepsilon$ of the maximum expected surplus requires transmitting an expected number of bits that is at least $c \exp\{m/(2n^2) - 5 \ln n\}$, for some fixed $c > 0$.

The distribution used in the above proposition may involve some correlation among the agents' valuations. NS also obtain a (weaker) lower bound on average-case approximation for independently distributed valuations:

Proposition 11.11 In the combinatorial allocation problem with $n = 2$ agents, there exists a probability distribution pair D_1, D_2 over valuations for each m such that realizing fraction c of the maximum expected surplus (for some fixed $c < 1$)[27] when the agents' valuations are distributed independently according to D_1, D_2, respectively, requires communication of an expected number of bits that is exponential in m.

These results leave open the possibility that for a "typical" probability distribution the communication problem may not be as hard. Sandholm and Boutilier (chapter 10 of this volume) simulate the average-case performance of several "preference elicitation schemes." For up to a dozen items, some of the proposed schemes achieve efficiency asking on average as little as 10 percent of the number of queries needed for full revelation. Unfortunately, the average-case communication burden still grows fast with the number of items, and would become prohibitive for a few dozen items. Also, it is hard to know what probability distributions over valuations should be used as typical: even if real-life bidders were willing to reveal their valuations honestly to a statistician, they may not be able to do so due to the very communication complexity problem studied in this chapter.

11.5.4 Incentives
So far we have ignored agents' incentives to follow the strategies suggested by the designer: even if the agents are obedient, in many cases the communication requirement *by itself* constitutes a "bottleneck," preventing exact or approximate efficiency. Yet it is still interesting to know how the requirement of incentive compatibility increases the communication burden.

Note that we cannot consider incentives in the framework of nondeterministic communication, because it does not stipulate what an agent can obtain by "rejecting" the oracle's message. For example, in a price equilibrium, an agent would not want to request a different allocation under the given prices, but may want to reject the oracle's message if this could bring about more favorable prices. In the course of *deterministic* communication finding a price equilibrium, agents may indeed be able to influence the prices to their advantage by deviating from the prescribed reporting strategies (see, e.g., Mas-Colell, Whinston, and Green 1995, example 23.B.2).

The additional requirement of incentive-compatibility *in itself* does not noticeably raise the deterministic communication burden of efficiency. Indeed, suppose that we have a communication protocol that realizes the surplus-maximizing allocation rule. After running the protocol, ask each agent i to report his payoff π_{ij} at the resulting allocation j, and give each agent i a transfer equal to sum of others' announcements, $t_i = \sum_{i' \neq i} \pi_{i'j}$. This transfer scheme, first proposed by Reichelstein (1984, pp. 45–46), gives each agent a payoff equal to the total surplus, and so the communication game becomes one of common interest (in the terminology of Marschak and Radner 1972, the agents become a "team"). Under the Reichelstein scheme, the prescribed strategies constitute an *ex post equilibrium*: no agent can be better off by deviating in any state of the world, because such a deviation could only reduce the total surplus, provided that the other agents adhere to the equilibrium strategies.[28] Thus, incentive compatibility is assured by communicating only n additional real numbers.

To be sure, an exactly efficient protocol may involve prohibitive amounts of communication (as discussed in this chapter) and computation (Lehmann, Müller, and Sandholm, chapter 12 of this volume). As Ronen notes in chapter 15, in a protocol that is only *approximately* efficient, agents may have the incentives to deviate from the proposed reporting strategy. However, under the Reichelstein transfer scheme, an agent will deviate only if the deviation raises his expectation of the total surplus. In general, this expectation will depend on the agent's beliefs about other agents' valuations and their strategies. Under the standard assumption that the agents have a common prior over the state space, a strategy profile that maximizes the expected total surplus constitutes a Bayesian-Nash equilibrium of the game induced by the Reichelstein transfer scheme.[29]

The Reichelstein transfer scheme is very costly: because each agent must receive the total surplus, the designer must pay out a total subsidy equal to $n - 1$ times the total surplus. The cost can be covered without affecting incentives by charging each agent a participation fee that depends on other agents' messages. The largest fee f_i that ensures agent i's voluntary participation is the surplus that could be achieved in his absence, and the resulting net transfer to the agent, called the *Vickrey-Groves-Clarke (VCG) transfer*, is $t_i - f_i$ (this equals to the externality imposed by agent i externality on the other agents; see Ausubel and Milgrom, chapter 1 of this volume).

Because f_i can be calculated by solving the maximization problem without agent i, VCG transfers can be revealed while multiplying the communication burden of efficiency by at most $n + 1$. However, it is often possible to calculate VCG transfers without solving the n additional subproblems. Lahaie and Parkes (2004) characterize efficient communication protocols that reveal VCG transfers using the following concept:

Definition 11.3   A pair $(p, j) \in \mathbb{R}^{nk} \times K$ is a *universal price equilibrium* if it is a price equilibrium and prices $(p_{i'})_{i' \neq i}$ constitute equilibrium prices upon the removal of any one agent $i \in N$.

A well-known example of a universal price equilibrium is given by a Walrasian price equilibrium in the limiting case of a "perfectly competitive" exchange economy, with so many agents that an individual agent cannot influence the prices, and so has no incentive to misrepresent his preferences. Parkes and Ungar (2002) show that the revelation of a universal price equilibrium (p, j) is sufficient for calculating the agents' VCG payments: indeed, in such an equilibrium all agents other than agent i are indifferent about removing agent i; hence, the agent's VCG transfer—the externality imposed by him—can be calculated as the revenue externality on the designer, $\sum_{i' \neq i} p_{i'j} - \max_{j' \in K} \sum_{i' \neq i} p_{i'j'}$. Moreover, Lahaie and Parkes (2004) show that revealing a universal price equilibrium is also *necessary* for finding VCG payments:

Proposition 11.12 (Lahaie-Parkes)   A communication protocol realizes VCG payments if and only if it reveals a universal price equilibrium.

The necessity part is proven by showing that if a message reveals VCG payments, then the supporting price equilibrium constructed by NS for this message (as described in 11.3) is a universal price equilibrium. Figure 11.3 illustrates the case of two agents. Suppose that message w reveals that agent 1's valuation is u_1 and that agent 2's valuation is either u_2' and u_2'', and therefore that allocation j is efficient. (As in figures 11.1 and 11.2, the agents' valuations for j are normalized to zero.) Recall from figure 11.2 that NS construct agent 2's price curve p_2 as the upper envelope of his possible valuation curves consistent with message w. By definition, agent 1's VCG payment in a given state is simply agent 2's maximum achievable value in this state. Figure 11.3 depicts a situation in which this maximum is revealed by message w, that is, it is

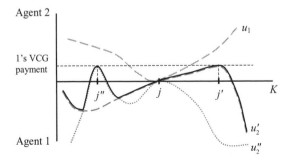

Figure 11.3
Revelation of universal prices.

the same for valuation u_2' (achieved by allocation j') and for valuation u_2'' (achieved by allocation j''). Then either allocation maximizes price p_2, and this price makes agent 2 indifferent about going to allocation j' when his valuation is u_2' or to allocation j'' when his valuation is u_2''. Hence, (p_2, j') is a price equilibrium in the problem with only agent 2 whose valuation is u_2', and (p_2, j'') is a price equilibrium in the problem with only agent 2 whose valuation is u_2''. Therefore, letting also $p_1 = u_1$, we see that (p_1, p_2, j) is a universal price equilibrium in both states consistent with message w.

Figure 11.3 also shows that a universal price equilibrium (p, j) need not reveal a solution to the subproblems obtained by removing a single agent (indeed, it does not reveal whether the problem with only agent 2 is solved by j' or j''). (Examples of protocols that yield a universal price equilibrium—and thus VCG payments—in specific allocation problems without yielding solutions to the subproblems obtained by removing a single agent can be found in Feigenbaum et al. 2003, Bikhchandani et al. 2002, and Parkes and Ungar 2002.)

11.5.5 Other Social Choice Problems

We may be interested in allocation problems in which monetary payments cannot be used to reallocate total surplus among the agents, because such payments may be constrained (e.g., by the agents' limited liquidity), or not allowed at all, or agents' utilities may not be quasilinear in the payments (i.e., they exhibit *wealth effects*). Also, we may be interested in achieving social criteria other than Pareto efficiency: for example, we may want the allocation to satisfy voluntary participation (i.e., be preferred to status quo by all agents), or to be immune to coalitional deviations (e.g., be in the core), or to satisfy some fairness criteria (e.g., that no agent should envy another agent's allocation).

Segal (2004) extends the analysis of NS to general social choice problems, which cover all such allocation settings and social goals. In a social choice problem, we are given a set N of agents, a set X of social alternatives, and a set $\mathscr{R}_i$ of preference relations that each agent $i \in N$ can have over X. Each agent's preference relation is his private type. The goal is to realize a *choice rule*, which is a correspondence $F : \mathscr{R}_1 \times \cdots \times \mathscr{R}_n \twoheadrightarrow X$.

One particular way to verify that alternative x is desirable (i.e., selected by F) is by asking each agent i to verify that x maximizes his own preferences within his *budget set* $B_i \subset X$. Such *budget protocols* naturally generalize price protocols to the general social choice setting. Not all choice rules can be verified with a budget protocol; it turns out that those that can are those that are either monotonic in the sense of Maskin (1999), or include a nonempty-valued monotonic subcorrespondence. Yet, just because a choice rule *can* be realized with a budget protocol does not mean that it cannot be realized in a different, perhaps more economical, way.

Segal (2004) generalizes proposition 11.1 by characterizing the choice rules that satisfy the following property: Any protocol verifying that alternative x is desirable verifies that some $(B_1, \ldots, B_n, x)$ is a budget equilibrium, which in itself verifies that x is desirable. These choice rules are characterized by the property of *intersection monotonicity*, which strengthens monotonicity, and is satisfied by such important rules as Pareto, approximate Pareto, the core, and no-envy rules. For such choice rules, any verification protocol must reveal supporting budget sets. Thus, the communication burden of such choice rules is exactly that of finding a supporting budget equilibrium. Furthermore, because some budget sets are less informative than others (e.g., smaller budget sets are less informative than larger ones), the verification burden can be minimized by using only minimally informative supporting budget equilibria.

To give one example, the efficient allocation problem described in subsection 11.2.1 can be viewed as a social choice problem in which an alternative is described by an allocation from K and by real-valued transfers of money (numeraire) among the agents that add up to zero. If agents' utilities are quasilinear in the transfers, Pareto efficiency coincides with total surplus-maximization. In this problem, we can restrict attention to budget sets that specify the prices of all allocations in terms of the numeraire. Restriction 11.2 on prices serves to ensure that such budget sets do verify efficiency. Furthermore, the minimally informative budget equilibria verifying efficiency obtain by having all inequalities (11.2) to hold with equality (which corresponds to shrinking the budget sets as much as possible while preserving restriction 11.2).

To give another example, consider the choice rule that approximates the maximum surplus within δ. Because this choice rule is also intersection-monotonic, we can again restrict attention without loss to budget protocols. Note that in order to verify that allocation j is approximately efficient within δ, the prices describing the budget sets must satisfy the following relaxation of condition 11.2: $\sum_{i \in N} p_{ij} \geq \sum_{i \in N} p_{ij'} - \delta$ for all $j' \in K \backslash \{j\}$. Furthermore, the minimally informative budget equilibria verifying surplus maximization within δ are obtained by requiring all these inequalities to hold with equality. Counting the number of distinct such price equilibria that must be used provides alternative proofs for the results on the communication burden of approximation.

Segal (2004) also uses the communication welfare theorem to identify the communication burden of the core in exchange economies in which *all* goods are indivisible (i.e., there is no divisible numeraire to compensate agents), and of stable many-to-one matching problems without transfers (Roth and Sotomayor 1990).

11.6 Conclusion

The communication problem discussed in this chapter is different from the so-called "winner determination problem" of *computing* an efficient or approximately efficient allocation given the agents' valuations expressed through their bids (Lehmann, Müller, and Sandholm, chapter 12 in this volume). Indeed, the computational complexity of a problem is defined relative to its input size, but in the WDP problem the input—a complete expression of the agents' valuations—is itself exponential in the number m of items. For this reason, the WDP problem has only been studied in cases in which the agents' valuations can be expressed using a small number of bids. Even in such simple cases from the viewpoint of communication, the WDP problem is typically NP-complete.

Nevertheless, the communication bottleneck appears to be more severe than the computational one. Recall that NP-completeness only suggests that the computation may need to be exponential *asymptotically* as the input size grows (and that only if $\mathcal{P} \neq \mathcal{NP}$, which is considered likely but not proven). In practice, as discussed in part III of this book, computational complexity can be handled for up to hundreds of items (and thousands of bids) optimally and thousands of items (with tens of thousand of bids) near optimally. In contrast, the lower bounds on communication complexity described in this chapter are *exact* for any given m. For example, with general valuations, exact efficiency requires communicating at least one price for each of the $2^m - 1$ nonempty bundles of items, and any improvement over the bundled auction with two bidders still requires communicating at least $\binom{m}{m/2}$ bits. Already with $m = 40$ items, any improvement would require the bidders to send at least $\binom{40}{20}$ bits $\simeq 16$ gigabytes of data, which would take 164 years of continuous typing (the average typist enters 200 keystrokes per minute, and each keystroke transmits eight bits). Considering the average case does not help matters much, at least for *some* probability distributions over valuations.[30]

These findings should not be taken to imply that all real-life combinatorial auctions are useless. Rather, by showing that there does not exist a practical auction design that works well for all possible combinatorial valuations, the findings should motivate auction designers to focus on specific classes of preferences or probability distributions over them. The burden should be on the proposer of a particular design to characterize the environments on which it works well. The tools described in this chapter may be useful for obtaining such characterizations.

Acknowledgments

Much of this survey is based on my joint work with Noam Nisan, and my intellectual debt to him should be evident. This work was supported by the National Science Foundation grants #0214500 and #0427770. Ronald Fadel and Hui Li provided excellent research assistance.

Notes

1. Another motivation for such indirect mechanisms, suggested by Parkes (2000), is to economize on the agents' cost of *computing* (rather than communicating) their valuations. However, in the absence of communication costs, the agents could reveal all the raw data for their computations and let the auctioneer perform them (or distribute them among the agents in a way that need not bear any relation to the initial allocation of the data).

2. Calsamiglia (1977) examined the communication burden in a convex economy with *divisible* goods, but failed to note the role of prices in this setting.

3. The general communication complexity problem, introduced by Yao (1979) and surveyed by Kushilevitz and Nisan (1997), is to compute a function (in our case, desirable allocation) whose inputs (in our case, agents' valuations) are distributed among agents. For comparisons between this literature and the economic literature on real-valued communication, see Marschak 1996 and Van Zandt 1999.

4. Although there exist "simple" mechanisms improving upon the bundled auction when m is not too large relative to n (Lehmann, O'Callaghan, and Shoham 2002, Holzman et al. 2004), the share of surplus they realize must still vanish as $m \to \infty$.

5. A *correspondence* $F : U \twoheadrightarrow K$ is a function from set U into the set 2^K of subsets of K.

6. Efficiency is equivalent to surplus maximization when agents can compensate one another with monetary transfers, and their utilities are quasilinear in the transfers. Other allocation rules are considered in subsections 11.4.2 and 11.5.5.

7. In fact, multistage communication may achieve exponential savings upon simultaneous communication (Kushilevitz and Nisan 1997, section 4.2). A CA problem with this property is described by Sandholm and Boutilier (chapter 10 of this volume), who call sequential communication "interleaving."

8. This is an established (if perhaps unfortunate), term in the economic literature, which refers to the fact that agents do not observe each other's types *initially*, but does not constrain the revelation of types in the course of communication.

9. This is merely a normalization, because a symbol in *any* finite alphabet could be coded with a fixed number of bits.

10. Formally, the distance is defined as

$$\rho_W(w, w') = \max\{d_W(\mu^{-1}(w), \mu^{-1}(w')), d_W(\mu^{-1}(w'), \mu^{-1}(w))\}, \quad \text{where}$$

$$d_W(A, B) = \sup_{u \in A} \inf_{u' \in B} \rho_U(u, u') \quad \text{for } A, B \subset U,$$

where the metric ρ_U on state space U is defined as

$$\rho_U(u, u') = \sup_{j \in K} \inf_{j' \in K} |[u(j) - u'(j)] - [u(j') - u'(j')]|.$$

11. dim W can be defined as the Hausdorff dimension, the box-counting dimension, or the packing index (Edgar 1990)—this would not affect the results in this survey.

12. The approach of NS stands in contrast to the previous literature on continuous communication, which took the topology on the message space as given, and ruled out dimension smuggling by imposing a continuity restriction on the communication protocol (e.g., Mount and Reiter 1974, Walker 1977, Abelson 1980, Luo and Tsitsiklis 1991). For example, Mount and Reiter (1974) require the message correspondence μ to be "locally threaded"—i.e., have a continuous selection on a neighborhood of any point. This restriction rules out some important communication protocols, e.g., the communication of discrete allocations (μ cannot have a continuous selection in a neighborhood in which the allocation switches).

13. Parkes (2002) establishes a similar result, but for a restricted communication language.

14. The communication burden is bounded above by $(n-1)(2^m - 1)$ (all agents but one fully reveal their valuations), but this bound is not tight. For example, efficient allocation of $m = 1$ item among any number n of agents can be verified by announcing just one number—the item's market-clearing price.

15. This is a "worst-case" definition, as it requires uniform approximation across all states. The weaker "average-case" approximation given some probability distribution over states is considered in subsection 11.5.3 below.

16. Note the role of B in ensuring that approximation can be achieved with finite communication. For example, consider the problem of allocating one object between two agents whose valuations lie in $[0, 1]$. Pick $r \in (0, 1)$, and consider the restricted problem in which both agents' valuations lie in the set $\{r^n\}_{n=0}^{\infty} \subset [0, 1]$. In this restricted problem, realizing an approximation ratio higher than r is equivalent to exact efficiency, and proposition 11.1 implies that this requires a countable message space. Because one can choose arbitrary $r \in (0, 1)$, this implies that no positive approximation can be achieved with finite communication. One reaches the same conclusion when the agents' valuations lie in $[1, \infty]$, by considering the restricted problem $\{r^{-n}\}_{n=0}^{\infty}$.

17. This result is stated only for nondeterministic protocols: it is not known whether a deterministic approximation scheme can be guaranteed when the original continuous protocol is deterministic.

18. See Edgar 1990.

19. Hurwicz and Marschak (2003a,b) report related results for discretizing the Walrasian protocol.

20. For ease of exposition let m be even whenever it is divided by 2. If m is odd, one item can be assigned zero marginal benefit to both players and be ignored, and so $m/2$ can be replaced with its integer part.

21. At each stage of the protocol, each agent i who is not yet allocated any items announces a subset S_i of yet unallocated items that maximizes the ratio $v_i(S_i)/\sqrt{|S_i|}$, along with the maximum ratio itself. The agent who announces the highest ratio receives the requested bundle and leaves. In the course of the protocol, agents announce no more than $n(n+1)/2$ valuations and bundles.

22. An equivalent definition is that

$$v(S \cup T) + v(S \cap T) \leq v(S) + v(T) \quad \text{for all } S, T \subset M.$$

23. For several equivalent definitions of the substitute property see Gul and Stacchetti 1999 and Milgrom 2000.

24. Calsamiglia (1977) restricts the valuation of agent 1 to be concave and that of agent 2 to be convex. Because the dual of a concave valuation is convex, the analysis goes through without modification. Similarly, the agents' valuations can be restricted to be arbitrarily smooth, because smoothness is preserved under duality.

25. One must be careful about the report of an agent who is indifferent among several bundles: if tie-breaking could depend directly on his valuation, then it could communicate arbitrary information about the valuation. Therefore, Nisan and Segal (2004) require that agents break ties using some a priori ordering over bundles (which may depend on the agents' previous reports).

26. These results also apply to protocols that use "value queries," which ask an agent to report his valuation for a given bundle S, since such a query is equivalent to the demand query with prices $p(\emptyset) = 0$, $p(S) = 1/2$, and $p(T) > 1$ for $T \neq S, \emptyset$.

27. NS do not optimize with respect to the constant c (their proof has $c = 99.5\%$).

28. In general, truthfulness will not be a dominant strategy: if agent i expects another agent to use a contingent strategy that is not consistent with any given type, agent i may prefer not to be truthful as well.

29. Taken to an extreme, this observation implies that agents need not be offered any protocol at all—it suffices to make them internalize the communication costs, along with others' utilities, using ex post payments. Then the protocol that maximizes the expected surplus net of communication costs will emerge as a Bayesian-Nash equilibrium of the "free-form" game in which agents can send any messages and implement an allocation. To be sure, this argument relies heavily on the agents' rationality—both individual (being able to calculate an optimal protocol) and collective (being able to coordinate on it). But if agents are not fully rational, it is not clear how to consider their incentives in the first place.

30. Also, although the computational burden may be distributed among the bidders, e.g., by asking them to suggest surplus-improving allocations (Land, Powell, and Steinberg, chapter 6 of this volume), the auctioneer bears the full communication burden.

References

Abelson, Harold (1980), "Lower Bounds on Information Transfer in Distributed Computations," *Journal of the Association for Computing Machinery*, 27, 384–392.

Ausubel, Lawrence and Paul Milgrom (2002), "Ascending Auctions with Package Bidding," *Frontiers of Theoretical Economics* 1, 1–42. Available at ⟨http://www.bepress.com/bejte/frontiers/vol1/iss1/art1⟩.

Babai, László, Péter Frankl, and János Simon (1986), "Complexity Classes in Communication Complexity Theory," *Proceedings of FOCS*, 337–347.

Bikhchandani, Sushil, Sven de Vries, Rakesh Vohra, and James Schummer (2002), "Linear Programming and Vickrey Auctions," in Brenda Dietrich and Rakesh V. Vohra, eds., *Mathematics of the Internet: E-Auction and Markets*, New York: Springer Verlag, 75–115.

Calsamiglia, Xavier (1977), "Decentralized Resource Allocation and Increasing Returns," *Journal of Economic Theory*, 14, 262–283.

Edgar, Gerald A. (1990), *Measure, Topology, and Fractal Geometry*, New York: Springer-Verlag.

Feigenbaum, Joan, Arvind Krishnamurthy, Rahul Sami, and Scott Shenker (2003), "Hardness Results for Multicast Cost Sharing," *Theoretical Computer Science*, 304, 215–236.

Gul, Faruk and Ennio Stacchetti (1999), "Walrasian Equilibrium with Gross Substitutes," *Journal of Economic Theory*, 87, 95–124.

Hayek, Friedrich (1945), "The Use of Knowledge in Society," *American Economic Review*, 35, 519–530.

Holzman, Ron, Noa Kfir-Dahav, Dov Monderer, and Moshe Tennenholtz (2004), "Bundling Equilibrium in Combinatorial Auctions," *Games and Economic Behavior*, 47, 104–123.

Hurwicz, Leo (1977), "On the Dimensional Requirements of Informationally Decentralized Pareto-Satisfactory Processes," in Kenneth J. Arrow and Leo Hurwicz, eds., *Studies in Resource Allocation Processes*, New York: Cambridge University Press, 413–424.

Hurwicz, Leo and Thomas Marschak (2003a), "Finate Allocation Mechanisms: Approximate Walrusian versus Approximate Direct Revelation," *Economic Theory*, 21, 545–572.

Hurwicz, Leo and Thomas Marschak (2003b), "Comparing Finite Mechanisms," *Economic Theory*, 21, 783–841.

Jordan, James S. (1982), "The Competitive Allocation Process is Informationally Efficient Uniquely," *Journal of Economic Theory*, 28, 1–18.

Kelso, Alexander S. and Vincent P. Crawford (1982), "Job Matching, Coalition Formation, and Gross Substitutes," *Econometrica*, 50, 1483–1504.

Kushilevitz, Eyal and Noam Nisan (1997), *Communication Complexity*, Cambridge: Cambridge University Press.

Lahaie, Sebastién and David Parkes (2004), "Applying Learning Algorithms to Preference Elicitation," *Proceedings of the 5th ACM Conference on Electronic Commerce*, 180–188.

Lehmann, Benny, Daniel Lehmann, and Noam Nisan (2001), "Combinatorial Auctions with Decreasing Marginal Utilities." In *Proceedings 3rd ACM Conference on Electronic Commerce*, New York: ACM Press, 18–28. To appear, *Games and Economic Behavior*.

Lehmann, Daniel, Liadan I. O'Callaghan, and Yoav Shoham (2002), "Truth Revelation in Approximately Efficient Combinatorial Auctions," *Journal of the ACM*, 49, 577–602.

Lovász, László (1975), "The Ratio of Optimal Integral and Fractional Covers," *Discrete Mathematics*, 13, 383–390.

Luo, Zhi-Quan and John N. Tsitsiklis (1991), "Communication Complexity of Algebraic Computation," *Proceedings of 31st IEEE Symposium on Foundations of Computer Science*, 758–765.

Marschak, Jacob and Roy Radner (1972), *Economic Theory of Teams*, New Haven: Yale University Press.

Marschak, Thomas (1996), "On Economies of Scope in Communication," *Economic Design*, 2, 1–30.

Mas-Colell, Andreu (1980), "Efficiency and Decentralization in the Pure Theory of Public Goods," *Quarterly Journal of Economics*, 94(4): 625–641.

Mas-Colell, Andreu, Michael D. Whinston, and Jerry R. Green (1995), *Microeconomic Theory*, New York: Oxford University Press.

Maskin, Eric (1999), "Nash Equilibrium and Welfare Optimality," *Review of Economic Studies*, 66, 23–38.

Milgrom, Paul (2000), "Putting Auction Theory to Work: The Simultaneous Ascending Auction," *Journal of Political Economy*, 108, 245–272.

Mount, Kenneth and Stanley Reiter (1974), "The Information Size of Message Spaces," *Journal of Economic Theory*, 28, 1–18.

Nisan, Noam (2002), "The Communication Complexity of Approximate Set Packing and Covering." *Proceedings of the 29th International Colloquium on Automata, Languages, and Programming*, 868–875.

Nisan, Noam and Ilya Segal (2003), "The Communication Requirements of Efficient Allocations and Supporting Prices," *Journal of Economic Theory*, To appear.

Nisan, Noam and Ilya Segal (2004), "Exponential Communication Inefficiency of Demand Queries," working paper, Stanford University.

Parkes, David (2000), "Optimal Auction Design for Hard Valuation Problems," in *Agent Mediated, Electronic Commerce II*, Alexandros Moukas, Carles Sierra, and Fredrik Ygge, eds., Springer-Verlag, 206–209.

Parkes, David C. (2005), "Price-Based Information Certificates for Minimal-Revelation Combinatorial Auctions," in *Agent Mediated Electronic Commerce Workshop IV*, Julian Padget, Onn Shehory, David Parkes, Norman Sadeh, and William El Walsh, eds., LNAI 2531, Heidelberg: Springer-Verlag, 103–122.

Parkes, David C. and Lyle H. Ungar (2002), "An Ascending-Price Generalized Vickrey Auction," Technical Report, Harvard University.

Reichelstein, Stephan (1984), "Incentive Compatibility and Informational Requirements," *Journal of Economic Theory*, 34, 32–51.

Roth, Alvin E. and Marilda A. Oliveira Sotomayor (1990), *Two-Sided Matching: A Study in Game-Theoretic Modeling and Analysis*, Cambridge: Cambridge University Press.

Segal, Ilya (2004), "The Communication Requirements of Social Choice Rules and Supporting Budget Sets," working paper, Stanford University.

Shannon, Claude E. (1948), "A Mathematical Theory of Communication," *Bell System Technical Journal*, 27, 379–423, 623–656.

van Zandt, Timothy (1999), "Decentralized Information Processing in the Theory of Organizations," in Murat Sertel, ed., *Contemporary Economic Issues, Volume 4: Economic Behaviour and Design*. London: MacMillan Press Ltd, 125–160.

Vazirani, Vijay V. (2001), *Approximation Algorithms*, Berlin: Springer-Verlag.

Walker, Mark (1977), "On the Informational Size of Message Spaces," *Journal of Economic Theory*, 15, 366–375.

Yao, Andrew Chi-Chih (1979), "Some Complexity Questions Related to Distributive Computing," *34th Annual ACM Symposium on Theory of Computing*, 209–213.

III Complexity and Algorithmic Considerations

12 The Winner Determination Problem

Daniel Lehmann, Rudolf Müller, and Tuomas Sandholm

12.1 Introduction

This part of the book provides a comprehensive overview of the computational challenges inherent in solving the winner determination problem (WDP): Given a set of bids in a combinatorial auction, find an allocation of items to bidders (the auctioneer can keep some of the items) that maximizes the auctioneer's revenue. The bids are expressions in a bidding language, by which bidders report valuations for subsets of items (see Nisan, chapter 9 of this volume). The auctioneer's revenue is maximized by choosing an allocation that maximizes the sum, over all bidders, of the bidders' valuations for the subset of items that they receive.

In this part of the book we do not discuss the concern that bidders might not report their true valuations because of strategic considerations. They can be *motivated* to tell the truth, under certain assumptions, by using the Vickrey-Clarke-Groves (VCG) mechanism, as discussed further by Ausubel and Milgrom (chapter 1 of this volume). We also do not discuss the issue that in some mechanisms, such as the VCG, the prices charged to winning bidders differ from the bids made, implying that the value of the optimal allocation is not equal to the revenue for the auctioneer. However, the WDP—exactly as discussed in this chapter—is the key to solving those problems as well: the VCG mechanism can be run by solving the WDP once overall, and once for each bidder removed in turn.

In this opening chapter we formally define the winner determination problem as a combinatorial optimization problem and present various alternative mathematical programming models for it. We derive several results stating that one cannot hope for a general-purpose algorithm that can efficiently solve every instance of the problem. We shall also see that significantly restricting the structure of the bids, such as allowing only bids of size of at most 3, does not help. However, negative complexity results do not exclude the ability to design algorithms that have a satisfactory performance for problem sizes and structures occurring in practice. The chapters of this part of the book will present many results in this direction: approximation methods for special cases, identification of polynomial solvable special cases, nonpolynomial but nevertheless fast exact solution methods, means to evaluate the empirical hardness, well-behaved practical cases and noncomputational approaches to circumvent the inherent computational complexity.

This chapter is organized as follows. Section 12.2 defines the winner determination problem as a combinatorial optimization problem, and lays out mathematical programming models that capture in detail variants of the problem related to specific bidding languages. Section 12.3 presents several computationally intractable versions of the WDP, discusses complexity implications of side constraints, and presents exhaustive algorithms that are effective when the number of items for sale is small. Section 12.4 illustrates negative results in terms of approximability, and reviews approximation algorithms. Section 12.5 concludes.

12.2 Problem Formulation

As elsewhere in the book, we use the following notation. The set of bidders is denoted by $N = \{1, \ldots, n\}$, the set of items by $M = \{1, \ldots, m\}$. A bundle S is a set of items: $S \subseteq M$. For a bundle S and a bidder i, we denote by $v_i(S)$ the package bid that bidder i makes for bundle S, that is, the maximal price that i announces to be willing to pay for S.

An allocation of the items is described by variables $x_i(S) \in \{0, 1\}$, where $x_i(S) = 1$ if and only if bidder i gets bundle S. An allocation $(x_i(S)|i \in N, S \subseteq M)$ is said to be feasible if it allocates no item more than once:

$$\sum_{i \in N} \sum_{S \subseteq M, S \ni j} x_i(S) \leq 1 \quad \text{for all } j \in M, \tag{12.1}$$

and at most one subset to every bidder

$$\sum_{S \subseteq M} x_i(S) \leq 1 \quad \text{for all } i \in N. \tag{12.2}$$

Definition 12.1 (Winner Determination Problem, WDP) Given bids v_i, $i = 1, \ldots, n$, the *winner determination problem* is the problem of computing

$$x \in \arg\max \left(\sum_{i \in N, S \subseteq M} v_i(S) x_i(S) | x \text{ is a feasible allocation} \right). \tag{12.3}$$

Definition 12.1 is not sufficient to discuss the algorithmic complexity of solving the WDP. It uses a number of decision variables and coefficients that is exponential in the number of items, and it does not specify how the bids are represented. The algorithmic complexity of an optimization problem is, however, measured in terms of the encoding length of the problem, that is, in terms of how many binary symbols are needed in order to store an instance of the problem in computer memory. An optimization problem is said to be solvable in polynomial time, or *tractable*, if the number of operations needed for any instance is bounded by a polynomial function in the encoding length of that instance. A naive representation of the WDP would store for every bidder i and for every subset S the bid value $v_i(S)$. With respect to this huge representation—the size is exponential in the number of items—dynamic programming would provide a polynomial method to solve the WDP (see section 12.3.4). Hence, in order to discuss the complexity of WDP we need to specify the representation of bids first.

Nisan (chapter 9 of this volume) introduces bidding languages as means to represent bids. We will focus here on the *OR* and *XOR* bidding languages, by which we define two refinements of WDP, called WDP_{OR} and WDP_{XOR}. In both frameworks, every bidder i provides atomic bids $v_i(S)$ for a set of bundles $S \subseteq M$. We use the notation $\mathscr{F}_i$ for the set of bundles for which bidder i submits an atomic bid. A bidding language may restrict $\mathscr{F}_i$ to subsets of items that have a particular combinatorial structure, which will have an influence on the algorithmic complexity of the WDP. This is briefly discussed later in this chapter and in depth in Müller (chapter 13 of this volume). For notational convenience we assume $\emptyset \in \mathscr{F}_i$ and $v_i(\emptyset) = 0$. We also make the common assumption of free disposal: for $S, S' \in \mathscr{F}_i$ such that $S \subseteq S' \Rightarrow v_i(S) \leq v_i(S')$.

In the OR bidding language the atomic bids by bidder i are interpreted as follows: i is willing to pay for any combination of pairwise disjoint atomic bids a price equal to the sum of the bid prices. By the free-disposal assumption, i's bid for any other set S is then the maximum sum of bid prices for pairwise disjoint atomic bids contained in S (see Nisan, chapter 9 of this volume).

Observe that in WDP_{OR}, constraint 12.2 can be omitted, because for every i, a solution with $x_i(T) = 1$ for exactly one $T \subseteq M$ has the same objective value as the solution $x_i(S) = 1$ for those $S \in \mathscr{F}_i$ that form a best packing of T. Observe also that we need only decision variables $x_i(S)$ for subsets $S \in \mathscr{F}_i$, and that for any i, j, $S_i \in \mathscr{F}_i$, $S_j \in \mathscr{F}_j$ with $S_i \subseteq S_j$ and $v_i(S_i) \geq v_j(S_j)$ we may drop the dominated bid $v_j(S_j)$. This leads to:

Definition 12.2 (WDP_{OR})   Given a set of bids in the *OR* bidding language, with atomic bids on sets in $\mathscr{F}_i$ for every bidder i, WDP_{OR} is the problem to compute

$$x \in \arg\max\left(\sum_{i \in N, S \in \mathscr{F}_i} v_i(S)x_i(S) | x \text{ satisfies } (12.1)\right). \tag{12.4}$$

In WDP_{XOR} the set of atomic bids by bidder i is interpreted as follows: bidder i is willing to receive at most one of the atomic bids. By the free-disposal assumption, i's bid for any other set S becomes then the maximum price for an atomic bid contained in S (see Nisan, chapter 9 of this volume).

Note that in the case of WDP_{XOR} we may not drop constraint 12.2, unless bids are superadditive; that is, for any two bundles S_1 and S_2 with $S_1 \cap S_2 = \emptyset$ we have $v_i(S_1 \cup S_2) \geq v_i(S_1) + v_i(S_2)$. Again we need only decision variables $x_i(S)$ for subsets $S \in \mathscr{F}_i$. This leads to:

Definition 12.3 (WDP_{XOR}) Given a set of bids in the XOR bidding language, with atomic bids on sets in $\mathcal{F}_i$ for every bidder i, WDP_{XOR} is the problem to compute

$$x \in \arg\max \left(\sum_{i \in N, S \in \mathcal{F}_i} v_i(S)x_i(S) \,\middle|\, x \text{ satisfies 12.1 and 12.2} \right). \tag{12.5}$$

WDP_{OR} and WDP_{XOR} are related in a way similar to that in which the OR and XOR bidding languages are related. On one hand, one can transform WDP_{XOR} to WDP_{OR} by transforming XOR bids to OR* bids (see chapter 9 of this volume). On the other hand, one can transform WDP_{OR} into an instance of WDP_{XOR} by generating an XOR bid from every OR bid. This transformation has a drastic impact on the encoding length as it calls for a potentially exponentially larger $\mathcal{F}_i$. Another reason to treat the two cases separately is that, with respect to the same family $\mathcal{F}_i$, WDP_{OR} and WDP_{XOR} can have different computational complexity (see section 12.3.2).

Sometimes several identical copies of the same type of item may be auctioned. We call this the multiunit WDP. Conceptually, the multiunit case is not of any impact because one can always consider the different copies as different items, and assume symmetric valuations. From a computational perspective, the assumption may well have an impact because the bidding language usually exploits the symmetry to derive a more compact bid representation. When we consider multiple copies, we shall assume that item $j \in M$ has multiplicity ω_j. A bundle $S = (\sigma_1(S), \ldots, \sigma_n(S))$ is, in this case, a multiset of items, where $\sigma_j(S)$ is the multiplicity of item j in S. Using this notation, we replace 12.1 by

$$\sum_{i \in N} \sum_{S \subseteq M} \sigma_j(S)x_i(S) \leq \omega_j \quad \text{for all } j \in M \tag{12.6}$$

to define the feasibility of an allocation. This generalizes naturally to the OR and XOR bidding languages.

The following subsections illustrate how one can use different classical optimization models from the field of mathematical programming to model (special cases of) the WDP: integer linear programming, weighted stable set in graphs, knapsack, and matching.

12.2.1 Integer Linear Programming and Knapsack

Problem WDP_{OR} can be modeled by the integer linear program

$$\max \quad \sum_{i=1}^{n} \sum_{S \subseteq M} v_i(S)x_i(S)$$

$$(WDP_{OR}) \qquad \sum_{i=1}^{n} \sum_{S \subseteq M, S \ni j} x_i(S) \leq 1 \quad \text{for all } j \in M$$

$$x_i(S) \in \{0, 1\}.$$

Based on our remarks above we need a variable $x_i(S)$ only for nondominated bids on sets $S \in \mathscr{F}_i$. We use summations over all $S \subseteq M$ for notational convenience.

This model for WDP_{OR} is identical to the integer linear programming model of the weighted set packing problem (Rothkopf, Pekeč, and Harstad 1998). In this problem we are given a collection of subsets of a set M, each with a weight, and the target is to find a subcollection of nonintersecting sets of maximal total weight.

Problem WDP_{XOR} can be modeled by the integer linear program

$$\max \quad \sum_{i=1}^{n} \sum_{S \subseteq M} v_i(S) x_i(S)$$

(WDP_{XOR})
$$\sum_{i=1}^{n} \sum_{S \subseteq M, S \ni j} x_i(S) \leq 1 \quad \text{for all } j \in M$$

$$\sum_{S \subseteq M} x_i(S) \leq 1 \qquad \text{for all } i \in N$$

$$x_i(S) \in \{0, 1\}.$$

Again it is sufficient to restrict to variables $x_i(S)$ for $S \in \mathscr{F}_i$, but for convenience we use again the full summation.

In the more general case of multiunit supply of items and multiplicities of items in bids, the above two integer linear programs get other than 0-1 coefficients.

Holte (2001) suggested to interpret in particular multi-item versions of WDP_{OR} and WDP_{XOR} as generalized knapsack problems. In the classical 0-1 knapsack problem we are given a set of objects with weights α_j and values β_j, and we try to find a set of objects of maximum value with total weight less than or equal to some capacity α_0. In the case of WDP_{OR} we get a multidimensional knapsack problem (sometimes also called multi-item knapsack problem), and in case of WDP_{XOR} a multidimensional multiple choice knapsack problem. Kellerer, Pferchy, and Pirsinger (2004) provide a comprehensive survey of the state of the art of research on knapsack problems. They also discuss the link to combinatorial auctions. Müller (chapter 13 of this volume) presents dynamic programming algorithms for WDP that stem from the connection to the knapsack problem.

12.2.2   Intersection Graphs

A second way of modeling WDP_{OR} and WDP_{XOR} is by intersection graphs. We use a graph $G = (U, E)$ consisting of a finite set of nodes and a set of undirected edges. The nodes in U are one-to-one to the bids $v_i(S)$, $i \in N$, $S \in \mathscr{F}_i$, and two nodes are connected by an edge if and only if there is a conflict between the bids, that is, an intersection of the sets of items, or, in WDP_{XOR} both bids are by the same bidder. A node u related to bid $v_i(S)$ gets a weight $w_u := v_i(S)$. Again we may restrict ourselves to relevant bids, in other words, the same bids as for which we have a column in one of the integer linear programming models above.

A subset U' of nodes in a graph is called a *stable set* if no two nodes in U' are connected by an edge. Synonyms for stable set found in the literature are *node packing* and *independent set*. The *(maximum) weighted stable set problem* is the problem to find a stable set of maximum total weight. It is obvious that WDP_{OR} and WDP_{XOR} coincide with weighted stable set on the intersection graph related to WDP_{OR} and WDP_{XOR}, respectively.

The *(maximum) weighted clique problem* in which we search for a maximum weighted set of nodes such that any two nodes *are* connected by an edge, is equivalent to stable set. Indeed, one can simply switch to the complement G^c of a graph G, which has an edge between two nodes if and only if the edge is not contained in G. The (unweighted) stable set as well as the (unweighted) clique problem can thus serve as reference point to answer algorithmic questions on WDP_{OR} and WDP_{XOR}, (see, for example, Sandholm 2002), as we will review later in this chapter. (In the unweighted case, all the weights are 1.)

12.2.3   Special Valuations

Special valuations allow for more succinct bidding languages, and lead also to special cases of the dicussed mathematical programming problems.

As a first example, we look at the downward sloping symmetric valuation introduced by Nisan (chapter 9 of this volume)—in other words, the case of homogenous items with decreasing marginal valuations. WDP can be solved by sorting all marginal values of all bidders, and allocating to every bidder as many items as many marginal valuations he has among the m highest.

As a second example, we mention unit demand valuation, where every bidder is only interested in winning at most one item. In this case, we can model WDP as weighted matching in a bipartite graph $G = (N, M, E)$ with an edge $e = (i, j) \in E$ if and only if bidder i makes a bid for item j. A graph is bipartite if its nodes can be partitioned into two disjoint subsets, such that all edges have a node in each of the two subsets. A matching is a subset of edges such that no two of them share a common node. This model, also called the assignment model, is the point of departure to study the connection between combinatorial auctions and Walrasian equilibria in exchange economies with indivisibilities (see Bikhchandani and Ostroy, chapter 8 of this volume).

Further models for specialized valuations appear in Müller (chapter 13 of this volume).

12.3   NP-Hardness of the Winner Determination Problem

Intuitively speaking, the WDP seems hard because one would need to check, *for each subset of the bids*, whether the subset is feasible (no bids within the subset share items) and how much revenue that subset of bids provides. A feasible subset that yields the highest revenue is an optimal solution. Unfortunately there are 2^k subsets of bids, k being the number of bids, so enumerating them is infeasible (except when there are fewer than thirty or so bids). The real question is: Can one do better than enumerating all the subsets of bids? To answer this question, we study the inherent complexity of the problem, that is, complexity that *any* algorithm would suffer from.

Before we present results on the computational complexity of the WDP, more precisely of different optimization models of WDP, we give a very brief introduction to complexity theory.

12.3.1 Complexity Theory in a Nutshell

We say that the (worst case) running time of an algorithm is given by a function $f(l)$, if $f(l)$ is equal to the maximum number of basic arithmetic operations needed by the algorithm, where the maximum is taken with respect to all instances that can be represented by l binary symbols. We may find it convenient to replace f by an asymptotic equivalent. The *big-O notation*, denoted $f \in O(g)$, is used to indicate an asymptotic upper bound $g(l)$ on some function $f(l)$, up to a constant factor. For example, if $f(l)$ is bounded by cl^2 for a constant c and l large, we say that f is of order $O(l^2)$. A *polynomial time algorithm* is an algorithm whose worst case running time is of order $O(g)$ for some polynomial g. The *big-Omega* notation, denoted $f \in \Omega(g)$, is used correspondingly to indicate an asymptotic lower bound.

An algorithm that is polynomial in the *unary encoding* of some optimization problem, that is, the length of an integer x is counted as x, is called *pseudo-polynomial*. If numbers involved are guaranteed to be small, a pseudo-polynomial running time may be practical. If an algorithm is polynomial, even if we measure the length of every number involved by 1, and if arithmetic operations involve only numbers that are polynomially bounded in this stricter measure, then the algorithm is said to be *strongly polynomial*.

Complexity theory investigates whether polynomial algorithms exist. It has been developed for *decision problems*, which are computational problems consisting of a class of instances and a definition of a property of these instances. The problem to be solved is to decide whether a given instance from the class has the property or not. For example, given a set of combinatorial bids and a target revenue w, is there an allocation of items to bidders with a total revenue of at least w. $\mathscr{P}$ is the class of decision problems that have a polynomial time algorithm. $\mathscr{P}$ is contained in $\mathscr{NP}$ (nondeterministic polynomial time). This is the class of decision problems for which there exists a polynomial time algorithm that can check the validity of the property in question, if it is given as input next to the instance a certificate for the validity (regardless of how hard it is to compute such certificates). Equivalently, it is the class of problems computable by a nondeterministic Turing machine in polynomial time. The decision versions of (special cases of) WDP are all members of the class $\mathcal{NP}$, because we can verify in polynomial time whether a particular solution is feasible and has an objective value larger than some value w.

It is generally believed, but never proven, that $\mathcal{P} \neq \mathcal{NP}$, i.e., there are problems in $\mathcal{NP}$ that cannot be solved in polynomial time. A problem in $\mathcal{NP}$ is NP-complete if any polynomial algorithm for it could be used as a polynomial algorithm for any other problem in $\mathcal{NP}$. Typically, one shows how to transform instances of any problem in polynomial time to instances of the NP-complete problem, in order to prove NP-completeness. This implies that NP-complete problems are the hardest problems within $\mathcal{NP}$. Cook (1971) proves the existence of an NP-complete problem by showing that any problem in $\mathcal{NP}$ can be transformed into the satisfiability problem. Based on Cook's theorem it became relatively easy to prove that other problems are NP-complete. We first have to show that they are in $\mathcal{NP}$, and second we have to define a polynomial transformation of an NP-complete problem to them.

A computational problem for which the existence of a polynomial time algorithm would imply tractability of all problems in $\mathcal{NP}$ is called NP-hard. By definition, NP-complete problems are NP-hard, but also problems not contained in $\mathcal{NP}$ can be NP-hard—for example, optimization problems whose decision version is NP-complete.

$\mathcal{ZPP}$ is a subclass of $\mathcal{NP}$ that we will mention in the context of approximation algorithms. It consists of those decision problems for which there exists a randomized algorithm, such that the algorithm terminates in expected polynomial time, and outputs 1 if and only if the correct answer to the decision problem is *yes*. A probabilistic algorithm chooses at some points randomly between a finite set of alternative next steps. The question of whether $\mathcal{NP} = \mathcal{ZPP}$ is as well an open question, related to the $\mathcal{P} = \mathcal{NP}$ question. $\mathcal{NP} = \mathcal{ZPP}$ is not known to imply $\mathcal{P} = \mathcal{NP}$.

12.3.2 Complexity of the Winner Determination Problem

Almost every paper on combinatorial auctions mentions that the winner determination problem is NP-hard. This can be simply derived by the fact that the NP-hard weighted set packing problem is equivalent to WDP_{OR} (Rothkopf et al. 1998). We take here a little closer look in order to convince the reader that the problem remains NP-hard if we restrict our attention to instances with rather simplistic bids.

Given some number w, we define the decision version of the winner determination problem as to decide whether there exists a feasible allocation of the items with total revenue greater than or equal to w.

Our first reductions make use of the intersection graph formulation of WDP from section 12.2.2. The decision version of the stable set problem is NP-complete (Garey and Johnson 1979). Given a graph $G = (U, E)$, we can construct an instance of WDP_{OR} as follows. We set $N = U$, $M = E$ and assume a bid $b_i(S) = 1$ for every $i \in N$ with $S = \{e \in E | i \in e\}$. Note that this is also an instance of WDP_{XOR}. It is obvious that G has a stable set of size k if and only if the instance of WDP_{OR} (or, equivalently, WDP_{XOR}) has an allocation with total bid value greater than or equal to k. This proves:

Theorem 12.1 The decision versions of WDP_{OR} and WDP_{XOR} are NP-complete, even if we restrict to instances where every bid has a value equal to 1, every bidder submits only one bid, and every item is contained in exactly two bids.

The same transformation can be used to prove the complexity of further special cases of WDP_{OR} and WDP_{XOR}. For example, the stable set problem remains NP-complete if we restrict ourselves to *planar cubic graphs* (Garey and Johnson 1979). Planar graphs are graphs that can be drawn in the plane such that edges become continuous curves that intersect only in their end nodes. In cubic graphs every node has exactly degree 3. Using this in the transformation we get NP-hardness of WDP_{OR} and WDP_{XOR} for the case that every bid offers a price of 1, every bid contains exactly three items, every item is contained in exactly two bids, and every bidder makes at most one bid.

The general pattern of such proofs is to take an optimization problem as restrictive as possible, but which is still NP-complete and to map instances of that problem to instances of winner determination. Other problems than stable set can be used, too. For example, Rothkopf, Pekeč, and Harstad (1998) use *three-set packing* to show

Theorem 12.2 (Rothkopf, Pekeč, and Harstad 1998) The decision version of WDP_{OR} is NP-complete even if we restrict to instances where every bid has a value equal to 1, and every bidder bids only on subsets of size of at most 3.

Similarly, van Hoesel and Müller (2001) transform *three-dimensional matching* to WDP_{XOR} to show:

Theorem 12.3 (van Hoesel and Müller 2001) The decision version of WDP_{XOR} is $\mathcal{NP}$-complete even if we restrict to instances where every bid has a value equal to 1, and every bidder bids only on subsets of size of at most 2.

Let us next assume that the items in M can be linearly ordered into a sequence $(i_1, \ldots, i_m)$, and that bidders bid only on subsets of items that are adjacent in this list. In Müller (chapter 13 of this volume) we will see that WDP_{OR} restricted to this case is solvable in polynomial time. However, the problem becomes NP-hard in case of WDP_{XOR}. Indeed, the problem is then identical to the *job interval selection problem*. In this problem we are given a number l, n jobs, and for every job l intervals on a discrete time scale in which this job may be scheduled on a single processor. Viewed as a combinatorial auction we may interpret jobs as bidders who bid for time intervals. A feasible allocation assigns at most one interval to every job, such that intervals do not overlap. Keil (1992) has shown that, even for the case $l = 3$, that is, three bids per bidder, the problem to decide whether n jobs can be assigned, is NP-complete (for further references on the complexity of this problem, see Spieksma 1999).

So far we restricted the instances by restricting the sets $\mathscr{F}_i$ for which bids are submitted. From an economic perspective it seems to be more natural to restrict bid values, because this better reflects a restriction of bidders' types. A prominent restriction in economics is to assume submodularity, which translates in the context of bids to the following condition. For any two subsets $S_1, S_2 \subseteq M$ we have

$$v_i(S_1 \cup S_2) \leq v_i(S_1) + v_i(S_2) - v_i(S_1 \cap S_2).$$

A special case of submodular bids is that of additive valuations with budget limits. Additive bids with budget constraint are OR bids for single items, with the additional constraint that the bid for a set S is never larger than the budget. Thus the bid for S is the minimum of the following two values: the sum of bids for individual items in S and the budget. Note that such bids can be represented very efficiently by OR bids for individual items together with the limit q_i. At the same time, it is a special case of WDP_{XOR}, although an explicit representation as an instance of WDP_{XOR} would be very large. The complexity of winner determination for additive valuations with budget limits, and thus for the case of submodular bids is as follows.

Theorem 12.4 (Lehmann, Lehmann, and Nisan 2001; Sandholm and Suri 2001)   The winner determination problem with two bidders, each submitting additive bids (that is, OR-bids on individual items only) with budget constraints is NP-hard.

Proof   We present the proof given in Lehmann, Lehmann, and Nisan 2003, where NP-hardness is proven by reducing the knapsack problem to this problem. (The decision version of the knapsack problem is NP-complete; see Garey and Johnson 1979.) An instance of the knapsack problem is given by a sequence of integers $a_1, \ldots, a_m$ and a desired total t. We want to decide whether there exists a subset T of the integers whose sum is equal to t. Let $A = \sum_{j=1}^{m} a_j$.

Given an instance of knapsack we construct the following bids on m items:

$$v_1(S) = \sum_{j \in S} a_j$$

$$v_2(S) = 2 \min\left(t, \sum_{j \in S} a_j\right).$$

We show that the answer to the decision is "yes" if and only if the winner determination instance has an allocation of value $A + t$.

If the answer is "yes," we can allocate the elements in T to bidder 2, and the elements in the set complement T^c to bidder 1, to obtain an allocation of value

$$\sum_{j \in T^c} a_j + 2t = A - t + 2t = A + t.$$

Assume the constructed winner determination problem has an allocation of value $A + t$. If bidder 2 would get a subset of value strictly less than t, say t', then the total value would be $A - t' + 2t' < A + t$, a contradiction. If bidder 2 would get a subset of value $t' > t$, then the total value would be $A - t' + 2t = A + t - (t' - t) < A + t$, again a contradiction. Thus the items allocated to bidder 2 exactly sum up to $A + t$, and the answer is "yes." ∎

Interestingly, with a similar constraint where the *number of items sold to each bidder* is constrained, WDP_{OR} is solvable in polynomial time (see Müller, chapter 13 of this volume). Other restricted versions of WDP_{OR} with certain types of structural side constraints are solvable in polynomial time as well, using b-matching (Penn and Tennenholtz 2000).

12.3.3 Complexity for Other Bidding Languages

Nisan (chapter 9 of this volume) discusses, next to OR and XOR, other bidding languages, as to combine OR and XOR. Most of them add *side constraints* to feasible allocations, either from the buyer or from the bid takers side. The bid taker (auctioneer) may have legal constraints, prior contractual obligations, or business rules that he may want to incorporate into the winner determination in the form of side constraints. A practical example is the one where the auctioneer does not want the hassle of dealing with more than a certain number of winners. Also, the budget constraint from theorem 12.4 is an example.

Sandholm and Suri (2001) provide a rich collection of results on the impact of side constraints on the complexity of winner determination. For example, they show that if at most k winners are allowed, WDP_{OR} is NP-complete even if bids are on individual items only. They also show that if we allow for arbitrary collections of XOR constraints, WDP is NP-complete even if bids are on individual items only. This case is a special case of WDP for bids submitted in the XOR-of-OR bidding language (see Nisan, chapter 9 of this volume). In both examples, the problem remains NP-complete even if bids could be accepted partially.

Specific side constraints (by the bid-taker) may induce a combinatorial structure with *favorable* algorithmic properties, as well. For example, Bikhchandani et al. (2001) and Nisan and Ronen (2001) study the setting of a reverse auction, where the auctioneer is interested to purchase a set of edges in a network that form a path from a source s to a target t. Such a path can be thought of as a communication link. Similarly,

Bikhchandani et al. (2001) study the case where the buyer wants to purchase a spanning tree. In both examples, bids are on individual items only and side constraints of the bid taker restrict the set of acceptable combinations of winning bids, but a rich combinatorial structure allows for efficient winner determination.

WDP_{OR} is solvable in polynomial time using linear programming if bids can be accepted partially. There are a host of practical side constraints that do not affect this. Examples are the budget constraint, not giving any bidders more than $k\%$ of the total dollar value in the auction, or making minority bidders win at least $k\%$ (Sandholm and Suri 2001). By contrast, XOR constraints and maximum winners constraints make WDP_{OR} NP-complete even if bids can be accepted partially.

Beyond side constraints, in some markets multiple *attributes* (such as reputation, weight, volume, color, delivery time, etc.) should affect the winner determination. Attributes can be integrated into market designs with package bidding and side constraints (Sandholm and Suri 2001), but that is not totally straightforward. The preceding discussion has omitted a number of important aspects of the WDP, including combinatorial reverse auctions and two-sided exchanges, removing the free-disposal assumption, and allowing of partial bid fulfilment. (See Kothari, Sandholm, and Suri 2003; Sandholm and Suri 2001; and Sandholm et al. 2005, for discussion of these issues.)

12.3.4 WDP_{OR} When the Number of Items Is Small or the Number of Bids Is Huge

Although WDP_{OR} is NP-complete, there are algorithms that always—that is, regardless of the number of bids—find an optimal allocation quickly if the number of items m is small. They also run in polynomial time in the size of the input if the number of bids is very large (exponential) compared to the number of items.

For example, WDP_{OR} can be solved by enumerating all partitions of items (Sandholm 2002), evaluate them, and pick the one of highest value. This yields an $O(m^{m+1})$ algorithm (Sandholm 2002).

Dynamic programming is a more efficient approach for achieving the same goals. Rothkopf, Pekeč, and Harstad (1998) suggest the following dynamic programming approach for WDP_{OR}. For all $S \subseteq M$ they compute the best allocation that allocates only elements out of S. This is done iteratively for increasing cardinality of S. For subsets of size 1, they get the information from the bids on single elements. For a subset S with size larger than 1, $w(S)$ is initialized by the largest bid for S, and then updated by the following formula:

$$w(S) = \max(w(S') + w(S\setminus S')|S' \subseteq S, |S'| \geq |S|/2).$$

The algorithm runs in $O(3^m)$ time (Rothkopf, Pekeč, and Harstad 1998). It can be improved by using in the recursion S' such that there exists a bid for S' (see Müller, chapter 13 of this volume). Interestingly, it constitutes an efficient algorithm (in the sense that it runs in polynomial time in the size of its input) if the number of bids l is very large in comparison to the number of items:

Theorem 12.5 (Sandholm 2002) Let l be the number of (nondominated) bids. If the dynamic program for WDP_{OR} runs in $O((l+m)^\rho)$ time for some constant $\rho > 1$, then $l \in \Omega(2^{m/\rho})$. If $l \in \Omega(2^{m/\rho})$ for some constant $\rho > 1$, then the dynamic program runs in $O(l^{\rho \log_2 3})$ time.

We may interpret this result as follows. If the auctioneer receives a number of bids that is very large in comparison to the number of items, then receiving the bids (and, accordingly, bidding for the bidders) is the computational bottleneck, and not solving the WDP. Müller (chapter 13 of this volume) gives further dynamic programming algorithms, in particular for multi-item versions of WDP.

12.4 Approximation

Because the winner determination problem cannot be solved in polynomial time to optimality unless $\mathscr{P} = \mathscr{NP}$, one may hope for efficient algorithms that compute an "almost" optimal solution. An approximation algorithm is a polynomial time algorithm with a provable performance guarantee. More precisely, let $\mathscr{I}$ be the set of instances of a maximization problem, $|I|$ the encoding length of $I \in \mathscr{I}$, $\mathscr{F}_{\mathscr{I}}$ the set of feasible solutions of $\mathscr{I}$, $c : \mathscr{F}_{\mathscr{I}} \to \mathbb{R}$ the objective, x^* the optimal solution, and $g : \mathbb{N} \to \mathbb{N}$. We say that an algorithm *approximates* the maximization problem *within* g if it finds for every instance $I \in \mathscr{I}$ a feasible solution $x \in \mathscr{F}_{\mathscr{I}}$ with $c(x^*) \le g(|I|)c(x)$.

12.4.1 Inapproximability Results

From the close relation between the winner determination problem and other combinatorial optimization problems we can derive several impossibility results with respect to approximation. The first was observed by Sandholm (2002) (and independently in Lehmann, O'Callaghan, and Shoham 2002) and is based on the following theorem:

Theorem 12.6 (Håstad 1999) If $\mathscr{NP} \ne \mathscr{ZPP}$, then for any $\varepsilon > 0$ there is no polynomial algorithm that approximates maximum clique for a graph $G = (V, E)$ within $|V|^{1-\varepsilon}$.

Corollary 12.1 (Sandholm 2002) If $\mathscr{NP} \ne \mathscr{ZPP}$, then for any fixed $\varepsilon > 0$ there is no polynomial algorithm that approximates WDP_{OR} or WDP_{XOR} within $\min(l^{1-\varepsilon}, m^{1/2-\varepsilon})$, where l equals the number of bids and m is the number of items, even when restricted to instances where every item is contained in at most two bids, and bid prices are all equal to 1.

Proof   Using the construction reviewed in section 12.2.2, we can first transform the maximum clique problem into a stable set problem by taking the complement of the edge set, then construct an instance of WDP_{OR} (or WDP_{XOR}) where all bid prices are 1. The later has $l = |V|$ bids. A polynomial time $l^{1-\varepsilon}$ approximation algorithm for the winner determination problem would thus immediately give rise to a $|V|^{1-\varepsilon}$ approximation algorithm for the maximum clique problem, which would contradict theorem 12.6. For $m^{1/2-\varepsilon}$ the proof is similar to Halldórsson, Kratochvíl, and Telle (2000) for maximum clique.   ∎

This negative result generalizes to a specific multi-unit case of WDP_{OR} and WDP_{XOR}.

Theorem 12.7 (Bartal, Gonen, and Nisan 2003)   For every fixed $k \geq 1$, consider the WDP_{OR} (or WDP_{XOR}) with $\sigma_i = k$ for all $i \in M$ and every bidder wants to obtain at most one unit of each type of item. For any fixed $\varepsilon > 0$, approximating this multiunit version of WDP_{OR} (or WDP_{XOR}) within a factor of $O(m^{(1-\varepsilon)/(k+1)})$ is NP-hard unless $\mathcal{NP} = \mathcal{ZPP}$.

A polynomial time approximation scheme (PTAS) for a maximization problem is a family of algorithms A_ε, $\varepsilon > 0$, such that A_ε approximates within a factor $1 + \varepsilon$, and such that, for fixed ε, A_ε is polynomial. Berman and Fujito (1999) show:

Theorem 12.8 (Berman and Fujito 1999)   Unless $\mathcal{P} = \mathcal{NP}$ there is no PTAS for the maximum stable set problem on graphs with degree at most 3.

Again by the same transformation this shows that

Corollary 12.2   Unless $\mathcal{P} = \mathcal{NP}$ there is no PTAS for WDP_{OR} or WDP_{XOR} even when restricted to instances with bids of size at most 3, and where every item is contained in at most two bids, and bid prices are all equal to 1.

12.4.2   Approximation Algorithms

Fast approximation algorithms for the WDP can be obtained by translating results for combinatorial problems related to winner determination (mainly the weighted set packing problem and the weighted stable set problem) to the context of winner determination (Sandholm 2002). Algorithms for these problems come very close to the bound of the inapproximability results.

The asymptotically best approximation algorithm for WDP_{OR} establishes a bound $O(l/(\log l)^2)$, where l is the number of bids (Halldórsson 2000).

From the same paper, we can establish a polynomial time algorithm for WDP_{OR} with a bound that depends only on the number of items, m. The auctioneer can choose the value for c. As c increases, the bound improves but the running time increases. Specifically, steps 1 and 2 are $O\left(\binom{l}{c}\right)$, which is $O(l^c)$, step 3 is $O(l)$, step 4 is $O(1)$, step 5 can be naively implemented to be $O(m^2 l^2)$, and step 6 is $O(1)$. So, overall the algorithm is $O(\max(l^c, m^2 l^2))$, which is polynomial for any given c.

Algorithm 12.1 (Greedy winner determination)   Given an integer c and a set of bids $\{v_i(S) | i \in N, S \subseteq M\}$:

1. Let $\mathscr{P}_c$ be the feasible allocations of bids consisting of no more than c bids.
2. Let $x_\mathscr{P}$ be the optimal alloction within $\mathscr{P}_c$.
3. Let $\mathscr{B}_c$ be the subset of bids $v_i(S)$ such that $|S| \leq \sqrt{m/c}$.
4. Compute a greedy feasible allocation $x_\mathscr{B}$ with respect to bids in $\mathscr{B}$ by sequentially selecting highest value bids which do not overlap with previously selected bids.
5. Choose the better of the allocations $x_\mathscr{P}$ and $x_\mathscr{B}$.

Another greedy algorithm for winner determination simply inserts bids into the allocation in largest $v(S)/\sqrt{|S|}$ first order (if the bid shares items with another bid that is already in the allocation, the bid is discarded) (Lehmann et al. 2002). This algorithm establishes a bound $\sqrt{m}$. If $c > 4$, the bound that algorithm 12.1 establishes is better than that of this algorithm ($2\sqrt{m/c} < \sqrt{m}$). On the other hand, the computational complexity of algorithm 12.1 quickly exceeds that of this algorithm as c grows.

The bound $m^{1/2-\varepsilon}$ is so high that it is likely to be of limited value for auctions. Similarly, so is the bound $2\sqrt{m/c} \geq 2$. Even a bound 2 would mean that the algorithm might only capture 50 percent of the available revenue. However, the bound that algorithm 12.1 establishes is about the best that one can obtain (recall corollary 12.1). If the number of items is small compared to the number of bids ($2\sqrt{m/c} < l$ or $\sqrt{m} < l$), as will probably be the case in most combinatorial auctions, then these algorithms establish a better bound than that of corollary 12.1.

One can do even somewhat better in special cases where the bids have special structure. For example, there might be some cap on the number of items per bid, or there might be a cap on the number of bids with which a bid can share items. For a detailed overview on specialized bounds available from the combinatorial optimization literature we refer to the review part in Sandholm 2002, or to the original literature (Chandra and Halldórsson 1999; Halldórsson and Lau 1997; Halldórsson 1998; Hochbaum 1983). Another family of restrictions that will very likely lend itself to approximation stems from limitations on the prices. We will next present two examples.

The first algorithm is due to Bartal, Gonen, and Nisan (2003) and approximates the WDP_{XOR} for a subclass of the multi-item case. Its approximation ratio is close to the best lower bound possible. The algorithm has to make two assumptions. The first is that bids are given such that valuation and demand oracle queries can be computed efficiently. Recall that a demand oracle for bidder i's bid v_i computes for item prices p_j, $j \in M$ a set

$$S \in \arg\max \left(v_i(S) - \sum_{j \in S} p_j \right).$$

The second assumption that has to be made says essentially that no bidder has a demand for a major share of the total number of items available of each type. More precisely we assume that there exists numbers $\Theta > \theta > 0$ such that the following hold. For each multiset S and every j for which $\sigma_j < \theta\omega_j$, $b_i(S) = b_i(S')$, where S' is the multiset with $\sigma'_k = \sigma_k$ for $k \neq j$, and $\sigma_j = 0$. Similarly, multisets with a $\sigma_j > \Theta\omega_j$ have the same valuation as the multiset in which we reduce the demand for item j to $\Theta\omega_j$. For example, if k copies of each item are in supply, and $\theta = \Theta = 1/k$, this models the case that each multiset for which a bidder makes a bid is an ordinary set—that is, all $\sigma_j = 1$.

The algorithm is parameterized by a price p_0 and a constant r. It works as follows:

Algorithm 12.2 (Approximate multiunit winner determination)

For each good j set $l_j = 0$.

For each bidder $i = 1, \ldots, n$

for each good j set $p_j = p_0 r^{l_j}$

choose $S' = (\sigma'_1, \ldots, \sigma'_m) \in \arg\max(b_i(S) - \sum_{j \in S} \sigma_j(S) p_j)$.

set bidder i's payment equal to $P_i = \sum_{j \in S'} \sigma'_j p_j$.

update $l_j = l_j + \sigma'_j$.

Thus, the basic idea is to increase prices fast enough such that the solution computed by the algorithm is feasible, that is, numbers of allocated items do not exceed supply. Bartal, Gonen, and Nisan (2003) show that for appropriate choices of p_0 (namely $np_0 \leq Opt/2$ and $r^{1-\Theta} \geq v_{\max}\theta p_0$) the solution computed is indeed feasible and achieves an approximation ratio of $2(1 + (r^{\Theta} - 1)/\Theta))$. They further show that with a small modification a sealed bid auction using this algorithm becomes incentive compatible. Furthermore, the algorithm can be modified to turn the auction into an incentive compatible online auction, an auction that can be used when bids arrive over time. Despite these achievements, a combinatorial auction based on this algorithm makes more a theoretical than a practical contribution to the auction literature because of the undesirable property that prices for later bidders are much higher than for earlier bidders, and that in practice an integer linear programming based heuristic certainly does better in terms of the value of the solution computed.

We show next that WDP_{XOR} can be approximated up to a factor of two if all $v_i : 2^M \to \mathbb{R}$ are submodular functions. We use the notation $v_i(j|S) := v_i(S \cup \{j\}) - v_i(S)$ for the marginal bid for item j given subset S is owned already by i. The following algorithm is due to Lehmann, Lehmann, and Nisan (2001).

Algorithm 12.3 (Approximate WDP algorithm for submodular bids)

1. Set $S_i = \emptyset$ for $i = 1, \ldots, n$, and $S = M$.
2. Let $(i, j) \in \arg\max(v_i(j|S_i) | i \in N, j \in S)$.
3. Set $S_i = S_i \cup \{j\}$, $S = S \setminus \{j\}$.
4. If $S = \emptyset$ stop, else go to 2.

Theorem 12.9 (Lehmann, Lehmann, and Nisan 2001) The above winner determination algorithm computes a 2-approximation for WDP_{XOR} with submodular bids.

Proof Our proof is by induction on the number of items. For $m = 1$ the claim is obvious.

For $m > 1$ let us assume w.l.o.g. that item m is assigned to bidder n. The algorithm can be thought of as being recursively invoked on the remaining instance. Bids become:

$$v_i'(S) = \begin{cases} v_i(S) & \text{if } 1 \leq i \leq n-1, \\ v_i(S|\{m\}) & \text{if } i = n. \end{cases}$$

We can easily show that v' is again submodular. Let us denote by $A(v)$ the revenue computed by the algorithm, and by $Opt(v)$ the optimal value. By the induction hypothesis we get

$$A(v) = v_n(m) + A(v') \geq v_n(m) + \frac{1}{2}Opt(v').$$

We are done if we can show: $Opt(v') \geq Opt(v) - 2v_n(m)$.

Let $T_1, \ldots, T_n$ be an optimal solution with respect to v. Assume $m \in T_k$. By deleting m from T_k we get a feasible solution T' with respect to bids v'. We show that this solution differs at most by $2v_n(m)$ from $Opt(v)$, from which the previous inequality follows.

If $k = m$, $Opt(v)$ and the value of solution T' differs at most $v_n(m)$. If $k \neq m$, we get by the definition of step 2 of the algorithm

$$v_k'(T_k \setminus \{m\}) = v_k(T_k \setminus \{m\}) \geq v_k(T) - v_k(m) \geq v_k(T) - v_n(m),$$

and by the definition of v':

$$v_n'(T_n) = v_n(T_n|\{m\}) = v_n(T_j) - v_n(m).$$

The claim follows now, because for all other i it is $v_i'(T_i) = v_i(T_i)$. ∎

Put together, considerable work has been done on approximation algorithms for WDP and for special cases of combinatorial optimization problems related to WDP. However, the worst case guarantees provided by the current algorithms are so far from optimum that they are of limited importance for auctions in practice, even if the approximation factor is 2.

12.5   Conclusion

The WDP is NP-complete and inapproximable. So, is there a useful way to tackle the WDP?

Since 1998, there has been a surge of research into addressing this. Researchers have pursued three fundamentally different approaches:

1. Designing algorithms that are provably fast (polynomial time in the size of the problem instance) but fail to find an optimal solution to some problem instances. We briefly reviewed work along this avenue in this chapter in the form of the approximation algorithms. Because the problem is inapproximable, such algorithms yield solutions that are extremely far from optimal (yielding less than 1 percent of the available revenue) in some cases. Approximation compromises economic value and generally also ruins the incentive properties of the auction. One can think of local search (and stochastic local search, e.g., Hoos and Boutilier 2000) algorithms as falling within this approach, too, except that they generally do not provide any guarantees on solution quality or run time.

2. Restricting the bundles on which bids can be submitted, or the bid prices, so severely that the problem can be solved optimally and provably fast. Müller discusses this approach in chapter 13 of the book. Although computationally attractive, this approach may suffer from similar economic inefficiencies, incentive problems, and exposure problems as noncombinatorial auctions because the bidders cannot fully express their preferences. In fact, they can only bid on a vanishingly small fraction of possible bundles: the number of allowable bundles has to be polynomial in m, whereas the total number of bundles is exponential in m (specifically, 2^m). Imposed restrictions by the auctioneer should therefore always be motivated by bidders' valuations.

3. Designing *tree search algorithms* that provably find an optimal solution. Sandholm discusses this approach in chapter 14 of this book. Because the problem is NP-complete, any optimal algorithm for the problem will be slow on some problem instances (unless $\mathcal{P} = \mathcal{NP}$). Even so, such algorithms can be fast in practice. Furthermore, most of them are *anytime algorithms*: they can be terminated early (if they happen to be taking too long) with usually a good feasible solution in hand. The use of commercial integer linear programming solvers also belongs to this class of approaches. Andersson, Tenhunen, and Ygge (2000) have investigated how well

such solvers scale. Similarly, we may employ algorithms for the multidimensional (multiple-choice) knapsack problem, as Holte (2001) suggested. It can be the case, however, that special-purpose solvers improve on the casual use of a general-purpose package (see Sandholm, chapter 14 of this volume).

References

Andersson, Arne, Mathias Tenhunen, and Fredrik Ygge (2000), "Integer Programming for Combinatorial Auction Winner Determination," in *Proceedings of the Fourth International Conference on Multi-Agent Systems*, 39–46.

Bartal, Yair, Rica Gonen, and Noam Nisan (2003), "Incentive Compatible Multi Unit Combinatorial Auctions," in M. Tennenholtz, ed., *Proceedings of the 9th Conference on Theoretical Aspects of Rationality and Knowledge*, 72–87.

Berman, Piotr and Toshihiro Fujito (1999), "On Approximation Properties of the Independent Set Problem for Low Degree Graphs," *Theory of Computing Systems*, 32, 115–132.

Bikhchandani, Sushil, Sven de Vries, James Schummer, and Rakesh R. Vohra (2001), "Linear Programming and Vickrey Auctions," in Brenda Dietrich, Rakesh R. Vohra, and Patricia Brick, eds., *Mathematics of the Internet—E-Auctions and Markets*, New York: Springer, 75–115.

Chandra, Barun and Magnús M. Halldórsson (1999), "Greedy Local Search and Weighted Set Packing Approximation," in *Proceedings of the 10th Annual SIAM-ACM Symposium on Discrete Algorithms (SODA)*, 169–176.

Cook, Stephen A. (1971), "The Complexity of Theorem Proving Procedures," in *Proceedings of the 3rd Annual ACM Symposium on Theory of Computing*, 151–158.

Garey, Michael R. and David S. Johnson (1979), *Computers and Intractability*, New York: W. H. Freeman and Company.

Halldórsson, Magnús M. (1998), "Approximations of Independent Sets in Graphs," in Klaus Jansen and José D.P. Rolim, eds., *Proceedings of the First International Workshop on Approximation Algorithms for Combinatorial Optimization Problems (APPROX)*, LNCS Vol. 1444, Berlin: Springer, 1–14.

Halldórsson, Magnús M. (2000), "Approximations of Weighted Independent Set and Hereditary Subset Problems," *Journal of Graph Algorithms and Applications*, 4(1), 1–16. Early versions appeared in *Computing and Combinatorics, Proceedings of the 5th Annual International Conference (COCOON)*, Tokyo, Japan, 1999, and in LNCS Vol. 1627, Berlin: Springer, 261–270.

Halldórsson, Magnús M. Jan Kratochvíl, and Arne Telle (2000), "Independent Sets with Domination Constraints," *Discrete Applied Mathematics*, 99, 39–54. Also appeared in *Proceedings of the 25th International Conference on Automata, Languages, and Programming (ICALP)*, LNCS 1443, pp. 176–187. Berlin: Springer.

Halldórsson, Magnús M. and Hong Chuin Lau (1997), "Low-Degree Graph Partitioning via Local Search with Applications to Constraint Satisfaction, Max Cut, and 3-Coloring," *Journal of Graph Algorithms and Applications*, 1, 1–13.

Håstad, Johan (1999), "Clique Is Hard to Approximate within $n^{1-\varepsilon}$," *Acta Mathematica*, 182, 105–142.

Hochbaum, Dorit S. (1983), "Efficient Bounds for the Stable Set, Vertex Cover, and Set Packing Problems," *Discrete Applied Mathematics*, 6, 243–254.

Holte, Robert C. (2001), "Combinatorial Auctions, Knapsack Problems, and Hill-Climbing Search," in Eleni Stroulia and Stan Matwin, eds., *Advances in Artificial Intelligence, Proceedings of 14th Biennial Conference of the Canadian Society for Computational Studies of Intelligence (AII 2001)*, LNCS 2056, Berlin: Springer, 57–66.

Hoos, Holger H. and Craig Boutilier (2000), "Solving Combinatorial Auctions Using Stochastic Local Search," in *Proceedings of the 17th National Conference on Artificial Intelligence*, 22–29.

Keil, J. Mark (1992), "On the Complexity of Scheduling Tasks with Discrete Starting Times," *Operations Research Letters*, 12, 293–295.

Kellerer, Hans, Ulrich Pferchy, and David Pirsinger (2004), *Knapsack Problems*, Berlin: Springer Verlag.

Kothari, Anshul, Tuomas Sandholm, and Subhash Suri (2003), "Solving Combinatorial Exchanges: Optimality via a Few Partial Bids," in *Proceedings of the ACM Conference on Electronic Commerce (ACM-EC)*, 236–237.

Kuhn, Harold W. (1955), "The Hungarian Method for the Assignment Problem," *Naval Research Logistics Quarterly*, 2, 83–97.

Lehmann, Benny, Daniel Lehmann, and Noam Nisan (2001), "Combinatorial Auctions with Decreasing Marginal Utilities," in *Proceedings 3rd ACM Conference on Electronic Commerce*, ACM Press, 18–28. To appear, *Games and Economic Behavior*.

Lehmann, Daniel, Liadan I. O'Callaghan, and Yoav Shoham (2002), "Truth Revelation in Approximately Efficient Combinatorial Auctions," *Journal of the ACM*, 49, 577–602.

Nisan, Noam and Amir Ronen (2001), "Algorithmic Mechanism Design," *Games and Economic Behavior*, 35, 166–196.

Penn, Michal and Moshe Tennenholtz (2000), "Constrained Multi-Object Auctions and b-Matching," *Information Processing Letters*, 75, 29–34.

Rothkopf, Michael H., Aleksander Pekeč, and Ronald M. Harstad (1998), "Computationally Manageable Combinational Auctions," *Management Science*, 44, 1131–1147.

Sandholm, Tuomas (2002), "Algorithm for Optimal Winner Determination in Combinatorial Auctions," *Artificial Intelligence*, 135, 1–54.

Sandholm, Tuomas and Subhash Suri (2001), "Side Constraints and Non-price Attributes in Markets," in *Proceedings of the IJCAI-2001 Workshop on Distributed Constraint Reasoning*, 55–61. To appear in *Games and Economic Behavior*.

Sandholm, Tuomas, Subhash Suri, Andrew Gilpin, and David Levine (2005), "CABOB: A Fast Optimal Algorithm for Winner Determination in Combinatorial Auctions," *Management Science*, 51, 374–390.

Spieksma, Frits C.R. (1999), "On the Approximability of an Interval Scheduling Problem," *Journal of Scheduling*, 2, 215–227.

van Hoesel, Stan and Rudolf Müller (2001), "Optimization in Electronic Markets: Examples in Combinatorial Auctions," *Netnomics*, 3, 23–33.

13 Tractable Cases of the Winner Determination Problem

Rudolf Müller

13.1 Introduction

Most versions of the WDP belong to the class of NP-hard optimization problems, meaning that we cannot expect to find a solution method that always has a running time polynomial in the size of the input. Lehmann, Müller, and Sandholm (chapter 12 of this volume) show that restrictions to bid sets of small size or bid values equal to 1 do not help to overcome this difficulty. To make WDP tractable we have to restrict bids or valuations in a way that gives the constellation of bids sufficient structure to allow for efficient solution methods. This chapter deals with such restrictions.

A tractable case is defined as a class of instances of WDP such that there exists an algorithm that optimally solves any instance in the class requiring a number of operations that is polynomially bounded in the encoding length of the instance. We assume, if not mentioned otherwise, a binary encoding of numbers. We focus on *theoretically* tractable cases, leaving aside *practically* tractable cases. For example, Lehmann, Müller, and Sandholm (chapter 12 of this volume) show that WDP in multi-item auctions can be modeled as a multidimensional knapsack problem, which opens the possibility for dynamic programming algorithms, with a polynomial running time for a fixed number of items. Furthermore, integer linear programming algorithms, or dedicated algorithms as Sandholm (chapter 14 of this volume) presents, are often capable of optimally solving theoretically intractable cases, also providing tractability in practice. Theoretically tractable cases are nevertheless relevant, for example, as building blocks in solvers for general cases (see Sandholm, chapter 14 of this volume), or as cases with superior economic properties, such as the existence of Walrasian pricing equilibria (see section 13.2.2). For the sake of simplicity we do not consider memory usage, knowing that required memory will always be polynomial if the running time is polynomial. In other words, we neglect some of the algorithmic fine tuning that we could get from a thorough computer science approach.

In the case of heterogeneous items, unit supply of each item, and OR bids, the WDP is identical to weighted set packing: find for a collection of weighted subsets of some set a subcollection of pairwise disjoint sets with maximum total weight. WDP is in this case also equivalent to the weighted stable set problem in a graph: find a maximum weight set of nodes that are pairwise nonadjacent. As an immediate consequence of this we get the equivalence of WDP with maximum weighted clique, where nodes are required to be pairwise adjacent. Such transformations of WDP to classic optimization problems provide us not only with easy NP-hardness proofs, but also with a large variety of algorithms (see, e.g., Babel 1994; Bomze et al. 1999; and Pardalos and Xue 1994 for maximum clique; and de Vries and Vohra 2003, with many further references to combinatorial optimization literature relevant for WDP). Indeed, these combinatorial optimization problems have been such a prominent subject of investigation that we may even claim that the majority of results on theoretical cases of the WDP *predate* the definition of the WDP.

Since Rothkopf, Pekeč, and Harstad (1998) pointed out in their influential paper on combinatorial auctions that tractable cases exist and can be of practical relevance, researchers have made a couple of specific contributions on theoretically tractable cases for WDP. However, results on set packing, stable set, or maximum weighted clique still provide a far richer source on the subject. It is impossible in a short chapter like this to summarize all these results, in particular because many of them require familiarity with concepts in combinatorial optimization or graph theory that goes beyond the scope of this book. I decided therefore not to give an exhaustive survey on what is known for these problems. Rather I will focus on the different *patterns* by which we can establish equivalence between the WDP and combinatorial optimization problems. I thereby keep the link with auction design by introducing patterns that have a meaningful auction interpretation. For each pattern, I will give a few representative examples of results from combinatorial optimization, leaving it to the interested reader to explore the richness of results that the pattern makes accessible.

As in Lehmann, Müller, and Sandholm (chapter 12 of this volume), we will start by looking at integer linear programming formulations of WDP. If the linear programming relaxation of a formulation has an integral optimal solution we get a tractable case for winner determination, and, in addition, the dual will provide us with a pricing equilibrium as Bikhchandani and Ostroy (chapter 8 of this volume) describe, which also distinguishes this approach economically from the other approaches. We will then approach the problem from the viewpoint of the intersection graph. In comparison to the linear programming approach, a treatment in terms of intersection graphs leads typically to faster algorithms, as we can benefit from algorithms that exploit specific combinatorial structures. Finally, we will illustrate that the WDP can be transformed into a surprisingly different combinatorial optimization problem, such as network flow models. We continue by setting a link to knapsack problems, before concluding with a pointer to literature on algorithmic issues of auctions with single item bids, but strong constraints on the combinations of items that may be accepted.

13.2 Tractable Integer Programs

For convenience, let us recall from Lehmann, Müller, and Sandholm (chapter 12) the integer linear programming models of the most prominent versions of the WDP, namely heterogeneous items, unit supply, and either OR or XOR bids on subsets of items:

$$\max \quad \sum_{i=1}^{n} \sum_{S \subset M} v_i(S) x_i(S)$$

$$(WDP_{OR}) \qquad \sum_{i=1}^{n} \sum_{S \subset M, S \ni j} x_i(S) \leq 1 \quad \text{for all } j \in M$$

$$x_i(S) \in \{0, 1\},$$

and

$$\max \quad \sum_{i=1}^{n} \sum_{S \subset M} v_i(S) x_i(S)$$

$$(WDP_{XOR}) \qquad \sum_{i=1}^{n} \sum_{S \subset M, S \ni j} x_i(S) \leq 1 \quad \text{for all } j \in M$$

$$\sum_{S \subset M} x_i(S) \leq 1 \qquad \qquad \text{for all } i \in N$$

$$x_i(S) \in \{0, 1\}.$$

Let LP_{OR} and LP_{XOR} be the linear programs that we get from WDP_{OR} and WDP_{XOR}, respectively, if we replace the constraints $x_i(S) \in \{0, 1\}$ by $x_i(S) \geq 0$. Furthermore, let A_{OR} and A_{XOR} be the coefficient matrices related to all other than the nonnegativity constraints in LP_{OR} and LP_{XOR}, respectively. In the following we focus on LP_{OR} unless there is a significant difference between LP_{OR} and LP_{XOR}.

We are interested in characterizing conditions under which LP_{OR} has an integral optimal solution. Practically this implies that one can use a linear programming solver to solve the WDP very efficiently. Theoretically it implies that WDP_{OR} is tractable in the encoding length of WDP_{OR}. Note that if LP_{OR} does not have an integral optimal solution, WDP_{OR} might still be tractable, however, not by simply employing a polynomial solution method for linear programming (see section 13.4.1). Note further that LP_{OR} might have an integral optimal solution just by chance. However, this is not really helpful. Rather we would like to *guarantee through the auction mechanism* that bidders submit only bids such that integrality of LP_{OR} is guaranteed.

Two ways to achieve this have been studied in the literature. The first is to enforce that bids are on subsets of items, such that the matrix A_{OR} belongs to a class of matrices that guarantees an integral optimal solution of LP_{OR}. A simple example would be that items are completely ordered and that bids are on sets of adjacent items with respect to this ordering. The second is to allow bids for any subset, but restrict to bid values that imply an integral optimal solution of LP_{OR}. A trivial example would be bid values that are completely additive in bid values for single items.

How can a mechanism guarantee restricted bid sets or bid values? First, it could be enforced as part of the bidding rules. In certain applications this might not even be considered to be restrictive, because restricted sets and values reflect bidders' valuations. For example, bidders might only be interested in sets of adjacent items, or their valuations might be completely additive. In these cases it may be sufficient that the mechanism gives incentives, rather than enforce by rules that bidders communicate "good" bids. In particular, if the mechanism is truth revealing, we can assume such behavior. We will not, however, elaborate further on this issue in this chapter. Rather, we assume restricted bid sets or bid values as being given.

13.2.1 Restriction of Bid Sets

As we said before, integrality of LP_{OR} just by chance is not helpful for a mechanism. Fortunately, a mechanism can allow for quite some flexibility in bid sets, while still guaranteeing integrality of LP_{OR} for whatever bid values have been submitted on these sets. Let us clarify this point.

Let $\mathcal{F} \subseteq 2^M$ be a system of subsets of M. We assume that bidders make bids only on $F \in \mathcal{F}$ (see also Lehmann, Müller, and Sandholm, chapter 12 of this volume). In the case of WDP_{OR} we can preprocess the bids by eliminating all but the highest bid on a specific subset F. By that we can assume the matrix A_{OR} to have one column for each $F \in \mathcal{F}$, that is, $A_{OR} = (a_{jF})_{j \in M, F \in \mathcal{F}}$, with $a_{jF} = 1$ if $j \in F$, and 0 otherwise. In the case of WDP_{XOR}, a similar preprocessing is not feasible. In this case A_{XOR} has a column for each combination (i, F), $i \in N$, $F \in \mathcal{F}$, that is, $A_{XOR} = (a_{l,(i,F)})_{l \in M \cup N, i \in N, F \in \mathcal{F}}$. For $l \in M$, $a_{l(i,F)} = 1$ if and only if $l \in F$. For $l \in N$, $a_{l(i,F)} = 1$ if and only if $l = i$. The question is then for which $\mathcal{F}$ belongs A_{OR} or A_{XOR} to a class of matrices that guarantees that LP_{OR} or LP_{XOR} have an integral optimal solution?

Restricting $\mathcal{F}$ such that A_{OR} is *totally unimodular* is the first candidate.

Definition 13.1 (totally unimodular matrix)   A $0, \pm1$-matrix A is *totally unimodular* if every square submatrix of A has determinant equal to $0, \pm1$.

The following classical result from integer programming establishes the importance of totally unimodular matrices:

Theorem 13.1 (Hoffman and Kruskal 1957) A $0, \pm 1$-matrix $A \in \mathbb{R}^{r,s}$ is totally unimodular if and only if $\{x \in \mathbb{R}^s : Ax \leq b, x \geq 0\}$ is an integral polyhedron for every integral vector b.

That gives the following corollary, which de Vries and Vohra (2003) have observed for WDP:

Corollary 13.1 (de Vries and Vohra 2003) Let $\mathscr{F} \subseteq 2^M$ such that A_{OR} (A_{XOR}) is totally unimodular, then for all bid values on subsets $F \in \mathscr{F}$ the linear program LP_{OR} (LP_{XOR}) has an integral optimal solution.

Note that by the fact that integrality of LP_{OR} does not depend on the right hand side b, total unimodularity of A_{OR} guarantees an integral optimal solution even if the supply of items is larger than 1, as long as we allow that bidders get multiple copies of the same set. Disallowing this requires additional constraints, such as the ones in WDP_{XOR}. In the case of A_{XOR}, the flexibility in choosing any right hand side covers again multiple supply in items, but now also the case of bounding the number of bids that are assigned to the same bidder is covered, in particular bounding this number to 1.

Let us provide two examples for collections $\mathscr{F}$ that guarantee total unimodularity. For the first example, recall that a $0, 1$ matrix is totally unimodular if ones in every column occur consecutively (see, e.g., Schrijver 1986). This coincides with WDP_{OR}, where we have a complete ordering on the items, and bidders bid only for sets of consecutive items with respect to this ordering. Observe that the number of bid sets is in this case at most $m(m+1)/2$, which implies that the winner determination problem is also polynomial in the number of items, and not only in the size of A_{OR}. Nevertheless, we would not necessarily use a linear programming solver, as there are very fast combinatorial algorithms (see section 13.3). Note that adding XOR constraints destroys the property of consecutive ones, which is consistent with the observation that the XOR version is NP-hard (see Lehmann, Müller, and Sandholm, chapter 12 of this volume).

For the second example, recall that the node-edge incidence matrix of a bipartite graph is totally unimodular. Given a graph $G = (U, E)$, the node-edge incidence matrix is the $0, 1$ matrix A with a row for every $u \in U$, a column for every $e \in E$, and $A_{u,e} = 1$ if and only if $u \in e$. The assignment model, that is, the case of WDP_{XOR} where every bidder submits bids for single items only, gives rise to a matrix A_{XOR} that belongs to this class (see also Bikhchandani and Ostroy, chapter 8 of this volume). Also in this case, a combinatorial algorithm provides us with a faster solution method than linear programming. Furthermore, changing the right hand side in this model is equal to allowing bidders to win multiple, but a restricted number of items, and to supplying multiple copies of the same item. As mentioned above, the WDP remains tractable with these modifications.

We observed above that total unimodularity of the constraint matrix implies tractability for any supply in items. For WDP_{OR} and WDP_{XOR} with unit supply, $0, 1$ matrices that satisfy a weaker condition are sufficient to guarantee integrality. In other words, it suffices to restrict to collections $\mathscr{F}$ of bid sets such that LP_{OR} and LP_{XOR}, respectively, are integral if the right hand side is equal to 1. Corresponding matrices A_{OR} and A_{XOR} are also well understood in combinatorial optimization. To explain this we need to introduce some terminology from graph theory.

A *node coloring* of a graph is a coloring of nodes such that no two adjacent nodes have the same color. In other words, nodes of the same color constitute stable sets. Given a graph G, let $\chi(G)$ be the minimum number of colors needed in a coloring, and let $\omega(G)$ be the maximum number of nodes in a clique in G. It is evident that $\omega(G) \leq \chi(G)$. An induced subgraph of a graph $G = (U, E)$ is a graph whose nodes U' form a subset of U, and which inherits all edges between nodes in U' from G.

Definition 13.2 (perfect graph) A graph G is called perfect if for all induced subgraphs H of G (including G itself), $\omega(H) = \chi(H)$.

Lovász (1972) showed that a graph is perfect if and only if its complement is perfect. In the complement of a graph, the stable sets become cliques, and the cliques become stable sets. Thus a graph is perfect if and only if for every induced subgraph the maximum size of a stable set is equal to the number of cliques necessary to cover the nodes of the graph.

The clique-node incidence matrix of a graph G is the $0, 1$ matrix with a row for every maximal clique in G, a column for every node in A, and $A_{ij} = 1$ if and only if node j is contained in clique i.

The main relevance of this is a result by Chvátal (1975), from which we derive a corollary similar to corollary 13.1.

Theorem 13.2 (Chvátal 1975) Let A be a $0, 1$ matrix. The linear program

max cx

$$Ax \leq 1$$

$$x \geq 0$$

has an integral optimal solution for every nonnegative vector c if and only if the nondominated rows of A form the clique-node incidence matrix of the maximal cliques of a perfect graph.

Recall that any instance of WDP_{OR} can be modeled as a stable set problem in an intersection graph. Every bid set induces a node in the intersection graph, and every item in the auction induces a clique in the intersection graph (the clique formed by all bids that contain that item), that is, A_{OR} is a submatrix of the clique-node incidence matrix of the intersection graph. Another way of stating Chvátal's theorem is thus:

Corollary 13.2 For a class $\mathscr{F}$ of bid sets, the following are equivalent:

1. LP_{OR} has an integral optimal solution for any bid values submitted for subsets $F \in \mathscr{F}$,
2. The intersection graph of $\mathscr{F}$ is perfect and all maximal cliques in the intersection graph of $\mathscr{F}$ are induced by items in M.

A similar equivalence holds for LP_{XOR}.

Let us give an example that falls under this category. Let T be a forest defined on M, that is, T is a graph whose nodes are identical to the set of items, and whose edges E are defined such that T does not contain any cycle. Let $\mathscr{F}$ be the set of subsets of M, such that every $F \in \mathscr{F}$ induces a connected subgraph (and thus subtree) of T. We know that the intersection graph G of $\mathscr{F}$ is a perfect graph (see theorem 13.6). Let A_{OR} be the matrix related to $\mathscr{F}$.

Let us demonstrate that the nondominated rows of A_{OR} are one-to-one to the maximum cliques in G. Let U' be a set of bids that form a maximum clique in the intersection graph. Then one can easily see that there exists an item that belongs to all bids in U'. Furthermore, there exists an item j that is contained in all bids in U' but in no other bid, because otherwise U' would not be maximal. Thus the maximum clique U' is represented by the row belonging to j. Now let j be a nondominated row in A_{OR}. The set of bids U' that contain j form a clique in the intersection graph. If that clique is not maximal there exists an item j' contained in all bids in U', and in at least some other bid. But then the row j would be dominated by row j'.

We can make two remarks here. First, although total unimodularity or perfectness of A_{OR} or A_{XOR} is an elegant way to prove that the winner determination problem can be solved in polynomial time, it does not imply that linear programming solvers provide the best possible algorithm. In most cases, faster algorithms can be found by exploiting more of the specific combinatorial structure of the problem.

Second, conditions such as total unimodularity and perfectness are helpful properties also if A_{OR} or A_{XOR} are not given explicitly but through a bidding oracle for every bidder. In particular it is sufficient to have an oracle that can determine for every price (and bidder surplus) vector (i.e., dual solution of LP_{OR} or LP_{XOR}) a subset $S \subset M$ that would give the bidder the highest revenue among all subsets at the current prices. Such an oracle provides us with a separation oracle for the feasible set of dual solutions.

By applying the equivalence between optimization and separation (Grötschel et al. 1981), we can thus optimally solve the dual, and by that also find an optimal primal solution.

13.2.2 Restriction of Bid Values

So far we have restricted the collection of subsets of items on which bidders may bid in order to achieve integrality of LP_{OR} and LP_{XOR}. We now turn to the other extreme, where we allow bids on any subset of items, but restrict the bid values. We focus on LP_{XOR}, because there is no essential difference between an instance of WDP_{OR} with bids for every subset and WDP_{XOR}. Furthermore, restricted bid values have only been investigated for this model.

Recall that in this case A_{XOR} has a column for every pair (i, S), $i \in N$, $S \subseteq M$, and we ask ourselves for which objectives does LP_{XOR} have an integral optimal solution. It turns out that the right condition on the objective, and thus the bid values, is the *(items are) substitutes* condition, introduced by Kelso Crawford (1982) (see also Ausubel and Milgrom, chapter 1 of this volume).

In order to define this property we define for a valuation $v : 2^M \to \mathbb{R}$, and prices $p_j \in \mathbb{R}$, $j \in M$ the *demand correspondence* of a bidder as the collection of sets of items with the largest net utility, given prices p:

$$D(v, p) = \{S \subseteq M | v(S) - p(S) \geq v(T) - p(T) \text{ for all } T \subseteq M\}.$$

Here, $p(S) := \sum_{j \in S} p_j$. The substitutes condition controls the change of the demand correspondence under price changes.

Definition 13.3 (substitutes condition) Given a set M, a set function $v : 2^M \to \mathbb{R}$ satisfies the *substitutes condition*, if for any pair of price vectors p, q with $p \leq q$, and $A \in D(v, p)$, there exists $B \in D(v, q)$ such that $\{j \in A | p_j = q_j\} \subseteq B$.

This means that by increasing prices on some items, the demand for other items does not decrease.

As Ausubel and Milgrom show in chapter 1, the substitutes condition is satisfied if and only if the indirect utility function is submodular. Furthermore, they show that the substitute condition is in some sense necessary and sufficient for good economic properties of the VCG mechanism. This coincides nicely with the computational implications of the substitutes condition:

Theorem 13.3 (Kelso and Crawford 1982) Let for all $i \in N$ the bid values $v_i(S)$, $S \subseteq M$ in an instance of WDP_{XOR} satisfy the substitutes condition. Then LP_{XOR} has an integral optimal solution.

Several authors have given other equivalent characterizations that we mention briefly. Gul and Stacchetti (1999) have proven the following equivalent characterization of *monotone* substitutes valuations:

Theorem 13.4 (Gul and Stacchetti 1999) Given a set M, a monotone set function $v : 2^M \to \mathbb{R}$ satisfies the substitutes condition if and only if it has the following single improvement property: for all price vectors p and all $S \notin D(v, p)$, there exists $T \subseteq M$, such that $v(T) - p(T) > v(S) - p(S)$ and $|T \backslash S| \leq 1$ as well as $|S \backslash T| \leq 1$.

Reijnierse, van Gellekom, and Potters (2002) gave two other characterizations. One of them is of particular relevance because it is independent of prices:

Theorem 13.5 (Reijnierse, van Gellekom, and Potters 2002) Given a set M and a set function $v : 2^M \to \mathbb{R}$, the following are equivalent:

1. v satisfies the substitutes condition.
2. There does not exist any price vector p such that
a. $D(v, p) = \{S \cup \{i, j\}, S\}$ for some $S, i, j \in M \backslash S$ or,
b. $D(v, p) = \{S \cup \{i, j\}, S \cup \{k\}\}$ for some $S, i, j, k \in M \backslash S$.
3. For all S, i, j, k the following conditions hold:
a. $v(S \cup \{i, j\}) - v(S \cup \{i\}) \leq v(S \cup \{j\}) - v(S)$,
b. $v(S \cup \{i, j\}) + v(S \cup \{k\}) \leq \max(v(S \cup \{i, k\}) + v(S \cup \{j\}), v(S \cup \{j, k\}) + v(S \cup \{i\}))$.

Note that 3a is equal to submodularity (and, as shown by Reijnierse, van Gellekom, and Potters 2002 equivalent to 2a), thus implying also that substitutes valuations are a special case of submodular valuations (see also Nisan, chapter 9 of this volume).

Danilov, Koshevoy, and Murota (2001) and Fujishige and Yang (2003) observed yet another characterization of substitutes that relates substitutes to $M^{\natural}$-concave functions. We skip the definition here, as it would require many additional details. We mention, however, two important algorithmic consequences.

First, it follows from a result on $M^{\natural}$-convex functions by Shioura (1998) that given a price vector p, a substitute valuation v, and a polynomial time oracle by which we can compute $v(S)$ for every $S \subseteq M$, we can compute a set $S \in D(v, p)$ in polynomial time. By applying the equivalence of optimization and separation (Grötschel, Lovász, and Schrijver 1981) to the dual of LP_{XOR} it follows that we can solve the winner determination problem for substitute valuations in polynomial time in the number of bidders and items if the valuations are given by polynomial time computable oracles (see Nisan, chapter 9 of this volume for a discussion of such bidding languages).

Second, Murota and Tamura (2001) show that solving WDP_{XOR} for substitutes bid values $v_i(S)$, $S \subseteq M$ can be modeled as a submodular flow problem, providing another

approach to solve WDP in polynomial time in the number of bidders and items, again
using an oracle to compute the valuations of subsets.

13.3   Tractable Stable Set in Intersection Graphs

The second approach by which we can model WDP_{OR} and WDP_{XOR} as a combinatorial
optimization problem is using the intersection graph of bids. For convenience we recall
the model from Lehmann, Müller, and Sandholm (chapter 12 of this volume). We use
a graph $G = (U, E)$ consisting of a finite set of nodes U and a set of undirected edges E.
The nodes in U are one-to-one to the bids $v_i(S)$, $i \in N$, $S \subseteq M$, and two nodes are
connected by an edge if and only if there exists a conflict between the bids, that is,
an intersection of the sets of items. In addition to this, in the case of WDP_{XOR}, two
bids intersect also if they are both by the same bidder. Every node gets a weight
$w_u := v_i(S)$.

A subset U' of nodes is called a *stable set* if no two nodes in U' are connected by an
edge. The (*maximum*) *weighted stable set problem* is the problem of finding a stable set of
maximum total weight. It is obvious that WDP_{OR} and WDP_{XOR} are equivalent to the
weighted stable set problem on their intersection graphs.

Grötschel, Lovász, and Schrijver (1981) have shown that a maximum weighted stable set can be solved in polynomial time if the intersection graph is perfect; however,
their algorithm uses the ellipsoid method as a subroutine and therefore does not provide a practical algorithm. Special classes of perfect graphs typically come with specific
combinatorial algorithms for weighted stable set. Often these algorithms exploit the
fact that the graphs in the class are intersection graphs of geometric objects, in which,
every node relates to some regularly shaped object in the plane, say, and two nodes are
connected if the corresponding objects intersect. We will describe an $O(n \log n)$ algorithm for a stable set of an intersection graph of n intervals, which models WDP_{OR} for
interval bids (see Lehmann, Müller, and Sandholm, chapter 12, for the definition of
the *big-O notation*). Although in the case of interval bids the integer linear programming formulation provides a totally unimodular matrix, which is stronger than perfect,
the case of subtree bids in the previous section provides a matrix that is "only" perfect.
Similarly for this case, one is able to give a very efficient combinatorial algorithm.

13.3.1   Interval Bids
We discuss here the case WDP_{OR} where items are completely ordered and bids are submitted for sets of consecutive items with respect to this ordering. Because the identity
of a bidder is not crucial, we may assume that all bids are from different bidders, providing us the convenience to number them from 1 to n.

The interpretation of such bids might be the following. The items are unit time
intervals that are available on some processor. Bids are submitted for consecutive time

intervals by owners of tasks who need processing time. Every time interval can be allocated to at most one task.

Let us denote the bid sets by $[l_j, u_j]$, $j = 1, \ldots, n$, and the bid value of the j-th bid by v_j. It is convenient to use for the values l_j and u_j not the item numbers, but instead half integer numbers; that is, if bid j is on the interval of items $\{i, \ldots, k\}$, then we represent this bid by $l_j = i - 1/2$ and $u_j = k + 1/2$.

Let us look at the lower and upper bounds of the intervals. They may be partly identical. Assume for a moment that we have sorted them as a nondecreasing sequence of numbers $a_1, \ldots, a_{2n}$, where each a_l coincides with some l_j or u_j. We make the additional assumption that whenever an end of an interval is equal to the start of another interval, the end precedes the start in our sort sequence. That is, if $a_l = a_k$, $l < k$, and a_l is equal to the start of some interval, then a_k is also equal to the start of some interval.

With this assumption the following dynamic programming algorithm computes an optimal solution of the winner determination problem. Let $W(l)$ be the optimal solution of the winner determination problem with respect to all bids i such that $u_i = a_k$, for some $k \leq l$. We initialize $W(0) := 0$, and compute $W(l)$ for $0 < l \leq 2n$ by:

$$W(l) = \begin{cases} W(l-1) & \text{if } a_l = l_j \text{ for some } j \\ \max(W(l-1), v_j + W(k)) & \text{if } a_l = u_j \text{ for some } j \text{ and } l_j = a_k. \end{cases}$$

To construct the solution we memorize with each l how $W(l)$ has been computed. Note that the algorithm has a running time that is linear in the number of bids.

What remains to be done is the construction of the sequence a_i, $i = 1, \ldots, 2n$. Sandholm and Suri (2003) suggest *bucket sort*, which yields an $O(m + n)$ algorithm. If the number of items is large in relation to the number of bids, we should instead adapt any of the well-known efficient sorting procedures based on pairwise comparison to get an $O(n \log n)$ algorithm.

Rothkopf, Pekeč, and Harstad (1998) introduced the case where bid sets are nested, that is, two bid sets are either disjoint or contained in each other. Obviously, this is a special case of interval bids, and can be solved in linear time as well, as long as bids are represented by intervals. Rothkopf, Pekeč, and Harstad (1998) gave an $O(m^2)$ algorithm that is based on a representation of bids as nodes in a tree. Given this representation one can compute the optimal winner assignment in $O(k)$ time, where k is the number of nodes in the tree. Note that after deleting dominated bids, there are at most $O(m^2)$ bids.

Felsner, Müller, and Wernisch (1997) extend the geometry based dynamic programming approach to compute stable sets to other graph classes that can be defined by intersections of geometric objects, including so-called circular-arc graphs, for which de Vries and Vohra (2003) observe that WDP_{OR} is tractable. Circular-arc graphs come from bids on neighbored items on a circle (e.g., bidding for shifts in a round-the-clock schedule in a personnel planning application). We note that circular-arc graphs are no longer perfect, providing us with an example where the combinatorial approach reaches further than the integer linear programming approach.

There are numerous other classes of intersection graphs; however, many of them are of limited value for combinatorial auctions as the underlying objects can hardly be interpreted as representing exactly the subsets of items on which a bidder would like to bid.

13.3.2 Subtree Bids

We saw in section 13.2.1 that LP_{OR} is integral when bid sets are restricted to subtrees of a tree, because A_{OR} coincides with the clique-node incidence matrix of a perfect graph. From the viewpoint of the intersection graph, we know that the intersection graphs of subtrees are exactly the chordal graphs. A graph is chordal if every cycle of length of at least four contains at least one chord.

Theorem 13.6 (Gavril 1974)   The intersection graphs of subtrees in a tree are exactly the chordal graphs.

The interpretation of subtree bids is as follows. We might be given a tree-like communication network. Bids are made for connected parts of this communication network. Another interpretation is that of a tree-like representation of relations between items in such a way that with any two items bidders always will desire all items in between.

Similar to the case of intervals, dynamic programming provides us with an efficient algorithm to solve WDP_{OR} in this case. Instead of traversing the sequence of items from left to right, thereby taking more and more intervals into account, we process the items from the leaves toward the root of the tree. To do so, we choose an arbitrary item as root item r of the tree. This also defines for every bid T_j, $j = 1, \ldots, n$, a root item, namely the item that is closest to r, which we call r_j. Let $R(i) := \{j \in \{1, \ldots, n\} | i = r_j \text{ for some } j\}$. Further, let $S(i) = \{i' | i \text{ adjacent to node } i' \text{ on the path from } i' \text{ to } r\}$; in other words, $S(i)$ are the neighbors of i on paths from i to leaves. Finally, let $SL(j) = \{i' | i' \in S(i) \backslash T_j \text{ for some } i \in T_j\}$.

We next label the nodes of the tree, starting with leaves, ending with the root, such that every item i has a higher label than all items in $S(i)$. Let $W(i)$ be the maximum weighted stable set with respect to trees that are contained in the subtree rooted in i. Set $W(i) := 0$ for all leaves that are not the root of some tree T_j, and $W(i) := V_j$, otherwise. One easily verifies the following formula for items with a higher label:

$$
W(i) = \max \left(\sum_{i' \in S(i)} W(i'), \max_{j \in R(i)} \left(v_j + \sum_{i' \in SL(j)} W(i') \right) \right).
$$

The total number of operations (with respect to all items) needed to compute the first sum in this formula is $O(m)$. The number of operations we need for the second maximum in this formula is nm, because we have to process every subtree T_j exactly once (when $i = r_j$) and $|SL(j)| \leq m$.

This algorithm is a little different from the interval algorithm above. Here the dynamic program iterates over all items, whereas above we iterated only over the beginnings and the ends of intervals. We can do the same here, should it be more efficient. Basically, we would skip items that are neither root nor neighbors of trees.

Sandholm and Suri (2003) suggest the described algorithm for combinatorial auctions. It also appears in Golumbic 1980, next to many other combinatorial algorithms for weighted stable sets for subclasses of the class of perfect graphs.

13.4   Combinatorial Models

In the previous two sections of this chapter our points of departure were the most obvious models for WDP: integer linear programming and intersection graphs. We exploited the fact that restricting bid sets or bid values might directly translate into a special class of integer programs or intersection graphs, and by that make WDP tractable. In this section we will show that other models might sometimes be more suited to show tractability. We start with a case of restricted bid sets, and proceed with a case of special bid values on arbitrary bid sets.

13.4.1   Weighted Matching

We observed earlier that in the case of bids for single items only, the matrix A_{XOR} is totally unimodular. WDP_{XOR} is in this case also equivalent to the maximum weight bipartite matching problem. The equivalence extends to so-called OXS-bids (Lehmann, Lehmann, and Nisan 2001). In XS-bids the bidder makes bids for singletons, and the bid for a subset is the exclusive or-bid defined by these singleton bids (see Nisan, chapter 9 of this volume). This is equivalent to bids for single items only. OXS-bids are defined as or-bids over such bids, and lead from a computational perspective to the same WDP as XS-bids from different bidders.

Maximum weight matching in *non*-bipartite graphs can also be used to solve special cases of WDP_{OR}. Rothkopf, Pekeč, and Harstad (1998) observe that it can be used to model WDP_{OR} if bids are restricted to a size of at most two. They mention airline take-off and landing slot auctions as a possible application. In this model, the graph has a node for every item in M, and an edge for every bid set of size 2, connecting the two items in the bid. Bids of size 1 are modeled by adding a dummy node for each such bid, and connecting the item in the bid with this dummy node. Giving each edge a weight equal to the bid, WDP_{OR} becomes equivalent to maximum weight matching in this graph. The first polynomial algorithm for general matching is due to Edmonds (1965).

Note that neither is the integer linear program related to this special case integral nor is the intersection graph perfect. This can be simply seen by taking five items and defining bids such that the edges in the matching model form a 5-cycle.

13.4.2 Cardinality Based Subadditivity

We can also use combinatorial models to solve the WDP efficiently in cases where bids on arbitrary sets are allowed, but where we restrict the bid values. We say that bid values are *additive with convex discounts* if for every bidder i there exists an increasing, convex function $d_i : \mathbb{R} \to \mathbb{R}$ such that for all $S \subset M$

$$v_i(S) = \max\left(0, \sum_{j \in S} v_i(\{j\}) - d_i(|S|)\right).$$

Let us further assume that bidder i wants to win at most r_i items, and that we are in the multiunit case with ω_j units available of item j. In this case the WDP can be modeled as a min-cost flow problem with a convex cost function on the arcs as follows.

The flow network has a source node s and a target node t, a node u_i for every bidder i, and a node w_j for every item j. It has arcs (s, u_i) for all i, arcs (u_i, w_j), for all $i \in N$, $j \in M$ for which $v_i(\{j\}) > 0$, and arcs (w_j, t) for all $j \in M$.

The cost for δ units of flow through arc (s, u_i) is determined as $d_i(\delta)$, the cost per unit of flow through arc (u_i, w_j) is equal to $-v_i(j)$. Cost of flow through other arcs is equal to 0. The capacities of arcs are: arcs (s_i, u_i) have 0 as lower and r_i as upper capacity, arcs (u_i, w_j) have 0 as lower and 1 as upper capacity, arcs (w_j, t) have 0 as lower and ω_j as upper capacity.

One can easily see that a minimum cost flow in this network coincides with an optimal solution of the WDP instance. Minimum cost flow with convex cost can be done in polynomial time (see Ahuja, Magnanti, and Orlin 1993, chapter 14). This model generalizes the results by Tennenholtz (2000) on quantity constrained multiobject auctions, almost additive multiobject auctions, and auctions with subadditive symmetric bids for triplets. Furthermore, using theorem 13.5, one can easily convince oneself that the valuations satisfy the substitute condition.

13.4.3 Multiunit Auctions for a Limited Number of Distinct Items

If all items are identical, winner assignment in a combinatorial auction becomes equal to the classical knapsack problem. In the case of WDP_{OR}, we can use dynamic programming, which has a running time that is polynomial in the total number of items (and some other terms).

The dynamic programming approach has been extended in two directions. Tennenholtz (2000) gives a dynamic programming algorithm for a fixed number of types of item, and van Hoesel and Müller (2001) consider the case of XOR bids for a single type of item. As a common generalization of both we state the following theorem for the case of XOR bids for multisets $S = (\sigma_j | j \in M)$. The algorithm is essentially a dynamic programming algorithm for the multicriteria, multidimensional knapsack problem (see also Holte 2001; Kellerer, Pferchy, and Pirsinger 2004).

Theorem 13.7 Given an instance of WDP with m types of items, ω_j copies of item j in supply, and XOR bids on multisets S. Let $l = \max(\omega_j | j \in M) + 1$. Then WDP can be solved in $O(l^m mnr)$ time, where r is the maximum number of bids made by the same bidder.

Proof Let $W(i, \alpha_1, \ldots, \alpha_k)$ be the maximum value of an allocation if the bidders are restricted to $1, \ldots, i$ and for every item j no more than α_j copies are allocated. Then

$$W(1, \alpha_1, \ldots, \alpha_m) = \max(v_1(S) | \sigma_j \leq \alpha_j),$$

and for $i > 1$:

$$W(i, \alpha_1, \ldots, \alpha_m) = \max v_i(S) + W(i - 1, \alpha_1 - \sigma_1, \ldots, \alpha_m - \sigma_m)$$

$$s.th. \ (\sigma_1, \ldots, \sigma_m) \leq (\alpha_1, \ldots, \alpha_m),$$

where we take the maximum over all S such that $\sigma_j \leq \alpha_j$, $j = 1, \ldots, m$.

Note that we have to determine at most $l^m n$ variables $W(i, \alpha_1, \ldots, \alpha_m)$, each of which is computed by comparing at most r values, and subtracting as part of this m numbers from each other.   ∎

This is only a pseudo-polynomial algorithm if the number l is much larger than the number of bids, even when the number of different types of items is small. Indeed, the encoding for the number of items requires in total only $m \log l$ memory. In the single unit case, l would be 2, in which case the number of different items is crucial for the running time.

13.5 Conclusion

We have shown in this chapter several approaches by which the winner determination problem becomes polynomial. In all approaches we had to restrict either the sets for which bids may be submitted, or the bid values. In many applications this might be well motivated from the application: bidders do not value other subsets of items, or their types are restricted such that only such bid values are necessary.

Another class of WDP, which we left out in our discussion, further supports the claim that such assumptions can be valid and meaningful. Let us briefly sketch them at the end of this chapter. We assume now a reverse auction in which the auctioneer wants to purchase a bundle of items. Bidders are only interested in selling single items, and all bidders compete for different items in the bundle. The auctioneer wants to purchase particular combinations. Typically, such combinations are the solutions of a combinatorial optimization problem. A prominent example is that of items equal to links in a communication network where the buyer wants to purchase sets of links that together connect two nodes in the network, or that form a spanning tree that connects a source node with every node in the network. In this case, simple bidding languages are sufficient, and the winner determination problem can be solved easily if the underlying combinatorial optimization problem, such as shortest path, is theoretically tractable. We refer to Bikhchandani et al. (2001) and Nisan and Ronen (2001) for further reading on this topic, and to Hershberger and Suri (2001) for accelerated computing of Vickrey prices in procurement auctions for shortest paths.

Acknowledgments

Special thanks go to Terence Kelly for valuable comments on an earlier version of this chapter.

References

Ahuja, Ravindra K., Thomas L. Magnanti, and James B. Orlin (1993), *Nework Flows*, Upper Saddle River: Prentice Hall.

Babel, Luitpold (1994), "A Fast Algorithm for the Maximum Weight Clique Problem," *Computing*, 52, 31–38.

Bikhchandani, Sushil, Sven de Vries, James Schummer, and Rakesh R. Vohra (2001), "Linear Programming and Vickrey Auctions," in Brenda Dietrich, Rakesh V. Vohra, eds., *Mathematics of the Internet—E-Auction and Markets*, New York: Springer, 75–115.

Bomze, Immanuel M., Marco Budinich, Panos M. Pardalos, and Marcello Pelillo (1999), "The Maximum Clique Problem," in Ding Zhu Du and Panos M. Pardalos, eds., *Handbook of Combinatorial Optimization*, volume 4, Boston: Kluwer Academic Publishers, 1–74.

Chvátal, Vašek (1975), "On Certain Polytopes Associated with Graphs," *Journal on Combinatorial Theory Series B*, 13, 138–154.

Danilov, Vladimir, Gleb Koshevoy, and Kazuo Murota (2001), "Discrete Convexity and Equilibria in Economies with Indivisible Goods and Money," *Mathematical Social Sciences*, 41, 251–273.

de Vries, Sven and Rakesh V. Vohra (2003), "Combinatorial Auctions: A Survey," *INFORMS Journal on Computing*, 15, 284–309.

Edmonds, Jack (1965), "Paths, Trees and Flowers," *Canadian Journal of Mathematics*, 17, 449–467.

Felsner, Stefan, Rudolf Müller, and Lorenz Wernisch (1997), "Trapezoid Graphs and Generalizations, Geometry and Algorithms," *Discrete Applied Mathematics*, 74, 13–32.

Fujishige, Satoru and Zaifu Yang (2003), "A Note on Kelso and Crawford's Gross Substitutes Condition," *Mathematics of Operations Research*, 28, 463–469.

Gavril, Fanica (1974), "The Intersection Graphs of Subtrees in Trees Are Exactly the Chordal Graphs," *Journal Combinatorial Theory B*, 16, 47–56.

Golumbic, Martin C. (1980), *Algorithmic Graph Theory and Perfect Graphs*, New York: Academic Press.

Grötschel, Martin, Laszlo Lovász, and Alexander Schrijver (1981), "The Ellipsoid Method and Its Consequences in Combinatorial Optimization," *Combinatorica*, 1, 169–197.

Gul, Faruk and Ennio Stacchetti (1999), "Walrasian Equilibrium with Gross Substitutes," *Journal of Economic Theory*, 87, 95–124.

Hershberger, John and Subhash Suri (2001), "Vickrey Pricing in Network Routing: Fast Payment Computation," in *Proceedings of the 42nd IEEE Symposium on Foundations of Computer Science*, 252–259.

Hoffman, Alan J. and Joseph B. Kruskal (1957), "Integral Boundary Points of Convex Polyhedra," in Harold W. Kuhn and Albert William Tucker, eds., *Linear Inequalities and Related Systems*, Princeton: Princeton University Press, 223–246.

Holte, Robert C. (2001), "Combinatorial Auctions, Knapsack Problems, and Hill-Climbing Search," in Eleni Stroulia and Stan Matwin, eds., *Proceedings AI'2001, the 14th Biennial Conference of the Canadian Society for Computational Studies of Intelligence*, volume 2056 of *Springer Lecture Notes in Artificial Intelligence*, 57–66.

Kellerer, Hans, Ulrich Pferchy, and David Pirsinger (2004), *Knapsack Problems*, Berlin: Springer Verlag.

Kelso, Alexander S. and Vincent P. Crawford (1982), "Job Matching, Coalition Formation and Gross Substitutes," *Econometrica*, 50, 1483–1504.

Lehmann, Benny, Daniel Lehmann, and Noam Nisan (2001), "Combinatorial Auctions with Decreasing Marginal Utilities," in *Proceedings 3rd ACM Conference on Electronic Commerce*, ACM Press, 18–28. To appear, *Games and Economic Behavior*.

Lovász, Lazlo (1972), "Normal Hypergraphs and the Weak Perfect Graph Conjecture," *Discrete Mathematics*, 2, 253–267.

Murota, Kazuo and Akihisa Tamura (2001), "Application of m-Convex Submodular Flow Problem to Mathematical Economics," in Peter Eades and Tadao Takaoka, eds., *Algorithms and Computation, Proceedings of 12th International Symposium, ISAAC 2001*, Christchurch, New Zealand, December 19–21, 2001, volume 2223 of *Springer Lecture Notes in Computer Science*, 14–25.

Nisan, Noam and Amir Ronen (2001), "Algorithmic Mechanism Design," *Games and Economic Behavior*, 35, 166–196.

Pardalos, Panos M. and Jue Xue (1994), "The Maximum Clique Problem," *SIAM Journal of Global Optimization*, 4, 301–328.

Reijnierse, Hans, Anita van Gellekom, and Jos A.M. Potters (2002), "Verifying Gross Substitutability," *Economic Theory*, 20, 767–776.

Rothkopf, Michael H., Aleksander Pekeč, and Ronald M. Harstad (1998), "Computationally Manageable Combinational Auctions," *Management Science*, 44, 1131–1147.

Sandholm, Tuomas and Subhash Suri (2003), "BOB: Improved Winner Determination in Combinatorial Auctions and Generalizations," *Artificial Intelligence*, 145, 33–58.

Schrijver, Alexander (1986), *Theory of Linear and Integer Programming*, New York: John Wiley and Sons.

Shioura, Akiyoshi (1998), "Minimization of an m-Convex Function," *Discrete Applied Mathematics*, 84, 215–220.

Tennenholtz, Moshe (2000), "Some Tractable Combinatorial Auctions," in *Proceedings of National Conference on Artifical Intelligence (AAAI)*, 98–103.

van Hoesel, Stan and Rudolf Müller (2001), "Optimization in Electronic Markets: Examples in Combinatorial Auctions," *Netnomics*, 3, 23–33.

14   Optimal Winner Determination Algorithms

Tuomas Sandholm

14.1   Introduction

This chapter discusses optimal winner determination algorithms for combinatorial auctions (CAs). We say the auctioneer has a set of items, $M = \{1, 2, \ldots, m\}$, to sell, and the buyers submit a set of package bids, $\mathscr{B} = \{B_1, B_2, \ldots, B_n\}$. A package bid is a tuple $B_j = \langle S_j, p_j \rangle$, where $S_j \subseteq M$ is a set of items and $p_j \geq 0$ is a price. (Note that in this chapter, n denotes the number of such bids, not the number of bidders.) The *winner determination problem* (WDP) is to label the bids as winning or losing so as to maximize the sum of the accepted bid prices under the constraint that each item is allocated to at most one bid:

$$\max \sum_{j=1}^{n} p_j x_j \quad \text{s.t.} \quad \sum_{j|i \in S_j} x_j \leq 1, \quad \forall i \in \{1 \ldots m\}$$

$x_j \in \{0, 1\}$.

This problem is computationally complex (NP-complete and inapproximable, see Lehmann, Müller and Sandholm, chapter 12 of this volume). Since 1997, there has been a surge of research addressing it. This chapter focuses on search algorithms that provably find an optimal solution to the general problem where bids are not restricted (e.g., Sandholm 2002a; Fujishima, Leyton-Brown, and Shoham 1999; Sandholm and Suri 2003; Andersson, Tenhunen, and Ygge 2000; Gonen and Lehmann 2000; Leyton-Brown, Tennenholtz, and Shoham 2000; Sandholm et al. 2005; Lehmann and Gonen 2001; van Hoesel and Müller 2001; Boutilier 2002; de Vries and Vohra 2003).[1] Because the problem is NP-complete, any optimal algorithm for the problem will be slow on some problem instances (unless $\mathscr{P} = \mathscr{NP}$). However, in practice, modern search algorithms can optimally solve winner determination in the large.[2]

The goal is to make a set of decisions (e.g., for each bid, deciding whether to accept or reject it). In principle, tree search algorithms work by simulating all possible ways of making the decisions. Thus, once the search finishes, the optimal set of decisions will have been found and proven optimal.

However, in practice, the space is much too large to search exhaustively. The science of search is in techniques that *selectively* search the space while still provably finding an optimal solution. The next section—the bulk of the chapter—studies different design dimensions of search algorithms for winner determination. Section 14.3 discusses state of the art algorithms in that framework. Section 14.4 discusses winner determination under fully expressive bidding languages where substitutability is expressed using XOR-constraints between bids. Finally, section 14.5 provides pointers to further reading.

14.2   Design Dimensions of Search Algorithms

We can classify search algorithms for winner determination under the following high-level design dimensions:

- search formulation
- search strategy
- upper bounding techniques (including cutting planes)
- lower bounding techniques and primal heuristics
- decomposition techniques (including upper and lower bounding across components)
- techniques for deciding which question to branch on
- techniques for identifying and solving tractable cases at search nodes
- random restart techniques
- caching techniques.

The following subsections study these dimensions in order.

14.2.1   Search Formulations

The most fundamental design dimension is the *search formulation*: what class of questions is the branching question for a node chosen from?

Branching on Items   First-generation special-purpose search algorithms for winner determination were based on the branch-on-items search formulation (Sandholm 2002a; Fujishima, Leyton-Brown, and Shoham 1999). At any node, the question to branch on is: "What bid should this item be assigned to?" Each path in the search tree consists of a sequence of disjoint bids, that is, bids that do not share items with each other.

The set of items that are already used on the path is

$$USED = \bigcup_{j|\text{bid } j \text{ is on the path}} S_j \qquad\qquad (14.1)$$

and let A be the set of items that are still available: $A = M - USED$. A path ends when no bid can be added to it: for every bid, some of the bid's items have already been used on the path.

As the search proceeds down a path, a tally, g, is kept of the sum of the prices of the bids accepted on the path:

$$g = \sum_{j|\text{bid } j \text{ is accepted on the path.}} p_j \qquad (14.2)$$

At every search node, the revenue g from the path is compared to the best g-value found so far in the search tree to determine whether the current path is the best solution so far. If so, it is stored as the new *incumbent*. Once the search completes, the incumbent is an optimal solution.

However, one must take care to treat the possibility that the auctioneer's revenue can increase by keeping items (Sandholm 2002a). Consider an auction of items 1 and 2. Say there is no bid for 1, a \$5 bid for 2, and a \$3 bid for $\{1,2\}$. Then it is better to keep 1 and sell 2 than it would be to sell both.

The auctioneer's possibility of keeping items can be implemented by placing *dummy bids* of price zero on those items that received no one-item bids (Sandholm 2002a). For example in figure 14.1, if item 1 had no bids on it alone and dummy bids were not used, the tree under 1 would not be generated and optimality could be lost.

A naïve method of constructing the search tree would include all bids (that do not include items that are already used on the path) as the children of each node. Instead,

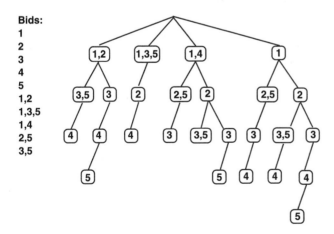

Bids:
1
2
3
4
5
1,2
1,3,5
1,4
2,5
3,5

Figure 14.1
This example search space corresponds to the bids listed on the left. For each bid, the items are shown but the price is not.

the following proposition enables a significant reduction of the branching factor by capitalizing on the fact that the order of the bids on a path does not matter.

Proposition 14.1 (Sandholm 2002a)   At each node in the search tree, it suffices to let the children of the node be those bids that

- include the item with the smallest index among the items that are still available ($i^* = \min\{i \in \{1, \ldots, m\} : i \in A\}$), and
- do not include items that have already been used on the path.

Formally, for any node, θ, of the search tree,

$$\text{children}(\theta) = \{j \in \{1, \ldots, n + n_{dummy}\} | i^* \in S_j, S_j \cap USED = \emptyset\}^3 \tag{14.3}$$

Figure 14.1 shows the use of that restriction.

Theorem 14.1 (Sandholm 2002a)   The number of leaves in the tree is no greater than $((n + n_{dummy})/m)^m$. Also, #leaves $\in O(m^m)$. The number of nodes is no greater than $m \cdot$ #leaves $+ 1$.

So, even in the worst case, the size of the tree is polynomial in the number of bids, but exponential in the number of items.

Branching on Bids   Instead of branching on items, newer, faster winner determination algorithms use the *branch-on-bids* search formulation (Sandholm and Suri 2003). At any node, the question to branch on is: "Should this bid be accepted or rejected?" When branching on a bid, the children in the search tree are the world where that bid is accepted (IN, $x_j = 1$), and the world where that bid is rejected (OUT, $x_j = 0$), figure 14.2, right.

The branching factor is 2 and the depth is at most n. (The depth of the left branch is at most $\min\{m, n\}$.) No dummy bids are needed: the auctioneer keeps the items that are not allocated in bids on the search path. Given the branching factor and tree depth, a naïve analysis shows that the number of leaves is at most 2^n. However, a deeper analysis establishes a drastically lower worst-case upper bound:

Theorem 14.2 (Sandholm and Suri 2003)   Let κ be the number of items in the bid with the smallest number of items. The number of leaves is no greater than

$$\left(\frac{n}{\lfloor m/\kappa \rfloor} + 1\right)^{\lfloor m/\kappa \rfloor}. \tag{14.4}$$

The number of nodes in the tree is $2 \cdot$ #leaves $- 1$.

Branch-on-items formulation   Branch-on-bids formulation

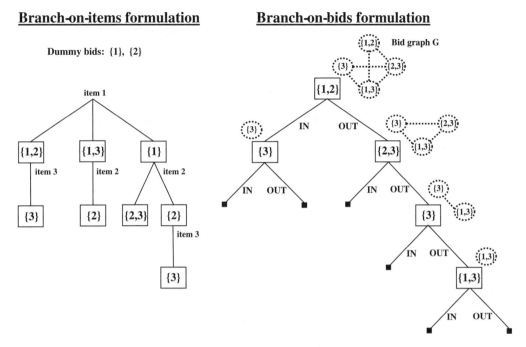

Figure 14.2
Branching on items vs. branching on bids. Bids in this example (only items of each bid are shown; prices are not shown): $\{1,2\}, \{2,3\}, \{3\}, \{1,3\}$.

Although this is exponential in items, it is polynomial in bids—unlike the naïve upper bound 2^n would suggest. This is desirable because the auctioneer can usually control the items that are for sale (if there are too many, he can split the CA into multiple CAs), but does not want to restrict the number of bids submitted.[4] Furthermore, the average performance tends to be significantly better than the worst case.

Sometimes the branch-on-bids formulation leads to a larger tree than the branch-on-items formulation (see figure 14.2). Opposite examples can also be constructed, by having items on which no singleton bids have been submitted; dummy bids would be added for them in the branch-on-items formulation.

The main advantage of the branch-on-bids formulation is that it is in line with the *principle of least commitment* (Russell and Norvig 1995). In a branch-on-items tree, all bids containing an item are committed at a node, whereas in the branch-on-bids formulation, choosing a bid to branch on does not constrain future bid selections (except that accepting a bid precludes later accepting bids that share items with it). Therefore, the branch-on-bids formulation allows more refined search control—in particular, better bid ordering. At any search node, the bid to branch on can be chosen in an unconstrained way using information about the subproblem at that node. Many techniques capitalize on that possibility, as we will see later in this chapter.

Multivariate Branching The integer programming literature shows that search algorithms can be made to branch on questions that include multiple variables. We can apply that idea to winner determination as follows (Gilpin and Sandholm 2004). The algorithm can branch on the sum of the values of a set of variables.[5] The branching question could then be, for instance: "Of these eleven bids, are at least three winners?"

Consider the remaining problem at a node (it includes only those bids that do not share items with bids that are already accepted on the path). Relaxing the integrality constraints $x_j \in \{0, 1\}$ of that remaining winner determination problem to $x_j \in [0, 1]$ yields a linear program (LP), and it can be solved quickly. Given a set $\mathcal{X}$ of variables and the LP solution $\hat{x}$, one can generate the following two branches:

$$\sum_{i \in \mathcal{X}} x_i \leq k \quad \text{and} \quad \sum_{i \in \mathcal{X}} x_i \geq k+1, \tag{14.5}$$

where $k = \lfloor \sum_{i \in \mathcal{X}} \hat{x}_i \rfloor$. No other value of k should be considered: any other integer value would cause one child to be exactly the same as the node, entailing infinitely deep search on that branch if that branch is ever explored. Similarly, no set of variables $\mathcal{X}$ where $\sum_{i \in \mathcal{X}} \hat{x}_i$ is integral should be a branching candidate: one of the branches will not exclude the current LP solution, so that child will be identical to the node.

Although branching on more than one variable at a time may feel less powerful than branching on individual variables because the branch does not seem to make as specific a commitment, we have:

Proposition 14.2 (Gilpin and Sandholm 2004) The search tree size (measured in terms of the number of nodes or number of leaves) is the same regardless of how many (and which) variables are used in different branches (as long as trivial branches where a child is identical to its parent are not used).

Thus theorem 14.2 applies to multivariate branching as well.

Proposition 14.2 is for exhaustive search. If one uses additional techniques (discussed later in this chapter), such as upper bounding, then search tree size can differ based on how many (and which) variables are used for branching at nodes. Experimentally, multivariate branching tends to lead to smaller trees than the other two search formulations discussed above, but it spends more time at each search node (deciding which set $\mathcal{X}$ should be branched on).

The different types of branching question classes could also be merged. For example, a search algorithm could branch on an item at a node, branch on a bid at another node, and branch on a multivariate question at yet another node.

14.2.2 Search Strategies

The second important design dimension of a search algorithm is the *search strategy*: what order is the tree searched in? The following subsections cover the most pertinent search strategies.

Depth-First Search   The first special-purpose search algorithm for winner determination (Sandholm 2002a) used the branch-on-items formulation and the *depth-first search* strategy, where the search always proceeds from a node to an unvisited child, if one exists. If not, the search backtracks. Depth-first search is desirable in that only the nodes on one search path (and their children) need to be kept in memory at any one time. So, $O((n + n_{dummy}) \cdot m)$ nodes are in memory.

The strategy yields an *anytime algorithm*: the algorithm is able to output a feasible solution at any time, and solution quality improves over time (because the algorithm keeps track of the best solution found so far [incumbent]). The user can stop the algorithm and use the incumbent if the algorithm is taking too long. In experiments, most of the revenue was generated early on as desired: there were diminishing returns to computation.

Search strategies that are *informed* by upper bounds yield faster winner determination. Specifically, a heuristic function h gives an upper bound on how much revenue the items that are not yet allocated on the current search path can contribute. The following subsections discuss search strategies that use such upper bounding. Later, section 14.2.4 presents different ways of computing such bounds.

Depth-First Branch-and-Bound Search   The simplest informed search strategy is *depth-first branch-and-bound (DFBnB)*. It creates the search tree in depth-first order, but prunes (discontinues) a path if the node's $g + h$ value is no greater than the value of the incumbent. (Recall that g is the sum of the prices of the bids accepted on the path.) This is valid because the condition guarantees that a better incumbent cannot exist in the subtree whose creation was omitted by pruning. The memory usage of DFBnB is as low as that of depth-first search, and pruning leads to significantly smaller search trees. Fujishima, Leyton-Brown, and Shoham (1999) present DFBnB experiments in the branch-on-items formulation, and Sandholm et al. (2005) in the branch-on-bids formulation.

A* and Best-Bound Search   The most famous informed search strategy is A^* *search* (Hart, Nilsson, and Raphael 1968). When a search node is expanded, its children are generated and stored in memory. The node itself is removed from memory. The node to expand next is always the node from memory that is *most promising*, as measured by having the highest value of $g + h$. Once a node that has no children (because all bids are decided) comes up for expansion from memory, that is an optimal solution, and the search ends.

A* leads to the smallest possible search tree: no tree search algorithm can provably find an optimal solution without searching all the nodes that A* searches (Dechter and Pearl 1985). A downside is that A* often runs out of memory because the fringe of the search tree is stored. (With depth d and branching factor b, the number of nodes in memory is $O(b^d)$.)

Best-bound search, a common search strategy in the integer programming literature (Wolsey 1998), is identical to A*, except that the following refinements are often used in practice.

• Approximate child evaluation   In order to avoid having to carefully compute upper bounds on a node's children at the time when the children are first generated, only approximate upper bounds (that sometimes underestimate) for the children are used in practice. Therefore, the children come up for expansion from memory in *approximate* order of $g + h$. Thus, unlike in A*, once a node with no undecided bids comes up for expansion from memory, that might not be an optimal solution. Rather, the search must continue until all potentially better nodes have been expanded.

• Diving bias   A child of the current node is expanded instead of expanding the most promising node if the latter is not too much more promising. Although this increases tree size, it can save search time because expanding a child is usually drastically faster than expanding a nonadjacent node. The reason is that data structures (e.g., LP-related ones) can be incrementally updated when moving between a node and a child, whereas they require significant reconstruction when moving to a nonadjacent node.[6] (All of the search strategies that proceed in depth-first order automatically enjoy the benefits of diving.)

Iterative Deepening A* Search   Like DFBnB, *iterative deepening A* (IDA*)* search (Korf 1985), achieves the same low memory usage, enjoys the benefits of diving, and takes advantage of upper bounds for pruning. IDA* guesses how much revenue (f-limit) can be obtained, and runs a depth-first search where a path is pruned if $g + h <$ f-limit. If a solution is not found, the guess was too optimistic, in which case a less optimistic guess is carefully made, depth-first search is executed again, and so on.

The following pseudocode shows how Sandholm (2002a) applied IDA* to winner determination. Instead of using depth-first search as the subroutine, this variant uses DFBnB (with an f-limit). The difference manifests itself only in the last IDA* iteration. That is the first iteration where an incumbent is found, and this variant of IDA* saves some search by using the incumbent's value for pruning.

Global Variable   f-limit

Algorithm 14.1 IDA*
// Returns a set of winning bids that maximizes the sum of the bid prices

1. f-limit := ∞
2. Loop
(a) winners, new-f := DFBNB-WITH-F-LIMIT($M, \emptyset, 0$)
(b) if winners ≠ null then return winners
(c) f-limit := min(new-f, $0.95 \cdot$ f-limit)[7]

Algorithm 14.2 DFBNB-WITH-F-LIMIT(A, winners, g)
// Returns a set of winning bids and a new f-cost

1. If $g + h(A) <$ f-limit then return null, $g + h(A)$ // Pruning
2. If the current node has no children, then // End of a path reached
a. f-limit := g // DFBnB rather than depth-first search
b. return winners, g
3. maxRevenue := 0, bestWinners := null, next-f := 0
4. For each bid $b \in$ children of current node
a. solution, new-f := DFBNB-WITH-F-LIMIT($A - S_b$, winners $\cup \{b\}, g + p_b$)
b. If solution ≠ null and new-f > maxRevenue, then
i. maxRevenue := new-f
ii. bestWinners := solution
c. next-f := max(next-f, new-f)
5. If bestWinners ≠ null then return bestWinners, maxRevenue else return null, next-f.

Experimentally, IDA* is two orders of magnitude faster for winner determination than depth-first search. By setting f-limit to 0 instead of ∞, IDA* turns into DFBnB. IDA* can lead to fewer search nodes than DFBnB because the f-limit allows pruning of parts of the search space that DFBnB would search. Conversely, DFBnB can lead to fewer nodes because IDA* searches nodes close to the root multiple times.

Exotic Search Strategies   IDA* and DFBnB explore a larger number of nodes than A*. Their run time can be improved by using more memory, while still using much less than A* does. Search strategies that do that include *SMA** (Russell 1992) and *recursive best-first search* (Korf 1993). A downside of SMA*, like A*, is that it requires node-related data structures to be laboriously reconstructed. A downside of recursive best-first search is that it leads to significant amounts of redundant search on problems where the edge costs of the search tree are mostly distinct numbers, as is the case in winner determination.

14.2.3   An Example Algorithm: CABOB

Let us now consider an example algorithm within which we can specifically discuss the other design dimensions of search algorithms for winner determination. The *CABOB (Combinatorial Auction Branch On Bids)* (Sandholm et al. 2005) algorithm is a DFBnB search that branches on bids.

The value of the best solution found so far (i.e., the incumbent) is stored in a global variable $\tilde{f}^*$. Initially, $\tilde{f}^* = 0$.

The algorithm maintains a conflict graph structure called the *bid graph*, denoted by G (see figure 14.2). The nodes of the graph correspond to bids that are still available to be appended to the search path, that is, bids that do not include any items that have already been allocated. Two vertices in G share an edge whenever the corresponding bids share items.[8,9] As vertices are removed from G when going down a search path, the edges that they are connected to are also removed. As vertices are reinserted into G when backtracking, the edges are also reinserted.[10]

For readability, the following pseudocode of CABOB only shows how values are updated, and omits how the incumbent (set of winning bids) is updated in conjunction with every update of $\tilde{f}^*$.

As discussed later, CABOB uses a technique for pruning across independent subproblems (components of G). To support this, it uses a parameter, *MIN*, to denote the minimum revenue that the call to CABOB must return (not including the revenue from the path so far or from neighbor components) to be competitive with the incumbent. The revenue from the bids that are winning on the search path so far is called g. It includes the lower bounds (or actual values) of neighbor components of each search node on the path so far.

The search is invoked by calling $CABOB(G, 0, 0)$.

Algorithm 14.3 $CABOB(G, g, MIN)$

1. Apply cases COMPLETE and NO_EDGES (explained later)
2. Run depth-first search on G to identify the connected components of G; let c be number of components found, and let $G_1, G_2, \ldots, G_c$ be the c independent bid graphs
3. Calculate an upper bound U_i for each component i
4. If $\sum_{i=1}^{c} U_i \leq MIN$, then return 0
5. Apply case INTEGER (explained later)
6. Calculate a lower bound L_i for each component i
7. $\Delta \leftarrow g + \sum_{i=1}^{c} L_i - \tilde{f}^*$
8. If $\Delta > 0$, then

$$\tilde{f}^* \leftarrow \tilde{f}^* + \Delta$$

$$MIN \leftarrow MIN + \Delta$$

9. If $c > 1$ then goto (11)

10. Choose next bid B_k to branch on (use articulation bids first if any)

10.a. $G \leftarrow G - \{B_k\}$

10.b. For all B_j s.t. $B_j \neq B_k$ and $S_j \cap S_k \neq \emptyset$,

$$G \leftarrow G - \{B_j\}$$

10.c. $\tilde{f}^*_{old} \leftarrow \tilde{f}^*$

10.d. $f_{in} \leftarrow CABOB(G, g + p_k, MIN - p_k)$

10.e. $MIN \leftarrow MIN + (\tilde{f}^* - \tilde{f}^*_{old})$

10.f. For all B_j s.t. $B_j \neq B_k$ and $S_j \cap S_k \neq \emptyset$,

$$G \leftarrow G \cup \{B_j\}$$

10.g. $\tilde{f}^*_{old} \leftarrow \tilde{f}^*$

10.h. $f_{out} \leftarrow CABOB(G, g, MIN)$

10.i. $MIN \leftarrow MIN + (\tilde{f}^* - \tilde{f}^*_{old})$

10.j. $G \leftarrow G \cup \{B_k\}$

10.k. Return $\max\{f_{in}, f_{out}\}$

11. $F^*_{solved} \leftarrow 0$

12. $H_{unsolved} \leftarrow \sum_{i=1}^{c} U_i, L_{unsolved} \leftarrow \sum_{i=1}^{c} L_i$

13. For each component $i \in \{1, \ldots, c\}$ do

13.a. If $F^*_{solved} + H_{unsolved} \leq MIN$, return 0

13.b. $g'_i \leftarrow F^*_{solved} + (L_{unsolved} - L_i)$

13.c. $\tilde{f}^*_{old} \leftarrow \tilde{f}^*$

13.d. $f^*_i \leftarrow CABOB(G_i, g + g'_i, MIN - g'_i)$

13.e. $MIN \leftarrow MIN + (\tilde{f}^* - \tilde{f}^*_{old})$

13.f. $F^*_{solved} \leftarrow F^*_{solved} + f^*_i$

13.g. $H_{unsolved} \leftarrow H_{unsolved} - U_i$

13.h. $L_{unsolved} \leftarrow L_{unsolved} - L_i$

14. Return F^*_{solved}.

14.2.4   Upper Bounding Techniques

As discussed, in all of the informed search methods, upper bounds on how much the unallocated items can contribute are used to prune the search (e.g., in CABOB in steps 3 and 4). Pruning usually reduces the search time by orders of magnitude.

First-generation special-purpose winner determination algorithms (Sandholm 2002a; Fujishima, Leyton-Brown, and Shoham 1999) used special-purpose upper bounding techniques. The main idea was to use as an upper bound the sum over unallocated items of the item's maximum contribution (Sandholm 2002a):

$$\sum_{i \in A} c(i), \quad \text{where } c(i) = \max_{j | i \in S_j} \frac{p_j}{|S_j|}. \tag{14.6}$$

Tighter bounds are obtained by recomputing $c(i)$ every time a bid is appended to the path—because all bids j that share items with that bid can be excluded from consideration (Sandholm 2002a).[11]

The value of the linear program (LP) relaxation of the remaining winner determination problem gives another upper bound.

LP	DUAL
$\max \sum_{j=1}^{n} p_j x_j$	$\min \sum_{i=1}^{m} y_i$
$\sum_{j \mid i \in S_j} x_j \leq 1, \forall i \in \{1..m\}$	$\sum_{i \in S_j} y_i \geq p_j, \forall j \in \{1..n\}$
$x_j \geq 0$	$y_i \geq 0$
$x_j \in \mathbb{R}$	$y_i \in \mathbb{R}$

The LP can be solved in polynomial time in the size of the input (which itself is $\Theta(nm)$) using interior point methods, or fast on average using, for example, the simplex method (Nemhauser and Wolsey 1999). Alternatively, one can use the DUAL because its optimal value is the same as LP's. Often the DUAL is used in practice because as the search branches, the parent's DUAL solution is feasible for the child's DUAL and can usually be optimized using a relatively small number of pivots.[12] (The parent's LP solution is infeasible for the child's LP, so the child's LP takes relatively long to solve.)

It is not always necessary to run the LP/DUAL to optimality. The algorithm could look at the condition in step 4 of CABOB to determine the threshold revenue that the LP (DUAL) has to produce so that the search branch would not (would) be pruned. If the threshold is reached, LP/DUAL can stop. However, CABOB always runs the LP/DUAL to completion because CABOB uses the solutions for several other purposes beyond upper bounding, as discussed later.

Linear programming-based upper bounding usually leads to faster search times (Sandholm et al. 2005) than any of the other upper bounding methods previously proposed for winner determination (Sandholm 2002a; Fujishima, Leyton-Brown, and Shoham 1999; Sandholm and Suri 2003). This is likely due to better bounding, better bid ordering, and the effect of the INTEGER special case, described below. The time taken to solve the linear program is greater than the per-node time with the other bounding methods, but the reduction in tree size usually amply compensates for that. However, on a nonnegligible portion of instances the special-purpose bounding heuristics yield faster overall search time (Leyton-Brown 2003).

Branch-and-Cut Algorithms   The LP upper bound can be tightened by adding *cutting planes* (aka *cuts*). These are additional constraints that do not affect the solution of the integer program, but do constrain the LP polytope. For example, if the bid graph G contains a set of nodes H that form an odd-length cycle longer than 3, and no nonadjacent pair of nodes in H share an edge (the nodes in H are said to form an odd hole), then it is valid to add the *odd-hole cut* $\sum_{j \in H} x_j \leq (|H| - 1)/2$. There are also cut families, for example *Gomory cuts* (Wolsey 1998), that one can apply to all integer programs, not just winner determination.

It is largely an experimental art as to which cuts, if any, are worth adding. That depends not only on the problem, but also on the instance at hand. The more cuts one adds, the fewer nodes the search takes due to enhanced upper bounding. On the other hand, as more cuts are added, the time spent at each node increases due to the time it takes to generate the cuts and solve the LP that now has a larger number of constraints. There is a vast literature on cuts (see, for example, Garfinkel and Nemhauser 1969; Loukakis and Tsouros 1983; Pardalos and Desai 1991; and the textbooks by Nemhauser and Wolsey 1999; and by Wolsey 1998). One principle is only to add cutting planes that cut off the currently optimal point from the LP.

Some cuts are *global*: it is valid to leave them in the LP throughout the search. (Nevertheless, it is sometimes worth removing global cuts because they may slow down the LP too much.) Other cuts are *local*: they are valid in the subtree of the search rooted at a given node, but might not be valid globally. Such cuts can be added at the node, but they have to be removed when the search is not within that subtree.

A cut can also be made to constrain the LP polytope more, by carefully moving the cut deeper into the polytope (by including a larger number of the variables in the cutting plane and setting their coefficients), while guaranteeing that it does not cut off any integer solutions. This is called *lifting* (see, for example, Wolsey 1998). Again, there is a tradeoff: the more the algorithm lifts, the fewer search nodes are explored due to improved upper bounding, but the more time is spent per search node due to the time it takes to lift.

14.2.5 Lower Bounding Techniques and Primal Heuristics

Lower bounding techniques are another design dimension of search algorithms. At a search node (e.g., in CABOB in step 6) a lower bound is computed on the revenue that the remaining items can contribute. If this bound is high, it allows the incumbent value, $\tilde{f}^*$, to be updated, leading to more pruning in the subtree rooted at that node. Generating good incumbents early is also desirable from an anytime perspective.

One famous lower bounding technique is rounding (Hoffman and Padberg 1993). CABOB uses the following rounding technique. In step 3, CABOB solves the remaining LP anyway, which gives an "acceptance level" $x_j \in [0, 1]$ for every remaining bid j. CABOB inserts all bids with $x_j > 1/2$ into the lower bound solution. It then tries to insert the rest of the bids in decreasing order of x_j, skipping bids that share items with bids already in the lower bound solution. Experiments showed that lower bounding did not help significantly.

Other techniques for constructing a good feasible solution for a node include *local branching*, where a tree search of at most k variable changes is conducted from some feasible solution to improve it (Fischetti and Lodi 2002), and *relaxation-induced neighborhood search*, where variables that are equal in the feasible solution and LP are fixed, and a search is conducted to optimize the remaining variables (Danna, Rothberg, and Le Pape 2005) (the search can be restricted to k changes). In either method, k can be increased based on allowable time.

Additional lower bounds cannot hurt in terms of the number of search nodes because the search algorithm can use the best (i.e., highest) of the lower bounds. However, there is a tradeoff between reducing the size of the search tree and the time spent computing lower bounds.

14.2.6 Decomposition Techniques

Decomposition techniques are another powerful tool in search algorithms. The idea is to partition the bids into sets (aka connected components) so that no bid from one set shares items with any bid from any other set. Winner determination can then be conducted in each set separately (and in parallel if desired).

At *every* search node, in step 2 CABOB runs an $O(|E| + |V|)$ time depth-first search in the bid graph G. (Here, E is the set of edges in the graph, and V is the set of vertices.) Each tree in the depth-first forest is a connected component of G. Winner determination is then conducted in each component independently. Because search time is superlinear in the size of G, a decomposition leads to a time savings, and experiments have shown that the savings can be drastic (Sandholm et al. 2005).

Upper and Lower Bounding *across Components* Perhaps surprisingly, one can achieve further pruning by exploiting information across the components (Sandholm et al. 2005). When starting to solve a component, CABOB checks how much that component would have to contribute to revenue in the context of what is already known about bids on the search path so far *and the connected components that arose from decompositions on the path*. Specifically, when determining the *MIN* value for calling CABOB on a component, the revenue that the current call to CABOB has to produce (the current *MIN* value) is decremented by the revenues from solved neighbor components and the lower bounds from unsolved neighbor components. (A neighbor component is a connected component that arose at the same decomposition.) The use of the *MIN* variable causes the algorithm to work correctly even if on a single search path there are several search nodes where decomposition occurred, interleaved with search nodes where decomposition did not occur.

Every time a better global solution is found and $\tilde{f}^*$ is updated, all *MIN* values in the search tree are incremented by the amount of the improvement because now the bar of when search is useful has been raised. CABOB handles these updates without separately traversing the tree when an update occurs: CABOB directly updates *MIN* in step 8, and updates the *MIN* value of any parent node after the recursive call to CABOB returns.

CABOB also uses lower bounding across components. At any search node, the lower bound includes the revenues from the bids that are winning on the path, the revenues from the solved neighbor components of search nodes on the path, the lower bounds of the unsolved neighbor components of search nodes on the path, and the lower bound on the revenue that the unallocated items in the current search node can contribute.[13]

14.2.7 Techniques for Deciding Which Question to Branch On

The search formulations, search strategies, and the CABOB pseudocode leave open the question: "Which question should the search algorithm branch on at this node?" Although any choice maintains correctness, different choices yield orders of magnitude difference in speed in the informed search methods. This section discusses techniques for making that choice.

Forcing a Decomposition via Articulation Bids   In addition to checking whether a decomposition has occurred, CABOB strives for a decomposition. In the bid choice in step 10, it picks a bid that leads to a decomposition, if such a bid exists. Such bids whose deletion disconnects G are called *articulation bids*. Articulation bids are identified in $O(|E| + |V|)$ time by a slightly modified depth-first search in G (Sandholm and Suri 2003). If there are multiple articulation bids, CABOB branches on the one that minimizes the size of the largest connected component.

The strategy of branching on articulation bids may conflict with price-based bid ordering heuristics (which usually suggest branching on bids with high price and a low number of items). Does one of these schemes dominate the other?

Definition 14.1   In an *articulation-based bid choosing scheme*, the next bid to branch on is an articulation bid if one exists. Ties can be resolved arbitrarily, as can cases where no articulation bid exists.

Definition 14.2   In a *price-based bid choosing scheme*, the next bid to branch on is

$$\arg \max_{j \in V} v(p_j, |S_j|), \tag{14.7}$$

where V is the set of vertices in the remaining bid graph G, and v is a function that is nondecreasing in p_j and nonincreasing in $|S_j|$. Ties can be resolved arbitrarily, for example, preferring bids that articulate.

Theorem 14.3 (Sandholm and Suri 2003)   For any given articulation-based bid choosing scheme and any given price-based bid choosing scheme, there are instances where the former leads to less search, and instances where the latter leads to less search.

However, experiments showed that in practice it pays off to branch on articulation bids if they exist (because decomposition tends to reduce search drastically).

Even if a bid is not an articulation bid, and would thus not lead to a decomposition if rejected, it might lead to a decomposition if it is accepted (because that removes the bid's neighbors from G as well). This is yet another reason to try the IN branch before the OUT branch (*value ordering*). Also, in bid ordering (*variable ordering*), we can give first preference to articulation bids, second preference to bids that articulate on the winning branch only, and third preference to bids that do not articulate on either branch (among them, the price-based bid ordering could be used).

During the search, the algorithm could also do shallow lookaheads—for the purpose of bid ordering—to identify *combinations* (aka cutsets) of bids that would disconnect G. Bids within a small cutset should be branched on first. (However, identifying the smallest cutset is intractable.)

To keep the computation at each search tree node small, CABOB simply gives first priority to articulation bids, and if there are none, uses other bid ordering schemes, discussed in the next three subsections.

Should an Algorithm Branch on Confidence or on Uncertainty?   It has become clear to me that different search strategies are best served by different branching heuristics, and perhaps surprisingly, the best branching heuristics for A* and DFBnB abide to *opposite* principles.

If one desires good anytime performance, it makes sense to use the DFBnB search strategy. In that context it is best to generate promising branches first because that yields good solutions early, and as a side effect, better pruning of the search tree via upper bounding. So, the principle is that the algorithm should always *branch on a question for which it knows a good answer with high confidence*. For example, in the context of the branch-on-items formulation, Fujishima, Leyton-Brown, and Shoham (1999) renumbered the items before the search so that the items i were in descending order of $\max_{j|i \in S_j} p_j/|S_j|$, and that was the branching order. Even better item ordering could be accomplished by *dynamically* reordering the remaining items for every subtree in the search—in light of what bids and items are still available.

By contrast, if provable optimality is desired, A* tends to be preferable over DFBnB because it searches fewer nodes before proving optimality. Good variable ordering heuristics for A* are the opposite of those for DFBnB: the principle is that the algorithm should *branch on a question about whose correct answer the algorithm is very uncertain*! For example, the best-known branching heuristic in the operations research literature (e.g., Wolsey 1998, p. 99) is the *most fractional variable heuristic*. In the branch-on-bids formulation of winner determination this translates to the *most fractional bid heuristic*: branching on a bid whose LP value, x_j, is closest to $1/2$ (Sandholm et al. 2005). The idea is that the LP is least sure about these bids, so it makes sense to resolve that uncertainty rather than to invest branching on bids about which the LP is "more certain." More often than not, the bids whose x_j values are close to 0 or 1 tend to get closer to those extreme values as search proceeds down a path, and in the end, LP will give an integer solution. Therefore those bids never end up being branched on.

In both algorithm families, to enhance pruning through upper bounding, it is best to visit the children of a node in most-promising-first order. (In A* this happens automatically due to the order in which nodes come up for expansion from memory, as discussed.) For example, within the branch-on-items formulation, Fujishima, Leyton-Brown, and Shoham (1999) use a child ordering heuristic where bids j are always visited in descending order of $p_j/|S_j|$. Even better child ordering could be accomplished by *dynamically* reordering the children at each search node—in light of what bids and items are still available. (For the particular child ordering metric above, there is no difference between static and dynamic.)

Sophisticated Numeric Bid Ordering Heuristics   An elaborate study has been conducted on bid ordering heuristics for the branch-on-bids formulation with the DFBnB search strategy in the context of CABOB (Sandholm et al. 2005).[14] Experiments were conducted with the following bid ordering heuristics:

• Normalized Bid Price (NBP) (Sandholm and Suri 2003)   Branch on a bid with the highest $p_j/(|S_j|)^\alpha$.[15]
• Normalized Shadow Surplus (NSS) (Sandholm et al. 2005)   The problem with NBP is that it treats each item as equally valuable. It could be modified to weight different items differently based on static prices that, for example, the seller guesses before the auction. A more sophisticated approach is to weight the items by their "values" *in the remaining subproblem*. The *shadow price*, y_i, from the linear program DUAL of the remaining problem serves as a proxy for the value of item i.[16] We branch on the bid whose price gives the highest surplus above the value of the items[17] (normalized by the values so the surplus has to be greater if the bid uses valuable items):

$$\frac{p_j - \sum_{i \in S_j} y_i}{\left(\sum_{i \in S_j} y_i\right)^\alpha}. \tag{14.8}$$

Experimentally, the following modification to the normalization leads to faster performance:

$$\frac{p_j - \sum_{i \in S_j} y_i}{\log(\sum_{i \in S_j} y_i)}. \tag{14.9}$$

We call this scheme NSS.
• Bid Graph Neighbors (BGN) (Sandholm et al. 2005)   Branch on a bid with the largest number of neighbors in the bid graph G. The motivation is that this will allow the search to exclude the largest number of still eligible bids from consideration.

- Number of Items (Sandholm et al. 2005) Branch on a bid with the largest number of items. The motivation is the same as in BGN.
- One Bids (OB) (Sandholm et al. 2005) Branch on a bid whose x_j-value from LP is closest to 1. The idea is that the more of the bid is accepted in the LP, the more likely it is to be competitive.
- Most fractional bid, described in the previous section. Branching heuristics of this type are most appropriate for A*-like search strategies (where the search strategy itself drives the search toward promising paths), whereas CABOB uses DFBnB.

Researchers conducted experiments on several problem distributions using all possible pairs of these bid ordering heuristics for primary bid selection and tie-breaking, respectively. They also tried using a third heuristic to break remaining ties, but that never helped. The speed difference between CABOB with the best heuristics and CABOB with the worst heuristics was greater than two orders of magnitude. The best composite heuristic (OB+NSS) used OB first, and broke ties using NSS.

Choosing the Bid Ordering Heuristic *Dynamically* On certain distributions, OB+NSS was best, whereas on distributions where the bids included a large number of items, NSS alone was best. The selective superiority of the heuristics led to the idea of choosing the bid ordering heuristic *dynamically based on the characteristics of the remaining subproblem*. A distinguishing characteristic between the distributions was LP density:

$$\text{density} = \frac{\text{number of nonzero coefficients in LP}}{\text{number of LP rows} \times \text{number of LP columns}}. \tag{14.10}$$

OB+NSS was best when density was less than 0.25, and NSS was best otherwise. Intuitively, when the LP table is sparse, LP is good at "guessing" which bids to accept. When the table is dense, the LP makes poor guesses (most bids are accepted to a small extent). In those cases the price-based scheme NSS (that still uses the shadow prices from the LP) was better. Therefore, in CABOB, at every search node the density is computed, and the bid ordering scheme is chosen dynamically (OB+NSS if density is less than 0.25, NSS otherwise).

Solution Seeding As a fundamentally different bid ordering methodology (Sandholm et al. 2005), stochastic local search (e.g., Hoos and Boutilier 2000)—or any other heuristic algorithm for winner determination—could be used to come up with a good solution fast, and then that solution could be forced to be the left branch (IN-branch) of CABOB's search tree. (The technique could be applied at the root, or also at other nodes.) Committing (as an initial guess) to the entire set of accepted bids from the approximate solution in this way would give CABOB a more global form of guidance in bid ordering than conducting bid ordering on a per-bid basis. To refine this method further, CABOB could take hints (for example, from the approximation algorithm) as to how "surely" different bids that are accepted in the approximate solution should be accepted in the optimal solution. In the left branch (IN-branch) of CABOB, the "most sure" bids should then be assigned closest to the root of the search tree, because bids near the root will be the last ones to be backtracked in the search. This ordering will allow good solutions to be found early, and (mainly due to upper bounding) avoids unnecessary search later on.

Lookahead A famous family of techniques for deciding what question to branch on is lookahead. Some potentially promising subset of candidate branching questions are considered, and a shallow search below the node is conducted for each one of those questions. The question with the highest "score" is then chosen to be the question to branch on.

Motivated by the goal of getting to a good solution quickly, a traditional scoring method is to take the weighted average of the leaves' values where more promising leaves are weighted more heavily (a leaf's value is $g + h$ where g is the sum of the prices of the accepted bids on that path, and h is an upper bound on how much remaining items can contribute) (Applegate et al. 1994). This is called *strong branching*. A recent alternative idea, motivated by the role of branching as a means of reducing uncertainty, is to set the score to equal the expected reduction in *entropy* of the leaves' LP values (Gilpin and Sandholm 2004). This is called *information-theoretic branching*. Depending on the problem instance, either method can be superior.

One can use these approaches in all of the search formulations: branch-on-items, branch-on-bids, and multivariate branching.

14.2.8 Identifying and Solving Tractable Subproblems at Nodes

A general approach to speeding up the search is, at each search node, to solve the remaining problem in polynomial time using some special-purpose method rather than continuing search below that node, if the remaining problem happens to be tractable (Sandholm and Suri 2003).[18]

COMPLETE Case In step 1, CABOB checks whether the bid graph G is complete: $|E| = n(n-1)/2$. If so, only one of the remaining bids can be accepted. CABOB thus picks the bid with highest price, updates the incumbent if appropriate, and prunes the search path.

NO_EDGES Case If G has no edges, CABOB accepts all of the remaining bids, updates the incumbent if appropriate, and prunes the search path.

INTEGER Case A classic observation is that if the LP happens to return integer values ($x_j = 0$ or $x_j = 1$) for all bids j (this occurs surprisingly frequently), that solution can be used as the actual solution for the node in question (rather than having to search under that node). CABOB does this in step 5. (If only some of the x_j values are integral, one cannot simply accept the bids with $x_j = 1$ or reject the bids with $x_j = 0$) (Sandholm et al. 2005).

Müller (chapter 13 of this volume) reviews sufficient conditions under which the LP provides an integer-valued solution. For some of those classes there exist algorithms for identifying and solving the problem faster than LP, for instance the NO_EDGES class above, and the class where items can be numbered so that each remaining bid is for consecutive items (possibly with wraparound) (Sandholm and Suri 2003).

Tree-Structured Items   If the remaining items can be laid out as nodes in a graph so that each remaining bid is for a connected component in the graph, then winners can be determined in time that is exponential only in the treewidth of the graph (and polynomial in the number of items and the number of bids) (Conitzer, Derryberry, and Sandholm 2004). A polynomial algorithm for identifying whether such a graph with treewidth 1 (i.e., a tree) exists has been developed (Conitzer, Derryberry, and Sandholm 2004), so handling of that case can be integrated into tree search algorithms. The question of whether such graphs with treewidth greater than 1 can be identified in polynomial time remains open. (The requirement that each bid is for one component is sharp: even in line graphs, if two components per bid are allowed, winner determination is NP-complete.)

Technique for Exploiting *Part* of the Remaining Problem Falling into a Polynomially Solvable Class   Polynomial solvability can be leveraged even if only *part* of the problem at a search node falls into a tractable class (Sandholm and Suri 2003). This section demonstrates this for one polynomially solvable class.

Bids that include a small number of items can lead to significantly deeper search than bids with many items because the latter exclude more of the other bids due to overlap in items (Sandholm 2002a). Furthermore, bids with a small number of items are ubiquitous in practice. Let us call bids with one or two items *short* and other bids *long*.[19] Winners can be optimally determined in $O(n^3)$ worst case time using a weighted maximal matching algorithm (Edmonds 1965) if the problem has short bids only (Rothkopf, Pekeč, and Harstad 1998).

To solve problems with both long and short bids efficiently, one can integrate Edmonds's algorithm with search as follows (Sandholm and Suri 2003). We restrict the branch-on-bids search to branching on long bids only, so it never needs to branch on short bids. At every search node, Edmonds's algorithm is executed using the short bids whose items have not yet been allocated to any accepted long bids on the search path so far. Edmonds's algorithm returns a set of winning short bids.

Those bids, together with the accepted long bids from the search path, constitute a candidate solution. If it is better than the incumbent, the candidate becomes the new incumbent.

This technique can be improved further by using a dynamic definition of "short" (Sandholm and Suri 2003). If an item x belongs to only one long bid b in the *remaining* bid graph G, then the size of b can, in effect, be reduced by one. As search proceeds down a path, this method may move some of the long bids into the short category, thereby further reducing search tree size. (When backtracking, the deleted items are reinserted into bids.)

14.2.9 Random Restart Techniques

Random restarts have been widely used in local search algorithms, but recently they have been shown to speed up tree search algorithms as well on certain problems (Gomes, Selman, and Kautz 1998). The idea is that if (mainly due to unlucky selection of branching questions) the search is taking a long time, it can pay off to keep trying the search again with different randomly selected branching questions. Sandholm et al. 2005 tested whether sophisticated random restart techniques, combined with careful randomized bid ordering, help in winner determination. The experiments showed that these techniques actually slow CABOB down.

14.2.10 Caching Techniques

Another technique commonly used in search algorithms is *caching*, which one can also apply to search algorithms for winner determination. For example, Fujishima, Leyton-Brown, and Shoham (1999) used caching in the branch-on-items formulation. Here I present how to use caching in the branch-on-bids formulation, but the same ideas apply to other search formulations.

If the remaining bid graph is the same in different nodes of the search tree (this occurs if the same items are used up, but by different sets of bids), then the remaining subproblems under those nodes are the same. The idea in caching is that the answer from solving the subproblem is stored (aka cached) in memory so that when that subproblem is encountered again, it does not have to be solved anew—rather, one can look the answer up from the cache.

One subtlety is that usually the subproblem is not searched completely when it is encountered, due to pruning through upper bounding. Therefore, in many cases only an upper bound h on the subproblem's value is stored in the cache rather than the exact value of the subproblem. The algorithm should therefore also store in the cache, with each solution, whether the value is exact or an upper bound. Then, if the same subproblem occurs in a search node elsewhere in the tree, there are several cases, to be checked in order:

- If the cached value is exact, it can be used as the value of the subproblem, and the search does not need to continue into the subtree. The remaining cases are for cached values that are not exact.
- If the new node has a greater (or equal) *MIN*-value than the node where the value of the same subproblem was cached (that is, the path to the new node is less promising than the path to the old node was), then the subtree can be pruned.[20] The following cases pertain if the new node has a lesser *MIN*-value than the old node.
- If the cached *h*-value is less than (or equal to) the *MIN*-value, the subtree can be pruned.
- If the cached *h*-value is greater than the *MIN*-value, then it is not valid to use the cached value because the optimal solution might be found in the subtree. In that case, the search has to continue into the subtree. (Once the subtree is solved deeply enough to allow for pruning with that *MIN*-value—or an exact solution is found—the new solution to the subtree is stored in the cache in place of the old.)

For large search trees, there is not enough memory to cache the values of all subtrees. It is important to decide which subtree solutions the algorithm should cache (and which it should remove from the cache when the cache becomes full). There are at least three principles for this: (1) cache subproblems that are encountered often, (2) cache subproblems that represent a large amount of search effort, and (3) cache subproblems that can be indexed rapidly (i.e., quickly retrieve the value or determine that it is not in the cache).

14.3   State of the Art

Despite the fact that winner determination is NP-complete, modern search algorithms can optimally solve large CAs in practice. The time it takes to solve a problem depends not only on the number of items and bids, but also on the specific structure of the problem instance: which bids include which items, and what the prices of the bids are. The rest of this section summarizes some of the performance results; more detail appears in Sandholm et al. 2005.

So far in the literature, the performance of winner determination algorithms has been evaluated on problem instances generated randomly from a variety of distributions (Sandholm 2002a; Fujishima, Leyton-Brown, and Shoham 1999; Andersson, Tenhunen, and Ygge 2000), most of which strive to be realistic in terms of how many items package bids tend to include, and in terms of bid prices. In some of the distributions (such as the CATS distributions in Leyton-Brown, Pearson, and Shoham 2000; see also chapter 18 of this volume), the choice of items for each package bid is motivated by potential application domains.

On easier distributions (such as CATS and certain less structured distributions), optimal winner determination scales to hundreds or thousands of items, and tens of thousands of bids in seconds. On hard distributions (such as one where each package bid includes five randomly selected items and has price $1), optimal winner determination only scales to tens of items and hundreds of bids in a minute.

It is interesting to see how the state of the art general-purpose mixed integer program solvers, CPLEX and XPress-MP, fare against state of the art algorithms specifically designed for winner determination such as CABOB. All three use the branch-on-bids search formulation (but could be modified to use other formulations), and LP-based upper bounding. CPLEX and XPress-MP use cutting planes, whereas vanilla CABOB does not. None of the three use random restarts (except some versions of CABOB not compared here) or caching. CPLEX and XPress-MP only have general methods for deciding which variable to branch on, whereas CABOB uses custom schemes discussed above. CABOB has several techniques for identifying and solving tractable cases at search nodes; the other two use only the INTEGER case. CPLEX and XPress-MP use algebraic preprocessing, whereas CABOB only uses a domination check between bids. (Sandholm 2002a discusses sophisticated preprocessing techniques specifically for winner determination.)

CPLEX and XPress-MP often run out of memory on hard instances because their default strategy is best-bound search (with approximate child evaluation and diving bias). CABOB does not run out of memory due to its DFBnB search strategy.[21] The depth-first order and the tailored variable ordering heuristics also cause CABOB to have significantly better anytime performance than CPLEX. When measuring time to find the optimal solution and to prove its optimality, CPLEX tends to be somewhat faster on many random problem distributions, but CABOB is faster on other random problem distributions. On structured instances that are somewhat decomposable (even if they are not decomposable at the root of the search), CABOB is drastically faster than CPLEX due to its decomposition techniques, identifying and branching on articulation bids, and upper and lower bounding across components. XPress-MP tends to perform similarly to CPLEX.

On real-world winner determination problems—which usually have forms of expressiveness beyond package bids, such as side constraints from the bid taker and bidders, and price-quantity discount schedules—special-purpose search algorithms can be orders of magnitude faster than general-purpose solvers because there is more domain-specific knowledge that the former can capitalize on. Those problems also tend to lead to other important issues such as insufficient numeric stability of CPLEX and XPress-MP (telling whether a real number is an integer, equals another real, or exceeds another number), yielding incorrect answers in terms of feasibility and optimality. Simply tightening the tolerance parameters does not solve this: for certain purposes in those solvers the tolerances must be sufficiently loose.

Interestingly, Schuurmans, Southey, and Holte (2001) recently showed that optimal search algorithms perform favorably in speed on winner determination even against incomplete search algorithms such as stochastic local search (e.g., Hoos and Boutilier 2000) that do not generally find the optimal solution.

14.4 Substitutability and XOR-Constraints

The winner determination methods discussed so far in this chapter, and most other work on winner determination (e.g., Rothkopf, Pekeč, and Harstad 1998; Kwasnica et al. 2005), are based on a setting where any number of a bidder's package bids may get accepted. This is called the *OR bidding language WDP$_{OR}$* (in Lehmann, Müller and Sandholm, chapter 12 of this volume). It suffices when the items are *complementary*, that is, each bidder's valuation function is superadditive. However, when some of the items exhibit *substitutability* (valuations are subadditive), this language is insufficient. Say an agent bids $4 for an umbrella, $5 for a raincoat, and $7 for both. The auctioneer could allocate both to that agent separately, and claim that the agent's bid for the combination would value at $5 + $4 = $9 instead of $7.

This problem was addressed in the context of the *eMediator* Internet auction server prototype (see ⟨http://www.cs.cmu.edu/~amem/eMediator⟩), where the *XOR bidding language* was introduced (Sandholm 2002a, b) (*WDP$_{XOR}$* in Lehmann, Müller and Sandholm, chapter 12 of this volume). In effect, each bidder submits exclusive-or (XOR) constraints among all his package bids, so at most one can be accepted. This enables bidders to express general preferences (with complementarity and substitutability): any valuation function $v : 2^m \rightarrow \mathbb{R}$. For example, a bidder in a 4-item auction may submit the following:

$(\{1\}, \$4)$ XOR $(\{2\}, \$4)$ XOR $(\{3\}, \$2)$ XOR $(\{4\}, \$2)$ XOR

$(\{1, 2\}, \$8)$ XOR $(\{1, 3\}, \$6)$ XOR $(\{1, 4\}, \$6)$ XOR

$(\{2, 3\}, \$6)$ XOR $(\{2, 4\}, \$6)$ XOR $(\{3, 4\}, \$3)$ XOR

$(\{1, 2, 3\}, \$10)$ XOR $(\{1, 2, 4\}, \$10)$ XOR $(\{1, 3, 4\}, \$7)$ XOR

$(\{2, 3, 4\}, \$7)$ XOR $(\{1, 2, 3, 4\}, \$11)$.

Full expressiveness is important because it allows the bidders to express their valuations exactly, and winner determination uses that information to determine an optimal allocation of items. Without full expressiveness, economic efficiency is compromised. Full expressiveness is also important because it is a necessary and sufficient property of a bidding language for motivating truthful bidding (Sandholm 2002a, b). Without it, a bidder may not be able to express his preferences even if he wanted to. With it, the VCG mechanism can be used to make truthful bidding a dominant strategy. (Ausubel and Milgrom describe VCG in chapter 1 of this volume.) In the VCG, winners are determined once overall, and once per winning agent without any of that agent's bids. That makes fast winner determination even more crucial. Note that just removing one winning bid at a time would not constitute a truth-promoting mechanism, and truth promotion can also be lost if winner determination is conducted approximately (Sandholm 2002a, b).

Although the XOR bidding language is fully expressive, representing one's preferences in that language often requires a large number of package bids. To maintain full expressiveness, but at the same time to make the representation more concise, researchers introduced the *OR-of-XORs bidding language* (Sandholm 2002b). In this language, a set of bids can be combined with XOR, forming an *XOR-disjunct*. These XOR-disjuncts are then combined with nonexclusive ORs to represent independence. For example, a bidder who wants to submit the same offer as in the example above, can submit the following more concise expression:

$[(\{1\}, \$4)]$

OR

$[(\{2\}, \$4)]$

OR

$[(\{3\}, \$2) \text{ XOR } (\{4\}, \$2) \text{ XOR } (\{3, 4\}, \$3)].$

The XOR bidding language is a special case of the OR-of-XORs bidding language. Therefore, the shortest way to represent a value function in the OR-of-XORs bidding language is never longer than in the XOR bidding language.

Another fully expressive bidding language is the *OR* bidding language* (Nisan 2000): items are thought of as nodes in a graph, and exclusion edges (i.e., XOR-constraints) can be submitted between arbitrary pairs of nodes. An equivalent encoding is to use the OR bidding language, and have mutual exclusion between a pair of bids encoded by a dummy item that each bid in the pair includes (Fujishima, Leyton-Brown, and Shoham 1999). (However, the latter does not work if [some] bids can be accepted partially.) Nisan discusses bidding languages in detail in chapter 9 of this volume.

One can easily adapt search algorithms for winner determination to handle XOR-constraints between bids (Sandholm 2002a; Sandholm and Suri 2003), be it in the XOR bidding language, the OR-of-XORs language, or the OR* language. If two bids are in the same XOR-disjunct, and one of them is accepted on the search path, the other should not be accepted on that path. This is easy to accomplish. For example, if using the bid graph method, we simply add an extra edge into the graph for every pair of bids that is combined with XOR.

Constraints actually *reduce* the size of the search space. However, in practice they tend to make winner determination slower because many of the techniques (e.g., upper bounding) in the search algorithms do not work as well: a larger fraction of the search space ends up being searched. This is the case even when the upper bounding is improved by adding to the LP an extra constraint for each XOR-disjunct:

$\sum_{j\in D} x_j \leq 1$, where D is the set of bids within the XOR-disjunct. Furthermore, the technique that avoids branching on short bids does not apply with explicit XOR-constraints, nor does the technique for tree-structured items. If XOR-constraints are encoded using dummy items, those techniques apply, of course, but their effectiveness is compromised.

14.5 Conclusion

Optimal winner determination is important for economic efficiency and procedural fairness. Optimal winner determination, together with a fully expressive bidding language, is also needed to motivate truthful bidding. Although winner determination is NP-complete, modern tree search algorithms can provably optimally solve the problem in the large in practice. Therefore, CAs are now technologically feasible, and have started to be broadly fielded.

One practical issue in iterative CAs is that winners have to be determined multiple times (at the end of each "round," or in some designs even every time a new bid is submitted). In such settings, it is not desirable to solve winner determination anew every time. Instead, *incremental* algorithms use results from earlier winner determinations to speed up the current winner determination (Sandholm 2002a; Parkes and Ungar 2000; Kastner et al. 2002).

Another desideratum of an iterative CA is the ability to provide quotes: "What would I have to bid in order to win bundle S (assuming no further bids are submitted)?" Quotes are subtle in CAs because there generally are no accurate item prices (so bundles have to be priced), and as further bids are submitted, the quote on a given bundle can increase *or decrease* (Sandholm 2002a). Furthermore, computing a quote for a given bundle is NP-complete. Sandholm (2002a) presents algorithms for quote computation, incremental quote computation, and for computing upper and lower bounds on quotes.

Many of the techniques of this chapter apply to related and generalized combinatorial markets as well, such as CAs where there are multiple indistinguishable units of each item (Sandholm 2002b; Sandholm and Suri 2003; Leyton-Brown, Tennenholtz, and Shoham 2000; Gonen and Lehmann 2000; Lehmann and Gonen 2001; Sandholm et al. 2002), *combinatorial reverse auctions* (where there is one buyer who tries to fulfill his demand using combinatorial bids from multiple sellers) (Sandholm et al. 2002), and *combinatorial exchanges* (where there are multiple buyers and multiple sellers) (Sandholm 2002b; Sandholm and Suri 2003; Sandholm et al. 2002). Many of the techniques can also be generalized to capture reserve prices on items, on bundles, and with substitutability (Sandholm and Suri 2003). Many of them can also be used when there is no free disposal (Sandholm 2002a; Sandholm and Suri 2003), but winner determination becomes harder (Sandholm et al. 2002). Finally, the algorithms can be generalized to markets with side constraints (from buyers and/or sellers) and non-price attributes (Sandholm and Suri 2001; Davenport and Kalagnanam 2000). Interesting winner determination issues arise also in the setting where bids can be accepted fractionally (Kothari, Sandholm, and Suri 2003).

Acknowledgments

Parts of this research were funded by CombineNet, Inc., and parts by NSF CAREER Award IRI-9703122 and NSF grants IIS-9800994, ITR IIS-0081246, ITR IIS-0121678, and ITR IIS-0427858.

Notes

1. These algorithms inherit ideas from search algorithms for related problems such as weighted set packing, weighted maximum clique, and weighted independent set (e.g., Balas and Yu 1986; Babel and Tinhofer 1990; Babel 1991; Balas and Xue 1991; Nemhauser and Sigismondi 1992; Mannino and Sassano 1994; Balas and Xue 1996; Pardalos and Desai 1991; Loukakis and Tsouros 1983).

2. Search algorithms only construct those parts of the search space that are necessary to construct in light of the bids submitted. The method of enumerating exhaustive partitions of items and (at least the naïve execution of) the dynamic programming method—discussed by Lehmann, Müller and Sandholm in chapter 12—construct, in effect, the entire search space as if each combination of items had been bid on. That is drastically slower (except when the number of items is tiny).

3. The correct children can be found quickly using a secondary search in a binary trie data structure (Sandholm 2002a), or using binning techniques (Garfinkel and Nemhauser 1969; Fujishima, Leyton-Brown, and Shoham 1999). The latter approach requires items to be numbered statically, thus reducing the efficiency of item ordering heuristics (discussed later).

4. Due to limited time and effort of the bidders, the number of bids in all but the tiniest CAs is much smaller than the number of possible bundles in practice.

5. More generally, one could use any hyperplane—with (positive or negative) coefficients on the variables—as the branching question.

6. In principle, one could avoid such reconstruction by maintaining a copy of the data structures with each search node, but that usually causes the search to run out of memory rapidly, and is thus not done in state of the art mixed integer programming solvers.

7. There is no reason to use an f-limit that is higher than the highest value of f that was lower than the f-limit in the previous IDA* iteration. The 0.95 criterion was used to decrease the f-limit even more quickly. If it is decreased too rapidly, search time increases because the last iteration will have a large number of search nodes in DFBNB-WITH-F-LIMIT. If it is decreased too slowly, search time increases because each iteration repeats a large portion of the search from the previous iteration.

8. The bid graph can be constructed incrementally as bids are submitted.

9. The bid graph can be prohibitively large to store if the problem is huge. One can address this by generating the graph explicitly only for those subtrees of the search tree where the graph is small (Sandholm et al. 2005).

10. Sandholm and Suri (2003) present data structures for representing the bid graph in a way that supports efficient removal and addition of a bid's neighbors (and the connecting edges). Atamtürk, Nemhauser, and Savelsbergh 2000 present efficient conflict graph data structures for cut generation.

11. Sandholm and Suri (2003) discuss fast ways of maintaining such upper bounds, and approximations of this heuristic appear in Fujishima, Leyton-Brown, and Shoham 1999.

12. CABOB does not make copies of the LP table. Instead, it incrementally deletes (reinserts) columns corresponding to the bids being deleted (reinserted) in the bid graph G as the search proceeds down a path (backtracks).

13. Due to upper and lower bounding across components (and due to updating of $\tilde{f}^*$), the order of tackling the components can potentially make a difference in speed.

14. In terms of ordering the answers to try for a given question (aka *value ordering*), the basic version of CABOB always tries the IN-branch first. The reason is that it tries to include good bids early so as to find good solutions early. This enables more pruning through upper bounding. It also improves the anytime performance. On the other hand, the most prominent general-purpose mixed integer program solvers, CPLEX and XPress-MP, (being variants of best-bound search) sometimes try the OUT-branch first. Future research could experiment with that in CABOB as well.

15. $\alpha = 0$ (selecting a bid that has highest price) gives too much preference to bids with many items. Such bids are likely to use up a large number of items, thus reducing significantly the revenue that can be collected from other bids. Conversely, it seems that $\alpha = 1$ (selecting a bid with the highest per-item price) gives too much preference to bids with few items. If there are two bids with close to equal per-item price, it would be better to choose a bid with a larger number of items so that the high per-item revenue could be obtained for many items. Experimentally, $\alpha \in [0.8, 1]$ yields fastest performance (Sandholm et al. 2005).

16. In the binary case (where bids have to be accepted entirely or not at all), individual items cannot generally be given prices (in a way that would motivate bidders to self-select packages so that the overall optimal allocation is achieved), but each y_i value from the continuous DUAL gives an upper bound on the price of item i. (The solution to DUAL is generally not unique.)

17. A similar numerator can be used for a different purpose in another technique called *column generation*, which is sometimes used in other search applications (Barnhart et al. 1998). It is best suited when the problem is so huge that not even a single LP fits in memory. CAs of that magnitude do not exist currently.

18. If the identification and solving using the special-purpose method is still slow, one could use it in selected search nodes only.

19. We define *short* in this way because the problem is $\mathcal{NP}$-complete already if three items per bid are allowed (Rothkopf, Pekeč, and Harstad 1998).

20. One could generalize the application of caching using the observation that an upper bound on a set of bids is also an upper bound on any subset of those bids (and a lower bound is also a lower bound on any superset).

21. CPLEX and XPress-MP also support DFBnB, but that option usually makes them slower.

References

Andersson, Arne, Mattias Tenhunen, and Fredrik Ygge (2000), "Integer Programming for Combinatorial Auction Winner Determination," in *Proceedings of the Fourth International Conference on Multi-Agent Systems*, 39–46.

Applegate, David, Robert Bixby, Vasek Chvátal, and William Cook (1994), "The Traveling Salesman Problem," Discussion paper, DIMACS.

Atamtürk, Alper, George Nemhauser, and Martin Savelsbergh (2000), "Conflict Graphs in Solving Integer Programming Problems," *European Journal of Operational Research*, 121, 40–55.

Babel, Luitpold (1991), "Finding Maximal Cliques in Arbitrary and Special Graphs," *Computing*, 46, 321–341.

Babel, Luitpold and Gottfried Tinhofer (1990), "A Branch and Bound Algorithm for the Maximum Weighted Clique Problem," *ZOR—Methods and Models of Operations Research*, 34, 207–217.

Balas, Egon and Jue Xue (1991), "Minimum Weighted Coloring of Triangulated Graphs, with Application to Maximum Weighted Vertex Packing and Clique Finding in Arbitrary Graphs," *SIAM Journal on Computing*, 20, 209–221.

Balas, Egon and Jue Xue (1996), "Weighted and Unweighted Maximum Clique Algorithms with Upper Bonds from Fractional Coloring," *Algorithmica*, 15, 397–412.

Balas, Egon and Chang Sung Yu (1986), "Finding a Maximum Clique in an Arbitrary Graph," *SIAM Journal on Computing*, 15, 1054–1068.

Barnhart, Cynthia, Ellis Johnson, George Nemhauser, Martin Savelsbergh, and Pamela Vance (1998), "Branch-and-Price: Column Generation for Solving Huge Integer Programs," *Operations Research*, 46, 316–329.

Boutilier, Craig (2002), "Solving Concisely Expressed Combinatorial Auction Problems," in *National Conference on Artificial Intelligence*, Edmonton, 359–366.

Conitzer, Vincent, Jonathan Derryberry, and Tuomas Sandholm (2004), "Combinatorial Auctions with Structured Item Graphs," in *National Conference on Artificial Intelligence*, San Jose, 212–218.

Danna, Emilie, Edward Rothberg, and Claude Le Pape (2005), "Exploring Relaxation Induced Neighborhoods to Improve MIP Solutions," *Mathematical Programming*, 102, 71–90.

Davenport, Andrew J. and Jayant R. Kalagnanam (2000), "Price Negotiations for Procurement of Direct Inputs," in *Proceedings of the IMS "Hot Topics" Workshop: Mathematical of the Internet: E-Auction and Markets*, 27–44.

de Vries, Sven and Rakesh V. Vohra (2003), "Combinatorial Auctions: A Survey," *INFORMS Journal on Computing*, 15, 284–309.

Dechter Rina and Judea Pearl (1985), "Generalized Best-First Search Strategies and the Optimality of A*," *Journal of the ACM*, 32, 505–536.

Edmonds, Jack (1965), "Maximum Matching and a Polyhedron with 0,1 Vertices," *Journal of Research of the National Bureau of Standards*, B, 125–130.

Fischetti, Matteo and Andrea Lodi (2002), "Local Branching," *Mathematical Programming*, 98, 23–47.

Fujishima, Yuzo, Kevin Leyton-Brown, and Yoav Shoham (1999), "Taming the Computational Complexity of Combinatorial Auctions: Optimal and Approximate Approaches," in *Proceedings of the IJCAI'99*, 548–553.

Garfinkel, Robert and George Nemhauser (1969), "The Set Partitioning Problem: Set Covering with Equality Constraints," *Operations Research*, 17, 848–856.

Gilpin, Andrew and Tuomas Sandholm (2004), "Information-Theoretic Approaches to Branching in Search," Mimeo.

Gomes, Carla, Bart Selman, and Henry Kautz (1998), "Boosting Combinatorial Search Through Randomization," in *National Conference on Artificial Intelligence*, Madison, 431–437.

Gonen, Rica and Daniel Lehmann (2000), "Optimal Solutions for Multi-Unit Combinatorial Auctions: Branch and Bound Heuristics," in *ACM Conference on Electronic Commerce*, 13–20.

Hart, Peter, Nils Nilsson, and Bertram Raphael (1968), "A Formal Basis for the Heuristic Determination of Minimum Cost Paths," *IEEE Transactions on Systems Science and Cybernetics*, 4, 100–107.

Hoffman, Karla and Manfred Padberg (1993), "Solving Airline Crew-Scheduling Problems by Branch-and-Cut," *Management Science*, 39, 657–682.

Hoos, Holger H. and Craig Boutilier (2000), "Solving Combinatorial Auctions using Stochastic Local Search," in *Proceedings of the 17th National Conference on Artificial Intelligence*, 22–29.

Kastner, Ryan, Christina Hsieh, Miodrag Potkonjak, and Majid Sarrafzadeh (2002), "On the Sensitivity of Incremental Algorithms for Combinatorial Auctions," in *IEEE Workshop on Advanced Issues of E-Commerce and Web-Based Information Systems*, 81–88.

Korf, Richard (1985), "Depth-First Iterative-Deepening: An Optimal Admissible Tree Search," *Artificial Intelligence*, 27, 97–109.

Korf, Richard (1993), "Linear-Space Best-First Search," *Artificial Intelligence*, 62, 41–78.

Kothari, Anshul, Tuomas Sandholm, and Subhash Suri (2003), "Solving Combinatorial Exchanges: Optimality via a Few Partial Bids," in *Proceedings of the ACM Conference on Electronic Commerce (ACM-EC)*, 236–237.

Kwasnica, Anthony M., John O. Ledyard, Dave Porter, and Christine DeMartini (2005), "A New and Improved Design for Multiobject Iterative Auctions," *Management Science*, 51, 419–434.

Lehmann, Daniel and Rica Gonen (2001), "Linear Programming Helps Solving Large Multi-Unit Combinatorial Auction," Mimeo, Leibniz Center for Research in Computer Science, Hebrew University.

Leyton-Brown, Kevin (2003), "Resource Allocation in Competitive Multiagent Systems," Ph.D. thesis, Stanford University.

Leyton-Brown, Kevin, Mark Pearson, and Yoav Shoham (2000), "Towards a Universal Test Suite for Combinatorial Auction Algorithms," in *ACM Conference on Electronic Commerce*, 66–76.

Leyton-Brown, Kevin, Moshe Tennenholtz, and Yoav Shoham (2000), "An Algorithm for Multi-Unit Combinatorial Auctions," in *National Conference on Artificial Intelligence*, 52–61.

Loukakis, Emmanuel and Constantine Tsouros (1983), "An Algorithm for the Maximum Internally Stable Set in a Weighted Graph," *International Journal of Computer Mathematics*, 13, 117–129.

Mannino, Carlo and Antonio Sassano (1994), "An Exact Algorithm for the Maximum Stable Set Problem," *Computational Optimization and Application*, 3, 242–258.

Nemhauser, George and Gabriele Sigismondi (1992), "A Strong Cutting Plane/Branch-and-Bound Algorithm for Node Packing," *Journal of the Operational Research Society*, 43, 443–457.

Nemhauser, George and Laurence Wolsey (1999), *Integer and Combinatorial Optimization*, New York: John Wiley & Sons.

Nisan, Noam (2000), "Bidding and Allocation in Combinatorial Auctions," in *Proceedings of the 2nd ACM Conference on Electronic Commerce*, 1–12.

Pardalos, Panos and Nisha Desai (1991), "An Algorithm for Finding a Maximum Weighted Independent Set in an Arbitrary Graph," *International Journal of Computer Mathematics*, 38, 163–175.

Parkes, David C. and Lyle H. Ungar (2000), "Iterative Combinatorial Auctions: Theory and Practice," in *Proceedings of the 17th National Conference on Artificial Intelligence*, 74–81.

Rothkopf, Michael, H. Aleksandar Pekeč, and Ronald M. Harstad (1998), "Computationally Manageable Combinational Auctions," *Management Science*, 44, 1131–1147.

Russell, Stuart (1992), "Efficient Memory-Bounded Search Methods," in *European Conference on Artificial Intelligence*, Vienna, 1–5.

Russell, Stuart and Peter Norvig (1995), *Artificial Intelligence: A Modern Approach*, New York: Prentice Hall.

Sandholm, Tuomas (2002a), "Algorithm for Optimal Winner Determination in Combinatorial Auctions," *Artificial Intelligence*, 135, 1–54.

Sandholm, Tuomas (2002b), "eMediator: A Next Generation Electronic Commerce Server," *Computational Intelligence*, 18, 656–676.

Sandholm, Tuomas and Subhash Suri (2001), "Side Constraints and Non-Price Attributes in Markets," in *Proceedings of the IJCAI-2001 Workshop on Distributed Constraint Reasoning*, 55–61. To appear in *Games and Economic Behavior*.

Sandholm, Tuomas and Subhash Suri (2003), "BOB: Improved Winner Determination in Combinatorial Auctions and Generalizations," *Artificial Intelligence*, 145, 33–58.

Sandholm, Tuomas, Subhash Suri, Andrew Gilpin, and David Levine (2005), "CABOB: A Fast Optimal Algorithm for Winner Determination in Combinatorial Auctions," *Management Science*, 51, 374–390.

Sandholm, Tuomas, Subhash Suri, Andrew Gilpin, and David Levine (2002), "Winner Determination in Combinatorial Auction Generalizations," in *Proceedings of the International Conference on Autonomous Agents and Multi-Agent Systems*, 69–76.

Schuurmans, Dale, Finnegan Southey, and Robert C. Holte (2001), "The Exponentiated Subgradient Algorithm for Heuristic Boolean Programming," in *International Joint Conference on Artificial Intelligence*, 334–341.

van Hoesel, Stan and Rudolf Müller (2001), "Optimization in Electronic Marketplaces: Examples from Combinatorial Auctions," *Netnomics*, 3, 23–33.

Wolsey, Laurence (1998), *Integer Programming*, New York: John Wiley & Sons.

15 Incentive Compatibility in Computationally Feasible Combinatorial Auctions

Amir Ronen

15.1 Introduction

A major achievement of mechanism design theory is the VCG method for the construction of incentive compatible mechanisms. The method is general and thus applicable to many variants of combinatorial auctions. VCG mechanisms are economically efficient, very simple from the agents' perspective, individually rational, and, above all, incentive compatible in dominant strategies. To date, (weighted) VCG is the only known general method for the construction of mechanisms that are incentive compatible in dominant strategies. For certain classes of problems, VCG is provably the sole available method (Roberts 1979; Lavi, Mualem, and Nisan 2003; Green and Laffont 1977). Ausubel and Milgrom (chapter 1 of this volume) discuss the pros and cons of VCG mechanisms.

Unfortunately, VCG mechanisms are computationally infeasible. Consider a combinatorial auction (CA) of m items. A VCG mechanism requires each agent to report his valuation function to the auctioneer. Based on these declarations, the auctioneer computes the optimal allocation and the payment due to each agent. This mechanism is clearly intractable. First, winner determination is very hard to compute (Lehmann, Müller, and Sandholm, chapter 12 of this volume). Second, the valuation of each agent consists of $2^m - 1$ values. Therefore, even approximating the optimal allocation requires an exponential amount of communication (Segal, chapter 11 of this volume).

One possible approach to handling these computational problems is to look for natural assumptions under which the optimal welfare can be found or at least approximated by incentive compatible, polynomial time mechanisms. Section 15.7 describes several sophisticated non-VCG approximation mechanisms for restricted CAs. It focuses on two major cases: CAs in which a large number of copies of each item are available and CAs where each agent is only interested in a specific subset of the items.

Another natural approach to the intractability of VCG mechanisms is to modify them in the following way: 1) Replace the optimal exponential allocation algorithm with a suboptimal but polynomial one. 2) Let the agents use a bidding language for the description of their valuations (see Nisan, chapter 9 of this volume, for an extensive discussion). Note that no matter what bidding language one uses, there are always valuations that cannot be communicated in feasible time. We term such a modified mechanism *non-optimal VCG*.

Most of this chapter is devoted to the study of the game theoretic properties of non-optimal VCG mechanisms. It contains both bad and good news. On the bad side, it shows that in general, non-optimal VCG mechanisms are neither individually rational nor incentive compatible. These are severe problems. Without individual rationality, the participants in a CA may lose large amounts of money. The loss of incentive compatibility is likely to lead to poor economic efficiency due to agents' manipulations. On the bright side, this chapter offers a general method for overcoming these bad phenomena. This method is called *second chance*. Second chance mechanisms are modifications of VCG mechanisms, in which the agents are allowed accurately to describe their valuations by oracles, and are given the chance to improve the result of the allocation algorithm. We show that under reasonable assumptions *the* rational strategy for the agents is faithfully to follow the auctioneer's instructions. When the agents do so, the allocation that the mechanism outputs is *at least as good* as the allocation that the algorithm computes. Second chance mechanisms satisfy individual rationality as well. The method is very general. It is not limited to CAs and can be applied whenever VCG, weighted VCG (Roberts 1979), or compensation and bonus (Nisan and Ronen 2000) mechanisms are applicable.

We should stress that all mechanisms presented in this chapter are aimed to maximize the total *welfare* of the agents, not the revenue of the auctioneer. Currently, not much is known about revenue maximization in CAs. Note that second chance mechanisms have not yet been tested on real environments.

This chapter is primarily an exposition of the following papers: Nisan and Ronen 2001; Ronen 2001; Archer et al. 2003; Bartal, Gonen, and Nisan 2003; Lehmann, O'Callaghan, and Shoham 2002; and Mu'alem and Nisan 2002. Most of the technical details have been sacrificed for clarity. The interested reader is pointed to the original papers.

Section 15.2 describes the basic notions of this chapter. Section 15.3 studies VCG mechanisms with limited computation but unlimited communication. Section 15.4 introduces the second chance mechanism. Effects of limited communications are studied in Section 15.5. Sections 15.6 and 15.7 briefly discuss alternative approaches to the design of computationally feasible mechanisms for CAs. In particular, it describes several truthful non-VCG approximation mechanisms for restricted CAs. The chapter concludes in section 15.8.

15.2   Basic Definitions

For completeness we briefly describe some basic notions and terms. The introduction to this book describes most of these notions.

A mechanism is called *incentive compatible* (in dominant strategies) if each agent has a weakly dominant strategy. In a revelation mechanism, the agents are simply required to declare their valuations. Such a mechanism is called *truthful* if truth telling is a dominant strategy equilibrium. A simple argument known as the revelation principle shows that for each incentive compatible mechanism there exists a truthful equivalent mechanism. Therefore, we treat these two terms as synonyms. A truthful mechanism is called *individually rational* if the utility of a truthful agent is guaranteed to be nonnegative.

Unless otherwise stated, the phrase *combinatorial auction* (CA) refers to the following variant of the problem. The valuations of the agents are privately known to them; there are no externalities, that is, the valuation of each agent depends only on his own bundle, free disposal is assumed, and the valuation of the empty set is assumed to be 0. Agents' utilities are quasi-linear; that is, for each agent i, $u_i(x, p_i) = v_i(x) + p_i$ (x denotes the chosen outcome and p_i the payment of agent i). Normally, p_i is nonpositive, meaning that the agents pay the auctioneer and not vice versa.

Throughout this chapter we use the following vector notation. We denote the tuple $(v_1, \ldots, v_{i-1}, v_{i+1}, \ldots, v_n)$ by v_{-i}. We let (v_i, v_{-i}) denote the tuple $(v_1, \ldots, v_n)$.

15.3   Effects of Limited Computation

15.3.1   VCG with Non-Optimal Allocation Algorithms

The standard VCG method uses optimal but intractable allocation algorithms. In this section we generalize VCG to allow non-optimal allocations. We then demonstrate that the game theoretic virtues of VCG may be destroyed as a result of this non-optimality.

A *VCG-based mechanism* for combinatorial auctions is a protocol of the following form: each agent reports his valuation to the auctioneer; let $k(.)$ denote an allocation algorithm, not necessarily optimal, and let $w = (w_1, \ldots, w_n)$ denote the vector of the agents' declarations. Based on these declarations, the mechanism computes the allocation $k(w)$ and the payment $p_i(w)$ of each agent. The payment of each agent i is the sum of the welfare of the *other* agents and any function $h_i(w_{-i})$, which is independent of the agent's declaration. Formally, $p_i(w) = \sum_{j \neq i} w_j(k(w)) + h_i(w_{-i})$. When the allocation algorithm $k(.)$ is optimal, this definition coincides with the standard VCG mechanism. Note that the payment functions depend on the allocation algorithm. Different algorithms yield different payment functions.

The idea behind the VCG method is to identify the utility of a truthful agent with the declared total welfare. The following equation gives the utility of each agent i:

$$u_i(w) = v_i(k(w)) + \sum_{j \neq i} w_j(k(w)) + h_i(w_{-i}). \tag{15.1}$$

This is exactly the total welfare of the allocation $k(w)$ according to the *actual* valuation of agent i and the reported valuation of the others (plus $h_i(.)$, which is independent of agent i's declaration). Let $w[i]$ denote the vector (v_i, w_{-i}). Suppose that $k(w[i])$ is optimal w.r.t. $w[i]$. When agent i is truthful, the input to the allocation algorithm is $w[i]$ and it computes an allocation $k(w[i])$ that maximizes the total welfare according to it. Lying to the algorithm can only cause the algorithm to compute an inferior allocation (w.r.t. $w[i]$), decreasing the agent's own utility.

Alternatively, suppose that $w[i]$ is a vector of valuations such that $k(w[i])$ is non-optimal. It is likely that there exists a nontruthful declaration $w_i \neq v_i$ which causes the algorithm to compute a better allocation (in terms of $w[i]$). As we shall see, non-optimal algorithms indeed yield nonincentive compatible mechanisms.

A VCG mechanism of particular note is that of Clarke. In this mechanism, the payment of each agent i equals the loss of welfare that he causes to the other agents. Let v_i^0 denote a valuation that is always zero. We call a VCG-based mechanism *Clarke-based* if agent i's payment $p_i(w)$ equals $\sum_{j \neq i} w_j(k(w)) - \sum_{j \neq i} w_j(k((w_{-i}, v_i^0)))$. In other words, the payment of each agent is the damage it causes to the welfare of the others. When $k(.)$ is optimal this mechanism coincides with Clarke's mechanism. In addition to incentive compatibility, Clarke's mechanism satisfies individual rationality. Both properties might break down when one uses a non-optimal algorithm.

In order to illustrate potential problems of non-optimal VCG-based mechanisms, consider a CA with two items, A and B, and two agents, Alice and Bob. Table 15.1 describes the valuations of the agents. The standard Clarke mechanism will allocate both items to Bob for the price of $300. Let $k(.)$ be an allocation algorithm that greedily allocates item A to the agent who values it most, and then allocates item B similarly. Consider Clarke's mechanism, which is based on $k(.)$. This mechanism will allocate both items to Alice for the price of $400, causing her a disutility of $100! By declaring a zero valuation, Alice can increase her utility to $0. Thus, the mechanism satisfies neither incentive compatibility nor individual rationality.

Table 15.1
Two agents and two items

	A	B	A,B
Alice	150	150	300
Bob	100	100	400

15.3.2 Characterization of Incentive Compatible Non-Optimal VCG-Based Mechanisms

In light of the example in the previous section, we would like to characterize the class of incentive compatible VCG-based mechanisms. One method for the construction of such mechanisms is to limit the set of allocations that the algorithm can output (its range), and always to choose a welfare-maximizing allocation from this range. For example, the algorithm can bundle all the items together and give the bundle to the agent who has the highest declared value for it. We call such an algorithm *optimal in its range*. Nisan and Ronen (2000) show that, except perhaps for a zero measured subspace of the valuation functions, any incentive compatible VCG-based mechanism for combinatorial auctions is optimal in its range. In particular, for every such mechanism, there exists an equivalent mechanism that is optimal in its range on the whole space of valuation functions. Formally:

Theorem 15.1 (k, p) is an incentive compatible VCG-based mechanism for combinatorial auctions if and only if there exists an allocation algorithm $\tilde{k}$, optimal in its range, such that for every vector v of valuation functions, $\sum_i v_i(k(v)) = \sum_i v_i(\tilde{k}(v))$.

In other words, every incentive compatible VCG-based mechanism is equivalent to a VCG-based mechanism in which the allocation algorithm is optimal in its range. Currently, it is not known whether a similar theorem holds for other mechanism design problems. (Nisan and Ronen, 2000, showed a different and much worse phenomenon for cost minimization problems.) In particular, if the valuation functions are known to be bounded, then the existence of incentive compatible VCG-based mechanisms that are not optimal in their range has not yet been ruled out. A corollary from theorem 15.1 is that incentive compatible VCG-based mechanisms suffer from the following anomaly. There exist situations where only one agent desires an item but this agent does not receive it. This abnormal behavior might cause agent dissatisfaction. A more severe problem is that standard algorithmic techniques (e.g., greedy methods, LP relaxation) do not yield this anomaly. Thus, it might be difficult to develop allocation algorithms that can be plugged into incentive compatible VCG-based mechanisms.

Researchers have not yet studied agents' behavior in non-optimal VCG-based mechanisms. It is conceivable that the agents will still behave truthfully, in particular when the allocation algorithm is not too far from optimal.

15.4 The Second Chance Mechanism

To date, VCG is the only general method available for the construction of incentive compatible mechanisms. Thus, the results of the previous section do not leave much hope for the construction of polynomial time, truthful mechanisms for CAs. The goal of this section is to develop mechanisms that are "almost" incentive compatible.

Given any algorithm for the WDP, we define the *second chance* mechanism based on it. This mechanism is a modification of the VCG-based mechanism where, in addition to their type declarations, the agents are allowed to submit appeal functions. An appeal function gives the agent an opportunity to express his knowledge of the underlying allocation algorithm. We show that, under reasonable assumptions, truth telling is *the* rational strategy for the agents. When the agents are truthful, the allocation computed by the mechanism is at least as good as the one computed by the algorithm. Subsections 15.4.1 and 15.4.2 describe the second chance mechanism. Subsection 15.4.3 explains the rationale for truth telling.

15.4.1 The Idea behind the Mechanism

Consider a non-optimal VCG-based mechanism. Let us examine carefully when lying to the mechanism can be beneficial for an agent. Consider equation 15.1. Let $w[i]$ denote the vector (v_i, w_{-i}) obtained from the actual valuation of agent i and the declared valuation of the other agents. When agent i is truthful, his utility (ignoring $h_i(.)$) equals the total welfare of the allocation $k(w[i])$ measured according to $w[i]$. When he lies, he may cause the algorithm to produce another allocation $k(w)$. His utility will be the welfare of $k(w)$ measured with respect to the *same* vector $w[i]$. Therefore, the only reason for the agent to lie to the mechanism is to *help* the algorithm to compute a better allocation. Therefore, if the agent does not know how to improve the results of the underlying algorithm, he can do no better than being truthful!

Our goal is to devise an algorithm with the property that no agent knows how to improve upon it. In a mechanism that is based on such an algorithm, the agents will not have an incentive to lie. To achieve this we let the agents merge their knowledge of the algorithm into it, by using appeal functions. Instead of declaring a falsified valuation, the appeals give the agents the opportunity of asking the mechanism to check whether this falsified declaration would cause the algorithm to compute a better allocation. In this case, the algorithm will use the falsified declaration. When such a lie decreases the total welfare, the mechanism will simply ignore it. In what follows we formalize the mechanism, provide examples, and explain the rationale for truth telling.

15.4.2 The Mechanism

In this subsection we define the second chance mechanism. We start with the definition of an appeal function.

Definition 1 (appeal function) Let $V = \prod_i V_i$ denote the type space of the agents. An *appeal* is a partial function $l : V \to V$.

Declaration Each agent sends a type declaration w_i and an appeal function l_i to the mechanism.

Allocation Let $w = (w_1, \ldots, w_n)$. The mechanism computes $k(w), k(l_1(w)), \ldots, k(l_n(w))$ and chooses among these outputs the one that maximizes the total welfare (according to w).

Payment Let $\hat{o}$ denote the chosen output. The mechanism calculates the payments according to the VCG formula: $p_i = \Sigma_{j \neq i} w_j(\hat{o}) + h_i(w_{-i}, l_{-i})$ (where $h_i(.)$ is any real function).

Figure 15.1
The second chance mechanism.

The semantics of an appeal l is: "When the agents' type is $v = (v_1, \ldots, v_n)$, I believe that the output algorithm $k(.)$ produces a better result (w.r.t. v) if it is given the input $l(v)$ instead of the actual input v." The next subsection discusses the actual representation of the appeals.

Figure 15.1 defines the second chance mechanism. It is a modification of VCG in which the agents are allowed to submit appeal functions as well.

A strategy in a second chance mechanism consists of both a type declaration w_i and an appeal function $l_i(.)$. A strategy is called *truthful* if the agent declares his actual valuation, that is, $w_i(.) = v_i(.)$. When the agents are truthful, the chosen allocation $\hat{o}$ is *at least as good* as the allocation $k(v)$ that the algorithm computes. In addition, when the running time of both the algorithm and the appeal functions is limited to a constant T, the overall running time is bounded by $O(n \cdot T)$. In subsection 15.4.3 we justify why, under a reasonable time limit T, truth telling is *the* rational strategy for the agents.

Representing the Appeal Functions An implementation of the second chance mechanism relies on tools that will help the agents conveniently to represent their appeal functions. Such tools must also limit the computation time of the appeals. Although such "engineering" issues are outside the scope of this chapter, some comments are in order.

One way of implementing the concept of appeal functions is simply to let the agents compute their appeals by themselves and send the results to the mechanism in a second round. The drawback of this method is that the valuation of each agent is revealed to all the others. This is undesirable for many applications. Another natural implementation is to supply the agents with a language for the description of their appeals and to perform the computation on the mechanism's machine.

In both methods it is not difficult to impose a time limit on the agents or to ask them to pay for additional computational time. However, an arbitrary time limit may prevent the existence of feasible dominant actions (see section 15.4.3).

An interesting direction is to represent the appeal functions in a way that will force them to reflect the agents' knowledge. One such possible representation is a decision tree where the agents are required to supply for each leaf α, a vector of valuations t_α, such that the algorithm's result is improved when it is given $l(t_\alpha)$ instead of the actual input t_α. In other words, each leaf in the decision tree must come with an example demonstrating that the input manipulation suggested in this leaf is indeed justified. Such a method enables each agent to get exactly the amount of computation he needs in order to represent his knowledge—not too small, but also not unjustifiably high.

Obtaining Individual Rationality   A basic desirable property of our mechanism is that the utility of a truthful agent is guaranteed to be nonnegative. In order to satisfy this property we construct the functions $h_i(.)$ similarly to Clarke's mechanism. Because our allocation algorithm is not optimal, this construction has to be done with care.

Definition 15.2   Given an allocation algorithm $k(w)$, we define its *low type closure* $\tilde{k}$ as the best (according to w) among the allocations $k(w), k(v_1^0, (w_{-1})), \ldots, k(v_n^0, (w_{-n}))$. ($v_i^0$ denotes the zero type of agent i.)

In other words, the result of $\tilde{k}$ is at least as good as the result of every invocation of $k(.)$, which excludes one of the agents.

If the allocation algorithm is polynomial, then so is its low type closure. Clarke's version of the second chance mechanism uses a low type closure as its allocation algorithm. The payment function is defined as $p_i = \sum_{j \neq i} w_j(\tilde{k}(w)) - \sum_{j \neq i} w_j(k((w_{-i}, v_i^0)))$. The utility of a truthful agent is therefore $u_i = \sum_j w_j(\tilde{k}(w)) - \sum_{j \neq i} w_j(k((w_{-i}, v_i^0)))$. Because the welfare obtained by $\tilde{k}(w)$ is at least the welfare that is obtained by $k(w_{-i}, v_i^0)$, the utility of a truthful agent is nonnegative.

A Note about the Agents' Payment   The main goal of VCG mechanisms is to obtain economic efficiency. However, for most applications, the revenue of the mechanism is of great importance. In general, little is currently known about the payment properties of mechanisms for CAs. In general, inefficiency results in low revenue because the total welfare is an upper bound on the possible revenue. The converse is not true, and the payment properties, even of VCG, are yet to be explored. (Interesting anomalies of

VCG and incentive compatible mechanisms in general appear in Archer and Tardos 2002, and Elkind, Sahai, and Steiglitz 2004.)

It is important to note that non-optimal VCG-based mechanisms might suffer from payment anomalies. In particular, a VCG-based mechanism for CA may result in negative payment. This means that the auctioneer might end up paying the agent instead of the reverse. Technically, it may be that $p_i = \sum_{j \neq i} w_j(\tilde{k}(w)) - \sum_{j \neq i} w_j(k((w_{-i}, v_i^0)))$ > 0. Second chance mechanisms suffer from the same anomaly.

We believe that, in practice, one can easily avoid these anomalies. One approach is simply to rule them out. Another is to prevent them by using reserve prices. The effect of such heuristics has not yet been studied.

An Example In order to demonstrate the second chance mechanism, consider the example in section 15.3.1. The example's VCG-based mechanism allocates both items to Alice. Bob's utility is, therefore, $0. Bob can guess that because his utility is superadditive, he might be better off declaring a higher valuation, say $160, on each item. This way, Bob will win both items for the price of $300, obtaining a utility of $100. However, such a declaration puts Bob at risk. If Alice's value for one of the items is higher than his, Bob will get only one item for the price of $150. This will cause Bob a disutility of $50. A similar problem exists in the simultaneous ascending auction (see Cramton, chapter 4 of this volume). The second chance mechanism prevents this problem. Instead of lying, Bob can ask the mechanism to *check* whether declaring a valuation of, say, $\{160, 160, 320\}$ would cause the algorithm to compute a better result. In our example, this appeal causes Bob to get both items for the price of $300, as in optimal VCG. In other cases in which this declaration does not improve the allocation, the mechanism will simply ignore it. In these cases, the damage to both the total welfare and Bob's own utility is prevented. In fact, Bob is not limited to modifying his own declaration, but can modify Alice's as well. This gives Bob the power to express all his knowledge of the algorithm in his appeal function.

15.4.3 The Rationale for Truth Telling

As in VCG, the utility of an agent is identified with the overall welfare. Unlike VCG, we claim that truth telling is *the* rational strategy for the agents. The rationale is that whenever the agent is *aware* of circumstances in which a falsified declaration is beneficial for him, he has the option of asking his appeal function to *check* this falsified declaration. In a second chance mechanism, an agent can always lose because of a falsified declaration. The reason is twofold. First, such a declaration may mislead the allocation algorithm. Second, it might cause the mechanism to prefer the wrong allocation when comparing between the outputs of the various appeals. Therefore, the agent is better off declaring his true valuation and expressing his algorithmic knowledge via his appeal function. In the following sections we formalize the above rationale. We introduce a notion of *feasible dominance* that captures the limitation on agents imposed by their own computational limits. We then show that under reasonable assumptions about the agents, truth telling is indeed feasibly dominant.

Feasibly Dominant Actions   The basic models of equilibria in game theory are justified by the implicit assumption that the agents are capable of computing their best response functions. In many natural games, however, the action space is huge and this function is too complex to be computed, even approximately, within a reasonable amount of time. In such situations the above assumption seems no longer valid.

In this section we re-formulate the concept of dominant actions (strategies) under the assumption that agents have a limited capability of computing their best response. Our concept is meant to be used in the context of revelation games. We assume that each of the agents chooses his action according to some *knowledge* he has at the beginning of the game. We define an action to be feasibly dominant if, when the agent has chosen his action, he was not *aware* of *any* circumstances where another action is better for him.

An action in the second chance mechanism is a valuation declaration and an appeal function. We denote the space of possible actions for each agent i by A_i.

We now define the concept of strategic knowledge in a game. Knowledge is a function by which the agent describes (for himself) how he would like to respond to any given situation.

Definition 15.3 (strategic knowledge)   *Strategic knowledge* (or *knowledge* for short) of agent i is a partial function $b_i : A_{-i} \rightarrow A_i$.

The semantics of $a_i = b_i(a_{-i})$ is "when the others' actions are a_{-i}, the best action I can think of is a_i." Naturally we assume that each agent is capable of computing his own knowledge and, henceforth, that b_i can be computed in a reasonable amount of time.

We now define the concept of a feasible best response. This is a generalization of the classical notion of best response.

Definition 15.4 (feasible best response)   An action a_i for agent i is called a *feasible best response* to a_{-i} w.r.t. $b_i(.)$ if either a_{-i} is not in the domain of the agent's knowledge $b_i(.)$ or $u_i((b_i(a_{-i}), a_{-i})) \leq u_i(a)$.

In other words, a_i is a feasible best response to the actions of the other agents, if agent i does not know how to respond better to the others' actions. Note that when the agent's knowledge $b_i(.)$ is optimal, this definition coincides with the standard one.

Note also that if a_{-i} is not in the domain of b_i, then any action a_i is a feasible best response to it.

The definition of feasibly dominant actions now follows naturally.

Definition 15.5 (feasibly dominant action)   An action a_i for agent i is called *feasibly dominant* if it is a feasible best response to any a_{-i}.

An agent who has a feasibly dominant action is not aware of any circumstances where he can do better against the strategies of the others. The paper argues that when such a strategy is available, this is *the* rational choice for the agent.

We will call the second chance mechanism *feasibly truthful* if there exist truthful actions for the agents that are feasibly dominant.

Let us reconsider the toy example in the previous section. Suppose that all Bob notices is that there are cases in which it is good for him to raise his price for single items by 10 percent. Instead of lying to the mechanism, Bob can report his true type and ask his appeal to check whether this manipulation is beneficial. Because this is the only phenomenon Bob has detected, this strategy is feasibly truthful for him. In other words, Bob is not aware of any circumstances in which it is beneficial for him to choose another strategy. Therefore, he does not have any reason to lie to the mechanism.

When Is the Mechanism Feasibly Truthful?   When the agents are allowed to use unlimited computation, they can submit optimal appeals. An optimal appeal causes the mechanism to be optimal in its range. Therefore, with unlimited time, the agents have dominant strategies. In reality, of course, the computational time of the appeals must be limited. In this case, theorem 15.1 implies that the existence of feasibly truthful strategies *must* depend on the type of knowledge that the agents have.

Nisan and Ronen (2000) describe three classes of knowledge under which truth telling is feasibly dominant for the agents. This section describes only the most basic class: appeal independent knowledge. Appeal independent knowledge does not consider the appeals of the other agents. Its semantics are: "When the others declare w_{-i}, I would like to declare w_i and submit an appeal $l_i(.)$." Formally:

Definition 15.6 (appeal independent knowledge)   Knowledge $b_i(.)$ is called *appeal independent* if it is of the form $b_i : W_{-i} \rightarrow A_i$.

Nisan and Ronen claim that in practice, the knowledge of the agents is likely to be appeal independent. The reason is that the space of appeals of the other agents is so huge and complex that it is not reasonable to expect any single agent to have significant knowledge of it. This claim has not yet been verified experimentally.

If $b_i(.)$ is appeal independent knowledge, it naturally defines an appeal function $l(.)$ of similar complexity. Nisan and Ronen (2000) show that the (truthful) action $(v_i(.), l_i(.))$ is feasibly dominant. Consider the case where the agents have appeal independent knowledge. Let $\bar{T}$ be a bound on the computational time of the agents' knowledge functions. If the agents' appeals are allowed to use at least $\bar{T}$ units of time, the resulting second chance mechanism is feasibly truthful. An alternative approach, discussed in the paper, is to enforce the appeals to represent the agents' knowledge of the algorithm. In this way the computational time of the mechanism is bounded by the computational limitations of the agents. Again, the resulting mechanism is feasibly truthful. A more general form of knowledge discussed in the paper is knowledge obtained by exploring not only the allocation algorithm but a polynomial size family of appeals for the other agents.

15.5 Effects of Limited Communication

15.5.1 VCG with Incomplete Bidding Languages

The standard VCG method relies on the agents' ability fully to describe their valuation function to the mechanism. Unfortunately, for CAs, a full description of the valuation requires exponential time and space and is therefore infeasible. In this section we reformulate VCG to allow the agents to communicate their valuations via a bidding language. Unfortunately, no matter what language we use, there are always valuations that cannot be communicated in polynomial time. Because in reality the communication must be limited (implicitly or explicitly), we call such languages *incomplete*. We demonstrate that both the individual rationality and the incentive compatibility of standard VCG may be destroyed as a consequence of this lack of communication.

A bidding language is any language by which the agents can describe their valuations. We distinguish between an actual valuation $v_i(.)$ and its description d_i. In order for d_i to be meaningful in the context of VCG, the mechanism must assign a valuation function $\hat{w}_i(.) = \hat{w}_i(d_i)$ to it. When the agents are limited to polynomial communication, there are valuations that cannot be described. In other words, $v_i(.) \neq \hat{w}_i(d_i)$ for any feasible description d_i.

A VCG-based mechanism with a bidding language L may be described as follows. Each agent describes his valuation to the mechanism; let $d_i \in L$ denote agent i's declaration, and let $d = (d_1, \ldots, d_n)$. The mechanism computes the allocation $k(d)$ and the payment $p_i(d)$ of each agent. The payment is computed according to the VCG formula. Formally, $p_i(d) = \sum_{j \neq i} \hat{w}_j(k(d)) + h_i(d_{-i})$. Let v_i^0 denote the zero valuation. Clarke's mechanism is obtained by defining $h_i(.)$ to be $-\sum_{j \neq i} \hat{w}_j(k((d_{-i}, v_i^0)))$; that is, the negation of the total welfare when no item is allocated to agent i. The allocation algorithm $k(.)$ can be any algorithm, not necessarily optimal. We say that a VCG mechanism with a bidding language is *incentive compatible* if the agents have dominant strategies $d_i(v_i)$.

Example: VCG with OR Bids We now demonstrate the problems that may occur as a result of the agents' inability to communicate their valuations.

Let S denote the auctioned set of items. We define an *atomic bid* to be a pair (s, p) where $s \subseteq S$ is a set of items and p is a price. The semantics of such a bid is "my maximum willingness to pay for s is p." A description in this language consists of a polynomial number of atomic bids. Given a sequence of pairs (s_j, p_j), we define for every set s, the price p_s to be the maximal sum of a partial partition of s. (For the sake of the example we ignore the fact that computing this maximum is NP-hard.) Nisan discusses this so-called OR language in chapter 9 of this volume.

Proposition 15.1 (Nisan 2000, chapter 9) OR bids can represent only superadditive valuation functions.

The OR language assumes that if an agent is willing to pay up to P_A for item A and P_B for item B, then he is willing to pay at least $(P_A + P_B)$ for both.

Consider a CA with two items, A and B, and two agents, Alice and Bob. Table 15.2 describes the agents' valuations. (The numbers in the brackets represent the value that the OR language assigns to the set $\{A, B\}$.) Consider a VCG mechanism with OR bids and assume that its allocation algorithm is optimal w.r.t. the assigned valuations $\hat{w}(d)$. When the agents are truthful, Alice gets both items for the price of $160. Unfortunately, this gives her a disutility of $35. By declaring a low value on each item, Alice can increase her utility to $0. Thus, despite the optimality of its allocation algorithm, the mechanism satisfies neither individual rationality nor incentive compatibility! Section 15.5.2 suggests a method for preventing these bad phenomena.

Incentive Compatible VCG with Bidding Languages The utility of an agent in a VCG mechanism with a bidding language equals his welfare resulting from his actual valuation and the assigned declared valuations of the other agents. Formally, $u_i(.) = v_i(k(d)) + \sum_{j \neq i} \hat{w}_j(k(d)) + h_i(d_{-i})$. Let $\mathcal{O}$ denote the range of the mechanism. Theorem 15.1 implies that if the mechanism is incentive compatible, there exists an equivalent mechanism such that the following holds. For every vector of valuations $v = (v_1, \dots, v_n)$, let $\hat{v} = (\hat{v}_1, \dots, \hat{v}_n)$ denote the assigned valuations corresponding to the

Table 15.2

OR bids

	A	B	A,B
Alice	100	100	125 (200)
Bob	80	80	120 (160)

agents' dominant strategies; for every agent i, the chosen allocation $k(d)$ must maximize the welfare $v_i(k(d)) + \sum_{j \neq i} \hat{w}_j(k(d))$ within the range $\mathcal{O}$. We argue that it is very hard, if not impossible, to construct a (nontrivial) VCG mechanism with an incomplete bidding language that satisfies the above property.

15.5.2 Second Chance Mechanisms with Bidding Languages

As we saw, VCG mechanisms with incomplete languages are neither incentive compatible nor individually rational. Our goal in this section is to develop feasibly truthful mechanisms for CAs. Even with unlimited communication, section 15.4.3 shows that the feasible truthfulness of a mechanism must depend on further assumptions on the agents' knowledge. Luckily, feasible truthfulness can be obtained under reasonable assumptions about this knowledge. As we shall see, the inability of the agents to communicate their valuations raises additional difficulties on the design of feasibly truthful protocols. In this section we extend the second chance mechanism to allow the usage of a bidding language. We then describe reasonable assumptions on the agents under which the mechanism is feasibly truthful.

Building Blocks of the Mechanism   Before we describe extended second chance mechanisms, let us consider their basic building blocks.

A VCG mechanism with limited communication is unable to measure the total welfare correctly. This can easily be fixed by the use of oracles.

Definition 15.7 (oracle)   An *oracle* is a function $w : 2^S \rightarrow R_+$. It is called *truthful* for agent i if $w_i(s) = v_i(s)$ for every set s.

An oracle is a program that can be queried on the agent's valuation. We assume that agents are capable of preparing such programs and that their oracles can be queried in polynomial time. The mechanism uses the agents' oracles to *measure* the total welfare of allocations.

As mentioned earlier, it is hard for allocation algorithms to work with oracles. In addition to oracles, our mechanisms require the agents to describe their valuations in some bidding langauge. The mechanism uses these descriptions to *compute* allocations.

In order to verify that the agent's description is consistent with his oracle, the mechanism uses a consistency checker. Semantically, a consistent description complies with the designer's instructions. Consider a mechanism that uses the OR language. The auctioneer can instruct the agents to declare their true valuations on all singletons. The consistency checker will verify that every singleton is an atomic bid and that the values of the description and the oracle are in agreement. Instead of disqualifying agents with inconsistent descriptions from participating in the mechanism, the checker simply augments their oracles.

Definition 15.8 (consistency checker) A *consistency checker* is a function $\psi(w,d)$, which gets an oracle w and a description d, and returns an *augmented oracle*, i.e., an oracle w' such that $w' = \psi(w',d)$.

We say that d is a *valid description* of w, if $w = \psi(w,d)$. Whenever there is an inconsistency between the value of a bundle according to the description and the oracle, the mechanism can simply prefer the value calculated according to the description. This produces an augmented oracle. For example, in the OR language, whenever a value of a bundle is less than the minimum of all its singletons, we can set the bundle's value to this minimal value. Therefore, from now on, we assume that the agents' descriptions are valid.

We now redefine the notion of an appeal function to allow the usage of a bidding language.

Definition 15.9 (extended appeal) An *extended appeal* function gets as input the agents' oracles and valid descriptions and returns a tuple of alternative descriptions. That is, it is of the form: $l(w_1, \ldots, w_n, d_1, \ldots, d_n) = (d'_1, \ldots, d'_n)$ where d_i is a valid description of w_i.

The semantics of an extended appeal $l(.)$ is: "When the vector of valuations (oracles) is $w = (w_1, \ldots, w_n)$ and its description is $d = (d_1, \ldots, d_n)$, I believe that the output algorithm $k(\ )$ produces a better result if it is given d' instead of the actual description d." For the rest of the chapter, the word "appeal" refers to extended appeal. Note that the d'_i do not need to be valid.

In our example (section 15.5.1), an appeal for Alice might try to reduce her value for either item A or B. She may try to apply a similar transformation to the valuations of the other agents as well.

The Mechanism We are now in a position to extend the second chance mechanism to include a bidding language.

Definition 15.10 (extended second chance) Given an allocation algorithm $k(.)$, and a consistency checker for the underlying bidding language, we define the *extended second chance* mechanism as follows:

1. Each agent submits to the mechanism:
• An oracle $w_i(.)$
• A (valid) description d_i
• An appeal function $l_i(.)$.

2. Let $w = (w_1, \ldots, w_n)$, $d = (d_1, \ldots, d_n)$. The mechanism computes the allocations $k(d), k(l_1(w, d)), \ldots, k(l_n(w, d))$ and chooses among these allocations the one that maximizes the total welfare (according to the oracles).

3. Let $\hat{o}$ denote the chosen allocation. The mechanism calculates the payments according to the VCG formula: $p_i = \sum_{j \neq i} w_j(\hat{o}) + h_i(w_{-i}, d_{-i}, l_{-i})$. ($h_i(.)$ can be any real valued function).

We do not require the allocation algorithm $k(.)$ to be optimal. It can be *any* polynomial time approximation or heuristic. When the appeal functions, the allocation algorithm, and the functions $h_i(.)$ are computable in polynomial time, then so is the mechanism.

An agent is said to be *truthful* if his (augmented) oracle is truthful. The following observation is a key property of the mechanism:

Proposition 15.2 Consider an extended second chance mechanism with an allocation algorithm $k(.)$. Let $d = (d_1, \ldots, d_n)$ denote the agents' descriptions. If all the agents are truth telling, the allocation chosen by the mechanism is *at least as good* as $k(d)$. ∎

As in section 15.4.2, we can define the function $h_i(.)$ in a way that ensures that the mechanism satisfies individual rationality.

Existence of Feasibly Truthful Strategies   Nisan and Ronen (2000) show that if the agents' knowledge is appeal independent, then feasibly truthful strategies of complexity similar to their knowledge exist.

How justified is the appeal independence assumption? Without limitation on the communication, such knowledge encapsulates all the agent's knowledge of the underlying algorithm. This is not true when the agents cannot communicate their valuations. Consider the example described in table 15.2. Suppose that Alice notices that the results of the algorithm improve when, instead of truthful descriptions, the assigned valuations $\hat{w}_i$ minimize the distance $\max_{s \subseteq S} |\hat{w}_i(s) - v_i(s)|$ (where S denotes the set of items for sale). Alice is probably capable of finding the best description for her own valuation (one that minimizes the above distance). Similarly, Bob can find the best description for his valuation. Unfortunately, in order to compute the best description for Bob's valuation, Alice must query Bob's oracle exponentially many times. Therefore, Alice may have an incentive to violate the auctioneer's instructions in order to help Bob's appeal to compute a better result. As we already commented, such violations may result in poor total welfare.

Ronen (2001) proposes two heuristics aimed at overcoming this problem. The first is to let the agents pass additional information on their valuations to the others' appeals. This information is of the form of additional descriptions, not necessarily valid. The second heuristic is to allow the agents to improve upon the others' appeals. These heuristics significantly broaden the class of knowledge under which the mechanism is feasibly truthful. Their drawbacks are increased computational time and potentially less simplicity for the agents. Because second chance mechanisms have not yet been demonstrated experimentally, it is not known whether this problem will occur in practice.

An Example of an Extended Second Chance Mechanism   Consider an extended second chance mechanism that uses the OR language. Suppose that the auctioneer instructs the agents to declare their true values on singletons. Consider Bob, who is participating in the auction. What must Bob do? First, Bob should describe his valuation in the OR language. It is possible, however, that his valuation is not always subadditive. In order to fix this, Bob is preparing a small program (an oracle) that accurately describes his valuation. It is not worthwhile for Bob to misreport his oracle, because this can only cause the mechanism to choose inferior allocations. Suppose that Bob thinks it is better for him to submit a description that is not prepared according to the auctioneer's instructions. If he would do so, he will have to submit a falsified oracle as well. Instead of doing this, Bob can ask his appeal to check whether a falsified description would actually help him. Reasoning similar to that of section 15.4.3 shows that under reasonable assumptions this strategy is feasibly dominant for Bob. In other words, Bob is not aware of any circumstances in which another strategy is better for him.

In reality, we expect bidding languages to be more expressive than the OR language. Yet, no matter which langauge we use, there will always be agents that will not be able to communicate their valuations in feasible time. As we saw, this destroys the truthfulness of the mechanism and thus can severely damage its efficiency. The second chance mechanism is aimed at overcoming this problem.

15.6   Alternative Approaches to the Intractability of VCG

This chapter offers a general method for handling the intractability of VCG mechanisms for CAs. There exist various alternative approaches to this problem, most of which are reflected in this book. We can divide these approaches into three categories: the design of alternative mechanisms, the identification of tractable cases, and methods shifting the need to cope with the complexity of CAs to the agents.

Various mechanisms for CAs have been proposed in the literature. Many of these are extensively discussed in this book (see Ausubel and Milgrom, chapter 1; Parkes, chapter 2; Ausubel and Milgrom, chapter 3; and Land, Powell, and Steinberg, chapter 6). Most of these mechanisms are multiround ascending auctions. The success of these mechanisms relies on the assumption that agents will behave myopically during the protocol (i.e., at each round respond optimally to the current state of the auction). Note that myopic behavior is an ex post equilibrium when it causes the mechanism to compute the optimal allocation. In this case, the payments are usually equivalent to those of VCG.

Another approach to the intractability of VCG is to identify reasonable assumptions under which the problem is tractable. Several results, both positive and negative, appear in this book (most notably, in Segal, chapter 11, and Müller chapter 13). Pekeč and Rothkopf (chapter 16) describe various heuristic methods for coping with the intractability of CAs. The next section of this chapter discusses incentive compatible approximation mechanisms for several special cases.

An interesting approach is developed by Holzman, et al. (2004) and Holzman and Monderer (2004). This work studies the equilibria that may occur in standard VCG mechanisms. Surprisingly, except for the obvious truthful equilibrium, many others are possible. One example of such an equilibrium is when each agent declares his true valuation of the whole set of items but declares $0 for any other subset. Obviously, such an equilibrium requires only a very small amount of communication. This work characterizes the set of possible equilibria and studies the tradeoffs between the communication and the efficiency of the equilibria. Unfortunately, as is the case in many economic models, in order for this approach to be practical, the agents have to somehow agree on the chosen equilibrium. Currently, there is no known way of doing so.

15.7 Incentive Compatible Approximation Mechanisms for Restricted CAs

The second chance method is very general but compromises the incentive compatibility of the mechanism. As previously explained, this compromise seems unavoidable in the general case. For many applications of interest, various assumptions on the valuation of the agents are natural. Sometimes, such assumptions facilitate the construction of incentive compatible, polynomial time non-VCG mechanisms that approximate the optimal welfare. This section describes four such mechanisms. It is divided into two parts. The first part is dedicated to the fairly general case of multiunit CAs with bounded demands. The second part describes mechanisms for single-minded bidders, that is, agents who are interested in one specific subset of the available items.

This section is based on the following papers: Bartal, Gonen, and Nisan 2003; Lehmann, O'Callaghan, and Shoham 2002; Mu'alem and Nisan 2002; and Archer et al. 2003. It only outlines the basic construction and main ideas of each paper. The interested reader is pointed to the original articles for more details.

Let m and n denote the number of items and number of bidders, respectively. A truthful mechanism is called an $\alpha(m, n)$-*approximation* if for every type vector, when the agents are truth telling, the welfare obtained by the mechanism is at most $\alpha(m, n)$ times worse than the optimal welfare. Note that this is a worst case definition. Typically, an approximation algorithm or mechanism yields an allocation that is much better than its worst case guarantee. Also, there exists an empirical correlation between the approximation ratio of an algorithm and its performance in practice. Under standard complexity assumptions, no polynomial time algorithm for CAs can obtain an approximation ratio better than $m^{1/2-\varepsilon}$ (see Lehmann, Müller, and Sandholm, chapter 14 of this volume). All mechanisms presented in this section have polynomial computation time and yield nearly tight approximation ratios.

15.7.1 Multiunit CAs with Bounded Demands

CAs in which multiple identical copies of each item are available are called *multiunit*. Bartal, Gonen, and Nisan (2003) study such auctions with an additional assumption that each bidder is either not interested in an item at all or has a bounded demand for it. This assumption is natural for many applications. Surprisingly, the paper constructs a mechanism with a good approximation ratio for this fairly general problem.

Let V_{max} denote a bound on the maximal valuation of any bidder. Let k_j denote the number of units available of each item j. The paper assumes that each agent i is either not interested in item j at all, or wants a quantity no less than $\theta \cdot k_j$ and no more than $\Theta \cdot k_j$ of it. For example, suppose that 100 VCRs and 200 TV sets are available for sale. If every bidder is only interested in up to five TVs and ten VCRs, then Θ equals $1/20$, and θ equals $1/200$.

The basic mechanism of Bartal, Gonen, and Nisan (2003) assumes that the designer knows the bounds V_{max}, θ, and Θ. The logic of the mechanism is simple. The agents are ordered arbitrarily. Each item has a price that is adjusted to every agent. Each agent, in his turn, chooses the bundle that is most desirable for him, given the current prices. The main idea of the mechanism is to *increase* the price of any sold item by an exponential rate. Figure 15.2 describes the mechanism. Its parameters are the vector of

---

For each good $i = 1, ..., m$

    $l_1^{(i)} = 0$

For each agent $j = 1, ..., n$

    For each good i

        $P_j^{(i)} = P_0 \cdot r^{l_j^{(i)}}$

    Query agent j for his most desired bundle of items $(x_j^{(1)}, ..., x_j^{(m)})$

    Determine agent j's payment to be $\Sigma_i x_j^{(i)} \cdot P_j^{(i)}$

    Update $l_j^{(i)} = l_j^{(i)} + x_j^{(i)}$

Figure 15.2

The basic mechanism of Bartal, Gonen, and Nisan.

initial prices P_0, and the rate r. The variables $l_j^{(i)}$ indicate how many copies of each item i are sold to bidders $(1, \ldots, j-1)$.

This mechanism is clearly incentive compatible. It is very simple and can be used in online settings as well. The mechanism only needs to know the most desired set of each agent, and henceforth preserves the privacy of the agents. Obviously, this mechanism is polynomial time computable, provided that the agents can efficiently compute their desired sets. The paper shows that with the right parameters r and P_0, the mechanism approximates the optimal welfare within a factor of $O(1/\Theta \cdot (n/\theta)^{\Theta/(1-2\cdot\Theta)})$. Note that when there are $K = O(\log n)$ copies available of each item, and the agents demand at most one unit of each item, the approximation ratio of this mechanism is $O(\log n)$. The paper shows that the approximation ratio of the basic mechanism is nearly tight for the case where the same number of units of each item are available.

The basic mechanism assumes a bound V_{max} on the valuations of the agents. The paper shows how to circumvent this assumption without decreasing the approximation ratio of the mechanism (except by a multiplicative constant). The main idea is to offer a second price type of mechanism to the agent with the maximal valuation and apply the basic mechanism to the others.

15.7.2 CAs with Single-Minded Agents

An agent is called *single minded* if he is interested in one particular subset of the available items. Formally, there exists a subset s and a value $r \geq 0$, such that the valuation of the agent is of the form $v(s') = r$ if $s \subseteq s'$ and $v(s') = 0$ otherwise. This subsection describes mechanisms for single-minded agents. Lehmann, O'Callaghan, and Shoham (2002) bring several examples for applications where the assumption of single-minded bidders is natural. Among the examples are auctions conducted for selling timber harvesting rights in New Zealand, auctions for pollution rights, and various electronic trading applications.

The single-mindedness assumption significantly facilitates the development of truthful, non-VCG mechanisms as the valuation of the agents can be embedded in R_1. Usually, for one-dimensional problems, a wide range of truthful mechanisms exist.

It should be stressed that from a computational point of view, the problem of finding a welfare maximizing allocation for single-minded agents is no easier than the general problem. Under standard complexity assumptions it is NP-hard to approximate it within a factor of $m^{-1/2+\varepsilon}$ for any $\varepsilon > 0$ (Lehmann, Müller, and Sandholm, chapter 14 of this volume).

An agent is called *known* single minded if the subset s in which he is interested is known to the designer. As we shall see, one can obtain better approximation ratios when these sets are known.

This section describes three mechanisms for single-minded agents: Lehmann, O'Callaghan, and Shoham (2002) for the general case, Mu'alem and Nisan (2002) for known single-minded bidders, and Archer et al. (2003) for multiunit CAs with known single-minded bidders.

Lehmann, O'Callaghan, and Shoham's Mechanism   Lehmann, O'Callaghan, and Shoham (2002) pioneered the study of single-minded bidders. They show a general way of transforming greedy algorithms into truthful mechanisms, and use this method for the construction of an $\sqrt{m}$-approximation mechanism for the problem. They also characterize the family of truthful mechanisms for single-minded bidders.

Perhaps the most natural way of finding allocations in combinatorial auctions is by a greedy algorithm. Such an algorithm operates in stages. At each stage, it selects a bid according to some criterion, removes all the bids that collide with it (i.e., including items in its bundle), and continues recursively. We now describe a specific greedy mechanism that yields an approximation ratio of $O(\sqrt{m})$. Note that this is almost the best ratio that any polynomial time mechanism can obtain.

Let $b_i = (s_i, v_i)$ denote the bid of the i'th agent. We define the *norm* of the bid as $r_i = v_i/\sqrt{|s_i|}$, and its *average amount per good* as $v_i/|s_i|$. We say that b_i and b_j collide if $s_i \cap s_j \neq \emptyset$. The allocation algorithm of the mechanism is very simple:

- The bids are sorted according to their norm. Without loss of generality, assume that $b_1 \geq b_2, \ldots, \geq b_n$ where the order refers to the norm of the bids.
- For each bid b_i on the list, (starting from b_1—the bid with the highest norm), accept b_i if and only if it does not collide with the previously satisfied bids.

When an agent is rejected, his payment is defined to be 0. We now describe the payment of an accepted agent i. Let $j \geq i$ denote the first bid in the list, which is *rejected* because agent i is accepted. (If such an agent does not exist, i's payment is defined to be 0 as well.) Let r_j be the norm of the bid b_j. The payment p_i is defined as the value that will cause the norm of b_i to be equal to r_j, that is, $p_i = \sqrt{|s_i|} \cdot r_j$. In other words, p_i is the critical value for agent i. If his bid had been below this value, agent j would have preceded his in the sorted list and his bid would have been rejected.

It is not difficult to see that this mechanism can be computed in polynomial time. Surprisingly, the approximation factor of this mechanism is almost tight.

Theorem 15.2 (Lehmann, O'Callaghan, and Shoham 2002)   The greedy mechanism approximates the optimal allocation within a factor of $\sqrt{m}$.

The paper shows that the norm $r_i(.)$ could be replaced by many other functions without destroying the incentive compatibility of the mechanism. Therefore, the construction described here is fairly general. The approximation ratio of the resulting mechanism is typically not preserved.

Mu'alem and Nisan's Mechanism   Mu'alem and Nisan (2002) study the problem of CAs with *known single-minded* bidders. In this problem, the designer not only knows that the agents are single minded, but he also knows in which subset of the items each agent is interested. The paper shows that this assumption facilitates the development of a set of algorithmic techniques for the construction of truthful mechanisms. In particular, it develops several operators for *combining* truthful mechanisms. (For most problems, it is not known how to combine truthful mechanisms in a way that preserves truthfulness. This makes the construction of polynomial time truthful mechanisms very difficult.) Mu'alem and Nisan use their techniques to obtain the following constructions:

- An $\varepsilon \cdot \sqrt{m}$-approximation for the general case for any fixed $\varepsilon > 0$. (m denotes the total number of items available.)
- A simple 2-approximation for the homogeneous (multiunit) case.
- An $(l + 1)$-approximation for multiunit combinatorial auctions with l types of goods.

An allocation algorithm of a truthful mechanism must maintain the following monotonicity property. For every agent i, and bid vector v_{-i} for the other agents, if agent i wins the auction with a bid (s_i, v_i), and $v_i' > v_i$, then he must also win when his bid increases to (s_i, v_i'). It is well known that monotonic allocation algorithms can be transformed into truthful mechanisms. Specifically, for every agent i, given the declaration of the other agents v_{-i}, either i never wins, or there exists a threshold $p_i = p_i(v_{-i})$ such that under this threshold the agent does not win, and above it i's bid is accepted. In this case, p_i must be the payment of agent j. Note that if the allocation algorithm is polynomial, the payments can be computed in polynomial time using a simple binary search.

Mu'alem and Nisan (2002) focus on monotonic allocation algorithms that satisfy an additional natural property called *bitonicity*.

Definition 15.11 (Bitonic Allocation Algorithm)   A monotonic allocation algorithm A is *bitonic* if for every bidder i and a type vector v_{-i} for the other agents, the welfare $w_A(v_{-i}, v_i)$ is a nonincreasing function of v_i for $v_i < p_i$ and a nondecreasing function of v_i for $v_i \geq p_i$. (p_i denotes the threshold of agent i.)

The paper shows several basic techniques allowing the development of bitonic algorithms: a greedy technique, a technique based on linear programming, and a bounded exhaustive search. It then develops two operators that allow the combination of bitonic algorithms, a Max construct and an If–Then–Else construct. Given two bitonic algorithms A_1 and A_2, $Max(A_1, A_2)$ is defined as follows: given a bid vector v, the allocations $A_1(v)$ and $A_2(v)$ are computed. The Max operator returns the allocation with a better welfare w.r.t. v. The If–Then–Else construct gets two algorithms A_1 and A_2 and a condition *cond*(*v*) where *v* is a bid vector. Given *v*, the operator tests *cond*(*v*). If the test succeeds, he chooses the allocation $A_1(v)$. If it fails, the operator returns $A_2(v)$. The condition function *cond*(.) must adhere to a certain monotonicity requirement.

Based on their basic techniques and combination operators, the paper develops polynomial time, bitonic approximation algorithms for the problems mentioned above. These algorithms, as explained, can be transformed into truthful, polynomial time, approximation mechanisms.

Archer, Talwar, Papadimitriou, and Tardos's Mechanism Archer et al. (2003) consider multiunit combinatorial auctions with known single-minded bidders. They further assume that there exist enough copies of each item. (Formally, $\Omega(\log K)$ where K is the maximal cardinality of any subset desired by one of the agents.) Given an arbitrary constant $1 > \varepsilon > 0$, the paper constructs a sophisticated $(1 - \varepsilon)$ approximation mechanism for this case. In this subsection we only describe the main stages of the construction.

The mechanism discussed in this section is randomized. Therefore, several definitions of truthfulness are natural. The mechanism satisfies truthfulness both in expectation and with high probability.

Successful design of a truthful randomizing mechanism must tackle two major problems: first, the allocation algorithm of the mechanism must be monotonic, that is, the winning probability of an agent must increase with his bid. In general, approximation algorithms do not satisfy this condition. Second, the payment of the agents must be computed in polynomial time. Although this computation is easy for deterministic mechanisms, it is not clear how to do this when the allocation algorithm is randomized.

We first begin with the construction of the monotonic approximation allocation algorithm. Figure 15.3 describes the algorithm.

1. Solve the linear program defined in (15.2)

2. Round each variable x_i to 1 with probability x_i. Set to 0 otherwise

3. Select all agents i with $x_i = 1$ and for whom the constraints for all the items in their bundle S_i are satisfied

4. Drop each agent with some additional probability θ_i

Figure 15.3
The allocation mechanism of Archer, Talwar, Papadimitriou, and Tardos.

Let k_j denote the number of units available from each commodity j, and let $k'_j = \lfloor (1 - \varepsilon) \cdot k_j \rfloor$. The first step is to solve the linear program 15.2.

$$\text{Maximize } \sum_i v_i \cdot x_i$$

$$\text{Subject to: } \sum_{i | j \in S_i} x_i \le k'_j \quad \text{(for each item } j\text{)} \tag{15.2}$$

$0 \le x_i \le 1$.

This program finds the optimal fractional allocation under the constraint that at most k'_j are sold of each item. The next step of the algorithm is to do a standard trick, which is to treat the variables x_i as probabilities. The algorithm then probabilistically rounds the variables x_i to either 0 or 1. It is not difficult to see that with high probability no item is oversold, and that the algorithm (so far) is monotonic. If there exist oversold items, the algorithm rejects all the bids that contain them. It then satisfies every nonrejected agent i with $x_i = 1$.

From a practical point of view, this algorithm might suffice (together with the payment function that we will describe later) to ensure the truthfulness of the agents. Nevertheless, there is still a small probability that agents will not be satisfied because of an over-sale. Moreover, this probability may depend on the agents' bids in a nonmonotonic way. The paper shows that if each agent i is dropped with some additional small probability θ_i, then the resulting algorithm is indeed monotonic.

We now turn to the computation of the payments. Let $p_i = p_i(v_i)$ denote the probability that agent i wins with a bid v_i (suppressing the bids of the other agents). It can be shown that the payment function $R_i(v_i) = v_i - 1/p_i \cdot \int_{u=0}^{v_i} p_i(u) \, du$ guarantees the truthfulness of the mechanism. The problem is that both $1/p_i$ and the integral might be hard to compute. One possible way of overcoming this is to evaluate both quantities by unbiased estimators. However, this might create anomalies such as the possibility of negative payments. The paper describes a payment schema that avoids such anomalies. This schema is nontrivial and we omit it from this exposition.

We summarize the properties of the mechanism in the following theorem.

Theorem 15.3 Given any $1 < \varepsilon < 0$, the mechanism of Archer, Talwar, Papadimitriou, and Tardos is truthful (both in expectation and with high probability), is computable in polynomial time, and approximates the optimal welfare within a factor of $1 + O(\varepsilon)$.

15.8 Conclusion

To date, VCG is the only general method available for the construction of incentive compatible mechanisms. Unfortunately, VCG mechanisms are computationally infeasible. This chapter studies VCG mechanisms where (1) the optimal allocation algorithm is replaced by a tractable one, and (2) the amount of communication is limited and the agents communicate their valuations via a bidding language. We show that, in general, such mechanisms satisfy neither individual rationality nor incentive compatibility.

Second chance mechanisms aim to overcome these bad phenomena. Under reasonable assumptions, *the* rational strategy for the agents is to follow faithfully the auctioneer's instructions. When they do so, the allocation that the mechanism computes is at least as good as that of the underlying algorithm. Second chance mechanisms satisfy individual rationality as well.

It is important to stress that the second chance method has not yet been tested. Its implementation relies on several tools to be developed, and the predicted good behavior of the participants has not yet been verified experimentally. As with most mechanisms for CAs, the payment properties of second chance mechanisms require further study.

For many applications of interest, various assumptions on the valuations of the agents are natural. Sometimes, these assumptions facilitate the construction of truthful, polynomial time mechanisms that approximate the total welfare. We described several such mechanisms in this chapter.

Acknowledgments

The author was supported in part by grant number 53/03–10.5 from the Israel Science Foundation. The author thanks Inbal Ronen and two anonymous reviewers for their comments on early drafts of this chapter.

References

Archer, Aaron and Éva Tardos (2002), "Frugal Path Mechanisms," *Proceedings of the 13th Annual ACM-SIAM Symposium on Discrete Algorithms*, 991–999.

Archer, Aaron, Christos Papadimitriou, Kunal Talwar, and Éva Tardos (2003), "An Approximate Truthful Mechanism for Combinatorial Auctions with Single Parameter Agents," *Proceedings of the 14th Annual ACM-SIAM Symposium on Discrete Algorithms (SODA 2003)*, 205–214.

Bartal, Yair, Rica Gonen, and Noam Nisan (2003), "Incentive Compatible Multi Unit Combinatorial Auctions," *Proceedings of the 9th Conference on Theoretical Aspects of Rationality and Knowledge*, 72–87.

Elkind, Edith, Amit Sahai, and Ken Steiglitz (2004), "Frugality in Path Auctions," *Proceedings 15th ACM-SIAM Symposium on Discrete Algorithms (SODA 2004)*.

Green, Jerry and J.J. Laffont (1977), "Characterization of Satisfactory Mechanisms for the Revelation of Preferences for Public Goods," *Econometrica*, 427–438.

Holzman, Ron, Noa Kfir-Dahav, Dov Monderer, and Moshe Tennenholtz (2004), "Bundling Equilibrium in Combinatorial Auctions," *Games and Economic Behavior*, 147, 427–438.

Holzman, Ron and Dov Monderer (2004), "Characterization of Ex Post Equilibria in VCG Combinatorial Auctions," *Games and Economic Behavior*, 47, 87–103.

Lavi, Ron, Ahuva Mualem, and Noam Nisan (2003), "Towards a Characterization of Truthful Combinatorial Auctions," *Proceedings of the 44th Annual IEEE Symposium on Foundations of Computer Science (FOCS 2003)*, 574–583.

Lehmann, Daniel, Liadan I. O'Callaghan, and Yoav Shoham (2002), "Truth Revelation in Approximately Efficient Combinatorial Auctions," *Journal of the ACM*, 49, 577–602.

Mu'alem, Ahuva and Noam Nisan (2002), "Truthful Approximation Mechanisms for Restricted Combinatorial Auctions," in *Proceedings of the Eighteenth National Conference on Artificial Intelligence (AAAI 2002)*, 379–384.

Nisan, Noam (2000), "Bidding and Allocation in Combinatorial Auctions," in *Proceedings of the 2nd ACM Conference on Electronic Commerce*, 1–12.

Nisan, Noam and Amir Ronen (2000), "Computationally Feasible VCG Mechanisms," in *Proceedings of the Second ACM Conference on Electronic Commerce (EC 00)*, 242–252.

Nisan, Noam and Amir Ronen (2001), "Algorithmic Mechanism Design," *Games and Economic Behaviour*, 35, 166–196.

Roberts, Kevin (1979), "The Characterization of Implementable Choice Rules," in Jean-Jacques Laffont, ed., *Aggregation and Revelation of Preferences*, 321–349. Amsterdam: North-Holland. Papers presented at the First European Summer Workshop of the Econometric Society.

Ronen, Amir (2001), "Mechanism Design with Incomplete Languages," in *Proceedings of the Third ACM Conference on Electronic Commerce (EC 01)*, 105–114.

16 Noncomputational Approaches to Mitigating Computational Problems in Combinatorial Auctions

Aleksandar Pekeč and Michael H. Rothkopf

16.1 Introduction

Hikers encountering a fallen tree blocking a trail can climb over it, cut a path through it, or walk around it. In general, obstacles can be overcome, reduced, or avoided. Often, reducing or avoiding the obstacle is a preferable choice. The computational problems in combinatorial auctions are no different. The previous four chapters have been largely devoted to describing ways of overcoming them. Although it is important to have the ability to overcome unavoidable computational difficulties, good combinatorial auction design will certainly want to take advantage of appropriate ways to reduce or avoid them. That is the topic of this chapter.

This section of this chapter sets the context by briefly reviewing the computational issues in combinatorial auction design, the context of auction design including the information available to the designer, and properties that the auction designer must trade off in selecting the auction format and procedures. The following four sections then look at mitigation opportunities prior to bid submission, at the time of bid submission, after bid submission but prior to announcing a tentative set of winning bids, and after the announcement of a tentative set of winning bids.[1] A final section concludes with a discussion of the implications of these opportunities for auction design.

16.1.1 Computational Issues

A distinguishing feature of combinatorial auctions is the computational complexity of tasks considered trivial and mundane in noncombinatorial auctions. The central problem that has gathered considerable attention in recent years is that of winner determination, to which the first three chapters of part III of this book are devoted. The winner determination problem is discussed in detail in Lehmann et al. (chapter 12), as well as in Müller (chapter 13) and Sandholm (chapter 14). Here, we briefly note that the winner determination problem in its simplest form is equivalent to the set packing problem (as pointed out by Rothkopf, Pekeč, and Harstad 1998).[2] Thus, the winner determination problem is one of the basic NP-complete problems and the fundamental source of potential computational difficulties in combinatorial auctions.

In this chapter, we focus on combinatorial bids that are "package bids" only, that is, we will assume that all bids are simple "all or nothing" bids. Our observations readily generalize to the more general case of Boolean combinations of "package bids" (defined as "combinatorial bids" in this book).[3]

Although it is fundamental, the winner determination problem is not the only issue that could bring computational difficulties. Among other problems that could be of computational concern is calculating how much more a losing bidder must bid in order for his bid to become a winning one, the problem of resolving ties, and determining minimum bid increments in an iterative auction. However, most of these problems, regardless of the approach, are inherently related to the winner determination problem and its complexity. For example, methods for determining bid increments have to revolve around calculations of the gap (see glossary) for each losing bid. As Rothkopf, Pekeč, and Harstad (1998) show, the complexity of calculating gap for any losing bid is equivalent to the complexity of the winner determination problem.[4] Similarly, resolving ties by random selection (e.g., FCC 2002) is essentially equivalent to solving a winner determination problem.[5] Thus, most of the potentially difficult computational problems in combinatorial auctions are equivalent or closely related to the winner determination problem. Hence, without serious loss of generality, one can focus on addressing complexities of the winner determination problem.

16.1.2 Context

When designing an auction and dealing with computational complexity, an auction designer has to take into account the importance of various potentially desirable properties of an auction and, if necessary, make appropriate tradeoffs. Some of desirable properties are:[6]

- allocative efficiency, that is, maximizing the total value to the winners of the items being auctioned;
- revenue maximization (or payment minimization);
- low transaction costs and auction speed as both the bidders and the bid-taker care about their costs of participating in the auction;
- fairness, that is, concern about equal treatment of competitors (and the appearance of it);
- failure freeness, as failures should be minimized and their impact mitigated;
- transparency;
- scalability is important in design of auctions that will be used repeatedly.

An important concern in government auctions doesn't have to be one in commercial procurement auctions, and vice versa. For example, a government auction might have to pay special attention to allocative efficiency, whereas cost minimization could be a primary goal in corporate procurement; a government might not be in position to appear unfair or afford settling for a suboptimal allocation (as it could face lengthy lawsuits), whereas corporate auctions could aim at speeding up the auction procedure at the price of possibly failing to find the optimal allocation. Regardless of the goals of the particular situations, some noncomputational auction design approaches discussed in this chapter could reduce the complexity burden while preserving (most of) the other desirable properties.

Another concern to the auction designer is the potential informational burden. One aspect of such a burden is mere handling information that could be massive given that there are up to $2^m - 1$ potential packages of m items that could be bid on. Clearly, eliciting bidder valuations for all possible packages (or all possible allocations) could be even more informationally demanding.[7] A different aspect of informational burden arises when the auction designer wants to or has to release comprehensive but aggregated information about the auction, such as the gap for all bids or minimum bid increments for all biddable combinations in every round of an iterative auction.[8] Therefore, auction design choices on the auction format, including the information flow from bidders to the bid-taker and vice versa, could affect the implementability of the auction from the information management point of view. This chapter discusses some possibilities at the disposal of an auction designer.

16.2 Mitigating Complexity Prior to Bid Submission

There are many tasks that need to be done before an auction begins. This section discusses how these tasks can mitigate computational complexity. The possibilities discussed below include the choice of definition of the items to be sold, the definition of a metric to make items comparable, and the definition of which combinations are to be biddable.

Sometimes the definition of an "item" is obvious. Often, however, there is considerable discretion involved in defining the items to be auctioned. For example, when the U.S. Federal Communications Commission decides to sell the rights to use 30 MHz of radio spectrum, it could offer one 30-MHz license, two 15-MHz licenses, a 20-MHz license and a 10-MHz license, three 10-MHz licenses, or thirty 1-MHz licenses. It can also divide the licenses geographically, and sell five regional licenses, fifty state licenses, or 500 local licenses. Clearly, the way the assets to be sold are divided up into items can have a profound effect on the computational problems of winner determination. An artless choice, for example, selling 15,000 local 1-MHz licenses when economic use of the spectrum requires regional aggregations and at least 10 MHz, could unnecessarily lead to horrendous computational difficulties. Sellers need to use their knowledge of the desires and the economic situation of their potential buyers to make sensible definitions of items. Sellers normally have much such knowledge and potential buyers often have incentive to provide or improve it. Indeed, a seller who does not have and cannot get any knowledge of what his potential buyers want should probably sell his assets competitively in one lot to the potential resellers who best know the market.

There is little that can be said in general about the decision about how to divide assets for sale into lots. However, even though it depends upon the particulars of the situation, it is a critical auction design issue. There are some possibilities worth mentioning that are of potential value.

One of these is defining some sort of measure that can be used, perhaps with adjustments, to make items fungible. This greatly simplifies the computational problem of selecting winners. An example of this is daily electricity supply auctions. In the best of these, a megawatt of power injected into the electricity grid over a given hour at point A is equivalent to a megawatt injected into the grid that hour at point B, except for an adjustment designed to take account appropriately of the costs of transmission congestion. This is called "locational marginal pricing." Electricity auctions that ignored this congestion effect and assumed that congestion-free zones could be predefined have run into difficulties. Recently, there has been a proposal to auction both energy and transmission rights simultaneously.[9]

Another one is to predefine biddable combinations in a way that reflects the underlying economics and will simultaneously mitigate potential computational difficulties during the course of an auction. For example, bids for takeoff and landing slots at an airport could be limited to pairs involving one landing slot and one takeoff slot. This would meet the economic need of airlines to takeoff any plane that they land at an airport while leading to a computationally tractable auction.[10] The next three subsections discuss these possibilities in more detail.

16.2.1 Defining Items for Sale

The issue of defining items for sale is not specific to combinatorial auctions. For example, what has to be sold and how it should be sold depends on physical nature of the items for sale, (dis)synergetic valuations that the bidders have over potential items that could result in either bundling or unbundling of such items, as well as on the practical considerations of conducting an auction in a timely and efficient manner. In many situations, the basic physical units that cannot reasonably be further decomposed are clear. For example, well-running used cars should not normally be sold as used car parts. However, there are many other important situations where such atoms do not exist, such as radio frequencies, electricity contracts, and undeveloped land division. As for possible synergies and dissynergies, if these occur naturally or are common to all bidders, a good auction design will define auction items by appropriately bundling or unbundling in order to accommodate such situations. Thus, trying to bundle objects that are synergetic to every bidder into an auction item, and unbundling them into separate auction items when dissynergies are common, could be a general rule of thumb. However, one has to consider possible budget constraints and differences in individual bidder valuations, because in such situations forced bundling might be inefficient and revenue deficient.[11] Similarly, even if bundling some objects is not synergetic, such "inefficient" bundling could make the total number of items to be auctioned small and the auction process fast and manageable. For example, an auctioneer selling off the property of a bankrupt restaurant might well chose to lump together into a single lot all of the pots and pans rather than sell them separately, reasoning that any possible lost revenue will be more than offset by savings in transaction costs.

In general, bidders might not agree on synergies and dissynergies. Thus, perfect, noncontroversial bundling or unbundling in defining auction items might be difficult. One approach to such situations would be for all bidders to agree on the items that should not be further decomposed, and then to allow bids on any combination of such items.[12] This approach could be useful for defining items when there is no obvious physical description or limitation. The drawback is that bidders might have infinite numbers of objects they would consider buying[13] and, even in the finite case, the resulting number of items could be unmanageably huge. Thus, perfect, noncontroversial item definitions may not be possible or practical.

However items to be auctioned end up being defined, an auction designer has to decide whether to allow bids on combinations of items (provided that there is more than one item). As many chapters of this book discuss (e.g., Nisan, chapter 9, Segal, chapter 11, Lehmann et al., chapter 12, and Leyton-Brown et al., chapter 19) and as briefly discussed in the introduction, combinatorial bidding could introduce complexities and potentially insurmountable obstacles in conducting an auction.

If many combinatorial bids are placed in an auction, this could mean (among other things) that bidders have serious conflicting synergetic valuations and/or that some items could have been bundled before being auctioned off. Taking this observation to the extreme, the final pricing and allocation, if done prior to the auction, could eliminate the need for the auction itself and lead to optimal posted prices because it would eliminate any interest for bidding except exactly for the winning bidders submitting the winning bids. So, in addition to allocation and price discovery, combinatorial auctions are mechanisms for optimal bundling discovery. The process of discovering the optimal bundling of items is the one that differentiates combinatorial from noncombinatorial auctions, and the one that is responsible for inherent complexities of combinatorial auctions. Thus, to the extent possible, auction designers should aim toward understanding likely optimal bundles. This understanding could be more critical to the auction success than understanding likely auction prices and likely auction winners. In turn, this suggests that an auction designer should put an effort into properly defining auction items in order to manage implementation complexities of combinatorial bidding.[14]

For example, consider an auction of three items, a, b, c, with highest valuations (all from different bidders) as follows: $v(a) = 3$, $v(b) = 4$, $v(c) = 5$, $v(ab) = 10$, $v(bc) = 10$, $v(ac) = 10$, $v(abc) = 13$, and with second highest valuations being exactly one less (and placed by a completely different set of bidders). Then, by posting the following prices, $p(a) = p(b) = p(c) = 5$, $p(ab) = 10$, $p(bc) = p(ac) = 11$, $p(abc) = 14$, the seller can bundle and allocate the items optimally by a simple posted price mechanism, instead of running the combinatorial auction. Of course, this assumes that the seller has guessed these prices correctly or that he has some information on optimal bundles and prices, that is, the type of information usually discovered by the auction mechanism. Note that knowing high valuations without the knowledge of specific structure is not sufficient to find an optimal allocation; all two-item bundles are valued at 10, but the optimal pricing has to price discriminate in order to clear the market in an optimal allocation that requires bundling a and b. Also note that with the assumed high valuations, the seller could simply decide to accept only bundled bids on ab and bids on c, and not lose anything by limiting bidding in this way. Thus, discovering optimal bundling is valuable for market mechanisms that allow combinatorial bids.

It is worth mentioning that even when packages can be divided among bidders, how this is done can have a major impact on the effectiveness of the auction. The original California day-ahead electricity auctions purchased twenty-four commodities, electricity in each of the hours of the next day. No bids on combinations of hours were allowed, and fractions of bids could be accepted. This is an awkward definition for a potential bidder with a generating plant that has start up costs, minimum run levels, and requires four hours to start or stop. A better design proposed by Elmaghraby and Oren (1999) would have bidders offering electricity from hour A to hour B. Note that the acceptance of a fraction of a bid in this auction would affect the allocation of start up costs but not the feasibility of starting and stopping the generating plant. An even better approach, actually used by the New York system operator and the operator of the Pennsylvania-New Jersey-Maryland system, considers bids involving start up costs and minimum run levels, solves a mixed integer program to find the optimum feasible dispatch for the day, uses hourly market clearing prices based on variable costs, and then further compensates bidders whose fixed costs would not be covered so that they will not lose money at the optimum dispatch.[15]

In summary, the way auction items are defined has direct impact on the level of complexities of a combinatorial auction. Even if items seem to be naturally defined, choosing to bundle or unbundle some of such items could significantly aid the process of optimal bundle discovery. Thus, if combinatorial bidding is to be allowed and if the computational complexity of running an auction is an issue, defining auction items should be looked at as an opportunity to mitigate effectively the potential for encountering computational nightmares while running the auction.

16.2.2 Defining Units

Bids on different combinations are usually incomparable,[16] and this incomparability is one of the core issues in combinatorial auctions. One potential way to simplify this problem is to define an underlying measure on all possible biddable combinations and use this measure when solving the winner determination problem and other computational tasks such as determining minimum bid increments in multiround auction formats.

For example, in the latest FCC combinatorial auction, the MHzPop measure, that is, the bandwidth of the spectrum multiplied by the population covered by the geographical scope of the license, is used in calculating minimum bid increments. The bid value is divided by the MhzPop value of the underlying combination and in this way all bids can be compared on the one-dimensional scale of $/MhzPop. Electricity auctions use $/MWh (dollars per megawatt hour)—adjusted by location for transmission congestion in the better auction designs and within predefined zones in others—as a common measure.[17]

In fact, many iterative combinatorial auction proposals suggest use of some underlying measure to define minimum bid increments.[18] The use of an underlying measure can be exact or approximate. If it is exact, then the items are truly fungible, as with treasury bonds, and individual items need not be differentiated at all. Use of an approximate simplification in determining minimum bid increments might not be viewed as too problematic, especially in iterative mechanisms where there are multiple chances to remedy the effects of any approximations. However, even in iterative mechanisms, there may be exceptions, such as when auction activity is coming to a close and the simplification proposes a minimum bid increment that is too high and that eliminates potential bidders who could drive up the price.

The one-dimensionality that results from introducing an underlying measure to compare bids can simplify the winner determination problem, too.[19] For example, there is a proposal (Rothkopf and Bazelon 2003) for auctioning residual spectrum subject to the limited rights of existing licensees. Because the existing rights holder has a strangle hold on the use of the residual rights, there will tend to be only one bidder for a given license's residual rights. The proposal is to take bids on many such licenses but sell only those getting the highest bid per MhzPop. Because spectrum of high frequencies is considerably less valuable per MhzPop than spectrum of lower frequencies that can penetrate buildings, the proposal is to auction low and high frequencies separately.

The key to introducing bidding units through an underlying measure on biddable combinations is that such a measure is widely accepted and appropriate for the situation in hand, such as KWhs adjusted for transmission congestion and MhzPops for spectrum with sufficiently similar frequencies, and that everyone involved in the process, especially bidders and the auctioneer, is aware of the potential to reach a suboptimal outcome. In that sense, choice of the underlying measure that is aligned with bidders' values is critical for the success of such an approach. Thus, situations in which a measure that is acceptable to all bidders exists are prime candidates for this approach.

16.2.3   Defining Biddable Combinations

Allowing bids on prespecified combinations of items can mitigate the difficulty of the winner determination problem, as well as that of other potentially computationally intractable issues that have to be resolved during the course of a combinatorial auction. Müller (chapter 13 of this volume) is devoted to structures of biddable combinations that ensure computational tractability for the winner determination problem.[20] Two things are worth noting. First, in most situations, it is not the size of the biddable combinations nor their number, but rather their structural properties (how they intersect, complement, and supplement each other) that is the main determinant of the complexity of the winner determination problem. Second, most other computational problems in combinatorial auctions involve solving some sort of a winner determination problem, so focusing on complexity of the winner determination is of primary importance.

An important concern in limiting biddable combinations is that such limits could give an unfair advantage to bidders who are able to express their synergies using biddable combinations over bidders whose synergies lie across combinations that are not biddable. This again points to the importance of properly defining auction items and of understanding bidders' synergies, as careful choices there could allow for restricting combinatorial bids in a way that won't be perceived as *unduly* limiting or unfair. Keep in mind that if computational complexity is an issue, there may be no set of usable rules that is completely neutral. In particular, allowing no combinations at all may greatly favor some bidders over others.

It is also worth noting that decisions on limiting biddable combinations interact strongly with decisions on defining items. It may be fairer and more efficient to have more items with bidding allowed on a limited but well-chosen set of combinations than to lump the items into a few biddable "super-items" and allow bidding on any possible combination of these super-items.

16.3   Mitigating Complexity during Bid Submission

One way for the bid taker to deal with the computational complexities of a combinatorial auction is to request that bidders submit bids together with information that will help in the computational process. This section discusses two specific ideas of this type. One approach is completely to shift the computational burden from the auctioneer to the bidders. In the other, the auctioneer is completely responsible for computation but allows bidders to guide the process; in this way, a heuristic can find a suboptimal solution that is aligned with bidders' preferences expressed at the time of bid submission.

16.3.1 Relegating Complexity to Bidders

The auctioneer could choose to take a passive role and let bidders not only submit their bids, but also prove to the auctioneer that their bids ought to be winning ones. Some of the very first and successful combinatorial auction designs, such as AUSM (Banks, Ledyard, and Porter 1989) have this feature. Examples of such policies include standard auction designs that relegate computational burden to bidders such as AUSM and PAUSE (see Land et al. chapter 6). The general idea here is that the auctioneer expects bidders to present a collection of (nonintersecting) bids that improves on the current best collection. (Usually, the measure is the revenue for the auctioneer.) Thus, it is the bidders who have to solve the winner determination problem in such designs. There are variants of such procedures that might generate better auction results. Bidders could be allowed to submit bids without having to demonstrate that their bid could be combined with other bids into the best available collection of bids. In this way, even bidders without any computational abilities could participate in an auction. Then the auctioneer (and perhaps other entities, e.g., those who have an interest in particular rivals not winning) could compute the best collection among available bids.

Relegating computational burden to the bidders is an option that does not really mitigate the computational complexities of combinatorial auctions, but it does relieve the auctioneer at the expense of participating bidders. The advantage of such a scheme is that the bidders know which combinations are of interest to them, whereas the auctioneer may be less well informed and have to be prepared to consider combinations that will not be bid. When designing such auction procedures, one has to be careful about the possible burden of managing, in a timely manner, what may turn out to be massive amounts of information. Also, this approach assumes continuous bidding or multiple rounds of bidding as bidders have to be aware of all bids currently in the system when composing and submitting their proposals.

16.3.2 Bidder Prioritization of Combinations

Park and Rothkopf (2005) propose a fundamentally different approach. They suggest that the bidders be allowed to bid on as many combinations of whatever kind they like but that they be required to prioritize their combinations. They propose that the bid-taker evaluate the bids, starting with no combinations, then including each bidder's top priority combination, then including each bidder's two top priority combinations, and so on, until either all combinations have been included or the time for computation has expired. This approach takes advantage of the bidders' knowledge of which combinations are important. It assures a measure of fairness when computational considerations do not allow all desired combinations to be considered, and it takes advantage of the fact that integer programming algorithms often perform much better in practice than worst-case based bounds. Note that the Park and Rothkopf approach need not be limited to giving an equal number of allowable combinations to each bidder. It could be generalized to accommodate any prespecified construction of the lists of combinations to be considered based on the bidders' input preferences lists. For example, in an iterative auction, bidders who are more active could be favored by being allowed to have more combinations considered.

A potential concern with this method, as well as with any other limited search method (as discussed in section 16.4.1) is that bidders might have incentives to submit bids with a primary goal of complicating computational process in order to limit search and perhaps influence the final, possibly suboptimal, allocation that favors them.

16.4   Mitigating Complexity Prior to Allocation Decisions

Sandholm (chapter 14 of this volume) discussed methods that do not guarantee finding an optimal solution to the winner determination problem or do not guarantee finding it in a reasonable time. The previous section discussed how the problem of solving the winner determination problem can be relegated to the bidders or how solving it could be guided based on bidder input. This section focuses on possibilities of mitigating complexities after bids are submitted.

16.4.1   Limited Search

A simple general method to deal with the complexity of solving the winner determination problem or any other complex problem during the course of an auction is for the bid-taker to announce (prior to the auction start) an upper bound in terms of computational time and/or other resources to be devoted to solving any particular problem. For example, in an iterative combinatorial auction, the time for solving the winner determination problem between two rounds could be limited, and the best available solution when the time expires could determine the provisional winners.

This approach is almost uniformly used in determining minimum bid increments in iterative combinatorial auctions. Instead of basing the increment value on the value of the gap (which would involve solving as many winner determination problems as there are biddable combinations), one could abandon any computational effort and prescribe a simple fixed increment amount (e.g., as in one of the first commercially implemented procurement combinatorial auctions; see Ledyard et al. 2002) or could use the linear programming relaxation of the winner determination problem in order to provide an approximation.[21]

Resorting to a limited search option opens up several issues:

• Should bidders know the details of the algorithm used to solve the winner determination problem (or another problem) under time/resource constraint, and should bidders be able to replicate the procedure used by the bid-taker?

• The very fact that one could select a suboptimal solution potentially allows for a new gaming dimension. At least in theory, bidders might submit bids aimed at slowing the algorithm down and potentially bringing it to settle for a suboptimal solution that favors them. However, in order to implement such a strategy in any limited search approach to the winner determination problem, one would have to know intricate details of the winner determination problem computation, have a very good idea about high bids on all relevant biddable combinations, and have considerable computing resources and expertise, likely beyond those available to the bid-taker. Thus, except maybe in specific narrow situations,[22] it is likely that such malicious bidding with a primary goal of hindering computation would not be a serious problem. The following two observations explain why one might so conclude. If a bid is close to being includable in an optimal solution, then its maker risks it being accepted. Hence, it would be risky to make it if it were insincere. However, if it is not close to being acceptable, it may well be easily eliminated in any branch and bound calculation of the winning bids. Furthermore, outsourcing computation, as suggested in section 16.4.2, could eliminate any computational advantage a bidder has over the bid taker making such an approach even more problematical.

• Given limited resources, the auction designer can choose a heuristic or an approximation algorithm that doesn't guarantee finding an optimal solution but does have some performance guarantees (e.g., that the solution found is not too far in some measure from the optimal one). If such an algorithm finds its solution before all resources are exhausted, for example, before time expires, should the remaining resources be used to attempt to improve on the proposed solution (if it is not provably optimal)?

• What if several problems, for example, the winner determination problem and the minimum bid increment problem, have to be solved within a joint resource constraint? How should resources be allocated?[23]

• How should complaints of bidders who would be winners in an optimal solution but are not winners in the limited search solution be handled?

16.4.2 Outsourcing Search

A compromise approach between relegating complexity to bidders and the limited search option is to allow but not require bidders and, perhaps, other parties to participate in the computational effort. This approach, first proposed by Pekeč (2001), aims at separating computation from the allocation decision. An auction mechanism could treat computation as a transaction service that the auctioneer can outsource. For example, the auctioneer could find an initial solution of the winner determination problem and invite everyone (bidders and perhaps others) to submit alternative solutions. Note that this approach requires the public release of bids (but not necessarily identification of the bidders). In some contexts, as when bidders' bids could reveal sensitive commercial information, this might be a disadvantage (see Rothkopf, Teisberg, and Kahn 1990).

There are several incentives issues that might complicate implementation of this approach. First, the auction-designer could try to set some incentives for computation contributors. Perhaps the auctioneer could pay a fee to whoever finds the best solution to the winner determination problem by, for example, awarding the party that first submits the best solution (hopefully, a provably optimal one), some combination of a fixed monetary award and a percentage of the improvement that the submitted solution made relative to the initial one. Second, as discussed above, participants interested in winning items in the auction might have incentives to submit bids that are aimed at complicating computation, while at the same time having no chance to become winning bids. Similarly, some concern might arise with respect to those interested in collecting computation fees.

In summary, limiting resources for computation surely brushes away potential computational disasters, but it does raise incentive issues.

16.5   Mitigating Complexity after Preliminary Allocation Decisions

A key goal of auctions is often fairness. Perfect efficiency, although desirable, is unlikely to be achieved in large, complicated combinatorial auctions. Indeed, efficiency may well be traded off against the transaction costs associated with conducting the auction. Although perfect efficiency may be unattainable, good efficiency and fairness can be obtained even if it proves impossible to get a provably optimal solution to the winner determination problem. One way to do this is the "political" solution suggested by Rothkopf, Pekeč, and Harstad (1998). The essence of such a political solution to the winner determination problem is to give an opportunity to bidders (and, perhaps, other parties) to challenge and improve upon a proposed allocation before it is made final. Not only will providing such an opportunity for challenges provide a chance to improve the solution to the winner determination problem, it assures fairness. The essence of this is that it will be impossible for a bidder to challenge suboptimal auction results as unfair if the bidder himself has had a fair opportunity to suggest an improved solution. The reason simple auctions are deemed fair is that a bidder who had a fair opportunity to bid cannot credibly complain about the price received by a rival whom he failed to outbid. Similarly, a bidder who has a fair opportunity to improve upon a proposed but possibly suboptimal solution to the winner determination problem cannot credibly complain if, later, a better solution is found. Because he had a fair chance to find it, it was clearly too difficult to find in the time and with the optimization technology available.

It is worth noting that this "political" approach to solving the winner determination problem is likely to be highly effective. It can be thought of as a decomposition approach in which each bidder is assigned the task of finding a way to have some of his tentatively excluded bids included in the final allocation. If the values at stake matter, each of the bidders with tentatively excluded bids will be highly motivated. Bidders, of course, are free to retain optimization experts as auction consultants just as they now hire economists.

Although allowing bidders the chance to improve upon a potentially suboptimal solution to the winner determination problem will assure fairness, it is not necessary to limit the parties who may suggest improvements to bidders. In particular, it may at times make sense for the bid taker to allow any party to suggest improvements. As discussed above, it could motivate such participation by offering whoever supplies the best solution a portion of the improvement in the objective function achieved. This can be thought of as an "economic" solution to the winner determination problem.

16.6 Conclusion

Combinatorial auction design, like many other design problems, is an art. Its practitioners must make choices that affect conflicting design objectives, and its results must be evaluated in the context of the facts of the particular situation. In this chapter, we have attempted to describe a variety of ways that combinatorial auction designers can achieve good auction results when computational issues are potentially intractable. There are quite a few possibilities, and some of them have attractive features of potential use in important contexts.

The items that serve as the underlying atoms of the auction can (and need to) be defined artfully so as to make computation and other aspect of the auction workable. Where bid-takers have knowledge of bidders' preferences, and they normally will, this needs to be taken into account in defining the items. These preferences also need to be taken into account in deciding which combinations will be biddable, and the item definition decision and the biddable combination decision need to be made together. When possible, one should take advantage of ways of making items fungible, either exactly or approximately.

If computation is a problem, its burden can be left with the auctioneer or shifted to the bidders during the course of the auction. If the auctioneer retains it, the bidders may be asked to prioritize bids on combinations so that if the computation cannot consider all of the combinations, it will have considered all of the most important ones. The auctioneer can outsource post-bidding computation to computational experts or to the bidders themselves. Further, the auctioneer can prevent potential problems that could arise from suboptimal allocations by allowing for challenges by third parties.

The combination of the possibilities discussed in this chapter with the computational capabilities discussed in many of the others will allow much better designs for combinatorial auctions in a wide variety of challenging contexts.

Notes

1. There is no section on using aftermarkets to avoid computational problems. If perfect aftermarkets were to exist, there would be no need for combinatorial auctions. With imperfect aftermarkets, bidders' values in the combinatorial auction should reflect the opportunities that do exist in these aftermarkets. Given the results of a combinatorial auction, even imperfect aftermarkets may present opportunities to mitigate the effects of misallocations in the auction. To the extent that this can happen, it can tip the balance in the combinatorial auction design tradeoff between efficient allocation and lower transaction costs toward lower transaction costs. Note also that aftermarkets can not only deal with misallocations caused by the auction design, but also by misallocations caused by changed circumstances and by bidder errors.

2. We refer the reader to chapters 12–14 to learn more about variations of the winner determination problem.

3. The "all-or-nothing" feature that can be represented by the AND Boolean operation, and not other Boolean operators such as OR and XOR, is a fundamental generator of complexities. Suppose Boolean combinations using OR clauses of XOR clauses of single items are allowed (but AND clauses that could create "packages" are not allowed). Then "winner determination" becomes almost trivial computationally as the problem reduces to the max weight system of distinct representatives, i.e., max weight bipartite matching, which is an optimization problem solvable in polynomial time.

4. Given the computational demands of calculating gap for all losing bids in a combinatorial auction in which solving the winner determination problem is not easy, researchers have developed several approximate approaches (e.g., see Hoffman et al., chapter 17; and Kwasnica et al., 2005). For example, Hoffman (2001), reported that in the simulations of one of the earlier versions of the FCC's combinatorial auction, more than 99 percent of the computational time was spent on calculating the gap for all losing bids; this problem eventually resulted in the change of the auction rules (FCC 2002).

5. There are other approaches to resolving ties. Pekeč and Rothkopf 2003 discuss several such approaches.

6. Following Pekeč and Rothkopf 2003.

7. See Segal, chapter 11 of this volume.

8. In fact, as Hoffman (2001) reported, the burden of precisely calculating the gap for all bids can be overwhelming in the context of the FCC combinatorial auction.

9. For that proposal, see O'Neill et al. 2002. For earlier discussions of alternative definitions of transmission rights, see Hogan 1992; Chao and Peck 1996; Baldick and Kahn 1997; and Chao et al. 2000.

10. See Rothkopf, Pekeč, and Harstad 1998. Also note that one of the first papers on combinatorial auctions, Rassenti, Smith, and Bulfin 1982 focuses on this potential application. See also Ball et al., chapter 20 of this volume.

11. For example, consider two objects, a and b, where bidder 1 has values $v_1(a) = 4$, $v_1(b) = 4$, $v_1(ab) = 9$; bidder 2 has $v_2(a) = 1$, $v_2(b) = 5$, $v_2(ab) = 7$, bidder 3 has $v_3(a) = 5$, $v_3(b) = 1$, $v_3(ab) = 7$. Suppose also that each bidder has a budget constraint of 8. If bidding on ab only is allowed, bidder 1 could win with bid $7 + \varepsilon$, whereas if bids on unbundled objects a and b are allowed, bidders 2 and 3 will win with bids of $4 + \varepsilon$ on each of a and b.

12. These items would be atoms of the algebra generated by the union of all objects (each object is a set) that any of the bidders might be interested in bidding on. For example, if each bidder provides a finite list of frequency ranges they would consider buying, one can define auction items to be all nonempty intersections of any collection of such frequency ranges (possibly from different bidders).

13. For example, a bidder could be interested in any 20-MHz range in the 600–700 MHz band.

14. As discussed in subsection 16.2.3, not all combinatorial bids are equally cumbersome during the course of an auction. The informational burden on the auctioneer is also a factor (as discussed in 16.1.2).

15. O'Neill et al. (2005) show that such equilibrium market-clearing prices always exist to support the MIP solution. The rules for the day-ahead and real-time energy auctions (as well as those for other products, such as operating reserves) are in an almost constant state of refinement. For the latest rules in these electricity markets, see ⟨www.pjm.com⟩ and ⟨www.nyiso.com⟩.

16. Suppose $b(ab) = 5$ and $b(bc) = 7$. Although, in isolation, the bid on ab is smaller than the bid on bc, in the presence of other bids, say $b(a) = 2$ and $b(c) = 5$, one could argue that the bid on ab is "better" than bid on bc.

17. There is a substantial literature on this. See, for example, Chao et al. 2000; Baldick and Kahn 1997; and especially O'Neill et al. 2002.

18. For example, the RAD mechanism described in Kwasnica et al. (2005) and the FCC combinatorial auction mechanism (FCC 2002).

19. Some relevant theoretical analysis is in chapter 13 of this volume, by Müller.

20. This is a well-defined and general combinatorial optimization question. However, there is little practical reason to dwell on the analysis of structures that have little chance of being relevant to any auction. Richer payoffs will be found in the exploration of structures of potential practical use.

21. See Hoffman et al., chapter 17 of this volume.

22. For example, government auctions with a dominant corporate bidder could exhibit all such properties: government might have to be very open about the computational process while at the same time bidders could have overwhelming resources and have good ideas of rivals' valuations.

23. For example, suppose that the winner determination problem is solved by a suboptimal solution and, based on that solution, minimum bid increments get calculated optimally without exhausting all resources. Suppose further that not enough resources are left to recalculate the minimum bid increments in case the leftover resources are used for improving the solution to the winner determination problem. Should this further improvement be attempted?

References

Baldick, Ross and Edward P. Kahn (1997), "Contract Paths, Phase Shifters, and Efficient Electricity Trade," *IEEE Transactions on Power Systems*, 12(2): 749–755.

Banks, Jeffrey S., John O. Ledyard, and David P. Porter (1989), "Allocating Uncertain and Unresponsive Resources: An Experimental Approach," *RAND Journal of Economics*, 20, 1–25.

Chao, Hung-Po and Stephen Peck (1996), "A Market Mechanism for Electric Power Transmission," *Journal Regulatory Economics*, 10, 25–59.

Chao, Hung-Po, Stephen Peck, Shmuel Oren, and Robert Wilson (2000), "Flow-Based Transmission Rights and Congestion Management," *The Electricity Journal*, 13, 38–58.

Elmaghraby, Wedad and Shmuel Oren (1999), "The Efficiency of Multi-Unit Electricity Auctions," *The Energy Journal*, 20, 89–116.

FCC (2002), *The Federal Communications Commission Public Notice DA02-260*. Available at ⟨http://wireless.fcc.gov⟩.

Hobbs, Benjamin F., Michael H. Rothkopf, Laurel C. Hyde, and Richard P. O'Neill (2000), "Evaluation of a Truthful Revelation Auction for Energy Markets with Nonconcave Benefits," *Journal Regulatory Economics*, 18(1): 5–32.

Hoffman, Karla (2001), "Issues in Scaling up the 700 MHz Auction Design," Presented at *2001 Combinatorial Bidding Conference*, Wye River Conference Center, Queenstown, MD, October 27.

Hogan, William W. (1992), "Contract Networks for Electric Power Transmission," *Journal Regulatory Economics*, 4, 211–242.

Kwasnica, Anthony M., John O. Ledyard, David Porter, and Christine DeMartini (2005), "A New and Improved Design for Multi-Object Iterative Auctions," *Management Science*, 51, 419–434.

Ledyard, John O., Mark Olson, David Porter, Joseph A. Swanson, and David P. Torma (2002), "The First Use of a Combined Value Auction for Transportation Services," *Interfaces*, 32, 4–12.

O'Neill, Richard P., Udi Helman, Benjamin F. Hobbs, William R. Stewart, Jr., and Michael H. Rothkopf (2002), "A Joint Energy and Transmission Rights Auction: Proposal and Properties," *IEEE Transactions on Power Systems*, 17, 1058–1067.

O'Neill, Richard P., Paul M. Sotkiewicz, Benjamin F. Hobbs, Michael H. Rothkopf, and William R. Stewart, Jr. (2005), "Efficient Market-Clearing Prices in Markets with Nonconvexities," *European Journal of Operational Research*, 164, 269–285.

Park, Sunju and Michael H. Rothkopf (2005), "Auctions with Endogenously Determined Allowable Combinations," RUTCOR Research Report 3-2001, Rutgers University, To appear in the *European Journal of Operational Research*, 164, 399–415.

Pekeč, Aleksandar (2001), "Tradeoffs in Combinatorial Auction Design," Presented at *2001 Combinatorial Bidding Conference*, Wye River Conference Center, Queenstown, MD, October 27.

Pekeč, Aleksandar and Michael H. Rothkopf (2000), "Making the FCC's First Combinatorial Auction Work Well," An official filing with the Federal Communications Commission, June 7, 2000. Available at ⟨http://wireless.fcc.gov/⟩.

Pekeč, Aleksandar and Michael H. Rothkopf (2003), "Combinatorial Auction Design," *Management Science*, 49, 1485–1503.

Rassenti, Stephen J., Vernon L. Smith, and Robert L. Bulfin (1982), "A Combinatorial Auction Mechanism for Airport Time Slot Allocation," *Bell Journal of Economics*, 13, 402–417.

Rothkopf, Michael H. and Coleman Bazelon (2003), "Spectrum Deregulation without Confiscation or Giveaways," Presented at *New America Foundation*, Washington, DC, September.

Rothkopf, Michael H., Aleksandar Pekeč, and Ronald M. Harstad (1998), "Computationally Manageable Combinational Auctions," *Management Science*, 44, 1131–1147.

Rothkopf, Michael H., Thomas J. Teisberg, and Edward P. Kahn (1990), "Why Are Vickrey Auctions Rare?" *Journal of Political Economy*, 98, 94–109.

IV Testing and Implementation

17 Observations and Near-Direct Implementations of the Ascending Proxy Auction

Karla Hoffman, Dinesh Menon, Susara van den Heever, and Thomas Wilson

17.1 Introduction

Chapter 3 of this volume describes the ascending proxy auction mechanism of Ausubel and Milgrom (2002), and presents its proven desirable economic properties. However, major obstacles arise in its practical implementation. The primary implementation obstacles are that the mechanism requires a bidder explicitly to enumerate all combinations of interest (for more on communications requirements, see chapter 11 of this volume), and that the mechanism theoretically assumes very small incremental increases in the minimum acceptable bid prices for each of the proxy rounds. This chapter is concerned with the calculation of the final prices without the need to perform all of the calculations associated with a direct implementation of the ascending proxy algorithm, as the number of rounds that would be required to complete such a direct implementation would be very large when a high level of accuracy is desired. For example, using an increment of $1,000 in a simulated auction of only ten bidders and six licenses where the auction terminated at about $3.5 million (starting at initial prices of $0), the total number of rounds in the ascending proxy auction was often over 3,000. Yet, without very small incremental increases in prices, many of the proven properties of the ascending proxy auction may not hold. This chapter presents the testing and analysis done on various suggested methods to accelerate the ascending proxy auction without losing its desired economic properties. Each of the methods discussed in the chapter assume that bidders have enumerated all combinations of interest.

Section 17.2 outlines the ascending proxy auction mechanism, provides the notation and definitions of properties that are essential to understanding the characteristics of the core outcomes of the ascending proxy auction, and presents observations of various properties of the mechanism. Section 17.3 summarizes three prior approaches to accelerating the ascending proxy auction suggested by Wurman, Cai, Zhong, and Sureka (2003), Parkes (2003), and Ausubel (2003); we conclude section 17.3 with a short description of Parkes' direct method (Parkes 2003) for calculating buyer-optimal core outcomes.

Section 17.4 presents three new approaches for accelerating the ascending proxy auction. The first approach works backwards from the efficient outcome using the concept of *"safe"* prices. This approach is referred to as *"safe start."* The second approach starts with a very large increment, runs the ascending proxy auction to completion, and then iteratively reduces the increment by a factor of ten, repeating the process until prices are calculated to a specified tolerance. This second algorithm is referred to as *"increment scaling."* The third approach combines the safe-start and incremental-scaling algorithms and is referred to as *"increment scaling with safe start."* The number of combinatorial optimization problems needed to achieve the efficient outcome with this combined approach is considerably fewer than any of the other approaches described in the chapter. In addition, this algorithm is capable of providing prices to any specified accuracy.

Section 17.5 presents several propositions that characterize the outcomes implemented by the proposed safe-start increment-scaling algorithm for speeding up the ascending proxy calculations and presents bounds on the computational requirements. Section 17.6 and the appendix present several examples to illustrate the outcomes of the various approaches. Finally, the chapter contains conclusions and recommendations for further research.

17.2   Background

This section contains a brief overview of the ascending proxy auction mechanism, definitions necessary to understand the outcomes of the auction, and observations of the various properties of the auction.

17.2.1   Mechanism Overview

Chapter 2 of this volume describes iterative ascending mechanisms, and chapter 3 provides a complete description of the ascending proxy mechanism. In chapter 2, Ausubel and Milgrom demonstrate that the ascending proxy mechanism converges to a core outcome with straightforward bidding. This auction mechanism converges to the VCG outcome when the buyer submodularity[1] condition holds and the authors show that semisincere equilibrium can be achieved even when this condition does not hold. When one incorporates Parkes and Ungar's (2000a) iBundle(3) with a proxy mechanism, the design is exactly that which Ausubel and Milgrom describe in chapter 3. The main thrust of this chapter is to show how the price allocations of that mechanism can be computed without requiring the computation of each round of proxy bidding. We first summarize the basic design aspects of the ascending proxy auction:

1. Each bidder provides a value at the beginning of the auction for each of their desired packages.

a. Bidders cannot revise the values they provided at the beginning of the auction.

b. Each bidder's valuation vector assumes a quasi-linear utility function, i.e., the change in utility of a package is proportional to the magnitude of the change in value for that package.

c. Each bidder's valuation vector assumes free disposal, i.e., there is no cost in receiving additional items at zero prices.

2. All packages of a bidder are considered mutually exclusive, thus a bidder can win at most one of its bids.

3. All bidders are forced to bid in a straightforward manner through a proxy bidding agent.

4. The auction progresses through a series of proxy bidding rounds and ends when no proxy agent places new bids.

5. In a proxy bidding round, the following events occur:

a. Each proxy agent of a nonprovisionally winning bidder computes the current profit for each desired package of the bidder. Profit is defined as the difference between the value that the bidder has placed on the package and the price that the auctioneer has currently set for the package. At the beginning of the auction, the price of every package is set to epsilon. The auctioneer raises the price of each nonwinning bid by a very small amount each round.

b. Each proxy agent of a nonprovisionally winning bidder then submits a bid at the current price on the bidder's package with the maximum profit. If more than one package has the maximum profit, bids are submitted on all such packages at the current price.

c. The auctioneer then takes all bids placed thus far in the auction and determines a set of provisionally winning bids such that revenue is maximized subject to the restrictions that each item is awarded at most once and that all bids of a bidder are mutually exclusive. The first solution found by the optimization software is the one used, i.e., there is no separate mechanism for choosing among ties.

d. New prices are calculated for each nonwinning package. In both the Parkes and Ungar (2000b) (iBundle(3)) auction and the Ausubel-Milgrom design, the price for a package is calculated by adding a fixed small increment, ε, to the highest previous bid amount placed on the package by the bidder. If the bidder has not previously bid on the package, the increment is added to the opening price for that package. Note that prices are non-anonymous, i.e., in any round of the auction the price for a given bundle is bidder specific. The Wurman-Wellman design, by contrast, formulates a linear program in each round to determine nonlinear, anonymous prices for the next round.

6. All bids are firm offers. A bidder can never reduce the bid amount of a bid submitted by its proxy agent or withdraw the bid.

7. The auction ends when there are no new bids. At the end of the auction, the provisionally winning bids become the winning bids of the auction.

Because all nonwinning bids are incremented by a fixed small *epsilon* amount each round, all nonwinning bidders will increase their bid by epsilon on all bids already made, until these bids are no longer profitable. New bids may be added to the set of "myopic best response" bids when they tie the current set. At some point, a proxy agent will no longer bid for that bidder because the prices on all of the packages of interest are greater than the valuations for those packages. Because all bids remain in the system throughout the auction, one of the already placed bids may become a winning bid. Because a winning bidder will have the price increased by epsilon on all bids *except* his winning bid, all bids other than this winning bid will have profitability less than the already placed winning bid. The proxy will therefore submit no new bids for this bidder until the current winning bid is no longer winning.

Limiting the bidders to straightforward myopic bidding restricts signaling, parking, and other strategic opportunities that can have negative effects on auction efficiency. Similar to a sealed-bid Vickrey auction, bidders have incentives to reveal the true relative values of the different combinations of items they wish to obtain. In its purest form, the effort required to compute the final allocation and the winning prices in a proxy bidding auction requires that the auctioneer run a forward auction with very small bid increments, computing the provisionally winning bidders in each round by solving a combinatorial optimization problem.

17.2.2 Definitions

We provide some definitions and well-known characterizations of the ascending proxy auctions in this section. Throughout this chapter we will use the following notation: A is the set of all agents with $a \in A$ an agent. The set of winning bidders is denoted as A^*, the value of package S to agent a is denoted as $v_a(S)$, and $w(A)$ is the value of the winner determination problem when the valuations on the packages are used as the objective function coefficients.

Free disposal Proxy mechanisms assume the property of free disposal. That is, any agent's value on any superset of items, S, is at least as great as his value for a set $T \subseteq S$. In other words, there is no cost in receiving additional items at zero prices.

Competitive equilibrium: An allocation, S, prices, p, and valuations v, are in competitive equilibrium if and only if the following two conditions hold:

$$v_a(S_a) - p_a(S_a) = \max_{S' \in X}(v_a(S'_a) - p_a(S'_a)), \quad \forall a \in A$$

$$\sum_{a \in A} p_a(S_a) = \max_{S' \in X} \sum_{a \in A} p_a(S'_a)$$

where S_a represents a's package in the allocation S, and X denotes the space of feasible allocations. That is, (S, p) is at competitive equilibrium if allocation S maximizes the payoffs for all agents including the seller, at the prices, p.

See chapters 1 and 3 of this volume for definitions of VCG mechanism, payoffs, and payments. For these VCG payoffs to have desired properties in a combinatorial auction, the "agents-are-substitutes" property must be satisfied. We define this property next.

Agents-are-substitutes (AAS): Based on bidder preferences, this is a condition whereby the following holds for all coalitions of bidders:

$$w(A) - w(A \backslash K) \geq \sum_{a \in K}[w(A) - w(A \backslash a)], \quad \forall K \subset A, 0 \notin K.$$

The AAS condition is a necessary condition for the VCG payments to be supported in the core, and for the existence of a unique buyer-optimal core payoff vector. However, this is not a sufficient condition for an ascending proxy auction to terminate with VCG payments. For this to occur, the stronger condition of buyer submodularity must hold.

Buyer submodularity (BSM): The condition of buyer submodularity requires that the VCG payoff is in the core for all subcoalitions that include the seller:

$$w(L) - w(L \backslash K) \geq \sum_{a \in K}[w(L) - w(L \backslash a)], \quad \forall K \subset L, 0 \notin K, \textit{for all } L \subseteq A, 0 \in L$$

where L represents subcoalitions of all agents, A, that include the seller. This stronger condition is sufficient for truthful, straightforward bidding and for an ascending proxy auction to terminate with the unique buyer Pareto-dominant Vickrey outcome.

Pareto-dominant allocation   An allocation, x', is said to Pareto-dominate an allocation, x, if every agent prefers x' to x. A *buyer Pareto-dominant* allocation is one where every winning bidder prefers x' to x.

If the VCG outcome is in the core, then it is a buyer Pareto-dominant allocation. Also, the core contains the buyer Pareto-dominant point if and only if the VCG payment is in the core (theorem 6, Ausubel and Milgrom 2002).

Failure of BSM condition could result in a winning bidder paying more than the VCG payment, by following a straightforward bidding strategy in an ascending proxy auction. In this chapter, we will present a method, which we label the *safe-start increment-scaling* implementation, that will end with VCG payoffs whenever the AAS condition holds, regardless of whether the BSM condition holds.

When the AAS condition does not hold, the VCG payoff vector may not be in the core. In this case, truthful bidding is not an equilibrium strategy. Parkes et al. (2001) proposed a threshold scheme to use when no such unique Pareto-dominant core outcome exists. This scheme is based on Parkes' studies of the incentive properties of allocations, and essentially minimizes the maximum deviation of payoffs from the VCG payoffs. Payment allocation using this scheme minimizes the bidder's freedom to manipulate the outcome of the bargaining problem by misstating valuations. For more on the price-based allocations, see chapter 2 of this volume.

17.2.3 Observations

In this section, we explain how a straightforward implementation of this mechanism allows for inefficiencies that may result in a solution that, although in the core, could result in payments to the seller that are larger than the Pareto-optimal payments. This inefficiency is due to the nature of the competition the bidders experience in each round and due to the effect of the size of the increment on the prices paid at the close of the auction.

Competition Induced Inefficiencies   The adjustment process in the ascending proxy auction requires that the payoff profile is unblocked in every round; that is, in every round, a bidder is forced to bid an increment higher every time he is not in a winning coalition in that specific round, due to the straightforward bidding strategy. However, some of these winning coalitions in the early rounds cannot be sustained as the prices rise above the valuations of these bidders, and they eventually stop bidding. Such competition in the early rounds results in convergence to a point in the core that may not be buyer Pareto-dominant; that is, straightforward bidding strategy forces the prices higher than the minimum required for winning. This is due to the failure of the BSM condition, according to which the marginal contribution of a specific bidder in a coalition decreases with the size of the coalition. In the process that we describe, we have eliminated this unnecessary competition by first determining an efficient allocation, and therefore both the set of winning and losing bidders, respectively. We then place all bids of losing bidders at their valuations and determine the competition that may exist between these losing bids of nonwinning bidders and all bids of winning bidders.

Increment-Induced Inefficiencies   A practical implementation of an ascending proxy auction requires the specification of a bid increment that is sufficiently larger than the theoretical requirement for small 'ε'. However, this larger increment size can result in two kinds of inefficiencies:

1. The winning bidder might end up paying significantly more than the minimum required to win.
2. A package may get assigned to a bidder who values it less than a losing bidder. This could happen if the increment applied to a standing bid by an agent makes the new minimum acceptable bid amount higher than the maximum valuation on the package. The agent with a lower valuation on the same package, but with a current high standing bid, wins.

17.3   Prior Approaches to Accelerating Proxy Auctions

In this section, we describe three approaches previously proposed to accelerate the ascending proxy mechanism. Each of these approaches involves identifying inflection points that define the path of convergence to final prices, and using the information to adjust prices while avoiding the small incremental steps. Identifying these defining inflection points could be computationally challenging and the number of such points could be exponential, depending on the number of items and agents in an auction. Thus, it is unlikely these approaches are scalable. However, they do provide insight and understanding of the nature of competition among coalitions in an ascending proxy mechanism and demonstrate an improvement in required computational effort over the pure ascending proxy implementation. We end this section with a short description of an approach, proposed by Parkes (2003), that considers the core conditions directly to arrive at the prices obtained by the accelerated proxy method.

17.3.1   Wurman et al.'s Inflection Point Approach

Wurman, Cai, Zhong, and Sureka (2003) plotted the change in the prices of each bid of each bidder throughout the course of the ascending proxy auction and noticed that for many rounds of the auction, the prices progress in a steady fashion. At certain points, however, the rate at which the package prices increase changes. They noticed that these inflection points occur when some bidder (a) adds a package to the packages that he is currently bidding on—that is, the point at which the profit (value – price) of this new package is equal to the profit that he could obtain on his current set of package bids, or (b) when a bidder drops out of the auction (equivalent to the bidder submitting a null bid because nothing is profitable) and (c) when an allocation that was not competitive becomes competitive.

Wurman et al.'s algorithm partitions time into *intervals* during which the demand sets for all agents remain constant. They then calculate a trajectory of the price of a given package in the interval, and from that calculate the next point in time at which an inflection in the package's trajectory will occur. They call a point at which an agent will change his trajectory a *collision* point. Looking among all agents, they find the first collision point. At each collision point, a mixed-integer optimization is solved and new slopes are computed.

In addition to considering bidders separately, the algorithm must compute the proportion of time that a bidder is winning/nonwinning so that it can determine the length of the noncollision interval. To determine when a bid can be part of a winning coalition, the algorithm must maintain information about the set of feasible coalitions. They hypothesize that the algorithm does not need to consider all such feasible coalitions, but only the *single best* allocation for any given coalition of agents.

Agents in an ascending auction will place new bids whenever they have no winning bids, and pass otherwise. Thus, agents that are not part of the winning allocation will continue to increase their bids on previously submitted packages and may also add additional packages to their demand set, at the point where such bids become as profitable as those already bid. One must therefore compute when a new item will be added to the set, as well as determine the most profitable coalition for each package of each bidder. In addition, one must know the allocations that will compete with this coalition. One can then use this information to determine the *inflection points* at which a new coalition becomes competitive with the existing coalitions. This information is also sufficient to determine the prices at these inflection points. At the last inflection point, one has obtained the competitive prices.

Wurman, Zhong, and Cai (2004) extend the above work to cases where an arbitrary number of bundles can be added to the demand sets and where several allocations become competitive simultaneously. In these cases, one must worry that bundles that were previously in the demand sets may be dropped and that there are more alternative coalitions to consider. Their auction rules differ from the Ausubel and Milgrom auction rules in that in the Wurman, Zhong, and Cai (2004) paper, a bidder randomly selects one element in its demand set on which to bid, whereas in the Ausubel and Milgrom design, bidders raise their offers on *all* elements of the best-response set. The authors provide an example that we use in the test cases discussed in section 17.5.

The authors acknowledge that they have not yet studied the computational complexity of the process. Rather than solving the standard winner determination problem, they must instead compute the allocation of attention by calculating the interval computations as comparisons between all combinations of elements in the set and those not in the set. Clearly, as problems increase in size, such calculations can increase dramatically. It is also hard to make a comparison on computational effort because the mixed-integer linear program that they solve is very different from the winner determination problems that we must solve. Our winner determination problem has the "nice" structure of a set-partitioning problem, and may be significantly easier to solve.

We do not present any direct comparisons with the Wurman et al. algorithm, because we have not coded that algorithm. We do know that the computational effort required by the algorithm is dependent on:

- The number of items in the demand set for each agent
- The number of collision points among all agents
- The number of relevant feasible allocations
- The number of times such competitive allocations collide.

17.3.2   Parkes' Indirect Implementation of Core Outcomes

Parkes (2002, revised 2003) proposed a staged implementation of the ascending proxy auction. The basic idea involves identifying the subset of coalitions that contribute to price competition in an ascending auction, and implementing the ascending phase in stages, where each stage involves a competing set of *active* coalitions. A coalition is considered active if every agent in the coalition has its bundle or package in its best response set. The price changes in a stage are computed as the maximal price changes that (a) retain the best response sets of agents and (b) retain competition between all active coalitions. The end of a stage is triggered when a coalition drops out of the active set. This coalitional structure enables large, discrete increments in seller revenue in each stage. The two steps involved in this accelerated implementation are:

Step 1   The first step is to compute the interesting coalitions and the interesting packages for each agent. The set of interesting coalitions, C^*, are those subcoalitions of agents that might be involved in dynamic price competition during the auction. Parkes defines a recursive combinatorial algorithm to construct the sets of interesting coalitions. Let T_i denote the set of interesting packages of agent i that correspond with a coalition $x \in C^*$, with $i \in x$. For every singleton coalition $\{i\}$, the interesting bundle is $\max_S v_i(S)$. Reduced valuations are determined for agents. This reduced valuation function is just an XOR valuation defined over an agent's values for packages in its interesting set.

Step 2   The second step of the staged proxy implementation involves the following computations:

a. At the beginning of each stage, $t \geq 1$, agent i has a current payoff, π_i^t, which is initially $\pi_0^1 = 0$ for the seller, and $\pi_i^1 = \max_{S \in T_i} v_i(S)$, for all $i \in A \backslash 0$. Let $\mathrm{MBR}_i(\pi_i^t)$, labeled the "best response set for agent i at round t, denote the set of packages that are most profitable for agent at the stage t. This is computed as

$$MBR_i(\pi_i^t) = \{S | S \in T_i, v_i(S) - \pi_i^t \geq 0\}.$$

Initially, this best response set includes only the bundle with maximal value, but as payoffs decrease this set monotonically increases. Let δ_i^t denote the best response *slack* for agent i at the start of stage t. This is computed as

$$\delta_i^t = \min[\pi_i^t, \{\pi_i^t - v_i(S) | S \notin MBR_i(\pi_i^t), S \in T_i\}].$$

The *slack* is therefore the maximal possible decrease in π_i^t that will leave the agent's best response set unchanged. An agent is *active* in stage t while $\delta_i^t > 0$. Otherwise, the agent is facing prices that are equal to its value on all packages.

b. Given the best response information, each stage of this accelerated mechanism is implemented as an LP. Let k index into the interesting coalitions C^*, and let C^t denote the set of indices for active coalitions at the start of stage t. These are the coalitions for which all packages are receiving bids and also have at least one agent still active. All dominated coalitions are pruned from C^t, where x is dominated by any $x' \supset x$. Given the active coalitions in a stage, the LP is formulated with decision variables, $x = \{x_k : k \in C^t\}$, where $x_k \geq 0$ is the bidding share for active coalition k, and interpreted as the minimal drop in payoff to agents bidding in coalition k during the stage. The LP formulation is

$$[STAGE]: \quad \pi_0^{t+1} = \max_x[\ldots] \min_{k \in C^t}\{V_k\}$$

Subject to:

$$V_k \geq \pi_0^t + \sum_{i \in C^*(k), bid^t(k,i)} \left[\max_{l:i \in C^*(l), l \in C^t} x_l \right] \quad \forall k \in C^t \tag{17.1}$$

$$\delta_i^t \geq \max_{l:i \in C^*(l), l \in C^t} [x_l] \quad \forall i \in I \backslash 0, \text{ with } \delta_i^t > 0 \tag{17.2}$$

$$x_k \geq 0 \quad \forall k \in C^t$$

where agent i bids, $bid^t(k,i)$, in coalition k during stage t if there is at least one other active coalition that does not include the agent. The objective is to find the payoff changes that maximize the minimal adjusted revenue across all active coalitions. The LP is solved iteratively to break ties so that all active coalitions have the same adjusted revenue.

c. Finally, at the end of the stage, the agent payoffs are adjusted as follows:

$$\pi_i^{t+1} = \pi_i^t - \max_{l:i \in C^*(l), l \in C^t} [x_l].$$

The auctioneer's revenue is updated to π_0^{t+1}, the objective value of [STAGE].

The next stage of the auction is initialized by updating the myopic best response bid sets, the myopic best response slack values, and the active coalitions. The auction terminates when all remaining active agents are included in the same (and active) coalition. The outcome in the final stage is implemented and the agent payments are based on their payoffs in the final stage. The semidirect proxy auction exactly implements the iBundle and Ausubel-Milgrom proxy outcomes. The complexity of these calculations is dependent on the computation needed to identify the interesting coalitions and the interesting packages for each agent. The set of interesting coalitions, C^*, are those subcoalitions of agents that might be involved in dynamic price competition during the auction. There may be an exponential number of such coalitions, and thus the algorithm may not be computationally feasible for large auctions. No computational studies have taken place for this approach.

17.3.3 Ausubel's Method for Accelerating the Ascending Proxy Auction

Ausubel (2003) also identified that the size of the bid increment should only affect the efficiency at moments in the bidding when *change events* occur. He refers to change events as moments in the bidding when a bidder begins bidding on a new package and when a bidder stops bidding on all packages because the proxy's set of profitable bids is empty.

Ausubel notes that when the bidding is not close to a change event it can proceed with very large bid increments, at essentially no cost. However, when the bidding is approaching a change event, the bid increment should be reduced to a very small epsilon, to avoid the inefficiencies and revenue losses of large increments. After the bidding goes past a change event, the bid increments can be drastically increased again until bidding approaches another change event. Because these change events are determined by the valuations provided, the auction system can switch on and off between very large bid increments and very small bid increments, depending on whether or not there exists a bidder who is approaching a change event.

The other issue to model, as it relates to change events, is the determination of when a bidder must raise his bid prices, that is, when the bidder no longer has a winning package in a given round. If one can identify a repeating cycle of events where within a cycle one can predict the sequence of bids that will win in each round, then one can also use larger increments during this entire cycle. Ausubel also notes that not all "change events" are consequential. A change event is consequential only if a bidder introduces a new positive bid *and* if the new bid becomes a provisionally winning bid. Hence, in a situation where the provisionally winning bids are cycling, the auction system can use the following procedure: Allow the bidder to introduce the new bid and re-compute the solutions to the optimization problems for one full cycle. If the new bid never becomes a provisional winner during this cycle, then the change event was inconsequential. In this case, the previously identified cycle will continue to hold, and the auction system can revert to not computing the solution to the optimization problem. However, if the new bid becomes a provisional winner sometime during the cycle, then the change event was consequential, and a new cycling pattern needs to be identified.

In order to implement this approach, one needs to determine the coalitions that impact the cycle of solutions. The challenge is to identify these "interesting" coalitions without incurring too much computation cost. In a large auction, the potential exists for the method to encounter an exponential number of such interesting coalitions. Little computational study has been done to determine how to implement these ideas.

17.3.4 Alternative Approaches

We note that each of the approaches described above are implementations to replicate *exactly* the end results of a proxy auction and mirror the significant change points that occur during that auction. They therefore simulate the bargaining problem that occurs whenever the BSM condition does not hold. As an alternative, Parkes in the same paper as the indirect approach (Parkes 2002, revised 2003) proposes a direct mechanism for obtaining core outcomes without simulating any auction rounds. He first provides an optimization problem that directly determines the buyer-optimal core prices. He labels this the "buyer-optimal core problem." He then uses an observation similar to that which we use in our semidirect approach, namely that the only coalitions that need to be considered are coalitions for subsets of winners. He also shows that many of the "core" constraints among winning coalitions are dominated by other core constraints and need not be explicitly provided to the optimization problem. This second observation is used to define an algorithm for constructing the core constraints needed in the buyer-optimal core problem. He acknowledges that the computational properties of this direct implementation are untested. Future research should determine the size of the problem each of the approaches described above is capable of handling.

17.4   Near-Direct Implementations of Proxy Auction

We now present new algorithms that have all of the attributes of the Ausubel-Milgrom algorithm, but speed up the calculations and improve the prices obtained. We begin by summarizing our assumptions.

We assume that bidders supply a maximum bid amount for all packages they are interested in winning. These bids can have overlapping items, and can have superadditive, additive or subadditive valuations. All bids of a bidder will be treated as mutually exclusive; each bidder can win at most one bid. Our assumptions are consistent with those made by Ausubel-Milgrom in their ascending proxy implementation:

1. Bidders are free to make as many mutually exclusive bids as they wish.
2. Each bidder has private valuations for the items being auctioned (each bidder knows the value of each good and this valuation does not change with information about other bidders willingness to pay).
3. Bidders have quasi-linear utility values without externalities (thereby limiting the bidders' payoffs to be linear in money).
4. Free disposal (i.e., there is no cost in receiving additional items at zero price).
5. Bidders have agreed to have proxy agents bid on their behalf in a straightforward manner.

In this section we propose some relatively easy to implement near-direct ascending implementations that when combined avoid the excessive number of rounds specified by a direct implementation of the Ausubel-Milgrom design. We assure that the allocation is (a) efficient, (b) in the core, and (c) accurate to whatever precision the auctioneer prescribes. When the AAS condition holds, we also show that the prices we obtain are buyer Pareto-dominant VCG payments.

We begin by describing an implementation that accelerates the ascending auction by first determining the efficient outcome and then using this information to jump start the auction at prices that are both *"safe"* and close to the final prices. We then present an alternative implementation that uses ideas of *increment scaling*, similar to that proposed by Bertsekas (1992) and Bertsekas and Castanon (1992) for solving network problems via an auction mechanism. Finally, we merge these two ideas into a *combined safe-start increment-scaling algorithm*.

17.4.1 Safe Start

This algorithm exploits the fact that we have complete knowledge of each agent's valuation vector. These valuations can be used to determine the set of winning bidders in the efficient solution. Thus, by solving the winner determination problem using the agent valuation vectors, we can divide the bidders into two sets: the winning and losing bidders, respectively. We can then determine nontrivial starting prices[2] for each bid of each bidder. Such starting prices can greatly reduce the number of rounds that are necessary to implement core outcomes.

We first present the concept of a "safe start." At the conclusion of the ascending proxy auction, all nonwinning agents have zero profitability. Consequently, each agent in the efficient allocation must bid at least as much as the highest value of any nonwinning agent on his allocated package. This nonwinning high value establishes a safe price for the winning agent's allocated package and can subsequently be used to determine the winning agent's initial profitability and price vector. We argue, similarly, that the initial price vector for every nonwinning agent can be set equal to its valuation vector. We describe this algorithm in further detail below.

Step 1 Solve for the efficient allocation   The efficient allocation is determined by solving the winner determination problem using the complete set of agent valuation vectors. The solution to this problem allows each agent to be categorized as either winning or nonwinning.

Step 2 Initialization step   The bid increment is set to a user-specified required accuracy and all valuations are rounded (down) to that accuracy.

Step 3 Determine safe prices   For each package in the efficient allocation, the safe price is determined by finding the maximal valuation on that package from all nonwinning agents. We call this the *safe price* of the package, denoted s_a^*. Alternatively, one can obtain better safe prices by calculating the Vickrey prices for the winning packages. When the AAS condition holds, the prices obtained are the buyer Pareto-optimal prices. When this property is not satisfied, the Vickrey price may not be in the core and will be lower than the buyer Pareto-optimal prices. Regardless, the Vickrey prices are very good prices with which to start the algorithm.[3] When there are only a few winning bids, we calculate the Vickrey price for each bidder's winning bid and use these prices as our safe start prices. When there are many winning bids, we calculate Vickrey prices only on the larger winning packages, because it is these packages that are likely to not satisfy the AAS condition.

Step 4 Calculate each agent's initial profitability   For each winning agent, profitability π_a is calculated as the difference between their valuation and the safe price of their winning package, where $\pi_a = v_a - s_a^*$. Every nonwinning agent has an initial profitability of zero.

Step 5 Create initial price vectors   The price of every other package for this bidder is set so that the profitability of all packages will be equal to π_a. Thus, $p_i = v_i - \pi_a$, where i is some nonwinning package of winning bidder a. Each losing bidder's initial price vector is equal to his valuation vector.

Step 6 Execute the ascending proxy auction   The ascending proxy auction starts with the initial price vector.

When valuation information is richly defined, the safe-start algorithm provides significant runtime improvements. Simulations have shown that auctions that had run up to two hours could be executed within two minutes by using the safe-start algorithm. Furthermore, this algorithm can eliminate some of the dynamic competition that often leads to outcomes that are not buyer Pareto-dominant due to competition between winning and losing bidders that takes place prior to the losing bidders leaving the auction.

17.4.2   Increment Scaling

One of the greatest challenges to the practical implementation of the ascending proxy auction is finding an acceptable balance between the size of the increment that is used and the runtime that is necessary to execute the auction. We have observed that as the increment is decreased linearly the runtime grows exponentially. However, by iteratively executing the ascending proxy auction with smaller increments,[4] using the outcome of one execution as the basis for the next, it is possible greatly to improve the overall runtime and still implement core outcomes. Furthermore, by applying some corrective measures to this scaled-increment algorithm it is also possible to counteract the increment-induced inefficiencies.

The increment-scaling algorithm attempts to exploit the known properties of the final allocation of the ascending proxy auction to provide a near-optimal starting point for a subsequent iteration. Specifically, all nonwinning agents are at zero profitability and are thus, at best, within one increment of becoming a winning agent. For all winning agents a possibility exists of having bid above that which is necessary.[5] We therefore reduce the current prices for all winning agents by an amount equal to the increment, and maintain the current prices for all nonwinning agents. These new prices provide a starting point for the subsequent iteration of the ascending proxy auction where the increment has been scaled down, in our examples, by a factor of ten. This process continues until the increment is reduced to within a desired threshold. We describe this algorithm in further detail below.

Step 1 Initialize the ascending proxy auction   The "increment threshold" is set equal to the user-supplied accuracy specified. Thus, it is equivalent to the epsilon increment set in step 1 of the safe-start algorithm. The starting increment for the auction (a much larger increment than this epsilon) is set based on the order of magnitude of the valuations submitted. The auction is provided the trivial starting point.

Step 2 Execute the ascending proxy auction   Provided the starting point, the ascending proxy auction is executed until a final outcome is achieved. All packages whose profits lie within the range of the current increment size are submitted in each round. This is achieved by rounding the valuations to the current increment, thus insuring equal profitability for all packages within the range of the current increment.

Step 3 Evaluate the final outcome

Step 3.1 Check if the current increment satisfies the increment threshold. If the increment threshold has been met the increment scaling algorithm terminates, else continue to step 3.2.

Step 3.2 Determine the starting point for the next iteration. Every winning agent's price vector is set equal to their final bid amount in step 2, less the amount of the current increment. Every nonwinning agent's price vector is set equal to his prior bid amount. Go to step 3.3.

Step 3.3 Scale down the current increment. Scale down the current increment by a factor of ten, and return to step 2.

This algorithm always implements a core outcome, but is subject to increment-induced inefficiencies caused by some winning bidder not being able to meet the increment required at some stage. Thus, another winning bidder may make up the difference and will therefore pay more than his fair share. Interestingly, it is possible to recognize when inefficiencies arise during the evaluation of the final outcome from any iteration. As a result, corrective measures can be employed to eliminate the inefficiencies before proceeding to the subsequent iteration.

Corrective Rollback   When winning bids exist in the final outcome of any iteration at a value equal to that agent's starting price on that package and that agent was winning at the conclusion of the prior iteration, then that agent continues to be in a position where he may have overbid. This can be corrected by returning to the starting point of the current iteration and reducing the price vector of the over-extended agent by an amount equal to the prior iteration's increment. This modified starting point is then used to rerun the current iteration. This process continues until the current iteration arrives at an outcome where no agent has been over-extended. The process of adjusting the current iteration's starting point is called a *corrective rollback*. The maximum number of rollbacks possible is equal to the number of digits of precision required. The algorithm changes only in step 3, where the corrective rollback is now step 3.1.

Step 3 Evaluate the final outcome

Step 3.1 Outcome evaluated for agent overextension. If an agent is winning a bundle in the final outcome at the starting price from the current iteration and that agent was winning at the conclusion of the prior iteration, then perform a corrective rollback, and return to *step 2*. Else, continue to step 3.2.

Step 3.2 Check if the current increment satisfies the increment threshold. If the increment threshold has been met, the increment-scaling algorithm terminates. Else, continue to step 3.3.

Step 3.3 Determine the starting point for the next iteration. Every winning agent's price vector is set equal to their final bid amount in step 2 less the amount of the current increment. Every nonwinning agent's price vector is set equal to his prior bid amount. Go to step 3.4.

Step 3.4 Scale down the current increment. Scale down the current increment by a factor of ten, and return to step 2.

17.4.3 Combined Algorithm – Increment Scaling with Safe Start

The combined algorithm uses two aspects of the safe-start algorithm. First, it solves for the efficient outcome. Given the efficient outcome, one can set the profitability of all of the bids of nonwinning bidders to zero. As in the safe-start algorithm, all bids of nonwinning bidders will be provided to the system at their valuations. The bids of winning bidders are also provided to the system for round one, such that all bids of a winning bidder have equal profitability (equal to the difference between the valuation of the winning bid and the safe price for that package). Calculating the efficient solution provides one other bit of information to the combined algorithm: it indicates an upper bound on the revenue for the auction and, therefore, a reasonable start for the increment-scaling algorithm. To determine this initial increment, we find the bidder with maximum profitability (value − safe price). We determine the order of magnitude of this profitability (k) and we set the initial increment equal to 10^k.

With this information as starting information, we perform the increment-scaling algorithm as described above. This algorithm will terminate when the increment threshold has been met. The entire algorithm is shown below:

Step 1 Solve for the efficient allocation Determine the efficient allocation by solving the winner determination problem using the complete set of agent valuation vectors.

The solution to this problem allows each agent to be categorized as either winning or nonwinning.

Step 2 Initialization step   Set the bid increment to a user-specified required accuracy and all valuations are rounded (down) to that accuracy.

Step 3 Determine safe prices   Determine the safe price for each package in the efficient allocation by finding the maximal valuation on that package from all nonwinning agents. We call this the *safe price* of the package, denoted s_a^*. Alternatively, one can obtain a better safe price by calculating the Vickrey price for this winning package.

Step 4 Calculate each agent's initial profitability   For each winning agent profitability, calculate π_a as the difference between their valuation and the safe price of their winning package, where $\pi_a = v_a - s_a^*$. Every nonwinning agent has an initial profitability of zero.

Step 5 Create initial price vectors   Set the price of every other package for this bidder so that the profitability of all packages will be equal to π_a. Thus, $p_i = v_i - \pi_a$, where i is some nonwinning package of winning bidder a. Each losing bidder's initial price vector is equal to his valuation vector.

Step 6 Initialize the increment scaling ascending proxy auction   Set the "increment threshold" equal to the user-supplied accuracy specified. Calculate the initial increment (based on the most profitable bidder's profitability).

Step 7 Execute the ascending proxy auction for the increment specified   Note that in this combined algorithm, bids are not considered on all packages whose profitabilities fall in the range of the current increment, i.e., no rounding of valuations to the current increment occurs. Instead, package bids are based on the profitability calculated using safe prices and the valuations rounded to the increment threshold.

Step 8 Evaluate the final outcome

Step 8.1 Outcome evaluated for agent overextension. If an agent is winning a bundle in the final outcome at the starting price from the current iteration and that agent was winning at the conclusion of the prior iteration then perform a corrective rollback, and return to step 7.

Step 8.2 Check if the current increment satisfies the increment threshold. If the increment threshold has been met, the increment-scaling algorithm terminates. Else, continue to step 8.3.

Step 8.3 Determine the starting point for the next iteration. Every winning agent's price vector is set equal to their final bid amount less the amount of the current increment. Every nonwinning agent's price vector is set equal to his prior bid amount.

Step 8.4 Scale down the current increment. Scale down the current increment by a factor of ten, and return to step 7. By using the corrective measures and the safe start, the combined algorithm produces an outcome that is buyer Pareto-optimal.

17.5   Economic Properties of Near-Direct Implementations

In this section we will show that by using the combined safe-start increment-scaling algorithm, we can achieve all of the desired properties of the Ausubel-Milgrom auction. In addition, when the AAS condition holds but BSM fails, the safe-start increment-scaling algorithm achieves VCG prices.

Specifically, we will show that:

1. The auction ends with an efficient allocation, i.e., the items are awarded to those who value them the most (proposition 17.1).
2. The auction ends with buyer Pareto-optimal payments by winners when the AAS condition holds (proposition 17.2).
3. The auction ends with buyer Pareto-optimal payments in the core even when the BSM property does not hold (proposition 17.3).
4. The auction design has the same properties of not being vulnerable to shill bidding and collusion as the Ausubel-Milgrom proxy auction, because it works off the same premises (proposition 17.4).
5. Our algorithm requires far fewer integer optimizations than a direct application of the ascending proxy auction. We also show that the number of optimizations is bounded by a polynomial in the digits of accuracy required and the number of packages in the optimal allocation (propositions 17.5 and 17.6).

Proposition 17.1   The safe-start increment-scaling algorithm ends with an efficient outcome.

Proof   The first step of this algorithm determines the efficient outcome. The next step sets the bid prices of a winning bidder so that all bids have equal profitability. Thus, the system will consider all bids at every step in the auction. These two features assure that the outcome will be efficient.

Proposition 17.2   The final payoff allocation is in the core.

Proof   Because the last winner determination problem solved by the safe-start increment-scaling algorithm included the bids of all of the nonwinning bidders at their valuations, and presented all bids of winning bidders to the system, the auction cannot stop until the winning coalition is unblocked.

Proposition 17.3   The auction ends with prices that are buyer Pareto-dominant, when the AAS condition holds.

Proof   All bids of nonwinning bidders are provided to the system with bid prices equal to their valuations. At the last round of the last stage of our algorithm, the winner determination problem considered these bids and determined that they were not part of the winning set. Thus, there are no bids of nonwinning bidders that could compete with the winning bids at the final prices. The algorithm also stops with prices such that if any winning bidder reduced their bid by ε (where ε is the required accuracy specified by the auction), then the winning set would no longer be winning. In addition, the rollback process assures that the increment size during a given iteration does not force a winning bidder to subsidize other winning bidders. Thus, the prices are Pareto-dominant for the winners.

We note that a direct implementation of the Ausubel-Milgrom auction could end with prices that are higher than the Pareto-dominant price when the AAS condition holds but the BSM property does not. One essential difference between the two approaches is that the safe-start increment-scaling algorithm eliminates the interim bargaining that may take place between winning and losing bidders prior to the losing bidders leaving the auction. Example 17.1 shows the results of the safe-start increment-scaling algorithm and that of a direct implementation of the Ausubel-Milgrom auction (labeled "pure proxy"). The appendix provides other such examples. In all these examples, the packages with the asterisks represent the optimal allocation and the increment used in each case is 0.01.   ∎

Example 17.1

Agent	1	2	3	4	5
Package	AB*	CD	CD*	BD	AC
Value	10	20	25	10	10

Method	Rounds	Prices paid by winning agents	
		Agent 1, {AB}	Agent 3, {CD}
Pure Proxy	3250	7.51	20.01
Safe Start	1	0.01	20.01
Increment Scaling	18	0.01	20.01
Increment Scaling with Safe Start	1	0.01	20.01
VCG Payments	–	0.00	20.00

We note that a *unique* set of Pareto-optimal prices may not exist when the AAS condition does not hold. Example 17.2 illustrates that there can be many such price sets. We present Parkes' threshold payments to illustrate the payments that are weighted toward the VCG Payments.

Example 17.2

Agent	1	2	3	4
Package	AB	BC*	AC	A*
Value	20	26	24	16

		Prices paid by winning agents	
Method	Rounds	Agent 2, {BC}	Agent 4, {A}
Pure Proxy	3100	12.01	12.01
Safe Start	801	16.01	8.01
Increment Scaling	20	17.01	7.01
Increment Scaling with Safe Start	15	16.01	8.01
VCG Payments	–	8.00	0.00
Threshold Payments	–	16.00	8.00

Proposition 17.4 The safe-start increment-scaling implementation does not have vulnerability to shill bidding and collusion by losing bidders, even when items do not satisfy the AAS condition.

Proof   This result was proven for the Ausubel-Milgrom framework. Our algorithm has the same characteristics as that of the Ausubel-Milgrom ascending proxy auction.

Proposition 17.5 The number of optimizations that are required by the safe-start increment-scaling algorithm is:

$$(d \cdot k \cdot 10^2) + c$$

where d is the number of digits of accuracy required, k is the number of winning bidders, and c is a constant.

Proof   To begin the algorithm, one must first solve the winner determination problem considering all bids with their maximum bid amount. The solution to this problem determines (a) an upper bound on the revenue of the problem, and (b) the set of winners that compose the winning set and the size of this set, k. The solution also determines the size of ε for the initial stage of the proxy auction. The safe-start increment-scaling algorithm proceeds in stages. In the first stage, one chooses an increment size based on the size of the theoretical maximum profitability of the winning bids. Given the increment size, one can determine the maximum number of steps that this stage would require by examining the number of possible bids that each winning bidder must make to go from the "safe start" price to his maximum valuation. Totaling all such steps determines an upper bound on the rounds that occur in this stage. If one finds that the possible number of steps is too large, then one can increase the increment size, knowing that the algorithm might require more rollbacks with a larger beginning increment.

After this initial stage, each additional stage provides one additional digit of accuracy, because we reduce the increment at each stage by a factor of ten. Thus, to obtain d additional digits of accuracy from the first increment size, one must perform d stages. Each stage comprises a number of auction rounds. For each round, any bids that are nonwinning and not at their maximum bid amount are raised by the increment size. Because we decrement the size by a factor of ten in each stage, the maximum number of times any bid could be raised in a given stage is ten. And because all bids of nonwinning bidders are at their maximum bid amount, only the winning bidders can change their bids from round to round. Thus, in the worst case, only one bidder is nonwinning in each round and, therefore, in each round, at worst only one bidder must raise all of his bids by the increment. Each such bidder can make such changes at most ten times, resulting in the maximum number of bids made in a stage of $k * 10$. However, because there may be as many as ten rollbacks in a stage (highly unlikely, but a worst-case bound), we increase the number of winner determination problems by a factor of ten to $k * 10^2$. Thus, the total number of rounds in the staged auction is $d * k * 10^2$ and the total number of optimizations performed is $(d * k * 10^2) + c$, where c denotes the number of winner determination problems that occur in the first round. This number is dependent upon the initial increment and on the number of optimization problems required to compute safe prices for each winning package.

We end this section by noting that when the BSM property holds, the prices obtained through the ascending proxy auction are VCG prices that are buyer Pareto-optimal in the core. However, there may be prices *not in the core* that buyers may prefer. Consider the example below (case 17.3 in the appendix):

Agent	1	2		3	4	
Package	AB*	AB	C*	AB	AB	C
Value	15	14	5	9	10	4

In this example, agent 2 cannot win package AB because agent 1 has a higher valuation. The VCG prices are 13 (for package AB won by agent 1) and 4 (for package C won by agent 2). However, if one removes the competition of nonwinning bids of winning bidders from consideration, then the prices would reduce to $10 (for agent 1 on package AB) and remain $4 (for agent 2 on package C). The reason for this reduction is that we have removed the competition of agent 2 from consideration (because agent 2 could never win package AB over agent 1). Notice that this example shows how a winning bidder can have an impact on what another winning bidder will pay for the items won.

Proposition 17.6 The prices obtained can be accurate to whatever precision is needed.

Proof   The safe-start increment-scaling algorithm works in stages, refining the winning bid set and the associated second prices. The accuracy required is specified up-front and determines the number of stages of the auction. Each stage of the auction provides one additional digit of accuracy, when the increment factor is set to ten.

17.6   Examples from the Literature

This section present results from a few examples found in the literature. Example 17.3 shows results from the example in the Wurman, Zhong, and Cai (2004) paper. We note again that the rules these authors use are slightly different from those used in the Ausubel-Milgrom paper (see section 17.3.4). Also, under the column heading "Rounds," we are reporting the number of mixed integer optimizations performed in the Wurman, Zhong, and Cai (2004) method. Because we perform one integer optimization in each round, this is a direct comparison of the number of optimization problems performed by each method. However, one should keep in mind that the structure of the optimization problems we compute are pure set-partitioning problems, whereas the integer optimization problems proposed by Wurman, Zhong, and Cai (2004) are more complicated and likely to be harder to solve. Thus, we provide only a weak comparison of computational effort. (For more on computational complexity of specific set-partitioning structures, see chapter 19 of this volume). We also alert the reader to the fact that a tie exists and there are two solutions with equal revenue of 25.02, namely {1-A, 2-BC} and {1-A, 2-B, 3-C}.

Example 17.3

Optimal Allocation {1–A, 2–BC}; Optimal Value = $28.00; Optimal Revenue = $25.00

Method	Rounds	Allocation {Agent-Package}	Prices ($)	Revenue ($)	Value ($)
Pure Proxy	3234	{1–A; 2–B; 3–C}	{8.01; 8.01; 9.00}	25.02	28.00
Safe Start	51	{1–A; 2–BC}	{7.51; 17.51}	25.02	28.00
Increment Scaling	39	{1–A; 2–BC}	{7.51; 17.51}	25.02	28.00
Increment Scaling with Safe Start	11	{1–A; 2–BC}	{7.51; 17.51}	25.02	28.00
Zhong et al.'s Approach	11	{1–A; 2–BC}	{8.00; 17.00}	25.00	28.00
VCG Payments	–	{1–A, 2–BC}	{7.00; 17.00}	24.00	28.00
Threshold Payments	–	{1–A, 2–BC}	{7.50; 17.50}	25.00	28.00

In appendix 17.7.1, we present a few additional small test cases. Appendix 17.7.2 shows the results from a collection of ten problems that were generated previously to test linear pricing algorithms. For more information on how these problems were generated, see Dunford et al. 2003. These cases constitute larger simulations involving six items and ten bidders, and consist of problems that simulate an auction for FCC spectrum licenses where synergies are the natural result of adjacent markets creating additional value to the bidder. In these instances, the auction had a total value between $3.1 and $4.4 million.

Figure 17.1 graphs the number of winner determination problems that have to be solved using each of the proxy algorithms for the ten larger profiles. Note that a logarithmic scale is used. Notice that on these problems, the combined safe-start increment-scaling algorithm often requires more computational effort than the safe-start algorithm. This can occur when the safe prices are either equal to or nearly equal to the second prices. Because the increment scaling technique starts with a much larger increment, additional winner determination problems have to be solved until the increment is scaled down to the desired resolution. The additional computational effort is required to prove that the safe prices represent the true second prices. The small examples (cases 17.4, 17.5, and 17.6) show instances where the safe-start increment-scaling method performs significantly better than the safe start method. In each of these cases, the AAS condition does not hold.

In appendix 17.7.3, we present four profiles provided to us by David Porter. These profiles are based on experiments with human subjects that were designed to test their

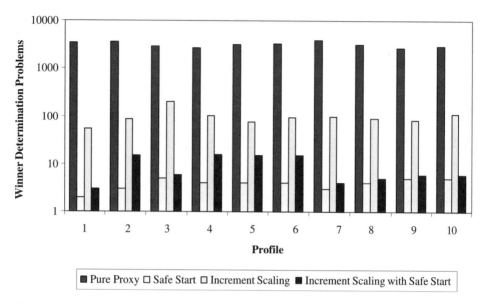

Figure 17.1
Number of winner determination problems for each algorithm.

combinatorial clock auction design (see Porter et al. 2003). For each of these profiles, three separate experiments were performed. The auction used a 10 percent increment rule—if an item has excess demand in the current round, the price of that item will increase by 10 percent for the next round. One notices that these clock auctions ended in very few rounds, but with prices consistently above the minimal second prices. We conjecture that the reason for this greater revenue is due to the increment size. With smaller increments, the number of rounds required to complete the auction would increase, but the combinatorial clock auction would likely end with prices closer to the minimal second prices.

17.7 Conclusion

In this chapter we have described a new algorithm that yields prices having all of the desirable properties of the Ausubel-Milgrom ascending proxy auction design while significantly reducing the number of integer optimizations required to obtain the desired second prices. The algorithm is easy to implement and allows the auctioneer to obtain payment amounts that are accurate to any desired precision. They provide buyer Pareto-dominant results (VCG payments) whenever the AAS condition holds, even if the BSM condition does not. However, when the AAS condition fails, the allocation of the payments among buyers is likely to be different even when each of the implementations arrives at the same total (core) auction revenue.

Direct implementations of the Ausubel-Milgrom ascending proxy auction and our near-direct proxy algorithm have an added attribute. Assume that the winning bidders expect that their valuations will be kept secret from other participants after the termination of the auction. In addition, assume that the auction has the added requirement that the bidders must be provided with sufficient information to validate that the auction's outcomes were properly determined (i.e., bidders can replicate the results of the auction). The ascending proxy mechanisms and the near-direct implementation described in this paper allow such validation. When these mechanisms are rerun with the winning bidders' highest bid on each package replacing the valuation on the package, the same outcome is obtained. Thus, transparency can be achieved *without* giving other bidders access to the valuations. Neither the VCG mechanism nor the direct mechanism of Parkes' has this attribute.

In this chapter, we provided limited computational testing. Future testing is required to ascertain how viable this approach is for auctions with a much larger number of items.

We note that all of the designs investigated in this chapter assume that the bidders have complete knowledge of their package valuations at the beginning of the auction; that is, they do not allow for price discovery. Future research could investigate a multi-stage implementation of the proxy auction that enables bidders to revise their valuations between stages. For more on dynamic proxy auctions, see chapter 5 of this volume.

Acknowledgments

This research was partially funded by the Federal Communications Commission under a contract to Computech Inc. All views presented in this research are those of the authors and do not necessarily reflect the views of the Federal Communications Commission or any of its staff.

17.8 Appendix

17.8.1 Small Test Cases

The increment for this group of test cases was set to 0.01. In all cases, the optimal allocation, value and revenue reported at the top of the results table correspond to the proposed combined safe start and increment scaling algorithm.

Case 17.1   AAS condition satisfied, BSM satisfied

Agent	1	2		3	4	
Package	AB*	AB	C*	AB	AB	C
Value	15	14	5	9	10	4

Optimal Allocation {A1–AB, A2–C}; Optimal Value = 20; Optimal Revenue = 17.02

Method	Rounds	Revenue	Prices paid by winning agents	
			Agent 1, {AB}	Agent 2, {C}
Pure Proxy	2450	17.02	13.01	4.01
Safe Start	1	17.01	13.00	4.01
Increment Scaling	31	17.02	13.01	4.01
Increment Scaling with Safe Start	1	17.02	13.01	4.01
VCG Payments	–	17	13.00	4.00
Threshold Payments	–	17	13.00	4.00

Case 17.2   AAS condition satisfied, BSM not satisfied

Agent	1	2	3	4	5
Package	AB	BC	C	C*	AB*
Value	21	35	14	20	22

Optimal Allocation {A4–C, A5–AB}; Optimal Value = 42; Optimal Revenue = 35.02

Method	Rounds	Revenue	Prices paid by winning agents	
			Agent 4, {C}	Agent 5, {AB}
Pure Proxy	4025	36.76	15.75	21.01
Safe Start	1	35.02	14.01	21.01
Increment Scaling	38	35.01	14.00	21.01
Increment Scaling with Safe Start	1	35.02	14.01	21.01
VCG Payments	–	35	14.00	21.00
Threshold Payments	–	35	14.00	21.00

Case 17.3   AAS condition satisfied, BSM not satisfied

Agent	1	2	3	4	5
Package	AB*	CD	CD*	BD	AC
Value	10	20	25	10	10

Optimal Allocation {A1–AB, A3–CD}; Optimal Value = 35; Optimal Revenue = 20.02

Method	Rounds	Revenue	Prices paid by winning agents	
			Agent 1, {AB}	Agent 3, {CD}
Pure Proxy	3250	27.52	7.51	20.01
Safe Start	1	20.02	0.01	20.01
Increment Scaling	18	20.02	0.01	20.01
Increment Scaling with Safe Start	1	20.02	0.01	20.01
VCG Payments	–	20.00	0.00	20.00

Case 17.4   AAS condition not satisfied

Agent	1		2		3
Package	A*	B	A	B*	AB
Value	16	16	8	8	10

Optimal Allocation {A1–A, A2–B}; Optimal Value = 24; Optimal Revenue = 10.02

Method	Rounds	Revenue	Prices paid by winning agents	
			Agent 1, {A}	Agent 2, {B}
Pure Proxy	1500	10.02	5.01	5.01
Safe Start	401	10.02	6.01	4.01
Increment Scaling	19	10.02	5.01	5.01
Increment Scaling with Safe Start	9	10.02	6.01	4.01
VCG Payments	–	2	2.00	0.00
Threshold Payments	–	10	6.00	4.00

Case 17.5   AAS condition not satisfied

Agent	1		2		3		4	5
Package	AB*	C	BC	B	AC	C	AB	C*
Value	15	5	15	5	12	3	12	6

Optimal Allocation {A1–AB, A5–C}; Optimal Value = 21; Optimal Revenue = 17.02

			Prices paid by winning agents	
Method	Rounds	Revenue	Agent 1, {AB}	Agent 5, {C}
Pure Proxy	1890	17.02	12.01	5.01
Safe Start	101	17.00	13.00	4.00
Increment Scaling	23	17.01	12.00	5.01
Increment Scaling with Safe Start	6	17.02	13.01	4.01
VCG Payments	–	15	12.00	3.00
Threshold Payments	–	17	13.00	4.00

Case 17.6   AAS condition not satisfied

Agent	1	2	3	4
Package	AB	BC*	AC	A*
Value	20	26	24	16

Optimal Allocation {A2–BC, A4–A}; Optimal Value = 42; Optimal Revenue = 24.02

			Prices paid by winning agents	
Method	Rounds	Revenue	Agent 2, {BC}	Agent 4, {A}
Pure Proxy	3100	24.02	12.01	12.01
Safe Start	801	24.02	16.01	8.01
Increment Scaling	20	24.02	17.01	7.01
Increment Scaling with Safe Start	15	24.02	16.01	8.01
VCG Payments	–	8.00	8.00	0.00
Threshold Payments	–	24.00	16.00	8.00

17.8.2 Larger Simulations

The increment for this group of larger simulations was set to $1,000. In all cases, the optimal allocation, value, and revenue reported at the top of the results table correspond to the proposed combined safe-start and increment-scaling algorithm. All dollar amounts are in thousands.

Profile 17.1 AAS condition satisfied

Optimal Allocation {6–6057}; Optimal Value = $3,477; Optimal Revenue = $3,305

Method	Rounds	Prices (Agent–$ Payment)	Revenue ($)
Pure Proxy	3429	{6–3,306}	3,306
Safe Start	1	{6–3,306}	3,306
Increment Scaling	53	{6–3,305}	3,305
Increment Scaling with Safe Start	1	{6–3,306}	3,306
VCG Payments	–	{6–3,305}	3,305

Profile 17.2 AAS condition not satisfied

Optimal Allocation {1–1005, 8–6041}; Optimal Value = $3,405; Optimal Revenue = $3,391

Method	Rounds	Prices (Agent–$ Payment)	Revenue ($)
Pure Proxy	3542	{1–535; 8–2,856}	3,391
Safe Start	1	{1–535; 8–2,856}	3,391
Increment Scaling	88	{1–535; 8–2,857}	3,392
Increment Scaling with Safe Start	13	{1–535; 8–2,857}	3,392
VCG Payments	–	{1–535; 8–2,856}	3,391

Profile 17.3   AAS condition satisfied

Optimal Allocation {1–6007, 4–1003, 6–1005, 8–1006}; Optimal Value = $3,822; Optimal Revenue = $3,481

Method	Rounds	Prices (Agent–$ Payment)	Revenue ($)
Pure Proxy	2973	{1–2,057; 4–490; 6–487; 8–450}	3,484
Safe Start	1	{1–2,056; 4–490; 6–488; 8–450}	3,484
Increment Scaling	203	{1–2,057; 4–491; 6–487; 8–449}	3,484
Increment Scaling with Safe Start	1	{1–2,056; 4–490; 6–488; 8–450}	3,484
VCG Payments	–	{1–2,056; 4–489; 6–487; 8–449}	3,481

Profile 17.4   AAS condition not satisfied

Optimal Allocation {1–1002, 2–6035, 6–6015}; Optimal Value = $3,169; Optimal Revenue = $3,085

Method	Rounds	Prices (Agent–$ Payment)	Revenue ($)
Pure Proxy	2633	{1–505; 2–1,569; 6–1,013}	3,087
Safe Start	1	{1–506; 2–1,568; 6–1,012}	3,086
Increment Scaling	101	{1–506; 2–1,570; 6–1,012}	3,088
Increment Scaling with Safe Start	13	{1–506; 2–1,568; 6–1,013}	3,087
VCG Payments	–	{1–505; 2–1,568; 6–1,011}	3,084

Profile 17.5   AAS condition not satisfied

Optimal Allocation {4–6053, 6–1003}; Optimal Value = $3,451; Optimal Revenue = $3,398

Method	Rounds	Prices (Agent–$ Payment)	Revenue ($)
Pure Proxy	3162	{4–2,919; 6–479}	3,398
Safe Start	2	{4–2,920; 6–479}	3,399
Increment Scaling	77	{4–2,920; 6–479}	3,399
Increment Scaling with Safe Start	13	{4–2,920; 6–479}	3,399
VCG Payments	–	{4–2,919; 6–477}	3,396

Profile 17.6   AAS condition not satisfied

Optimal Allocation {6–6049, 10–1004}; Optimal Value = $3,426; Optimal Revenue = $3,409

Method	Rounds	Prices (Agent–$ Payment)	Revenue ($)
Pure Proxy	3361	{6–2,898; 10–511}	3,409
Safe Start	2	{6–2,899; 10–510}	3,409
Increment Scaling	92	{6–2,897; 10–511}	3,408
Increment Scaling with Safe Start	13	{6–2,901; 10–508}	3,409
VCG Payments	–	{6–2,897; 10–508}	3,405

Profile 17.7   AAS condition satisfied

Optimal Allocation {1–1006, 10–6026}; Optimal Value = $4,412; Optimal Revenue = $4,141

Method	Rounds	Prices (Agent–$ Payment)	Revenue ($)
Pure Proxy	3995	{1–694; 10–3,447}	4,141
Safe Start	1	{1–694; 10–3,448}	4,142
Increment Scaling	99	{1–694; 10–3,447}	4,141
Increment Scaling with Safe Start	1	{1–694; 10–3,447}	4,141
VCG Payments	–	{1–694; 10–3,447}	4,141

Profile 17.8   AAS condition satisfied

Optimal Allocation {1–1002, 3–1003, 6–6051}; Optimal Value = $3,312; Optimal Revenue = $3,221

Method	Rounds	Prices (Agent–$ Payment)	Revenue ($)
Pure Proxy	3182	{1–506; 3–473; 6–2,245}	3,224
Safe Start	1	{1–506; 3–473; 6–2,245}	3,224
Increment Scaling	90	{1–506; 3–472; 6–2,245}	3,223
Increment Scaling with Safe Start	1	{1–505; 3–473; 6–2,245}	3,223
VCG Payments	–	{1–505; 3–472; 6–2,244}	3,221

Profile 17.9   AAS condition satisfied

Optimal Allocation {1–6050, 6–1003, 8–1001, 10–1002}; Optimal Value = $3,140; Optimal Revenue = $3,097

Method	Rounds	Prices (Agent–$ Payment)	Revenue ($)
Pure Proxy	2654	{1–1,632; 6–478; 8–487; 10–503}	3,100
Safe Start	1	{1–1,632; 6–478; 8–487; 10–504}	3,101
Increment Scaling	83	{1–1,632; 6–478; 8–487; 10–503}	3,100
Increment Scaling with Safe Start	1	{1–1,631; 6–478; 8–487; 10–504}	3,100
VCG Payments	–	{1–1,631; 6–477; 8–486; 10–503}	3,097

Profile 17.10   AAS condition satisfied

Optimal Allocation {1–1002, 3–6034, 6–6015, 8–1001}; Optimal Value = $3,086; Optimal Revenue = $3,025

Method	Rounds	Prices (Agent–$ Payment)	Revenue ($)
Pure Proxy	2911	{1–506; 3–1,024; 6–1,012; 8–487}	3,029
Safe Start	1	{1–506; 3–1,024; 6–1,012; 8–486}	3,028
Increment Scaling	111	{1–505; 3–1,023; 6–1,011; 8–487}	3,026
Increment Scaling with Safe Start	1	{1–506; 3–1,023; 6–1,012; 8–487}	3,028
VCG Payments	–	{1–505; 3–1,023; 6–1,011; 8–486}	3,025

17.8.3   Comparisons with Clock Mechanism

The following test cases correspond to case 1 from Porter et al. 2003, where the authors distinguish instances by characterizing "join" and "own" factors. For further explanation of these factors, please refer to that paper. The increment for the comparisons with the clock mechanism was, where applicable, set to 1. The clock mechanism increased prices by 10 percent per round. In all cases, the optimal allocation, value, and revenue reported at the top of the results table correspond to the proposed combined safe start and increment scaling algorithm.

Case 17.1 (Join = 70; Own = No)

Optimal Allocation {1–6022, 2–6520, 3–6288, 4–6192, 5–1010}; Optimal Value = $430; Optimal Revenue = $304

Method	Rounds	Prices (Agent–$ Payment)	Revenue ($)	Value ($)
Pure Proxy	359	{1–84; 2–30; 3–77; 4–62; 5–50}	303	430
Safe Start	51	{1–71; 2–80; 3–51; 4–51; 5–50}	302	430
Increment Scaling	54	{1–81; 2–32; 3–79; 4–61; 5–49}	302	430
Increment Scaling with Safe Start	18	{1–99; 2–67; 3–59; 4–44; 5–33}	302	430
Porter's Clock Mechanism (10% increment)	14	{1–116; 2–76; 3–73; 4–36; 5–73}	374	430
	8	{1–90; 2–60; 3–60; 4–60; 5–30}	300	430
	9	{1–99; 2–66; 3–66; 4–66; 5–33}	330	430
VCG Payments	–	{1–20; 2–30; 3–0; 4–0; 5–0}	50	430

Case 17.1 (Join = 70; Own = Yes)

Optimal Allocation {1–6022, 2–6520, 3–6288, 5–1010, 6–6192}; Optimal Value = $430; Optimal Revenue = $246

Method	Rounds	Prices (Agent–$ Payment)	Revenue ($)	Value ($)
Pure Proxy	314	{1–85; 2–36; 3–66; 5–50; 6–29}	266	430
Safe Start	28	{1–94; 2–42; 3–41; 5–27; 6–44}	248	430
Increment Scaling	121	{1–85; 2–42; 3–51; 5–41; 6–32}	251	430
Increment Scaling with Safe Start	28	{1–87; 2–37; 3–49; 5–30; 6–46}	249	430
Porter's Clock Mechanism (10% increment)	14	{1–116; 2–76; 3–73; 5–36; 6–73}	374	430
	8	{1–90; 2–60; 3–60; 5–30; 6–60}	300	430
	9	{1–99; 2–66; 3–66; 5–33; 6–60}	324	430
VCG Payments	–	{1–85; 2–14; 3–23; 5–8; 6–24}	154	430

Case 17.1 (Join = 81; Own = No)

Optimal Allocation {1–6022, 2–6520, 3–6288, 4–6192, 5–1010}; Optimal Value = $430; Optimal
Revenue = $352

Method	Rounds	Prices (Agent–$ Payment)	Revenue ($)	Value ($)
Pure Proxy	415	{1–104; 2–37; 3–80; 4–81; 5–50}	352	430
Safe Start	47	{1–87; 2–77; 3–63; 4–73; 5–50}	350	430
Increment Scaling	66	{1–101; 2–41; 3–79; 4–81; 5–48}	350	430
Increment Scaling with Safe Start	20	{1–103; 2–69; 3–61; 4–80; 5–41}	354	430
Porter's Clock Mechanism (10% increment)	20	{1–120; 2–76; 3–76; 4–73; 5–44}	389	430
	13	{1–99; 2–76; 3–73; 4–69; 5–36}	353	430
	12	{1–120; 2–66; 3–73; 4–80; 5–40}	379	430
VCG Payments	–	{1–40; 2–30; 3–16; 4–26; 5–24}	136	430

Case 17.1 (Join = 81; Own = Yes)

Optimal Allocation {1–6022, 2–6520, 3–6288, 5–1010, 6–6192}; Optimal Value = $430; Optimal
Revenue = $280

Method	Rounds	Prices (Agent–$ Payment)	Revenue ($)	Value ($)
Pure Proxy	336	{1–86; 2–45; 3–76; 5–50; 6–25}	282	430
Safe Start	32	{1–114; 2–45; 3–53; 5–38; 6–27}	277	430
Increment Scaling	72	{1–85; 2–47; 3–75; 5–44; 6–24}	275	430
Increment Scaling with Safe Start	23	{1–107; 2–43; 3–62; 5–40; 6–28}	280	430
Porter's Clock Mechanism (10% increment)	14	{1–116; 2–76; 3–73; 5–36; 6–73}	374	430
	10	{1–109; 2–73; 3–73; 5–36; 6–60}	351	430
	10	{1–109; 2–73; 3–73; 5–36; 6–60}	351	430
VCG Payments	–	{1–85; 2–14; 3–23; 5–8; 6–24}	154	430

Notes

1. Definitions of the submodularity condition appear in section 17.2.2.

2. A starting point is defined by a collection of initial price vectors assigned to the respective agents. A trivial starting point sets all prices equal to ε.

3. We thank Larry Ausubel for suggesting the use of Vickrey prices as a "best" safe price.

4. The idea of an increment scaling algorithm is similar to that employed by Bertsekas (1992), and Bertsekas and Castanon (1992).

5. The increment effect can be as large as k-times the increment, where k is the number of packages in the final allocation. Additionally, the effect of dynamic competition can result in inefficiencies that are unknown a priori.

References

Ausubel, Lawrence M. (2003), "On Accelerating the Calculations of the Ascending Proxy Auction," E-mail communication.

Ausubel, Lawrence M. and Paul Milgrom (2002), "Ascending Auctions with Package Bidding," *Frontiers of Theoretical Economics*, 1, 1–42. Available at ⟨http://www.bepress.com/bejte/frontiers/vol1/iss1/art1⟩.

Bertsekas, Dimitri P. (1992), "Auction Algorithms for Network Flow Problems: A Tutorial Introduction," *Computational Optimization and Applications*, 1, 7–66.

Bertsekas, Dimitri P. and D. A. Castanon (1992), "A Forward Reverse Auction Algorithm for Asymmetric Assignment Problems," *Computational Optimization and Applications*, Vol. 1, 277–297.

Dunford, Melissa, Karla Hoffman, Dinesh Menon, Rudy Sultana, and Thomas Wilson (2003), "Price Estimates in Ascending Combinatorial Auctions," Technical Report, George Mason University, Systems Engineering and Operations Research Department.

Milgrom, Paul (1998), "Putting Auction Theory to Work: The Simultaneous Ascending Auction," *Journal of Political Economy*, 108, 245–272.

Parkes, David C. (1999), "iBundle: An Efficient Ascending Price Bundle Auction," *Proceedings of the 1st ACM Conference on Electronic Commerce*, 148–157.

Parkes, David C. (2003), "Notes on Indirect and Direct Implementations of Core Outcomes in Combinatorial Auctions," Technical Report, Harvard University.

Parkes, David C. and Lyle H. Ungar (2000a), "Iterative Combinatorial Auctions: Theory and Practice," *Proceedings of the 17th National Conference on Artificial Intelligence (AAAI-00)*, 74–81.

Parkes, David C. and Lyle H. Ungar (2000b), "Preventing Strategic Manipulation in Iterative Auctions: Proxy Agents and Price Adjustment," *Proceedings of the 17th National Conference on Artificial Intelligence (AAAI-00)*, 82–89.

Parkes, David C., Jayant R. Kalagnanam, and Marta Eso (2001), "Achieving Budget-Balance with Vickrey-Based Payment Schemes in Exchanges," *Proceedings of the 17th International Joint Conference on Artificial Intelligence (IJCAI-01)*, 1161–1168.

Parkes, David C. and Lyle Ungar (2002), "An Ascending-Price Generalized Vickrey Auction," Technical Report, Harvard University.

Porter, David, Stephen Rassenti, Anil Roopnarine, and Vernon Smith (2003), "Combinatorial Auction Design," *Proceedings of the National Academy of Sciences*, 100, 11153–11157.

Wurman, Peter R. and Michael P. Wellman (1999), "Equilibrium Prices in Bundle Auctions," *Proc. AAAI-99 Workshop on Artificial Intelligence for Electronic Commerce*, 56–61.

Wurman, Peter R., Gangshu Cai, Jie Zhong, and Ashish Sureka (2003), "An Algorithm for Computing the Outcome of Combinatorial Auctions with Proxy Bidding," *Fifth International Conference on Electronic Commerce (ICEC-03)*, 1–8.

Wurman, Peter R., Jie Zhong, and Gangshu Cai (2004), "Computing price Trajectories in Combinatorial Auctions with Proxy Bidding," *Electronic Commerce Research and Applications*, To appear.

18   A Test Suite for Combinatorial Auctions

Kevin Leyton-Brown and Yoav Shoham

Many researchers have proposed algorithms for determining the winners of general combinatorial auctions, with encouraging results. (Chapter 14 of this book describes some of these algorithms.) This line of research has given rise to another problem, however. In order to evaluate—and thus to improve—such algorithms, it is necessary to use some sort of test data. Unfortunately, there is little data recording the behavior of real bidders upon which such test data may be built; furthermore, even as such data becomes available, algorithmic testing will require benchmarks that permit arbitrary scaling in the problem size. It is thus necessary to generate artificial data that is representative of the sort of scenarios one is likely to encounter. This chapter describes such a test suite.

18.1   Past Work on Testing CA Algorithms

18.1.1   Experiments with Human Subjects

One approach to experimental work on combinatorial auctions has used human subjects. These experiments assign valuation functions to subjects, then have them participate in auctions using various mechanisms (Banks, Ledyard, and Porter 1989; Ledyard, Porter, and Rangel 1997; DeMartini et al. 1998). Such tests can be useful for understanding how real people bid under different auction mechanisms; however, they are less suitable for evaluating the mechanisms' computational characteristics. In particular, this sort of test is only as good as the subjects' valuation functions, which in the above papers were hand-crafted. As a result, this technique does not easily permit arbitrary scaling of the problem size, a feature that is important for characterizing an algorithm's performance. In addition, this method relies on relatively naive subjects to behave rationally given their valuation functions, which may be unreasonable when subjects are faced with complex and unfamiliar mechanisms.

18.1.2 Particular Problems

A parallel line of research has examined particular problems to which CAs seem well suited. For example, researchers have considered auctions for real estate (Quan 1994), the right to use railroad tracks (Brewer and Plott 1996), pollution rights (Ledyard and Szakaly 1994), airport time slot allocation (Rassenti, Smith, and Bulfin 1982), and distributed scheduling of machine time (Wellman et al. 1998). Most of these papers do not suggest holding an unrestricted general CA, presumably because of the computational obstacles. Instead, they tend to discuss alternative mechanisms that are tailored to the particular problem. None of them proposes a method of generating test data, nor do any of them describe how the problem's difficulty scales with the number of bids and goods. However, they still remain useful to researchers interested in general CAs because they give specific descriptions of problem domains to which CAs may be applied.

18.1.3 Artificial Distributions

A number of researchers have proposed algorithms for determining the winners of general CAs. In the absence of test suites, some have suggested novel bid generation techniques, parameterized by number of bids and goods (Sandholm 1999; Fujishima, Leyton-Brown, and Shoham 1999; Boutilier, Goldszmidt, and Sabata 1999; de Vries and Vohra 2003). Other researchers have used one or more of these distributions (e.g., Parkes 1999; Sandholm et al. 2005), whereas still others have refrained from testing their algorithms altogether (e.g., Nisan 2000; Lehmann, O'Callaghan, and Shoham 1999). Parameterization represents a step forward, making it possible to describe performance with respect to the problem size. However, there are several ways in which each of these bid generation techniques falls short of realism, concerning the selection of which goods and how many goods to request in a bundle, what price to offer for the bundle, and which bids to combine in an XORed set. More fundamentally, however, all of these approaches suffer from failing to model bidders explicitly, and from attempting to represent an economic situation with a non-economic model.

Which Goods First, each of the distributions for generating test data discussed above has the property that all bundles of the same size are equally likely to be requested. This assumption is clearly violated in almost any real-world auction: most of the time, certain goods (for which "natural" complementarities exist) will be more likely to appear together than others.

Number of Goods Likewise, each of the distributions for generating test data determines the number of goods in a bundle completely independently from determining *which* goods appear in the bundle. Although this assumption may appear more reasonable, there are many domains in which the expected number of items in a bundle will be related to which goods it contains. To give an example, in an electronics domain, people buying computers might tend to make long combinatorial bids, requesting monitors, printers, and so on, whereas those buying refrigerators might tend to make short bids.

Price   Next, there are problems with the schemes for generating price offers used by all four techniques. Prices cannot make an easy distribution hard (consider the tractable cases discussed in chapter 13 of this volume); however, if prices are not chosen carefully then an otherwise hard distribution can become computationally easy.

Sandholm (2002) draws prices randomly from either $[0, 1]$ or from $[0, g]$, where g is the number of goods requested. The first method is clearly unreasonable (and computationally trivial) because price is unrelated to the number of goods in a bid—note that one bid for a large bundle and another for a small subset of the same bundle will have the same expected price. The second method is better, but has the disadvantage that mean and range are parameterized by the same variable.

Boutilier, Goldszmidt, and Sabata (1999) distribute prices of bids normally with mean 16 and standard deviation 3, giving rise to the same problem as the $[0, 1]$ case above.

Fujishima, Leyton-Brown, and Shoham (1999) draw prices from $[g(1 - d), g(1 + d)]$, $d = 0.5$. Although this scheme avoids the problems described above, prices are simply additive in g and are unrelated to *which* goods are requested in a bundle, both strong and often unrealistic assumptions.

More fundamentally, Anderson, Tenhunen, and Ygge (2000) note a critical pricing problem that arises in several of the schemes discussed above. As the number of bids to be generated becomes large, a given short bid will be drawn much more frequently than a given long bid. Because the highest priced bid for a bundle dominates all other bids for the same bundle, short bids end up being much more competitive. Indeed, for extremely large numbers of bids, a good approximation to the optimal solution is simply to take the best singleton bid for each good. One solution to this problem is to guarantee that only the first bid for each bundle will be retained. However, this solution has the drawback that it is unrealistic: different real bidders *are* likely to place bids on some of the same bundles.

The best way of addressing this problem is to make bundle prices superadditive in the number of goods they request—indeed, the fact that bidders' valuations satisfy this property is often a motivation for holding a combinatorial auction in the first place. De Vries and Vohra (2003) take this approach, making the price for a bid a quadratic function of the prices of bids for subsets. (However, this pricing scheme makes it difficult to control the amount of the increase in price as a function of bundle length.) Where appropriate, the distributions presented in this chapter will include a pricing scheme that may be configured to be superadditive or subadditive in bundle length, parameterized to control how rapidly the price offered increases or decreases as a function of bundle length.

XOR Bids Finally, although most of the bid-generation techniques discussed above permit bidders to submit sets of bids XORed together, they have no way of generating meaningful sets of such bids. As a consequence, the computational impact of XORed bids has been very difficult to characterize.

18.2 Generating Realistic Bids

Although the lack of standardized, realistic test cases does not make it impossible to evaluate or compare algorithms, it does make it difficult to know what magnitude of real-world problems each algorithm is capable of solving, or what features of real-world problems each algorithm is capable of exploiting. This second ambiguity is particularly troubling: it is likely that algorithms would be designed *differently* if they took the features of more realistic[1] bidding into account. (As we will see, chapter 19 of this volume discusses one such algorithm-design approach.)

18.2.1 Prices, Price Offers, and Valuations

Researchers have traditionally used the term "price" when constructing artificial distributions to describe the amount offered for a bundle. However, this term really refers to the amount a bidder is made to pay for a bundle, which is of course mechanism-specific and often not the same as the amount offered. The distributions described in this chapter aim to model bidders' valuations, which are of course mechanism-independent. For consistency with past literature we will continue to use the term *price offer* to refer to the numeric portion of a bid; this may be understood as referring to bids placed in the VCG mechanism, in which it is a dominant strategy for bidders to make price offers equal to their true valuations (see chapter 1 of this volume). Researchers wanting to model bidding behavior in other mechanisms can still use our distributions by transforming the generated valuation according to bidders' equilibrium strategies in the given mechanism.

18.2.2 The Combinatorial Auction Test Suite

In this chapter we present the combinatorial auction test suite (CATS), a set of distributions that attempt to model realistic bidding behavior. This suite is grounded in previous research on specific applications of combinatorial auctions, as described in section 18.1.1. At the same time, all of our distributions are parameterized by numbers of goods and bids, facilitating the study of algorithm performance. This suite represents a move beyond previous work on modeling bidding in combinatorial auctions because we provide an economic motivation for both the contents and the valuation of a bundle, deriving them from basic bidder preferences. In particular, in each of our distributions:

- Certain goods are more likely to appear together than others.
- The number of goods appearing in the bundle is often related to which goods appear in the bundle.
- Valuations are related to which goods appear in the bundle. Where appropriate, valuations can be configured to be subadditive, additive, or superadditive in the number of goods requested.
- Sets of XORed bids are constructed in meaningful ways, on a per-bidder basis.

The CATS suite also contains a legacy section including all bid generation techniques described above, so that new algorithms may easily be compared to previously published results. More information on the test suite, including executable versions of our distributions for Linux and Windows, appear on the CATS website.

In section 18.3, we present distributions based on five real-world situations. For most of our distributions, the mechanism for generating bids involves first building a graph representing economically motivated relationships between goods, and then using the graph to generate sets of substitutable bids, each of which requests bundles of complementary goods. Of the five real-world situations we model, the first three concern complementarity based on adjacency in a graph, whereas the final two concern complementarity based on correlation in time. Our first example (section 18.3.1) models shipping, rail, and bandwidth auctions. Goods are represented as edges in a nearly planar graph, with agents submitting an XORed set of bids for paths connecting two nodes. Our second example (section 18.3.2) models an auction of real estate, or more generally of any goods over which two-dimensional adjacency is the basis of complementarity. Again the relationship between goods is represented by a graph, in this case strictly planar. In section 18.3.3 we relax the planarity assumption from the previous example in order to model arbitrary complementarities between discrete goods such as electronics parts or collectables. Our fourth example (section 18.3.4) concerns the matching of time slots for a fixed number of different goods; this case applies to airline takeoff and landing rights auctions. In section 18.3.5 we discuss the generation of bids for a distributed job-shop scheduling domain, and also its application to power generation auctions. Finally, in section 18.3.7 we provide a legacy suite of bid generation techniques, including all those discussed in section 18.1.3.

In the descriptions of the distributions that follow, let $rand(a,b)$ represent a real number drawn uniformly from $[a,b]$. Let $rand\_int(a,b)$ represent a random integer drawn uniformly from the same interval. With respect to a given graph, let $e(x,y)$ represent the proposition that an edge exists between nodes x and y. All of the distributions are parameterized by the number of goods (num_goods) and number of bids (num_bids).

18.3 CATS in Detail

18.3.1 Paths in Space
There are many real-world problems that involve bidding on paths in space. Generally, this class may be characterized as the problem of purchasing a connection between two points. Examples include truck routes (Sandholm 1993), natural gas pipeline networks (Rassenti, Reynolds, and Smith 1994), network bandwidth allocation, and the right to use railway tracks (Brewer and Plott 1996).[2] In particular, spatial path problems consist of a set of points and accessibility relations between them. Although the distribution we propose may be configured to model bidding in any of the above domains, we will use the railway domain as our motivating example because it is both intuitive and well understood.

More formally, we will represent this domain by a graph in which each node represents a location on a plane, and an edge represents a connection between locations. The goods on auction are therefore the edges of the graph, and bids request a set of edges that form a path between two nodes. We assume that no bidder desires more than one path connecting the same two nodes, although the bidder may value each path differently.

Building the Graph   The first step in modeling bidding behavior for this problem is determining the graph of spatial and connective relationships between cities. One approach would be to use an actual railroad map, which has the advantage that the resulting graph would be unarguably realistic. However, it would be difficult to find a set of real-world maps that could be said to exhibit a similar sort of connectivity and would encompass substantial variation in the number of cities. Because scaling the size of input data is of great importance to the testing of new CA algorithms, we have chosen to generate such graphs randomly. Figure 18.1 shows a representative example of a graph generated using our technique.

We begin with *num_cities* nodes randomly placed on a plane. We add edges to this graph, G, starting by connecting each node to a fixed number of its nearest neighbors. Next, we iteratively consider random pairs of nodes and examine the shortest path connecting them, if any. To compare, we also compute various alternative paths that would require one or more edges to be added to the graph, given a penalty proportional to distance for adding new edges. (We do this by considering a complete graph C, an augmentation of G with the new edges weighted to reflect the distance penalty.) If the shortest path involves new edges—despite the penalty—then the new edges (without penalty) are added to G, and replace the existing edges in C. This process models our simplifying assumption that there will exist uniform demand for shipping between any pair of cities, though of course it does not mimic the way new links would actually be added to a rail network. The process continues until slightly more edges

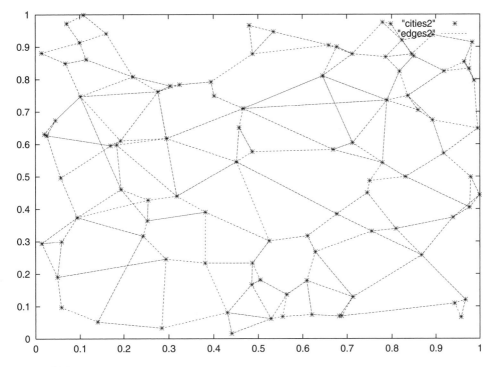

Figure 18.1
Sample "railroad" graph.

have been created than the number of goods in the auction being modeled. (This is achieved by the "1.05" in the first line of figure 18.2.) The reason more edges than are necessary are created is that some edges will not ultimately appear in bids.

Our technique produces slightly nonplanar graphs—graphs on a plane in which edges occasionally cross. We consider this to be reasonable, as the same phenomenon may be observed in real-world rail lines, highways, network wiring, and so on. Of course, determining the "reasonableness" of a graph is a subjective task unless quantitative metrics are used to assess quality.

Generating Bids Once we have constructed a map of cities and the connectivity between them, we must next use this map to generate bids. We propose a method that generates a set of substitutable bids from a hypothetical agent's point of view. We start with the value to an agent for shipping from one city to another and with a shipping cost that we make equal to the Euclidean distance along the path. We then place XOR bids on all paths for which the agent has positive utility. The path's value is random, in (parameterized) proportion to the Euclidean distance between the chosen cities, and

Let $num\_cities = num\_goods \div edge\_density \times 1.05$
Randomly place nodes (cities) on a unit box
Connect each node to its *initial_connections* nearest neighbors
While $num\_edges < num\_cities \times edge\_density$
    $C = G$
    For every pair of nodes $n_1, n_2 \in G$ where $\neg e(n_1, n_2)$
        Add an edge to C of length
          building_penalty $\cdot$ *Euclidean_distance*(n_1, n_2)
    End For
    Choose two nodes at random, and find the shortest path
     between them in C
    If shortest path uses edges that do not exist in G
        For every such pair of nodes $n_1, n_2 \in G$ add an edge to G
        with length *Euclidean_distance*(n_1, n_2)
    End If
End For

Figure 18.2
Paths in space: Graph-building technique.

with a minimum value of this distance. (Bidders with smaller values would never be able to place bids.)

We aim to generate bids over a desired number of goods; however, in this distribution the number of goods (edges in the graph) is not a parameter that can be set directly. Thus we must do some extra work to ensure that we hit our target.

First, there are some generated edges that we choose to remove. Some edges are useful only for shipping directly between the two cities they connect. These edges are somewhat unrealistic; also, because they will only be selected for singleton bids, they will not increase the size of the search space. A similar argument can be made about any small disconnected component of the graph: these goods would be better modeled as a separate auction, and contribute very little to the difficulty of the winner determination problem. At some point in the bid generation process—usually before we have generated all of the bids—the total number of goods requested across all bids will meet our target. (Recall that we started out with more goods than we want to generate.) At this point we check for edges that are used only in singleton bids or isolated groups of bids, and delete those bids. Once we reach the target number of goods without deleting any bids, we delete all goods that are uninvolved in the bids we have generated so far, and continue with bid generation.

Second, it is possible that we will reach our target number of bids *without* making use of the target number of goods. In this case, we must generate a new graph, increasing the number of cities in order to increase the expected number of different goods used as a fraction of bids generated.

```
finished = true
Do
    While num_generated_bids < num_bids
        Randomly choose two nodes, n₁ and n₂
        d = rand(1, shipping_cost_factor)
        cost = Euclidean_distance(city₁, city₂)
        value = d · Euclidean_distance(city₁, city₂)
        Make XOR bids of value − cost on every path from city₁ to
          city₂ having cost < value
        If there are more than max_bid_set_size such paths, bid
          on the max_bid_set_size paths that maximize value − cost.
        If number of goods receiving bids ≥ num_goods
            remove isolated singleton bids and isolated bid
              groups
            remove from the city map all edges that do not
              participate in any bid
        End If
    End While
    If number of goods receiving bids < num_goods
        delete all bids
        delete graph
        num_cities = num_cities + 1
        run graph generation
        finished = false
    End While
While finished not false
```

Figure 18.3
Paths in space: Bid-generation technique.

Note that this distribution, and indeed all others presented in this chapter, may generate slightly more than *num_bids* bids. This occurs because we only check to see whether we have generated enough bids after we have generated an entire XOR set of bids. In our experience, CA optimization algorithms tend not to be highly sensitive to the number of bids, so we judged it more important to build economically sensible sets of substitutable bids. If generating a precise number of bids *is* important, it is a simple matter to remove an appropriate number of bids after generation is complete.

CATS default parameter values: *initial_connections* = 2, *building_penalty* = 1.7, *shipping_cost_factor* = 1.5, *max_bid_set_size* = 5.

Multiunit Extensions: Bandwidth Allocation, Commodity Flow This model may also be used to generate realistic data for multiunit CA problems such as network bandwidth allocation and general commodity flow. The graph may be created as above, but with a number of units (capacity) assigned to each edge. Likewise, the bidding technique remains unchanged except for the assignment of a number of units to each bid.

18.3.2 Proximity in Space

There is a second broad class of real-world problems in which complementarity arises from adjacency in two-dimensional space. An intuitive example is the sale of adjacent pieces of real estate (Quan 1994). Another example is drilling rights, where it is much cheaper for an oil company to drill in adjacent lots than in lots that are far apart. In this section, we first propose a graph-generation mechanism that builds a model of adjacency between goods, and then describe a technique for generating realistic bids on these goods. Note that in this section nodes of the graph represent the goods on auction, whereas edges represent the adjacency relationship.

Building the Graph   There are a number of ways we could build an adjacency graph. The simplest would be to place all the goods (locations, nodes) in a grid, and connect each to its four neighbors. We propose a slightly more complex method in order to permit a variable number of neighbors per node (corresponding, for example, to non-rectangular pieces of real estate). As above we place all goods on a grid, but with some probability we omit a connection between goods that would otherwise represent vertical or horizontal adjacency, and with some probability we introduce a connection representing diagonal adjacency (figure 18.4). (We call horizontally or vertically adjacent nodes *hv-neighbors* and diagonally adjacent nodes *d-neighbors*.)

```
Place nodes at integer vertices (i, j) in a plane, where
  1 ≤ i, j ≤ ⌈√(num_goods)⌉
For each node n
    If n is on the edge of the map
        Connect n to as many hv-neighbors as possible
    Else
        If rand(0, 1) ≤ three_prob
            Connect n to a random set of three of its four
              hv-neighbors
        Else
            Connect n to all four of its hv-neighbors
        While rand(0, 1) ≤ additional_neighbor
            Connect g to one of its d-neighbors, provided that
              the new diagonal edge will not cross another
              diagonal edge
        End While
End For
```

Figure 18.4
Proximity in space: Graph-building technique.

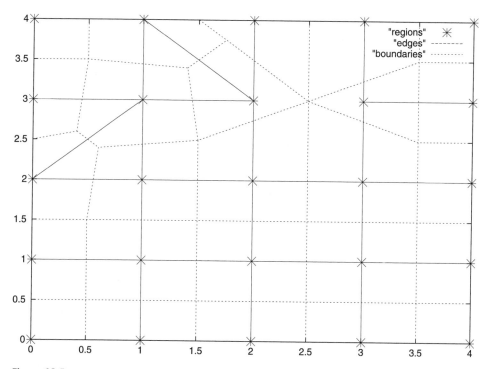

Figure 18.5
Sample real estate graph.

Figure 18.5 shows a sample real estate graph, generated by the technique described in figure 18.4. Nodes of the graph are shown as asterisks, and edges are represented by solid lines. The dashed lines show a set of property boundaries that could be represented by this graph. Note that one node falls inside each piece of property, and that two pieces of property border each other if and only if their nodes share an edge.

Generating Bids To model realistic bidding behavior, we generate a set of common values for each good, and private values for each good for each bidder. The common value represents the appraised or expected resale value of each individual good. The private value represents the amount that a given bidder values that good, as an offset to the common value (e.g., a private value of 0 for a good represents agreement with the common value). We use these private valuations to determine both a value for a given bid and the likelihood that a bidder will request a bundle including that good. There are two additional components to each bidder's preferences: a minimum total common value for which the bidder is prepared to bid, and a budget. The former reflects the idea that a bidder may only wish to acquire goods of a certain recognized value. The latter reflects the fact that a bidder may not be able to afford every bundle that is of interest to him.

To generate bids, we start with a random good, chosen with probability weighted by a bidder's preferences. Next, we determine whether another good should be added by drawing a value uniformly from $[0, 1]$, and adding another good if this value is smaller than a threshold. This is equivalent to drawing the number of goods in a bid from a decay distribution.[3] We must now decide which good to add. Ordinarily, we select only goods from the set of nodes bordering the goods in B. However, we assign a small probability to "jumping" to a new node of the graph: in this case we add a new good selected uniformly at random from the set of goods, without the requirement that it be adjacent to a good in the current bundle B. This permits bundles requesting un-connected regions of the graph: for example, a hotel company may only wish to build in a city if it can acquire land for two hotels on opposite sides of the city.

In the case where we do not "jump," the probability that some adjacent good n_1 will be added depends on how many edges n_1 shares with the current bundle, and on the bidder's relative private valuations for n_1 and n_2. For example, if nodes n_1 and n_2 are each connected to B by one edge and the private valuation for n_1 is twice that for n_2, then the probability of adding n_1 to B, $p(n_1)$, is $2p(n_2)$. Further, if n_1 has three edges to nodes in B, whereas n_2 is connected to B by only one edge, and the goods have equivalent private values, then $p(n_1) = 3p(n_2)$.

Once we have determined all the goods in a bundle we set the price offered for the bundle, which depends on the sum of common and private valuations for the goods in the bundle, and also includes a function that is superadditive (depending on our parameter settings) in the number of goods (figure 18.6).[4] Finally, we generate additional bids that are substitutable for the original bid, imposing the constraint that each bid in the set must request at least one good from the original bid (figure 18.7).

CATS default parameter values: *three_prob* $= 1.0$, *additional_neighbor* $= 0.2$, *max_good_value* $= 100$, *max_substitutable_bids* $= 5$, *additional_location* $= 0.9$, *jump_prob* $= 0.05$, *additivity* $= 0.2$, *deviation* $= 0.5$, *budget_factor* $= 1.5$, *resale_factor* $= 0.5$, and $S(n) = n^{1+additivity}$. Note that *additivity* $= 0$ gives additive bids, and *additivity* < 0 gives subadditive bids.

Spectrum Auctions   A related problem is the auction of radio spectrum, in which a government sells the right to use specific segments of spectrum in different geographical areas (Plott and Cason 1996; Ausubel et al. 1997). It is possible to approximate bidding behavior in spectrum auctions by making the assumption that all complementarity arises from spatial proximity. (This assumption would be violated, for example, if some bidders wanted to secure the right to broadcast at the same frequency in several adjacent areas.) In cases where this assumption is acceptable, our

```
For all  g, c(g) = rand(1, max_good_value)
While  num_generated_bids < num_bids
      For each good, reset  p(g) =
      rand(−deviation · max_good_value, deviation · max_good_value)
```

$$pn(g) = \frac{p(g) - deviation \cdot max\_good\_value}{2 \cdot deviation \cdot max\_good\_value}$$

```
      Normalize  pn(g) so that  ∑_g pn(g) = 1
      B = {}
      Choose a node  g at random, weighted by  pn( ), and add it to
       B
      While  rand(0, 1) ≤ additional_location
            Add_Good_to_Bundle(B)
```

$value(B) = \sum_{x \in B}(c(x) + p(x)) + S(|B|)$

```
      If  value(B) ≤ 0 on  B, restart bundle generation for this
       bidder
      Bid  value(B) on  B
```

$budget = budget\_factor \cdot value(B)$

$min\_resale\_value = resale\_factor \cdot \sum_{x \in B} c(x)$

```
      Construct substitutable bids. For each good  g_i ∈ B
            Initialize a new bundle,  B_i = {g_i}
            While  |B_i| < |B|
                  Add_Good_to_Bundle(B_i)
            Compute  c_i = ∑_{x ∈ B_i} c(x)
      End For
      Make XOR bids on all  B_i where  0 ≤ value(B) ≤ budget and
       c_i ≥ min_resale_value.
      If there are more than  max_substitutable_bids such bundles,
       bid on the  max_substitutable_bids bundles having the largest
       value
End While
```

Figure 18.6
Proximity in space: Bid-generation technique.

```
Routine Add_Good_to_Bundle(bundle  B)
      If  rand(0, 1) ≤ jump_prob
            Add a good  g ∉ B to  B, chosen uniformly at random
      Else
            Compute  s = ∑_{x ∉ B, y ∈ B, e(x,y)} pn(x)
            Choose a random node  x ∉ B from the distribution
             ∑_{y ∈ B, e(x,y)} \frac{pn(x)}{s}
            Add  x to  B
      End If
End Routine
```

Figure 18.7
Proximity in space: Add good to bundle.

spatial proximity model is nearly sufficient for generating bidding distributions for spectrum auctions, given two modifications. First, in a spectrum auction, each good may have multiple units (frequency bands) for sale. It is insufficient to model this as a multiunit CA problem, however, if bidders have the constraint that they want the same frequency in each region.[5] Instead, the problem can be modeled with multiple distinct goods per node in the graph, and bids constructed so that all nodes added to a bundle belong to the same "frequency." With this method, it is also easy to incorporate other preferences, such as preferences for different types of goods. For instance, if two different types of frequency bands are being sold, one 5 megahertz wide and one 2.5 megahertz wide, an agent only wanting 5-megahertz bands could make substitutable bids for each such band in the set of regions desired (generating the bids so that the agent will acquire the same frequency in all the regions). Second, our current scheme for generating price offers may be inappropriate for the spectrum auction domain. Research indicates that although price offers will still tend to be superadditive, this superadditivity may be quadratic in the population of the region rather than exponential in the number of regions (Ausubel et al. 1997); see section 18.3.6. Finally, we should note some very recent work on modeling bidder behavior in spectrum auctions, albeit with restrictions to specific auction mechanisms under consideration by the FCC (Dunford et al. 2004; Porter et al. 2003).

18.3.3 Arbitrary Relationships

Sometimes complementarities between goods will not be as universal as geographical adjacency, but some kind of regularity in the complementarity relationships between goods will still exist. Consider an auction of different, indivisible goods, for example, for semiconductor parts, collectables, or distinct multiunit goods such as the right to emit some quantity of different pollutants produced by an industrial process. In this section we describe a general way of modeling such arbitrary relationships.

Building the Graph   We express the likelihood that a particular pair of goods will appear together in a bundle as being proportional to the weight of the appropriate edge of a fully connected graph (figure 18.8). That is, the weight of an edge between n_1 and n_2 is proportional to the probability that, having only n_1 in our bundle, we will add n_2. Weights are only proportional to probabilities because we must normalize them so that the sum of all weights from a given good sum to 1.

```
Build a fully-connected graph with one node for each good
Label each edge from n₁ to n₂ with a weight  d(n₁, n₂) = rand(0, 1)
```

Figure 18.8
Arbitrary relationships: Graph-building technique.

Generating Bids Our technique for modeling bidding is a generalization of the technique used for proximity in space (section 18.3.2), applied to the complete graph constructed above. We choose a first good and then proceed to add goods one by one, with the probability of each new good being added depending on the current bundle. Unlike in the proximity in space distribution, the graph is fully connected here; thus there is no need for the "jumping" mechanism described above. The likelihood of adding a new good g to bundle B is proportional to $\sum_{y \in B} d(x, y) \cdot p_i(x)$. The first term $d(x, y)$ represents the likelihood (independent of a particular bidder) that goods x and y will appear in a bundle together; the second, $p_i(x)$, represents bidder i's private valuation of the good x. We implement this new mechanism by providing a modified routine *Add_Good_to_Bundle( )* (figure 18.9); otherwise, we use the bid-generation technique described in figure 18.6.

CATS default parameter values: *max_good_value* = 100, *additional_good* = 0.9, *max_substitutable_bids* = 5, *additivity* = 0.2, *deviation* = 0.5, *budget_factor* = 1.5, *resale_factor* = 0.5, and $S(n) = n^{1+additivity}$.

18.3.4 Temporal Matching

We now consider real-world domains in which complementarity arises from a temporal relationship between goods. In this section we discuss matching problems, in which corresponding time slices must be secured on multiple resources. The general form of temporal matching includes m sets of resources, in which each bidder wants one time slice from each of $j \le m$ sets subject to certain constraints on how the times may relate to one another (e.g., the time in set two must be at least two units later than the time in set three). Here we concern ourselves with the problem in which $j = 2$, and model the problem of airport takeoff and landing rights.

At present, the FAA allocates takeoff and landing slots through an administrative process. However, there has been much discussion of using a combinatorial auction to perform this allocation, in which certain high-traffic airports would require airlines to purchase the right to take off or land during a given time slice. Rassenti, Smith, and Bulfin (1982) made the first study of auctions in this domain. The problem has been

```
Routine Add_Good_to_Bundle(bundle B)
    Compute s = ∑_{x∉b, y∈B} d(x, y) · pn(x)
    Choose a random node x ∉ B from the distribution
    ∑_{y∈B} d(x, y) · pn(x)/s
    Add x to B
End Routine
```

Figure 18.9
Arbitrary relationships: Add good to bundle.

the topic for much other work, such as by Grether, Isaac, and Plott (1989), who include detailed experiments and an excellent characterization of bidder behavior. The foreword to this volume and chapter 20 also discuss this domain.

Single-good auctions are not adequate for this domain because an airline that buys the right for a plane to take off at one airport must also be guaranteed the right for the plane to land at its destination an appropriate amount of time later. Thus, complementarity exists between certain pairs of goods, where goods are the right to use a runway at a particular airport at a particular time. Substitutable bundles are different departure/arrival packages; therefore bundles will only be substitutable within certain limits.

Building the Graph   Departing from our graph-generating approach above, we ground this example in the map of high-traffic U.S. airports for which takeoff and landing right auctions have been proposed (Grether, Isaac, and Plott 1989). These are the four busiest airports in the United States: La Guardia International, Ronald Reagan Washington National, John F. Kennedy International, and O'Hare International. Figure 18.10 shows

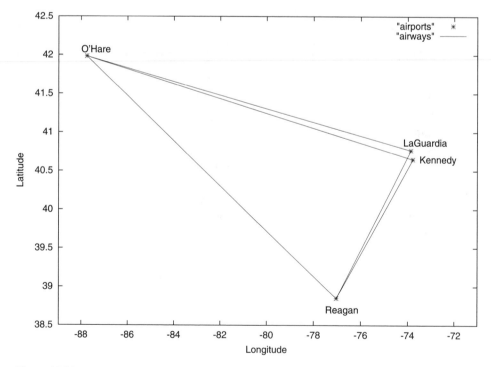

Figure 18.10
Map of airport locations.

this map. We chose not to use a random graph in this example because the number of bids and goods is dependent on the number of bidders and time slices at the given airports; it is not necessary to modify the number of *airports* in order to vary the problem size. Thus, *num_cities* = 4 and *num_times* = $\lfloor num\_goods/num\_cities \rfloor$.

Generating Bids Our bidding mechanism presumes that airlines have a certain tolerance for when a plane can take off and land (*early_takeoff_deviation, late_takeoff_deviation, early_land_deviation, late_land_deviation*), as related to their most preferred takeoff and landing times (*start_time, start_time + min_flight_length*). We generate bids for all bundles that fit these criteria. The value of a bundle is derived from a particular agent's utility function. We define a utility u_{max} for an agent, which corresponds to the utility the agent receives for flying from $city_1$ to $city_2$ if it receives the ideal takeoff and landing times. This utility depends on a common value for a time slot at the given airport, and deviates by a random amount. Next we construct a utility function which reduces u_{max} according to how late the plane will arrive, and how much the flight time deviates from optimal (figure 18.11).

```
Set the average valuation for each city's airport:
  cost(city) = rand(0, max_airport_value)
Let max_l = length of longest distance between any two cities
While num_generated_bids < num_bids
    Randomly select city₁ and city₂ where e(city₁, city₂)
    l = distance(city₁, city₂)
    min_flight_length = round(longest_flight_length · 1/max_l)
    start_time = rand_int(1, num_times − min_flight_length)
    dev = rand(1 − deviation, 1 + deviation)
    Make substitutable (XOR) bids. For takeoff =
    max(1, start_time − early_takeoff_deviation) to
    min(num_times, start_time + late_takeoff_deviation)
        For land = takeoff + min_flight_length to min(start_time +
        min_flight_length + late_land_deviation, num_times)
            amount_late =
            min(land − (start_time + min_flight_length), 0)
            delay = land − takeoff − min_flight_length
            Bid dev · (cost(city₁) + cost(city₂)) · delay_coeffᵈᵉˡᵃʸ
            amount_late_coeffᵃᵐᵒᵘⁿᵗ_ˡᵃᵗᵉ for takeoff at time
            takeoff at city₁ and landing at time land at city₂
        End For
    End For
End While
```

Figure 18.11
Temporal matching: Bid-generation technique.

CATS default parameter values: *max_airport_value* = 5, *longest_flight_length* = 10, *deviation* = 0.5, *early_takeoff_deviation* = 1, *late_takeoff_deviation* = 2, *early_land_ deviation* = 1, *late_land_deviation* = 2, *delay_coeff* = 0.9, and *amount_late_coeff* = 0.75.

18.3.5 Temporal Scheduling

Wellman et al. (1998) proposed distributed job-shop scheduling with one resource as a CA problem. We provide a distribution that mirrors this problem. Although there exist many algorithms for solving job-shop scheduling problems, the distributed formulation of this problem places it in an economic context. Wellman et al. describe a factory conducting an auction for time slices on some resource. Each bidder has a job requiring some amount of machine time, and a deadline by which the job must be completed. Some jobs may have additional, later deadlines that are less desirable to the bidder and so for which the bidder is willing to pay less.

Generating Bids   In the CA formulation of this problem, each good represents a specific time slice. Two bids are substitutable if they constitute different possible schedules for the same job. We determine the number of deadlines for a given job according to a decay distribution, and then generate a set of substitutable bids satisfying the deadline constraints. Specifically, let the set of deadlines of a particular job be $d_1 < \cdots < d_n$ and the value of a job completed by d_1 be v_1, superadditive in the job length. We define the value of a job completed by deadline d_i as $v_i = v_1 \cdot d_1/d_i$, reflecting the intuition that the decrease in value for a later deadline is proportional to its "lateness." As Wellman et al., we assume that all jobs are eligible to be started in the first time slot. Our formulation of the problem differs in only one respect—we consider only allocations in which jobs receive continuous blocks of time. However, this constraint is not restrictive, because for any arbitrary allocation of time slots to jobs there exists a new allocation in which each job receives a continuous block of time and no job finishes later than in the original allocation. (This may be achieved by numbering the winning bids in increasing order of scheduled end time, and then allocating continuous time blocks to jobs in this order. Clearly no job will be rescheduled to finish later than its original scheduled time.) Note also that this problem cannot be translated to a trivial one-good multiunit CA problem because jobs have different deadlines (figure 18.12).

CATS default parameter values: *deviation* = 0.5, *prob_additional_deadline* = 0.9, *additivity* = 0.2, and *max_length* = 10. Note that we propose a constant maximum job length, because the length of time a job requires should not depend on the amount of time the auctioneer makes available.

18.3.6 Legacy Distributions

To aid researchers designing new CA algorithms by facilitating comparison with previous work, CATS includes the ability to generate bids according to all previous pub-

```
While num_generated_bids < num_bids
    l = rand_int(1, max_length)
    d₁ = rand_int(l, num_goods)
    dev = rand(1 − deviation, 1 + deviation)
    cur_max_deadline = 0
    new_d = d₁
    To generate substitutable (XOR) bids. Do
        Make bids with price offered = dev · l^(1+additivity) · d₁/new_d
            for all blocks [start, end] where start ≥ 1, end ≤ new_d,
            end > cur_max_deadline, end − start = l
        cur_max_deadline = new_d
        new_d = rand_int(cur_max_deadline + 1, num_goods)
    While rand(0, 1) ≤ prob_additional_deadline
End While
```

Figure 18.12
Temporal scheduling: Bid-generation technique.

lished test distributions of which we are aware, subject to the requirement that the distributions be able to generate arbitrary numbers of goods and bids. Each of these distributions may be seen as answering three questions:

- What number of goods should be requested in a bundle?
- Which goods should be requested?
- What price should be offered for the bundle?

We begin by describing different techniques for answering each of these three questions, and then show how they have been combined in previously published test distributions.

Number of Goods

Uniformly   Uniformly distributed on $[1, num\_goods]$
Normal   Normally distributed with $\mu = \mu\_goods$ and $\sigma = \sigma\_goods$
Constant   Fixed at $constant\_goods$
Decay   Starting with 1, repeatedly increment the size of the bundle until $rand(0, 1)$ exceeds α

Binomial   Request n goods with probability $p^n(1 − p)^{num\_goods−n} \binom{num\_goods}{n}$

Exponential   Request n goods with probability $C \exp(−n/q)$.

Which Goods

Random   Draw n goods uniformly at random from the set of all goods, without replacement.[6]

Price Offer

Fixed Random   Uniform on $[low\_fixed, hi\_fixed]$
Linear Random   Uniform on $[low\_linearly \cdot n, hi\_linearly \cdot n]$
Normal   Draw from a normal distribution with $\mu = \mu\_price$ and $\sigma = \sigma\_price$
Quadratic[7]   For each good k and each bidder i set the value $v_k^i = rand(0, 1)$; then i's price offer for a set of goods S is $\sum_{k \in S} v_k^i + \sum_{k,q} v_k^i v_q^i$.

18.3.7   Previously Published Distributions

The following is a list of the distributions used in all published tests of which we are aware. In each case we describe first the method used to choose the number of goods, followed by the method used to choose the price offer. In all cases the "random" technique was used to determine which goods should be requested in a bundle. Each case is labeled with its corresponding CATS legacy suite number; very similar distributions are given similar numbers and identical distributions are given the same number.

[L1] Sandholm   Uniform, fixed random with $low\_fixed = 0$, $hi\_fixed = 1$
[L1a] Anderson et al.   Uniform, fixed random with $low\_fixed = 0$, $hi\_fixed = 1000$
[L2] Sandholm   Uniform, linearly random with $low\_linearly = 0$, $hi\_linearly = 1$
[L2a] Anderson et al.   Uniform, linearly random with $low\_linearly = 500$, $hi\_linearly = 1500$
[L3] Sandholm   Constant with $constant\_goods = 3$, fixed random with $low\_fixed = 0$, $hi\_fixed = 1$
[L3] de Vries and Vohra   Constant with $constant\_goods = 3$, fixed random with $low\_fixed = 0$, $hi\_fixed = 1$
[L4] Sandholm   Decay with $\alpha = 0.55$, linearly random with $low\_linearly = 0$, $hi\_linearly = 1$
[L4] de Vries and Vohra   Decay with $\alpha = 0.55$, linearly random with $low\_linearly = 0$, $hi\_linearly = 1$
[L4a] Anderson et al.   Decay with $\alpha = 0.55$, linearly random with $low\_linearly = 1$, $hi\_linearly = 1000$
[L5] Boutilier et al.   Normal with $\mu\_goods = 4$ and $\sigma\_goods = 1$, normal with $\mu\_price = 16$ and $\sigma\_price = 3$
[L6] Fujishima et al.   Exponential with $q = 5$, linearly random with $low\_linearly = 0.5$, $hi\_linearly = 1.5$
[L6a] Anderson et al.   Exponential with $q = 5$, linearly random with $low\_linearly = 500$, $hi\_linearly = 1500$
[L7] Fujishima et al.   Binomial with $p = 0.2$, linearly random with $low\_linearly = 0.5$, $hi\_linearly = 1.5$
[L7a] Anderson et al.   Binomial with $p = 0.2$, linearly random with $low\_linearly = 500$, $hi\_linearly = 1500$
[L8] de Vries and Vohra   Constant with $constant\_goods = 3$, quadratic.

Parkes (1999) used many of the test sets described above (particularly those described by Sandholm and Boutilier et al.), but tested with fixed numbers of goods and bids rather than scaling these parameters.

Since the publication of Leyton-Brown, Pearson, and Shoham (2000), the CATS distributions have also been widely used (e.g., Sandholm et al. 2005; Gonen and Lehmann 2000, 2001; Holte 2001; Schuurmans, Southey, and Holte 2001; Kastner et al. 2002; Zurel and Nisan 2000).

18.4 Tuning Distributions

Our main goal in this work has been to generate realistic artificial test data, even if this data turns out not to be as computationally difficult as other, less realistic benchmarks. After all, combinatorial auction researchers should care more about optimizing WDP algorithm performance on realistic problems than on tackling arbitrary set packing problems that cannot easily be interpreted as combinatorial auctions. This should not make us entirely unconcerned with the hardness of our distributions, however. In this section we present evidence about how hard the CATS distributions really are, and show how to tune them so that the hardest possible instances are generated from a given distribution.

18.4.1 Removing Dominated Bids

For the WDP, it is known that problems become harder as the number of goods and bids increases.[8] For this reason, researchers have traditionally reported the performance of their WDP algorithms in terms of the number of bids and goods of the input instances. Although it is easy to fix the number of goods, holding the number of bids constant is not as straightforward as it might seem. Most special-purpose algorithms make use of a polynomial-time preprocessing step that removes bids that are strictly dominated by one other bid. More precisely, bid i is dominated by bid j if the goods requested by i are a (nonstrict) superset of the goods requested by j, and the price offer of i is smaller than or equal to the price offer of j. It is thus possible for the size of problems given as input to the WDP algorithm to vary even if all generated instances had the same number of bids.

It is not obvious whether this domination procedure ought to remove many bids, or whether the relationship between the average number of nondominated bids and total bids ought to vary substantially from one distribution to another, so we set out to measure this relationship. Figure 18.13 shows the number of nondominated bids as a function of the total number of bids generated. In these experiments, with each line representing an average over twenty runs, bids were generated for an auction with sixty-four goods, and the program stopped after 2,000 nondominated bids had been made. We observe that some of the legacy distributions are considerably more likely

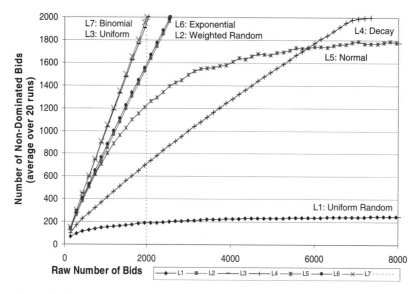

Figure 18.13
Nondominated bids vs. raw bids.

than others to generate nondominated bids; we do not show the CATS distributions in this graph as all five generated virtually no dominated bids.

Of course, many other polynomial-time preprocessing steps are possible, for example, a check for bids that are dominated by a pair of other bids. Indeed, sophisticated solvers such as CPLEX employ many much more complex preprocessing steps before initiating branch-and-bound search. Our own experience with algorithms for the WDP has suggested that other polynomial-time preprocessing steps offer much poorer performance in terms of the number of bids discarded in a given amount of time. In any case, the results above suggest that strict domination checking should not be disregarded, because distributions differ substantially in the ratio between the number of nondominated bids and the raw number of bids.

For this reason, the CATS software has the ability to generate instances for all CATS and legacy distributions with a specified number of *nondominated* bids: the software iteratively generates bids and removes dominated bids until the specified target is reached. Observe that if we want to be able to generate any given number of nondominated bids then we will be unable to use the distributions L1 and L5, because they often fail to generate a target number of nondominated bids even after millions of bids have been created. As an aside, this observation helps to explain why other researchers have found L1 and L5 empirically easy, and suggests that they are a poor choice for computational benchmarking.

18.4.2 Sampling Parameters

In our original paper on CATS (Leyton-Brown, Pearson, and Shoham 2000), we suggested default values for the parameters of each generator. This chapter also gave default values in section 18.3. However, the parameter space is large and the computational characteristics of the different CATS distributions vary substantially throughout this space. An alternative ensures that the whole parameter space is explored: reasonable ranges for each parameter are established, and then each time an instance is generated, these ranges are sampled uniformly at random. The CATS software now supports this sort of parameter sampling.

18.4.3 Making CATS Harder

There has been discussion in the combinatorial auctions literature about whether CATS is computationally hard (see, e.g., Gonen and Lehmann 2000; Sandholm et al. 2005). We performed tests on both CATS and legacy distributions with ILOG's CPLEX 7.1 solver,[9] sampling parameters as described above. Figure 18.14 shows the results of 500 runs for each distribution on problems with 256 goods and 1,000 nondominated bids, indicating the number of instances with the same order-of-magnitude runtime— that is, $\lfloor \log_{10}(\text{runtime}) \rfloor$. We ran these experiments on a cluster of Pentium III Xeon 550-Mhz machines with 4 GB of RAM each, and spent over a CPU-year gathering the data.

We can see that several of the CATS distributions are quite easy for CPLEX, and that others vary from easy to hard. It is interesting that most distributions had instances that varied in hardness by several orders of magnitude, despite the fact that all instances had the same problem size. This gives rise to the question of whether we can tune CATS so that in addition to generating "realistic" instances, it also generates the hardest possible instances. It turns out that the answer is yes: in chapter 19 of this volume, we show that even the easiest CATS distributions can be made orders of magnitude harder.

Our interest in generating the hardest possible instances notwithstanding, we should not be discouraged by the fact that some CATS distributions are computationally easy. On the contrary, this evidence suggests that realistic bidding patterns may often lead to much more tractable winner determination problems than the hardest unrealistic distributions such as "uniform" (L3). This is good news for those who hope to run practical combinatorial auctions.

18.5 Conclusion

In this chapter we introduced CATS, a test suite for combinatorial auction optimization algorithms. The distributions in CATS represent a step beyond earlier CA testing techniques because they are economically motivated and model real-world problems. We

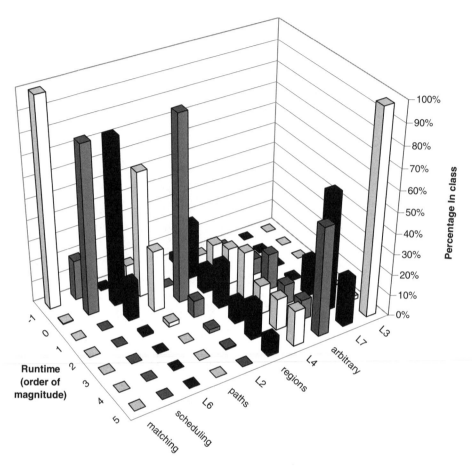

Figure 18.14
Gross hardness.

hope that CATS will continue to facilitate the development and evaluation of new CA optimization algorithms.

Acknowledgments

This chapter is based on work first presented in Leyton-Brown et al. 2000 and Leyton-Brown et al. 2002. We would like to acknowledge Mark Pearson, who was involved in the creation of the original test suite and co-wrote Leyton-Brown et al. 2000; Galen Andrew, who has helped to maintain the test suite since the publication of Leyton-Brown et al. 2000 and was responsible for many of the enhancements described here; and Eugene Nudelman, who was our coauthor on Leyton-Brown et al. 2002.

Notes

1. There does exist a body of previous work characterizing hard cases for weighted set packing, which is of course equivalent to the combinatorial auction problem. Real-world bidding is likely to exhibit various regularities, however, as discussed throughout this chapter. A data set designed to include the same regularities may be more useful for predicting the performance of an algorithm in a real-world combinatorial auction.

2. Electric power distribution is a frequently discussed real-world problem that is superficially similar to the problems discussed here. However, many of the complementarities in this domain arise from physical laws governing power flow in a network. Consideration of these laws becomes very complex in networks of interesting size. Also, because these laws are taken into account during the construction of power networks, the networks themselves are difficult to model using randomly generated graphs. For these reasons, we have not attempted to model this domain.

3. We use Sandholm's (1999) term "decay" here, though the distribution goes by various names—for a description of the distribution, see section 18.3.6. There are two reasons we use a decay distribution here. First, we expect that more bids will request small bundles than large bundles. Second, we require a distribution where the expected bundle size is relatively insensitive to changes in the total number of goods.

4. Recall the discussion in section 18.1.3 motivating the use of superadditive valuations.

5. To see why this cannot be modeled as a multiunit CA, consider an auction for three regions with two units each, and three bidders each wanting one unit of two goods. In the optimal allocation, b_1 gets one unit of g_1 and one unit of g_2, b_2 gets one unit of g_2 and one unit of g_3, and b_3 gets one unit of g_3 and one unit of g_1. In this example there is no way of assigning frequencies to the units so that each bidder gets the same frequency in both regions.

6. Although in principle the problem of *which* goods to request could be answered in many ways, all legacy distributions of which we are aware use the random technique.

7. De Vries and Vohra (2003) briefly describe a more general version of this price offer scheme, but do not describe how to set all the parameters (e.g., defining which goods are complementary); hence we do not include it here. Quadratic price offers may be particularly applicable to spectrum auctions; see Ausubel et al. 1997.

8. Recall the exception discussed in section 18.1.3: when distributions favor small bundles and lack sufficiently superadditive pricing then the problem generally becomes easier as the number of bids grows very large.

9. CPLEX has become faster with every version released, and so newer versions of CPLEX will most likely exceed the performance reported here. We reran a subset of these problems using CPLEX 8.0, but found that the qualitative shape of the distribution was unchanged. Due to the investment of machine time that would have been required to regenerate figure 18.14 we elected not to rerun the entire dataset, and report only our CPLEX 7.1 results here.

References

Andersson, Arne, Mattias Tenhunen, and Fredrik Ygge (2000), "Integer Programming for Combinatorial Auction Winner Determination," *Proceedings of the Fourth International Conference on Multi-Agent Systems*, 39–46.

Ausubel, Lawrence M., Peter Cramton, R. Preston McAfee, and John McMillan (1997), "Synergies in Wireless Telephony: Evidence from the Broadband PCS Auctions," *Journal of Economics and Management Strategy*, 6, 497–527.

Banks, Jeffrey S., John O. Ledyard, and David P. Porter (1989), "Allocating Uncertain and Unresponsive Resources: An Experimental Approach," *RAND Journal of Economics*, 20, 1–23.

Boutilier, Craig, Moisés Goldszmidt, and Bikash Sabata (1999), "Sequential Auctions for the Allocation of Resources with Complementarities," *IJCAI*, 527–534.

Brewer, Paul J. and Charles R. Plott (1996), "A binary Conflict Ascending Price (BICAP) Mechanism for the Decentralized Allocation of the Right to Use Railroad Tracks," *International Journal of Industrial Organization*, 14, 857–886.

de Vries, Sven and Rakesh V. Vohra (2003), "Combinatorial Auctions: A Survey," *INFORMS Journal on Computing*, 15, 284–309.

Dunford, Melissa, Karla Hoffman, Dinesh Menon, Rudy Sultana, and Thomas Wilson (2004), "Testing Linear Pricing Algorithms for Use in Ascending Combinatorial Auctions," Working paper, George Mason University.

Fujishima, Yuzo, Kevin Leyton-Brown, and Yoav Shoham (1999), "Taming the Computational Complexity of Combinatorial Auctions: Optimal and Approximate Approaches," *Proceedings of the IJCAI'99*, 548–553.

Gonen, Rica and Daniel Lehmann (2000), "Optimal Solutions for Multi-Unit Combinatorial Auctions: Branch and Bound Heuristics," *ACM Conference on Electronic Commerce*, 13–20.

Gonen, Rica and Daniel Lehmann (2001), "Linear Programming Helps Solving Large Multi-Unit Combinatorial Auctions," Technical Report TR-2001-8, Leibniz Center for Research in Computer Science.

Grether, David M., R. Mark Isaac, and Charles R. Plott (1989), *The Allocation of Scarce Resources: Experimental Economics and the Problem of Allocating Airport Slots*, Boulder, CO: Westview Press.

Holte, Robert C. (2001), "Combinatorial Auctions, Knapsack Problems, and Hill-Climbing Search," in Eleni Stroulia and Stan Matwin, eds., *Advances in Artificial Intelligence, Proceedings of the 14th Biennial Conference of the Canadian Society for Computational Studies of Intelligence (AI'2001)*, LNCS 2056, Berlin: Springer, 57–66.

Kastner, Ryan, Christina Hsieh, Miodrag Potkonjak, and Majid Sarrafzadeh (2002), "On the Sensitivity of Incremental Algorithms for Combinatorial Auctions," in IEE Workshop on Advanced Issues of E-Commerce and Web-Based Information Systems, 81–88.

Kwasnica, Anthony M., John O. Ledyard, Dave Porter, and Christine DeMartini (2005), "A New and Improved Design for Multiobject Iterative Auctions," *Management Science*, 51, 419–434.

Ledyard, John O., David Porter, and Antonio Rangel (1997), "Experiments Testing Multiobject Allocation Mechanisms," *Journal of Economics & Management Strategy*, 6, 639–675.

Ledyard, John O., and Kristin Szakaly (1994), "Designing Organizations for Trading Pollution Rights," *Journal of Economic Behavior and Organization*, 25, 167–196.

Lehmann, Daniel, Liadan I. O'Callaghan, and Yoav Shoham (1999), "Truth Revelation in Approximately Efficient Combinatorial Auctions," *Journal of the ACM*, 49, 577–602.

Leyton-Brown, Kevin, Eugene Nudelman, and Yoav Shoham (2002), "Learning the Empirical Hardness of Optimization Problems: The Case of Combinatorial Auctions," LNCS 2470, 556–572.

Leyton-Brown, Kevin, Mark Pearson, and Yoav Shoham (2000), "Towards a Universal Test Suite for Combinatorial Auction Algorithms," *ACM Conference on Electronic Commerce*, 66–76.

Nisan, Noam (2000), "Bidding and Allocation in Combinatorial Auctions," *Proceedings of the 2nd ACM Conference on Electronic Commerce*, 1–12.

Parkes, David C. (1999), "iBundle: An Efficient Ascending Price Bundle Auction," *Proceedings of the 1st ACM Conference on Electronic Commerce*, 148–157.

Plott, Charles R. and Timothy N. Cason (1996), "EPA's New Emissions Trading Mechanism: A Laboratory Evaluation," *Journal of Environmental Economics and Management*, 30, 133–160.

Porter, David, Stephen Rassenti, Anil Roopnarine, and Vernon Smith (2003), "Combinatorial Auction Design," *Proceedings of the National Academy of Sciences*, 100, 11153–11157.

Quan, Daniel C. (1994), "Real Estate Auctions: A Survey of Theory and Practice," *Journal of Real Estate Finance and Economics*, 9, 23–49.

Rassenti, Stephen J., Stanley S. Reynolds, and Vernon Smith (1994), "Cotenancy and Competition in an Experimental Auction Market for Natural Gas Pipeline Networks," *Economic Theory*, 4, 41–65.

Rassenti, Stephen J., Vernon Smith, and Robert L. Bulfin (1982), "A Combinatorial Auction Mechanism for Airport Time Slot Allocation," *Bell Journal of Economics*, 13, 402–417.

Sandholm, Tuomas (1993), "An Implementation of the Contract Net Protocol Based on Marginal Cost Calculations," *Eleventh National Conference on Artificial Intelligence*, 256–262.

Sandholm, Tuomas (2002), "Algorithm for Optimal Winner Determination in Combinatorial Auctions," *Artificial Intelligence*, 135, 1–54.

Sandholm, Tuomas, Subhash Suri, Andrew Gilpin, and David Levine (2005), "CABOB: A Fast Optimal Algorithm for Winner Determination in Combinatorial Auctions," *Management Science*, 51, 374–390.

Schuurmans, Dale, Finnegan Southey, and Robert C. Holte (2001), "The Exponentiated Subgradient Algorithm for Heuristic Boolean Programming," in *International Joint Conference on Artificial Intelligence*, 334–341.

Wellman, Michael P., William R. Walsh, Peter R. Wurman, and Jeffrey K. MacKie-Mason (1998), "Auction Protocols for Decentralized Scheduling," *Games and Economic Behavior*, 35, 271–303.

Zurel, Edo and Noam Nisan (2000), "An Efficient Approximate Allocation Algorithm for Combinatorial Auctions," *3rd ACM Conference on Electronic Commerce*, 125–136.

19 Empirical Hardness Models for Combinatorial Auctions

Kevin Leyton-Brown, Eugene Nudelman, and Yoav Shoham

19.1 Introduction

In this chapter we consider the empirical hardness of the winner determination problem. We identify distribution-nonspecific features of data instances and then use statistical regression techniques to learn, evaluate, and interpret a function from these features to the predicted hardness of an instance, focusing mostly on ILOG's CPLEX solver. We also describe two applications of these models: building an algorithm portfolio that selects among different WDP algorithms, and inducing test distributions that are harder for this algorithm portfolio.

Figure 18.14 demonstrates that runtimes of WDP algorithms can vary by many orders of magnitude across different problems of the same size, and even across different instances drawn from the same distribution. In particular, this figure showed CPLEX runtimes for WDP instances of the same size varying from about a hundredth of a second to about a day. This raises a puzzling question: what characteristics of the instances are responsible for this enormous variation in empirical hardness? Because an understanding of the amount of time an auction will take to clear is a requirement in many combinatorial auction application areas, an answer to this question would greatly benefit the practical deployment of WDP algorithms.

It is not altogether surprising to observe significant variation in runtime for a WDP algorithm, as such variation has been observed in a wide variety of algorithms for solving other NP-hard problems. Indeed, in recent years a growing number of computer scientists have studied the *empirical* hardness of individual instances or distributions of various NP-hard problems, and in many cases have managed to find simple mathematical relationships between features of the problem instances and the hardness of the problem. The majority of this work has focused on decision problems: that is, problems that ask a yes/no question of the form, "Does there exist a solution meeting the given constraints?" The most successful approach for understanding the empirical hardness of such problems—taken, for example, in Cheeseman, Kanefsky, and Taylor

1991 and Achlioptas et al. 2000—is to vary some parameter of the input looking for an easy-hard-easy transition corresponding to a phase transition in the solvability of the problem. This approach uncovered the famous result that 3-SAT instances are hardest when the ratio of clauses to variables is about 4.3 (Selman et al. 1996); researchers have also applied it to other decision problems, such as quasigroup completion (Gomes and Selman 1997). Another approach rests on a notion of backbone (Monasson et al. 1998; Achlioptas et al. 2000), which is the set of solution invariants.

For optimization problems, experimental researchers have looked at reductions to decision problems, or related the backbone of an optimization problem to its empirical hardness (Slaney and Walsh 2001). It is also possible to take an analytic approach, although this approach typically requires strong assumptions about the algorithm and/or the instance distribution (e.g., that the branching factor is constant and node-independent and that edge costs are uniform throughout the search tree) (Zhang 1999; Korf and Reid 1998).

Some optimization problems do not invite study by existing experimental *or* theoretical approaches. Existing experimental techniques have trouble when problems have high-dimensional parameter spaces, as it is impractical to explore manually the space of all relations among parameters in search of a phase transition or some other predictor of an instance's hardness. This trouble is compounded when many different data distributions exist for a problem, each with its own set of parameters. Theoretical approaches are also difficult when the input distribution is complex or is otherwise hard to characterize; moreover, they tend to become unwieldy when applied to complex algorithms, or to problems with variable and interdependent edge costs and branching factors. Furthermore, standard techniques are generally unsuited to making predictions about the empirical hardness of *individual* problem instances, instead concentrating on average (or worst-case) performance on a class of instances.

The empirical properties of the combinatorial auction winner determination problem are difficult to study for all of the reasons discussed above. Instances are characterized by a large number of apparently relevant features. Many different input distributions exist, each with its own large set of parameters. There is significant variation in edge costs throughout the search tree. Finally, it is desirable to predict the empirical hardness of individual problem instances. Thus, a new approach is called for.

19.1.1 Methodology

Instead of using any of the approaches mentioned above, we suggested an experimental methodology for constructing hardness landscapes for a given algorithm (Leyton-Brown, Nudelman, and Shoham 2002). Such models are thus capable of predicting the running time of a given algorithm on new, previously unseen problem instances. The methodology is as follows:

1. Choose one or more algorithms.

2. Select a problem instance distribution, and sample the distribution to generate a set of problem instances.

3. Define and choose a problem size. Hold problem size constant to focus on unknown sources of hardness.

4. Select a set of fast-to-compute, distribution-independent features.

5. For each problem instance, measure the running time of each optimization algorithm, and compute all features.

6. Eliminate redundant or uninformative features.

7. Learn a function of the features to predict each algorithm's running time, and analyze prediction error.

The application of machine learning to the prediction of running time has received some recent study (see, e.g., Horvitz et al. 2001; Ruan, Horvitz, and Kautz 2002; Lagoudakis and Littman 2000, 2001); however, there is no other work of which we are aware that uses a machine learning approach in order to understand the empirical hardness of an NP-hard problem. There have been some reports in the literature about the relation of particular features or parameters of input distributions to the hardness of WDP instances (e.g., Sandholm 2002), but to our knowledge no systematic study has been attempted. Finally, as is common with hard problems, empirical evaluations have focused on scaling behavior of algorithms on different distributions rather than on structural differences at a fixed size.

As described above, our main motivation for proposing this methodology has been the problem of *understanding* the characteristics of data instances that are predictive of long running times. However, empirical hardness models have other more practical uses, making them important for CA practitioners as well as for academic researchers. These applications of empirical hardness models include:

- predicting how long an auction will take to clear
- tuning benchmark distributions for hardness
- constructing algorithm portfolios
- designing package bidding rules to reduce the chances of long clearing times
- efficiently scheduling auction clearing times
- improving the design of WDP algorithms.

19.2 Building Hardness Models for WDP

19.2.1 Optimization Algorithm

In recent years, researchers working on the WDP have converged toward branch-and-bound search, using a linear-programming relaxation of the problem as a heuristic. There has thus been increasing interest in the use of ILOG's CPLEX software to solve the WDP, particularly since the mixed integer programming module in that package improved substantially in version 6 (released 2000), and again in version 7 (released 2001). In version 7.1, this off-the-shelf software has reached the point where it is competitive with the best academic special purpose software. In this chapter we selected CPLEX 7.1 as our WDP algorithm,[1] although we do consider some special-purpose software in section 19.4. Sandholm (chapter 14 of this volume) gives a survey describing the architecture of special-purpose WDP algorithms.

19.2.2 Instance Distribution

There are a variety of widely used benchmark generators for CAs (see chapter 18 of this volume). To avoid bias, we used all Legacy and CATS generators that are able to generate instances with arbitrary numbers of goods and undominated bids, and created the same number of instances with each generator. Our instance distribution can thus be understood as sampling uniformly from instances created by the following generators:[2]

- Uniform (L2)
- Constant (L3)
- Decay (L4)
- Exponential (L6)
- Binomial (L7)
- Regions (CATS)
- Arbitrary (CATS)
- Matching (CATS)
- Scheduling (CATS).

Most of these generators have one or more parameters that must be assigned values before instances can be generated. As described in section 4.2 of chapter 18, for each parameter of each instance generator we established a "reasonable" range, and then before creating an instance sampled uniformly at random from this range. This helped us to explore more of the parameter space.

19.2.3 Problem Size

Some sources of empirical hardness in NP-hard problem instances are well understood. For the WDP—an NP-hard problem, as discussed by Lehmann, Müller, and Sandholm (chapter 12 of this volume)—it is known that instances generally become harder as the problem gets larger: that is, as the number of bids and goods increases. Furthermore, as argued in chapter 18, the removal of dominated bids can have a significant effect. Our goal is to understand what *other* features of instances are predictive of hardness, so we hold these parameters constant, concentrating on variations in other features. We therefore defined problem size as the pair (*number of goods, number of nondominated bids*).

19.2.4   Features

As described above, we must characterize each problem instance with a set of features. There is no known automatic way of constructing such a feature set: researchers must use domain knowledge to identify properties of the instance that appear likely to provide useful information. We do restrict the sorts of features we will use in two ways, however. First, we only consider features that can be generated from *any* problem instance, without knowledge of how that instance was constructed. (For example, we do not use parameters of the specific distribution used to generate an instance.) Second, we restrict ourselves to those features that are computable in low-order polynomial time, as the computation of the features should scale well as compared to solving the optimization problem.

We determined thirty-five features that we thought could be relevant to the empirical hardness of WDP, ranging in their computational complexity from linear to cubic time. After having generated feature values for all our problem instances, we examined our data to identify redundant features. After eliminating these, we were left with twenty-five features, which figure 19.1 summarizes. We describe our features in more detail below, and also mention some of the redundant features that we eliminated.

There are two natural graphs associated with each instance; examples of these graphs appear in figure 19.2. First is the *bid-good graph* (BGG): a bipartite graph having a node for each bid, a node for each good, and an edge between a bid and a good node for

Bid-Good Graph Features:

1–3. **Bid node degree statistics:** max and min degree of the bid nodes, and standard deviations.

4–7. **Good node degree statistics:** average, maximum, minimum degree of the good nodes, and their standard deviations.

Bid Graph Features:

8. **Edge Density:** number of edges in the BG divided by the number of edges in a complete graph with the same number of nodes.

9–11. **Node degree statistics:** the max and min node degrees in the BG, and their standard deviation.

12–13. **Clustering Coefficient and Deviation.** A measure of "local cliquiness." For each node calculate the number of edges among its neighbors divided by $k(k-1)/2$, where k is the number of neighbors. We record average (the clustering coefficient) and standard deviation.

14. **Average minimum path length:** the average minimum path length, over all pairs of bids.

15. **Ratio of the clustering coefficient to the average minimum path length:** One of the measures of the smallness of the BG.

16–19. **Node eccentricity statistics:** The eccentricity of a node is the length of a shortest path to a node furthest from it. We calculate the maximum eccentricity of BG (graph diameter), the minimum eccentricity of BG (graph radius), average eccentricity, and standard deviation of eccentricity.

LP-Based Features:

20–22. $\ell_1, \ell_2, \ell_\infty$ norms of the integer slack vector.

Price-Based Features:

23. **Standard deviation of prices among all bids:** $stdev(p_i)$

24. **Deviation of price per number of goods:** $stdev(p_i/|S_i|)$

25. **Deviation of price per square root of the number of goods:** $stdev(p_i/\sqrt{|S_i|})$.

Figure 19.1

Four groups of features.

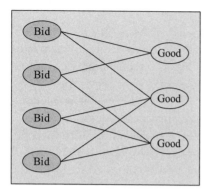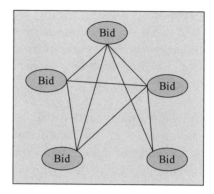

Figure 19.2
Examples of the graph types used in calculating. Features 1–19: bid-good graph (left); bid graph (right).

each good in the given bid. We measure a variety of BGG's properties: extremal and average degrees and their standard deviations for each group of nodes. The average number of goods per bid was perfectly correlated with another feature, and so did not survive our feature selection.

The *bid graph* (BG) has an edge between each pair of bids that cannot appear together in the same allocation (thus it is the constraint graph for the associated constraint satisfaction problem [CSP]). As is true for all CSPs, the BG captures a lot of useful information about the problem instance. Our second group of features are concerned with structural properties of the BG.[3] We originally measured the first, second, and third quartiles of the BG node degrees, but they turned out to be highly correlated with edge density. We also measured the average number of conflicts per bid, but as the number of bids was held constant this feature was always proportional to edge density. We considered using the number of connected components of the BG to measure whether the problem is decomposable into simpler instances, but found that virtually every instance consisted of a single component.[4]

The third group of features is calculated from the solution vector of the linear programming relaxation of the WDP. Recall that WDP can be formulated as an integer program, as described in chapter 12 of this volume. In our notation, S_i stands for the set of goods in bid i, p_i for the corresponding price, and a variable x_i is set to 1 if and only if bid i is part of an optimal allocation.

We calculate the *integer slack* vector by replacing each component x_i with $|0.5 - x_i|$. These features appeared promising both because the slack gives insight into the quality of CPLEX's initial solution and because CPLEX uses LP as its search heuristic. Originally we also included median integer slack, but excluded the feature when we found that it was always zero.

Our last group of features is the only one that explicitly considers the prices associated with bids. Observe that the scale of the prices has no effect on hardness; however, the spread is crucial, because it impacts pruning. We note that feature 25 was shown to be an optimal bid-ordering heuristic for certain greedy WDP approximation schemes in Gonen and Lehmann 2000.

19.2.5 Running Experiments

We generated three separate data sets of different problem sizes, to ensure that our results were not artifacts of one particular choice of problem size. The first data set contained runs on instances of 1,000 bids and 256 goods each, with a total of 4,500 instances (500 instances per distribution). The second data set, with 1,000 bids and 144 goods, had a total of 2,080 instances; the third data set, with 2,000 bids and sixty-four goods, contained 1,964 instances. Where we present results for only a single data set, we always used the first data set. We collected all of our runtime data by running CPLEX 7.1 with minimal preprocessing. We used a cluster of four machines, each of which had eight Pentium III Xeon 550-MHz processors and 4G RAM and was running Linux 2.2.12. Because many of the instances turned out to be exceptionally hard, we interrupted CPLEX runs once they had expanded 130,000 nodes (reaching this point took between two hours and twenty-two hours, averaging nine hours). Overall, solution times varied from as little as 0.01 seconds to as much as twenty-two hours. We estimate that we consumed approximately three years of CPU time collecting the runtime data described here. We also computed thirty-five features for each instance. (Recall that feature selection took place after all instances had been generated.) Each feature in each data set was normalized to have a mean of 0 and a standard deviation of 1.

19.2.6 Learning Models

Because we wanted to learn a continuous-valued model of the features, we used statistical regression techniques. (A large literature addresses the statistical techniques we used; for an introduction see, e.g., Hastie, Tibshirani, and Friedman 2001.) We used the logarithm of CPLEX running time as our response variable (dependent variable). In a sense, this equalizes the effort that the regression algorithm spends on fitting easy and hard instances—taking the log essentially corresponds to penalizing the relative prediction error rather than absolute error. Without this transformation, a 100-second prediction error would be penalized equally on an instance that took 0.01 seconds to run as on an instance that took 10,000 seconds. Our use of log runtime as the response variable also allows us to ask the question of how accurately our methods would be able to reconstruct the gross hardness figure (figure 18.14) for unseen instances, without any knowledge of the distribution from which each instance was drawn.

We performed regression on a training set consisting of 80 percent of each of our datasets, and then tested our model on the remaining 20 percent to evaluate its ability to generalize to new data. Regression was performed using the open-source R package.

Linear Regression One of the simplest and most widely studied regression techniques is linear regression. This technique works by finding a hyperplane in the feature space that minimizes root mean squared error (RMSE), which is defined as the square root of the average squared difference between the predicted value and the true value of the response variable. Minimizing RMSE is reasonable because it conforms to the intuition that, holding mean absolute error constant, models that mispredict all instances equally should be preferred to models that vary in their mispredictions. Although we go on to consider nonlinear regression, it is useful to consider the results of linear regression for two reasons. First, one of our main goals was to understand the factors that influence hardness, and insights gained from a linear model are useful even if other, more accurate models can be found. Second, our linear regression model serves as a baseline to which we can compare the performance of more complex regression techniques.

Overall, we found that even linear models have a surprising ability to predict the amount of time CPLEX will take to solve novel WDP instances: in our experiments most instances were predicted very accurately, and few instances were dramatically mispredicted. Overall, our results show that our linear model would be able to do a good job of classifying instances into the bins shown in figure 14 in chapter 18, even without knowledge of the distribution from which each instance was drawn: 93 percent of the time the log running times of the data instances in our test set were predicted to the correct order of magnitude (i.e., with an absolute error of less than 1.0).

Our experimental results with linear models are summarized in table 19.1 and figures 19.3 and 19.4. In table 19.1, we report both RMSE and mean absolute error, as the latter is often more intuitive. A third measure, adjusted R^2, is the fraction of the original variance in the response variable that is explained by the model, with an adjustment

Table 19.1
Linear regression: test set error and adjusted R^2

Data Set	Mean Abs. Err.	RMSE	Adj-R^2
1000 Bids/256 Goods	0.399	0.543	0.938
1000 Bids/144 Goods	0.437	0.579	0.909
2000 Bids/64 Goods	0.254	0.368	0.912

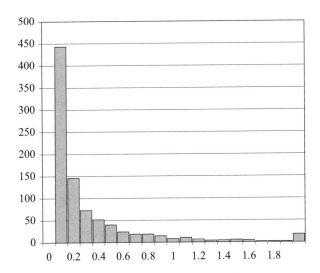

Figure 19.3
Linear regression: Histogram of test set root mean squared error.

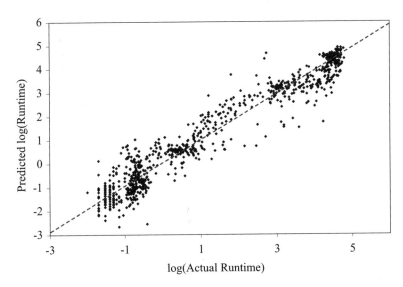

Figure 19.4
Linear regression: Error scatterplot.

Table 19.2
Quadratic regression: test set errors and adjusted R^2

Data Point	Mean Abs. Err.	RMSE	R^2
1000 Bids/256 Goods	0.183	0.297	0.987
1000 Bids/144 Goods	0.272	0.475	0.974
2000 Bids/64 Goods	0.163	0.272	0.981

penalizing more complex models. Despite this penalty, adjusted R^2 is a measure of fit to the training set and cannot entirely correct for overfitting; nevertheless, it can be an informative measure when presented along with test set error. Figure 19.3 shows a histogram of the RMS error, with bin width 0.1. Figure 19.4 shows a scatterplot of predicted log runtime versus actual log runtime.

Nonlinear Models   Although our linear model was quite effective, we expected nonlinear interactions between our features to be important and therefore looked to nonlinear models. A simple way of performing nonlinear regression is to compute new features based on nonlinear interactions between the original features and then to perform linear regression on the union of both sets of features. We added all products of pairs of features to our linear model, including squares of individual features, which gave us a total of 350 features. This meant that we chose our model from the space of all second-degree polynomials in our twenty-five-dimensional feature space, rather than from the space of all hyperplanes in that space as in section 19.2.6. For all three of our datasets this model gave considerably better error measurements on the test set and also explained nearly all the variance in the training set, as table 19.2 shows. As above, figures 19.5 and 19.6 show a histogram of root mean squared error and a scatterplot of predicted log runtime versus actual log runtime. Comparing these figures to figures 19.3 and 19.4 confirms our judgment that the quadratic model is substantially better overall.

19.3   Analyzing Hardness Models

The results summarized above demonstrate that it is possible to learn a model of our features that very accurately predicts the log of CPLEX running time on novel WDP instances. For some applications (e.g., predicting the time it will take for an auction to clear; building an algorithm portfolio) accurate prediction is all that is required. In some other cases, however, we are interested in *understanding* what makes an instance empirically hard. In this section we discuss the interpretation of our models.

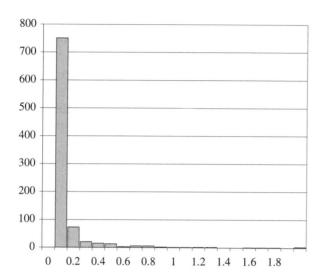

Figure 19.5
Quadratic regression: Histogram of test set root mean squared error.

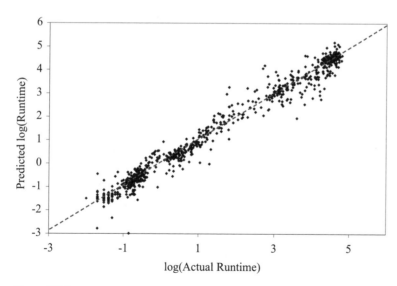

Figure 19.6
Quadratic regression: Error scatterplot.

19.3.1 Cost of Omission

It is tempting to interpret a model by comparing the coefficients assigned to the different features; because all features have the same mean and standard deviations, more important features should tend to have larger coefficients. Indeed, this will often be the case. However, this simplistic analysis technique ignores the effects of correlation between features. For example, two perfectly correlated but entirely unimportant features can have large coefficients with opposite signs in a linear model. In practice, because imperfect correlation and correlations among larger sets of variables are common, it is difficult to untangle the effects of correlation and importance in explaining a given coefficient's magnitude. One solution is to force the model to have smaller coefficients and/or to contain fewer variables. Requiring smaller coefficients reduces interactions between correlated variables; two popular techniques are ridge regression and lasso regression. We evaluated these techniques—using cross-validation[5] to estimate good values for the shrinkage parameters—and found no significant improvement on either accuracy or on interpretability of the model. Thus we do not discuss these results further.

Another family of techniques allows interpretation *without* the consideration of coefficient magnitudes. These techniques attempt to select good subsets of the features, with the number of features in the subset given as a parameter. Small models are desirable for our goal of analyzing hardness models because they are easier to interpret directly and because a small, optimal subset will tend to contain fewer highly covariant features than a larger model. (Intuitively, when subsets get small enough then the optimal model will not be able to afford to spend its feature choices on a highly correlated set of features.) If the number of original features is relatively small, it is possible to determine the optimal subset by exhaustively enumerating all feature subsets of the desired size and evaluating the quality of each corresponding model. However, most of the time such an exhaustive enumeration is infeasible and some incomplete optimization approach must be used instead.

In order to choose the size of the subset to analyze, we plotted subset size (from 1 to the total number of variables) versus the RMSE of the best model involving a subset of that size. We then analyzed the smallest subset size at which there was little incremental benefit gained by moving to the next larger subset size. We examined the features in the model, and also measured each variable's cost of omission—the (normalized) difference between the RMSE of the model on the original subset and a model omitting the given variable. It is very important to note that our technique identifies a set of features that is *sufficient* to achieve a particular level of accuracy, not a set of features that is *necessary* for this degree of performance. It is entirely possible that many different subsets will achieve nearly the same RMSE—when many correlations exist between features, as in our WDP dataset, this is quite likely. Thus, we must be careful not to draw overly general conclusions from the particular variables appearing in the best subset of a given size, and even more careful about reasoning about the absence of a particular feature. The strength of our approach is in providing a conceptual picture of the sorts of features that are important for predicting empirical hardness; the substitution of one feature for another highly covariant feature is irrelevant when the inclusion of either feature in the model has the same intuitive meaning. It is also worth noting that subset selection and cost of omission were both evaluated using the test set, but that all model selection was evaluated using cross-validation, and all analysis was performed after our models had been learned.

19.3.2 Experimental Results

Figure 19.7 shows the RMSE of the best subset containing between one and twenty-five features for linear models; because we had only twenty-five features in total we selected the best subsets by exhaustive comparison. We chose to examine the model with seven features because it was the first for which adding another feature did not cause a large decrease in RMSE, which suggested that the features in the eight-feature model were more highly correlated. Figure 19.8 shows the seven features in this model and their respective costs of omission (scaled to 100).

The most overarching conclusion we can draw from this data is that structural features are the most important. Edge density of BG is essentially a measure of the

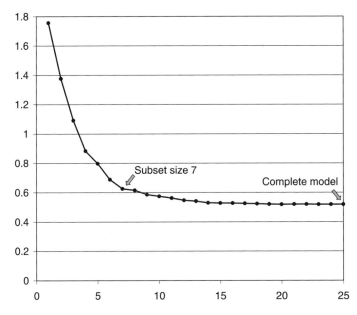

Figure 19.7
Linear regression: Subset size vs. RMSE.

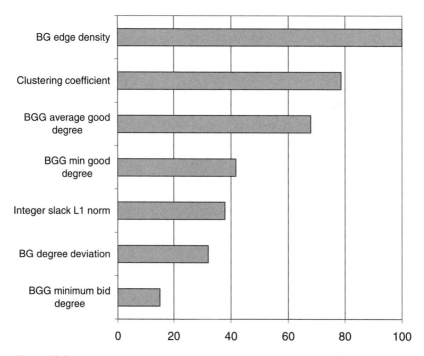

Figure 19.8
Linear regression: Cost of omission for subset size 7.

constrainedness of the problem, so it is not surprising to find that this feature is the most costly to omit. Clustering coefficient, the second feature, is a measure of average cliquiness of BG; this feature gives an indication of how local the problem's constraints are. All but one of the remaining features concern node degrees in BG or BGG; the final feature is the ℓ_1 norm of the linear programming slack vector.

We now consider second-order models, where we had 350 features and thus exhaustive exploration of feature subsets was impossible. Instead, we used three different greedy subset selection methods (forward selection, backward selection, sequential replacement) and at each size chose the best subset among the three. Figure 19.9 describes the best subsets containing between one and sixty features for second-order models. Due to our use of greedy subset selection techniques, the subsets shown in figure 19.9 are likely not the RMSE-minimizing subsets of the given sizes; nevertheless, we can still conclude that subsets of these sizes are *sufficient* to achieve the accuracies shown here. We observe that allowing interactions between features dramatically improved the accuracy of our very small subset models; indeed, our five-feature quadratic model outperformed our twenty-five-feature linear model.

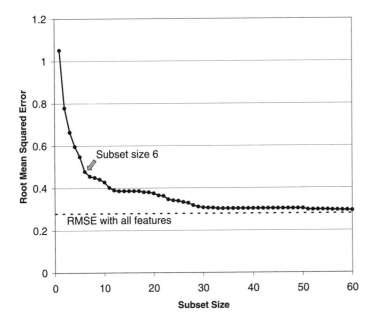

Figure 19.9
Quadratic regression: Subset size vs. RMSE.

Figure 19.10 shows the costs of omission for the variables from the best six-feature subset. As in the case of our linear model, we observe that the most critical features are structural: edge density of BG, the clustering coefficient, and node degrees. Overall many second-order features were selected. The ℓ_1 norm becomes more important than in the linear model when it is allowed to interact with other features; in the second-order model it is also sufficiently important to be kept as the only first-order feature.

We can look at the features that were important to our quadratic and linear models in order to gain understanding about how our models work. The importance of the ℓ_1 norm is quite intuitive: the easiest problems can be completely solved by LP, yielding an ℓ_1 norm of 0; the norm is close to 0 for problems that are almost completely solved by LP (and hence usually do not require much search to resolve), and larger for more difficult problems. The BG edge density feature describes the overall constrainedness of the problem. Generally, we would expect that very highly constrained problems would be easy, as more constraints imply a smaller search space; however, our experimental results show that CPLEX takes a long time on such problems. It seems that either CPLEX's calculation of the LP bound at each node becomes much more expensive when the number of constraints in the LP increases substantially, or the accuracy of the LP relaxation decreases (along with the number of nodes that can be pruned); in

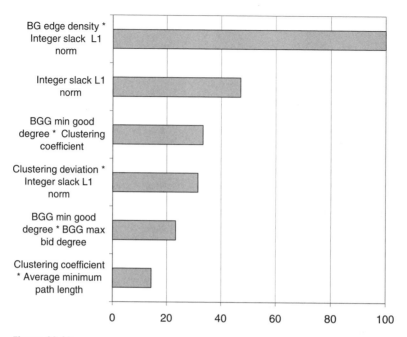

Figure 19.10
Quadratic regression: Cost of omission for subset size 6.

either case this cost overwhelms the savings that come from searching in a smaller space. Some other important features are intuitively similar to BG edge density. For example, the node degree statistics describe the max, min, average, and standard deviation of the number of constraints in which each variable is involved; they indicate how quickly the search space can be expected to narrow as variables are given values (i.e., as bids are assigned to or excluded from the allocation). Similarly, the clustering coefficient features measure the extent to which variables that conflict with a given variable also conflict with each other, another indication of the speed with which the search space will narrow as variables are assigned. Finally, we can now understand the importance of the feature that was by far the most important in our six-feature quadratic model: the product of the BG edge density and the integer slack ℓ_1 norm. Note that this feature takes a large value only when both BG edge density and ℓ_1 norm are large; the explanations above show that problems are easy for CPLEX whenever either of these features has a small value. Because BG edge density and ℓ_1 norm are relatively uncorrelated on our data, their product gives a powerful prediction of an instance's hardness.

It is also interesting to notice which features were consistently *excluded* by subset selection. In particular, it is striking that no price features were important in either our first- or second-order models (except implicitly, as part of LP relaxation features). Although price-based features do appear in larger models, they seem not to be as critically important as structural or LP-based features. This may be partially explained by the fact that the removal of dominated bids eliminates the bids that deviate most substantially on price (indeed, it led us to eliminate the "uniform random" [L1] distribution in which average price per good varied most dramatically across bids). Another group of features that were generally not chosen for small subsets were path length features: graph radius, diameter, average minimum path length, and so on. It seems that statistics derived from neighbor relations in constraint graphs are much more meaningful for predicting hardness than other graph-theoretic statistics derived from notions of proximity or connectedness.

19.4 Using Hardness Models to Build Algorithm Portfolios

When algorithms exhibit high runtime variance, one is faced with the problem of deciding which algorithm to use for solving a given instance. In 1976, Rice dubbed this the "algorithm selection problem" (Rice 1976). Though Rice offered few concrete techniques, all subsequent work on algorithm selection (e.g., Gomes and Selman 2001; Lagoudakis and Littman 2000, 2001; Lobjois and Lemaître 1998) falls into his framework. Despite this literature, however, the overwhelmingly most common approach to algorithm selection remains measuring different algorithms' performance on a given problem distribution, and then always selecting the algorithm with the lowest average runtime. This approach, which we dub "winner-take-all," has driven recent advances in algorithm design and refinement, but has resulted in the neglect of many algorithms that, although uncompetitive on average, offer excellent performance on particular problem instances. Our consideration of the algorithm selection literature, and our dissatisfaction with the winner-take-all approach, has led us to ask the following two questions. First, what general techniques can we use to perform per-instance (rather than per-distribution) algorithm selection? Second, once we have rejected the notion of winner-take-all algorithm evaluation, how should we evaluate novel algorithms? We address the first question here, and the second question in section 19.5.

Given our existing technique for predicting runtime, we propose the following simple approach for the construction of algorithm portfolios:

1. Train a model for each algorithm, as described above.
2. Given an instance:
a. Compute feature values
b. Predict each algorithm's running time using runtime models
c. Run the algorithm predicted to be fastest.

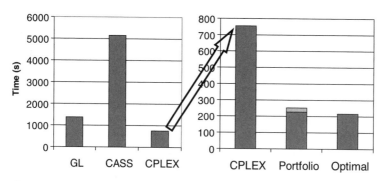

Figure 19.11
Algorithm and portfolio runtimes.

19.4.1 Experimental Results

In order to build an algorithm portfolio, we needed more algorithms for solving the WDP. In addition to CPLEX, we considered two special-purpose algorithms from the combinatorial auctions literature for which a public implementation was available: GL (Gonen and Lehmann 2001), a simple branch-and-bound algorithm with CPLEX's LP solver as its heuristic, and CASS (Fujishima, Leyton-Brown, and Shoham 1999), a more complex branch-and-bound algorithm with a non-LP heuristic. We used the methodology described in section 19.1.1 to build regression models for GL and CASS; for the results in this section all models were learned using simple linear regression, without a log transformation on the response variable.[6]

Figure 19.11 compares the average runtimes of our three algorithms (CPLEX, CASS, GL) to that of the portfolio (note the change of scale on the graph, and the repeated CPLEX bar). Note that CPLEX would be chosen under winner-take-all algorithm selection. The "optimal" bar shows the performance of an ideal portfolio where algorithm selection is performed perfectly and with no overhead. The portfolio bar shows the time taken to compute features (light portion) and the time taken to run the selected algorithm (dark portion). Despite the fact that CASS and GL are much slower than CPLEX on average, the portfolio outperforms CPLEX by roughly a factor of three. Moreover, neglecting the cost of computing features, our portfolio's selections take only 5 percent longer to run than the optimal selections.

Figures 19.12 and 19.13 show the frequency with which each algorithm is selected in the ideal portfolio and in our portfolio. They illustrate the quality of our algorithm selection and the relative value of the three algorithms. Observe that our portfolio does not always make the right choice (in particular, it selects GL much more often than it should). However, most of the mistakes made by our models occur when both algorithms have very similar running times; these mistakes are not very costly, explaining why our portfolio's choices have a running time so close to optimal.

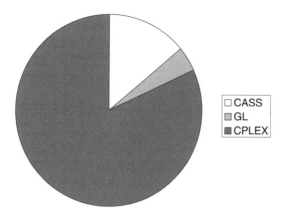

Figure 19.12
Optimal.

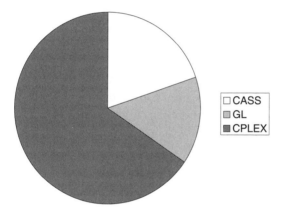

Figure 19.13
Selected.

Observe that our variable importance analysis from section 19.3.2 gives us some insight about why an algorithm such as CASS is able to provide such large gains over algorithms like CPLEX and GL on a significant fraction of instances.[7] Unlike CASS, both GL and CPLEX use an LP relaxation heuristic. It is possible that when the number of constraints (and thus the bid graph edge density feature) increases, such heuristics become less accurate, or larger LP input size incurs substantially higher per-node costs. On the other hand, additional constraints reduce feasible search space size. As with many search algorithms, CASS often benefits whenever the search space becomes smaller; thus, CASS can achieve better overall performance on problems with a very large number of constraints.

We can also compare the performance of our portfolio to an alternative portfolio that task-swaps among its constituent algorithms, described, for example, by Gomes and Selman (2001). Portfolios built using this approach always take time equal to the number of algorithms in the portfolio times the runtime of the optimal portfolio. Thus, on this dataset running the alternative portfolio would have been only very slightly faster than running CPLEX alone. If we observe that GL is rarely chosen by the optimal portfolio and that it contributes little over CPLEX when it is chosen, we can conclude that GL should be dropped from the task-swapping portfolio. Even if we do so, however, the alternate portfolio still takes nearly twice as long to run as the portfolio built using our techniques.

19.5   Using Hardness Models to Induce Hard Distributions

Once we have recognized the value of selecting among existing WDP algorithms using a portfolio approach, it is necessary to reexamine the data we use to design and evaluate our algorithms. When the purpose of designing new algorithms is to reduce the time that our portfolio will take to solve problems, we should aim to produce new algorithms that *complement* that existing portfolio. First, it is essential to choose a distribution D that reflects the problems that will be encountered in practice. Given a portfolio, the greatest opportunity for improvement is on instances that are hard for that portfolio, very common in D, or both. More precisely, the importance of a region of problem space is proportional to the amount of time the current portfolio spends working on instances in that region. (For previous work on generating hard test data on a different problem domain, see e.g., Selman, Mitchell, and Levesque 1996.)

19.5.1   Inducing Harder Distributions

Let H_f be a model of portfolio runtime based on instance features, constructed as the minimum of the models that constitute the portfolio. By normalizing, we can reinterpret this model as a density function h_f. By the argument above, we should generate instances from the product of this distribution and our original distribution, D. However, it is problematic to sample from $D \cdot h_f$: D may be non-analytic (an instance generator), whereas h_f depends on features and so can only be evaluated after an instance has been created.

One way to sample from $D \cdot h_f$ is rejection sampling (Doucet, de Freitas, and Gordon 2001): generate problems from D and keep them with probability proportional to h_f. Furthermore, if there exists a second distribution that is able to guide the sampling process toward hard instances, rejection sampling can use it to reduce the expected number of rejections before an accepted sample. This is indeed the case for parameterized instance generators: for example, all of the CATS (and legacy) distributions have some tunable parameters $\vec{p}$, and although the hardness of instances generated with the same parameter values can vary widely, $\vec{p}$ is (weakly) predictive of hardness. We can generate instances from $D \cdot h_f$ in the following way:[8]

1. Create a hardness model H_p with features $\vec{p}$, and normalize it to create a pdf, h_p.
2. Generate a large number of instances from $D \cdot h_p$.
3. Construct a distribution over instances by assigning each instance s probability proportional to $H_f(s)/h_p(s)$, and select an instance by sampling from this distribution.

Observe that if h_p turns out to be helpful, hard instances from $D \cdot h_f$ will be encountered quickly. Even in the worst case where h_p directs the search away from hard instances, observe that we still sample from the correct distribution because the weights are divided by $h_p(s)$ in step 3.

In our case, D is factored as $D_g \cdot D_{p_i}$, where D_g is a uniform distribution over the CATS and legacy instance generators in our dataset, each having a different parameter space, and D_{p_i} is a distribution over the parameters of the chosen instance generator i. In this case it is difficult to learn a single H_p. A good solution is to factor h_p as $h_g \cdot h_{p_i}$, where h_g is a hardness model using only the choice of instance generator as a feature, and h_{p_i} is a hardness model in instance generator i's parameter space. Likewise, instead of using a single feature-space hardness model H_f, we can train a separate model for each generator $H_{f,i}$ and normalize each to a pdf $h_{f,i}$.[9] The goal is now to generate instances from the distribution $D_g \cdot D_{p_i} \cdot h_{f,i}$, which can be done as follows:

1. For every instance generator i, create a hardness model H_{p_i} with features $\vec{p_i}$, and normalize it to create a pdf, h_{p_i}.
2. Construct a distribution over instance generators h_g, where the probability of each generator i is proportional to the average hardness of instances generated by i.
3. Generate a large number of instances from $(D_g \cdot h_g) \cdot (D_{p_i} \cdot h_{p_i})$
a. select a generator i by sampling from $D_g \cdot h_g$
b. select parameters for the generator by sampling from $D_{p_i} \cdot h_{p_i}$
c. run generator i with the chosen parameters to generate an instance.
4. Construct a distribution over instances by assigning each instance s from generator i probability proportional to $H_{f,i}(s)/(h_g(s) \cdot h_{p_i}(s))$, and select an instance by sampling from this distribution.

19.5.2 Experimental Results
Due to the wide spread of runtimes in our composite distribution D (seven orders of magnitude) and the high accuracy of our model h_f, it is quite easy for our technique to generate harder instances. Figure 19.14 presents these results. Because our runtime data was capped, there is no way to know if the hardest instances in the new distribution are harder than the hardest instances in the original distribution; note, however, that very few easy instances are generated. Instances in the induced distribution came predominantly from the CATS "arbitrary" distribution, with most of the rest from L3.

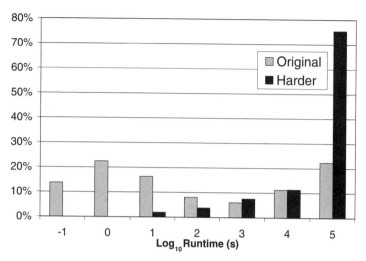

Figure 19.14
Inducing harder distributions.

To demonstrate that our technique also works in more challenging settings, we sought a different distribution with small runtime variance. As described in chapter 18 of this volume, there has been ongoing discussion in the WDP literature about whether those CATS distributions that are relatively easy could be configured to be harder. We consider two easy distributions with low variance from CATS, *matching* and *scheduling*, and show that they can indeed be made much harder than originally proposed. Figures 19.15 and 19.16 show the histograms of the runtimes of the ideal portfolio before and after our technique was applied. In fact, for these two distributions we generated instances that were (respectively) 100 and fifty times harder than anything we had previously seen! Moreover, the *average* runtime for the new distributions was greater than the observed *maximum* running time on the original distribution.

19.6   Conclusion

In this chapter we showed how to build models of the empirical hardness of WDP, and discussed various applications for these models. First, we identified structural, distribution-independent features of WDP instances and showed that they contain enough information to predict CPLEX running time with high accuracy. Next, we showed that these models can be effective for straightforward prediction of running time, gaining deeper insight into empirical hardness through the analysis of learned models, the construction of algorithm portfolios, and tuning distributions for hardness.

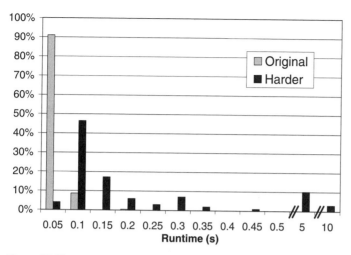

Figure 19.15
Matching.

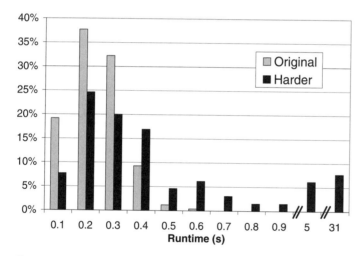

Figure 19.16
Scheduling.

Acknowledgments

This chapter is based on work first presented in Leyton-Brown, Nudelman, and Shoham 2002 and Leyton-Brown et al. 2003a,b. We would therefore like to acknowledge the contributions of Galen Andrew and James McFadden, who were coauthors on Leyton-Brown et al. 2003a,b.

Notes

1. We must note that CPLEX is constantly being improved. Unfortunately, it is not easy to rerun three CPU-years worth of experiments. The results presented here are specific to version 7.1, and might change in future versions. We emphasize, however, that both the techniques and features that we introduce here are quite general, and can be applied to any WDP solver. Furthermore, limited experiments with CPLEX 8.0 suggest that the qualitative runtime distribution and our models' accuracy remain very similar to the results presented here, at least for our WDP benchmark distributions.

2. The attentive reader will notice the omission of the CATS Paths generator from this list. Indeed, we did initially include instances from this generator in our experiments. However, the definition of this generator changed substantially from version 1.0 of the CATS software (Leyton-Brown, Pearson, and Shoham 2000) to version 2.0 (chapter 18). To avoid confusion we dropped these instances, though we note that the change did not make a significant difference to our experimental results.

3. We thank Rámon Béjar for providing code for calculating the clustering coefficient.

4. It would have been desirable to include some measure of the size of the (unpruned) search space. For some problems branching factor and search depth are used; for WDP neither is easily estimated. A related measure is the number of maximal independent sets of BG, which corresponds to the number of feasible solutions. However, this counting problem is hard, and to our knowledge does not have a polynomial-time approximation.

5. Cross-validation is a standard machine learning technique that provides an unbiased estimate of test set error using only the training set. First, the training set is split into k different subsets. Validation set errors are then computed by performing learning in turn on each of $k - 1$ of those subsets and evaluating resulting model on the remaining subset. The average of these k validation set errors is then used as an approximation of a model's performance on test data.

6. We argued above that applying a log transform to the response variable leads to regression models that minimize relative rather than absolute error. This is useful when building models with the goal of understanding why instances vary in empirical hardness. In this section, by contrast, we care about building portfolios that will outperform their constituent algorithms in terms of average runtime. This implies that we are concerned with absolute error, and so we do not perform a log transform in this case.

7. Observe that, in order to maintain continuity with other parts of the chapter such as this variable importance analysis, we have described the construction of algorithm portfolios optimized for fixed-size inputs. We have observed (both with combinatorial auctions and in other domains such as SAT) that it is possible to build accurate runtime models with variable-size data and hence that our portfolio approach is not restricted in any way to fixed-size inputs. It is therefore worth emphasizing that our methodology for building both empirical hardness models and algorithm portfolios can be applied directly to the construction of models for variable-size data.

8. In true rejection sampling, step 2 would generate a single instance that would be then accepted or rejected in step 3. Our technique approximates this process, but doesn't require us to normalize H_f and guarantees that we will output an instance after generating a constant number of samples.

9. However, the experimental results presented in figures 19.14–19.16 use hardness models H_f trained on the whole dataset rather than using models trained on individual distributions. Learning new models would probably yield even better results.

References

Achlioptas, Dimitris, Carla P. Gomes, Henry A. Kautz, and Bart Selman (2000), "Generating Satisfiable Problem Instances," *AAAI*, 256–261.

Cheeseman, Peter, Bob Kanefsky, and William M. Taylor (1991), "Where the Really Hard Problems Are," *IJCAI-91*, 331–337.

Doucet, Arnaud, Nando de Freitas, and Neil Gordon (eds.) (2001), *Sequential Monte Carlo Methods in Practice*. New York: Springer-Verlag.

Fujishima, Yuzo, Kevin Leyton-Brown, and Yoav Shoham (1999), "Taming the Computational Complexity of Combinatorial Auctions: Optimal and Approximate Approaches," *Proceedings of the IJCAI'99*, 548–553.

Gomes, Carla P. and Bart Selman (1997), "Problem Structure in the Presence of Perturbations," *AAAI/IAAI*, 221–226.

Gomes, Carla P. and Bart Selman (2001), "Algorithm Portfolios," *Artificial Intelligence*, 126, 43–62.

Gonen, Rica and Daniel Lehmann (2000), "Optimal Solutions for Multi-Unit Combinatorial Auctions: Branch and Bound Heuristics," *ACM Conference on Electronic Commerce*, 13–20.

Gonen, Rica and Daniel Lehmann (2001), "Linear Programming Helps Solving Large Multi-Unit Combinatorial Auctions," Technical Report TR-2001-8, Leibniz Center for Research in Computer Science.

Hastie, Trevor, Robert Tibshirani, and Jerome Friedman (2001), *Elements of Statistical Learning*. New York: Springer.

Horvitz, Eric, Yongshao Ruan, Carla P. Gomes, Henry A. Kautz, Bart Selman, and David M. Chickering (2001), "A Bayesian Approach to Tackling Hard Computational Problems," *UAI*, 235–244.

Korf, Richard E. and Michael Reid (1998), "Complexity Analysis of Admissible Heuristic Search," *AAAI-98*, 305–310.

Lagoudakis, Michail and Michael Littman (2000), "Algorithm Selection Using Reinforcement Learning," *ICML*, 511–518.

Lagoudakis, Michail and Michael Littman (2001), "Learning to Select Branching Rules in the DPLL Procedure for Satisfiability," *LICS/SAT*.

Leyton-Brown, Kevin, Eugene Nudelman, Galen Andrew, James McFadden, and Yoav Shoham (2003a), "Boosting as a Metaphor for Algorithm Design," *Principles and Practice of Constraint Programming*, LNCS, 2833, 899–903.

Leyton-Brown, Kevin, Eugene Nudelman, Galen Andrew, James McFadden, and Yoav Shoham (2003b), "A Portfolio Approach to Algorithm Selection," *IJCAI-03*, 1542–1543.

Leyton-Brown, Kevin, Eugene Nudelman, and Yoav Shoham (2002), "Learning the Empirical Hardness of Optimization Problems: The Case of Combinatorial Auctions," *CP*, 556–572.

Leyton-Brown, Kevin, Mark Pearson, and Yoav Shoham (2000), "Towards a Universal Test Suite for Combinatorial Auction Algorithms," *ACM Conference on Electronic Commerce*, 66–76.

Lobjois, Lionel and Michel Lemaître (1998), "Branch and Bound Algorithm Selection by Performance Prediction," *AAAI*, 353–358.

Monasson, Rémi, Riccardo Zecchina, Scott Kirkpatrick, Bart Selman, and Lidror Troyansky (1998), "Determining Computational Complexity for Characteristic 'Phase transitions,'" *Nature*, 400, 133–137.

Rice, John R. (1976), "The Algorithm Selection Problem," *Advances in Computers*, 15, 65–118.

Ruan, Yongshao, Eric Horvitz, and Henry Kautz (2002), "Restart Policies with Dependence Among Runs: A Dynamic Programming Approach," LNCS, 2740, 573–586.

Sandholm, Tuomas (2002), "Algorithm for Optimal Winner Determination in Combinatorial Auctions," *Artificial Intelligence*, 135, 1–54.

Selman, Bart, David G. Mitchell, and Hector J. Levesque (1996), "Generating Hard Satisfiability Problems," *Artificial Intelligence*, 81, 17–29.

Slaney, John and Toby Walsh (2001), "Backbones in Optimization and Approximation," *IJCAI-01*, 254–259.

Zhang, Weixiong (1999), *State-Space Search: Algorithms, Complexity, Extensions, and Applications*. New York: Springer.

V Applications

20 Auctions for the Safe, Efficient, and Equitable Allocation of Airspace System Resources

Michael O. Ball, George L. Donohue, and Karla Hoffman

20.1 Introduction

Most countries attempt to design their air transportation system so that it is economically viable, safe, and efficient. As the system evolves, changes are necessary to assure that these goals continue to be met. Although air transportation in the United States has a comparable safety record to that of automobile travel (on an exposure to risk time basis, see Royal Society 1992), the margin of safety is slowly eroding under the demands for more enplanement opportunities. The 1978 deregulation of the U.S. route structure was intended to increase competition within the airline industry and thereby improve efficiency, decrease cost to travelers, and expand the overall flying opportunities. This policy initially provided increased enplanement opportunities at reduced prices because there was sufficient capacity in the system to allow such growth. However, the current policies and procedures do not produce a similar effect in a capacity-limited system. In fact, these policies impede the need to build additional airports and overhaul the technology both within air traffic control and on airplanes. Without such expansion, more system elements are likely to become capacity limited. In such a system it is essential to use system resources efficiently. We therefore provide suggestions for mechanisms both to expand the capacity and to assure that the current, limited capacity is used both safely and efficiently.

As the U.S. National Air Transportation System (NATS) becomes highly capacity constrained along multiple dimensions, it requires feedback mechanisms that can react along multiple time scales to adjust system behavior (Fan and Odoni 2002). Today, more than a quarter of a century after airline deregulation in 1978, strategic airspace management exercises little or no control over the number of aircraft that are scheduled to land and depart from various airports. It can only react when the system is overloaded. Thus, the U.S. airlines implicitly are responsible for setting constraints on airport operations as part of their scheduling process. The policies of the U.S. Department of Transportation (DOT) and the Federal Aviation Administration (FAA) effectively encourage these airlines to overbook and then cancel or delay flights, leaving

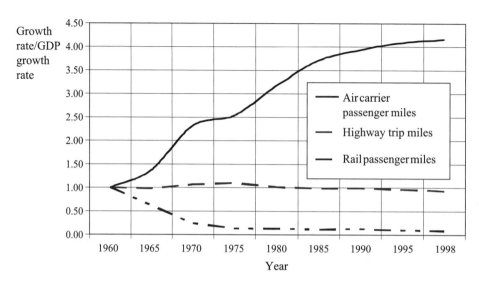

Figure 20.1
Major transportation modal growth normalized to 1960 and GDP growth.

the system regularly in crisis mode, with re-scheduling the norm rather than the exception. Similarly, regional governments that wish to determine their demographic growth patterns are powerless to shape, or even to suggest, how the airspace in their region is used. The driving forces behind this chapter are two questions: what forces led to this situation, and what policy changes might be made to improve the U.S. national air transportation system crisis?

We begin by providing a description of the history of the U.S. aviation system and then proceed to explain how market-clearing mechanisms might be able to rectify many of the shortcomings of the current system (see Mineta 1997 and the Commission on the Future of the U.S. Aerospace Industry 2002 for background).

20.1.1 History of U.S. Aviation

From 1938 to 1978, the Civil Aviation Board (CAB) managed the nation's air transportation route (and industry) structure (Gleimer 1996). Many economists felt this administrative process did an inefficient job of providing transportation services (Rochester 1976; Preston 1987). Figure 20.1 shows how the growth rate of revenue passenger miles (RPMs), normalized by Gross Domestic Product, was stagnating just prior to 1978 (data taken from DOT/BTS 2001). Prior to 1978, air travel was relatively expensive and considered by many to be only for the upper echelons of society. The 1978 deregulation of the airline industry led to a decrease in prices and a dramatic increase in industry productivity and frequency of service. Figure 20.2 illustrates how deregulation

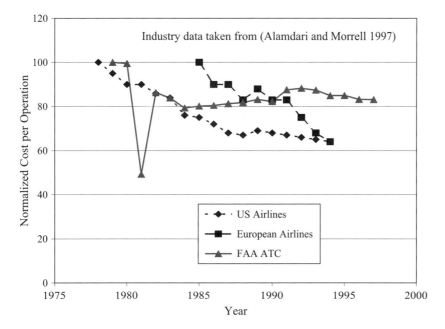

Figure 20.2
Productivity trends for the US ATC System, U.S. and European airlines.

in both the United States and Europe initially increased airline productivity (Alamdari and Morrel 1997), even though FAA productivity did not change (with the exception of the effect caused by the air traffic controllers strike in 1981). However, after 1990, there was a leveling off of airline productivity (Donohue 2002). Some factors limiting growth include the lack of incentives to adopt new technology and the political inability to add new airport infrastructure; and an inevitable rise in queuing delays occurred as the system approached the maximum demand to capacity ratio (Donohue and Shaver 2000).

20.1.2 Airport Capacity and Slot Controls

Even prior to 1978, however, some airports were already congested. Four airports had been arrival slot controlled since 1968 under the High Density Rule (HDR): New York's Kennedy (JFK) and LaGuardia (LGA), Chicago O'Hare (ORD), and Washington's Reagan National (DCA).

Today, the air transportation situation looks very different than it did in 1978. Many U.S. airports are becoming scheduled at levels that exceed the FAA's estimate of a maximum safe operational rate (DOT/BTS 2001; Haynie 2002). The major domestic U.S. air carriers use the hub-and-spoke system, which brings passengers from smaller cities to

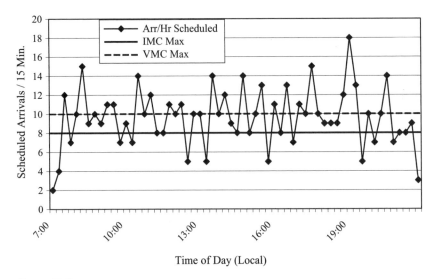

Figure 20.3
LaGuardia scheduled arrivals vs. FAA capacity estimates.

hubs that will then transport them in an economical way to their final destination. Hub operations tend to concentrate very large numbers of flight arrivals and departures over short periods. In some cases, airlines maintain near monopoly control over hub airports so that newer airlines face significant barriers to entry into these airports.

On April 5, 2000, the semi-deregulation of the slot controls went into effect with the enactment of the AIR-21 bill (Federal Register 2000), which among other things directed the DOT to eliminate totally slot controls at the four U.S. HDR airports by 2007, and to increase immediately the number of slots allocated for regional service at LaGuardia. This act led to the immediate and extreme congestion of air traffic activity at LaGuardia (Fan and Odoni 2002). Strong "network effects" meant that the LaGuardia delays induced additional delays throughout the NATS.

LaGuardia has been arrival slot controlled (approximately thirty-two arrivals per runway per hour) since 1968, due to concerns about congestion and community noise at that airport. These slot controls were maintained even after the Civil Aviation Board was abolished in 1978. Figure 20.3 shows the scheduled number of flights at LaGuardia in 2000. The schedule consists of both arrivals and departures in fifteen-minute intervals from 7 am to 10 pm. LaGuardia has one arrival runway and one orthogonal crossing departure runway. The FAA officially considers the maximum safe level of operations under favorable weather conditions to be forty arrivals and forty departures per hour (i.e., ten arrivals per fifteen-minute epoch) under visual conditions. Under reduced visual conditions (instrument flight rules, or IFR), this airport is supposed to

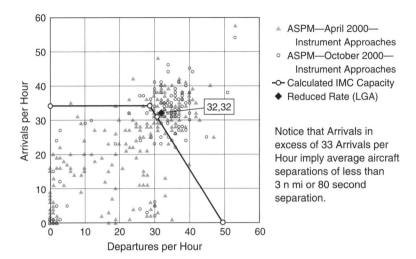

Figure 20.4
LaGuardia IMC operation rates for April and October 2000 (FAA 2001).

be reduced to thirty-two arrivals and thirty-two departures per hour (i.e., eight arrivals per fifteen-minute epoch). Figure 20.4 shows that the actual operational rates under the more restrictive, and slightly more hazardous IFR conditions frequently exceed the (thirty-two, thirty-two) rate (DOT/BTS 2001). Section 20.2.1 will show that this rate was set by runway occupancy time (ROT) considerations and not aircraft wake vortex separation standards, which are more restrictive. The wake vortex problem was unknown in 1968, when most commercial aircraft were of medium size. With the introduction of both wide-body aircraft (heavy) and small regional jets (RJs) in a highly dynamic mixture, this safety problem is of growing concern (Haynie 2002).

The fact that there are two different capacity levels, one for good weather conditions and another for inclement conditions, further complicates the process of scheduling. Also, FAA regulated separation rates change depending upon whether a small aircraft follows a large aircraft (in which case the separation must be larger), due to aircraft wake vortex encounter concerns. These alternative landing and takeoff separation rules are quite complex and are not considered in the FAA determination of the maximum number of scheduled operations.

20.1.3 Scheduling Practices

A question naturally arises: Why do the airlines schedule operations that exceed the safe departure/arrival rate that an airport can support, thus generating excessive flight delays, cancellations, and loss-of-separation violations? The answer is competition. If airline A acts responsibly and does not increase its schedule at a congested airport, it will have voluntarily provided another airline with the opportunity to schedule more flights at that airport. Conversely, if airline B decides to increase its schedule in an attempt to increase city pair options and flight frequency (but in reality only increasing congestion and delay for all airlines), airline A may lose market share. Under policies currently in effect, if scheduled flights at that airport are, at some time in the future, legislatively or procedurally reduced through re-regulation, then the airline with the greatest number of scheduled flights is likely to argue and receive more of the available flights. Thus, the risk is not only the reduction of current market share, but also the risk of a permanent market share reduction. In addition, at an airport not dominated by a single carrier (e.g., LaGuardia), when an airline adds another flight the delay experienced by that flight may be small relative to the total delay to other flights caused by that additional flight. Thus, only a small portion of the "delay cost" of adding the flight may be internalized by the initiating airline.

LaGuardia may be the extreme case, but many U.S. airports and airlines are experiencing similar situations. Table 20.1 shows the demand to capacity ratio of twenty major U.S. airports. The demand/capacity (D/C) ratio is based upon FAA computed good weather capacity calculations and measured average operational rates. When the D/C ratio approaches 1, queuing theory predicts that the delay will grow exponentially.

20.1.4   Impact of Level of Competition

We now view the congestion issue relative to a measure of competition at a given airport. The Herfindahl-Hirschman Index (HHI) is a measure of industry competition. Higher HHI values indicate more concentration of business activity among fewer participants and thus less competition. According to Cooper (2000), studies of the hub system within the United States have shown that fare revenues are higher on average for trips to and from major hub airports, with a few concentrated hub airports showing significant premiums over a decade; also, the higher premiums are realized by the dominant carrier in that hub, whereas fares charged by the other carriers in that hub are similar to the fares charged in less concentrated airports. The hub airports that have a dominant carrier typically have a high HHI.

One could argue, on a theoretical basis, that the more competition at an airport, the greater tendency there would be to over-schedule (i.e., monopolists will totally internalize the cost penalty of the delays they cause themselves and therefore not over-schedule). Thus, under current procedures, from the perspective of driving down prices, one would like competition, but from the perspective of keeping congestion at a reasonable level one would like to discourage competition but only if the monopolist would internalize all delay costs and therefore operate at the optimum delay value. Unfortunately, the data in table 20.1 does not support this hypothesis. Airports with both high market concentration (Atlanta) and low market concentration (Newark and LaGuardia) are experiencing similar delays. Even the current slot controlled airports are

Table 20.1

Airport operations/year vs. delays, competition and demand management

City	Airport	Operations per year (in thousands)	Delays > 15 mins. per thousand	HHI Index	Demand to Capacity	Slot Controlled
LaGuardia	LGA	392	156	<1800	.68	yes
Newark	EWR	457	81	3600	.66	no
Chicago	ORD	909	63	3200	.72	yes
San Francisco	SFA	431	57	3500	.67	no
Philadelphia	PHL	484	45	3100	.67	no
Kennedy	JFK	359	38	<1800	.42	yes
Atlanta	ATL	913	31	5500	.78	no
Dallas-Ft Worth	DFW	866	24	4500	.52	no
Los Angeles	LGA	784	22	<1800	.78	no
Dulles	IAD	480	20	2700	.54	no
St. Louis	STL	484	18	3800	.72	no
Detroit	DTW	554	18	3600	.53	no
Minneapolis	MSP	522	13	4500	.68	no
Seattle	SEA	445	11	<1800	.71	no
Baltimore	BWI	315	7	1900	.42	no
Charlotte	CLT	460	6	5200	.52	no
Pittsburgh	PIT	448	4	5300	.47	no
Denver	DEN	528	2	4200	.41	no

experiencing high delays because they are operating near the maximum capacity level. If the current slot controls on these high demand airports expire in 2007, they will undoubtedly become even more congested, as seen at LaGuardia in 2001. This argues for the need for slot allocation measures.

20.1.5 Reduction in Average Aircraft Size

The mixture of aircraft types has changed significantly in recent years. Airlines are moving toward flying smaller aircraft for several reasons, including lower labor costs, higher average load factors, ability to provide higher frequency service to a given market, fuel efficiency, aircraft maintenance costs, and so on. Each aircraft arrival or departure consumes approximately the same amount of airport capacity. Thus, as average aircraft size decreases, airspace throughput in terms of passengers decreases. Hansen (2002) noted that 31 percent of the daily flights into Los Angeles International airport (LAX) in 1998 provided only 8 percent of the seats available for passenger enplanement. From a network operator viewpoint, these flights caused a substantial increase in delays and overall costs at LAX with very little marginal transportation benefit. The combination of competitive pressures to provide more frequency discussed earlier, as well as the fact that a single flight can cause much more delay than it experiences, means that there are little or no natural economic pressures to arrest the trend toward smaller aircraft.

20.1.6 Safety Impact of Scheduling Practices

Perhaps the most compelling argument for a new slot control system is the safety impact of operating at a high demand to capacity ratio. The recent data and analysis by Haynie (2002) indicate that loss of the regulated safe separation distance of aircraft is positively correlated to the aircraft arrival demand to runway capacity ratio (figure 20.5). Table 20.1 shows that ten of the largest airports in the United States have demand to capacity ratios above .6. The next section will further discuss the relationship between airport capacity and separation standards.

20.2 Current Procedures for Allocating Landing Time Slots

20.2.1 Capacity Determination and Safety Standards

There is a long-standing, internationally recognized safety principle that two aircraft should never be on an active runway at any one time. The concern is that the leading aircraft may not be able to exit the active runway for a variety of reasons and the following aircraft must not land until the active runway is clear in order to avoid a potential high-speed collision. In general, aircraft deceleration times vary and larger aircraft approach a runway at a higher speed than do small aircraft, so minimum separation times and runway capacities will vary with aircraft mix.

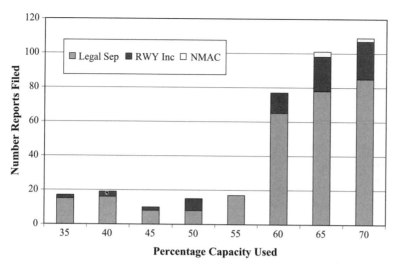

Figure 20.5
Airport incidents for 13 years (1988–2001) vs. the capacity fraction at occurrence.

With the introduction of the Boeing 747 wide-body aircraft into commercial service in the 1970s, the aviation community became aware of a new hazard for smaller, lighter-weight aircraft following very heavy aircraft. The lift required to support any aircraft ultimately gets left in its wake in the form of both turbulence and a set of counter-rotating vortex pairs. Aircraft are generally designed to withstand a significant amount of turbulence, but the coherent induced rolling encounter of a significantly smaller aircraft in the wing-tip vortex of a wide-body heavy aircraft can be fatal.

In the 1970s and 1980s, conservative safe aircraft separation times were estimated (based upon wake vortex knowledge at the time) and established as separation times for adverse weather conditions when air traffic control had responsibility for separation. Generally these times were in excess of the standards-based runway occupancy times. In good weather, when the aircraft pilot has separation responsibility, the pilot is warned when he is following a heavy aircraft and the wake should be avoided (however, the wake vortex is invisible most of the time). Table 20.2 shows aircraft separation time estimates taken from a study on the aircraft mixture and maximum arrival rate at LAX based upon wake vortex separation times (Hansen 2001). This table illustrates that many aircraft pairs should maintain separation times in excess of the ROT separation standard of ninety seconds. In a study for Atlanta airport, Haynie (2001) showed that under certain VFR scenarios, when pilots assumed responsibility for separation, almost 50 percent of the flights had separation times less than the minimum specified by the wake vortex standard. The ability to meet this standard and, at the same time, produce

Table 20.2
Representative aircraft separation time estimates for wake vortex separation

Leading	Trailing Aircraft			
	Small	Large	B757	Heavy
Small	80	68	66	64
Large	160	73	66	64
B757	200	120	100	100
Heavy	240	150	140	100

Note: Shading indicates wake vortex standard exceeds ROT standard.

high throughput, is hampered by the inherent variability in the joint air traffic control/ pilot process for spacing aircraft. In particular, the higher the variability in the process, the lower the throughput must be set in order to insure a minimum separation standard is met. Technology, which places greater control in cockpit, exists (Green et al. 2001) (Ballin et al. 2002) to reduce the variance of this process. This technology would significantly increase the effective capacity of airports. However, implementation of this technology requires that the airlines purchase and install new equipment on aircraft and that the FAA certify new procedures. In general, significant benefits to any airline will not be accrued until *all* airlines are equipped. Thus, there is little incentive for a single airline to make the required investment unless that airline can be assured that all airlines will make a similar investment, and this has so far impeded the introduction of such technology (Commission on the Future of the U.S. Aerospace Industry 2002).

20.2.2 Administrative Procedures and Property Rights

The definition of a slot is somewhat ambiguous. In general, the concept refers to the ability to access a resource over a particular time. Title 49 of the United States Code (USC) subtitle VII (49USC41714) defines the term "slot" to mean "a reservation for an instrument flight rule takeoff or landing by an air carrier of an aircraft in air transportation."

In the United States, prior to 1969, the concept of an arrival or departure slot essentially did not exist. Rather, airlines interested in providing service simply published schedules at the airports of interest and, on a given day of operations, requested access to runways as needed. There were other resources, of course, that had to be arranged to support such services, including gates, ticketing facilities, and baggage handling capabilities.

When the FAA instituted the high density rules (HDR) in 1969 at Kennedy, LaGuardia, Chicago, and Washington's National, it assumed responsibility for determining the appropriate number of slots and of overseeing their allocation. Slots were divided into three categories: air carriers, commuter airlines, and general aviation. The separate allocation at each of the four airports was accomplished via airport-based scheduling committees, which were granted limited antitrust immunity. The FAA intervened when committee deliberations became deadlocked. Slot ownership was ceded to the incumbent operators at the HDR airports in 1985. However, "use it or lose it" rules were established to ensure that each allocated slot was used. Slot exchange among owners has been allowed over the years.

On April 5, 2000, through the so-called "Air-21" Act, Congress made additional slots available at LaGuardia airport (Federal Register 2000). The restrictions placed on the usage of these slots effectively directed their use toward small aircraft providing access to small communities. By the end of September 2000, there were 192 additional operations scheduled at LaGuardia based on the Air-21 exemptions. Because the additional slots made available were not based on an actual increase in physical capacity, the increase in operations lead to substantial performance degradations in the form of extreme delays and numbers of flight cancellations (Fan and Odoni 2002). To address these performance problems, limitations on the number of Air-21 slots were instituted and these slots were allocated based on a lottery. The lottery is considered a temporary measure and replacement mechanisms are under investigation (Federal Register 2001).

Internationally, slot allocation activities are essentially similar to the U.S. experience. Administrative procedures are used to allocate slots (see DotEcon Ltd. 2001). Generally, there are provisions to encourage new entrants and access to small communities; however, grandfather rights predominate and limit the effect of such provisions. Although there appears to be interest in exploring the use of market mechanisms, there has been little or no use to date. In fact, in the United Kingdom, although the exchange of slots on a one-for-one basis is allowed, buying and selling slots is prohibited. Two IATA conferences, held each year in June and November, provide a forum for airlines to coordinate slot assignments relative to international schedules. At these conferences airport schedule coordinators and airlines confirm and possibly renegotiate slot assignments. Airlines also engage in slot exchanges. These activities are essential in order for airlines properly to coordinate schedules and to optimize ground, maintenance, and other operations. They can continue after the conferences as airlines and airport coordinators continue to refine schedules.

When considering options relative to market mechanisms for allocating slots and, possibly related airport resources, a number of ambiguous legal questions arise. Regional airport authorities and municipalities typically own the airports in the United States and Europe. Because these authorities are almost always public agencies, they are typically restricted in that their charges for services can only achieve cost recovery.

Thus, the prospect of generating revenue streams from auctions that are well in excess of costs may be legally prohibited. In the Unites States, virtually all of these airports have received federal aviation trust funds to partially fund infrastructure investments and have therefore agreed to abide by a number of federal regulations governing access to and the safe operation of the airport. Most major airports have also funded numerous landside infrastructure investments with municipal bond debt financing. Many airlines have long-term leases with the municipal airport authorities on gates that give them exclusive rights to the gates. In fact, in many cases, the airlines have paid for the construction of these gates. The owner airlines can effectively use these long-term rights to exclude new entrants. These local gate ownership arrangements represent a major impediment to the prospect of auctioning gate access.

Currently, one might consider landing fees the charge most similar to a fee one might pay to lease a slot. However, landing fees represent a component of an airport's revenue stream that is used to recover overall airport costs. Conceptually, this fee pays for the cost required to maintain, and possibly construct, runways, taxiways, and related infrastructure. By contrast, the FAA has exclusive and unambiguous rights to all aircraft use of the airspace. Title 49 of the United States Code, subtitle VII (49USC40103) states, "The administrator of the Federal Aviation Administration shall develop plans and policy for the use of the navigable airspace and assign by regulation or order the use of the airspace necessary to ensure the safety of aircraft and the efficient use of airspace." This authority is exercised daily with the routine practice of aircraft departure denial under ground delay programs (GDPs). GDPs, the LaGuardia lotteries, and other activities have clearly established the precedent for network-wide government control of scheduled airline flights. Thus, the FAA "owns" the airspace immediately above airport runways and, consequently, has the authority to allocate the use of that airspace.

20.3   Slot Allocation and Reallocation on the Day of Operations

In an ideal world, airport capacity could be partitioned into well-defined slots and market or administrative mechanisms used to determine owners (or renters) of each slot. On any given day, slot ownership would afford an airline with the rights to carry out an operation within the precise time limits specified by the lease or ownership agreement. If the airline failed to exercise this right for any particular slot, then no offsetting compensation would be granted. A variety of factors render this ideal impractical or impossible. Uncertainty on several levels necessitates a more flexible approach. We use the term *demand uncertainty* to categorize effects that can cause flights to fail to meet planned departure or arrival time slots and the term *capacity uncertainty* to categorize effects that cause changes to the number and/or timing of slots. Examples of factors contributing to demand uncertainty include problems in loading passengers onto an aircraft, mechanical problems, queues on the airport surface or in the air, and en-route weather problems. Examples of factors contributing to capacity uncertainty include weather conditions at the airport and changes in flight sequences that cause the need to alter flight departure or arrival spacing.

In the United States, under normal conditions, there are essentially no controls placed on an airline to adhere to "scheduled slot assignments." Airlines have total control over when flights push back from their gates and, within the safety constraints imposed by ATC, control over when flights arrive. Within this framework, the stated FAA policy is to provide access to National Airspace System (NAS) resources on a first-come, first-served basis. That is, as aircraft push back from gates, they are placed in queues and given access to departure runways based on their place in the queue. Similarly, flights are placed in arrival sequences as they approach the airspace of their destination airports.

FAA traffic flow management (TFM) procedures in many cases make exceptions to this policy for safety and efficiency reasons. For example, flights routed toward congested airspace with restrictions on flow rates (miles-in-trail) might not be given sequential access to a departure runway in order to delay their arrival to a portion of airspace. On the arrival side, flights can be sequenced to maximize airport arrival throughput using the capabilities of the Center Tracon Automation System (CTAS) (Erzberger 1995). It is noteworthy that IATA guidelines explicitly recognize a decoupling of schedules and the actual timing of operations (IATA 2000): "The Conferences deal with adjustments to planned schedules to fit in with the slots available at airports. This activity has nothing to do with adjustments to schedules on the day of operation for air traffic flow management. The two types of slot allocation are quite different and unrelated."

In the United States, the most significant TFM adjustments to operations occur during ground delay programs (GDPs). FAA traffic flow managers institute a GDP whenever the anticipated arrival demand is significantly greater than the estimated arrival capacity at an airport. This most often occurs when degraded weather conditions at an airport cause a change from visual flight rules (VFR) to instrument flight rules (IFR). Under IFR, the pilot depends on air traffic control and aircraft instruments for separation and guidance so, more conservative procedures are used reducing capacity.

The FAA has used GDPs for close to twenty years now. Recently, however, the emergence of a new paradigm for TFM has led to significant changes in the implementation of GDPs. This paradigm, called *collaborative decision making* (CDM), is based on the recognition that improved data exchange and communication between the FAA and airlines will lead to better decision making (see Wambsganss 1996; Ball et al. 2000). In particular, the CDM philosophy emphasizes that decisions with a potential economic impact on airlines should be decentralized and made in collaboration with the airlines whenever possible. The GDP enhancements introduced under CDM are numerous, and include improved data exchange, better situational awareness tools, and increased flexibility for the airlines. All major U.S. airlines participate in CDM. An extranet connects the airline operational control centers with the Air Traffic Control System Command Center (ATCSCC), and all participants have a common decision support tool, the flight schedule monitor (FSM). The most significant improvements from CDM derive through using different procedures for allocating ground delays. Under CDM, arrival capacity is allocated to the airlines by a procedure called ration-by-schedule (RBS), based on the consensus recognition that airlines have claims on the arrival schedule based on the original flight schedules. In addition, CDM has introduced a new reallocation procedure called compression. This procedure aims to ensure optimal capacity utilization in the presence of delays and cancellations.

Figure 20.6 illustrates the overall allocation process. Note that in addition to RBS and compression, there is a third significant process, *cancellations and substitutions*, that is totally controlled by the airlines. Under this process, each airline may cancel flights and interchange slot-to-flight assignments for its own flights. Thus, although RBS in concept allocates slots to flights, the cancellation and substitution process effectively converts the slot-to-flight assignment into a slot-to-airline assignment.

The principal output of either RBS or compression is a controlled time of departure (CTD) for each flight in the GDP. Calculation of a CTD is accomplished by assigning a controlled time of arrival (CTA) to each flight and then computing a CTD by subtracting the estimated enroute time from the CTA. The assignment of CTAs by RBS can be viewed as a simple priority rule. A set of arrival slots consistent with the degraded capacity is created. Using the OAG arrival order as a priority order, each flight in the OAG is assigned the next available arrival slot. If this rule was applied to all flights and there were no cancellations or substitutions, then the flights would arrive in their original sequence but generally later. There are two groups of flights exempted from this basic allocation scheme: (1) flights that are currently airborne (clearly these cannot be assigned ground delay), and (2) a set of flights characterized by the distance of their departure airports from the GDP (arrival) airport (see Ball and Lulli 2004). The motivation for the second exemption is to include in the allocation scheme flights close to the airport and to exempt flights further away from the airport. Flights a greater distance

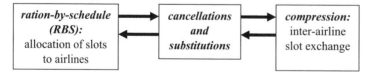

Figure 20.6
CDM resource allocation.

away must be assigned ground delays well in advance of their actual arrival, for example, four or five hours. So far in advance of arrival, there tends to be a greater level of uncertainty regarding weather and, as a consequence, airport arrival capacity. There is a significant likelihood that these flights could unnecessarily be assigned the ground delay. Thus, distance-based exemptions constitute a mechanism for improving expected airport throughput.

After a round of substitutions and cancellations the utilization of slots can usually be improved. The reason for this is that an airline's flight cancellations and delays may create "holes" in the current schedule; that is, there will be arrival slots that have no flights assigned to them. The purpose of the compression algorithm is to move flights up in the schedule to fill these slots. The basic idea behind the compression algorithm is that airlines are "paid back" for the slots they release, so as to encourage airlines to report cancellations.

To illustrate the compression algorithm, let us consider the example in figure 20.7. The leftmost figure represents the flight-slot assignment prior to the execution of the compression algorithm. Associated with each flight is an earliest time of arrival, and each slot has an associated slot time. Note that there is one cancelled flight. The rightmost figure shows the flight schedule after execution of the compression algorithm: as a first step, the algorithm attempts to fill AAL's open slot. Because there is no flight from AAL that can use the slot, the slot is allocated to UAL, and the process is repeated with the next open slot, which, using the same logic, is assigned to USA. The process is repeated for the next open slot, which is assigned to AAL. The AAL receives the earliest slot that it can use.

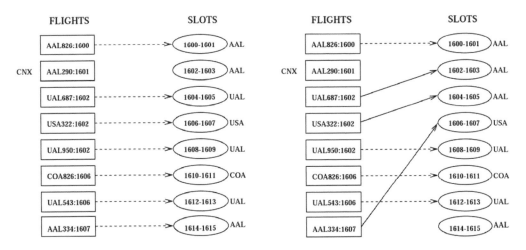

Figure 20.7
Execution of compression algorithm.

The compression algorithm results in an exchange among airlines of the initial RBS allocation. One could interpret this result as a reallocation. However, there is also a natural interpretation of compression as an inter-airline trading or bartering process (see Vossen and Ball 2005b). For example, in figure 20.7, American Airlines "traded" the 1600–1601 slot, which it could not use, for the 1607–1607 slot, which it could use, and United Airlines reduced its delay by trading the 1604–1605 slot for the earlier 1602–1603 slot. Vossen and Ball show that a bartering process can be structured so as to produce a result essentially equivalent to compression. This view of compression suggests many possible extensions. For example, Vossen and Ball (2005) define a more complex two-for-two bartering mechanism and show that there is a substantial potential for improved economic performance from using this mechanism. Probably the most intriguing enhancement is to allow "side payments" with any exchange as well as the buying and selling of slots. Section 20.8 discusses and analyzes such a process, which can be viewed as a day-of-operations aftermarket. It is noteworthy that experience with the current process can provide insights into the design of future market mechanisms and, also, that the CDM IT infrastructure can potentially serve as a basis for implementing such a market.

20.4   Objectives and Fundamental Issues Associated with the Design of Auctions within Aviation

The concept of creating a market-clearing mechanism for the allocation of takeoff and landing rights at airports is not new. Rassenti, Smith, and Bulfin (1982) provided the first general package-bidding framework for slot auctions. They suggested a combinatorial auction design that allowed bidders to be able to couple takeoff and landings in a single bid of the form "I want to purchase the right to take off from airport A at time X and also have the right to land at airport B at time Y for a total price of $Q." Even more complicated expressions of uses and related values may be needed. For example, an airline may need to express a collection of arrivals and takeoffs in a single bid to ensure that arrivals at a given airport are coupled with a takeoff from that airport and each takeoff is coupled with a landing at some other airport. The need for alternative collections, describing different business plans, also argues for a bidding language that allows bidders to say that two packages are mutually exclusive (the bidder is willing to win either package A or package B, but not both). With this type of expressive language, a bidder does not experience the concern that he will win only part of what he needs to create a commercially viable schedule of flights, or conversely, that he will win more than expected (the "exposure" problem) (a very detailed and excellent account of the issues and benefits associated with auctions for slot allocation appears in DotEcon, Ltd. 2001). We begin this section with a short summarization of some of these issues.

The current process for slot allocation whereby airlines have landing and takeoff rights grandfathered for decades at capacity-limited airports leads to inefficiencies, inertia, and distorted incentives (e.g., use available slots so as to keep competition at bay). When slots are allocated through an administrative process, the cost of ownership is only the cost of acquiring the slot. This is true whether there are many competitors wanting this slot or whether only one. When the slot is scarce, the decision of assigning new slots must be somewhat subjective and vulnerable to legal challenge. Such decisions often limit entrance or expansion of new carriers into a given market because they have less ability to impact the outcome of the administrative process.

By contrast, there are a number of benefits to the airline industry to using an administrative process. Grandfathering slots (a) allows a maximum degree of certainty over future slot holdings, thereby helping an airline with its long-term investment decisions; (b) makes the job of determining the allocation less cumbersome, because it is done infrequently, and (c) helps the airline do long-term planning, because it can predict most of its competition over long periods of time. Finally, the management of the overall airspace is less complex because the activities at a given airport, or over the entire airspace, are predictable and change little over time. Each of these benefits, however, also highlights how such allocation impedes competition and change over long periods.

We believe that using an alternative market-based allocation system, such as auctions, for the allocation of slots for a finite specified period of time, is more likely to provide a system that is efficient, that is, produces an allocation that results in maximizing the benefits to the consumer and the economy by allocating them to those that can generate the greatest benefit from their use. The knowledge that the slots will be re-auctioned in the future assures that the industry must actively evaluate the market and the value of ownership of such slots.

Because an auction allocates items by determining the bidder that will pay the most for the good, the auction-clearing price resolves the conflicting demands on the use of the resource without subjective arbitration. Another benefit of the use of auctions is that the process is both transparent and is less open to legal challenges.

One argument against auctions is that they are an easy mechanism for the government to raise revenues. Auctions do raise revenue, but the revenues raised are no more than a reflection of the market value associated with a scarce resource. How the revenue generated is used warrants discussion. It is our belief that the revenue can help pay for the infrastructure necessary to safely administer and expand airspace use. Because such costs must be incurred somehow, one can argue that the revenues generated are in lieu of other taxes that would be required if they were not generated from the auctioning of slots. However, we note that careful auction design often works *not* to maximize the revenue from high value bidders, but rather chooses objectives that encourage new entries and discourages or disallows monopolistic control over markets.

Thus, the revenue generated is a consequence of ensuring efficient outcomes but need not generate any more than the minimum necessary to do so.

There are a number of design issues that one must consider for an auction that allocates slots at airports. We discuss many of these issues prior to providing the details of a basic auction framework.

Capacity issues   Because airport slots cannot be considered separately from the other resources that will be used with the slot, one must consider runway, gating, baggage, and terminal capacity when determining the number of slots that might be available within a given time period. One must also know how the slots are to be used, that is, what is the distribution of aircraft types that will use the slots, because such distribution impacts the capacity of the system. The number of the items (e.g., arrival slots between 9:00 am and 9:15 am) to be auctioned may vary depending on the type of aircraft that will use these arrival slots (see section 20.2.1). Thus the *number* of slots may be dependent on demand characteristics that are unknown prior to the auction. Thus, the auctioneer—when determining winners—must consider the physical limitations of the airport when choosing a feasible allocation set.

Property rights   Currently, airlines receive rights that they expect to be able to renew indefinitely if they adhere to conditions of usage specified by the FAA. In fact, these "use it or lose it" requirements have encouraged carriers inefficiently to use allocated slots in order to assure that they would continue to own them in the future and to preclude competition from other carriers. Although allocation exercises take place semiannually, the turnover of slots is very small. When airports expand, new slots become available and an administrative process measures the value of providing these slots to new entrants versus expanding the slots of the major existing carriers at that airport.

Although carriers currently enjoy what they consider "perpetual right of usage," this usage does not confer any future property rights. Indeed, the law indicates that the DOT has exclusive rights to determine the takeoffs and landings at all airports in the continental United States. Because the government has exclusive airside rights, we believe that auctioning off arrival time slots at airports would provide a mechanism for acquiring the infrastructure needed to grow the industry (new technology allows closer separation and safer skies) while also assuring a fair mechanism for growth of smaller carriers and the entrance of new carriers.

Property rights would need to be carefully specified. One approach would allow the buyer of a slot to have exclusive use of the slot during a given time window (e.g., within a fifteen-minute period) every day. The owner of this slot would keep this right over a relatively long period, thereby providing the owner with the ability to create long-term plans and schedules. For example, if 20 percent of the slots were auctioned each year, then the duration of the property rights for any given slot could be a five-year period. Research to determine the optimal period for the right is necessary.

In addition to these yearly auctions, we perceive the need for a secondary auction that would allow trades of slots among carriers. Thus, the carrier acquires an assumable lease for the given lease period. That carrier has the right to trade or sell this slot for any subset of the leasing period to any other carrier contingent upon regulatory conditions specified by the DOT/FAA (e.g., proof that the buyer-carrier can operate in this market safely and that this carrier adheres to any limitation on market share).

Finally, there is a need for a third trading mechanism for the day of operations. This market is a classic "trade" exchange among carriers having rights to take off and land at a given airport to accommodate issues of weather, maintenance, and other problems that cause planes to be delayed in departure or landing.

Thus, if the FAA decides to allocate long-term rights to departures and landings through a market clearing mechanism, then the FAA must also stipulate how carriers can trade these slots during the period of that lease. In sections 20.5, 20.6, and 20.7, we will discuss the differences in auction design necessary for each of these three situations.

Valuation issues   Currently, the value of a takeoff or landing slot is unknown. This is consistent with many other government administrative processes. For example, prior to the Federal Communication Commission auctioning off spectrum rights, the value of this spectrum was unknown but perceived to be quite valuable. When the first personal communications service (PCS) auction was held (an auction for wireless cell phone communications) and brought over $7 billion into the U.S. Treasury, the value of spectrum was no longer questioned. Similarly, because the values of airline slots are not well understood at present, we believe that one should choose an auction design that allows price discovery.

Market power   Auctions allocate markets efficiently when there is sufficient competition within the market. In this case, competitors bid against each other and the market is allocated to the bidder that values the market the most and is, therefore, willing to pay the associated price of acquiring the market. However, for markets where the goods are scarce and where the goal is to assure competition within the industry, the auction rules must ensure that an airline does not bid based on the airlines' willingness to buy a monopoly. Without rules to preclude this situation, an auction can lead to insufficient monopolistic control of an airport or region by an airline. One can avoid this pitfall by placing ownership restrictions both on the entire airspace, within any given airport, and even within an airport by time of day. Carriers may need a certain amount of activity at given airports to optimize their hub/spoke system, but no airline needs to control a majority of the airport. Rules similar to those imposed by the FCC on spectrum can control the total ownership of slots within regions, airports, and within time windows.

Implementation issues   There must be a transition period that moves the airline industry from an administrative process to a market-clearing process. As discussed earlier, we
would expect only some small percentage of the slots to be auctioned in any given
year; our initial suggestion is 20 percent per year. The question of where to start must
be studied (see Rothkopf and Bazelon 2003 for a general approach to this problem). It
would seem quite attractive to start with the most congested airports, thereby relieving
some of the safety and delay issues that exist at these airports, most notably LaGuardia.
Similar logic suggests auctioning slots at those airports during the most congested time
interval periods. We expect that peak-demand slots will command higher prices than
off-peak hour schedules. Choosing them as the first to be auctioned will force airlines
to reexamine the sizing of flights that take off during these high-demand times. Thus,
we expect that, although flight operations might decrease (for safety reasons), the
number of passengers being serviced during these time periods may remain the same
or increase. Similarly, the less demanded flights are likely to move to alternative times
where it makes sense to have smaller planes taking off and landing.

We emphasize that the definition of a "slot" is either a takeoff or a landing within
a given time interval. This "slot right" provides the airline with the right to schedule
a published arrival or departure during that time window. We believe that a "time window" of fifteen minutes is reasonable given the physical limitations of aircraft movements. A larger window could allow airlines to "bunch" takeoffs and landings into a
smaller portion of this larger window, thereby resulting in significant delays and safety
concerns (e.g., if the window were for one hour, then airlines might still list most of
the departures to take off during the first fifteen minutes of this period).

If one "wins" a slot in this auction, then one must also acquire commensurate rights
to terminal space, for example, ticketing, baggage, and gating facilities. Thus, it is essential that the winner be able to obtain such rights, for example, by paying the "going
rate" for these facilities as computed based on the current long-term contracts with the
local airport authority. Dominant carriers have historically limited rivals from entering
the market by limiting the available gates at the peak demand periods. When dominant carriers lose their ability to control gates and ticketing counters, competition during these periods is likely to increase at capacity-limited airports. The gradual transition
over a five-year period will allow dominant carriers to continue to have their hub presence, as no more than 20 percent of the flights at the airport would change during a
given year.

We emphasize that in order for a slot market mechanism to work, one must ensure
that open, fair access to complementary airport resources is provided. All must be
linked in order for a successful market exchange.

In the next few sections, we highlight some of the specifics of auction design relevant to this application.

20.5   Design Principles and Research Questions for Long-Term Lease Auctions

When considering the design principles for the long-term lease auction, one must first be certain that all property rights are well defined. Such rights must include the length of the right (e.g., for x years), the right itself (arriving at runway y at airport A between x and y time on an aircraft of size b), the transfer rights, and the obligations (safety, adhering to restrictions on market concentration, etc.). One must also determine what happens if the airline cannot use the slot at the time allocated. We are presuming that the airline must either cancel the flight or bid in the same-day auction for a different time slot. We also note that rules must specify what happens if the airline wishes to substitute an alternative aircraft type into that slot. We only mention these "same day" issues here because any ambiguity in the overall process can create bad outcomes. Similarly, rules that specify the maximum amount of slot ownership at any airport, region or globally, must be carefully considered. Once property rights have been completely and unambiguously specified, a one-sided combinatorial auction can be designed. This auction design is one-sided because the U.S. government is the seller and is selling a collection of slots. Thus, there is only one seller and multiple buyers.

Because the success of an auction design is dependent on all of the details "fitting," we next present a "straw man" for discussion and study.

20.5.1   General Framework
We believe that the overall framework for this auction should be a simultaneous multiple round ascending bid auction. Because the items being auctioned are scarce commodities with both private and common values (i.e., the value to a buyer is based partially on the value that others place on this item and partially based on the buyer's own business plan), there is a strong need for price discovery. Such auctions also have the added attribute that they close at slightly over second highest prices. Because all items are awarded simultaneously, buyers can alter their business plans as they collect information about prices and competition among slots. Because of the complexity of an airline's overall business plan, there is a strong need for an expressive language that allows bids to be treated as mutually exclusive.

Because there have been few combinatorial auctions, we believe that careful study—both empirically and computationally—is necessary to assure its success. We present some of the components below:

1. Activity   We argue that activity rules similar to those set by the FCC in simultaneous multiround auctions be considered.

2. Bidding language   The literature presents a number of expressive bidding languages. The general XOR language allows complete expressivity but at the cost of requiring the bidder to place an extraordinary number of bids. Alternatively, other bidding languages are compact but only appropriate for specific kinds of bidders. (Ledyard et al.

2002) describes the need to express mutual exclusive bids based on his experience in transportation auctions. For more on bidding languages, see Nisan, chapter 9 of this volume.

3. Bidder's aid tools   A number of tools would make a package bidding auction easier. They include tools that a) help the bidder estimate a competitive price for his package, b) help the bidder determine his *best bids* based on his business plans and the current prices of the various slots, and c) help the bidder to identify "partnering" bids (i.e., bids that fit with his bid to create a winning set).

4. Pricing   In a combinatorial auction, it is hard to infer the prices of the individual pieces from the winning prices of packages. Yet, this information is critical to a bidder being able to create new packages that have some hope of "winning" in future rounds. There are a number of papers that discuss both *linear* pricing and *nonlinear* pricing (Hoffman et al., chapter 17 of this volume). Pricing information is critical to both the overall outcome (efficiency) and speed of the auction.

5. Winner determination calculations   Because a slot allocation auction is likely to have many objects auctioned simultaneously, the size of the winner determination problem can get very large. The federal government must weigh the benefits of speeding up these calculations against the issues associated with fairness and transparency. Indeed, the FCC chose not only to solve the winner determination problem to proven optimality but also to choose among *all tied solutions* randomly. These calculations are expensive, but may be necessary to assure that the results of the auction are not contested in court. A compromise may be that the auction performs less careful optimizations (e.g., to within 1 percent of optimality) in the early stages of the auction, and more careful optimizations late in the auction. We also note that the winner determination problem may be harder than for other auctions because additional constraints that assure a safe distance between planes and restrict carrier concentration may be required.

6. Length of time bids are kept   In order to assure sincere bidding, we believe that bids should be kept active throughout the auction. This rule plays substantially with the rules about expressive languages, in determining the complexity of the winner determination problem. More study must be done to understand how they interact.

7. Setting the minimum bid increment   The minimum bid increment determines the allowable new bids for the next round. If this increment is set too small, then the overall length of the auction will be extended significantly. If, on the other hand, the increment is too large, efficiency can be lost. One should use smoothing procedures that use a relatively large bid increment when there is considerable competition and a relatively small increment when there is little competition.

8. Proxies   Many auctions employ either an optional or a mandatory computerized facility that bids for the bidder within an auction, called "proxies." Proxies allow bidders to participate in multiple rounds without the cost of continuing to monitor the system. Forced proxy bidding can eliminate much signaling and gaming, because the

proxy will always engage in straightforward bidding (see Ausubel and Milgrom, chapter 3 of this volume, for details). We believe that for the slot-allocation auction, such designs would require modification to allow "stages" whereby bidders could re-adjust their maximum bid prices and set of bids. With stages, eligibility and activity rules would need to be imposed. Little experience with such an auction system exists, and careful study of these systems is warranted due to their ability to reduce disruptive bidding.

9. Stopping rule   In a multiple round auction, the stopping rule must be coordinated with the eligibility and activity rules of the auction. The rule that the auction ends when no new bids are placed encourages activity. However, in package bidding, there can be many rounds with new bids but with little or no change. An alternative with promise is to consider merging an ascending bid auction with a "last proxy stage." In this stage, bidders provide the "maximum bid amount" for every bid they might wish to win and the proxy works with these bids to determine the winners.

Clearly, for an application as critical as slot allocation, one must be careful in choosing the auction design. The problem is sufficiently important to warrant extensive experimental and computational study of the alternatives.

20.6   Design Principles and Research Questions for Medium-Term Exchange of Slots

In order for a market-clearing strategy to work, airlines must have the right to reassign their lease to another airline for the remaining lease period. The only regulatory oversight of such transactions would be to insure that airlines do not, by such transactions, violate any of the rules of aggregation originally specified for the long-term auction. Thus, the FAA would specify rules restricting the overall leasing of slots at (a) a given airport, (b) within a given region, and (c) throughout the U.S. airspace. Trades must not violate these rules. Within this overall restriction, the industry can determine the market trading mechanism that they feel most suits their needs.

Because the FAA should specify the rights associated with a slot-allocation lease (takeoff or landing, gate access, ticket space, baggage-claim area, duration) and the obligations associated with that right, any entity in possession of such a right is free to transfer this right to another entity as long as that new entity can comply with the obligations imposed on the slot holder. We believe that airlines should be free to trade these rights through all forms of trading. These trades can then be performed by bilateral negotiation or through an organized market (auction) mechanism. If the airline industry chooses an auction mechanism, the choices are large: the mechanism can be a simple one-sided exchange mechanism whereby one lists slots for sale, and an auctioneer then sells these for the airlines. Alternatively, one can create a two-sided combinatorial exchange whereby one can create packages of items for sale where items are exchanged either (a) whenever a seller's ask price "matches" a buyer's bid price, or (b) at the end of a full combinatorial exchange whereby bidders provide complicated buy and sell bundles and trades take place simultaneously with the surplus from those trades being allocated based on a given set of rules (a summary of issues associated with combinatorial exchanges appear in Parkes et al. 2001; Wurman and Wellman 2002; Ledyard et al. 2002).

The auction design for this application is likely to evolve over time. We believe that as long as property rights are established and the industry is free to exchange these rights in the market place, the industry will determine the exchange that works best.

We now move onto the issues associated with what occurs on day of operations, given the fact that weather conditions, mechanical breakdowns, and other operational conditions might significantly alter an airline's ability to adhere to its published schedule.

20.7   Design Principles and Research Questions for Day of Operations Slot Exchange

The current CDM exchange mechanism, the compression algorithm, together with the CDM data communications infrastructure provides a firm foundation for structuring and understanding a possible "day of operations" slot exchange market. Viewed most simply, one "only" needs to convert this non-monetary exchange into a monetarily based exchange. Prior to pursuing this approach, it is worthwhile to step back and consider the basic premise for such a market so that one can consider more fundamental changes.

20.7.1   Issues to Consider in Evaluating a Market-Based Day of Operations Exchange
Currently slot rationing and slot exchange are employed for arrival slots during periods when the arrival capacity at an airport is reduced usually as a result of poor weather conditions. These operations occur before the departure of the impacted flights. The arrival slot allocated to each flight is converted into a departure slot by subtracting an estimate of the en-route time. The difference between the revised departure time and original departure time of a flight is the ground delay assigned to a flight. Thus, control is ultimately exercised through the assignment of ground delays, whereas planning and allocation are carried out in terms of arrival slots. No constraints are placed on the revised departure times, so there is an implicit assumption that departure capacity is unconstrained. When considering more general market structures, some questions naturally come to mind.

Should a Day of Operations Slot Exchange Market Only Exist During Conditions of Reduced Arrival Capacity?   Air carriers routinely enter into conditions of irregular operations. Under such conditions there can be large deviations from normal schedules, so the set of required slots can substantially deviate from the set "owned" by the

carrier. Clearly this suggests the usefulness of market mechanisms to achieve a reallocation under a broad set of circumstances. On the other hand, today it is only deemed
necessary to carry out an explicit allocation during times of reduced capacity because
relatively few delays result from exercising a basic first-come, first-served rule. It seems
clear that some expansion over the current practice is warranted; however, the extent
of such an expansion deserves additional consideration.

Should Both Arrival and Departure Slots be Exchanged in the Market? At this time it
is difficult to provide a definitive answer this question. It certainly is clear that there are
times of significant congestion with respect to departure slots, which strongly suggests
the need for allocation mechanisms. By contrast, the notion of dynamically coordinating NAS-wide arrival and departure slot allocation, for example, through a NAS-wide
auction with package bidding, would seem to be extremely onerous and perhaps over-
kill. Thus, we will proceed here with the development of a day of operations slot exchange for arrival slots. At the same time, we view this as an open question worthy of
study.

**Should the Basic Control via Departure Times Remain the Same or Should Other
Control Mechanisms be Used?** The current approach to controlling arrivals may
seem rather convoluted, in that *arrival slots* are allocated and this allocation is implemented by controlling when flights *depart*. The logic of this strategy might seem especially dubious when one considers the high degree of uncertainty associated with
departures and en-route traffic flows as described in section 20.3. In fact, one of the
goals of CDM development activities has been to migrate to the so-called "control by
CTA." This concept states flights should be given a CTA (controlled time of arrival) and
that the responsibility to meet the CTA rests with the airline/pilot. No restrictions
would be placed on departure times. In fact, we do not believe this to be a desirable
method of control for CDM, nor do we believe it is desirable under a future day of
operations auction scenario. The principal disadvantage of such an approach rests in
the fundamental difference in how to handle flights on the ground and flights in the
air. Once a flight is airborne, by necessity, it must be granted certain priorities and priv-
ileges. For example, the fuel on board would represent a hard constraint on the degree
to which it could absorb airborne delay. Of even greater concern is that prospect that if
significant penalties were attached to either early or late arrivals into the terminal area,
then it is likely that the added pressures placed on pilots and air traffic controllers to
meet certain time windows would lead to a degradation in safety. Thus, our answer
to this question is that the current approach of allocating arrival slots and controlling
access to those slots via departure time modifications should be continued.

To summarize, we conclude that a basic "conversion" of the current system to a
monetarily based system is the best alternative to pursue at this time.

20.7.2 Value Proposition and Need

Section 20.1 of this chapter argued the merits of the general use of market mechanisms within air traffic management. Here we would like specifically to consider whether market mechanisms might provide significant added value when compared with the current CDM procedures.

If one examines the two types of offers associated with the bartering model described at the end of section 20.3 as well as figure 20.8, it becomes apparent that the current slot exchange procedure addresses a very specific, limited scenario. That is, compression and/or the bartering process are driven by one or more slots that have become unusable by their owner-airlines. As figure 20.8i illustrate, airline A owning an unusable slot, [x], places a value of $0 on [x] but say a value of $1,000 on a slightly later slot [y]. By contrast, airline B might place a value of $800 on [y] and a value of $900 on [x]. An exchange of ownership provides an added value of $1,000 to A and an added

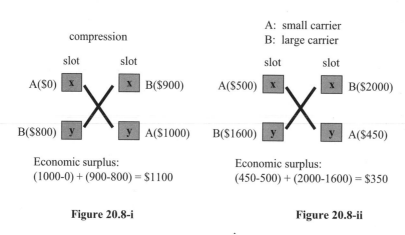

Figure 20.8-i   Figure 20.8-ii

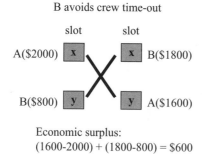

Figure 20.8
Illustration of value proposition for day of operations market for slot exchange.

value of $100 to B for a total economic surplus of $1,100. It would seem clear that many other types of scenarios are not only possible but also likely. In figure 20.8ii, airline A's flight has a relatively small number of passengers and airline B's has a much larger number, leading to A's valuations of [x]: $500, [y]: $450, and B's valuations of [x]: $2,000, [y]: $1,600, for a total economic surplus of $350. In figure 20.8iii, by switching from slot [y] to slot [x], airline B is able to avoid a timing out of its crew, thus saving a much larger incremental amount than A incurs. The second and third scenarios are quite realistic, but would not be addressed under the current CDM procedures.

Recent research on non-monetary extensions of the current CDM exchange mechanism provides further evidence of the potential value of a day of operations market. Vossen and Ball (2005a) describe an extension from the current one-for-one bartering model, compression, to a two-for-two bartering model. Experimental results show that airlines can derive substantial additional value from using such a system.

Because of the high degree of uncertainty in daily NAS operations there is always a need dynamically to adjust schedules. The evidence just provided clearly indicates that during time of severe or even moderate disruptions, substantial value can be derived from a day of operations slot exchange market.

20.7.3 Design Principles and Research Questions

We now discuss fundamental questions that must be addressed in designing a day of operations exchange for arrival slots. Based on the preceding discussion, we will specifically address the conversion of the current non-monetary CDM exchange process into a monetarily based exchange. Thus, the exchange will allow airlines to trade rights to arrival slots on a particular day of operations. The right to an arrival slot is translated into the right to depart from an origin airport within a specified time window a certain amount of time in advance. The departure time window will be based on an estimated en-route travel time from the origin to the destination airport, which in turn is based on the flight plan filed by the airline.

Exchange Markets A key property of these slot-trading markets is that each airline is potentially both a buyer and seller. In fact, the natural extension of the current exchange system suggests simply adding the possibility of side payments to the current trades. Of course, once exchanges with side payments are supported, outright slot buying and selling would seem to be a small additional step. One might then ask whether the entire process could be simplified by only supporting buy/sell transactions. Thus, each trade illustrated in figure 20.8 would be replaced by two individual buy/sell transactions. In a static environment with no budget constraints, complete information, and equilibrium prices this would probably be reasonable. However, during the trading process, each airline will be managing a flight schedule and will generally be seeking a set of slots to provide high quality service for some subset of its flights. With this in mind, in a dynamic environment, few airlines would accept the uncertainty of executing separate sell and buy transactions in order to reduce the delay on an important flight. Thus, we feel it is essential that the market support true exchange transactions. This is, of course, equivalent to supporting conditional buy/sell transaction, for example, "I will only sell slot x if I can buy slot y so that my net payment is no more than $UU." Unconditional buy/sell transactions should also be supported.

Package Bidding   In general, airlines will be interested in insuring good performance for a set of flights. Furthermore, the relative position of groups of flights can be of great interest especially in the context of airline banking operations. The results of Vossen and Ball (2005a) show that the use of complex—for example, two-for-two, trades— can lead to substantially improved performance under certain assumptions. These facts point to the possible advantages of exchanges involving sets of slots. Although such a system is worthy of study, we do not see clear evidence of a need. For example, it is likely that an exchange supporting side payments would achieve performance improvements over a one-for-one bartering system at least as good as those achieved by the two-for-two. That is, the added flexibility provided by two-for-two trades might not be necessary if side payments are allowed. We certainly do not wish to absolutely rule out package trades, but only suggest that there is not obvious overwhelming evidence of their merit.

Dynamic Bidding vs. Discrete Cycles   Currently the slot exchange mechanism, compression, is executed periodically, for example, every half hour. A more dynamic, transaction oriented system (slot credit substitution) has been accepted by the CDM constituency and has recently been brought into operation. Similarly, in the case of a slot trading market, either or both of these options could be employed. A transaction-based system would operate in a manner similar to a stock exchange. Such a system would give airlines immediate feedback on proposed trades. Fast response to such proposals could help improve the overall timeliness of airline operations. A system based on discrete cycles could potentially lead to better system-wide performance in that large sets of offers would be considered simultaneously giving a larger feasible region over which to optimize. We do not see a clear resolution of this issue and suggest it as a topic for further research.

20.8   Conclusion

Airport arrival and departure slots at certain critical airports have become scarce commodities that have substantial intrinsic value. In spite of recent downturns in demand for air transportation, demand for the most desirable slots remains greater than supply.

Further, there is little doubt that this condition will remain in the near term and most likely will worsen in the long term.

The effective provision of scheduled air transport services requires the acquisition of multiple coordinated slots as well as related airport resources, including access to gates and terminal facilities. Complementary slots are required both at a single airport and at multiple airports.

In the United States, the FAA has statutory authority to control access to the airspace and consequently has authority over the allocation of slots. At many airports, certain airlines hold implicit or explicit grandfather rights to certain slots. Airport resources, most notably gates, are typically owned and managed by local public airport authorities. However, in many cases, airlines own long-term leases to gates. Slots cannot be effectively used without corresponding gate resources, so any approach to slot allocation must allow for the allocation or reallocation of corresponding gate resources.

At many airports, the airport capacity, that is, number of available slots, depends on the weather. This dependency implies a high degree of "supply" variability and uncertainty. Variability in a variety of airline and air traffic control processes makes it difficult to achieve precise timing in the delivery of aircraft to departure and arrival slots. This "demand" uncertainty coupled with the supply uncertainty make it necessary to employ a flexible approach to the rights associated with slot ownership on a particular day of operations. Furthermore, a day of operations reallocation or exchange of slots can produce substantial improvement in overall system and market efficiency. Such a reallocation is currently used under the collaborative decision making procedures for planning and controling ground delay programs.

The various circumstances of the aviation slot allocation setting suggest the possible use of three types of market mechanisms. First, an auction of long-term leases of arrival and/or departure slots at capacity constrained airports. Second, in order to refine the initial allocation and achieve market efficiency, a market that allows inter-airline exchange of such long-term leases. Third, a near-real-time market that allows inter-airline exchange of slots on a particular day of operation.

The absence of an effective slot allocation mechanism has led to the gradual degradation of safety levels as well as instances of excessive delays. The use of market mechanisms offers the prospect of addressing these issues as well as providing a number of other economic benefits, including use of existing slots by air carriers who can most productively make use of them, easier entry into markets by new and emerging carriers, breaking up monopolistic "fortress hubs," and disclosure of true market value of slots. Of course, auctions of long-term slot leases will generate additional revenue. This most naturally should be used to invest in NAS infrastructure and aircraft equipage. Identifying funds or economic necessity for such investments has been difficult in the past.

The successful use of auctions for telecommunication spectrum, energy, and other commodities provide valuable insight into how to design auctions for NAS resources.

Furthermore, this experience provides ample evidence that effective auctions can be designed and implemented in the aviation setting. A number of issues and problems need to be addressed before effective auctions for NAS resources can be designed. These include determining the number of slots offered per time period at an airport, defining the property rights associated with slot ownership, transition issues related to current implicit and explicit airline property rights, and handling the need for airlines to acquire groups of slots and related airport resources, through package bidding and/or after-markets. Auction design for both long-term slot leases and for slot exchange on the day-of-operations, although fundamentally similar to other cases previously tackled, present a number of challenges, some of which represent interesting research questions.

We believe that market mechanisms should play a fundamental role in any comprehensive approach to the management of an air transportation system. Furthermore, such mechanisms show strong promise for improving the safety, delay performance, and economic efficiency of today's NAS.

Acknowledgments

The work of the first author was supported in part by NSF Grant: ITR0205489. Many of the ideas for this chapter grew out of the workshop, "National Airspace System Resource Allocation: Economics and Equity" organized by the authors. The workshop was supported by George Mason University, NEXTOR, the National Center of Excellence for Aviation Operations Research, and the University of Maryland.

References

Air Transport Action Group (1998), Airport *Capacity/Demand Profiles*, database on CDROM published by the International Air Transport Association, London.

Alamdari, Fariba E. and Peter Morrell (1997), "Airline Labor Cost Reduction: Post-Liberalism Experience in the USA and Europe," *Journal of Air Transport Management*, 3, 53–56.

Aviation Week and Space Technology (2002), "Justice Dept. Backs Slot Auctions at LGA," July 15, 37–38.

Ball, Michael O., Robert L. Hoffman, David Knorr, James Wetherly, and Michael Wambsganss (2000), "Assessing the Benefits of Collaborative Decision Making in Air Traffic Management," in *Proceedings of 3rd USA/Europe Air Traffic Management R&D Seminar*.

Ball, Michael O. and Guglielmo Lulli (2002), "Ground Delay Programs: Optimizing over the Included Flight Set Based on Distance," *Air Traffic Control Quarterly*, 12, 1–25.

Commission on the Future of the U.S. Aerospace Industry (2002), *Final Report of the Commission*, Washington DC: USGPO.

Cooper, Mark N. (2000), "The Proposed United Airlines-U.S. Airways Merger," Testimony before the Antitrust Committee, Unites States Senate, June 14.

Donohue, George L. (2002), "The U.S. Air Transportation System: A Bold Vision for Change: A White Paper Prepared for the Commission on the Future of the U.S. Aerospace Industry," George Mason University.

Donohue, George L. and Russell Shaver (2000), "United States Air Transportation Capacity: Limits to Growth Part I (Modeling) and Part II (Policy)," National Research Council Transportation Research Board 79th Annual Meeting, Washington DC, Papers Numbered 00-0582 and 00-0583.

DOT/BTS (2001), U.S. Department of Transportation, Bureau of Transportation Statistics website ⟨http://www.bts.gov/⟩.

DotEcon Ltd. (2001), "Auctioning Airport Slots, A Report for HM Treasury and the Department of the Environment, Transport and the Regions." Available at ⟨http://www.dotecon.com⟩.

Erzberger, Heinz (1995), "Design Principles and Algorithms for Automated Air Traffic Management," *AGARD Lecture Series 200 Presentation*; Madrid, Spain; Paris, France; Moffett Field, California. Available at ⟨http://ctas.arc.nasa.gov⟩.

Fan, Terrence P. and Amadao R. Odoni (2002), "A Practical Perspective on Airport Demand Management," *Air Traffic Control Quarterly*, 10, 285–306.

Federal Aviation Administration (2001), "Airport Capacity Benchmark Report". Available at ⟨http://www.faa.gov/events/benchmarks/⟩.

Federal Register, Department of Transportation, Federal Aviation Administration (2000), "High Density Airports; Notice of Lottery of Slot Exemptions at LaGuardia Airport," Docket Number [FAA2000-8278], vol. 65, no. 221.

Federal Register, Department of Transportation, Federal Aviation Administration (2001), "Notice of Alternative Policy Options for Managing Capacity at LaGuardia Airport and Proposed Extension of the Lottery Allocation," Docket Numbers [FAA2001-9852], [FAA2001-9854], vol. 66, no. 113.

Gleimer, Eileen (1996), "Slot Regulation at High Density Airports: How Did We Get Here and Where Are We Going?" *Journal of Air Law and Commerce*, 10, 877–931.

Goetz, Andrew R. (2002), "Deregulation, Competition and Antitrust Implications in the U.S. Airline Industry," *Journal of Transport Geography*, 10, 1–19.

Green, Steve M., K. D. Billimoria, and M. G. Ballin (2001), "Distributed Air/Ground Traffic Management for En Route Flight Operations," *Air Traffic Control Quarterly*, 9, 259–285.

Haynie, Richard C. (2002), "An Investigation of Capacity and Safety in Near-Terminal Airspace for Guiding Information Technology Adoption," Ph.D. Dissertation, George Mason University.

Hansen, Mark (2002), "Micro-Level Analysis of Airport Delay Externalities Using Deterministic Queuing Models: A Case Study," *Journal of Air Transport Management*, 8, 73–87.

IATA (2000), *Worldwide Scheduling Guidelines*, 3rd *Edition*, International Air Transport Association, Montreal, Canada.

Ledyard, John O., Mark Olson, David Porter, Joseph A. Swanson, and David P. Torma (2002), "The First Use of a Combined-Value Auction for Transportation Services," *Interfaces*, 32, 4–12.

Mineta, Norman Y. (1997), *Avoiding Aviation Gridlock & Reducing the Accident Rate: A Consensus for Change*, National Civil Aviation Review Commission. Available at ⟨http://www.faa.gov/ncarc⟩.

Parkes, David C., Jayant R. Kalagnanam, and Marta Eso (2001), "Achieving Budget-Balance with Vickrey-Based Payment Schemes in Exchanges," *Proceedings of the 17th International Joint Conference on Artificial Intelligence (IJCAI-01)*, 1161–1168.

Preston, Edmond (1987), *Troubled Passage: The Federal Aviation Administration during the Nixon-Ford Term 1973–1977*, Washington, DC: US DOT USGPO.

Rassenti, Stephen J., Vernon L. Smith, and Robert L. Bulfin (1982), "A Combinatorial Auction Mechanism for Airport Time Slot Allocation," *Journal of Economics*, 13, 402–417.

Rochester, Stewart I. (1976), *Takeoff at Mid-Century: Federal Civil Aviation Policy in the Eisenhower Years 1953–1961*, Washington, DC: US DOT USGPO.

Rothkopf, Michael H. and Coleman Bazelon (2003), "Combinatorial Interlicense Competition: Spectrum deregulation without confiscation or giveaways," Technical Report. Rutgers University. 23 pp.

Royal Society (1992), *Risk: Analysis, Perception and Management*, Report of a Royal Society Study Group, London, fifth Printing 2002.

Vossen, Thomas and Michael O. Ball (2005a), "Slot Trading Opportunities in Collaborative Ground Delay Programs," to appear in *Transportation Science*.

Vossen, Thomas and Michael O. Ball (2005b), "Optimization and Mediated Bartering Models for Ground Delay Programs," to appear in *Naval Research Logistics*.

Wambsganss, Michael (1996), "Collaborative Decision Making Through Dynamic Information Transfer," *Air Traffic Control Quarterly*, 4, 107–123.

Welch, Jerry D. (2002), "Assessing Capacity Needs of Congested Airports," AIAA.

Wurman, Peter R. and Michael P. Wellman (2002), "Equilibrium Prices in Bundle Auctions," Technicla Report #99-09-064, Santa Fe Institute. 12 pp.

21 Combinatorial Auctions for Truckload Transportation

Chris Caplice and Yossi Sheffi

21.1 Introduction

This chapter explores how combinatorial auctions are being used for the procurement of freight transportation services. It focuses on those attributes of transportation that make combinatorial auctions especially attractive and describes some of the unique elements of transportation auctions. We concentrate on the United States truckload (TL) market, because the characteristics of this mode are the most compelling for using combinatorial auctions and therefore it is where most combinatorial auctions in transportation are taking place.

The actors in the transportation market consist of shippers and carriers. The shippers are the retailers, manufacturers, distributors, and other companies that need to move freight. They are the auctioneers in the procurement of transportation services. In many cases a third party, such as a software vendor, consultant, or third-party logistics provider (3PL) will conduct the auction on the shipper's behalf and thus act as the auctioneer. The carriers are the trucking companies that own the transportation assets and are the bidders in the process. This chapter looks at reverse procurement auctions in which typically one shipper is the auctioneer and many carriers are the bidders looking to win contracts to haul the shipper's freight over a specified future period.

The differences between transportation services auctions and other auctions described in the literature and in this book include the importance of defining the items to be auctioned, the level of uncertainty in the resulting contracts, and the number and variety of business conditions considered in the final winner determination problem (WDP). We describe the nature of shipper-carrier interactions and illustrate how it affects transportation service auctions.

21.1.1 The Freight Transportation Market

The United States commercial freight transportation market exceeded $701 billion in 2003, representing approximately 6.3 percent of the U.S. gross domestic product

(Standard & Poor's 2004). Although the industry includes a myriad of transportation modes, such as railroad, heavy air, parcel, pipeline, and water, the predominant mode in the United States is trucking. Truck transportation represents 86.9 percent of all commercial freight revenues (Standard & Poor's 2004).

Trucking, and indeed most all transportation operations, fall into two major categories: direct and consolidated. In direct operations, the cargo (or people) move(s) on a single conveyance directly from origin to destination, whereas in consolidated operations the cargo has to be unloaded and reloaded to a different conveyance at a terminal. Examples of direct transportation include taxi cabs, charters in all modes, and unit trains. Examples of consolidated transportation include busses, most traditional commercial airlines, rail, less than truckload (LTL) trucking, and package delivery. The dichotomy is very clear in trucking; less than truckload (LTL) operations use break-bulk terminals to consolidate (and break) the shipments, whereas truckload (TL) carriers move in full trailers from origin directly to destination. The operations, economics, and markets differ significantly between these two segments—all of which influence the extent and type of procurement and bidding methods that shippers use.

The TL segment, both private and for-hire, comprises over 78 percent of the total trucking transportation market and is the focus of this chapter.

21.1.2 Literature Review

The first reported use of optimization to solve the winner determination problem (WDP) for a transportation service auction can be traced to the Reynolds Metals Company in the late 1980s. Moore, Warmke, and Gorban (1991) describe how Reynolds centralized its transportation management system and how it bid out and assigned lanes[1] of traffic to carriers. They developed a mixed integer program (MIP) model that minimized transportation costs by assigning carriers to specific shipping locations and traffic taking into consideration individual carrier capacity constraints, equipment commitments, and other transportation specific concerns. Although it allowed for simple bids with volume constraints (see section 21.5), it did not permit package or combinatorial bids.

Porter et al. (2002) describe combinatorial auctions (which they referred to as *combined value auctions*) run in 1992 by Sears Logistics Services, in what was probably the first application of package bidding in the transportation context. They reported savings of 6 percent to 20 percent. Although the model allowed package bids, it did not permit the use of any business specific side constraints as model Moore, Warmke, and Gorban (1991) developed did.

The use of combinatorial auctions for transportation services (incorporating both package bids and business side constraints) increased dramatically throughout the 1990s, as Caplice and Sheffi (2003) and Elmaghraby and Keskinocak (2002) described. The first commercially available software specifically designed for combinatorial auctions for transportation services, OptiBid®, was released in 1997, using formulation and approach from Caplice (1996). Other software companies have followed suit, and by 2003 approximately half a dozen transportation procurement software packages that incorporate package bids were available in the market. These include Manugistics Inc. (RFQ Optimizer®[2]), Manhattan Associates Inc. (OptiBid®[3]), i2 Inc. (Transportation Bid Collaborator®), Baan Inc. (BidPro®), Saitech Inc. (SBids®), and Schneider Logistics Inc. (SUMIT CVA®). Additionally, other nontransportation-specific auction software from CombineNet Inc., Freemarkets Inc., Tigris Inc., and others have been used for transportation services. We estimate that from 1997 to 2003, over one hundred companies have run a total of several hundred combinatorial auctions using these software tools. These companies include Procter & Gamble, Sears, Roebuck and Corporation, Kmart, Wal-Mart, Best Buy, The Home Depot, Bridgestone, Ford Motor Company, Compaq Computer Corporation, Staples, Limited Brands, Ryder System, Rite Aid, and many others.

Although the majority of the research and commercial interest has focused on solving the shipper's problem (WDP), the carrier's (bidder's) problem has received some attention. Song and Regan (2005), for example, develop several optimization-based strategies for carriers to construct package bids. Although ignoring the uncertainty both in the strategic bidding process and in carrier operations, they nevertheless develop a mathematical framework for thinking about the bidders' issues in this very complicated auction setting. Caplice (1996) presents heuristic-based algorithms that carriers can use to create open loop tours, closed loop tours, inbound-outbound reload packages, and short haul packages using potential savings estimates based on historical load volumes.

The insights within this chapter are partially based on the authors' firsthand experience[4] in designing and conducting well over a hundred auctions for transportation services as part of LogiCorp Inc., PTCG Inc., Sabre Inc., Logistics.com Inc., and Chainalytics LLC. Over the last six years, more than fifty of these were combinatorial auctions. These auctions were generally conducted to obtain trucking services for large retailers and manufacturers, but they also included smaller shippers and covered rail, intermodal, and ocean transportation modes. These combinatorial procurement efforts involved more than $8 billion in transportation services and have documented combined savings to the shippers in excess of $500 million.

21.2 The Shippers' (Auctioneer's) Perspective

Since the United States surface transportation industry was deregulated in the 1980s, the transportation procurement process has settled into a fairly standard procedure, with most shippers conducting auctions every one to two years. This section outlines the auction practice and explains the uncertainty associated with the process.

21.2.1   The Auction Process

Transportation procurement generally follows a standard three-step process consisting of pre-auction, auction, and post-auction activities. We highlight those steps that are unique or particular to transportation service auctions.

During the pre-auction stage, the following tasks are completed:

- The shipper forecasts the demand for the upcoming period's transportation needs, which is then translated into a set of expected weekly flows on individual lanes, by period (see section 21.2.3). Shippers have a fair amount of discretion in the exact definition of the lanes and the network in general. Thus, there are tradeoffs involved in the development and communication of the shipper's business (see section 21.4.1).
- The shipper determines which carriers to invite to the auction. Often, shippers will allow certain carriers only to participate in specific regions or portions of an auction. Common practice is to include most incumbents plus a small number of new carriers. Thus, in transportation auctions, most carriers have at least some private information concerning the shipper's business.
- The shipper determines what information the carrier is required to submit back. This usually includes the form of the rate (flat rate per move, rate per mile, rate per hundredweight moved, etc.), service details (days of transit, capacity availability, equipment type, etc.), and the types of bid allowed (bid types such as simple bids, static package bids, flexible package bids, etc.; see section 21.5).

During the auction stage, the following steps are performed:

- The freight network is communicated to the carriers through the use of faxed lists, spreadsheets, online web pages, or direct EDI connections. Email is the most common form of communication tool used for transportation auctions (Caplice, Plummer, and Sheffi 2004).
- The carriers conduct their own analysis on the network and determine the rates to offer. For transportation, the bidder valuation, or carrier problem, is extremely complicated due to cost interdependencies and uncertainty (see section 21.3.3).
- The carriers will then submit their bid rates, and depending on whether the format of the auction involves single (most common) or multiple rounds may receive feedback information and have to resubmit updated rates.

During the post-auction stage, the following tasks are performed:

- The shipper receives the carriers' bids, converts them into a common format and database, and solves the WDP. In transportation auctions, this typically involves creating several dozen "what-if" scenarios by applying different business rules to the WDP (see section 21.6).
- In a multiple round auction, the shipper would send back to the carriers selected information on where they stand. The specific feedback information differs from shipper

to shipper but can include the carriers' rank on each lane, the leading rate on each lane, identification of package bids that are leading, etc.

· Once the shipper solves the WDP, the results are uploaded to the downstream planning, execution, auditing, and payment systems. The transition to a completely new carrier base can take upwards of several months to complete.[5] (The description of this process is out of scope of this chapter, however, and is omitted.)

21.2.2   Characteristics of Transportation Auctions

Table 21.1 provides summary information on the relative size and scope of the several dozens of TL transportation procurement involving combinatorial auctions designed and managed by the authors between 1997 and 2001. We believe it to be representative of combinatorial auctions conducted for transportation services during this time.

The duration of the auctions is measured from the start of the auction process, after all data has been gathered, until the award decisions are made. It does not include the pre-auction data collection efforts or the post-auction process of updating the shipper's systems.

Table 21.1

Characteristics of transportation auctions, 1996–2001

	Minimum	Median	Average	Maximum
Number of lanes	136	800	1,800	~5,000
Number of annual shipments	~6,000	88,000	~200,000	~1,500,000
Annual value of transportation services	$3M	$75M	$175M	$700M
Number of incumbent carriers	5	100	162	700
Number of carriers participating in the auction	15	75	120	470
Number of carriers assigned business from the auction	5	40	64	300
Reduction in the size of the carrier base	17%	48%	52%	88%
Base reduction in transportation costs (without considering service factors)	3%	14%	13%	24%
Final reduction in transportation costs (considering service factors and other business constraints)	0%	6%	6%	17%
Duration of procurement process (months)	<1	3	3	6+

We should point out four observations from the data in table 21.1. First, note that in all auctions, the shippers significantly reduced the number of carriers being used. In fact, "core carrier" programs have flourished in the 1990s, motivated by the desire to give more business to fewer carriers, thereby becoming a more important customer to these carriers. Many of these auctions have been used to establish core carrier programs.

Second, optimization-based procurement for transportation services tended to be used primarily by large shippers. The average auction size for this period was about $175 million in annual TL transportation expenditures, which is quite large.[6] The cost and effort required to run one of these auctions was not insignificant.

Third, the shippers are, on average, reducing their cost of transportation services by 13 percent—before taking service considerations into account. This is in line with the results that Porter et al. (2002) reported for its Sears auctions. Note, however, that transportation combinatorial auctions permit both simple and package bids, so it is never clear how much of the total savings in any such auction is due to package bids versus other more standard aspects of the process. Current research is aimed at separating and quantifying each of these factors.

Fourth, shippers, on average, forgo 50 percent of the potential savings in order to obtain a better engineered solution. This is done by adding constraints representing service requirements and other business issues into the WDP. These business constraints and performance factors are, in effect, costing the shippers 7 percent of their total annual transportation costs on the average. This points out the importance that shippers place on nonprice factors when solving the WDP.

Table 21.1 does not imply that the number of carriers bidding is related to the number of lanes or size of the network being auctioned. In fact, figure 21.1 shows that there is little correlation between the number of bidders and the number of lanes being auctioned for the same data set.

We have observed over the last several years that more shippers are conducting auctions of smaller magnitude more frequently. It seems that many shippers are replacing network-wide carrier reassignments with regional auctions—but we do not have sufficient longitudinal statistics fully to support or explain this observation.

21.2.3 Uncertainty in Shipper-Carrier Relationships

Many procurement auctions do not result in a transfer of goods, but rather the winner is awarded the right to sell its products or services in the future. For example, if a tire supplier wins the right to furnish an automobile manufacturer with tires for an upcoming model, it will sell the car manufacturer only five tires per car manufactured and no more; there is no absolute a priori tire volume commitment made on the manufacturer's part. It all depends on how many cars are made. Similarly, in the process of procuring transportation services, the winning carrier on a particular lane wins the right to haul traffic—but will only be called when and if there is a load to haul.

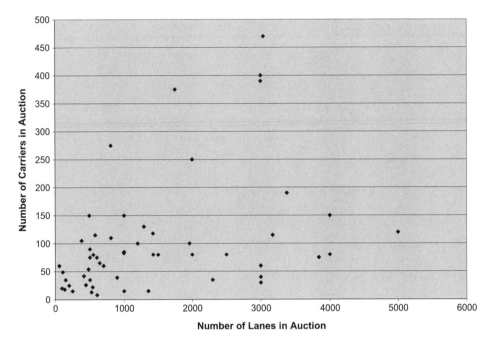

Figure 21.1
Size of transportation auctions, 1997–2001.

The uncertainty with transportation services, however, is even more pronounced due to forecasting uncertainties and prevalent shipper behavior.

Shippers have difficulties forecasting the lane flows that define the items in the auction due to the freight flows being highly disaggregated. It is not enough, for example, for a shipper to know that it will need, say, 3,000 trucks to carry 3,000 loads next year; for auction design purposes the shipper needs to know how many trucks it will need on each lane for each week (or in some cases, at the daily level). The coefficient of variation is very high at this disaggregated (loads per week per lane) level. In addition, most transportation departments, although responsible for buying the transportation services, are not always privy to their own company's marketing, promotion, and manufacturing plans, further adding to the uncertainty.

It is also accepted practice for shippers to capitalize on short-term opportunities. For example, suppose a carrier is hauling an inbound load to the shipper's facility, and that shipper has an outbound load that needs to be picked up later that day from the same facility. The shipper can create a *continuous move* by offering the new load to the inbound carrier, thus reducing or eliminating the carrier's dwell time and *deadhead* miles. A deadhead move is a movement where the carrier does not have a paying load. They are typically used for repositioning a truck from a destination to its next origin for a pickup. A carrier will typically reduce its line haul rate by 5 percent to 8 percent for a continuous move. So, even if another carrier was assigned to the outbound lane in the strategic bidding process, the shipper may choose to tender the load to an alternative carrier for a specific load. Not only is this accepted behavior for shippers, most analysts and transportation management software packages consider such opportunistic continuous move optimization a key capability.

Given the uncertainty caused by both forecasting errors and shipper behavior, it is well understood and accepted by carriers that the freight they will actually haul may differ significantly from the freight patterns they were awarded in the bid. In that sense, the contract is no more than *an option* that the carriers grant the shippers. That is, the shippers have the *right but not the obligation* to use the carriers as determined in the WDP. Most of the contracts specify the line haul rates, any potential accessorial rates (prices for services beyond hauling, such as collect on delivery, inside delivery, special loading requirements, etc.), and contingency remedies (in case of haulage problems, service failures, or nonpayment, not for lack of business from the shipper), which will be used if loads materialize. Specific volume commitments are rarely included— and if so they are usually expressed as percentages of the traffic flow rather than as an absolute number of shipments.

Shippers, however, cannot abuse this option too badly because freight transportation contracts are negotiated frequently and shippers that get a reputation for not living up to their commitments are not likely to see aggressive bidding the next time around (see section 21.4.3).

Because carriers cannot be expected to hold trucks and drivers in reserve, waiting for a shipper's call, shippers do not expect carriers to respond to every call for a truck ("tendering" a load) once a load materializes. Instead, carriers are generally expected to accept a high percentage (typically 70–80 percent) of the tendering requests. In fact, the acceptance rate is one of the performance metrics that shippers use to evaluate carriers. In addition, most transportation contracts specify the percentage of the time that carriers are allowed to bring in a subcontract operator (which they sometimes use instead of their own equipment).

This means that the contract is somewhat nonbinding on both sides. The contract may oblige shippers to tender the load to a specific carrier, but only when there is a load, something not known at the time of the auction. And the carriers are obliged to provide a truck at the agreed terms, "most of the time." Naturally, carriers understand that a shipper, during an auction, might award them a set of lanes in a package bid that mimics a continuous move, for example, traffic lanes from A to B, B to C, and C to A, but that in execution, they may be called to haul a load from A to B when there will be no load waiting at B to go to C (or anywhere else). Thus, carriers apply a certain probability of a follow-on load to each bundle of lanes during the auction process (see section 21.3.4). The net effect of this uncertainty is a damping of the potential value and usefulness of package bids in transportation service auctions.

Interestingly, although the high levels of uncertainty are well known within the industry, we know of no use of recourse models or other stochastic programming techniques in practice for transportation auctions. This is a topic of ongoing research by the authors, as discussed in section 21.7.3.

21.3 The Carrier's (Bidder's) Perspective

Although the daily operations of TL carriers are deceptively simple, they result in some rather complicated interdependencies and uncertainties that impact how a carrier can place a value on a shipper's freight. Additionally, carriers operate in a highly competitive market. This section discusses the carrier market, daily TL carrier operations, cost interdependencies, and the carrier valuation process.

21.3.1 Truckload Carrier Market

The TL transportation industry is close to a perfectly competitive market. The barriers to entry (and exit) are very low—mainly the cost of a tractor and trailer, which many lenders are happy to finance using the equipment as collateral.[7] Their service is essentially a commodity—a box on wheels—with the exception of some smaller specialty equipment submarkets. The more than 50,000 U.S. TL firms (ATA 2002) are distributed over the entire nation, making geographic monopolies rare. Switching costs for shippers are generally low.

The TL industry is very fragmented, with 75 percent of the firms owning fewer than six power units (ATA 2002). Most large shippers, however, will deal primarily with relatively large operators that not only can supply additional capacity when demand picks up, but also can comply with an increasing number of information and communication technology requirements, such as electronic data interchange (EDI) for sending advanced shipping notices and invoices, ability to accept automatic electronic fund transfers, automatic provision of GPS-based status reports and digital delivery proofs, and so on. There are only several hundred players like this in the U.S. TL market, many of which use sophisticated information technology tools to optimize their operations and can respond to relatively intricate bidding schemes. The vast majority of the remaining firms subcontract to these larger trucking firms, work through brokerage houses, or serve as regional or local spot capacity for individual shippers. It is these few hundred leading firms who are the active participants in combinatorial auctions.

21.3.2 Truckload Carrier Operations

TL carrier operations generally follow the steps outlined below:

• A customer (shipper) calls for a shipment pickup. Typically shippers do not give carriers advance notice of impending loads.

- The carrier assigns a specific truck and driver to that load, who picks the load up from the origin. Usually, the truck will drive to the origin empty.
- The truck departs and drives directly to the final destination. A typical truck can drive 400–500 miles in a day, and the average length of haul for a shipment is approximately 750 miles.
- At the destination, the truck is unloaded. In some cases, the trailer is dropped in a shipper's facility (a trailer yard) to wait future unloading and the driver picks up an empty trailer (or a full one in the case of a continuous move tied to a trailer pool) to haul away.
- The truck then either holds in a local terminal for the next load, drives empty (deadheading) to a region from which more loads typically emanate (a repositioning movement), or drives directly to the next pick up point. The process then repeats.

The challenge of operating TL carriers is in coordinating the movements of hundreds or thousands of trucks simultaneously. As implied by the last bullet point, freight flows are not symmetric: some regions of the country produce many more shipments than there are shipments destined there (or consumed), and vice versa. And even geographically balanced operations may not be time balanced, in that they require drivers to wait until an appropriate load is available.

Adding to these structural imbalances is the uncertainty of the operation—shippers typically do not tender the loads well ahead of time. TL operations, therefore, entail significant uncertainty regarding follow-on loads. When a truck is sent to a given destination, in most cases neither the driver nor the carrier knows where it will go next.

21.3.3 Cost Interdependency

The basic unit of service that shippers are interested in is a unidirectional flow from a given origin to a given destination, or lane flow. Trucking operations, however, depend on getting the equipment and the operators back to certain fixed points at regular intervals. The reasons are that trucks need to be maintained at certain base terminals and drivers need to get home. The last point is particularly relevant—some TL carriers experience a 100 percent operator turnover annually. Costello (2003) estimates the cost of recruiting and training a new driver at $9,000. With thousands of drivers and razor-thin margins, carriers compete with each other for drivers by providing reasonable working conditions. The most important attribute of job satisfaction for long-haul drivers is getting home frequently and predictably.[8] This is difficult to provide in the uncertain environment of TL transportation, as discussed in section 21.2.3.

The most obvious example of cost interdependency is a round trip, including head-haul and back-haul lanes. If a carrier has the contract to haul both from A to B and from B to A, it can base operations and recruit drivers at one end of the tour and operate its trucks back and forth. Not only will the drivers get home but, if the timing is right, there will be little dwell time and little or no deadheading.

In general, the cost of serving a lane is strongly affected by the probability of finding a follow-on load out of that destination. Securing a balanced network reduces the uncertainty in connection costs and can lower the carrier's overall costs. Thus a carrier may offer a lower price for hauling a given number of loads from A to B if it also hauls loads from B to A.

In most cases, however, it is not obvious which package of lanes and flows make sense for a particular carrier. Some sets may look disjoint to the shipper but when combined with the carrier's other traffic make perfect sense. For example, it is intuitive that a single carrier hauling ten loads per week from Boston to Detroit may have a lower cost if it can also haul ten loads from Detroit to Boston. A carrier, however, may be able to offer a lower price for hauling from Boston to Detroit conditional on, say, hauling ten loads per week from Philadelphia to New York. Such a carrier may have "power lanes"[9] between Detroit and Philadelphia as well as between New York and Boston, and the extra business complements and balances its network. Requiring that carrier to also haul the ten loads per week from Detroit to Boston, in this example, may actually increase the carrier's cost per load because this creates more of an imbalance out of Detroit.

In summary, the economics of direct transportation carriers imply the following:

• A carrier's cost structure for hauling on one lane of traffic is highly influenced by the remainder of its business across its network.
• Carriers can reduce their total costs by intelligently selecting which lanes to serve and at what volume level.
• The effect that a set of potential lanes of traffic has on a carrier's bid valuation consists of both a common information component (due to the prevailing flows in the marketplace) and a private information component (due to the carrier's other business).

In the auction process, these factors imply that the shipper should

• enable and encourage the carriers' preference elicitation in terms of specific lanes, bundles of lanes, and traffic volume
• not bother spending too much time preparing "shipper specific" potential bundles ahead of time
• be able to analyze and evaluate the large number and types of complex bids that will be submitted.

21.3.4 Individual Lane Pricing—Dealing with Uncertainty

As mentioned in section 21.2.3, carriers consider, explicitly or implicitly, the uncertainty of follow-on connectivity when determining the value or price for each shipment. This can be done explicitly by calculating the total system contribution of each shipment hauled for a given type of equipment, in a given time frame (say, a day) $\Pi_{i,j}^{q}$, as follows:

$$\Pi_{i,j}^q = R_{i,j}^q - D_{i,j} + P_j^q - P_i^q \qquad\qquad\qquad\qquad (21.1)$$

where:

- $\Pi_{i,j}^q$ is the total system contribution that the carrier receives for hauling the qth shipment from region i to region j in the time frame under consideration.
- $R_{i,j}^q$ is the rate that the carrier under consideration quotes for hauling the qth shipment from region i to region j in the time frame under consideration.
- $D_{i,j}$ is the direct cost of hauling a load from i to j (including fuel, driver wages, tire wear, etc.). Note that this is the same for all loads from i to j.
- P_j^q is the expected contribution of the extra truck carrying the qth shipment at region j.
- P_i^q is the expected lost contribution from one less truck (the qth shipment) at region i.

The regional potentials, P_j^q and P_i^q, imbed all the information about future loading opportunities out of regions i and j. Naturally, carriers should agree to haul a load only if $\Pi_{i,j}^q > 0$, that is, if the system contribution of a load is positive. Similarly a carrier should haul the loads with the highest $\Pi_{i,j}^q$ if more than one is available.

When moving from an area, i, that has many hauling opportunities to an area that does not, j (a head-haul move), P_i^q is high whereas P_j^q is low, and may even be negative (because the destination region may require the carrier to move empty out of there or wait a long time for a follow-on load). Given that $D_{i,j}$ is only a function of the distance, the carrier has to charge a high price, $R_{i,j}^q$, in order ensure that the move is worthwhile, that is, that $\Pi_{i,j}^q > 0$. In back-haul lanes, P_i^q is low, and P_j^q is high. Consequently, the carrier can charge a low price, $R_{i,j}^q$ to haul a shipment from i to j. In fact, if P_i^q is low enough and P_j^q is high enough, the carrier can move the truck empty, with $R_{i,j}^q = 0$. This is the rationale for a repositioning move.

The calculation of the regional potential involves recursive computations (see, for example, Powell et al. 1988). When making real-time decisions about dispatching and spot market pricing, some of the future shipments to be moved are known, and in many cases the carrier is committed to haul them. Thus, they have to be accounted for in the calculations. Furthermore, the short-term regional potentials vary by day of week, week of month, month of quarter, season, and specific holidays and events.

When participating in a strategic auction, carriers typically calculate the regional potentials for each location in the network simply as the average direct contribution of outbound loads over the last year. Thus:

$$P_i = \sum_{\forall m \text{ last year}} \sum_{\forall j} (R_{i,j}^m - D_{i,j}), \qquad\qquad\qquad\qquad (21.2)$$

where $R_{i,j}^m$ is the revenue of shipment m. Note that in this case the regional potentials are not indexed by the shipment due to the uncertainty involved.

The value of a lane (or the minimum price at which the carrier will haul the freight, with zero expected system contribution) is then:

$$R'_{i,j} = D_{i,j} - P_j + P_i. \tag{21.3}$$

Regional potentials capture the costs related to the uncertainty of incurring *deadhead* miles or dwell time at a shipper's facility. Carriers often use a formula such as 21.3 to establish pricing guidelines for bids on each lane before factoring in desired margins, competitive pressures, and other considerations.

To be more accurate, a carrier should recalculate the regional values every time it determines the price of a bid because, if won, the business represented by the auction will impact the regional potentials. Furthermore, they should factor in the probability that the loads will actually occur. We do not dwell on this issue further; it is the subject of an ongoing research effort.

Package bids conceptually enable carriers to engineer and modify the regional values by controlling the number of loads in or out of a region. Note that closed loop tour packages would, at this level of analysis, have no impact on the regional values (subject, of course, to the uncertainty mentioned above). Package bids comprising a group of lanes out of a given region increase its regional potential and thus make lanes coming into it more attractive, whereas lanes emanating from it may become less attractive.

21.4   Nature of Contracts and Auctions

The relationships between shippers and carriers, and the contracts that govern them, have certain characteristics that distinguish them somewhat from auctions for electromagnetic spectrums or durable goods. This section looks at some of these differences, and explains why sealed bids are the predominant form of auctions in this market.

21.4.1   Lane Definition

In most auctions, it is pretty clear what the items are. This, however, is not the case in transportation procurement auctions where each shipper may define the items differently.

Actual movements between origins and destinations go from a shipping point to a receiving point. In order to minimize the effort required to create, upload, and manage the large number of potential rates that could be collected, shippers aggregate the individual ship-to and ship-from locations into regions.[10] The aggregation depends on the volumes between regions and can typically range from a single shipping point (a plant or a warehouse), a five-digit postal code area, a three-digit postal code area, to an entire state. The lane can be defined as any combination of these (state-to-state, point-to state, three-digit postal code to five-digit postal code, etc.), depending on the volume. Using larger origin and destination regions can result in higher planned lane flows and a more stable forecast of such flows as compared to smaller regions. It also means fewer lanes in the network, which makes it easier to analyze. Unfortunately, it also increases the uncertainty in terms of deadhead miles *within* a region. Due to the uncertainty in the loads actually materializing, carriers tend to include only lanes with higher volume in their package bids.

Interestingly, using larger origin and destination regions also means that incumbents have a bigger advantage because the distribution of actual shipping points and consignees within regions is fairly stable over time. Although the detailed intra-region distribution of actual shipping locations is typically not included in the auction information, it is known by the incumbents.

21.4.2 Shipper Objectives

The main objective of every procurement auction is to determine the lowest total cost provider(s). Transportation auctions are no different. This main objective, however, is rarely the only one. Most shippers consider both lane-based and system-based objectives along with the total cost when solving the winner determination problem. Hohner, Bichler, Davenport, and Kalagnanam (chapter 23 of this volume) discuss similar issues with procurement auctions in other industries.

Lane-Based Shipper Objectives Lane-based objectives are business requirements that can be considered within the WDP on a lane-independent basis. That is, there are no cross-lane dependencies involved. For example, level of service delivered on each traffic lane can be considered within the WDP by applying a qualifying factor to each carrier-lane bid. This is typically done by allocating penalties and rewards to the bids based on various service attributes. For example, a shipper might consider a 90 percent "on time" performance to be a base level of service on a given lane. Bids from carriers with higher performance on that lane may be rewarded, say, $10 for each percentage point higher than 90 percent and $20 for each point higher than 95 percent, while being penalized by $10 for each percentage point below 90 percent and not being eligible to participate in the auction if the service is below 80 percent. This means that the carriers' bids will be adjusted before it is fed into the WDP to reflect their service level. A common use of lane-based objectives is favoring incumbent carriers by a small percentage to lower the churn of carriers. Many shippers consider the "utility exploration" process of agreeing on these factors across the organization to be one of the most important benefits of a structured auction process.

One of the primary benefits of lane-based objectives is that they can be applied without any modification to the underlying formulation used to solve the WDP; only the cost coefficients need to be adjusted.

System-Based Shipper Objectives System-based objectives are more complex in that they involve conditions that cross multiple lanes, bids, or carriers, and therefore require modification of the model formulation used to solve the winner determination problem. System-based objectives allow shippers to enforce external business rules within the strategic bidding process.

These can include things such as:

• Business guarantees whereby certain carriers, or sets of carriers, are guaranteed to be awarded a predetermined minimum or maximum number of loads or dollar value of business. Common examples include core carrier programs, incumbent carriers, or minority vendor initiatives.
• Size of carrier base the shipper might want to restrict the number of winning carriers (across the system or serving a given region) to simplify its daily operations and increase its visibility and importance to the winning carriers.
• Transit time where the shipper wants a certain percentage of the winning carriers to have specific transit times or specific level of service.
• Mix of carriers many shippers prefer to have a mix of different types of carriers, such as union and nonunion or regional and national in order to mitigate operational risks.

The introduction of these business considerations further complicates the strategic auction process. Each of these business rules has a cost and an impact on the final carrier awards. We discuss this in the context of common and private information in section 21.4.3.

Other Objectives In addition to achieving low cost, high service levels, and complying with other corporate policies, transportation auctions try to meet other objectives, such as efficiency of the auction results, robustness of the awards, and the speed of the process itself.

Efficiency Although efficiency is important in most auctions, another argument is at work in the procurement of transportation services. In an auction for transportation services, the quality of that future service depends on how well the business won in any auction fits with the winner's other business. If the new business does not really fit the winner's capability or its network, the service will likely be poor regardless of contract terms or past performance. Thus, the auctioneer has a vested interest in ensuring that the winners are truly those carriers that most value each of the lanes auctioned.

Robustness A criterion not typically used in standard auction theory is that of robustness. The auction results are robust if a change to the underlying freight flow network—such as a supplier or a customer going out of business, a major port closure, or total volume dramatically increasing or decreasing—does not result in a large cost increase. This criterion is particularly important in TL transportation auctions because many of the possible providers are small and financially unstable and the accuracy of the forecasts at the lane level is typically very low. In addition, the commodity nature of the industry and its meager profits mean that even larger carriers are not always financially secure. In fact, during 2001, over a thousand carriers per quarter filed for bankruptcy protection in the United States (see ATA 2002). Thus shippers would like to be in a situation where back-up carriers can pick up the slack with little cost increase if a primary carrier goes out of business.

Robustness is not easily handled within the WDP framework that virtually all shippers and software vendors use. Some shippers will conduct sensitivity analysis by making multiple optimization runs with modifications to the underlying network flows and the base of winning carriers, but this is not common practice. Creating and incorporating a workable metric of robustness for transportation service auctions is a ripe area for future research.

Simplicity and Speed   Many shippers have to conduct large and complicated transportation auctions fairly frequently. Such auctions can involve thousands of lanes (items) and dozens of carriers (bidders) and require significant work on the part of the auctioneer to prepare the items for bid, manage the auction process, and award the business.

The situation is even more critical for carriers who have to respond to many auctions. Over 80 percent of all carriers who participate in auctions receive, on average, at least one bid a week, with just under 50 percent receiving at least one bid a day, each of which require, on average, over a man-week of effort for analysis (see Caplice, Plummer, and Sheffi 2004).

Keeping on top of multiround bids is too time consuming for these carriers. A shipper that wants to increase carrier participation and response needs to simplify the process as much as possible by, for example, using only one round of bidding. Interestingly, even though the auction theory literature suggests that sealed bid auctions require more effort on the part of the bidders in terms of preparation and market research, in transportation procurement bids when bidders know the market, the administrative burden of multiple rounds more than offsets this consideration.

Consequently, simple formats that can be executed quickly are preferable for both shipper and carriers. Most transportation auctions include only a single round and are based on a sealed bid, first price format. This need for simplicity is also a negative influence on the use of combinatorial auctions because of the effort and energy required by carriers to design package bids. Even with a single round format, the transportation auction process typically takes from three to six months.

The literature has proposed other auction formats with beneficial theoretical properties. These include the Vickery-Clarke-Groves (VCG) design (Ausubel and Milgrom, chapter 1 of this volume) and iterative combinatorial auctions (Parkes, chapter 2). Although we have never actually seen any of these more sophisticated formats used in practice for transportation procurement, it is worthwhile considering why not. As Ausubel and Milgrom (chapter 1) note, three of the main drawbacks of the VCG design are the added complexity it brings to the bidders, the general reluctance of bidders to reveal their own values, and the low revenue generation for the auctioneer. Any one of these three design disadvantages is enough to discourage a shipper from employing a novel auction format outside of industry norms. Iterative CAs hold promise for use in transportation auctions, but the issue still remains on how to handle system-based shipper objectives. In our experience, whenever multiple round CAs have been run for transportation procurement (which is quite rare) the system-based shipper objectives were not considered until the final round. That is, the information feedback to the bidders never included the impact of these side constraints.

21.4.3 Types of Information
As in most other auctions, the value of the items being auctioned off has both private and common components. The common component consists primarily of the direct costs involved in hauling a shipment. The cost for a carrier to haul a certain distance is almost identical for all carriers—they all use the same technology, and driver wages are competitive across the industry. Studies have shown that 80 percent of the variability in TL carrier prices can be explained through the distance hauled (see, for example, Plummer 2003 or SABRE Group 1998).

The common information portion of the regional potentials, as discussed in section 21.3.4, captures freight flow imbalances at the national level; all carriers know that it is more difficult, for example, to find loads leaving the Southeast than to find loads leaving the industrial heartland of the U.S. Midwest. These macro-level geographic factors[11] to capture regional value effects increase the explanatory power of these pricing models by another 5 percent, as these references show.

The primary source of private information for transportation auctions is in the individual carrier's regional potentials. For example, suppose a carrier has a contract with a plant in Freeport, Florida (located in the far western section of the Florida panhandle) that tenders several loads a day outbound to, say, Chicago (a well-known source of potential follow-on loads). This is private information for that carrier that would enable it to bid more aggressively on inbound loads to the Freeport area because it has a reliable source of outbound loads in close proximity. We know of no studies that have attempted to quantify the influence of this private information on carrier's bid prices, even though we have seen its effects in practice.

Another type of information that is common to a set of the bidding carriers (the incumbents) but private from the nonincumbent carriers' perspective is rooted in the shipper's behavior. A carrier's costs, and therefore to some extent the prices charged, are influenced by the business terms and practices of the shipper, such as the speed of turning around loads, payment terms, gate checking and security procedures, handling of missing and damaged items, and so on. Regardless of what information the shipper presents to the carriers within an auction, the carrier will only learn of the *actual* practice after winning the bid and starting to serve the account. Incumbent carriers, then, have an advantage over the nonincumbent carriers in that they can price according to the behavior they have experienced rather than the shipper's purported behavior.[12]

In addition to the common and private information that each bidder has, transportation auctions have a third factor at work. Shippers tend to engineer the final solution by incorporating lane-based and system-based business objectives into the WDP. These objectives constitute a third type of information that influences the final assignment and can, therefore, influence the bidding behavior, if the carriers are aware of the specific objectives. Table 21.1 shows that on average, shippers are willing to pay an additional 6 percent over the lowest cost submitted bid solution (base case) in order to achieve a better engineered assignment. In other words, the impact of this private auctioneer information is greater than that of regional values at the macro level.

Although a carrier has no direct influence over how much a shipper values different business objectives, it can infer these objectives from shipper statements, corporate announcements, and past behavior. For example, if a shipper's new procurement department announces that one of its objectives is to reduce the number of vendors in general, a carrier that bids on many lanes can potentially be less aggressive than a smaller carrier that will only bid on a few lanes. The larger carrier in this example would be betting that the shipper values larger coverage more than their higher relative rates. Similarly, if a shipper has a history of taking incumbency into consideration, then the incumbents can probably hedge their bid prices. The impact and influence of these different types of information messages from the shipper to the carriers is part of an ongoing research effort.

In any case, the carriers utilize both private and common information in determining the value of the freight business and their bids, whereas the shipper uses business rules that are typically not communicated directly to the carriers[13] to modify the WDP outcome.

21.4.4 Long-Term Shipper-Carrier Relationships

Buyers and sellers (auctioneers and bidders) of transportation services develop long-term relationships in the sense that the large carriers and the large shippers depend on each other for business and capacity, respectively. The implications of this are the following:

Repetitive auctions   The auctions themselves are typically repeated every one to two years and carriers do get to know their customers' business and the strategies of their main competitors. As mentioned above, shippers also know the market and what to expect from carriers. Consequently, for example, reserve prices are typically used for providing "guidance of expectations" to carriers rather than to "avoid bad surprises," as is the case with some other auctions.

Asymmetric information   In every auction some carriers are incumbents on a significant portion of the business. This means that they understand many of the processes of the customer's operation, may have electronic data interchange links already established, or may be located nearby. In addition, they may be aware of contract details that may not be mentioned in the request for proposal, such as extra equipment requirements, the actual payment lead time, and so on. It is also well known in the industry that shippers understand that incumbents know the business and can start performing immediately, whereas new carriers have to learn the nuances of the new business. Thus, many shippers will prefer incumbents either by modifying their actual bid (lane-based objectives) or by using a constraint to place a minimum on the amount of business that incumbents are awarded (system-based objectives).

Auctioneer's reputation   Shippers do enjoy, or suffer from, reputation developed ex post. Auctioneers that do not stand by their commitments or are difficult to do business with find that carriers not only bid higher the next time around but also are not reluctant to share their experience across the industry. On the other hand, shippers who pay on time and are fair in dispute resolution may see more aggressive bids.

Collusion is not an important issue   By and large, TL carriers do not seem to collude, at least in the United States and Western Europe. The reasons are that the number of bidders is relatively large and the predominant form of bidding involves sealed bids, leaving less opportunity for collusion. Other reasons for the lack of widespread collusion may include: (1) the familiarity associated with the repeated nature of the auctions, (2) the expertise of the shippers who know more or less what to expect, and (3) the ease with which human resources can move between companies and the existence of whistle blowers, both of which make detection easy.

Although these issues are common in practice, very little has been written on them in the game-theoretic literature. An exception to this is Weber 1983.

21.5   Bidding Language

The communication language used during the auction determines how the carriers can respond to the shipper's request for bids. Traditional practice in transportation is for carriers to submit a "per load" (or per load-mile) rate for haulage on each lane, regardless of the volume of business that they might win on that lane or any other lane. We refer to this as a *simple bid*. This form of bid language leads to the carriers hedging their bid prices to cover those instances where they do not win any supporting business.

Combinatorial auctions allow carriers to make explicit their otherwise implicit pricing assumptions. They can provide a lower bid price, given certain that other conditions are met. In transportation, these are sometimes referred to as *conditional bids*. That is, the bid rates submitted are conditional on a predefined set of actions also taking place. Lane-based package bids are but one type of conditional bids.

Below we describe the different types of conditional bids that are currently in use within transportation auctions.

21.5.1 Simple Lane Bid

A bid rate applies to all shipments on that lane regardless of the volume awarded. The number of shipments awarded to the carrier on that lane is determined by the shipper. Each bid may include specific service capabilities (transit time, trailer size, weekend coverage, additional safety factors, etc.) that are only available if that bid at that rate is awarded.

This is the most widely type of bid used. Oftentimes shippers do not even provide carriers with lane volume estimates or forecasts. Carriers can include different service levels in multiple simple bids for the same business in order to "de-commoditize" their offerings.

21.5.2 Simple Lane Bid with Volume Constraint(s)

A bid rate applies to all shipments on a lane but only if the carrier is awarded at or above the *minimum commitment constraint* and at or below the *maximum capacity constraint* for that lane, region, set of lanes, or system—as specified.

Capacity (upper bound) constraints are more commonly submitted by carriers than minimum commitment constraints. They are equivalent to budget constraints in that they allow a carrier to submit a set of bids whose sum total capacity is greater than the carrier's total available capacity.

21.5.3 Static Package Bids (AND)

This is a set of individual lane bid rates that apply to each lane within that set, conditional on the shipper awarding the carrier all lanes within the set at the *exact volume levels* specified by the carrier. Most commercially available software tools handle static package bids.

21.5.4 Static Either/Or Package Bids (XOR)

This is where two or more package bids with rates that apply conditional on the shipper, 1) only awarding the carrier one of the bids and 2) awarding that carrier all lanes within that package bid.

This communicates the message, "give me this set of lanes, or that set of lanes, but not both." The message "Give me this set of lanes or that set of lanes or both" is referred to as an OR bid. It can be achieved through the use of nonoverlapping AND bids.

21.5.5 Flexible Package Bids

A set of individual lane bid rates apply to each lane within that set, conditional on the shipper awarding the carrier all lanes within the set *within volume ranges* specified by the carrier for each lane within the set. Note that with static package bids the shipper does not determine the specific volume level awarded on each lane within that package. The carrier determines the lane volume as part of the submission of the static package bid. With flexible package bids, by contrast, the shipper selects the specific volume level awarded on all lanes within the awarded package bid—as long as it adheres to the carrier's ranges. This means that although a carrier knows the total value of a static package bid at the time of bid submission, it only knows the potential range of values for a flexible package bid at that same time. Only after the WDP is solved will the carrier know the actual number of shipments and total dollar value of a flexible package bid.

The carrier specifies for each lane within the package both the rate per load and the minimum and maximum volume per week, month, or year. Additionally, the carrier can provide package level capacity ranges. If the shipper is awarding only one carrier per lane, then these bids are equivalent to static package bids.

21.5.6 Simple Reload Bids

A carrier specifies that the total number of awarded inbound loads to a facility is equal to (or within some parameter of) the number of awarded outbound loads from the same facility. The WDP model determines the actual volume awarded, so that the conditional bid only specifies the ratio of the awards. This is done to improve the balance at a specific site and increase the potential for *continuous moves* at that site. It differs from flexible package bids in that the condition is added that the balance between two sets of lanes must be met.

21.5.7 Tier Bids

A schedule of bid rates apply to a lane for a predetermined set of volume ranges on that lane. The relevant rate is applied to each shipment depending on the volume of loads processed that week or month. This captures the economies of scale effect on the lane level. Because the actual rate charged is determined during execution, it more accurately maps the carrier's costs.

Regardless of the type of conditional bid used, the end result is a rate per load for each lane that is used in execution. Although the total value of each bid is used for analysis, it is always divisible and easily allocated to each specific lane. In fact, the final upload to the downstream systems is a set of individual lane rates for each winning carrier. The conditions under which the carrier was awarded those rates are rarely included, or even tracked, in actual execution, thus increasing the uncertainty described previously in section 21.2.3.

21.6   Winner Determination Problem

Part III of this book discusses the winner determination problem (WDP) in depth. We will only relate what is being used in practice for transportation services, where this problem is generally referred to as the "carrier assignment" problem.

Shippers will either assign business to carriers by lane (a single carrier is responsible for hauling on each lane) or by load (each carrier is assigned a number of loads to haul on each lane awarded). In practice, most software applications use models that assign by load because this permits other network and business specific aspects to be considered.

21.6.1   Bid Types

The most straightforward carrier assignment model allows only simple bids with no side constraints:

$$\min \quad \sum_c \sum_k \sum_{i,j} {}_cc^k_{i,j\,c}x^k_{i,j} \qquad\qquad (21.4a)$$

subject to:

$$\sum_c \sum_k {}_cx^k_{i,j} = x_{i,j} \quad \forall i,j \qquad\qquad (21.4b)$$

$${}_cx^k_{i,j} \geq 0 \quad \forall i,j,c,k \qquad\qquad (21.4c)$$

where the notations are:

Indices
i Shipping origin region
j Shipping destination region
k Bid package identification
c Carrier identification.

Decision Variables
${}_cx^k_{i,j}$ number of loads per time unit (week, month), on lane i to j, assigned to carrier c, under package (which in this case is a simple bid) k.

Data

$x_{i,j}$ Volume of loads from shipper s, on lane i to j, that are being bid out

$_cc_{i,j}^k$ Bid price per load on lane i to j, for carrier c, as part of conditional bid k.

The objective function 21.4a minimizes the total price charged by carriers to haul loads over the shipper's network. The coefficient $_cc_{i,j}^k$ is the price per load submitted by carrier c under the terms of a specific bid k.[14] Constraints 21.4b ensure that the planned volume on each lane is covered.

Simple bids, $_cc_{i,j}^k$, allow the carrier to submit a rate per load and the shipper to determine the specific quantity of loads awarded to each carrier on each lane. This is the most common bid type used in transportation auctions. The k index permits the carriers to submit multiple bids (with correspondingly different rates) for the same lane but with potentially different service levels, equipment types, or other characteristics. So, although these are not package bids, we refer to them as conditional bids (or packages) nevertheless.

Permitting both simple bids and static package bids into the carrier assignment problem results in the formulation:

$$\min \quad \sum_c \sum_k \left[\left(\sum_{\forall i, j \in k} {_c}c_{i,j}^k {_c}\delta_{i,j}^k \right) {_c}y^k + \sum_{i,j} ({_c}c_{i,j}^k {_c}x_{i,j}^k) \right] \tag{21.5a}$$

subject to:

$$\sum_c \sum_k ({_c}x_{i,j}^k + {_c}\delta_{i,j}^k {_c}y^k) = x_{i,j} \quad \forall i, j \tag{21.5b}$$

$$_cx_{i,j}^k \geq 0 \quad \forall i, j, c, s, k \tag{21.5c}$$

$$_cy^k = [0, 1] \quad \forall c, k \tag{21.5d}$$

where the additional variables and data are:

$_cy^k$ $= 1$ if carrier c is assigned static package bid k, $= 0$ otherwise

$_c\delta_{i,j}^k$ Volume of loads on lane i to j, that carrier c is bidding on as part of package bid k.

The objective function 21.5a minimizes the cost of assigning carriers to haul loads over the shipper's network. The package bid cost coefficient is the total cost per planning time period for all volume on all of the lanes included in the package bid k submitted by carrier c. Constraints 21.5b ensure that the planned volume on each lane is covered—either by simple or static package bids. Note that the carrier must specify the exact number of loads requested for each lane within each static package bid, $_c\delta_{i,j}^k$. Static package bids are the most common form of package bids used in transportation auctions—the carrier specifies the lanes and the exact level of flow per each lane. Most of the commercial software programs use similar formulations.

More recently, flexible package bids are being discussed—both with and without capacity limits. By introducing flexible package bids, the model becomes:

$$\min \quad \sum_c \sum_k \sum_{i,j} (_c c_{i,j}^k {}_c x_{i,j}^k) \tag{21.6a}$$

subject to:

$$\sum_c \sum_k {}_c x_{i,j}^k = x_{i,j} \quad \forall i,j \tag{21.6b}$$

$$-_c M_{i,j}^k {}_c y^k + {}_c x_{i,j}^k \leq 0 \quad \forall c,k,i,j \tag{21.6c}$$

$$-_c LB_{i,j}^k {}_c y^k + {}_c x_{i,j}^k \geq 0 \quad \forall c,k,i,j \tag{21.6d}$$

$$-_c UB_{i,j}^k {}_c y^k + {}_c x_{i,j}^k \leq 0 \quad \forall c,k,i,j \tag{21.6e}$$

$$-_c PL^k {}_c y^k + \sum_{ij} {}_c x_{i,j}^k \leq 0 \quad \forall c,k \tag{21.6f}$$

$$_c x_{i,j}^k \geq 0 \quad \forall i,j,c,s,k \tag{21.6g}$$

$$_c y^k = [0,1] \quad \forall c,k \tag{21.6h}$$

where the additional variables and data are:

$_c M_{i,j}^k$ Large constant

$_c LB_{i,j}^k$ Lower bound in loads on lane i to j, that carrier c is bidding on as part of flexible package bid k

$_c UB_{i,j}^k$ Upper bound in loads on lane i to j, that carrier c is bidding on as part of flexible package bid k

$_c PL^k$ Lower bound in loads across all lanes, that carrier c is bidding on as part of flexible package bid k.

The objective function 21.6a sums the product of the individual lane bid prices and the awarded lane volume on each lane within each conditional bid. Constraints 21.6b ensure that the volume in each lane is covered by some carrier; 21.6c enforce the condition that any carrier assigned any volume on a lane within a flexible package bid is awarded the entire package bid; 21.6d and 21.6e enforce the conditions that if any volume is assigned to a lane within a flexible package bid it satisfies the carrier's specified minimum and maximum lane volume requirements for that bid; and 21.6f enforce the condition that if any volume is assigned to any lanes within a flexible package bid the total package volume awarded to that carrier under that bid package satisfies the carrier's minimum volume requirement for the entire package.

Note that 21.6 is a more general formulation than 21.5 in that it handles simple, static package and flexible package bids all within the same decision variables. Simple bids are modeled as flexible package bids consisting of just one lane. Static package bids are modeled as flexible package bids but with the upper and lower lane volume restrictions set equal to the same value. Thus, the same decision variable, $_c x_{i,j}^k$, can be used for all three of the primary conditional bid types.

Simple reload bids also can be incorporated into 21.6 by adding constraints 21.6i and 21.6j for each facility, j, that is subject to reload simple bid, k, for carrier c.

$$\beta_j \leq \sum_i {_c x_{i,j}^k} - \sum_i {_c x_{j,i}^k} \leq \beta_j' \quad \forall j, k, c \tag{21.6i}$$

$$\alpha_j \leq \sum_i {_c x_{i,j}^k} \bigg/ \sum_i {_c x_{j,i}^k} \leq \alpha_j' \quad \forall j, k, c. \tag{21.6j}$$

The terms β_j, β_j', α_j, α_j' are constants capturing the possible relationships between the outbound and inbound volumes. Shippers typically use either of these two sets of parameters, but rarely both. A simple reload bid would typically also contain minimum and maximum volume constraints at the lane and package levels.

21.6.2 Side Constraints

Section 21.4.2 discussed the different shipper objectives that are frequently considered in transportation auctions. This section illustrates the three most commonly used constraints, using formulation 21.6 as the basis.

Business Guarantee Constraints A shipper often wants to ensure that the amount of traffic that a carrier, or set of carriers, wins is within a certain bound. The shipper might not want to rely too heavily on a single carrier, thus setting a maximum coverage. Conversely, the shipper might want to give enough business to a carrier to remain a significant customer, thus setting a minimum. Coverage can be measured in terms of loads won or in total estimated dollar value. The constraints below ensure that all carriers within some set of carriers C' are awarded business within some preset volume (dollar value) bounds.

$$_{C'}\text{MinValue}_{N'}^{K'} \leq \sum_{c \in C'} \sum_{k \in K'} \sum_{ij \in N'} ({_c c_{i,j}^k} {_c x_{i,j}^k}) \leq {_{C'}}\text{MaxValue}_{N'}^{K'}, \tag{21.7a}$$

$$_{C'}\text{MinVolume}_{N'}^{K'} \leq \sum_{c \in C'} \sum_{k \in K'} \sum_{ij \in N'} ({_c x_{i,j}^k}) \leq {_{C'}}\text{MaxVolume}_{N'}^{K'}. \tag{21.7b}$$

Note that these constraints can apply to a specified set of carriers (C'), bid packages (K'), or geographies (N'). Some common constraints include guaranteeing that the core carrier group is awarded, say, at least 100 loads a week out of a facility; ensuring that at least half of the loads covered in the Northeast are awarded to carriers providing 53-foot trailers, setting a maximum of 20 percent of the total volume in the network to be awarded to intermodal services, and so on. These constraints are easy to explain and shippers tend to think of their business in these terms. Care needs to be taken when MinVolume or MinValue constraints are used to ensure feasibility. There is a tendency for some shippers to over-specify or over-engineer a final award using these types of constraints.[15]

Carrier Base Size Constraints   Another typical business constraint is the restriction of the total number of carriers winning—at the system, region, or lane levels. The number of carriers in the system or at a location can be restricted through the use of either hard or soft constraints. The system-based (or hard) approach adds the following constraints to limit the number of carriers assigned at the system and facility levels:

$$-_cM^k_{i,j c}w_i + _cx^k_{i,j} \leq 0 \quad \forall c,k,i,j \tag{21.8a}$$

$$\sum_c {_cw_i} \leq L_i \quad \forall i \tag{21.8b}$$

$$-_cM^k_{i,j c}z + _cx^k_{i,j} \leq 0 \quad \forall c,k,i,j \tag{21.8c}$$

$$\sum_c {_cz} \leq S \tag{21.8d}$$

$$_cw_i = [0,1] \quad \forall c,i \tag{21.8e}$$

$$_cz = [0,1] \quad \forall c \tag{21.8f}$$

where the additional variables and data are:

$_cw_i$ = 1 if carrier c is assigned to facility i, = 0 otherwise
$_cz$ = 1 if carrier c is assigned to the network, = 0 otherwise
L_i Location limit of carriers desired to serve facility i
S System limit of carriers desired to serve network as a whole.

The traditional approach of using a single large "M" variable, although creating more compact formulations, can result in extremely fractional LP solutions, making it very weak in solving the IP. Barnhart et al. (1993) show in most cases, disaggregating the model leads to tighter bounds when solving the IP as will minimizing the constant, M. Setting $_cM^k_{i,j}$ to the maximum of $(_cx^k_{i,j})$ for each carrier, bid identifier, and lane combination accomplishes this.

Although the hard constraints make sense at the facility or system levels, when applied to individual lanes it often results in one carrier winning the lion's share of the volume and the others winning the bare minimum to satisfy the constraint. This is less desirable in practice because many shippers want a more balanced distribution. A way to create more balance is simply to add in a maximum volume constraint for each carrier for the location or lane in question equal to the percentage of the business that the largest carrier is desired to haul using the business guarantee constraints shown earlier.

Soft constraints can also be used to discourage additional carriers being awarded business by modifying the objective function as follows:

$$\min \quad \sum_c \sum_k \sum_{i,j} (_c c_{i,jc}^k x_{i,j}^k) + \sum_c \sum_i F_{i\,c}^c w_i + \sum_c F_c^c z \tag{21.9}$$

where all variables are the same as previous models with the addition of:

F^c Cost of including carrier c into the system and
F_i^c Cost of including carrier c serve location i.

These fixed costs can be both carrier and location specific as shown above, or the same for all carriers and all locations. Essentially, these fixed costs act as penalties for adding additional carriers to the winning set.

The two most common uses of these constraints are to limit the total number of carriers awarded any business and to limit the number of carriers serving a facility on both the inbound and outbound sides so as to minimize the size of the required trailer pool. The latter consideration also encourages the use of continuous moves at that facility—because specific carriers will tend to win both inbound and outbound business.

If Then Constraints Shippers will often wish to guarantee that if a carrier is awarded any business, then it has to be of a certain minimum level. Constraints 21.10 below ensure that if a carrier is awarded any business across the network, then it must be at least $_cSV$ loads.

$$-_cSV_c z + \sum_k \sum_{i,j} (_c x_{i,j}^k) \geq 0 \quad \forall c \tag{21.10a}$$

$$-_c M_{i,jc}^k z + _c x_{i,j}^k \leq 0 \quad \forall c, k, i, j. \tag{21.10b}$$

21.7 Conclusion

Three observations from practice warrant discussion in this chapter: the lack of widespread adoption of package bids (or the incentive problem), the unexpected (by us) apparent value of solving the WDP, and the benefits of using CAs over traditional transportation auctions used in practice. We conclude this section and the chapter with some observations on future research directions.

21.7.1 The Incentive Problem

As detailed earlier in the chapter, package bids make clear economic sense for TL carriers and more shippers are running combinatorial auctions than ever before. Unfortunately, the number of carriers submitting package bids (static or flexible) has rarely exceeded a small minority in any single auction. Most carriers when presented with the opportunity to submit package bids opt to submit only simple bids. The question, then, is how can shippers provide incentives to carriers to create and submit more package bids?

We feel that there are two major reasons for the low use of package bids (and therefore two avenues of approach for increasing their use). The first is the lack of tools to assist carriers in formulating robust and worthwhile package bids. Unfortunately, many carriers and researchers approach the strategic problem of formulating package bids from an execution (truck by truck) perspective. In the very first uses of combinatorial auctions, it was not uncommon for carriers to submit package bids with upwards of a dozen lanes linked together in a closed loop tour with only one or two loads per week of volume on each lane. The carriers were trying to construct a real-time continuous move in a strategic auction. This practice is becoming less common among carriers, but many software solutions and researchers still take this approach. What carriers need is a methodology to incorporate the numerous levels of risk and uncertainty inherent in the planning problem and formulate those packages that provide the greater probability of retaining a balance of loads across their entire network.

Second, most shippers and carriers rarely even track, much less enforce, compliance of contracted volumes and rates. Frequently, carriers will win lanes in a strategic auction, but never be tendered any business on them. This can be caused by a change in business shipping patterns as well as local preferences in the transportation manager's decision process. The net result is that there is a significant gap between what is awarded and what is actually tendered to a carrier, which means that the effort spent formulating a package bid could go for naught—even if it is awarded—when the actual loads do not materialize.

Our experience suggests that providing carriers with more robust, probabilistic tools for forming package bids and improving the contractual compliance systems of shippers and carriers will lead to the wider acceptance of package bids by carriers.

21.7.2 Unexpected Value of the Winner Determination Problem

Although our initial research and model formulation in the early 1990s allowed for the insertion of constraints into the carrier assignment model, it was felt that they would not be widely used in practice. Similarly, the initial model in Porter et al. (2002) for Sears did not consider any business constraints besides covering the available volume.

The common thought was that there would be minimal use of these side constraints because the model would select the "optimal" assignment. Our experience has taught us otherwise. In fact, having the ability to model various business constraints and "philosophies" directly in the assignment problem is now viewed as the most valuable component of the procurement process. Shippers use the optimization model to price out various "what if" scenarios in order to conduct a value assessment. As discussed in section 21.4.3, the cost of including these business considerations averages 6 percent of the total lowest submitted bids.

It is not uncommon to run several dozen scenarios during an auction process, each of which features hundreds of specific business constraints. Shippers, once enabled with this type of decision support, typically spend a considerable amount of time exploring various assignments to maximize the fit to their business needs rather than just looking for the lowest cost. This "what if" analysis or scenario management capability is frequently used as a tool to drive consensus among different factions within a shipper (or among shippers in a multicompany engagement)[16] where the consequences of different business decisions are weighted against each other. The power of these "what if" analyses is that they are conducted with actual relevant and operational bids, not based on historical costs. Bichler, Davenport, Hohner, and Kalagnanam (chapter 23 of this volume) discuss similar benefits of running multiple scenarios within procurement auctions in other industries.

The increasing use of the WDP to estimate the financial impact of various business rules contributes to the growing use of sealed bid auctions. This is because the constraints used within the WDP are not visible to the bidders—only the final results are. Thus, the information provided to the bidders is not sufficient to make accurate or intelligent price adjustments in between rounds.

21.7.3 Benefits of Combinatorial Auctions over Traditional Auctions

The transportation industry has benefited tremendously from the introduction of CAs in the 1990s. Many of these benefits, however, are indirectly, rather than directly, the result of CAs.

The primary benefit is that CAs forced shippers to improve the quality and quantity of data that they provide to the carriers. The shippers realized that in order for a carrier to formulate a complex bid, they would need to have exceptionally accurate and detailed information. This is not the case in traditional transportation auctions where only origin and destination are typically provided.

Second, CAs forced shippers to recognize the underlying economics of their carriers. This manifested itself in shippers allowing, and encouraging, their carriers to "be creative" in engineering their proposed solutions. Shippers are more cognizant of the interplay between lanes and locations for carriers. Traditional transportation auctions ignore these complexities.

Third, because CAs require the use of optimization, the shippers were enabled to consider nonfinancial information when running a procurement auction. This has lead to the inclusion of level of service and other factors in most of the larger procurement auctions. Traditional transportation auctions ignore any factors aside from bid rate.

Overall, then, the introduction of CAs into the truckload transportation industry has led to more accurate, collaborative, and comprehensive interaction between shippers and carriers.

21.7.4 Areas for Future Research

The use of combinatorial auctions for transportation procurement offers many opportunities for future research. Although it has been used in practice for the better part of a decade, the adoption rate is not as large as the theory would indicate it should be. This leads to a large number of potential areas of investigation, including the following:

Carrier bidding behavior   The way in which carriers actually approach and participate in combinatorial auctions has not been studied to any significant degree. This could lead to better and more standardized auction rules.

Carrier bidding methodology   As mentioned earlier, carriers do not utilize very sophisticated systems or approaches when setting prices or creating package bids. A methodology that incorporates the stochastic nature of the underlying transportation services as well as the uncertainty of the actual award is sorely lacking.

Cross shipper auctions   Many shippers have attempted to form coalitions to better procure transportation services collectively. These have in general not been successful. It would be interesting to develop auction approaches and rules to enhance cross company auctions.

Improved robustness in the WDP   A key weakness of the traditional WDP approach is that it tends to over-concentrate the awards in order to minimize the planned cost. Unfortunately, the WDP does not take variability into account. This can result in assignments that are lowest cost for the assumptions made in the plan, but are highly susceptible to any operational changes. A better approach is needed so that shippers can measure, manage, and decide how much additional redundancy to secure in order to minimize total system risk. The use of real options in transportation contracting is a step in this direction.

This is just a short list of research topics that we and other researchers in the field are pursuing.

Acknowledgments

The authors would like to sincerely thank Pinar Keskinocak, Matthew Harding, Amelia Regan, and Amr Farahat for their helpful comments and recommendations on earlier drafts of this chapter.

Notes

1. A lane is an origin-destination pairing of freight flows; in other words: "X truckloads per week going from A to B." It is typically the item being auctioned off in TL transportation procurement engagements.

2. This product line was developed by Digital Freight, which was acquired by Manugistics in 2001.

3. The OptiBid product line was developed originally by PTCG. It was acquired by Sabre in 1996, Logistics.com in 2000, and Manhattan Associates in 2003.

4. The authors have no financial or commercial interests in the development, leasing, or sale of any of the software created or marketed by any of the companies mentioned in this chapter or others.

5. Although replacing a single carrier on a small subset of lanes has very low switching costs, the effort required for a wholesale change is quite high.

6. A manufacturer with such an annual TL transportation bill will probably have annual revenue of $5–15 billion.

7. In the late 1980s, North American Van Lines, one of the market leaders at the time, was accused of making a higher return from financing and repossessing trucks than from transportation operations.

8. When the flow of traffic is such that drivers spend too much time on the road, carriers will allow operators to drive home empty or even fly them home, just to ensure that they will visit their families.

9. A power lane for a carrier is an origin destination pair that has a very large number of reliable shipments.

10. For example, a medium sized shipper that has, say, 5,000 point-to-point movements may aggregate them into 1,000 three-digit zip code to three-digit zip code lanes or several hundred state-to-state lanes. There are generally orders of magnitude of difference between the number of point to point moves and the number of lanes used in an auction.

11. In both Plummer 2003 and SABRE 1998, the nation was divided into seven zones: Northeast, Southeast, Midwest, Southwest, Central, and Northwest. Separate regional values were estimated for both inbound and outbound effects.

12. In fact, one quality check that many auctioneers run in these bids is to compare the gap between the leading bid and the leading incumbent's bid on each lane. A large gap indicates the potential of some common "incumbent" information that should be investigated and potentially shared with the non-incumbents. This can reduce the incidence of the winner's curse that, due to the nonbinding nature of the relationships, can hurt both the carrier and the shipper.

13. In many cases, level of service preferences are communicated to the carriers but not other business constraints, for obvious reasons.

14. Note that although the carrier might submit a bid specifying a rate per mile or weight per hundredweight, this is typically converted to a cost per load for analysis within the WDP.

15. Interestingly, some traffic managers will try to use these constraints to force the model to assign the incumbents to their exact original lanes—in order to avoid any change while still adhering to the letter, if not the spirit, of a corporate directive to conduct an auction.

16. The software tools mentioned in this chapter enable and therefore encourage multiple shipper auctions, where several shippers combine their volume in order to exploit the carriers' economics across more freight to achieve lower costs and therefore lower prices.

References

ATA (2002), *American Trucking Trends 2002*, Alexandria, VA: American Trucking Association.

Barnhart, Cynthia, Ellis Johnson, George Nemhauser, G. Sigismondi, and Pamela Vance (1993), "Formulating a Mixed Integer Programming Problem to Improve Solvability," *Operations Research*, 41 (6), 1013–1019.

Caplice, Chris (1996), "Optimization-Based Bidding, a New Framework for Shipper-Carrier Relationships," Unpublished Ph.D. Dissertation, Massachusetts Institute of Technology, Cambridge, MA.

Caplice, Chris and Yosef Sheffi (2003), "Optimization Based Procurement for Transportation Services," *Journal of Business Logistics*, 24 (3), 109–128.

Caplice, Chris, Clint Plummer, and Yosef Sheffi (2004), "Bidder Behavior in Combinatorial Auctions for Transportation Services," Working Paper, Massachusetts Institute of Technology Center for Transportation & Logistics.

Costello, Robert (2003), "Motor Carrier Update," Presentation to Great West Casualty Company, Chief Economist of the American Trucking Association, March 20.

de Vries, Sven and Rakesh V. Vohra (2003), "Combinatorial Auctions: A Survey," *INFORMS Journal on Computing*, 15, 284–309.

Elmaghraby, Wedad and Pinar Keskinocak (2002), "Combinatorial Auctions in Procurement," Technical Report, School of Industrial and Systems Engineering, Georgia Institute of Technology.

Moore, E. William, Janice M. Warmke, and Lonny R. Gorban (1991), "The Indispensable Role of Management Science in Centralizing Freight Operations at Reynolds Metals Company," *Interfaces*, 21 (1), 107–129.

Plummer, Clint (2003), "Bidder Response to Combinatorial Auctions in Truckload Procurement," Unpublished Master of Engineering in Logistics Thesis, Massachusetts Institute of Technology, Cambridge, MA.

Porter, David, David P. Torma, John O. Ledyard, Joseph A. Swanson, and Mark Olson (2002), "The First Use of a Combined-Value Auction for Transportation Services," *Interfaces*, 32 (5), 4–12.

Powell, Warren B., Yosef Sheffi, Kenneth S. Nickerson, and Susan Atherton (1988), "Maximizing Profits for North American Van Lines' Truckload Division: A New Framework for Pricing and Operations," *Interfaces*, 18 (1), 21–41.

SABRE Group (1998), "Third Party Logistics Study for the Defense Logistics Agency," 001A— Technical Report—CRDL Sequence A001.

Song, Jeannette and Ameila Regan (2005), "Approximation Algorithms for the Bid Valuation and Structuring Problem in Combinatorial Auctions for the Procurement of Freight Transportation Contracts," *Transportation Research, Part B, Methodological*, To appear.

Standard & Poor's (2004), Industry Survey, *Transportation: Commercial*, 19 August, p. 7.

Weber, Robert (1983), "Multiple-Object Auctions," in Richard Engelbrecht-Wiggans, Martin Shubik, and Robert M. Stark (eds.), *Auctions, Bidding, and Contracting: Uses and Theory*, New York: New York University Press, 165–191.

22 Auctioning Bus Routes: The London Experience

Estelle Cantillon and Martin Pesendorfer

22.1 Introduction

The London bus routes market provides an early example of the use of a combinatorial auction format in public procurement. This market covers about 800 routes serving an area of 1,630 square kilometers and more than 3.5 million passengers per day. It is valued at £600 million per year (roughly US $900 million).

Prior to deregulation, bus services in the Greater London area were provided by the publicly owned London Buses Limited. The London Regional Transport Act of 1984 reorganized the sector. The act designated London Regional Transport (LRT) as the authority responsible for the provision and procurement of public transport services in the Greater London area, as well as for the development and operation of bus stations and for the operational maintenance. It also advocated a franchise system by empowering LRT to invite private operators to submit bids to carry out bus services.

In order to enhance competition, LRT, which by virtue of the Transport Act acted as the holding company for the original public operator London Buses Limited, created a separate tendering division, independent from its operational division. The operational division, London Buses Limited, was split into twelve operational subsidiaries. These were privatized in 1994.

In practice, the introduction of route tendering was gradual. There was an experimentation phase as LRT built up procurement expertise and identified the routes that represented the greatest potential for cost reduction and the least risk of disruption (Kennedy, Glaister, and Travers 1995). Hence, though the first auction took place in 1985, it was not until 1995 that half of the network was tendered at least once.[1] Since then, tendering has reached its steady state regime with 15–20 percent of the network tendered every year.

This chapter does several things. First, we describe the combinatorial auction format adopted by LRT and briefly discuss its properties (sections 22.2 and 22.3). Second, we describe the bidding patterns observed in the data that we collected for these auctions, with a special emphasis on package bidding and the effect of the auction size (section 22.4).

Finally, as in any practical design problem, LRT was faced with a range of options when deciding on the auction format. A critical input into any such analysis is a better understanding of bidders' preferences—in our case, their cost structure. In section 22.5, we summarize a new method that we have developed to analyze bid data from combinatorial first price auctions to do exactly this: infer bidders' cost structure. We illustrate this method and discuss our findings.

22.2 Auction Design

The choice of auction design in London was driven in part by circumstances and economic conditions. Early on, LRT came to the conclusion that the private sector in Britain was unlikely to have the expertise to provide full transportation services in a complex environment such as London (Kennedy, Glaister, and Travers 1995). As a result, it was decided to keep the design of the bus network and all related aspects of the transport supply such as frequencies, bus types, exact routing, cross route coordination, and so on, at the network level. Only the actual provision of bus services would be outsourced.

Nevertheless, this left several important design questions open. First, what "items" would be auctioned? A contract for a route? For a set of routes? Or less than a route? Second, how should LRT auction these contracts? Should LRT seek to tender the whole network at the same time? Route by route? Or groups of routes together? If so, which criteria should they use to decide which routes to auction at the same time? Also, how much should bidders be able to express in terms of their preferences over routes and bundles of routes? Third, who should be allowed to participate? Finally, which criteria should they use to award the contracts?

In the remainder of this section, we describe LRT's actual choices with respect to these options.

22.2.1 Pre-Auction Design

Definition of the Items Auctioned With two exceptions, the items auctioned are contracts for the operation of a bus route. First, "mobility routes," which are low-frequency services (one or two round trips per week) with buses especially equipped to accommodate wheelchairs, are usually auctioned as a bundle. The reason is that any such route by itself represents too small a contract. Second, the night and day portions of the same route are sometimes auctioned as separate contracts when they require different types of buses. The intention in both cases is to define an item as a self-standing homogeneous contract.

The contracts are usually for five years. LRT has experimented with several contractual forms over time. It has mainly used "gross cost" contracts, whereby the winner's compensation is the amount it bid, whereas all revenues collected on the bus accrue to LRT.

Packaging and Sequencing Decisions From the very beginning, designing the auctions to enhance competition and attract new entry to the London bus market was a clear concern. The choice of auctioned routes in the early years, peripheral and requiring a relatively small number of vehicles to operate, reflects this (Glaister and Beesley 1991). This concern may also have affected how LRT decided how many routes to auction at the same time. On the one hand, there are bundling benefits in terms of shared fixed costs and coordination efficiencies. This calls for auctioning a large amount of related routes together. On the other hand, larger auctions could discourage entry by smaller bus operators without the capacity to bid on all the routes in the auction.[2] The current practice may have reached a compromise between these two views. Today, LRT holds an auction every two or three weeks. An auction covers on average 3.77 routes, though the range in our data goes from one route to twenty-one routes in a single auction. Importantly, the routes tendered within one auction are usually in the same area of London.

Participation Only prequalified operators can participate in the auctions. Prequalification screens for financial stability and operational capacity of potential operators. There were about fifty-one such operators during our sample period. All prequalified operators are informed of upcoming auctions.

22.2.2 Auction Format

The auction format adopted in the London bus routes market is a variant of a combinatorial first price auction. In a standard combinatorial first-price auction, bidders simultaneously submit sealed bids on any individual items and on any packages of items; the auctioneer solves the winner determination problem (Lehmann, Müller, and Sandholm, chapter 12 of this volume) by determining the "best" bidder-item allocation based on these bids (because this is a procurement setting, the best allocation is the one that minimizes total cost); and the winners receive the amount they bid for the items they won.

As in the standard combinatorial first price auction, bidders in the LRT auction can submit bids on any number of routes and route packages. There is no restriction on the number of bids placed, nor is there an obligation to bid on some routes or route packages. In particular, a bidder can submit a bid on a package without submitting a bid on the individual routes that make up that package.

The distinctive feature of the LRT auction is that each bid is a firm but nonexclusive commitment of resources. This means that two bids on different routes implicitly define a bid for the package of these routes. An important consequence of this rule is that bidders are not allowed to bid more for a package than the sum of the bids on any partition of that package. In particular, this rules out bids expressing diseconomies of scale or scope.[3] The original motivation for this rule was the expectation that the market was mainly characterized by economies of scale and scope, and that by allowing bidders to express such synergies, LRT would lower its procurement costs and improve efficiency.

After verification that the bids satisfy the technical requirements of the auctioned contracts, LRT awards the contracts to the bidder allocation that delivers the best economic value. In practice, this means that the contract is awarded to the low bidder, but deviations at the margin are possible to account for operator quality, for example. The winner receives the amount he bid for the contract, indexed yearly. To allow winning operators to reorganize and order new buses if necessary, contracts start eight to ten months after the award date.

22.3 Motivations for Submitting a Package Bid

We have built a model to study the properties of the auction format adopted in London. Our goal was twofold: first, to investigate the motivations for submitting bids on packages in the first-price combinatorial auction, and their implications for welfare and efficiency;[4] second, to guide our analysis of the data by suggesting things to look for in the data.

An outline of the model is as follows. An agency seeks to procure m items from n risk neutral bidders. Each bidder i privately observes a cost draw, $c_s^i \in \mathbb{R}$, for each possible subset of the items, $s \subseteq S = \{1, \ldots, m\}$ (that is, s represents either a single item or a package of items). Contract costs are ex ante distributed according to some joint distribution $F((c_s^i)_{s \subseteq S, i=1,\ldots n} | X)$ where X denotes a vector of observable auction characteristics. Here F is common knowledge, it has bounded support, and has a well-defined strictly positive density everywhere, absolutely continuous with respect to the product of its marginals. This allows independence and correlation or affiliation in bidders' costs across bidders and contracts.

The rule for the auction replicates that of the LRT auction. Bidders may submit bids on all subsets of the set of items. Let b_s^i denote bidder i's bid on the subset of items $s \subseteq S$, and let $b^i = (b_1^i, \ldots, b_s^i, \ldots b_S^i) \in \mathbb{R}^{2^m-1}$. Bidders receive the value of their winning bids and the auctioneer selects the winner(s) based on the allocation that minimizes his total payment. Formally, the last restriction requires that $b_{s \cup t}^i \leq b_s^i + b_t^i$ for all s and t such that $s \cap t = \emptyset$. This captures the fact that package bids must be equal to or lower than the sum of the bids on any partition of the package.

A Bayesian Nash equilibrium in this environment is a n-tuple of vector-valued bidding functions, $b^i(c_1^i, \ldots, c_S^i) \in \mathbb{R}^{2^m-1}$, that maximize bidder i's expected payoff, for all i,

$$\sum_{s \subseteq S} (b_s^i - c_s^i) G_s(b^i | X) \tag{22.1}$$

where $G_s(b^i | X)$ denotes bidder i's probability of winning package s given his opponents' strategy and his submitted vector of bids b^i.

We have identified two distinct motivations for a bidder to submit a package bid at equilibrium. First, bidders may want to submit a bid on a package when the cost for the package differs from the sum of the costs. This is the standard synergy explanation and it motivates much of the use for combinatorial auctions.

But we also uncovered a more strategic motivation for submitting a package bid lower than the sum of the constituent bids. The reason is that the bids submitted by a bidder compete with one another in a combinatorial auction. For example, consider a two-item auction. Fix bidder i, and for each item or package of items s, define B_s^{-i} as the value of the cheapest allocation of s among i's opponents (from the perspective of bidder i, B_s^{-i} is a random variable; he does not know what his opponents are bidding). With two items, there are four possible winning allocations between bidder i and his opponents: bidder i wins item 1 (and one of his opponents wins item 2, if $b_1^i + B_2^{-i}$ is the cheapest allocation), he wins item 2 (and his opponents win item 1), he wins both items, or he does not win anything.

Now consider item 1. Holding the distribution of the opponents' best bids $(B_1^{-i}, B_2^{-i}, B_{12}^{-i})$ fixed, decreasing b_1^i increases bidder i's chance to win exactly that item by lowering the price of allocation $b_1^i + B_2^{-i}$ relative to the others. But it decreases bidder i's chance of winning the package because it could be the case that, *had bidder i not lowered b_1^i*, the cheapest bid allocation was b_{12}^i. Another way to look at this is in terms of the following tradeoff. The benefit to bidder i from lowering his bid on item 1 is that he wins item 1 more often. But the costs are twofold. First, it lowers his profit margin whenever he wins item 1. Second, it reduces his chance of winning the package of items 1 and 2.[5] At equilibrium of course, bidder i chooses bid b_1^i such that this marginal benefit and these marginal costs exactly balance one another.[6] One can carry out a similar analysis for bidder i's bid on item 2 and on the package.

The result of this strategic effect is that bidder i may be tempted to submit a package bid $b_{12}^i < b_1^i + b_2^i$, even when his costs are completely additive. A simple example may illustrate the idea. Suppose that bidder i is facing two other bidders. Bidder 1 is only interested in item 1; bidder 2 is only interested in item 2. All bidder i knows is that they might submit a bid of 7 or 15 on the item they are interested in, depending on whether they have a low or high cost. Moreover, whenever bidder 1 has a high cost and therefore bids 15 on item 1, bidder 2 has a low cost and bids 7 on item 2, and vice versa. Suppose finally that bidder i has a cost of 5 for each item. In this example, bidder i's best strategy is to submit a bid just below 22 for the package, and a bid higher or equal to 15 for each of the items. This way, he wins for sure both items at a profit of $(22 - 10) = 12$.[7] If instead he bid only on the individual items, his best strategy would be to bid slightly less than 15 on each item for an expected profit of $(15 - 5) = 10$. Clearly, it is best in this example to submit a bid for the package. Moreover, it is not in bidder i's interest to submit a bid on the individual items that has a chance of winning, exactly because of the strategic effect identified above. To see this, consider what happens if bidder i lowers his bid below 15 on item 1 when he also submits a package bid of 22. Now, with some probability p, bidder 1 bids 15 on item 1. In that case, the cheapest allocation is to give item 1 to bidder i for a price below 15, item 2 to bidder 2 for 7, for a total amount less than the package bid. Bidder i's profit now becomes less than $p(15 - 5) + (1 - p)(22 - 10)$, which is lower than his profit of 12 when he only submits a bid on the package. The reason is that the increased probability of winning item 1 comes at the cost of the decrease in the probability of winning the package.

This analysis generalizes. McAfee, McMillan, and Whinston (1989) proved that whenever bids by bidder i's opponents are independently distributed, it is also optimal for bidder i to submit a bid on the package that is strictly lower than the sum of the bids on the individual items. Armstrong and Rochet (1999) proved that submitting such a package bid is profitable whenever the correlation among opponents' bids is not too high.[8]

The normative implication of these two motivations—synergy and strategic—for auction design is ambiguous. In fact, there is no general theoretical result on whether a combinatorial first price auction is better than a series of independent first price auctions. It is easy to construct examples, especially when synergies are important, where a combinatorial auction is better. At the same time, Cantillon and Pesendorfer (2004) present a realistic example without cost synergy where a first price combinatorial auction leads to higher costs and lower efficiency than a simpler first price auction without package bidding.

There are several lessons from this analysis. First, we need to be careful when interpreting the data because a package bid is no guarantee that they are synergies between the items.

Second, the theory suggests a couple of observable factors likely to favor the use of package bids. Correlation or, more precisely, lack of correlation in the environment that bidders face is a driver of package bidding for strategic reasons. Underlying synergies will favor package bidding for synergy reasons.

Third, there is no clear a priori answer to the question of whether allowing package bids in the London bus routes market was a good idea or not. Any answer to this question must rely on a more careful analysis of the economic environment, in particular the drivers of costs. This is the purpose of the next two sections.

22.4 Practice

This section describes our data and provides summary statistics.

We have collected data on a total of 179 auctions held between December 1995 and May 2001. For each auction and for each route in the auction the data provide the following information: (1) route characteristics, including contract duration, the planned start of the contract, the start and end points of the route, the route type (day, night, school service, mobility route), the annual mileage, the bus type (single deck, midibuses, double deck, or routemaster), and the peak vehicle requirement.[9] For the routes auctioned after May 2000, we observe an internal cost estimate generated by LRT. (2) The bidders, their bids (including package bids), and the garage from which bidders plan to operate the route(s). Bids are expressed in June 1995 Pounds.

The auction format implies that bidders are committed by their route bids. Hence, route bids define implicitly a package bid with value equal to the sum of the route bids. We call a package bid "nontrivial" when it is strictly less than the sum of the component route bids. Otherwise, we call the package bid "trivial."

Most auctions consist of a few routes only. The average number of routes per auction in our data is 3.77.

Table 22.1 reports descriptive summary statistics. The table reveals that the distribution of the number of routes per auction is as follows: fifty auctions consist of a single route, thirty-six auctions have two routes, thirty-two auctions have three routes, thirteen auctions have four routes, ten have five routes, twelve have six routes, twelve

Table 22.1

Descriptive summary statistics by number of routes

No. of Routes	All	1	2	3	4–6	7–9	10–21
No. of Auctions	179	50	36	32	35	12	14
No. of bidders per auction	4.28	3.22	3.81	4.34	4.83	5.92	6.00
	(2.04)[a]	(1.52)	(1.82)	(1.79)	(2.01)	(2.54)	(1.84)
No. of bidders per route	2.71	3.22	2.88	2.85	2.39	2.48	2.78
	(1.40)	(1.52)	(1.68)	(1.52)	(1.20)	(1.12)	(1.33)
Log individual route bid	13.31	12.81	13.22	13.54	13.34	13.24	13.27
	(1.24)	(1.33)	(1.24)	(1.20)	(1.29)	(1.17)	(1.18)
No. of bids per bidder[b]	–	1.00	1.76	2.42	3.18	5.06	–
	–	(0.00)	(0.51)	(0.70)	(1.28)	(2.97)	–
No. of package bids per bidder[b]	–	0	0.24	0.41	0.84	1.45	–
	–	(0.00)	(0.30)	(0.36)	(0.78)	(2.13)	–

[a] Standard deviations are displayed in parenthesis.

[b] No. of bids per bidder and the no. of package bids per bidder exclude trivial package bids.

have between seven and nine routes, and fourteen auctions have more than nine routes. The total number of routes across all auctions equals 674.

On average, 4.28 bidders submit at least one bid on an auction. The number of bidders ranges between one and thirteen per auction. On average, 2.71 bidders submit a bid for an individual route on the auction and the number of bidders per route ranges between one and seven. In total, 1,818 individual route bids were submitted. The average individual route bid equals 13.31 in logarithm, which amounts to about £603,000.

Bidder Participation and Auction Size   The number of bidders per auction increases with the size of the auction. The average number of bidders equals 3.22 for single route auctions, 3.81 for two-route auctions, 4.34 for three-route auctions, and increases to six bidders for auctions of more than nine routes. This does not mean increased competition at the route level. Indeed, there is no correlation between the number of bidders per route and the number of routes in the auction. The number of bidders per route remains roughly constant across the range of the number of routes. Similarly, the log of individual route bids does not change significantly as the number of routes varies.

Number of Bids Submitted and Auction Size   The number of bids submitted per bidder equals 1.76 for two-route auctions, and increases to 2.42 for three-route auctions, 3.18 for four- to six-route auctions, 5.06 for seven- to nine-route auctions. This number underestimates the actual number of bids submitted because it does not count trivial package bids.[10]

We also looked more specifically at nontrivial package bids. The number of package bids per bidder increases with the size of the auction. It equals 0.24 for two-route auctions, it increases to 0.41 for three-route auctions, 0.84 for four- to six-route auctions, 1.45 for seven- to nine-route auctions.

Next, we report the relative frequencies of route bids, trivial package bids, and nontrivial package bids for two-, three-, and four-route auctions.

The first column in table 22.2 illustrates that for two-route auctions, 51 percent of all active bidders submitted a package bid. Nontrivial package bids account for 36 percent of all package bids submitted. All but one bidder who submitted a package bid also sub-

Table 22.2
Frequency of package bids by number of routes

No. of Routes	2	3	4
Percent of bidders submitting a package bid	51	63	52
Percent of nontrivial package bids of all package bids	36	59	55
Percent of bidders submitting a full set of bids	18	3	0

mitted a route bid. A full set of bids (individual route bids and nontrivial package bids) was submitted by 18 percent of active bidders.

The second column in table 22.2 shows that for three-route auctions, 63 percent of active bidders submitted a package bid and nontrivial package bids accounted for 59 percent of all package bids submitted. All bidders that submitted a package bid also submitted a route bid. A full set of bids was submitted by 3 percent of active bidders.

For four-route auctions, 52 percent of active bidders submitted a package bid and nontrivial package bids accounted for 55 percent of all package bids submitted. All bidders that submitted a package bid also submitted a route bid. No bidder submits a full set of bids.

Nontrivial Package Bids and Route Attributes   The operators invoke the possibility to share spare vehicles and depot overhead costs, and more efficient organization and coordination of working schedules when they offer discounts for packages. Therefore, the frequency of package bids may be related to the attributes of the routes offered at an auction. We examined this hypothesis by looking at the sample correlation in the data between the frequency of nontrivial package bids and the similarity of the routes for sale. Specifically, we looked at correlation between the frequency of nontrivial package bids and whether the routes at the auction require the same bus type or not. We found that the correlation coefficient between submitting a package bid and whether the routes require the same bus type or not is not significantly different from zero. Furthermore, there is no significant correlation between submitting a nontrivial package bid and whether the routes require the same bus type or not when we condition on the number of routes offered at the auction.

Package Bid Discount   We can calculate the markdown of a nontrivial package bid relative to the sum of route bids. We considered two measures: the total package bid discount calculates the discount equal to one minus the ratio of package bid to sum of route bids. For two, three, and four routes, the formula is given by:

$$1 - \frac{b_{12}}{b_1 + b_2}, 1 - \frac{b_{123}}{b_1 + b_2 + b_3}, 1 - \frac{b_{1234}}{b_1 + b_2 + b_3 + b_4}.$$

The discount equals zero if there is no package discount. It equals one half if the package bid costs half as much as the sum of route bids. If routes differ in size, then the total package bid discount will not adequately measure bid discounts. The reason is that total package bid discount measures the discount on the average route in the bid only. Hence, even if a package bid includes the smaller route for free, the total package bid discount will be almost zero, when the size difference between two routes is large.

Our second measure accounts for size heterogeneity among routes by looking at the marginal route bid. The marginal package bid discount determines the marginal

Table 22.3

Package bid discount by number of items in the package

No. of Items in the Package	All	2	3	4
No. of Observations	421	232	131	58
Total package bid discount	0.057	0.049	0.061	0.077
Marginal package bid discount	0.284	0.182	0.364	0.513

Note: We consider nontrivial package bids only.

discount on the smallest route bid in the package. To calculate the marginal package bid discount, we sorted bids in descending order. Then, we computed one minus the ratio of the marginal route price, calculated as the difference between the package bid and the route bids on the marginal route relative to the marginal route price of the marginal route. For two-, three-, and four-route auctions, the marginal package bid discount measure is given by:

$$1 - \frac{b_{12} - b_1}{b_2}, 1 - \frac{b_{123} - b_1 - b_2}{b_3}, 1 - \frac{b_{1234} - b_1 - b_2 - b_4}{b_4},$$

where b_1 denotes the largest route bid, b_2 the second largest route bid, and so on. The marginal package bid discount equals zero if there is no package bid discount. It equals one if the marginal route is offered for free in the package bid.

Table 22.3 depicts the package discount measures for two-, three-, and four-route package bids. Ignoring trivial package bids, the total package bid discount amounts to 5.7 percent, on average, for two-, three-, and four-route package bids. The marginal package bid discount is substantially higher and amounts to 28.4 percent.

Both the total package bid discount and the marginal package bid discount increase with the number of routes in the bid. The total package bid discount equals 4.9 percent for two-route bids, 6.1 percent for three-route bids, and 7.7 percent for four-route bids. The marginal package bid discount equals 18.2 percent for two-route bids, 26.4 percent for three-route bids, and 51.3 percent for four-route bids.

22.5   A Method to Infer Costs from Auction Data

The evidence presented so far suggests that bidders in the London bus routes market do have recourse to package bids (table 22.2) and offer economically significant discounts (table 22.3), even if they do not bid on all packages. Moreover, one factor suggested by the theory—the similarity between routes—did not seem to explain bidders' use of package bids much (there was no correlation between the frequency of nontrivial package bids and a measure of similarity between the routes). In this section, we go one step further and ask: Can we say anything about bidders' cost structure based on the bid data?

We have developed a method to infer the cost structure of bidders in combinatorial first price auctions that allows us to evaluate the presence of cost synergies. Our method is general and can be used to analyze any data generated from a combinatorial first price auction. It can be described heuristically as follows.

Bidders' cost structure (the cost of operating each route and each package of the routes tendered in the auction), their information (for example, about the participating bidders), together with the auction rules, describe a game of incomplete information. The information is incomplete because bidders do not know the costs of the other participating bidders in the auction. The equilibrium of such a game, that is, the bids submitted by each bidder given their costs, generates an (equilibrium) distribution of bids. If we make the assumption that the bidders in the London bus routes market are using equilibrium strategies, we can use the bids observed in our data to estimate this equilibrium distribution of bids.

Once we know the empirical distribution of bids, we can infer the probability of winning of any bid vector submitted by our bidders. Hence, we can replicate the optimization problem that each bidder in our data was facing when he submitted his bids. Because we assumed that our bidders followed equilibrium bid strategies, we can use the first order conditions of their optimization problem to infer their costs. A simple example may illustrate the idea. Suppose you are bidding in a single item auction and that we can estimate that your probability of winning depends on your bid according to the function $G(b)$, where b is your bid. Suppose we see you submit bid b^*. *If we assume that you are playing according to the equilibrium*, we can conclude that b^* maximizes your expected profit, that is, b^* solves $(b^* - c)G(b^*)' + G(b^*) = 0$. Now, of course, we do not know your cost, but if we reorganize this expression, we find that $c = b^* + G(b^*)/G(b^*)'$. Because we know everything in the right hand side of this equation, we have inferred your cost just by observing how you bid!

We now describe and illustrate each step of our approach on the subset of our data of two route auctions.[11]

22.5.1 Step 1: Choice of the Game That Describes the Data

Our first step is to choose an economic model describing bidders' behavior. We have chosen the constrained combinatorial first price auction with independent private values and risk neutral bidders as the model that we feel best represents the London bus routes auction.

The choice of the auction format deserves little comment given the description in section 22.2. We account for the fact that bidders are committed by their bids by placing the explicit constraint on strategies that bids on a package must be smaller than or equal to the sum of the bids on any partition of the package. An additional constraint that we have included in our modeling is a reserve price on each route and package s, R_s.

We consider each auction in our data as an independent observation and assume that bidders treat each of those as independent one-shot games. Given the frequency of the auctions, this may not hold exactly. However, a mitigating factor is the fact that auctions are held for routes in different parts of London, so that bidders' overlap may be limited across any sequence of auctions. For example, we computed that an average bidder in our data participates in an auction every five months.

Our assumption that costs are private values is driven by our interpretation that the main source of uncertainty in this market is bidders' opportunity costs. Indeed, although it is certainly true that a large fraction of the routes' costs are common to all bidders (the labor, fuel, and other material costs represent on the order of 52 percent of bidders' costs), asymmetries of information about these costs are unlikely because there are well-functioning markets for these inputs. By contrast, opportunity costs arising from the use of capital and rolling stock are likely to differ across bidders. Moreover, they are essentially private values.

Our assumption that costs are ex ante independently distributed across bidders, conditional on auction characteristics, is a simplifying assumption. It is mainly driven by the small size of our dataset.

Summarizing, the primitives of the model are: (1) the three-dimensional ex ante distribution of costs for each bidder i given the characteristics of the auction X^{it}, $f(c_1, c_2, c_{12}|X^{it})$,[12] and (2) bidders' profit conditional on winning route or package s, that is, the difference between their winning bid and their known cost of performing that contract, $b_s - c_s$. Neither the costs nor the distribution of costs are observed in the data. Only the bids and the auction characteristics are.

22.5.2   Step 2: Estimation of the Equilibrium Distribution of Bids

Our second step is to estimate the equilibrium distribution of bids. Because bidders' costs are independently distributed so must be their equilibrium bids. Moreover, we have assumed that, conditional on auction characteristics, each auction was independent. This means that an observation is our analysis is a bidder auction. Based on an analysis of bidder participation, we have considered that any bidder with a garage within five miles of one of the extremities of a route in an auction is a potential bidder for that auction. With this definition, we have 338 observations for the two-route auctions. Not all of these bidders submitted a full vector of bids. In fact, in our data, only 131 of those 338 bidders actually participated by submitting at least one bid.

Our objective is to estimate the distribution of bids based on this data. Because bids on route 1, route 2, and the package are related, we want to estimate them jointly. Denote this three-dimensional distribution by $h(b_1, b_2, b_{12}|X^{it})$, where the conditioning on X^{it} accounts for some auction characteristics. The marginal densities of submitted bids seemed lognormal, so we adopt the following parametric specification for our two route auctions. With probability p, latent bids are distributed lognormal:

$$\begin{bmatrix} \ln b_1 \\ \ln b_2 \\ \ln b_{12} \end{bmatrix} \sim N\left(\begin{bmatrix} \mu_1(X^{it}) \\ \mu_2(X^{it}) \\ \mu_{12}(X^{it}) \end{bmatrix}, \begin{bmatrix} \sigma_{11}(X^{it}) & \sigma_{12}(X^{it}) & \sigma_{13}(X^{it}) \\ \sigma_{12}(X^{it}) & \sigma_{11}(X^{it}) & \sigma_{13}(X^{it}) \\ \sigma_{13}(X^{it}) & \sigma_{13}(X^{it}) & \sigma_{33}(X^{it}) \end{bmatrix} \right) \tag{22.2}$$

and with probability $1 - p$, they are distributed with values higher than the reserve price and so they are not observed.[13]

There are several elements worth emphasizing in this specification. First, the p parameter allows the specification to follow closely the empirical distribution of observed bids, yet, at the same time, account for the fact that in the order of 40 percent of the bidders did not submit any bid. Second, the specification in 22.2 imposes some symmetry between route 1 and route 2, conditional on route characteristics. The reason is that nothing a priori distinguishes route 1 from route 2 in our sample. Both of them are single routes and therefore, conditional on route characteristics, the distribution of bids for those routes should be the same. This symmetry restriction appears in the specification of the means, $\mu_1(X^{it}) = \mu_2(X^{it})$, and in the covariance terms, $\sigma_{11}(X^{it}) = \sigma_{22}(X^{it})$, and $\sigma_{13}(X^{it}) = \sigma_{23}(X^{it})$. Third, many bidders did not submit a bid on all routes and route packages in the auctions. Our interpretation is that they did not find it worthwhile to submit a bid that would have had a positive probability of winning. Similarly, bids on packages higher than the sum of the bids for the individual items are also not observed in practice. So, referring back to 22.2, although we assumed that the log of the latent bid on the package was lognormal, we only observe those bids that satisfy the package bid constraint strictly.

As an illustration, table 22.4 reports our estimates of the parameters of the three-dimensional distribution of bids for the simplest specification where the covariance matrix is not a function of the covariates X^{it}, $\mu_s(X^{it}) = \mu_1 + \beta \ln(ice_{st})$ if s is a single route, and $\mu_s(X^{it}) = \mu_{12} + \beta \ln(ice_{st})$ if s is the package route (ice_{st} is the internal cost estimate for route s in auction t).[14] The parameters were estimated using the method of moments, which yields consistent and asymptotically normal estimates.[15]

In section 22.3, we noted that a key driver of package bidding is the correlation in the environment that bidders are facing. Table 22.4 allows us to say more about this. The coefficient of correlation between the log of the bids on route 1 and those on route 2, σ_{12}/σ_{11}, is equal to 0.09. This measure of correlation looks at one bidder only. What matters in the objective function of a typical bidder is not the correlation among individual bids of a bidder, but the correlation in the low bids from the set of opponents on each route. In our data, the average number of potential bidders is 8.44. We computed the coefficient of correlation between the opponents' lowest bid on route 1 and the opponents' lowest bid on route 2, conditional on being lower than the reserve price, for a representative auction with eight potential bidders and an internal cost

Table 22.4

Estimates for the lognormal distribution

	Estimate	Std[a]
μ_1 (the mean of a single bid)	−0.5041	(0.4412)
μ_{12} (the mean of a package bid)	−0.3127	(0.4610)
ln(internal cost estimate)	1.0299	(0.0329)
σ_{11}	0.1170	(0.0194)
σ_{12}	0.0104	(0.0041)
σ_{13}	0.0713	(0.0131)
σ_{33}	0.0805	(0.0152)
p	0.3785	(0.0262)

[a] Standard deviations refer to asymptotic standard deviations.

estimate for the individual routes of £1,002,553. The coefficient of correlation is 0.19. There is positive correlation in the environment that bidders are facing. We revisit this issue in step 4.

22.5.3   Step 3: Computation of the Probabilities of Winning

Now that we have estimated the distribution of bids, we can estimate the probabilities of winning. Consider an auction with n potential bidders and characteristics X^t. Fix bidder i. His probability of winning route or package s is the probability that

$$b_s^i + B_{S\setminus s}^{-i} < \min_{t \subseteq \{1,2\}, t \neq s} \{B_S^{-i}, b_t^i + B_{S\setminus t}^{-i}\}$$

where B_t^{-i} denotes the best bid by bidder i's opponents on package t.[16]

The distribution of low bids of bidder i's opponents and therefore the probability that bidder i wins package s given his bid vector, $G_s(b^i|X^{it})$, can be recovered from the individual distributions estimated in step 2 by integration.[17]

22.5.4   Step 4: Infer the Costs

Bidder i's optimization problem in each auction is to decide what bids to submit on each route and package in order to maximize his expected payoff. Formally, bidder i solves:

$$\max_{b_1, b_2, b_{12}} \sum_{s \subseteq \{1,2\}} (b_s - c_s) G_s(b_1, b_2, b_{12}|X^{it}) \tag{22.3}$$

subject to the constraint that $b_{12} \leq b_1 + b_2$, and that the bids must meet the reserve price, R_s, on each route and on the package.

This maximization problem is almost everywhere differentiable so optimal bids must solve the three first order conditions. Notice that the only "unknowns" in expression 22.3 are the three costs, c_1, c_2, and c_{12}. The same applies for the first order conditions. We can describe conditions under which this system of equations can be used to infer the costs as follows: if we observe a full set of bids, all bids have a positive probability of winning and the package bid constraint does not bind, then we can identify all the costs. The argument is similar to the one we made above concerning the single unit auction.

A binding constraint introduces a degree of underidentification. Specifically, if a bidder only submitted a bid on route 1 and route 2, say, but not on the package, we can only identify an upper bound on the individual route costs, a lower bound on the package cost, and therefore an upper bound on the amount of synergy. Intuitively, if the cost for the package were really much lower than the sum of the costs of the individual routes, $c_1 + c_2$, the bidder would be especially eager to win both routes rather than one only. Submitting a bid on the package lower than the sum of the two individual bids, $b_{12} < b_1 + b_2$, helps him achieve this. By contrast, if running both routes together is much more expensive, the bidder would prefer to win only one route. Because he cannot submit a bid on the package greater than the sum of the two, he will submit $b_{12} = b_1 + b_2$. The constraint is binding. This explains why we can bound the synergy from above ("it must be at most x%") when the constraint is binding.

Finally, if the reserve price is binding for the package or for an individual route *but not for the package*, then we can infer that the cost for that particular route or package was higher than the reserve price. Intuitively, submitting a bid just below the reserve price for this route or for the package would not affect much the probability of winning the other routes, but because the probability of winning that route is not close to zero,[18] the benefit of such a bid is positive as long as the cost is lower than the reserve price.[19]

Table 22.5 illustrates this cost inference method for one particular auction. Five bidders participated in this auction. Bidders 1 and 3 submitted a full set of bids. Bidder 2 only submitted a bid on the second route, and bidders 4 and 5 submitted a bid only on routes 1 and 2. Their package bid is defined by their bids on the individual routes.

The probabilities of winning were generated from the results of table 22.4. The first order conditions for optimal bids were then used to solve for the costs.[20] Because bidders 1 and 3 submitted a full set of bids, we can identify their costs for each route and the package. These are given in columns 6, 7, and 8. For bidder 2, we could only identify his cost for route 2 and conclude that his cost for the package was above the reserve price. We cannot say anything about his cost for route 1. Finally, because bidders 4 and 5 did not submit a nontrivial package bid, we could only identify bounds on their costs.

Table 22.5
A sample of cost estimates for one two-route auction

	Bids (June 1995 Pounds)			Package discount (%)	Costs			Cost synergy (%)
	b_1	b_2	b_{12}		c_1	c_2	c_{12}	
1	338,175	411,925	749,763	0.045	284,908 (6,596)[a]	347,927 (7,408)	664,733 (9,877)	−4.45 (0.80)
2	n/a	532,343	n/a	n/a	n/a	491,452 (6,504)	$>R_{12}$	n/a
3	334,457	429,771	759,174	0.661	282,993 (6,344)	368,259 (7,392)	678,515 (9,751)	−4.19 (0.75)
4	448,847	371,101	819,948	0	<402,689 (7,294)	<301,861 (7,472)	>740,197 (9,240)	<−5.06 (1.10)
5	381,939	439,280	821,219	0	<341,737 (5,329)	<384,967 (6,406)	>744,290 (8,832)	<−2.42 (0.58)

[a] Standard deviations in parenthesis. $R_1 = 838,626$; $R_2 = 1,867,646$.
< indicates that the number given is an upper bound to the true parameter.
> indicates that it is a lower bound.

For this particular auction, the mark-up over costs suggested by table 22.5 is on average 16.1 percent for the individual routes and 11.4 percent for the package (due to the bounds in table 22.5, this measure underestimates the mark-up on individual routes and overestimates the mark-up on packages). This is consistent with the announced mark-ups in bidding documents.[21] The mark-ups are higher for the individual routes than for the package.

The last column of table 22.5 reports the relative cost synergy estimate, $(c_1 + c_2 - c_{12})/(c_1 + c_2)$. A negative number indicates that the inferred cost for the package is higher than the sum of the individual costs. The relative synergy estimates are negative for bidders 1, 3, 4, and 5. The negative sign is somewhat surprising given the motivation for using a combinatorial auction in the London bus routes market. They suggest that for this particular auction at least, package bidding may have been driven by the strategic motivation.

We end with two important caveats concerning the empirical results reported in this section. First, the specification used in table 22.4 is for illustration purposes only. Second, table 22.5 looks at a single auction only. It permits us to illustrate the way in which we infer costs. Nevertheless, the selected auction may not be representative of our sample. We carry out a fuller analysis in our companion paper. The results also suggest that the synergies are negative.

22.6   Conclusion

In London, the local transportation authority has used a form of combinatorial auction for the allocation of bus routes services since the mid 1980s. The reason for this choice was expected economic synergies among routes located in the same area of London.

The London bus routes tendering is considered a success. It has led to increased quality of service and lower costs. However, there was a range of design options for LRT to choose from, from the size of the auction, the definition of the items, to the auction rule. It is unclear whether their actual choice was the most appropriate.

This chapter has documented bidding behavior in the LRT auctions and presented a new method for inferring bidders' cost structure. We did not find that auction size affected bidding behavior much: in fact, competition and prices at the item level seemed uncorrelated with the size of the auction. Moreover, when we applied our cost inference method to the data, we found evidence for slight negative synergies across routes.

These results can be used to choose the parameters in human subjects experiments (Smith, foreword to this volume) or computational experiments (Leyton-Brown and Shoham, chapter 18) to evaluate alternative auction formats. Obvious candidates given our data analysis are a combinatorial auction that allows bidders to make exclusive bids and independent parallel or sequential single item auctions.

Acknowledgments

Funding from the Division of Research at Harvard Business School and the National Science Foundation (SES 0214222) is gratefully acknowledged.

Notes

1. Non-tendered routes remained operated by the subsidiaries of London Buses Limited under a negotiated block grant. The private operators and the subsidiaries competed for the tendered services.

2. As a benchmark, a typical garage, which is necessary to operate a route, has capacity for 50–100 buses and serves about eight routes.

3. In practice, the bidders in our data start expressing unease with this restriction for the auctions of six routes and more.

4. With respect to other choices that LRT made, we have little to say from a theoretical perspective. However, the next section looks at bidder participation and prices as a function of the auction size.

5. Formally, the argument assumes that $b_{12}^i < b_1^i + b_2^i$ so that lowering b_1^i slightly still satisfies LRT's package bid constraint. This is also the reason why lowering b_1^i only affects the winning

chances of b_{12}^i and not that of b_2^i. To see this, suppose that originally, bidder i wins item 2, i.e., $B_1^{-i} + b_2^i \in \arg\min\{b_1^i + B_2^{-i}, b_2^i + B_1^{-i}, B_{12}^{-i}, b_{12}^i\}$. We claim it cannot be the case that, after sligthly lowering b_1^i to $b_1^i - \varepsilon$, the winning allocation now becomes to give item 1 to bidder i. Indeed, $B_1^{-i} + b_2^i < b_{12}^i$ by assumption, which itself is lower than $b_1^i + b_2^i$ by the package bid constraint. This means that $B_1^{-i} < b_1^{-i}$ both before and after the slight decrease. But then this means that $b_1^{-i} + B_2^{-i} > B_1^{-i} + B_2^{-i} > B_{12}^{-i}$, which, in turn, is greater than $B_1^{-i} + b_2^i$ by assumption. Hence, lowering b_1^i has no effect on the winning probability of b_2^i.

6. Interestingly, we can compare this with the tradeoff a bidder faces in a single item auction. The marginal benefit is the same, but the cost is only in terms of profit margin.

7. To simplify the argument, we are being slightly cavalier with the math. This is inessential for the argument. More formal analyses of this kind of problem appear in Adams and Yellen 1976, McAfee, McMillan, and Whinston 1989, and Armstrong 1996, for example.

8. These papers do not deal with the combinatorial first price auction proper but with the monopoly multiproduct pricing problem. As argued in our companion paper, the mathematical structure of the two problems is identical. Therefore the results also apply to the combinatorial first price auction.

9. The peak vehicle requirement determines how many buses the winning operator will need to commit to the contract.

10. We have not coded the data on package bids for auctions with more than nine routes. Hence the entry for the column 10–21 and the overall value are left blank.

11. Additional technical details appear in Cantillon and Pesendorfer 2004.

12. Auction characteristics for auction t are denoted by the vector X^t. We use the notation X^{it} to stress the fact that they are viewed from bidder i's perspective. Hence, $f(c_1, \ldots, c_S | X^{it})$ refers to $f_i(c_1, \ldots, c_S | X^t)$.

13. In the absence of a characterization result of the equilibrium in the combinatorial first price auction, we have no guarantee that the equilibrium takes exactly this shape. The objective here is to stay as close to the data as possible.

14. Because the log of the internal cost estimate explains 90 percent of the variation in the log of bids, the internal cost estimate is the most reasonable covariate to include in a sparse specification.

15. Specifically, we used the first and second moments of the distribution, conditional on the bids not being censored, as well as the probability of not submitting any bid. The first moment for the individual route bids was interacted with a dummy and with $\ln(ice_{st})$ as instruments, leading to a total of eight moment conditions, i.e., an exactly identified model. For estimation purposes, the reserve price was set equal to twice the internal cost estimate.

16. $S \backslash s$ denotes the set of both routes, S, minus the route(s) in s. By convention, $B_\emptyset^{-i} = 0$.

17. Practically, this involves multidimensional integrals that are difficult to evaluate numerically, so we implement this using Monte Carlo integration. Notice that our method requires that we solve the winner determination problem at each draw.

18. Indeed, there is always a chance that no other bidders submitted a bid on that route or package.

19. If the bidder submitted a bid on route 2 but not on route 1 and the package, we cannot say anything. Indeed, it may be that his cost for route 1 is lower than the reserve price but that his cost of operating both routes is very high. Submitting a bid on route 1 will define (through the package bid constraint) a bid on the package and run him the risk of winning both routes!

20. Given that the probabilities of winning were generated by Monte Carlo integration (step 3) and are therefore step functions, numerical differentiation was used. Due to the nature of the function for the first order condition, the delta method for computing the standard errors on the cost parameters could not be implemented numerically. Instead, we computed the standard errors on the basis of the cost estimates inferred from 250 draws from the bid distribution parameters. Errors due to the Monte Carlo integration contribute to an additional 1 percent error on the coefficients.

21. In their bidding documents, bidders were asked to provide an estimate of the costs associated with their bids. We did not have access to that information on a systematic basis as bidders report costs on a small sample only. Additionally, the measure may not be accurate as bidders may misreport costs. However, bidders' announced margins range between 10 percent and 15 percent.

References

Adams, William and Janey Yellen (1976), "Commodity Bundling and the Burden of Monopoly," *Quarterly Journal of Economics*, 90, 475–498.

Armstrong, Mark (1996), "Multi-Product Nonlinear Pricing," *Econometrica*, 64, 51–75.

Armstrong, Mark and Jean Charles Rochet (1999), "Multi-Dimensional Screening: A User's Guide," *European Economic Review*, 43, 959–979.

Beaumont, Helen and Michael Watson (1999), "Review of Bus Tendering in the Greater London Area," LRT Manuscript.

Cantillon, Estelle and Martin Pesendorfer (2004), "Combination Bidding in Multi-Unit Auctions," Working Paper, Harvard Business School and London School of Economics.

Kennedy, David, Stephen Glaister, and Tony Travers (1995), "London Bus Tendering, Greater London Group," Report, London School of Economics.

Glaister, Stephen and Michael Beesley (1991), "Bidding for Tendered Bus Routes in London," *Transportation Planning and Technology*, 15, 349–366.

McAfee, R. Preston, John McMillan, and Michael D. Whinston (1989), "Multiproduct Monopoly, Commodity Bundling and Correlation of Values," *Quarterly Journal of Economics*, 102, 371–383.

23 Industrial Procurement Auctions

Martin Bichler, Andrew Davenport, Gail Hohner, and Jayant Kalagnanam

23.1 Introduction

As illustrated in the previous chapters, combinatorial auctions have successfully been applied to various application domains, such as the allocation of airspace system resources (chapter 20), truckload transportation (chapter 21), and bus routes (chapter 22). Industrial procurement is potentially a huge application domain for combinatorial auctions, and it has turned into a topic of interest for software vendors and procurement managers in the business to business (B2B domain). A number of applications have been reported, but unfortunately, possibly because of efforts to protect proprietary information and competitive advantages, there is little documentation and public information on details of the design of combinatorial auctions in industrial procurement. The focus of this chapter is on describing current practice in this domain. We will also provide a case study of procurement auctions at Mars, Incorporated, in order to illustrate the particularities in this field.

Several authors have analyzed the dynamics of traditional procurement auctions (Dasgupta and Spulber 1989; Laffont and Tirole 1993). Although some firms, for example, GlaxoSmithKline, are already using electronic auctions for over a third of their spending (Hannon 2004), the average level of adoption is much lower. The Center for Advanced Purchasing Studies (CAPS) interviewed e-auction users, suppliers who have participated in e-auctions, technology and service providers, and firms that have rejected the use of e-auctions. The study found that more than 35 percent of firms who spend $100 million or more are using e-auctions. The level of spending users put through e-auctions is less than 5 percent, but growing steadily (Beall et al. 2003). Estimating the monetary value of goods awarded through electronic auctions is very difficult, and comprehensive quantitative data are not available. Below is a summary illustrating estimates of purchasing via electronic auctions.

- The 2004 global volume being purchased using electronic auctions is on the order of hundreds of billions of euros (Plant 2004).

• More than 40 percent of large firms (over $100 million in spending) surveyed in North America are using auctions for procurement up from 20 percent two years ago (Beall et al. 2003).

• Less than 3 percent of large firms (over $100 million in spending) surveyed in North America say that they have completed their adoption of e-procurement business processes (Beall et al. 2003).

Nearly all of the procurement auctions being run today in the private sector are single unit English auctions. The fact that it is very difficult to satisfactorily value the complex nature of business relationships in a single price parameter accounts for much of the negative press written about electronic auctions. Many procurement negotiations require the use of special auction protocols that allow for negotiation of multiple attributes, multiple units, or multiple items. Auctions with such complex bid types are also called *multidimensional auctions*. Combinatorial auctions have emerged as a powerful mechanism to automate complex procurement negotiations on multiple items.

Some of the first procurement applications of combinatorial auctions include Net Exchange's auction for Sears Logistics (Ledyard et al. 2002), a combinatorial auction at The Home Depot (Elmaghraby and Keskinocak 2002), a combinatorial auction for school meals in Chile (Epstein et al. 2002), and one for packaging materials and raw materials for different manufacturing locations at a large chocolate manufacturer (Hohner et al. 2003). Some companies already provide software platforms for conducting combinatorial procurement auctions, such as CombineNet (〈http://www.combinenet.com〉), Net Exchange[1] (〈http://www.nex.com〉), and TradeExtensions (〈http://www.tradeextensions.com〉), and these software vendors have reported several applications in press releases (P&G, Siemens, and Volvo). This chapter draws on information from these primary vendors of combinatorial auction software, as well as the practical experience of Mars, Incorporated with proprietary combinatorial auction software, developed with IBM's T.J. Watson Research Lab.

23.2   Procurement Operations

Industrial procurement managers are customarily responsible for the whole sourcing process. They determine specifications, choose a portfolio of possible suppliers, and negotiate price/conditions simultaneously through multiple bilateral bargaining. Typically, in the private sector, they commit to particular negotiation parameters such as quality, quantity, and price as late as possible. Prolonging commitment to any particular parameter is often seen as the best practice in that it allows all possible conditional offers from the supply pool. For a purchasing manager with a complex set of parameters and constraints, this iterative bargaining process allows them to find a feasible solution within their constraints while maximizing the number of bids received from their supply pool. In contrast, in the public sector, legal requirements often dictate a more formal process with commitment earlier on in the process: a completely defined specification, preferences for some supplier categories (e.g., minority owned businesses), written submissions of bids, and publication of all offers received.

23.2.1 Procurement Auctions

When industrial procurement managers use auctions, they need to commit to certain product specifications and constraints early in the process, which is similar to public sector negotiations. Procurement managers first need to define their requirements, analyze market conditions for the materials and service markets in which they operate, commit to a specification, and finally develop a portfolio of potential suppliers. Only then do they begin the process of requesting bids. Figure 23.1 illustrates the general process.

This process requires many industrial procurement managers to adapt their negotiation behavior considerably. For example, in combinatorial procurement auctions, buyers have to define exactly the items that need to be purchased, as well as various additional constraints on the number of winners, and so on (see section 23.3.5). In the private sector, precisely defining many goods and services for an auction may be a challenge. This is especially true when the items are complex or part of contracts that

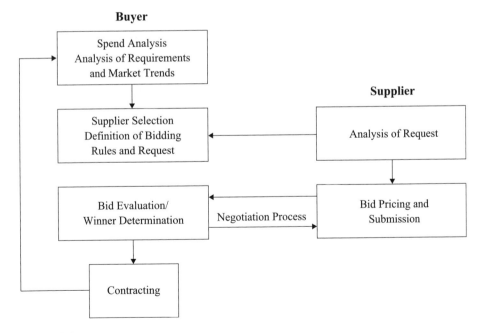

Figure 23.1
Sourcing cycle.

include extra non-quantifiable benefits. Complex items are often purchased from incomplete specifications. This is particularly true if the item has been developed with a single supplier. Standard practice within the supplier's operations sometimes are not codified in the specification. In large consumer packaging contracts, research and development support and product innovation are often included as noninvoiced benefits in the contract. Also, deciding on the granularity of items in a package auction can be a challenge.

In addition, a purchasing manager has to balance many competing business issues, such as:

- Significance of the material or service to the overall business
- Cost, and variance at risk, of the material or service
- Market power of suppliers
- Number of suppliers available
- Cost of switching suppliers
- Cost of managing additional suppliers
- Risk of reduced supply pool
- Assurance of long-term supply.

In a combinatorial auction, one can consider some of these issues as overall allocation constraints, but they need to be defined at the beginning. Also here, procurement managers have difficulties committing to particular constraints a priori. Therefore, in many cases in private industry, auctions are run without commitment on the buyer's side. In most cases, even the winner determination is not entirely automated, and there is some human judgment involved. This is often referred to as *scenario analysis*, where after each round the auctioneer performs some type of what if analysis and reveals his current preferred scenario. This scenario analysis can be performed manually by solving various winner determination problems, or can even be automated (Boutilier, Sandholm, and Shields 2004). As a consequence, software for combinatorial procurement auctions needs to be flexible in a variety of ways. First of all, it must support a rich bidding language (see section 23.3.3). Apart from simple package bids, purchasing managers use multiattribute bids, volume discount bids, and combinations of all three. Second, in order to reach implementable solutions, it is essential that procurement managers can easily define various types of allocation constraints to express legal, contractual, and business rules capturing strategic and operative considerations (see section 23.3.5).

23.2.2   The Use of Combinatorial Auctions in Procurement

Combinatorial auctions have been used for many varied materials and services including various types of packaging (bottles, cans, cartons, flexibles, etc.), chemicals, road construction and repair in different geographical areas, office supplies, and so on.

Goods and services purchased with combinatorial auctions tend to be comprised of large numbers of discrete items, some of which have strong complementarities (e.g., routes within a logistics network, or packaging materials fabricated on the same production equipment). Transportation (see chapter 21 of this volume) is a huge application area for all combinatorial auction providers. To date, most have involved high spending levels. In packaging and logistics, renegotiations incur high transaction costs, and switching costs from one supplier to another are high; therefore, it is standard practice to commit to long-term contracts of one year or more, in order to recoup the costs. However, software automating combinatorial auctions has the potential to reduce significantly the transaction costs of the renegotiation process.

In our survey of combinatorial auction software vendors, the number of items included in private procurement auctions ranged from ten to nearly 100,000. In public procurement, the span was more moderate, ranging from twenty to fifty items per auction. The number of bidders ranged from only a few up to several hundreds, but ten to twenty bidders were most common. This is also the maximum number of suppliers a buyer would negotiate with simultaneously. Using the automation of electronic auctions significantly lowers the time investment required per participating supplier; consequently, bids may be collected from a larger pool of suppliers. In this aspect, commitment is pushed to the end of the process by maintaining a larger supply pool into the bidding. More suppliers are active in the process for a longer period, increasing competition.

Over the last five years there has been a trend toward the reduction in the supply base for large companies. The control of allocation constraints (e.g., the number of suppliers receiving business, see section 23.3.5) in combinatorial auction software has been considered very useful in this respect. One vendor even reported an application with more than 130,000 constraints. In general, the size of problems (number of items and suppliers) reported varied considerably across the participating vendors. Often combinatorial auctions have led to high reductions in procurement costs. Some part of these reductions may accrue by using a small number of low-cost suppliers. Such extreme outcomes need to be managed using allocation constraints, as in most strategic sourcing exercises, maintaining a good supplier pool is an important goal. Table 23.1 provides a summary of responses from CombineNet, Net Exchange, and TradeExtensions.

23.3 Procurement Auction Design

In the following we summarize some of the particularities of designing combinatorial procurement auctions. We will discuss auction design goals, the protocols used, winner determination, and the allocation constraints typically used in procurement operations.

Table 23.1
Summary of data and estimates provided by selected software vendors

	Minimum	Average	Maximum
Number of items	10	250	90,000
Number of bidders	2	15	300
Transaction volume/auction	$50,000	$5 million	$1 billion
Reduction in procurement cost	0%	13%	75%
Reduction in size of supplier base	10%	25%	50%
Duration of the auctions (active bidding)	30 minutes	1 day	Several weeks

23.3.1   Auction Design

Part I of this book discussed mechanism design questions and various types of sealed bid and iterative auction formats. One goal in economic theory is the *allocative efficiency*, in which the auction mechanism maximizes the total payoff across all agents. Another goal is the *revenue maximization (cost minimization respectively)*, in which the auction maximizes the revenue to a particular participant, usually the auctioneer. Cost minimization is also considered a central design goal for purchasing managers.

In addition, procurement specialists involved in combinatorial auctions highlight design issues, which are less well defined. For example, *supplier perceived fairness* is rated very high. This is achieved through higher transparency of the negotiation, but also through additional *allocation constraints*, which guarantee that all suppliers are considered in the allocation, or that certain minority suppliers receive a particular share of the pie. The notion of fairness is considered critical in strategic procurement, in which long-term relationships are key. One specific notion of fairness that we will discuss in detail in later sections is related to time of bid arrival. In cases where there are multiple cost minimizing allocations, it is important that bids that arrived early are given some preference. This is in fact quite common, as in a competitive bidding situation there are often multiple solutions and tie-breaking policies need to be well thought out.

Some purchasing managers consider the *speed* of the auction important. After the initial savings have been accrued, efficiency of the process continues to deliver savings to the business. For example, without the use of formal protocols (such as auctions), the negotiation process itself might take weeks. However, the use of auction protocols often helps substantially to reduce the time to reach an outcome. Other design goals have to do with the software implementations in use. Combinatorial auction software needs to be *robust*, and *easy to use*. In addition it should be *flexible* and allow for various types of *allocation constraints* and various *types of bids*, which we will discuss in the next section. This is important, because the requirements tend to vary considerably across different procurement applications, depending on the type of good and the particular market structure.

23.3.2 Auction Protocol

Auction design can be described as a set of rules that motivate the bidders to reveal their true valuations to the extent that makes it possible for the auctioneer to solve for the cost minimizing allocation. We will categorize these auction rules as follows:

- The *auction protocol*, i.e., the syntax, semantics (i.e., bidding language), and sequence of messages exchanged throughout the auction.
- The *winner determination rules*, which include the overall objective of the allocation (i.e., efficiency vs. cost minimization), as well as additional allocation constraints.
- The *payment rules*, which determine the payment to the winner(s).

Part I of this book discusses a number of different auction protocols, including sealed-bid combinatorial auctions, Vickrey Clarke Groves (VCG) mechanisms, and various types of iterative auction formats. To our knowledge, the VCG mechanism has not been used for procurement auctions, because of the unreasonable demands it would place on bidders. First of all, bidders need to reveal their entire utility function, that is, to submit bids for all $2^m - 1$ possible bundles, where m is the number of items. This leads to a high valuation complexity for the bidders, but also to a large input size to the winner determination problem. In addition, the determination of the Vickrey payments itself becomes a computationally hard problem. Another problem is the need of a trusted auctioneer. The winner in a second price auction needs to be sure that the auctioneer does not reveal his valuations to other auction participants, or to the buyer, which might put him in a disadvantage in future negotiations. Finally, there is the issue of budget balance. If Vickrey payments are made to all participants including the buyer, then the total Vickrey payments might actually be less than the total revenue realized from the auction—this is clearly not acceptable and hence some modified versions of VCG that incorporate budget balance as a hard constraint need to be considered (see Parkes, Kalagnanam, and Eso 2001).

Generalizations of the *first-price sealed bid auction* have been used in public procurement, which is a huge application area. For example, European government spending on goods and services represents about 16 percent of the EU-wide GDP. For the future, the European Commission has proposed to allow for the implementation of more dynamic methods in public procurement, such as the use of iterative reverse auctions. The majority of procurement auctions in the private sector are run as *multiple-round auctions*. The main differences of these multiple-round formats lie in the information feedback that is given to the bidders in each round. Most vendors provide at least price information about the winning bid set. Some vendors also allow for the computation of linear prices (see Kwasnica et al. 2005), and some applications even use nonlinear prices. In particular, if the complementarities are considerable, the price feedback becomes more important. None of the vendors have mentioned clock auctions.

One observation is that many bidders are used to bidding in traditional request for quotes (RFQ), where the initial round of bidding is often followed by additional rounds of bilateral bargaining. Using straightforward sealed-bid combinatorial auctions often leads to the fact that bidders bid too high. This corresponds with the claim by some procurement specialists that iterative combinatorial auction formats induce competition among suppliers. Additionally, most bidders are not able or willing to bid on all possible combinations. In general, iterative combinatorial auctions avoid the need for the supplier to specify the entire cost structure at once, and are helpful for the bidders, in particular when the bidders' values are correlated, because they allow bidders to learn about the value of the good by seeing other bidders' bids (Milgrom and Weber 1982). In general, the burden of reporting entire cost might not be eliminated by an iterative procedure. However, in a well-designed auction the items and the price feedback are chosen in a way that reduces a chance of potentially having to elicit too many valuations. A frequently used argument for both the bidders and the auctioneer is that iterative combinatorial auctions lead to a more transparent market because the alternative to conducting combinatorial procurement auctions is usually simultaneous bilateral bargaining, where there is no transparency whatsoever. This way, suppliers get a better understanding of competitive market rates.

Iterative combinatorial auctions are the most common auction protocol for procurement applications. A number of issues need to be considered in iterative combinatorial auctions. One of these issues is *tie breaking*. Consider the following example: a combinatorial auction is created to purchase some quantities of items A, B, C. In the first round of the auction, supplier 1 makes a bid b1 for items A, B, C at a price of $100, and supplier 2 submits a bid b2 of $30 for item A. Finally, supplier 3 enters the auction with a bid b3 for items B, C at $70. There are two potential solutions to this winner determination problem: either bid b1 or the combination of bids b2, b3. In both cases the total cost to the buyer is $100. Time stamping is one method to deal with these situations. We refer the reader to Parkes (chapter 2 of this volume), Hohner et al. (2003), and Pekeč and Rothkopf (2003) for a discussion of tie breaking strategies and many other issues in iterative combinatorial auctions, such as the setting of minimal bid increments, reserve prices, and strategies for dealing with infeasibilities in initial auction rounds.

23.3.3 Bidding Languages

Procurement specialists in the field emphasize the importance of flexible bidding languages. The flexibility of the bidding language is important because it can enhance or hinder the ability of bidders to express their preferences. In addition, the expressiveness allowed has a considerable impact on the economic and computational properties of the auction. This has prompted research that examines bidding languages and their expressiveness and the impact on winner determination (see chapter 9 of this volume).

The bidding language is closely related with the type of goods and the market structure. For example, in markets where multiple units are being bought or sold it becomes necessary to allow bids that express preferences over multiple units. Some common bid types that have been examined in the literature in addition to package bids are:

- indivisible bids with price-quantity pairs, where the price is for the total amount bid and this is to be treated as an all-or-nothing bid, as is typically the case in multiunit auctions
- divisible bids with a price schedule, for example volume discounted bids, such as in Davenport and Kalagnanam 2000
- multiattribute bids, which specify various attribute levels and a price (Bichler 2001).

Volume discount auctions are specifically tailored to industries where volume discounts are common, for example, bulk chemicals and agricultural commodities. In a volume discount auction, suppliers provide bids that are specified as a curve with a quantity range associated with each price level (e.g., \$500/unit up to 100 units, \$450/unit over 100 units). These auctions may deal with one product or many. Multiattribute bids are used for the procurement of complex goods and services. These auctions allow bidding on price and qualitative attributes, where bids are evaluated by a scoring rule or function. Multiattribute auctions are useful if supplier offerings are close substitutes. We will refer to these different bid types as the bidding language and discuss some of the known types briefly.

With multiple items or multiattribute bids the preference structure of bidders can be exponentially large. As previous chapters already discussed, if there are m items and the bidder has superadditive preferences, then in general the bidder could specify 2^m bids. Multiattribute offers with multiple binary attributes lead to a similar informational complexity. Therefore an additional consideration is to provide a compact bid representation language that allows bidders easily to specify a large space of possible offers. Several researchers have proposed mechanisms for specifying bids logically. These combinatorial bids, also know as logical bidding languages, have two flavors:

- logical combinations of goods as formulae
- logical combinations of bundles as formulae

Nisan (chapter 9 of this volume) provides an overview focusing on combinatorial auctions. Bichler and Kalagnanam (2004) explore similar issues of concise representation of preferences over multiattribute items.

Software for combinatorial procurement auctions typically supports various logical combinations of package bids. Multiattribute bidding is common and is a way to incorporate qualitative attributes such as ISO certification, brand name, and so on. Threshold levels and weighted additive scoring functions are often used to evaluate these multiattribute bids (Keeny and Raiffa 1993). In addition, there are many cases where qualitative attributes are added to traditional package bids. Volume discount bids are less commonly available in commercial software.

23.3.4 Winner Determination

Part III of this book discussed winner determination in detail. Ideally, every time a new bid is received in an iterative procurement auction, bid evaluation could be triggered to identify the provisional winners. However, because winner determination in combinatorial auctions is NP-hard, this is usually impractical. In addition, the introduction of allocation constraints impacts the runtime to solve these problems, as Davenport and Kalagnanam (2000) show. As a result, it is difficult to identify the provisional winners with every new bid. The compromise is typically a multiround design where the new bids are accumulated within a certain time interval.

Although it might seem computationally expedient, approximate solutions are considered unacceptable in procurement auctions that are run with commitment, because the difference between an approximate solution and the real solution can significantly change how much and exactly which business a single supplier receives. For example, a supplier who receives an allocation in the optimal[2] solution might receive nothing in an approximate solution. These types of occurrences, if made public, could destroy the credibility of an auction mechanism. However, as indicated, in the private sector auctions are often run without commitment. In some cases (e.g., scenario analysis) the combinatorial optimization is used to perform an accurate dollar valued tradeoff analysis after each round of bidding, but buyers do not commit to any of the constraints until at some point they make a decision.

The winner determination depends essentially on the bidding language and the allocation constraints used. Many software vendors use their own custom code to solve these problems, but some also use commercial off-the-shelf mixed integer programming solvers. For scenario analysis, companies such as CombineNet offer complete packages that help the user analyze various allocations, mostly including multiple items and attributes (Boutilier, Sandholm, and Shields 2004; Sandholm and Suri 2001).

23.3.5 Allocation Constraints

There are many types of allocation rules that one needs to consider throughout an auction, such as eligibility, reservation prices, and so on. Some of them need to be considered while solving the winner determination problem. Winner constraints, budget limits, market share constraints, and quality constraints are general types of allocation constraints that appear in many procurement auctions.

Procurement experts typically distinguish between *single-sourcing* or *multisourcing*. This determines whether the goods are purchased from a single supplier or multiple ones. On a more general level, a *winner constraint* in a combinatorial auction determines the minimum and maximum allowable number of winning bids. For example, buyers want to make sure that the entire supply is not sourced from too few suppliers, because this creates a high exposure if some of them are not able to deliver on their promise. On the other hand, having too many suppliers creates a high overhead cost in terms of managing a large number of supplier relationships.

In long-term relationships with multiple suppliers, *market share constraints* on a group level are of considerable importance. For example, representation constraints specify that at least one minority supplier is included in the set of winners. Winner constraints can also be considered as a special case of market share constraints. This means the number of winners and market share that are required from different supplier groups can be restricted.

Another constraint is *volume-based budget limits*, which are often placed as an upper limit on the total volume of the transaction with a particular supplier. In a reverse auction, these limits could either be on the total spending or on the total quantity awarded to a supplier. These types of constraints are largely motivated (in a procurement setting) by considerations that the dependency on any particular supplier is managed. Similarly, often constraints are placed on the minimum amount or minimum spend on any transaction; that is, if a supplier is picked for sourcing, then the transaction should be of a minimum size. Such constraints reduce the overhead of managing a large number of very small contracts.

Some combinatorial reverse auctions also consider multiple attributes of a purchase, where it is necessary to restrict qualitative attributes of an allocation. Threshold levels for qualitative attributes can easily be checked at the time of the bid submission. Others need to be considered during the winner determination. For example, one constraint is to specify that all the winning bids must have the same value for some attributes. For example, if boxes are being bought from three different suppliers, then it is important that all boxes perform identically in the packaging equipment. Such constraints can be generalized to allow selection of winning bids such that for an attribute of interest all bids have values adjacent to each other.

Software vendors such as CombineNet or TradeExtension offer a wide variety of such constraints and distinguish among several dozens or hundreds of constraint classes (average capacity, attribute value, etc.). Most common are quality constraints, as well as winner constraints. Allocation constraints can impact the runtime of the winner determination considerably. Davenport and Kalagnanam (2000) offer a detailed discussion. See also Bichler and Kalagnanam 2004. The question whether to communicate allocation constraints to the bidders is an important design question, which could impact bidder behavior. Experimental analysis might help to analyze the impact of this and many other design choices in combinatorial auctions (e.g., limits on the number of bids per bidder, etc.).

23.3.6 Business Impact

There are a number of reasons why procurement managers use combinatorial auctions. The primary motivation is cost savings in complex negotiation scenarios. Using package bids, it is possible to represent complementarities or substitutabilities that occur as a consequence of production and/or transportation cost savings. As described in section 23.3.3, many complex auctions are not limited to package bids. Some vendors emphasize that their tools allow users accurately to model and analyze the thousands of price and nonprice attributes that influence the true cost of sourcing. The respective software packages are sometimes used more as decision analysis tools that allow procurement managers to understand the effects that their business rules and other constraints have on the total spent. A secondary benefit, which is shared by all participants, is time efficiency. Huge amounts of data can be uploaded and processed with greatly increased effectiveness.

In addition, combinatorial auctions provide an opportunity to impact the market structure. In price-only procurement auctions suppliers can only submit bids on the entire contract, restricting competition to big suppliers. Combinatorial auctions make it easier to split large contracts into smaller ones, allowing small bidders to compete. This is an important issue in some public procurement operations or for private firms developing their supply base.

From a supplier's point of view, the main advantage of package bids is the elimination of the exposure problem. Some bidders find it quite natural to submit package bids, others have problems with the new technology and do not make use of package bids at all. As a result, the calculation of market clearing prices is still an issue, as well as decision support for bidders to help them make better bids. Some suppliers emphasize the increased market transparency as compared to multiple bilateral bargaining, whereas others mention the high perceived fairness of the procedure, although there are different opinions on this issue. We will discuss some of these issues in the case study in the next section.

23.4 Case Study: Mars, Incorporated

In the following section, we will highlight some of the main aspects of combinatorial auctions used at Mars, Incorporated. These auctions are run with commitment and illustrate a number of typical features of procurement auction applications.[3]

23.4.1 Procurement Operations at Mars, Incorporated

Mars, Incorporated relies on a limited number of suppliers for each material and service it procures. Small supply pools may arise by necessity as well as design. For example, many agricultural inputs are available from a limited number of origins, a limited number of brokers, and/or under tariff regimes that limit the number of supplies. Buyers are responsible for existing supplier relationships and the development of new sources as well as contract conditions and price. A buyer may be responsible for up to fifty relationships. Many different buying techniques are used to address the large number of different purchasing situations. One-to-one bargaining and sealed bid tendering are the most common forms of negotiation. In addition, auctions have emerged as a popular mechanism for implementing negotiations. Procurement auctions take place with a set of precertified suppliers on an electronic private exchange.

Combinatorial auctions are used for strategic purchases, typically characterized by 1) small and fairly static supply pools, 2) long-term relationships, and 3) significant business integration. The contracts in strategic purchases typically are of high value, are renewed quarterly or annually, and require the use of special business rules to constrain the winner determination.

23.4.2 Procurement Auction Design

Over eighteen months beginning in early 2000 Mars, Incorporated worked together with IBM Research to create an electronic private exchange supporting a variety of multidimensional auction formats. The bidding language consists of:

- package bids
- volume discount bids, where suppliers could specify price schedules such as $3,000 for up to 125 units, $2,900 for 126–150 units, etc.
- multiattribute bids, where buyers predefined the attributes required for an item (e.g., payment terms, turnaround time, delivery schedule, product quality: material, color, etc.).

Of these types, volume discount bidding and multiattribute bidding have been the most utilized. In the following, however, we will focus on combinatorial auctions. The design goals were to support complex procurement auctions, in a "do it yourself" software environment for the buyer, to provide optimization of complex bids that buyers could not perform for themselves, to lower transaction costs, and to increase the transparency of the process.

Mars, Incorporated has a strong corporate culture of mutuality with its suppliers, which determined some of the auction design choices, and therefore, unlike many private industrial auctions, Mars chose to run auctions with commitment on both sides (as long as reserve prices were met). Mars chose an *iterative auction format* for the following reasons:

1. It mirrored the iterative nature of negotiations, a process the supply pool was familiar with and accepted.

2. It allowed suppliers to rethink and resubmit bids that were not competitive or submitted by mistake.

3. It was simple and time efficient. Suppliers submitted only bids on bundles they were interested in, as opposed to VCG mechanisms.

Another important aspect of the design was related to specific criteria for tie-breaking that was closely associated with the supplier perceptions of "fair allocations." It is often the case that in intermediate rounds new bids arrive that lead to multiple cost minimizing allocations. In these settings, it is very important that the allocation engine does not change the set of suppliers at the same cost level in subsequent allocations. These were handled by the engine by providing time stamps to the bids based on their time of arrival and evaluating the bids on the primary criteria of cost minimization and as a secondary criterion of choosing the allocation that arrived first. The next section discusses implications of this on the allocation engine.

The winning set of bids is announced to all participants. Nonwinning bids are only visible to the supplier who placed them. Although this methodology negates the possibility of suppliers formulating complementary package bids based on others' bids, the loss is not felt to be significant. Suppliers create package bids that reflect their own particular complementarities, and they create package bids for the purpose of volume aggregation, with accompanying price discounts. A particular aspect of this combinatorial procurement auction is that typically each bidder provides per unit prices for each of the items and typically provides package bids as discounting rules for allocations of multiple items. In each round, the lowest per unit prices for each item provides a basis for calculating the prices for nonwinning bundles. Up until now, there is very little evidence of strategic behavior among bidders. On average, less than 5 percent of the bids placed were package bids. There also has been a notable occurrence of superadditive bids (e.g., package bids where the price is below the sum of prices for single items). In contrast, during volume discount auctions, more than 80 percent of the bids placed utilized the ability to vary price with volume, rather than offering a constant price. This might be explained by that fact that the bid expression for volume discount bids is quite similar to standard price quoting practices in situations where it was utilized. In contrast, bid expression for package bidding was not familiar to any of our participants prior to the auction.

Suppliers may remain active throughout the auction without placing a bid. All bids placed must be a certain percentage lower than any previous bid placed by that supplier on the particular package.

The auctions run on the Mars, Incorporated private electronic exchange typically run for one hour (longer if the number of bids or value of the auction is particularly large). Once the stated end time has been reached, the active time is extended in ten-minute increments as long as bids are received. As soon as there is a ten-minute period without a new bid placed, the auction ceases.

23.4.3 Winner Determination and Allocation Constraints

The winner determination engine for Mars, Incorporated was developed as an independent optimization module in C++ that was then integrated with a web-based auction platform. Combinatorial optimization was used for this problem by modeling it as an integer program and using a commercial off-the-shelf MIP solver. The winner determination algorithms have later been extended and embedded in a Java object framework (Bichler et al. 2002) to include multiattribute auctions and volume discount auctions. In the following, we will describe a basic problem formulation used for winner determination in combinatorial procurement auctions and the most important allocation constraints. Davenport and Kalagnanam (2000) offer more detailed description including volume discount auctions.

We are given $j \in L$ bids, and a set of M items indexed with $k = 1, \ldots, m$. Each supplier $i \in N$ submits a set of L^i bids. We associate with each bid B_{ij} a zero-one vector a_{ij}^k, where $a_{ij}^k = 1$ if bid B_{ij} will supply the entire quantity demanded for item k, and zero otherwise. Each bid B_{ij} offers a price p_{ij} at which the bidder is willing to supply the combination of items in the bid. The basic mixed integer programming formulation for the reverse combinatorial auction can be written as follows:

$$\text{Minimize} \sum_{i \in N} \sum_{j \in L^i} p_{ij} x_{ij}$$

$$\text{subject to} \sum_{i \in N} \sum_{j \in L^i} a_{ij}^k x_{ij} \geq 1 \quad \forall k \in M, \tag{23.1a}$$

$$x_{ij} \in \{0, 1\} \quad \forall i \in N, \forall j \in L^i. \tag{23.1b}$$

The decision variable x_{ij} takes the value 1 if the bid B_{ij} is a winning bid in the auction, and 0 otherwise. Constraint 23.1a states that the total number of units of each item in all the winning bids must satisfy the demand the buyer has for this item. Note that an optimal supply solution may over-satisfy demand. If there is free disposal or no considerable holding costs, this might be acceptable or even desirable. A departure from the conventional combinatorial auction formulation is that the solver software considers a number of additional allocation constraints:

- The total number of winning suppliers must be at least a minimum number to avoid depending too heavily on just a few suppliers.
- The total number of winning suppliers must be at most a maximum number to avoid the administrative overhead of managing a large number of suppliers.

• The maximum amount procured from each supplier is bounded to limit exposure to a single supplier.
• The minimum amount procured from each supplier is bounded to avoid receiving economically inefficient orders (e.g., less than a full truck load).
• If there are alternative winning bid sets, then one needs to pick the set that arrived first.

The following winner constraints can be added to the MIP formulation as follows:

$$W_{i,min}y_i \leq \sum_{k \in M} \sum_{j \in L^i} a_{ij}^k Q^k x_{ij} \quad \forall i \in N \tag{23.1c}$$

$$\sum_{k \in M} \sum_{j \in L^i} a_{ij}^k Q^k x_{ij} \leq W_{i,max}y_i \quad \forall i \in N \tag{23.1d}$$

$$\sum_{j \in L^i} x_{ij} \geq y_i \quad \forall i \in N \tag{23.1e}$$

$$S_{min} \leq \sum_{i \in N} y_i \leq S_{max} \tag{23.1f}$$

$y_i \in \{0,1\} \quad \forall i \in N.$

For each item there is a demand for Q^k units of the item. The terms $W_{i,min}$ and $W_{i,max}$ define the minimum and maximum quantity that can be allocated to any supplier i. Constraints (23.1c) and (23.1d) restrict the total allocation to any supplier to lie within the range $(W_{i,min}, W_{i,max})$. Note that y_i is an indicator variable that takes the value 1 if supplier i is allocated any item. Notice that if $W_{i,min} = 0$, then y_i becomes a free variable. In order to fix this, a constraint (23.1e) is introduced which ensures that $y_i = 0$ if no bids from supplier i are chosen. S_{min} and S_{max} relate to the minimum and maximum number of winners required for the allocation. Constraint (23.1f) restricts the total number of winners to be within the range (S_{min}, S_{max}).

The impact of these allocation constraints is as follows: bid submissions for each supplier are restricted by the minimum/maximum quantity limits. If a bid is submitted by a supplier that violates this constraint, the bid is removed from consideration. An important auction design question is whether this constraint is made public to the supplier. If bidders know, or assume that there are additional allocation constraints, this can impact strategic bidding behavior and needs to be taken into consideration together with other design decisions. In the Mars case, a bidder knows all their own constraints, maximum allowed volume, and the minimum contract size globally and per lot. A bidder knows if Mars wants multiple suppliers, but he doesn't observe how many suppliers are bidding, or the exact minimum or maximum number of winners.

The maximal problem size is given as thirty suppliers and 400 items. Without allocation constraints these problem sizes can be solved within seconds. The consideration of allocation constraints makes a fundamental impact on the feasibility of the problem. With limits on the quantity allocated to each supplier and on the total number of winners, a feasible solution might not exist or might be difficult to find. These side constraints can also have significant impact on the cost of procurement—a tight constraint can often force the cost to be higher than a constraint free solution.

23.4.4 Business Impact

Increasing suppliers' margins and consistent cost savings to Mars have resulted from an improved matching of the company's needs to the suppliers' capabilities. Mars procurement managers have found that when buyers were willing to change the size of the supplier pool or shift large amounts of business, the auctions yielded greater savings. The payback time on Mars' investment into procurement auctions was much less than a year.

Once they were integrated into the business process, auctions took much less time than multiple bilateral bargaining. This is a benefit to both buyers and suppliers. Mars buyers, as a result, have more time to align businesses and to seek synergistic value from suppliers. No suppliers have refused to participate once an auction has been scheduled.

It usually takes a day or two to set up an auction in the software and train suppliers for auctions the first time they are run. As an auction is repeated, training times for suppliers drop from one hour for first-time users to less than ten minutes for repeat users. Although complex auctions may take weeks to design, auctions have never taken more time than the traditional ways of bargaining they replaced. In the most significant reported time savings, a forty-minute auction replaced a price-only negotiation process that had lasted over two weeks and required the buyer to make nine separate air trips to finalize only the prices and volumes of the contract.

23.5 Conclusion

Traditional price-only auctions are unable to handle indivisibilities and other real-world market complexities. Package bids and other types of multidimensional bidding enable suppliers to take advantage of their unique abilities and put forth their best offers. This stimulates competition by freeing the suppliers to express their strengths and competitive differences, as opposed to forcing them to compete as if they were the same.

A few aspects of industrial procurement auctions might be considered as distinct. First of all, due to the variety of goods and services that need to be purchased, it is important to allow for a rich bidding language. Second, allocation constraints are key to address the many strategic and operational issues a procurement manager faces, and to achieve implementable solutions.

Although combinatorial auctions have been used for industrial procurement for several years, their adoption process has been slow. A number of specialized software vendors provide combinatorial auctions, but they have not been picked up by large procurement or ERP software vendors yet. A number of reasons have been mentioned for this:

• Purchasing managers are not used to commitment early on in the process. This requires considerable change in the negotiators' behavior.
• Many private companies are still struggling to get their procurement processes organized and save money with restructuring and automating processing steps. Although there are a number of success stories, people are still struggling with the question of whether combinatorial auctions will improve their purchasing or not.
• Many private companies are concentrating on fully exploiting the relatively easy applications that can be purchased via price-only auctions.
• Combinatorial auctions are used for complex negotiation scenarios. In addition to a combinatorial optimization engine, their introduction requires a great deal of experience and know-how about how to set up a combinatorial auction properly. Not many people have experience with combinatorial auctions yet. In other words, there is a certain time and financial investment required to get an auction up and running (typically a couple of months for the first example). This is also an education exercise. Often inexperienced bidders have difficulties bidding in combinatorial auctions.

At this time, combinatorial auctions are mostly used for strategic sourcing, where the stakes are high, such as, for large and time-consuming purchases, where an automatic process incorporating optimization has undisputed advantages. Only when both buyers and suppliers become familiar with the process may more routine purchases warrant using this tool. Combinatorial auctions, however, are still very new to both suppliers and buyers. As with many new business processes, combinatorial auctions require time before they become a standard business practice.

Acknowledgments

We would like to thank Arne Anderson, John Ledyard, Tuomas Sandholm, and the anonymous reviewers for their valuable input to this chapter.

Notes

1. The focus of auctions conducted by Net Exchange and Schneider Logistics is primarily on transportation auctions.

2. This refers to optimality of the optimization, not to "optimality" in the sense of "optimal mechanism design."

3. An overview of the Mars, Incorporated procurement auction project appears in Hohner et al. 2003.

References

Beall, Stewart, Craig Carter, Phillip L. Carter, Thomas Germer, Thomas Hendrick, Sandy Jap, Lutz Kaufmann, Debbie Maciejewski, Robert Monczka, and Ken Petersen (2003), "The Role of Reverse Auctions in Strategic Sourcing," Center for Advanced Purchasing Studies (CAPS), Temple, AZ.

Bichler, Martin (2001), *The Future of eMarkets: Multi-Dimensional Market Mechanisms*, Cambridge, UK: Cambridge University Press.

Bichler, Martin and Jayant Kalagnanam (2004), "Configurable Offers and Winner Determination in Multi-Attribute Auctions," *European Journal of Operational Research*, 160, 380–394.

Bichler, Martin, Juhnyoung Lee, Ho Soo Lee, and Jayant Kalagnanam (2002), "Resource Allocation Algorithms for Electronic Auctions: A Framework Design," in Proceedings of the *3rd International Conference on Electronic Commerce and Web Technologies (EC-Web)*, Aix-en-Provence, France: Springer LNCS, 216–224.

Boutilier, Craig, Tuomas Sandholm, and Rob Shields (2004), "Eliciting Bid Taker Non-Price Preferences in (Combinatorial) Auctions," V. Khu-Smith and C.J. Mitchell (editors), in Proceedings of the *National Conference on Artificial Intelligence*, San Jose, CA, 204–211.

Dasgupta, Sudipto and Daniel F. Spulber (1989), "Managing Procurement Auctions," *Information Economics and Policy*, 4, 5–29.

Davenport, Andrew J. and Jayant R. Kalagnanam (2000), "Price Negotiations for Procurement of Direct Inputs," in Proceedings of the *IMA "Hot Topics" Workshop: Mathematics of the Internet: E-Auction and Markets*, 27–44.

Elmaghraby, Wedad and Pinar Keskinocak (2002), "Technology for Transportation Bidding at The Home Depot," in C. Billington, T. Harrison, H. Lee, and J. Neale (eds.), *The Practice of Supply Chain Management*, Boston: Kluwer, 245–258.

Epstein, Rafael, Lysette Henriquez, Jaime Catalan, Gabriel Weintraub, and Cristian Martinez (2002), "A Combinatorial Auction Improves School Meals in Chile," *Interfaces*, 32, 593–612.

Hannon, David (2004), "GSK Closes the Loop Using E-Sourcing Tools," *Purchasing Magazine*, Available at ⟨http://www.purchasing.com/article/CA422096.html⟩.

Hohner, Gail, John Rich, Ed Ng, Grant Reid, Andrew Davenport, Jayant Kalagnanam, Ho Soo Lee, and Chae An (2003), "Combinatorial and Quantity Discount Procurement Auctions with Mutual Benefits at Mars, Incorporated," *Interfaces*, 33, 23–35.

Keeny, Ralph L. and Howard Raiffa (1993), *Decision Making with Multiple Objectives: Preferences and Value Tradeoffs*, Cambridge, UK: Cambridge University Press.

Kwasnica, Anthony M., John O. Ledyard, David Porter, and Christine DeMartini (2005), "A New and Improved Design for Multiobject Iterative Auctions," *Management Science*, 51, 419–434.

Laffont, Jean-Jaques and Jean Tirole (1993), *A Theory of Incentives in Procurement and Regulation*, Cambridge, MA: The MIT Press.

Ledyard, John O., Mark Olson, David Porter, Joseph A. Swanson, and David P. Torma (2002), "The First Use of a Combined Value Auction for Transportation Services," *Interfaces*, 32, 4–12.

Milgrom, Paul R. and Robert J. Weber (1982), "A Theory of Auctions and Competitive Bidding," *Econometrica*, 50, 1089–1122.

Parkes, David C., Jayant Kalagnanam, and Marta Eso (2001), "Achieving Budget-Balance with Vickrey-Based Payment Schemes in Exchanges," in *Proceedings of IJCAI 2001*, 1161–1168.

Pekeč, Aleksandar and Michael H. Rothkopf (2003), "Combinatorial Auction Design," *Management Science*, 49, 1485–1503.

Plant, Judith (2004), "e-Auction: la révolution des appels d'offres," *le Journal du Management* ⟨http://managementjournaldunet.com/0406/040643_encheres.shtml⟩.

Sandholm, Tuomas and Subhash Suri (2001), "Side Constraints and Non-Price Attributes in Markets," *Proceedings of the IJCAI-2001 Workshop on Distributed Constraint Reasoning*, 55–61.

Combinatorial Auction Glossary

additive set function A set function f is *additive* if and only if $f(S \cup T) = f(S) + f(T)$ for all disjoint S and T.

activity A measure of the quantity of bidding in a round by a bidder in a simultaneous ascending auction. Activity includes both standing high bids and new bids in the round. In spectrum auctions, activity is measured in units of bandwidth times the number of people covered by the license (e.g., MHz-pop). In electricity auctions, the quantity is in energy units (e.g., MWh).

activity rule A restriction on allowable bids intended to maintain the pace and encourage price discovery in simultaneous ascending auctions. This is done by preventing the "snake in the grass" strategy, in which a bidder maintains a low level of activity early in the auction and then greatly expands his demand late in the auction. The activity rule forces a bidder to maintain a minimum level of activity to preserve current eligibility. Typically, the activity requirement increases in stages. For example, the activity requirement might be 60 percent in stage 1, 80 percent in stage 2, and 100 percent in stage 3 (the final stage). With a 60 percent activity requirement, each bidder must be active on a quantity of items, equal to at least 60 percent of the bidder's current eligibility. If activity falls below the 60 percent level, then the bidder's current eligibility is reduced to its current activity divided by 60 percent. With a 100 percent activity requirement, the bidder must be active on 100 percent of its current eligibility or its eligibility drops to its current activity. The lower activity requirement early in the auction gives the bidder greater flexibility in shifting among license aggregations early on when there is the most uncertainty about what will be obtainable. Typically, bidders are given some small number of waivers of the activity requirement.

affiliated The random variables $Z = \{S, T_1, \ldots, T_n\}$ are *affiliated* if the joint density $f(z)$ is such that for all $z, z' \in Z$, $f(z \vee z') f(z \wedge z') \geq f(z) f(z')$, where $z \vee z' = \max\{z, z'\}$ and $z \wedge z' = \min\{z, z'\}$.

affiliated values Model of bidder values in which bidder i's value $v_i(s, t_1, \ldots, t_n)$ depends on the state of world s and the realization of each bidder's private information $(t_1, \ldots, t_n)$, where the random variables determining the state of the world and each bidder's private information are *affiliated*. The affiliated values model is a general model, allowing both *private values* uncertainty and *common values* uncertainty. Affiliation implies that if one bidder has a high estimate of value it is more likely that the other's estimate of value is high. See *interdependent values*.

agent A party or computer program that acts on behalf of another. A player in a game. See *bidding agent*.

agents are substitutes See *bidders are substitutes*.

allocation An assignment of items to bidders as a result of the auction.

allowable bids Bids that bidders are allowed to submit. Auction rules may prevent bids on certain combinations, bids that are too low or too high, or that claim too many goods.

anonymous pricing Pricing that does not depend on bidder identity (in contrast with *nonanonymous pricing*).

approximation A solution to an optimization problem that is not necessarily optimal but that has a performance guarantee. See *heuristic*.

ascending auction An iterative auction in which bids on any biddable combination can only increase during the course of the auction.

auction design The process of defining the products being auctioned, as well as the auction rules and procedures.

auction designer One designing an auction.

auctioneer One conducting the auction.

Bayesian Nash equilibrium The extension of Nash equilibrium to games with incomplete information. Each player plays a best response to the strategies of the other players. Best responses are evaluated after a player learns his private information, but before he learns the private information of the other players. Hence, the player's strategy maximizes his expected utility given his private information, the joint distribution of others' private information, and the strategies of the other players. Private information is drawn from a common joint distribution and beliefs about strategies are consistent. See *Nash equilibrium* and *ex post equilibrium*.

bid An expression of preference by the bidder, indicating an interest in buying or selling particular items under certain conditions. Typically, bids are binding commitments, with the exception of *indicative bids*.

bid increment In an ascending auction, the minimum amount that a standing high bid must be raised for the bid to be valid. Typically, bid increments are set at the discretion of the auctioneer.

bid preparation The act of preparing a bid for an auction.

bid retraction In a discrete round auction, removing a bid before the bid submission period for the round has concluded. The bid becomes null and void, equivalent to as if it was never made. See *bid withdrawal*, which is fundamentally different.

bid withdrawal The situation under which a high bidder can withdraw his bid subject to a penalty. In such a case, the auctioneer is then listed as the high bidder and the minimum bid is then set at a lower level. Bid withdrawals typically are allowed in simultaneous ascending auctions without package bidding. A bid withdrawal occurs after the bid submission period of the round the bid was placed.

biddable combination A combination on which it is possible to place an allowable bid.

bidder A company or person participating in an auction.

bidder submodular A *coalitional value function* w where bidders are more valuable when added to smaller coalitions: for all $l \in L\backslash\{0\}$ (0 denotes the seller) and all coalitions S and S' satisfying $0 \in S \subset S'$, $w(S \cup \{l\}) - w(S) \geq w(S' \cup \{l\}) - w(S')$. Bidder submodular implies *bidders are substitutes* (or *agents are substitutes*). Bidder submodular requires the bidders are substitutes condition for every subset of the grand coalition (the set L of all bidders and the seller).

bidders are substitutes A coalitional value function w where the incremental value of a subset of bidders to the grand coalition is at least as great as the sum of the incremental contributions of each of its members: for all $K \subset I$ (the set of all bidders), $w(I) - w(I\backslash K) \geq \sum_{i \in K} w(I) - w(I\backslash\{i\})$. The Vickrey payoff is in the core if and only if bidders are substitutes. The stronger condition, bidder submodular, requires bidders are substitutes for every subset of the grand coalition. Hence, it assures the Vickrey payoff is in the core of the game with the reduced set of bidders.

bidding agent A party or computer program that submits bids on behalf of a bidder according to a predetermined procedure. See *proxy*.

bidding language The set of all allowable bids.

bid-taker See *auctioneer*.

bipartite graph An undirected graph whose nodes can be partitioned into two sets such that each edge connects nodes from different sets.

Boolean combination An expression using the primitive Boolean connectives AND, OR, and NOT, and possibly other logical connectives defined by these such as XOR (exclusive OR).

budget constraint An upper bound on the amount of money a bidder can spend in the auction.

bundle See *package*.

bundle prices Prices defined on bundles.

clock auction A type of *dynamic auction* used for identical items or divisible goods, in which the auctioneer announces prices and bidders respond with quantities desired at the announced prices. Bidding is continuous in a theoretical clock auction, although practical implementations have a discrete clock and discrete rounds.

coalitional value function A mapping from a set of players S to a real number $w(S)$, equal to the maximum value created by the set of players working together. In auctions, this is the total value from trade among the players S. See *cooperative game*.

collusion Cooperative behavior among bidders in an auction, which may be explicit (as in a bidding ring) or tacit (as in a shared understanding derived from past or current bidding behavior).

combination See *package*.

combinatorial bid A Boolean combination of package bids.

complement The set of all items that do not belong to a given combination.

complements Items such that the value of the items combined is greater than the sum of individual values. See *superadditive*.

combinatorial auction (CA) An auction that allows combinatorial bids, or, as a special case, package bids. See *package bid* and *combinatorial bid*.

common values Model of bidder values in which packages of items have the same value to all bidders. Typically, these values are unknown, and bidders only have estimates of the common value $v(S, s, t_1, \ldots, t_n)$, where S is the package of items, s is the state of the world (reflecting common uncertainty), and t_i is bidder i's private information. See *interdependent values* and *private values*.

communication complexity The minimum number of bits whose transmission is required in order to compute a given function.

computational complexity The intrinsic minimum amount of resources—such as time or storage capacity—needed to solve instances of a computational problem, measured as a function of the number of bits needed to represent an instance (input size).

computationally tractable A computational problem is *computationally tractable* if it is possible to provide an algorithm that solves each instance within a computation time that is bounded by a polynomial function of the size of the instance.

computationally intractable A computational problem is *computationally intractable* if it is not possible to provide an algorithm that has a computation time bounded by a polynomial function of the size of the instance.

conditional bid A bid that is valid only if a specified set of requirements are met, such as package, minimum volume, delivery, or payment requirements. See *multiattribute bid*.

continuous auction An auction that is not subdivided into rounds, allowing bid submission at any time. Often, trades occur on a continuous basis, as well as bids.

cooperative game A game in which players decide what group of players to work with (a coalition) and how to split up the maximum value created by their working together. The value by their working together is defined by a *coalitional value function*. Players can make binding commitments.

core A concept for cooperative games. For the case of transferable utility (utility is linear in money), the core is the set of value allocations among coalition members such that each member does at least as well within the coalition as in any subcoalition. For the case of non-transferable utility, the *NTU-core* is the set of feasible unblocked allocations. An allocation ω is *blocked* if there exists some coalition S and allocation ω' feasible for coalition S such that all the members of S strictly prefer ω' to ω.

correspondence A one-to-many mapping: every point in the domain is mapped to possibly many points in the range. In contrast, a function is a one-to-one mapping: every point in the domain is mapped to a single point in the range.

cost minimization A common objective in auctions to buy, such as procurement auctions, in which the auctioneer minimizes the cost of acquiring the items. See *revenue maximization*.

decision problem A computational problem consisting of a class of instances and a definition of a property of these instances. The problem to be solved is to decide whether a given instance from the class has this property or not. For example, given a set of combinatorial bids and a target revenue w, is there an allocation of items to bidders with a total revenue of at least w.

direct revelation mechanism   For games with private information, a mapping from player reports of private information into utility outcomes. For any game with private information, a direct revelation mechanism is the composition of the strategy functions (mapping private information into actions) and the utility functions (mapping actions and private information into payoffs). See *mechanism* and *incentive compatibility*.

discriminatory price   An auction where two bidders winning identical item combinations may nonetheless pay different prices for those bundles.

discriminatory auction   In economics, a format for auctioning multiple identical items (or divisible goods) where bidders simultaneously submit demand curves. Each bidder wins the quantity he demanded at the clearing price, paying the amount that he bid for each unit won. See *pay-as-bid auction*. Computer scientists sometimes refer to any auction with a discriminatory price as a discriminatory auction.

dominant strategy   A strategy that, for every possible realization of types of players, does at least as well as any other, regardless of what strategies are played by the other players. The strategy is a *strictly dominant strategy* if it does for every possible realization of types of players strictly better than all other strategies, regardless of the strategies chosen by others.

dominant strategy equilibrium   A refinement of *Nash equilibrium* (or *Bayesian Nash equilibrium* for games of incomplete information). Each player's strategy is a best response, regardless of the strategies of the other players. Behavior in dominant strategy equilibria is robust to uncertainty about what strategies the other players adopt and to uncertainty over the other players' private information. With private values, bidding one's value is a dominant strategy equilibrium in the *Vickrey auction*.

dual   Every *linear program* has a corresponding linear program called the *dual*, with the property that its objective is always a bound on the original linear program, called the *primal*. When a point is feasible to both the primal and the dual linear programming problems, the point is optimal to both problems.

Dutch auction   As used in auction theory, a format for auctioning a single item also known as a *descending clock auction*. The auctioneer starts at a high price and announces successively lower prices. The first bidder to bid wins the item, and pays the current price at the time of the bid. Unfortunately, the same term is sometimes used in the finance literature to refer to the *uniform-price auction* for multiple items.

dynamic auction   Any auction format that involves multiple opportunities to bid and where some information about the bidding is revealed to the bidders during the course of the auction. An English auction is the most common form of dynamic auction. Dynamic auctions can either have discrete rounds (as in an *iterative auction* or *multiround auction*) or continuous bidding, as in a *clock auction*.

(Pareto) efficiency   An assignment of resources such that it is impossible to make someone better off without making anyone else worse off. Equivalently, when the utility possibility set is convex, an assignment of resources that maximizes a weighted sum of players' utilities for some positive welfare weights. For games with incomplete information, there are several definitions of efficiency depending on the time at which efficiency is evaluated (*ex ante*—before players learn their private information, *interim*—after each player learns his own private information, but before he learns the others' private information, and *ex post*—after all information has been revealed), and whether incentive constraints are recognized. The most common form of efficiency applied to auction games is *ex post efficiency*, which examines efficiency after all private information is known and ignoring incentive constraints. For games with transferable utility (utility that is linear in money), this is the same as maximizing the ex post gains from trade; that is, assigning the items to those that value them the most.

electronic auction   An *electronic market* in which the market is conducted by auction.

electronic market   A market that is designed for or requires use of electronic communication and computation.

eligibility   The maximum quantity of items that a bidder may bid on. In a dynamic auction, eligibility may decline as a result of a bidder's failure to satisfy an activity rule. Eligibility is initially set based on a bidder's financial qualifications, its incumbent position, a bid deposit, or a letter of credit. See *activity rule*.

ending rule   The rule in iterative auctions defining the point at which the auction ends. A common ending rule is the point at which no bidder is willing to submit another bid.

equilibrium bidding   A set of bidding strategies, one for each bidder, such that each bidder's strategy is a best response to the other bidders' strategies. Typically, bidders have private information, in which case the best responses are calculated in expected terms. See *Bayesian Nash equilibrium*.

ex post equilibrium   A refinement of Bayesian Nash equilibrium for games with incomplete information, in which each player's equilibrium strategy remains an equilibrium even after learning the realization of each players' private information. An ex post equilibrium is robust to the distribution of private information; that is, ex post equilibrium strategies remain best responses regardless of the distribution of private information. Hence, the ex post outcome is invariant to the distribution of private information. Ex post equilibrium is a weakening of *dominant strategy equilibrium*. It typically arises in auction settings with interdependent values, because dominant strategy equilibria typically do not exist in these settings, but ex post equilibria may exist.

exposure problem   The problem of winning some—but not all—of a complementary collection of items in an auction without package bids. The bidder is "exposed" to a possible loss if his bids include synergistic gains that might not be achieved.

English auction   A format for auctioning a single item. Bidders submit successively higher bids for the item, until no bidder is willing to bid higher. The final bidder wins the item, and pays the amount of his final bid.

failure-freeness   The property that the auction procedure never fails to allocate and price items and combinations according to predetermined auction rules.

first-price (sealed bid) auction   A format for auctioning a single item. Bidders simultaneously submit sealed bids for the item. The highest bidder wins the item, and pays the amount of his bid.

free disposal A valuation function v satisfies free disposal if $v(S \cup T) \geq v(S)$ for all combinations S and T. In particular, disposing an item from a combination cannot increase the combination value.

gap The difference between the minimum bid on a combination that would be needed to make the bid a winning one under the assumption all other bids remain unchanged, and the current highest bid on that combination. The gap is zero if the current highest bid is a provisional winner; otherwise the gap is positive.

gross substitutes See *substitutes*.

heterogeneous items Items that are not identical. See *homogeneous items*.

heuristic An algorithm that is believed to be valuable but is not guaranteed to be optimal and is lacking in performance guarantees. An algorithm can be heuristic with respect to some properties (for example, running time) but not others (for example, correctness or optimality of the output). See *approximation*.

homogeneous items Identical items. See *heterogeneous items*.

incentive compatibility A direct revelation mechanism is *incentive compatible* if truthfully reporting private information is a Bayesian Nash equilibrium in the revelation game; that is, it is a best response truthfully to report private information assuming all other players report truthfully. A direct revelation mechanism is *incentive compatible in dominant strategies* if truthfully reporting private information is a dominant strategy equilibrium in the revelation game; that is, it is a best response, regardless of the reports of the other players. Every mechanism with a *Bayesian Nash equilibrium* has a corresponding direct mechanism that is incentive compatible. See *direct revelation mechanism*.

incumbent bidder A bidder who already has existing operations in the market.

independent private values A *private values* model for bidder values in which the bidders' values are independent random variables.

indicative bids A nonbinding indication of interest. This is used in certain auctions to identify a short list of bidders that are allowed to bid in the subsequent auction with binding bids.

integer program An optimization problem, typically with a linear objective and linear constraints, where one or more of the choice variables must take on integer values. See *linear program*.

integer programming A collection of techniques from mathematics, operations research, and computer science for solving integer programs. The problem of finding a solution to an arbitrary integer program is *NP-hard*. See *linear programming*.

item Basic unit of good or service offered at the auction. Equivalent terms include *product*, *property*, and *object*. See *unit*.

item prices See *linear prices*.

iterative auction A *dynamic auction* with discrete rounds.

interdependent values Model of bidder values with a general valuation function in which each bidder's value of a package depends on his private information as well as the private information of the other bidders. Typically, these values are unknown, and each bidder i only has estimates of the value $v_i(S, s, t_1, \ldots, t_n)$, where S is the package of items, s is the state of the world (reflecting common uncertainty), and t_i is bidder i's private information. See *common values* and *private values*.

jump bid   A bid in an ascending auction that is higher than the minimum bid required in the round. Jump bids are sometimes used to signal a strong interest in particular items. In auctions with package bids, jump bids can be used on large packages to exploit the *threshold problem*.

lattice   A lattice $(L, \geq)$ is a pair consisting of a nonempty set L and a partial order $\geq$ on L in which any two elements $a, b \in L$ have 1) a least common upper bound (join) $a \vee b$, and 2) a largest common lower bound (meet) $a \wedge b$.

linear pricing   Each item has a price that is the same for each bidder. The price for any package is the sum over all items in the package of the price of each item times the quantity of the item in the package.

linear program   An optimization problem with a linear objective and linear constraints, in which any real valued solutions are allowed. See *integer program*.

linear programming   A collection of techniques from mathematics, operations research, and computer science for solving linear programs. Linear programming is computationally tractable. See *integer programming*.

linear programming relaxation   A linear program obtained from a given integer program by removing the constraints that certain choice variables take on integer values.

linear valuation   A valuation function that is additive.

market   An opportunity for sellers and buyers of items to engage in trade.

market design   Defining the products to be traded, as well as the rules and procedures of trade, with the goal of maximizing an objective, often efficiency or revenues.

mechanism   A description of the possible actions for each agent, and a mapping from the agents' actions into an outcome. See *protocol* and *direct revelation mechanism*.

minimum bid   The smallest acceptable bid. In ascending auctions, this is one bid increment more than the prior bid. See *bid increment*.

monotone likelihood ratio property   A probability density function f satisfies the monotone likelihood ratio property if the ratio $f(v|t)/f(v|s)$ is weakly increasing in v for all $t > s$. Typically, $f(v|s)$ is the probability density of a bidder's value v conditional on the signal s (an estimate of value). Intuitively, the likelihood of high values increases with the estimate of value.

multiattribute bid   A bid in an auction, especially procurement auctions, where the bidder specifies several predefined attributes of an item, such as price, payment terms, delivery schedule, quality, and material.

multiple-round auction   A *dynamic auction* where bidders have a chance to modify their bids in a sequence of rounds.

multi-item auction   An auction for many items. Also called a multiple-object auction or multi-object auction. See *multiunit auction* for the special case where the items are identical.

multiunit auction   An auction for many identical items. Bidders express the quantity desired of each type of item.

Nash equilibrium   A set of strategies, one for each player of the game, such that each player's strategy is a best response to the others' strategies.

net substitutes   See *substitutes*.

non-anonymous pricing   A pricing rule in which two bidders may win the same set of items and yet pay different prices. See *anonymous pricing*.

nonlinear pricing   The price of a package does not equal the dot product of item prices times item quantities. Volume discounts are an example of nonlinear pricing. *Vickrey pricing* is an example of both nonlinear and *non-anonymous* pricing. See *linear pricing*.

NP (nondeterministic polynomial time)   A complexity class of *decision problems* for which there exists a polynomial time algorithm that can check the validity of the property in question, if it is given as input next to the instance a certificate for the validity (regardless of how hard it is to compute such certificates). Equivalently, it is the class of problems computable by a nondeterministic Turing machine in polynomial time. It is generally believed, but not known, that the class NP contains problems that are computationally intractable. See *NP-complete*.

NP-complete   Those problems in NP that are the hardest problems in NP in the following sense: any polynomial time algorithm that solves an NP-complete problem could be used to solve any other problem in NP. For this reason, it is generally believed, but not known, that NP-complete problems are computationally intractable.

NP-hard   The complexity class of computational problems that are intrinsically as hard as any in NP. By definition, NP-complete problems are NP-hard, but also problems not contained in NP can be NP-hard.

NP-complete (resp. hard) optimization problem   An optimization problem whose corresponding *decision problem* is NP-complete (resp. NP-hard). The decision version of an optimization problem "find for a given instance an optimal solution" takes the form "Is there a solution for this instance of quality at least …"

object   See *item*.

online auction   An auction conducted with electronic means, typically over the Internet.

quasilinear utility   Utility that is linear in money and the good: $u(S, p) = v(S) - p$, where $v(S)$ is the bidder's value for the package S and p is his payment.

package   A set collection of items. Also called *bundle* or *combination*.

package auction   An auction for multiple items, allowing package bids. A bid is interpretable as an all-or-nothing offer for the specified package at the specified price. See *combinatorial auction*.

package bid   A price for a specified collection of items. In the indivisible, single-unit case, the collection is simply the set of items. In the indivisible, multiunit case, the collection is the number of units of each good. In the divisible-good case, the collection is the fraction of each good.

pay-as-bid auction   A format for auctioning multiple identical items (or divisible goods) where bidders simultaneously submit demand curves. Each bidder wins the quantity demanded at the clearing price, paying the amount that he bid for each unit won. See *discriminatory auction.*

permitted bids   See *allowable bids.*

polynomial time algorithm   An algorithm that has an execution time that is no more than a polynomial function of the size of the input.

price discovery   A feature of dynamic auctions in which tentative price information is reported to bidders, giving bidders the opportunity to adjust subsequent bids based on the price information.

pricing rule   An auction rule defining prices for all allowable combinations at any given point of the auction procedure.

privacy preservation   A property that precludes bidders from making their valuations contingent on the valuations of other bidders.

private values   Model of bidder values in which each bidder's value does not depend on the private information of the other bidders. Bidder i's value for the package S is given by $v_i(S)$. See *common values* and *interdependent values.*

procurement auction   An auction to buy services or goods. Also called a *reverse auction.*

product   See *item.*

property   See *item.*

protocol   A specification for sequential contingent actions (such as communication or computation) by one or more agents. See *mechanism.*

provisional winner   In an interactive auction, a bidder that would be a winner if the auction were to end at that point. See *tentative winner.*

provisional winning bid   In an iterative auction, a bid that would be a winning bid if the auction were to end at that point.

proxy   An agent process that automatically submits bids for a bidder according to a predetermined procedure.

proxy auction   An auction in which bids are submitted by proxy. Most typically, real bidders submit preferences, and then the proxy agents iteratively submit bids using straightforward bidding. The use of a proxy speeds up the iterative auction and constrains how bidder preferences are translated into bids. See *straightforward bidding.*

reserve price   The minimum price at which the seller will sell an item. The amount is sometimes known to the bidders and is sometimes not known, in which case it is called a "secret reserve." In an auction to buy, the reserve price is the maximum price at which the buyer will buy an item.

reservation price   A bidder's valuation or willingness to pay. Also called *valuation* or *value.*

revelation principle   A principle of mechanism design, which states that under certain conditions, there is no loss in restricting attention to direct revelation mechanisms in which the players simply report their private information to the mechanism, and in equilibrium do so truthfully.

revenue maximization A common objective in auctions to sell, in which the auctioneer maximizes the revenue obtained for the items. See *cost minimization*.

reverse auction An auction to buy goods or services with one buyer and many competing sellers. This is "reverse" of the standard auction to sell goods or services with one seller and many competing buyers. See *procurement auction*.

scalable A property that the auction procedure would still be practically solvable if the number of items auctioned were increased significantly.

sealed-bid auction A single round auction where bids are simultaneously submitted by the bidders.

second-price (sealed-bid) auction A format for auctioning a single item. Bidders simultaneously submit sealed bids for the item. The highest bidder wins the item, and pays the amount bid by the second-highest bidder. See *Vickrey auction*.

set packing problem See weighted set packing problem.

shortfall See *gap*.

simultaneous ascending auction (SAA) A format for auctioning multiple items, commonly used for auctioning spectrum licenses. The auction is a natural generalization of the English auction, especially useful when selling many related items. The items are auctioned simultaneously in a sequence of rounds. In each round, each bidder can submit bids on any of the items, raising the standing high bids by at least the bid increment. The auction does not end until no bidder is willing to bid higher on any item. Typically, bidding is constrained by activity rules that force bidders to maintain a level of activity throughout the auction that is consistent with their desired winnings. An equivalent term is *simultaneous multiple round* (SMR) *auction*.

single-round auction An auction in which bidders have a single opportunity for bid submission. See *sealed-bid auction*.

sincere bidding See *straightforward bidding*.

straightforward bidding A bidding strategy in dynamic auctions in which, in each round, the bidder bids the minimum bid on the package of items that maximizes his net value given the current item and package prices. Such a strategy is optimal if this is the last bid placed by any bidder. However, in other cases straightforward bidding typically is not optimal. This is sometimes called *sincere bidding*.

subadditivity A set function f is locally subadditive at the disjoint sets S and T if $f(S \cup T) \leq f(S) + f(T)$. A set function f is subadditive if it is locally subadditive for all disjoint S and T. See *superadditivity*.

submodular A set function $f : 2^m \to \Re$ is submodular if for all sets S and T, $f(S \cap T) + f(S \cup T) \leq f(S) + f(T)$. A lattice function $f : L \to \Re$ is submodular if for all $a, b \in L$, $f(a \wedge b) + f(a \vee b) \leq f(a) + f(b)$. See *lattice* and *bidder submodular*.

substitutes Goods are substitutes when increasing the price of one does not reduce demand for the other. The modified terms "gross substitutes" and "net substitutes" are often used to distinguish between substitutes for uncompensated and compensated demand, respectively. With quasilinear utilities, there is no distinction between "gross" and "net."

superadditivity   A set function f is locally superadditive at the disjoint sets S and T if $f(S \cup T) \geq f(S) + f(T)$. A set function f is superadditive if it is locally superadditive for all disjoint S and T. See *subadditivity*.

synergy   When a player's valuation function is superadditive on a specified subset of items, the player is said to have a synergy for those items. See *complements*.

tentative winner   In an interactive auction, a bidder that would be the winner if the auction were to end at that point. See *provisional winner*.

tie   A situation in which there are distinct alternative solutions to the winner determination problem.

tie-breaking   A procedure for determining which of alternative sets of bids that solve the winner determination problem should be preferred.

threshold problem   Allowing package bids may favor bidders seeking larger packages, because small bidders do not have the incentive or capability to top the tentative winning bids of the large bidder.

tractable   See *computationally tractable*.

transparency   The property that, in any instance of the auction, the participants or the public can verify that the auction rules have been properly followed; for example, a losing bidder can see why he lost.

uniform-price auction   A format for auctioning multiple identical items. Bidders simultaneously submit demand curves. Each bidder wins the quantity demanded at the clearing price, and pays the clearing price for each item won.

unit   A measure of quantity in the identical good case or the divisible good case, as in multiunit auction. (However, in electricity auctions the term "unit" refers to a physical generator, as in "unit commitment.") See *item*.

valuation   See *reservation price*.

value   See *reservation price*.

valuation function   A function describing a bidder's valuation for all biddable packages.

VCG mechanism   See *Vickrey-Clarke-Groves mechanism*.

Vickrey allocation   An allocation defined by the VCG mechanism.

Vickrey auction   An auction format for multiple identical items. Bidders simultaneously submit demand curves. Each bidder wins the quantity demanded at the clearing price, and pays the opportunity cost of its winnings. For a single-item auction, the Vickrey auction is a *second-price auction*. When the approach is applied to the auction of non-identical items, the Vickrey auction is often referred to as the *generalized Vickrey auction* or the *Vickrey-Clarke-Groves mechanism*.

Vickrey-Clarke-Groves (VCG) mechanism   A format for auctioning multiple items. Bidders simultaneously submit sealed bids giving their value for each possible package. The auctioneer then determines an efficient assignment of the items based on the bids. Payments are determined so as to allow each bidder a payoff equal to the incremental surplus that he brings to the auction. See *Vickrey auction*.

Vickrey outcome   An allocation and pricing defined by the VCG mechanism.

Vickrey pricing   Pricing defined by the VCG mechanism.

Walrasian pricing process   A dynamic pricing process in which market participants express quantities in response to announced prices. Prices are increased in response to excess demand and decreased in response to excess supply. The process continues until supply equals demand for all items.

weighted set packing problem   The problem of finding a disjoint collection of weighted subsets of a larger set with maximal total weight. Weighted set packing is a classical *NP-hard* problem, and is closely related to the *winner determination problem*.

winner's curse   The insight that winning an item in an auction is bad news about the item's value $(E(v_i|i \text{ wins}) < E(v_i)$, where v_i is bidder i's uncertain value), because winning implies that no other bidder was willing to bid as much for the item. Hence, it is likely that the winner's estimate of value is an overestimate. Because a bidder's bid is only relevant in the event that the bidder wins, the bidder should condition the bid on the negative information winning conveys about value. Bidders that fail to condition their bids on the bad news winning conveys suffer from the winner's curse in the sense that they often pay more for an item than it is worth.

winner determination problem (WDP)   The computational problem of determining the winning bids in a combinatorial auction by labeling bids as either winning or losing so as to maximize the sum of the accepted bids under the constraint that each item can be allocated to at most one bidder. This is equivalent to the *weighted set packing problem*, a computationally intractable problem.

winning bid   The bid that is selected by the winner determination problem. A bidder placing a winning bid is assigned all items defining the combination on which the bid was placed.

Contributors

Lawrence M. Ausubel is Professor of Economics, University of Maryland, and president of Market Design Inc. He has authored several important articles in auction theory and he holds three patents for innovative combinatorial auction designs. Ausubel has applied his research in the design and implementation of practical auction markets worldwide.

Michael O. Ball is the Orkand Corporation Professor of Management Science in the Robert H. Smith School of Business at the University of Maryland. He is co-director of NEXTOR, the National Center of Excellence for Aviation Operations Research, and he leads the NEXTOR Collaborative Decision Making project.

Martin Bichler is professor at the Institute of Informatics at the Technical University of Munich, where he holds a chair of Internet-based Information Systems. He has been involved in research and development in the areas of decision support systems, distributed systems, and electronic auctions.

Sushil Bikhchandani is Professor of Policy at the Anderson School of Management at UCLA. He is interested in the economics of incentives and information and its application to the study of auctions, market institutions, and social learning.

Craig Boutilier is Professor and Chair of the Department of Computer Science, University of Toronto. His research includes decision making under uncertainty, preference elicitation, multiagent systems and economic models, and knowledge representation. He serves on the editorial or advisory boards of several journals, and on the Technical Advisory Board of CombineNet, Inc.

Estelle Cantillon is assistant professor at Harvard Business School and an FRNS Research Associate at ECARES, Université Libre de Bruxelles. She is also research fellow at the Center for Economic Policy Research. Her research interests are in auction and market design, including combinatorial auctions and multiattribute (scoring) auctions.

Chris Caplice is a principal research associate at the MIT Center for Transportation and Logistics. Prior to joining MIT, he held senior positions at Chainalytics,

Logistics.com, and SABRE, and managed over fifty optimization-based auctions. His Ph.D. dissertation on combinatorial bidding in transportation won the CLM Doctoral Dissertation Award.

Peter Cramton   is Professor of Economics, University of Maryland, and Chairman of Market Design Inc. His recent research studies auction theory and practice. Cramton has applied this research in designing auction markets worldwide. He has led the design and implementation of numerous auctions in telecommunications, electricity, and other industries.

Andrew Davenport   is a researcher in the Mathematical Sciences Department of IBM T. J. Watson Research Center. His work has included developing constraint programming technology to solve complex planning and scheduling problems in industry. He currently applies optimization and artificial intelligence technologies to customer problems in electronic commerce, production planning, and scheduling.

George Donohue   is Professor of Systems Engineering and Operations Research at George Mason University. He has been an associate administrator at the Federal Aviation Administration and a vice president of the RAND Corporation. He was named one of the top 100 decision makers in Washington DC (1997) by *The National Journal*.

Karla Hoffman   is Professor of Operations Research, George Mason University. Her areas of research include combinatorial optimization, computational issues in combinatorial auctions, and real-time scheduling and capital dispatching. Hoffman currently serves as a consultant to the Federal Communications Commission and Federal Aviation Administration on the testing of alternative auction mechanisms.

Gail Hohner   holds a co-appointment as the research director of Freight Traders Ltd., a Mars Incorporated subsidiary providing online tender services for the freight industry, and as the research manager for Strategic Sourcing within Mars' Catalyst Innovation group. She has been designing and running combinatorial procurement auctions since 1996.

Jayant R. Kalagnanam   is research staff member in the Mathematical Sciences Department at the IBM Watson Research Center. He has worked on developing optimization models for production planning and scheduling. His current work focuses on the design and analysis of electronic markets and their use for eProcurement.

Ailsa Land   is Emeritus Professor of Operational Research at the London School of Economics. After developing, in cooperation with Alison Doig, the branch and bound procedure to solve integer linear programming problems, her research interests have been largely in the application and development of methods for dealing with combinatorial problems.

Daniel Lehmann is Professor of Computer Science at Hebrew University, in Jerusalem. He has made fundamental contributions to the study of nonmonotonic logic, the way we reason in everyday life. He is currently investigating algorithmic aspects of mechanism design and mathematical economics, and also the logic of quantum mechanics.

Kevin Leyton-Brown is an assistant professor in the Department of Computer Science at the University of British Columbia, Vancouver. His research addresses problems in computational game theory, auction theory, and the empirical properties of algorithms.

Dinesh Menon is an operations research specialist at Decisive Analytics Corporation, Arlington, VA. He has a Masters in Electrical Engineering from Florida Tech and has recently conducted research on combinatorial auctions and exchanges at the FCC. His prior experience includes implementation of forecasting and revenue management systems for commercial airlines.

Paul Milgrom is the Ely Professor of Humanities and Sciences and professor of economics at Stanford University. A world-renowned economic theorist and auction consultant and a principal designer of the pioneering U.S. spectrum auctions, Milgrom has also co-founded three companies and been awarded a patent for innovative combinatorial auction designs.

Rudolf Müller is Professor of Quantitative Infonomics at Maastricht University. His research on auctions focuses on the interplay of computational complexity, communication complexity, and strategic properties. His workshops on market design have greatly stimulated the dialogue among computer scientists, economists, and operations researchers.

Noam Nisan is Professor of Computer Science at the Hebrew University. His research interests include computational complexity, electronic commerce, and the interface between computation and economic theory.

Eugene Nudelman is a Ph.D. candidate in Computer Science at Stanford University. He received his B.Sc. in computer science and mathematics from the University of Toronto. His research interests include empirical complexity of algorithms, computational game theory, multiagent systems, and artificial intelligence.

Joseph M. Ostroy is Professor of Economics, UCLA. His research interests are general equilibrium theory and mathematical economics, with particular emphasis on the connections among competition, incentives, and efficiency.

David C. Parkes is Associate Professor of Computer Science at Harvard University. He was awarded the prestigious NSF CAREER Award in 2002 and the IBM Faculty Partnership Award in 2002 and 2003. Parkes has published papers on electronic markets, computational mechanism design, auction theory, and multiagent systems.

Aleksandar Saša Pekeč is Associate Professor of Decision Sciences in the Fuqua School of Business at Duke University. His research focuses on design and analysis of choice, allocation, and pricing mechanisms in complex competitive environments, ranging from multi-item auction design to subset choice and valuation.

Martin Pesendorfer is Professor of Economics at the London School of Economics, as well as a research affiliate at the CEPR, and a research fellow at the NBER. His research interests are in industrial organization, auctions, information economics, and strategic interaction.

Susan Powell is senior lecturer in the Operational Research Department at the London School of Economics. Her general area of research is mathematical programming. Her current research focuses on computer-based algorithms and combinatorial auctions.

Amir Ronen is senior lecturer (assistant professor) in the Industrial Engineering and Management Faculty at the Technion. His main areas of interest are the interplay between game theory and computer science, theoretical computer science, game theory, electronic commerce, and the Internet.

Michael H. Rothkopf is professor at Rutgers University's Business School and RUT-COR, its Ph.D. program in operations research, and is president of INFORMS. He is a consultant on electricity auctions to the Federal Energy Regulatory Commission, and has worked on scheduling, queuing, energy economics, and extensively on modeling auctions.

Tuomas Sandholm Associate Professor of Computer Science at Carnegie Mellon University, has published two hundred papers and received numerous awards, including Computers and Thought. He built the first combinatorial market for trucking in 1990. As founder, chairman, and CTO of CombineNet, he has fielded over two hundred large-scale combinatorial auctions.

Ilya Segal is Roy and Betty Anderson Professor of Economics at Stanford University. His research is in contracting and auction design. He is a fellow of the Econometric Society, director of the Stanford Institute for Theoretical Economics, and founding editor of the *Berkeley Electronic Journals in Theoretical Economics*.

Yossi Sheffi is Professor of Engineering Systems and of Civil and Environmental Engineering and head of the Center for Transportation and Logistics at MIT. His work focuses on logistics and supply chain management. He founded Logistics.com, which developed the first commercial application using combinatorial auctions to procure transportation services.

Yoav Shoham is Professor of Computer Science at Stanford University. His research has spanned artificial intelligence (in particular, logic and multiagent systems), game theory, and electronic commerce. He is a fellow of the American Association of Artificial Intelligence, and a founding member of the International Game Theory Society.

Vernon L. Smith is Professor of Economics and Law at George Mason University, research scholar in the Interdisciplinary Center for Economic Science, and a fellow of the Mercatus Center. He works on capital theory, finance, natural resource economics, and experimental economics. He was awarded the 2002 Nobel Prize in Economics.

Richard Steinberg is Reader in Operations Management at the University of Cambridge. His research has included graph theory, transportation networks, cost allocation, and marketing-production joint decision making—an area that he helped to establish. In addition to combinatorial auctions, his current research includes pricing in communication networks.

Susara van den Heever is senior operations research analyst at Decisive Analytics Corporation. Her current research includes auction bidding strategies and bidder tools; past research includes strategic and supply chain planning. Van den Heever has applied her research in the energy, food and beverage, and telecommunication industries.

Thomas Wilson is a student at MIT Sloan School of Management. His past work with Decisive Analytics Corp. supported the Federal Communications Commission's combinatorial auction program. Wilson's contributions included development of a combinatorial auction simulation platform and algorithms that effect feasible implementations of theoretical proxy auction designs.

Makoto Yokoo is Professor of Information Science and Electrical Engineering at Kyushu University, Japan. His current research interests include multiagent systems, especially mechanism design and constraint satisfaction among multiple agents. He is the recipient of the 2004 ACM SIGART Autonomous Agents Research Award.

Author Index

Subject Index